The Fuzz Factor

A Fool's Guide to Reality

Second Edition

by

Jimmy Clair MB PhD

I

Published in the Republic of Ireland by:

Kolbe Ltd,

9 North Main Street,

Cork,

Ireland.

Front Cover Photo: Image in the sky taken at Knock Shrine, Mayo, Ireland, on July 8th 2016. Courtesy of Ciarán O Riordan.

On the same night, a group of teenagers saw another image in the sky of St Brigid holding the Church, with a Cross and Monstrance beside her.

ISBN: 978-0-9529627-6-2

Further Copies: https://www.facebook.com/benedictusbookshop/

Printed by: Carrick Print, Carrigtwohill, County Cork, Ireland.

Dedication

This book is dedicated to:

The Three Hearts of Jesus, Mary & Joseph

&

Diana

Maria & Nicolas

Sr Bernadette & Joseph

Jacinta & Robert

Ronan, James & Clovis

Foreword to the Second Edition

It is now almost a decade since the first edition of this title was published. I am glad to say that it was received very well and even though it was sold only in Ireland, lots of compliments came from other countries. It has been out of print for a number of years but we are still getting requests. Rather than opting for another reprint I thought it best to update the first edition and add about ten new chapters covering various topics of some current interest, such as Islam, homosexuality, world finance, UFOs and others. I hope that the extra chapters will make it a book that everybody will want to read. Like the first edition, the pages, I hope, are full of interesting facts which I hope the readers will enjoy. I have tried to write a book that, if you wish, you can open at random to read a few pages. These few pages, I hope will enrich you and help you in some way and above all help you to be a better person for others and for yourself. It is my hope also that this edition will be sold outside of Ireland.

It is with great sadness I recognize that the danger I saw looming for humanity and tried to highlight in some small way, in the first edition, has now progressed rapidly towards a major unavoidable and unstoppable world crisis. It is a crisis of confusion, a crisis of selfishness, a crisis of greed, a crisis of morality and a crisis caused by lack of love. Above all it is a crisis of the ascendancy of evil and a rejection of truth. It will be a crisis of social collapse and much suffering. There are now a number of International borders where tension is increasing with several global hot spots that could be the spark for a general upheaval. The collapse of global finance is likely to be a very early major contributing factor, if not the initiating factor. We will soon know.

In trying to get some understanding of the complex problems of modern society, I feel that I am standing on the shoulders of giants. Emeritus Pope Benedict XVI with Scott Hahn and others have contributed enormously, in recent decades, in promoting a new and more global understanding of Christian Sacred Scripture. Peter Kreeft and Robert J. Spitzer, S.J., in particular, are God's gift to thinking humanity at this time. Peter Kreeft for his sharp philosophical intellect and Fr Spitzer, not only for his philosophy and theology but also for his mathematical, physical, metaphysical, and cosmological insights. There are also many others who are helping to point out the inevitable consequences to the great errors of modern society. One of my relatively new favourites is Mark Mallett, who is a well-known Canadian singer and song writer. Mark also has an extraordinary gift with Christian Sacred Scripture and I have gained a lot of useful insights from his writings in recent years. These are just a few of the voices, now crying in the wilderness, pointing us towards the need to PREPARE. The mainstream media is now so controlled that it has become unreliable and very restricted as a source of serious news items. I now, therefore, tend to rely on alternative news sources. My favourite alternative news magazine at the moment is *Nexus*.

The topics covered in the first edition have been retained in this edition, with occasional adjustments and updates. This makes for a larger book, but I hope that it also makes for better value for money. I have also retained a reasonably large print size, as this was the choice of most people, when I asked. In order to prevent the book from getting too unwieldy, the line spacing was made a little more cramped. The chapters can again be read in any order, but may be most beneficial when read in the order chosen in the book. There is no doubt, however, that some will regard certain sections or chapters, heavy or boring, and in those situations these sections are best ignored or skipped over. Overall, I hope that you and yours enjoy reading this second edition and benefit from it.

Foreword to the First Edition

This book presents evidence indicating that the world is on the brink of a great catastrophe, which could eventually lead to the death of the greater part of humanity, unless attitudes change very rapidly. Most of the good evidence for this comes from Roman Catholic sources, so in order to appreciate it, some understanding of Catholic teaching is necessary. One cannot be expected to understand Roman Catholicism without some understanding of God and the supernatural. Evidence for this is, therefore, also presented. I have tried to do this as simply as possible, so that readers can begin to understand that the evidence is solid, believable, and pretty overwhelming in many respects, especially for those who want to investigate more. Different kinds of evidence and what can be accepted as solid and good evidence is an interesting aspect to all of this, which will be presented in various sections. In so far as our behaviour is evidence based, we are all largely restricted to evidence, which we have encountered on the way through life, but we also know that there are none so blind, as those who will not see, or none so deaf, as those who will not hear.

The attitude that we can do nothing about the future is false. I am convinced that we can prevent an enormous amount of unnecessary suffering for ourselves, our families and those around us, by taking action now. The first requirement is to be aware, and to be prepared to accept the truth and to act on it, whatever the cost. Pope John Paul II was once asked by a journalist, what in his opinion, was the most important word in the bible? The immediate reply which came was, "truth". All Christians will have heard that the truth will set you free, and that the way to fulfilment, happiness, and joy in life, will be found only in truth. We must also recognize, that this truth which sets us free, is the truth that many of us may not be interested in hearing. In the end each individual will have to decide for themselves, but we can help one another. I should warn you, that this book may upset you. The object is not to upset, but rather to share some facts, and maybe to break a mould of silence, on a very important subject.

The first chapter serves as an introduction and an overview of reality, with the consequent dangers facing the world at this time. Different aspects of this reality are elaborated on in the later chapters. Chapters 2 and 3 outline some support evidence for the truth of Roman Catholic belief and the logical consequences of this truth. Chapter 4 discusses the New Age and the One World Order. Chapter 5 deals with different levels of spirituality, ranging from the mystical heights reached by the saints, to evidence for the existence of Hell, demons, and demonic possession. No discussion on the subject matter of this book would be complete, without considering the contribution made by science and mathematics, towards our understanding of Reality, Truth, and the probability of the existence of God. Although the use of scientific evidence is mentioned in different sections of chapter 2 and 3, chapter 6 discusses the interaction of mathematics and science with religion in a lot more detail. Chapters 7 and 8, deal with Catholic prophecy and future events. You will appreciate as you read through this book, that Catholic prophecy has a good track record, and what is predicted for the near future is not pleasant. The good news, however, is that after this present crisis, the world will enter a great period of peace and prosperity. In this context, one of the objects of this book is to make people aware of what is coming, so that they can properly prepare. The final chapter tries to pull the different strands together in the form of a conclusion.

I hope that this book will be of particular interest for the sceptics and the confused. I have tried to cover a range of topics, which I hope will encourage readers to do more reading and investigations, on the information presented. I have chosen a particular order for the chapters, but they can be read separately in any order. All through the book I have referenced items within the book with page numbers, and for this reason you may find it easier to read the chapters in the order chosen. I hope that you will at least enjoy the read, and hopefully become a better and more fulfilled person for having read it.

Table of Contents

XV

1. Humanity & God

Turning and turning in the widening gyre
The falcon cannot hear the falconer:
Things fall apart: the centre cannot hold:
Mere anarchy is loosed upon the world,
The blood-dimmed tide is loosed, and everywhere
The ceremony of innocence is drowned:
The best lack all conviction, while the worst
are full of passionate intensity.
The Second Coming - William Butler Yeats

Humanity is living in a haze. Objective reality, like objective truth, is perceived as vague, illusive and nebulous. In the immortal words of John Henry Newman, however, the situation remains – "Truth cannot be divided".

Humanity is drifting towards turmoil. There are signs that social instability is growing in the world. This instability is being fuelled by a wide variety of problems such as increased crime, increased terrorism, global climate changes with accompanying extreme weather conditions, an apparent increase in seismic activity, the growth of new more aggressive infectious diseases, unpredictable oil prices and collapsing markets. Global military spending and arms sales occupy the highest position in world trade, while efforts to improve the lot of the world poor are making little progress. A new political polarization is developing with many countries now opposing the US. The Middle East and other world hot spots are getting more unstable. Behind the scenes, political tension is increasing between the US and some Muslim states as well as the other two great nuclear powers of China and Russia. Are battle lines, slowly being defined?

A more serious view is that humanity is descending into chaos. World secularism is now at war with God. It is often said that the first casualty of war is truth and never before has the world been so much exposed to deception, deceit, and lies. Secret societies have significant control of world finance, through a cabal of international bankers. A new *World Order* is being promoted in the media: but what we are getting is not more order, but more chaos.

The God Problem

Belief in God can be usefully looked at under three general groups or headings. The first group incorporates the views of Marxists, atheists and secular humanists. These profess either not to believe in God, or, in the case of humanists, to believe that as we can never be sure about God, we should regard God as irrelevant. This group proposes that laws and ideals for life should be worked out as we think best for humanity, separate from any religious beliefs. In the second group are religions which have developed from the ideas and teachings of individuals who try to know and reach God and a higher level of consciousness, from their own resources. This group encompasses the great Eastern religions of Hinduism, Buddhism, Confucianism, Taoism, Shinto and others. These religions generally promote belief in reincarnation but have a wide variety of opinions on God. Hinduism is described as polytheistic as it promotes a belief in many gods. Buddhism and Confucianism, on the other hand, promote more a philosophy of life, with strong links to spiritualism, rather than an allegiance to any specific deity. In the final group are the so called monotheistic religions. In monotheism, all believe in the same one God, who has been revealed directly to humanity, but there are different beliefs and understandings on the nature of this God. This group includes

Judaism and the two great religions which have developed from Judaism, namely, Christianity and Islam, as well as a number of other smaller religions.

In terms of using a religious belief system as a basis for morality and law making for world governments, the principles of secular humanism have now been widely accepted as the international norm. This is supported by most democratically elected governments and by a newly developing World Order, promoted by international bodies, such as the United Nations, World Parliament Association, European Union, World Health Organization, and International Planned Parenthood. Adhering to secular humanist principles as a basis for morality and law-making amounts to issuing a direct challenge to the Judeo-Christian-Islamic God who, according to revelation, teaches that the authority to decide what is good from what is evil, does not belong to man, but to God alone. Clearly, therefore, the existence of this monotheistic God, or at least the authority of this God to make laws, is being called into question. The perceived 'bluff of God' or The God Delusion, as Richard Dawkins puts it,[1] is being firmly challenged like never before, by this international drive to secularism. Humanity is saying, through the *One World Order* and through many elected governments, – "We will not serve, – we will make our own laws and we will decide what is moral and what is not". More bluntly, therefore, the majority view is that a belief in a personal Judaeo-Christian-Islamic God is a load of nonsense.

The ball is now definitely in this God's court and in the court of those who profess a belief in a unified personal God. The population of the world is roughly divided into two halves, on the basis of individual, family or national allegiance to monotheism. There are many lukewarm nominal believers, however, and so called "baptized non believers" are common, so that firmly convinced active believers are very much in a minority. This has profound implications for all of us at this time in history.

Is Global Turmoil Inevitable?

The risk of world turmoil is clearly growing. There are two major sources of world tension with increasing potential for conflict. The first is from new geopolitical alignments, with the American-Jewish axis on one side, and a neo-communism, combining with some Islamic states, forming an axis on the other. Political instability is now also spreading in other parts of the world, while financial markets are getting more uncertain. There are ominous signs that nuclear weapons, instead of being a deterrent to war, as was the case over the last sixty years, are now more likely to be a cause of war. The movement towards turmoil, at this global level, is now becoming clear to those who keep in touch with mainstream media.

The seriousness of the global situation, at the spiritual level, is not at all obvious to those who are informed by the mainstream media only. This is the second and far more significant reason, why global turmoil now seems to be inevitable. The Ten Commandments are well known basic laws for mankind, issued by divine revelation, and first recorded in the Old Testament (Exodus 20: 1 – 17). For mainstream Christianity, these commands of God are still promoted as core teaching. The One World Order approach of promoting secular humanist principles comes into direct conflict with these, in a number of significant and contentious issues. Compromise is not on the agenda as the fundamental difference is the truth about God, God's laws, and the consequences for humanity not abiding by these laws. Roman Catholic teaching suggests that major wars result from the collective evil in human hearts and a general rejection of God's laws, rather than from rash decisions by fools and madmen. Mother Teresa of Calcutta used to say, that the greatest danger to peace in the world came from evil deeds, especially the killing of unborn babies, and a number of other mystics have mentioned this same theme. The moral consequences of the direct killing of 150,000 unborn every day, which was labelled as an unspeakable evil by Pope John Paul II, is not something humanity can avoid. If we are to believe some recent Divine revelations, evil in the world has now reached a tipping point, which God cannot allow to continue (see page 151). It is not just the killing of the unborn, but also the abuse of children and elderly, the victimization of the poor and a long list, culminating with an increased public worship of Satan in many parts of the world.

Some believe that the prime objective of the One World Order is not peace and harmony among all peoples, as they would like us to believe, but rather, world-wide control of humanity, and in particular, control and suppression of monotheistic religions. Many political parties and governments, world-wide, now have members who support and promote the aims of the One World Order. They are already working hard at the political level, promoting laws and international agreements, which support the principles of secularism. Conflict now seems inevitable, therefore, because it is perceived as a major global spiritual battle between two opposing views on morality, on what should be regarded as good, and what should be called evil. The particular Islamic believers, who promote aggression against other faiths and nations, may get their wish for war, but unfortunately for all of us, it is likely to be on a much grander scale than even they would hope for. From the Roman Catholic point of view, world turmoil now also seems to be very close because God has said so, through his prophets, and in particular through The Virgin Mary, who has already given many details about this coming battle.

Catholic revelation further suggests that the final battle will also be between the secret societies and the Roman Catholic Church.

This is also probably the institution most hated by the secularists. It is also the only organization on the planet, which is interpreting and teaching morals, on the basis of natural law, that is, the law of reason and of rational beings. Natural law is the law written in every human heart which helps the individual distinguish what is good from what is evil. It is simply the law of human nature. Laws and morals that are not based on natural law, such as a legal right to kill the unborn, would be regarded by the Catholic Church as corrupt not meriting the name of law or moral. Therefore, if these revelations and prophecies are true, we are now on the threshold of a major world conflict between two opposing views on what is immoral and what is moral, between secularism and monotheism, between anti-God and God. There is also a promise of a certain outcome. The Church of Rome will survive and flourish like never before, after severe persecution, and near annihilation in some places.

Of course, if monotheism, or more specifically for Christians, the Holy Trinity, is not for real, then we may have little to worry about at the spiritual level. If the Ten Commandments really are from God, however, then suffering and turmoil are now unavoidable. The time is rapidly coming for all of us, whether we like it or not, that we will have to choose which side we are on. The time for sitting on the fence is rapidly passing and the change with the capital "**C**" is coming. The choice we have is, to follow the majority: accept secularism: reject God and carry on regardless: or repent and be serious about prayer.

The Truth

Ultimately the battle is for truth. In recent years, one of the most significant books on the subject of Truth was the "Splendour of Truth" (Veritatis Splendor)[2] published by Pope John Paul II, in 1993. This book discusses the very important relationship between truth, genuine human freedom, and natural law. The

Pope said that "although each individual has a right to be respected in his own journey in search of truth, there exists a prior moral obligation and a grave one at that, to seek the truth and to adhere to it once it is known". This is the duty of conscience. Human freedom can never create values which would be superior to truth. In other words, truth must be first, and the attainment of true freedom follows from and depends on truth. Otherwise truth would become a creation of freedom. Freedom thus finds its' authentic and complete fulfilment in the acceptance of moral law, which in turn is based on natural law. Therefore, the bottom line is, that if this natural law does really mark the boundary of freedom given by God to humanity, then accepting the principles of secularism as a basis for morality, is taking the road to falsehood, madness, and self-destruction.

Just before he became Pope Benedict XVI, Cardinal Joseph Ratzinger commented on the great changes in doctrines and ideologies which the world has experienced in recent decades. He said that we are, "flung from one extreme to another: from Marxism to liberalism, even to libertinism (no morals): from collectivism to radical individualism: from atheism to a vague religious mysticism: from agnosticism to syncretism (fusion of different beliefs) and so forth." He further said that, "We are building a dictatorship of relativism, that does not recognize anything as definitive, and whose ultimate goal consists solely of one's own ego and desires." Failure to recognize the responsibility that goes with freedom and the consequences of not basing our morality on natural law is, therefore, the great problem for our modern human society.

The Great Deception

The great deception for humanity is that, although the promoters of the One World Order appear to simply want to create a peaceful and prosperous world, based on a secular value system, which ignores God, they are very much aware of the major spiritual aspects of their plan. Preparations first began with Adam Weishaupt, who established a secret society called the Twelve Just Men, later known as the Illuminati, in Bavaria in 1776. The objectives of this society were:

1. The abolition of ordered government

2. Abolition of private property

3. Abolition of the family

4. Abolition of religion

5. Creation of a World Government

The Illuminati played a major role in organising the French revolution, through infiltration of Freemason lodges in France. The world-wide influence of this organization has grown dramatically since then. The insignia of the Order of the Illuminati first appeared on the reverse side of U.S. one-dollar bills in 1933 (see page 213). Gradually nationality is becoming less and less significant and the object now is a One World Order with total control of human affairs. Religious control is planned to come under the New World Religion, recently established with support from the UN, from a conglomeration of the major world religions.

While the Illuminati and other secret societies were making plans for a New World Order based on a rejection of God, the God of Christians was at the same time, encouraging humanity to reject these plans. Over the last two centuries many public and private revelations have been given regarding the time that we are now living in. The leader chosen, for this battle against this proposed One World Order, is The Blessed Virgin Mary, mother of Jesus. This is particularly apparent over the last half century through a great increase in Heavenly prophetic messages, especially from The

Virgin Mary. An army of Catholic priests (one estimate is 100,000) has been established under the banner of "The Marian Movement of Priests", who have been given specific details on the problems ahead, through locutions (A locution is a mystical concept, recognized by various religions, including the Roman Catholic Church, whereby an individual gets a direct communication from God) to Don Stefano Gobbi, in Italy. This movement is widely known and respected in Catholic circles throughout the world, with many lay supporters meeting quietly at regular weekly or monthly "Cenacles" to pray and read from the prophetic Blue Book.[3] Few non Catholics would be aware of these preparations.

It is notable, perhaps, as time goes on that, The Virgin Mary could be more easily accepted as a spiritual leader by followers of Islam, than by Jews, or many Protestant Christians, neither of which have any devotion to Mary. Many say that Mary, through her famous message at Fatima, Portugal, 1917 (Fatima was the daughter of the founder of Islam) and her appearances in Zeitun, Cairo, Egypt, 1968 (where a Muslim was the first person to receive a miraculous cure, (see page 152) and through a recent string of lesser manifestations of Mary to individuals in Islamic countries, will be a big influence in bringing followers of Islam and Christians together.

The Attitude of Rome

It is important to understand the attitude of the Roman Catholic Church leadership to recent well known alleged supernatural revelations. The Catholic Church would claim to deal with certainties rather than with probabilities or possibilities. Private revelations generally, are usually regarded as worthy of belief only after much detailed investigations, which usually take many years. This approach has come from centuries of experience, and the knowledge that sometimes, even the most authentic visionaries can make serious errors, or can drift into error, after starting out as authentic. It is, therefore, very rare for any revelation to get any kind of official approval, before well substantiated supernatural phenomena, in keeping with Church teaching, have accompanied these revelations. This is particularly true regarding the major revelations of the last half century, where there are two extra good reasons to be cautious. Firstly, these revelations deal with events which are so enormous, as to become world changing, in a manner never before experienced by humanity and secondly, there were suggestions that the behaviour of some clergy, which included Bishops and Cardinals, was leading many astray. The latter is hardly a pleasing message for the Church authority to promote. Presenting this kind of information publicly is also full of dangers for misunderstandings, misinterpretation and even manipulation. This explains the resistance of the official Catholic Church to make any statements on these events, and when statements are made, the language is very carefully measured. It would be wrong to assume on that basis, however, that there is no knowledge, no credence, or no conviction, from the higher Church authorities on these matters. They are very much aware of, and have studied in great detail, the many recent alleged Divine revelations, explaining what is to come in the near future.

Generally, it is true to say that the better informed, and the more senior the Church authority is, then the more understanding and credence that is likely to be given to these major modern prophetic messages. This is an important fact to recognize, not only for ordinary lay Catholics, but also for those outside the Church, who may be inclined to regard the phenomena of Medjugorje and lesser known Marian revelations, as of interest to the lunatic fringe only. There is no doubt that Pope John Paul II was convinced of the seriousness of these times. In Philadelphia, as a Cardinal, in 1976, he said:

"We are now standing in the greatest confrontation humanity has ever experienced. I do not think the wide circle of the

American Society, or the wide circle of the Christian Community, realise this fully. **We are now facing the final confrontation between the Church and the anti-church, between the Gospel and the anti-gospel, between Christ and the Antichrist. This confrontation lies within the plans of Divine Providence. It is therefore in God's plan, and it must be a trial which the Church must take up and face courageously".**[4] A few years later in Fulda, Germany after being elected Pope he said, **"We must prepare ourselves to suffer great trials before long, such as will demand a disposition to give up even life, with a total dedication to Christ and for Christ. With our prayers it is possible to mitigate the coming tribulation, but it is no longer possible to avert it, because only thus can the Church be effectively renewed. How many times has the renewal of the Church sprung from the shedding of blood? This time too, it will not be otherwise".**[5]

Pope Benedict XVI, from his previous position, as Cardinal in charge of the Doctrine of the Faith Office, was involved directly with the message of Akita in Japan, 1976, which is one of the most extraordinary supernatural warnings ever given to mankind directly from God (see page 172). He was also involved in the approval of Betania, Venezuela (see page 91) and in removing Medjugorje (see page 164) from the authority of the local Bishop. Pope Benedict was a close confidant of Pope John Paul II. He is well aware of the recent warnings of The Virgin Mary. He is also likely to be very aware that some Catholic prophecy suggests that he may have to leave Rome, "for fear of the wolves".

There is no doubt that Pope Francis is acutely aware of the "end times" battle between secularism and Christianity, which is going on at this time. He has encouraged, on a number of public occasions, the reading of the 1907 novel, *Lord of the World*, by Robert Hugh Benson. This book describes a final battle between Humanism and Catholicism or between the Antichrist and the

Pope. In the novel, the Antichrist is a political peace maker, who becomes the leader of Europe and then of the world, and is promoted as the only individual who can bring peace to a very troubled world. He then sets about destroying religion under the banner of tolerance and truth. Pope Francis recognizes that this novel corresponds with many aspects of the transformation of society which has gradually occurred over the last century. He also recognizes that it is an endgame from which there can be only one winner. He has not told us when he believes this final battle will reach a climax, or if he thinks that he personally will be involved in the final stages, but he did say a few years ago, that he only expected to survive a few short years.

Who Else Knows?

Only very few are aware of how serious the world situation is right now. It is difficult to believe that we are on the brink of the most incredible upheavals in the history of humanity and only a tiny minority have any idea of what is going on. These events will be world shattering and world transforming. Each individual will experience these extraordinary phenomena and will be profoundly changed by them. God is about to reclaim control of humanity, but this will be preceded by unprecedented natural and man-made disasters, combined with supernatural interventions.

There are many reasons for this lack of awareness. In the first place, the information is restricted largely to those of the Catholic believers who have an interest in this subject, and to those who access information on recent revealed supernatural Catholic messages. This is a relatively small number of people and who generally like to keep their own counsel on this subject. Although the official Church authorities are well aware of these predictions, little is said for reasons explained above. The information, by its nature, is complex and needs a lot of study to get some idea of the message being promulgated and the different layers of reliability, on the various issues. Even then, many will disagree. Many clergy will know and believe in various aspects of these messages, but due to the complexity and "the cloud of unknowing", which always prevents a clear view of the supernatural, they generally decide for silence in public, or maybe – a pray, hope and don't worry attitude.

Many Catholic lay people and others, who have heard of some of the details of these recent Catholic revelations, either show just a passing interest, or disregard the stories as nonsense, typical of extreme religious views, and peripheral to any serious thinking or teaching. Intellectuals, particularly if non-Catholic, would usually frown and scoff at the whole idea of private revelation, as nothing more than the imagination of fools, to be completely ignored. Others, who may be inclined to put some credence on these stories, ignore them due to the fear of becoming upset, which would result from concentrating on the predicted major problems ahead. The commonest attitude by far among lay Catholics, is that the future is too uncertain, and worrying about it will not help, as we can do nothing about it anyway. There are also the busy life styles which sap energy and leave little time for considering spiritual predictions. The lack of certainty about the timing of future predicted events also compares unfavourably with the more certain secular daily timetables. Finally the views and attitudes of the majority are usually fed by the mainstream media, which only rarely reports on these events, and then usually, with a strong anti-Catholic bias.

There is a great emphasis now, especially in industry, science, and medicine, to have important decisions based on evidence, rather than on vague opinions. Evidence based decisions, however, form only a very small part of most of life's routines. Attitudes towards God and religious beliefs, in particular, are unfortunately based more on a mixture of influences, such as, upbringing, emotions, mass media, and various life experiences, rather than any critical analysis of easily accessible evidence. Many drift through life, with no deep conviction on the need to be in tune with God. Most of us, in one way or another, tend to get stuck in ruts of routine work, routine thinking, and routine attitudes. These ruts usually get deeper as the hair gets greyer and our decisions become more and more automatic. The objective of most of us is to have hassle free living, in a comfortable environment, in so far as this is possible within life's lottery of circumstances. For most, the problems of tomorrow will not be very different from the problems of yesterday and a common view is that nothing important in the world ever really changes. This is wonderfully summarized in the old Irish proverb which says, "Imeoidh a dtiocfaidh mar a dimigh a dtáinigh riamh" (everything that will come will go, as everything which has ever come has gone). In this context Divine revelations, international conspiracy theories, and deep philosophical discussions on the difference between good and evil, are usually far from the minds of those who are trying to pay the bills, trying to make ends meet, or struggling to keep the children safe and happy.

There comes a time, however, when scepticism, complacency, lack of time, and lack of interest must give way to evidence and urgency. One of the principal reasons for writing this book is to try to convince readers that human society has now reached this critical time or tipping point, when, in order to survive, we need to start paying a lot more attention to the reality of God.

The mainstream media seems to be completely out of tune concerning the significance of this battle between secularism and belief in God. It is likely that the average reporter, trying to do a job, represents no more than a cross section of views and attitudes in society. At the editorial level, however, it would be foolish not to recognize that the media is very controlled. The masses are fed news fodder and reporting on many news items is very selective. The anti-Catholic bias is not hard to find, as for example the efforts made to portray Opus Dei as a secret society, which it is not, whereas the real secret societies, with world-wide control of finance, and with a very powerful influence on world media and politics, never get a mention. We are hearing a lot in the media now about a global food crisis with various factors being blamed. We are very unlikely, however, to hear mention of the GM terminator seeds which have been widely promoted in the poor countries by multinational corporations, (which will not reproduce, and thus have to be purchased each year, at great expense, by the poor farmers - Seeds of Destruction[6]), as a contributing factor to this food crisis (see page 223).We are also very unlikely to hear about the tetanus vaccine which contained the female hormone, Human Chorionic Gonadotrophin (HCG). This was promoted by the World Health Organization and others, for young females (not males) in some poor countries, ostensibly to prevent tetanus. This vaccine, however, also had the effect of making it difficult for these young women to bear children. This scandal was exposed by a Catholic Mexican prolife group, but was not reported in the mainstream media (see page 225). This control of the media by international secret groups is considered in some detail by Daniel Estulin in his book, *The true Story of the Bilderberg Group.*[7]

The vast majority, therefore, are now completely unaware of the enormous global implications which will result from world governments adopting secular principles, instead of natural law, as a basis for morality. I have tried to list some of the many reasons why something so important, and indeed catastrophic for humanity, is never discussed publicly, and only very rarely in private. I collectively refer to these reasons as the "Fuzz Factor", for want of a more appropriate term. In this fuzz factor, there is also a complex mixture of human behavioural traits, such as, pride, prejudice, fear, too much caution, lack of trust etc., which ultimately are creating a fog of confusion, hiding the truth, and locking humanity in a cul de sac of self-destruction. A significant part of this fuzz factor is just lack of knowledge, lack of insight and lack of faith. We are all deficient in these.

2. A Tale of Two Cities

*"It was the best of times, it was the worst of times, it was the age of wisdom, it was the age of foolishness, it was the epoch of belief, it was the epoch of incredulity, it was the season of Light, it was the season of Darkness, it was the spring of hope, it was the winter of despair, we had **everything before us, we had nothing before us, we were all going direct** to Heaven, we were all going direct the other way - in short, the period was so far like the present period, that some of its noisiest authorities insisted on its being received, for good or for evil, in the superlative degree of comparison only."*

Such were the opening words of the famous novel, *A Tale of Two Cities,* by Charles Dickens, written in 1859 and set in London and Paris before and during the French Revolution.

It seems to be a great irony of the struggle for human progress and development that many periods in the history of humanity can be described in this manner. There is always this struggle of contradictions between the right way and the wrong way, between confusion and insight, between success and failure, between greed and generosity, between light and darkness, and between good and evil. This should hardly surprise us, since society, at different times in history, is just a reflection and a collective summation within each individual as they struggle to achieve progress and fulfilment in life. There is a struggle and a searching drive in most of us to be a success rather than a failure, while at the same time to be happy and joyful in what we do. There is also in each of us an inbuilt conscience, which drives us to choose good rather than evil, but unfortunately, the good can often get sacrificed on the altar of success and greed, which results in a broken and confused society.

We are now in a time when change and the potential for change is becoming exponential. Never before have developments in science and medicine been so rapid, so innovative and so rewarding. The developments in new methods of communications have been mesmerizing, especially over recent decades. Rapid information retrieval is a product of these new communication technologies and this forms a great basis for further rapid developments in all fields of research. Human ability and ingenuity in various interest areas can now be channelled and combined to make the world a collection of global cyber villages, connected by information technology pathways. These cyber villages have experts in the various fields from various parts of the world collaborating and assisting each other as if working in the same room. The more humanity progresses in knowledge and technological development, therefore, so the more these forces create a uniting of thought processes and a development of new, better, and more efficient ways of doing things, which can be beneficial to everybody.

Meanwhile, as progress with new technology is exploding, so too a dark side is being manifested. At this time our world also seems to have reached new heights with greed, selfishness, dishonesty, and general disregard for law. It could be said that, for whatever reason, our standards of morality have never been as low. The general promotion of money and prosperity as the first requirement for success has driven this greed and selfishness at the expense of consideration for others. The growth in technology has also compounded this and the result is that, with the cut-throat or 'survival of the fittest' attitude operating in the global environment, more and more wealth and power is being channelled towards less and less organizations and less and less people. The few are becoming all powerful. The demon of money is bestowing enormous influence on select individuals and organizations. At the same time, through the ready access to information technology and military resources, the demon of war is bestowing frightening destructive power on those countries that are controlled by belligerent leaders, as well as to rogue organizations and terrorists. In recognizing, therefore, that this kind of progress is inevitable in our modern human global environment as information and knowledge is now collected and analysed at exponential speed, we must also recognize that the struggle between good and evil is ever present. Going forward in this 21st century this human struggle seems to be getting more acute and polarized. In many ways things have now never been as good, while in other ways things have never been so bad. The big question now must be: where will it all end? Quo Vadimus?

Where are we going?

There was another story written about a tale of two cities. This one was written almost fifteen hundred years before the tale by Charles Dickens and it has become even more famous. This was not just one book but a twenty two volume set, called *The City of God*, written by St Augustine of Hippo in the fifth century, after the conquest of Rome in 410 A.D. It was written at the time when Romans were blaming the Christians of that city for their defeat by the Visigoths. St Augustine argued that Christianity sustained Rome and that it was the failure of the population to respond appropriately to Christianity that led to the collapse of Rome. This book presents human history as the on-going struggle between good and evil and as a struggle between the City of God and the earthly City of Man. This large volume set of The City of God has become recognised over the centuries as one of the foundations for Western philosophical thought and today it speaks to us more loudly and clearly than at any time in history.

George Orwell once said that, "People can foresee the future only when it coincides with their own wishes, and the most grossly obvious facts can be ignored when they are unwelcome." This present day society is crumbling but it is surprising how few recognise the signs. Most think that it is business as usual but it is far from that. How bad it will get is difficult to say but there is a significant danger of implosion with complete global chaos. Over the last decade in particular, the final confrontation between secularism and Christianity will become global, more focused and more acute. Secularism is pushing moral relativism under the banner of tolerance and at the same time is becoming more and more intolerant of Christianity. In a talk given in Washington (May 2016), Cardinal Sarah said that we were witnessing the consummation of the efforts to build a utopian paradise on earth but without God. He said, "The death of God results in the burial of good, beauty, love and truth. Good becomes evil, beauty is ugly, love becomes the satisfaction of sexual primal instincts, and truths are all relative…. All manner of immorality is not only accepted and tolerated today in advanced societies, but even promoted as a social good. The result is hostility to Christians, and increasingly religious persecution… This is not an ideological war between competing ideas. This is about defending ourselves, our children, and future generations, from a demonic ideology that says children do not need mothers and fathers. It denies human nature and wants to cut off entire generations from God." At the same meeting Mr Paul Ryan, Speaker of the US House of Representatives said, "When faith is ruled out of bounds, then happiness itself is being placed out of reach. There is a spiritual void that needs be filled…"

Background to the Present

Western civilization and society was built on Christianity. Even during the so called Dark Ages, when monarchs, princes and powerful landlords tried to subdue the populace and keep them ignorant, the monasteries kept Christian principles and scholarship alive and later formed the basis for the beginnings of universities. The French Revolution was a national rejection of Christian worship and teaching. Separation of Church and State can be good but only provided that the state recognizes that for man-made laws to be valid, they must be subject to natural law, and inalienable human rights can never be abrogated by a state. This rejection by the French Revolution of the respect for inalienable human rights was taken one step further by Marxism, which proposed the abolition of all religions, abolition of rights of inheritance and putting all land and property under the control of the state.

After the Russian Revolution in 1917 efforts were made to export this communist revolution to Western Europe, but all these efforts were quickly crushed, especially in Poland and Germany. Two apostles of Marxism recognized the reason for this failure. The first was the Hungarian, Georg Lukacs. At that time, he was a commissioner for culture in Bella Kun's Hungarian government. He believed that the acceptance of Marxism could only come about by first annihilating the old Christian values and replacing them with new ones. He thus started what became known as "cultural terrorism" in Hungary. He concentrated particularly on radical sex education in the schools and he promoted prostitution in order to destroy family life. His ideas were not accepted in Hungary at that time but were enthusiastically promoted in Western countries fifty years later.

In 1921, four years after the Russian Communist revolution, an Italian Marxist, Antonio Gramsci, also tried to start a similar revolution in Italy but he too failed. He identified three main reasons for his failure. These were Christianity, nationalism and charity. He also realised that violence was not the answer. He recognized that after almost 2,000 years Christianity was embedded as the dominant moral and philosophical way of life in Europe and the Americas. He said that Marxists must first de-Christianize the West. The moral principles controlling the culture had to be changed for Communism to be accepted. Gramsci then set about planning a new way to conquer the West for Communism. His methods are now often referred to as *Cultural Marxism.* It was to depend on deception, infiltration and undermining the cultural pillars of society. Politics, media, education, the law, family and religion would be the prime focus for attention and infiltration. Gramsci asked for "a long march through the institutions to capture the citadels of the culture." This was to be a gentle, anonymous revolution, without arms or bloodshed. Everything should be done under the banner of human dignity, human rights and tolerance. He encouraged his Marxist associates to form links with Western intellectuals who had similar contempt for Christian teachings. The people should be trained eventually to despise the claims and constraints of Christianity.

The Frankfurt School

In 1923, Georg Lukacs, with the help of German Communists, established an Institute for Marxism in the University of Frankfurt. The name was later changed to the Institute for Social Research, to make it less provocative. The old approach to promoting power by the use of violence, as in the French and Russian Revolutions was now discarded. Marxists were now beginning to fight Western culture rather than Capitalism. In 1930, the Marxist, Max Horkheimer, became the director and under his direction the war against Western culture began seriously. Anything which promoted Marxism was promoted as moral and as President Ronald Reagan later famously said, referring to the Soviets, "They reserved to themselves the right to lie, steal and cheat." Horkheimer was joined by the music critic Theodor Adorno, by the psychologist Eric Fromm, and by the sociologist Wilhelm Reich. An early graduate student was Herbert Marcuse, who was to become one of the leaders in the US. This occurred after the Institute was forced to leave Germany in 1933 with the advent of Hitler, when Jews and Marxists became undesirables. Columbia University, in

New York City, became the new home for the Frankfurt school. Frankfurt and New York, therefore, are the two cities forever linked to this infamous and insidious Marxist propaganda school which over the last century, has played a major role in destroying the culture of Western Christianity. It was developed in Frankfurt and nurtured in New York.

In the US, Marcuse progressed rapidly from a teacher's aide in Columbia University, to being one of the heads of the secret service during World War II. When the Frankfurt school developed a new psychological discussion technique, known as the "Critical Theory", Marcuse became an enthusiastic promoter of this as a way of surreptitiously promoting Marxism. The Critical Theory was based on promoting a destructive criticism of all aspects of Western culture, with the object of encouraging everybody who took part in the studies to reject completely all traditional morality and values. Parental authority was undermined by encouraging children to accept the opinions of teachers and school psychologists rather than parents. Christianity, authority, the family, tradition, chastity, nationalism, patriotism, loyalty, etc. were all targeted. A critique of gender was used to encourage the perceived differences between sexes to be blurred. Male superiority in all its aspects was suppressed and radical feminism was promoted. Western society was accused of racism, fascism, Nazism, anti-Semitism, xenophobia, genocide etc. Critical Theory also promoted pessimism, hopelessness and despair, so that traditional ways of life would be rejected.

In his book, *Eros and Civilization*, Marcuse promoted sex and drugs and encouraged all to embrace the *pleasure principle*, in order to create a "polymorphous perversity". The abolition of the family became a prime objective as it was regarded as a dictatorship, promoting injustice and sexism. Feminists began to widely promote hostility to marriage and the family. By the 1960's,

Marcuse was a cult figure and he was known as the Father of the New Left. In 1968, French students carried banners through Paris with the slogan, "Marx, Mao and Marcuse".

In the meantime, Theodor Odorno worked on the cultural subversion of music, especially for films and television. Music, he said, should reflect the marginalized in society. A whole entertainment promotion was designed to promote Marxists ideas. It was not just drinking alcohol while at the late night clubs, but video games and artistic promotions associating music and violence were also developed. Psychedelic drugs were then also used to encourage this cultural revolution and the rejection of Christianity. Adorno also supported the view that what was needed for the success of Marxism was psychological conditioning rather than philosophical argument. Children in American schools were sensitized to accept a new morality. Teachers were directed to put more emphasis on teaching attitudes rather than facts or skills. So called, *Life Skills*, courses became premature sex education programmes, laden with psychological pornography, rather than teaching about first-aid, plumbing, electricity, carpentry, clothes design, public speaking, computer skills, financial management and a host of other subjects, all of which would offer useful skills for life. Eventually American graduates were the most *sexualized sensitized illiterates* in the world. Other countries would follow suit later.

Patrick J. Buchanan is well known in political and public affair circles in the US and ran for the Republican Presidential nomination in 1992 and 1996. In his book, *The Death of The West*[8], he details how the four individuals, Lukacs, Gramsci, Adorno and Marcuse, through the Frankfurt school, played a hugely significant role in promoting and building an anti – Western culture all over America. He listed four important reasons why he believed that this cultural Marxism promoted by the Frankfurt school was so successful in the US during the 1960's. I summarize these as follows:

1. The first was the flowering of anti-Capitalist and anti-Christian views among many intellectuals in American society at this time. Notable among these were the supporters of Margaret Sanger, founder of *Planned Parenthood* (*Planned Parenthood* has grown to become a global provider of abortion services and has reached new notoriety recently through revelations detailing its business of selling body parts, harvested from aborted babies). Sanger once said, "I look forward to see humanity free someday, from the tyranny of Christianity".

2. Universities were being filled at that time with affluent spoiled young people who never knew shortage, hardship, or war. Boredom encouraged sex, narcotics and revolution.

3. The advent and progression of television services was used to promote the tactics and triumphs of radicals and revolutionaries.

4. The Vietnam War. The young students had no interest in becoming war heroes and wanted nothing to do with sacrifice or bloodshed. Marcuse coined the slogan, "Make Love, Not War" and he gave the young intellectuals a moral reason for draft dodging and a respectable cover for cowardice.

Buchanan quotes Oscar Wilde who said that "America is the only country that has gone from barbarism to decadence without civilization in between." The kindness of the Americans, however, in accepting the refugees from the Frankfurt school was rewarded with the lethal poison of *Cultural Marxism.* This was later exported from the US, to other nations all over the world.

Feminine Cultural Marxism: Mallory Millett wrote an article for *Frontpage Magazine* in 2014, in which she described the damage done to family life in the US by her Marxist sister, Kate Millett, with the assistance of her radical feminist friends. This article was later highlighted by a book, *Their Angry Creed*, written by Herbert Purdy (herbertpurdy.com) in the UK (LPS publishing, June 2016) and by the *"Alive"* newspaper (December 2016, Dublin, Ireland). Mallory Millett described how she attended a radical feminist meeting referred to as a "conscious-raising-group" at the invitation of her sister, in the US, in 1969. The meeting began with the following litany:

"Why are we here today? To make revolution.

What kind of revolution? The Cultural Revolution.

And how do we make the Cultural Revolution? By destroying the American family.

How do we destroy the family? By destroying the American Patriarch.

And how do we destroy the American Patriarch? By taking away his power.

How do we do that? By destroying monogamy

How can we destroy monogamy? By promoting promiscuity, eroticism, prostitution and homosexuality."

They then continued to discuss how Western society could be deconstructed by invading every American institution with these radical feminist revolutionary ideas. Her sister, Kate Millett, wrote books promoting radical feminism and these books became required reading in women's study courses across the US nation. Young college girls were taught that their fathers were villains and that their mothers were fools for allowing men to enslave them into the barbaric practices of monogamy, family life, and motherhood, when they could be enjoying life to the fullest and having abortions when and if necessary. It is not difficult to see the similarity with the sexual promiscuity promoted by the Marxists, Georg Lukacs (in Hungary) and Gramsci (in Italy) in the early 1920s – (see above). Kate was promoted on the cover of Time magazine and celebrated as "the Karl Marx of the Women's movement". Radical feminism was and is nothing more than cultural Marxism, promoted by women, driven by misandry (hatred of men). Herbert Purdy argues that radical feminism is the most far-reaching, divisive, and socially corrosive ideology that civilized nations have ever encountered. He condemns it for what it is doing to children and especially for the damage it is doing to boys.

Saul Alinsky (1909 – 72)

Saul David Alinsky was an American who became famous for his community work within African-American ghettos, beginning in Chicago and then in New York, California and many other locations in the US. Although Alinsky was always *his own man* and he shied away from joining specific organizations, he was heavily influenced by Gramski's ideas. He developed many new unorthodox methods for changing society. His ideas on methods for changing the world from what it is to what he believed it should have been were widely promoted in some political circles. He is considered to have been one of the most influential community leaders in the US over the last century and influenced many well-known politicians in all parties. In 1971 he published the book, *Rules for Radicals,* describing new approaches to change, which he had learned through his life. He said that his book was written for radicals instructing them how to take away power from those who had it. These methods became very popular, particularly among the leaders of the Democrats in the US. Barak Obama and Hillary

Clinton were avid students of his methods. During the 1960's Hillary Clinton wrote a thesis on his work for Wellesley College. It is of interest that at the end of this book, Alinsky gave an "over the shoulder" acknowledgement to Lucifer, the greatest radical of all. In an interview with *Playboy* magazine he said that, if there was an afterlife, he would choose to go to Hell because he had spent all his life working for have-nots. In Hell the have-nots have no virtue and he would work for those. It is not for us to judge him and he may have started his early campaigns out of real concern for the poor and deprived, but let us hope for his sake, that his motives were based on love rather than hate, or that he appreciated his mistakes and repented before it was too late, and that his twisted thinking did not eventually lead him into Hell. He was of Jewish origin but was a non-believer.

Where are we now?

We are now at one of the most divisive periods of world history. The struggle between good and evil is about to reach an end game. Pope Benedict XVI pointed out that Judas Iscariot, who betrayed Jesus was "neither a master of evil or the figure of a demonical power of darkness but rather a sycophant (one who uses flattery to win favour with those who have power or influence), who bows down before the anonymous power of changing moods and current fashion." The same anonymous power of evil is now pushing our globalised society deeper and deeper into immorality. This anonymous power is driven by surreptitious Marxism, secularism, humanism, political and media manipulation, misinformation, religious extremism, political correctness, moral relativism, and above all by the power of money in promoting secret agendas driven by secret societies.

For a Marxist, Gramsci's ideas for cultural hegemony, which he expounded in his 800 page book called *The Prison Notebooks*, when he was put into prison by Mussolini, have now blossomed into a brilliant success story. Most of all, this is because Marxism is not now even recognised as the driving force behind the great anti-God and particularly anti-Christian transformation of the Western culture over the last century. Through this plan, promoted by the Frankfurt school, the Christian moral standards of society have now been virtually completely destroyed. Secularization and liberalization of the churches and society has progressed rapidly and humanistic and New-Age programmes are now advertised regularly in church halls and meeting rooms. God is being ignored, pushed aside, and replaced. The West is awash with Gramsci's new *Cultural Marxism* under various pseudonyms and the people love it. What Marx failed to do with force, Gramsci succeeded with psychology and subterfuge.

It is ironic that at this time also there are great signs that Russia has recognized the folly of Marxism. President Putin promotes Christianity openly and is rumoured to wear a scapular as a sign of consecration to The Virgin Mary. He attends religious conferences and goes on Orthodox Christian retreats. At this time in Russia, hundreds of Christian churches and monasteries are re-opening and new ones are being built. Crucifixes are appearing in classrooms, the new nuclear submarines have chapels for regular Mass services, and army chaplains are regularly seen in public blessing various aspects of Russian armed forces. Homosexual activity is rejected as immoral and abortion is being made illegal. It would be foolish to consider that President Putin is a saint, but for whatever reason, Christianity is being promoted at this time in Russia, rather than being repressed, as it was in the US (before Trump). The recent history of the largest Orthodox Cathedral in Moscow, as explained below, confirms this change of attitude.

Cathedral of Christ The Saviour in Moscow: On 25th December 1812, Emperor Alexander I announced his intention to build what was a magnificent edifice as a thanksgiving to Christ The Saviour for saving Moscow from Napoleon. It was demolished in 1930 by Stalin to make way for what was to be *The Palace of Soviets*, which was designed as the tallest building in the world at that time (415 metres going to 495 metres with an antenna). Despite many efforts, however, no structure was ever built in place of the cathedral and the site was subsequently used for many years as a large swimming pool. When Marxism was rejected by the recent Russian Government, the construction of a new cathedral was approved. This was opened on the feast of The Transfiguration, 19th August, 2000. President Putin was subsequently very upset when, on 21st February 2012, some young women desecrated this building by dancing and singing inappropriately in the sanctuary, - the so called "Pussy Riot" punk rock group. They rapidly found themselves with extended periods in prison for their misdeed. Putin said that they undermined the moral foundation of the state and got what they deserved.

Can the West be saved?

There are many signs given to us that confirm the truth of Christianity. Humanity, at this time, is largely blind to these signs. When individuals and nations reject Christian teaching, especially if they had already been Christian, then without repentance, the inevitable result will be destruction, pain, suffering, sorrow and war among nations. There is no other way back. The first nation to reject Christianity was Israel and it is still suffering because of it. Ireland is an example of a nation now rejecting Christianity, after many centuries of Catholicism, and it too will suffer for this rejection. We are called to love God and love each other, within the confines of natural law. *In the end, every knee will bow, and every tongue confess, that Jesus Christ is Lord.* Jesus Christ is a God of the "Beatitudes", a God of pure humility and love. We can take the easy way or the hard way. The West has chosen the hard way which is the way of suffering. It is amazing how many turn back to

God through suffering and pain but it is very sad that it has to be this way.

Things have now gone too far. The whole cultural edifice must now collapse. In the US, it took a depression and a war to stop the *Roaring Twenties*. It will probably take a bigger depression and a bigger war to stop the secular, selfish, corrupt, immoral, survival of the fittest, debt ridden, derivative driven, murderous and 'free for all' attitude, that we have at the moment. Everything will soon collapse and then will come the great rebuilding. This old order must pass away, hopefully even before it becomes the planned 'one world order'. The good will then have to task themselves with building a new society and a new culture from the bottom up. It will have to be a society based on truth, justice and goodness. The good news is that even in these times, when evil seems to be in the ascendancy on all fronts, there are still many reasons to hope and to be confident. In the end we will be rescued and as Pope Benedict XVI said during Easter 2012, "Life is stronger than death. Good is stronger than evil. Love is stronger than hate. Truth is stronger than lies."

3. Re-building Society

"It is a characteristic of any decaying civilization that the great masses of the people are unaware of the tragedy. Humanity in a crisis is generally insensitive to the gravity of the times in which it lives. Men do not want to believe their own times are wicked, partly because they have no standard outside of themselves by which to measure their times. If there is no fixed concept of justice, how shall men know it is violated? Only those who live by faith really know what is happening in the world: the great masses without faith are unconscious of the destructive processes going on, because they have lost the vision of the heights from which they have fallen."

Archbishop Fulton J. Sheen

A just society must be built on truth and charity, with a legal system which recognizes truth and promotes justice with charity. Truth is based on evidence and we all have an obligation in conscience to seek the truth. He who seeks, finds. It is now a very popular approach, in secular society, to promote actions and solutions to problems that are *evidence based*. When it comes to how our lives are lived, however, our feelings often take over from evidence. Many may feel that Hell does not exist, but is this just wishful thinking trying to answer the most crucial question of all for every person, and have those who don't believe in Hell looked at the evidence?

Two pillars which support a just society are:

A. **An appreciation why morality must be absolute rather than relative.**

B. **Sound philosophical principles which define, promote, and support authentic morality.**

A. Natural Law & Morality – Absolute or Relative?

Natural Law: Human nature is rational. An individual finds natural law by use of his reason in drawing conclusions about his own nature. Individuals are equipped by nature to form judgments on rules of conduct. Individuals can compare their own conduct and the conduct of others with their natural demands and the natural demands of others and decide what is morally good and what would make a good law for society to adopt. Natural law, therefore, consists of the judgments of practical reason on what should be done and what should not be done. The terms, "natural law" and "moral law" are often used interchangeably. When natural law is accepted in society and established in a legal framework it becomes positive law.

A problem arises, however, when there is a disagreement of opinion on matters of morality. The first step in solving this dilemma is to recognise that natural law has precepts, with different degrees of importance in relation to caring for the welfare of humanity. There will always be different levels of understanding and knowledge of these precepts or principles within society. The more general the principles are, then the more impossible it becomes for ordinary people to avoid knowing them. Thus the first moral principle which every individual will know directly from human nature and human reason is founded on the nature of "good". This means that the first principle of natural law, therefore, is all things must seek after good. Good must be promoted and done and evil must be avoided. The different levels of natural law are explained in some detail in the book, *Right and Reason*.[9]

There are other common principles which follow from the first principle that are commonly regarded as moral axioms. Examples of some of these would be, "Treat others fairly", "Do not kill",

"Care for your children", etc. No person of normal mental maturity can fail to know and understand these. Young children and adults with mental incapacity may fail to appreciate these principles. Adequate moral education can also be important, however, and some normal adults may be victims of defective or perverted moral training and fail to understand these moral axioms.

There are also other more subtle or hidden conclusions which are derived from the first principle of natural law by reason, but sometimes this can be a complicated process. The conclusions are certain, however, and the logic is perfect, but the reasoning can be long and involved. The mind can be easily side-tracked through confusion or prejudice. Such questions as suicide, euthanasia, polygamy, promiscuity, contraception, and divorce would fit into this category. Some modern writers call these tertiary precepts, while others, more in line with St Thomas Aquinas, call them secondary precepts. Others still just call them remote conclusions of natural law. Well educated individuals can sometimes be wrong in their conclusions from a study of statistics, medicine, science, history, etc. So we see likewise that well educated people can also be mistaken and confused in this area of understanding natural or moral law, when contradictory conclusions seem equally plausible. This is mainly due to defective moral education: hence a proper grounding in ethics, logic and philosophy should be the basis for a good education system.

Finally, it is important to understand that natural law is intrinsically unchangeable. There can never be an exemption or a dispensation from this law as it is part of human nature and is in complete harmony with it. No state or government can make laws that can be considered valid, but which are contrary to this natural or moral law. Laws contrary to natural law, which are enacted by governments, will, therefore, be a destructive force in efforts to create an honest, good, happy, and humane society.

A Refutation of Relativism

Pope Benedict XVI warned many times about moral relativism. Moral relativism proclaims that good and evil are man-made and therefore that there is no objective good or evil. Relativism rejects absolute truth and absolute morality. Peter Kreeft[10] believes that no society has survived after it has made the mistake of accepting moral relativism. He also says that an honest moral atheist is more religious than a relativistic churchgoer. The idea that you can do anything you wish if it feels good, is not acceptable, simply because doing evil deeds can feel good to some.

Kreeft has developed some arguments as to why morality must be absolute rather than relative. He listed these arguments as follows:

1. **Consequence**

2. **Consensus**

3. **Experience**

4. **Moral Argument**

5. **Logical Self Contradiction**

6. **Practical Self Contradiction**

Kreeft believes that although these arguments get more abstract as we progress from 1 to 6, they also get more forceful and stronger in the same order as they are more and more based on formal logic rather than on reason.

1. **Consequence:** Many believe that absolute moral values are wrong because that leads to intolerance, and this is a bad

consequence. Kreeft on the other hand believes that absolutism grounds tolerance better than relativism. He believes that relativism is tolerant of evil and not of people or contrary opinions. Those who may want to do evil must tolerate similar behaviour in others, lest they be accused of hypocrisy. He agrees with G. K. Chesterton who said that tolerance is the one value you have left when you have lost all principles. The consequences of moral absolutism is "doing the right thing", whereas the consequences of moral relativism is "do whatever you feel like" as the deterrent is removed. The former makes saints and the latter makes sinners. No saint has been a moral relativist and likewise no saintly society has ever been based on moral relativism.

2. **Consensus:** The second argument for moral absolutism given by Kreeft is consensus. Almost all who have ever lived, including all the wise and learned people of the past were moral absolutists. Only highly educated members of modern western society, that is, largely white, democratic, industrialized, urbanized, secularized society have become moral relativists. A theological view of this sociological group would be apostate Christendom. Even in America, the majority view is still absolutist but the educators and those who control the media are relativists. Traditional morality is absolutist.

3. **Experience:** This is an argument of data from moral experience. The data of philosophy is ordinary experience. This data is listed under four categories as follows:
   a. Personal moral experience. The words, *good, right and ought*, are recognized by everyone, as for example to be healthy, and to have reliable friends

is good, etc. We also know intuitively that it is right not to steal etc.

b. Interpersonal moral behaviour. This is represented in how we interact with one another. Praising for doing good, blaming for doing wrong, quarrelling, rewarding, punishing and counselling etc. Free will and moral responsibility distinguish us from animals.

c. Public moral language. This was the data which Socrates, the father of philosophy, always explored. The data is in the meaning of the words which we understand.

d. Human history, that is, handed down through tradition.

4. **Moral argument:** Even relativists have moral arguments and relativists generally accept the validity of some universal moral principles, such as: "It is wrong to murder innocent people for no reason". "That is not fair" or "What right have you to do that?" is said by relativists as well as absolutists. For those who accept relativism, moral argument should be impossible. If moral absolutism is not true, therefore, all moral argument is impossible and meaningless. Furthermore, if these premises are true and there is no logical fallacy, then the conclusion is true. Moral absolutism is true. That is logic.

5. **The logical self-contradiction argument:** Relativistic morality is like illogical logic, because absolutism is inherent in the very essence of morality. The alternative to absolute morality is **no morality at all.** Morality cannot be based on the soft approach of giving ideals or suggestions, just as God did not give Moses ten suggestions or ideals. Moral obligations are commands.

6. **The practical self-contradiction argument:** This is based on many aspects of the behaviour of relativists. They contradict themselves when they say that there are no absolute principles of right and wrong. Unless they have lost their humanity, for example, they would object to have their property stolen. They also try to convince humanity that relative morality is right and absolute morality is wrong. If nothing is ever right or wrong, then there can be nothing wrong in believing in absolute morality.

B. Philosophical Principles for a Just Society?

Robert J. Spitzer, S.J., Ph.D. in his book concerning a philosophy of life issues,[11] outlines ten fundamental principles on which cultures and civilisations are built. Three of these principles concern objectively verifiable truth, three concern personal ethics and virtue, three concern political justice and rights and one is concerned with personal dignity and the development of a great culture. Failure to practice any of these can lead to an under-estimation of human dignity and failure to practice several of these principles will lead to widespread abuse and a general decline in culture. Without these principles, democracy could vote away the rights of individuals, the legal system would have nothing on which to base laws, and court systems could legalize every form of indignity and harm. The absence, or even partial absence, of these principles, therefore, opens the way to corruption, deceit and injustice. These ten fundamental principles are listed as follows:

Principles of Reason:

(1) **Complete Explanation:** The best theory is the one that explains the most data.

(2) **Non-contradiction:** Valid theories have no internal contradiction.

(3) **Objective evidence:** Non-arbitrary opinions are based on publicly verifiable evidence.

These first three principles deal with the validation of truth. Truth is fundamental to everything we know and the only reason we want to believe something is because it is true. The philosopher, Peter Kreeft, puts it well when he says, "Truth Trumps Everything". These principles indicate three important ways for testing the truth of a statement, opinion or theory. Stated in another way, these are: the quantity of the evidence, the logical consistency of the arguments, and the quality of the evidence. They were established by Socrates, Plato, and Aristotle and have been used (unfortunately not nearly enough) down through the centuries to combat the arguments of those who oppose truth, such as **Sophists, Sceptics and Cynics.** Sophists construct complicated, confusing and illogical arguments with the intention of deceit. Sceptics support sophists in promoting all truth as relative and undermine truth as unreasonable and unfounded. Cynics promote negativity and openly reject what is good and true.

Evidence: Subjective evidence is accessible to one person only and Objective evidence is accessible to everyone. There are two categories of evidence which are considered to be publicly accessible, namely, a priori and a posteriori evidence. A priori evidence is the basis for mathematical, logical, and metaphysical truths and is based on the principle of non-contradiction. A posteriori evidence is described as sensorial, that is, it accessible to the five senses – touching, seeing, hearing, smelling, and / or tasting.

A number of examples are described by Robert J Spitzer S.J.[11] on the practical importance of these principles as, for example, in recognising the evils of Nazi and Stalinist propaganda. These principles can also be used in other less obvious ways such as, in developing an objective (non-arbitrary, publicly verifiable) definition of human personhood. This has many very significant legal implications in relation to major legal errors of judgment made in the past by various Supreme Courts, especially in cases of abortion and slavery. The definition of a human person proposed by Spitzer is: "The presence of a full human genome in a human organism, which in the vast majority of cases, can be expected to become fully actualized".

Principles of Ethics

(4) **Non-maleficence:** Avoid doing harm or minimize the harm as much as possible. Apply the so called Silver Rule, that is, "Do not do unto others, what you would not have them do unto you."

(5) **Consistent Ends and Means:** The end does not justify the means.

(6) **Full Human Potential:** Every human person should be valued according to the full potential of human development and not just according to the level of development already achieved.

Ethics is concerned with the pursuit of good and the avoidance of evil. The principle of non-maleficence is the foundation of all ethics and is as fundamental to ethics as the principle of non-contradiction is to the rules of evidence. If this principle is not accepted as a law for personal conduct then society will collapse. It is also recognised that evil means cannot be used to achieve a good end. There can, however, be an exception to this in what is sometimes called, "the lesser of two evils". There is also another qualification to the end not justifying the means known as, "the principle of double effect". This can be the situation when a pregnant mother is given life saving treatment, which will have the unintentional result of the death of the unborn baby.

The Principal of full human potential originated, in the middle of the sixteenth century, with the Dominican friar, Bartolomé de las Casas, who attempted to defend American Indians against Spanish slave traders. Peoples or races cannot be judged as "less than human", even though this rationale has been used to justify slavery and genocide all through history. This principal is important also in declaring that an unborn human being cannot be branded as "less than human". The well known Roe v. Wade court case in America, which approved abortion, broke this principle, as well as other principles, by deciding that the stage of development was the important issue in permitting the killing of the unborn.

Principles of Justice and Natural Rights

(7) **Natural Rights:** All human beings possess the inalienable rights of life, liberty and ownership of property, which no government can take away.

(8) **Fundamentality of Rights:** Where there is a conflict of rights, we should decide in favour of the most fundamental right, that is, the right on which others depend.

(9) **Limits of Freedom:** One person's freedom cannot impose undue burdens on others.

Civil liberties and laws that are just must be based on the principle of justice. Saint Thomas Aquinas, like Plato and Aristotle, recognised that laws should be based on justice in order to promote a right relationship between people. In the early seventeenth century the Spanish Jesuit, Francisco Suarez, promoted this need for right relationship between individuals and emphasised that it can only work properly when the natural rights of individuals are recognised. This view of individual "natural" rights was later enshrined in various national constitutions as the inalienable human rights of life, liberty, the pursuit of happiness, and the right to own property. In the American Declaration of

Independence, these inalienable rights are regarded as self-evident. States or governments do not confer these inalienable rights and therefore, under normal circumstances, cannot take them away. Furthermore, if any state fails to protect these rights, then the basis for the rule of law within the state is undermined and the government loses legitimacy to govern. Freedom, justice and peace cannot be maintained in any country without the protection of natural inalienable human rights.

When a person violates the rights of another, then he gives up his own rights. In these circumstances a state has the right to punish such behaviour for the good of society, in order to preserve natural rights and natural law. A law in a state protecting natural rights would be useless otherwise, that is, unless there was a legitimate human authority to enforce it.

The principle of fundamental rights is important in the resolution of rights conflicts. The right to life is necessary in order to have the right of liberty or the right to own property, so the right to life is, therefore, more fundamental than the other two. In any situation, if there are objective criteria to assess which right is the most fundamental, then everyone, including the legal system, especially Supreme Courts, have an obligation to uphold the fundamentality of rights, so that the principle of non-maleficence can be upheld.

In his book,[11] Robert Spitzer gives a big discourse on two major errors made by the US Supreme Court by breaking many of the above fundamental principles. These errors were made on the issues of slavery and abortion. The first case was the Dred Scott Decision of 1857 when the US Supreme Court declared people of African descent to be a "subordinate and inferior class of beings" leading to one of the greatest disgraces in the history of US court decisions. This declaration was a violation of a number of aspects of the universal principles of human rights, described above. Firstly, it denied that all human beings should be valued on the basis of their full human potential. Secondly, the declaration denied the existence of natural rights and this also led to the violation of the principle of non-maleficence. By assuming that all rights were derived from the US constitution, the Supreme Court justices denied the rights to life, liberty and property to non-citizens. The events that followed with Abraham Lincoln, the Civil War and the aftermath, revealed the errors associated with the Dred Scott Decision. In the words of Spitzer, "The consequences were so terrible, that one might think the Court would be careful not to make the same mistake again: yet it has decidedly done this in the Roe v. Wade Decision."

Roe v. Wade was the well-known decision in 1973, by the US Supreme Court, to legalise the killing of the unborn. There was a great similarity between the legal arguments used in Dred-Scott and Roe-Wade decisions. In both cases the principle of natural rights was ignored. In the Dred-Scott case, the court decided that blacks could not be citizens and only citizens had rights under the American Constitution. In the case of Roe-Wade the court decided that unborn humans are not persons as not all human beings deserve to be recognised as persons. Consequently the unborn have no rights, as only persons have rights (in this case the right to life) under the Constitution. The first duty of all governments and courts must be to protect natural rights and the rights cannot be superseded by the power of the state.

(10) Principle of Identity and Culture

This is the principle of beneficence, that is, to make the optimal contribution to others and to society generally. It can be referred to as the so called "Golden Rule", that is, "Do unto others as you would have them do unto you." This is also be referred to as ethical maximalism (do good to others) and it is superior to the so called "Silver Rule", which is ethical minimalism (do no harm to others). It is derived from the great teaching of Christianity and improves the biblical Old Testament teaching of, do no harm, by incorporating the new Christian command, Love one another and do good for others in all things. This command of loving one another is the most powerful ethical teaching in the history of humanity and it is aimed at transforming human culture towards goodness. It forms the primary inspiration and incentive for understanding the purpose of life and attaining higher levels of happiness and fulfilment. Ultimately it leads to an understanding and an incentive to live in The Divine Will (see chapter 15).

4. Signs and Supports for Catholicism

Life is only a kind of sowing time, and the harvest is not here.
Vincent van Gogh

In order to appreciate the evidence for the impending world crisis, which I will try to outline in this book, the reader will first need to have some understanding of the evidence supporting Catholic Church teaching. This evidence can be presented under several different headings, such as philosophical, theological, historical, biblical, scientific etc., but, as I am neither, a philosopher, a theologian, a historian, or a biblical scholar, I will try not to stray too much into these areas. The evidence which I will present will largely be from the accounts of experiences given by large numbers of witnesses, as well as some miraculous signs and supernatural events, where there are good records and good scientific support for their veracity. I believe that this is the most acceptable kind of evidence for this sceptical age. There is no implied effort to belittle other religious beliefs or those who practice these beliefs. On the contrary, all those in other religions, including humanism and atheism, who seek the truth, must be respected and supported in their journey. I do not regard it as being honest, however, to pretend that all religions are equally valid or true and for this reason, I occasionally try to defend the Catholic Church against religious opinions which are opposed to Catholicism. Generally, the purpose of this effort is to present this evidence, in a spirit of sharing believing as I do, that the teaching of the Catholic Church is based on the truth.

Before considering evidence supporting Catholic Church beliefs, it may be useful to first consider briefly some important related topics, such as, some aspects of the person of Jesus Christ in history, the supernatural, spirits, and the sometimes puzzling relation between faith and evidence.

Jesus Christ in History

Nicky Gumbel in his book, Questions of Life[12], points out that no historian, or classical scholar, disputes the evidence for Caesar's Gallic War, Livy's Roman history, Tacitus, or Thucydides, despite the fact that there are only a few manuscripts detailing these accounts available, with origins no earlier than the tenth century. By contrast, there are many thousands of manuscripts available giving evidence about the veracity of the New Testament, in Latin, Greek and other languages, from as early as the second century. As well as that, there are approximately 36,000 citings of New Testament accounts in the writings of the early Church fathers, so that the evidence for New Testament accounts stands unapproachably alone among ancient prose. There can be no doubt, therefore, that the authenticity and general integrity of the New Testament writings, detailing the life of Jesus, is a well-established fact.

Other than Jesus, there is no evidence for any other major historical figure, or religious leader, having been prophesied by many prophets, for hundreds of years, before their birth. Nicky Gumbel discusses this and goes on to say, "Yet in the case of Jesus, He fulfilled over 300 prophecies (spoken by different voices over 500 years), including twenty nine major prophecies fulfilled in a single day – the day He died ... .I suppose it could be suggested that Jesus was a clever con man who deliberately set out to fulfil these prophecies.... The problem with that suggestion is, first, the sheer number of them would have made it extremely difficult. Secondly, humanly speaking, he had no control over many of the events. For example the exact manner of His death was foretold in the Old Testament (Isaiah 53), the place of His burial and even the place of his birth (Micah 5:2). It would have been a bit late by the time he discovered the place in which he was supposed to be born."

Jesus never wrote a book, yet his words are quoted, copied and translated more than those of any other man. Nobody else has answered the fundamental questions of life so clearly and with so much authority. He explained the reason for our existence and the way to fulfilment, joy and happiness in life. He told his friends that He was the Son of God and confirmed this by His behaviour, His knowledge, His words, and the miraculous signs which He worked. C. S. Lewis said that if the message of Christ is false it is of no importance, but if it is true, it is of infinite importance. The one thing it cannot be is moderately important.[13] C. S. Lewis also said that, "A man who was merely a man and said the sort of things Jesus said, would not be a great moral teacher. He would either be a lunatic ...or else he would be the Devil of Hell. You must make your choice. Either this man was, and is, the Son of God, or else a madman or something worse ...You can spit at Him and kill Him as a demon, or can fall at His feet and call Him Lord and God. But let us not come with any patronising nonsense about His being a great human teacher. He has not left that open to us. He did not intend to."[14]

Finally, it is not without significance that the men he chose, who were to spread the message of Christianity after His death, were prepared to be martyred rather than deny that He was God or to deny that He came back from the dead. They obviously got to know Him and believed in Him.

The Natural & Supernatural

Much of this book deals with evidence for the supernatural. Supernatural is a word normally understood to mean that which is outside nature, or that which cannot be understood within the laws of nature, as we know them. Some say that if we can perceive and recognize events with our senses then it cannot be supernatural. An extension of this view is that everything has a natural explanation, even though we may not be able to understand it, at this stage of scientific development. After all, television could have been regarded as supernatural, a few hundred years ago. It is easy to understand this logic, which is often used by those who reject the supernatural, in their efforts to explain the unexplainable. Nevertheless, when individuals survive for many years without food or drink (as described below), it is reasonable to describe this as supernatural, as in the first place it is contrary to the laws of thermodynamics and physical energy. There are also a wide variety of other well substantiated "miraculous" events described within the Catholic Church which defy the natural laws of physics, chemistry and biology and in a similar way merit the term supernatural.

Preternatural: The term preternatural is sometimes used to describe something which is at the extreme or border of what we accept as natural. An example would be an extraordinary ability to hear sound at a particular frequency. The terms preternatural and supernatural are probably best understood, however, in Christian theological terms, where the power to order supernatural forces and gifts belong to God alone.

In theology, natural states are usually categorized into three major states, with the second of these in turn being divided into two. The first natural state is described as original justice and holiness. The second is the state of sin, followed by the state after the redemption by Christ. The final state is that of glorified nature (in Heaven after death). Preternatural gifts reflect the ordering of the natural powers of the intellect, will, emotions and body. Before sin these were infused knowledge in the intellect, loving obedience in the will, spontaneous enjoyment of the virtues in the emotions and no suffering or death for the body. After sin came ignorance, malice, concupiscence, with suffering and death for the body. It is a mistake to describe something preternatural, as supernatural.

Spirits

Accepting the supernatural is acknowledging the existence of a reality that is outside the natural physical material world which we experience and survive in. Appreciating the supernatural opens the door to an understanding of our spiritual nature and the spiritual forces that surround us. These forces can be good or evil and can lead to happiness, or sorrow. Christian prayer is one of the best ways of linking with good spiritual forces, while evil spiritual forces are often contacted through spiritualism. Spiritualism can be described as a religious movement that promotes a belief in the existence of personal spiritual entities and communicates with these spirits through individuals, called mediums. Spiritism is a more restricted form of spiritualism, which was established in France in the middle of the nineteenth century. Those involved in spiritism do not regard it as a religion, but rather, as a science that studies the relation between incorporeal beings (spirits) and humans. Individuals who try to contact the spirits of the dead are referred to as spiritualists. From the Christian point of view, spiritualism, spiritism and spiritualists all have evil connotations. The Roman Catholic Church, in particular, gives strict warnings about dabbling with unknown spiritual forces, or trying to contact personal spirits, especially those of the dead, because of the great dangers associated with this. The dangers associated with demons or evil spirits are discussed in more detail in chapters 7 and 8.

One of the most common encounters described between our natural world and the spirit world is in the form of ghosts. Although ghost stories were a common feature of fictional writing, before the advent of television it is surprising how many of these stories were based on fact. You will discover this if you ask your friends how many have experienced good first hand evidence of ghosts, haunted houses, and/or poltergeists. If you don't ask, however, you will not be aware of how common it is, as most of those with personal experiences of this kind, rarely speak about it publicly. C.S. Lewis, in his book, Miracles,[15] said that he only ever met one person who saw a ghost and seeing this ghost, had no impact in terms of this individual's belief in their immortal soul. In contrast, I have met many people who have seen ghosts, and who have encountered spirits of many different types. I work in an environment of approximately fifteen people. A colleague's sister is now living in a haunted house. A family, who live a few doors away from my home, described in detail to me their experiences of living, for two years, in their last home, which had been haunted. The house was relatively isolated but they often heard the noise of children playing in the house, even though nobody was there. On one occasion, the father encountered a young girl in a bedroom and when he spoke to her, he was naturally a little surprised to see her body float away through the wall.

I have met many others with a wide variety of experiences with ghosts and spirits. Accounts of poltergeists are very well recognized and relatively common. From contacts which my family had in Iceland, we were told that seeing ghosts in Iceland is well recognized. One friend used to say that she always knew when some individuals were coming to visit her, because their ghost friends came before them. One particular individual had three ghosts or spirit forms attached to him, that our friend could see and she was able to describe them in detail to us. These ghosts usually came dressed in period costume, from earlier centuries, some minutes before that particular individual would arrive. It is my belief therefore, that there is no difficulty finding good evidence for ghosts, spirits and haunted houses. Those who claim that these phenomena do not exist, or are just figments of the imagination, have not really looked for evidence, and are not living in the real world.

I do, however, agree with C. S. Lewis that, seeing is not necessarily believing. Seeing ghosts, apparitions, or fairies at the bottom of the garden (which Richard Dawkins often talks about), may have no impact on an individual's religious belief, or view of the supernatural. This message came to me very forcibly, on one occasion, when sharing some stories about the apparition of The Virgin Mary, in Knock, County Mayo, Ireland, with an old priest friend from Galway. We spoke, in particular, about two coincidental events at Knock at the time of the apparition. The first concerned the fact that the vision occurred on the evening which ended the hundred masses for holy souls, which the priest said every year. On that particular year, the priest of the parish had refused to take money from the parishioners for this novena, as they were very poor, and he had received enough money already from American donations. On the same weekend, this parish priest, of Knock, had also been sentenced by a secret court, to a severe punishment, for speaking out against secret illegal meetings held in the locality at the time. This sentence, however, was never carried out due to the commotion and excitement connected with the visions seen just beside the church. When my friend, Fr T Kelly, was a young priest, in the diocese of Galway, he was friendly with an older Priest in the Knock area. Fr. Kelly's older friend had the job, on one occasion, of interviewing one of the visionaries in Knock, who was ill and preparing for death. It was the common practice, when each visionary was nearing their death, to have them interviewed again officially by a priest on behalf of the local Bishop, regarding what they saw at the gable of the church, in Knock, in 1879. This particular visionary was very happy to confirm what they had said previously, with all the details correct. This particular individual, however, although born a Catholic, never went to Church and refused the last sacraments,

71

before death. Obviously, for this person, seeing a detailed and complicated vision at the church in Knock, lasting over an extended period of time, did little or nothing to support or confirm a belief, in Catholic Church teaching.

Faith and Evidence

When it comes to accepting a belief in God, Christianity, or any other religion, then faith is the fulcrum on which everything else hinges. Faith is a complex theological subject, which I am not competent to deal with in any detail. Nevertheless, because of its pivotal importance to the subject matter of this chapter and this book, a brief consideration is necessary.

In his book Expectant Faith,[16] Fr Pat Collins C.M., points out that there are two basic forms of Christian faith, namely, doctrinal and trusting. He quotes St Cyril of Jerusalem from the fourth century, who explained these two aspects of Christian faith. First of all, faith is concerned with doctrine and it denotes the assent of the soul to some truth: secondly, faith is a particular gift and grace of Christ. St Cyril went on to say that this gift of grace is a form of trust, which reaches its most intense form in mountain moving faith. The Catechism of the Catholic Church confirms and agrees with these two aspects of faith.

Fr Collins also points out, from his study of the epistles, how St Paul refers to at least five interrelated forms of faith, which are like five different facets of the same precious stone. These are creedal, saving, faith as a fruit of the Spirit, trusting faith and the charism of faith. He explains the charism of faith as, "an unhesitating trust of an expectant kind in the inspirations and promises of God, which often find expression in deeds of power, such as healings and miracle working... Through faith in Christ, a person is granted a Spirit given understanding, which reaches beyond the limitations of purely rational forms of knowledge."

It is a common opinion, among non-religious, that faith is belief without evidence, even to the extent of being irrational or contrary to reason. There is a problem with this view for the atheists, however, in that being an atheist probably requires even more blind faith in atheism, than being a believer in God! Evidence for the existence of God (and for the existence of Heaven and Hell), as I hope you will discover as you read through this book, is much easier to find than evidence for God's non-existence. St Thomas Aquinas, Martin Luther and John Calvin all denied that faith was a belief without evidence. Aquinas said that faith was a belief based on trustworthy testimony. According to Aquinas also, for a belief to be regarded as faith, it must be voluntary and confident. If something can be proven beyond doubt, then it cannot be regarded as voluntary when it becomes unreasonable not to believe it. That does not mean however, that what is believed in faith cannot be supported by good substantial evidence, but when the evidence reaches a point when there can be no doubt, then faith is no longer necessary to believe it. In a similar way, to the extent that there is doubt about a belief, to that measure also, there is no faith.

It is also the Christian view that true faith and reason can never be opposed, as both originate in God, who is truth. Cardinal Ratzinger, now Emeritus Pope Benedict XVI, made the following comments on faith and reason in his book, God and the World:[17]

"Faith speaks to our reason, our understanding, because it expresses truth – and because reason was created for the sake of truth. To that extent, faith without understanding is no true Christian faith. Faith demands to be understood…. Faith cannot be understood in the same sense that a mathematical formula might be for me entirely comprehensible, but reaches into ever deeper levels of being, into the eternal nature of God, into the mystery of love…. We are unable even to understand another man, because his person reaches down into depths more profound than our ability to conceptualize. We cannot, in the end, understand the structure of matter, but can only conceive of it up to a certain point... In this sense faith cannot be rationally demonstrated. I cannot say whoever does not accept this is just stupid. Faith has its own way of life, in which what we believe is gradually substantiated by experience and is shown to be meaningful as a whole. There are therefore convergences, from the point of view of reason, that make it right for me to enter into it. They give me the certainty that I am not handing myself over to some superstition. But an exhaustive demonstration, such as can be given for natural laws, does not exist."

How can you get faith? We sometimes hear people say, "I have no faith, but I envy those who have". The question we need to answer for those who would like to believe and cannot is, how can they get faith? To what extent faith is a gift or a voluntary intellectual act of saying, "I believe" based on evidence, is something which seems to be subject to great individual variation. If we assume that intelligence and insight is a gift of God then it is unlikely that individuals with these gifts would have an advantage over the simple minded in getting to know God. Cardinal Ratzinger touched on this when he said:[17]

"Even a simple person can know God quite well. It is not necessarily the case that a broad acquaintance with the scientific and historical knowledge we now have will make someone capable of understanding God better. You can drown understanding in facts ...A great amount of scientific knowledge can, on one hand, lead to someone being no longer able to see beyond the facts, so that he is hemmed in by facts ... and can no longer bring himself to make the leap into mystery. He sees only what is tangible, and from a metaphysical point of view, in this way a person becomes more stupid. The other side of it is that sometimes, precisely by the breadth of our vision, in that we can see so many glimpses of divine reason in reality, this really does add breadth and scope to our image of God, and we stand before him with greater reverence and even with humility and awe."

The gospel accounts are full of praise by Jesus for those who believe and full of warnings for those who do not. "Whoever denies me before men, I also will deny before my Father who is in Heaven" (Matt 10.33). We can also read what Jesus said to the apostle Thomas, who found it difficult to believe in the resurrection: "Have you believed because you have seen me? Blessed are those who have not seen, and yet believe" (John 20.29). Christians are always exhorted to, "Repent" (Act 2.38) and again we can read, "Unless you repent you will all likewise perish" (Lk 13.3). All of this indicates clearly that faith is an act of the will to say, "I believe", in the same way that repenting begins with, "I am sorry". In the New Testament there is also a strong admonishment for those who reject signs given by God, as in, "And you, Capernaum, will you be lifted up to Heaven? You will be thrown down to Hell! For if the miracles which were performed in you had taken place in Sodom, Sodom would still be in existence today." (Matt 11.23).

The Catechism of the Catholic Church describes true Christian faith as a theological virtue, but like all virtues, it is up to each individual to seek it out, work for it, cultivate and develop it. To get faith you must want to believe just as to be an atheist, to some extent, you must want to reject God. The first step in faith, therefore, is humbly accepting the possibility that God may exist and exploring the evidence for this. In a famous Oxford painting, Christ is depicted as standing at a door with a light and knocking. The door represented in this picture, is each human heart, which can only be opened from the inside. Each person, who wants to believe, must open this door and begin a dialogue with God, or in other words begin to pray. Prayer is an opening of the mind and heart to God. It is unlikely that any person can truly believe in God without prayer and the shortest way to faith is through prayer. Prayer can be very simple, even to the extent of the agnostic just saying, "God, if you are there, please give me some positive indication". Don't expect, however, that a two second prayer will sort out all your problems, but if you get serious about talking to God, you will get faith. The "signal graces" of prayer are a sure confirmation for Christian faith. God always answers sincere prayer and communicates with individuals in a very personal way, which they alone will recognize. Through prayer, there is a gradual growing into faith, hope and love. Those who are praying properly, sincerely and sufficiently will be growing in love.

Many will say that they only want to hear positive news and views. Deciding to say yes to God, in many ways, represents the ultimate in being positive about life. You can assume that God is for real and look for supporting evidence or you can reject the whole idea of God. The older we get the more embedded our attitudes become and the more difficult it is to change. Some who have a comfortable life style do not want the trouble of believing in God. Some just do not want to know. The world may be on the brink of self-destruction, but many do not want to even think about it. The masses still prefer to be deceived – Vulgus Vult Decepi – .

Faith can be the crossroads between scepticism and trust, between deception and truth and even between despair and hope. Faith can also be a crossroads for the proud and self-confident, who can become lowly when they acquire faith. On the other hand those who feel worthless or have low self-esteem can begin to appreciate their infinite value as part of the eternal family of God, with The Virgin Mary as a mother and St Joseph as a guardian. An often quoted remark of Mary to the children in

Medjugorje (see chapter 5) is, **"If you knew how much I love you, you would die of joy"**.

Most of those who find faith, appreciate that this is only the beginning. The typical Protestant view that Christians are saved or "justified" by faith only (sola fide) is not the Catholic view, but, as dialogue continues between Christian Churches, it now seems that this difference may be more about emphasis, than on substance, particularly on the interpretation of the word, "faith". In the Bible (Jas 2.17) it says, "Faith by itself, if it has no works, is dead". The Bible also says (1 Corin 13.2), "if I have faith great enough to remove mountains, but have not love, I am nothing." The ultimate test, therefore, is not just faith, but how much we love God and love others, and show this by our actions. After death we will be judged by our measure of love for God and love for others.

Finally, there are two very different types of modern prophetically revealed messages, which can be used to highlight both the trusting and believing aspects of faith, already described. The first concerns the aspect of faith dealing with complete trust in God. These messages are associated with the very extensive and profound revelations on Divine Mercy given to the Polish nun, St Faustina Kowalska (see page 450), and promoted by Pope John Paul II. These Polish messages are now continued in a different format by the prophet Anne, an American mother who was directed to come and live in Ireland (see page 454). Both series of messages strongly encourage everybody to have complete trust in God, without which there is no hope. These messages are also significant for two other important reasons. **Firstly, they are preparing humanity for the great tribulation and transformation of the world which is about to begin and which will lead humanity back to the true God. Secondly, both of these series of messages, dealing with complete trust in God, significantly, have support and approval from official Catholic Church authorities.**

The second set of revelations concerns extraordinary signs, which are predicted to occur in the near future and which will represent overwhelming support evidence for a belief in God and the truth of Catholic Church teaching. Among these predictions, are Permanent Signs which will appear at particular world locations. These sites have been selected, revealed and are already widely known. These signs will be directly from God and of God and will remain to the end of the world. It will be possible for all to see and photograph them. Should these signs occur as predicted, it will leave the evidence for the Catholic Church (which is already very strong, as described below), at that stage, beyond any reasonable doubt. This would obviously have enormous world implications. This predicted time is approaching rapidly and we are told that it will mark a major turning point in the history of humanity. Humanity has also been warned not to wait for these major signs to repent and convert as by then, time will be too short for many. After these signs, only those who stubbornly refuse to accept God will reject the implications of this evidence. These signs and events are discussed in much greater detail in chapters 5, 11, and 16.

The purpose of this section below is to describe some events and evidence, which you may not already be aware of, and which support the beliefs of Catholicism. This, I hope, will encourage non-believers in particular, to search more and to pray, so that their eyes may be opened and it becomes possible for them to say, "I believe".

The Catholic Church: is it from God?

To say that the evidence for the truth of Catholic Church teaching is very strong is an understatement. I never cease to be amazed at the amount of information that is available from scientifically supported observes of all kinds, intricately combining together, to give an amazing interconnecting and crosschecking library of evidence, that supports Catholic beliefs and teaching. I

78

have come across very large numbers of these occurrences and events over the years, most of which remain hidden to the average believer and non-believer alike. This is largely because few have an interest in searching them out. One has only to read some of the large volumes written on Eucharistic miracles, to get a glimpse at the immensity of this evidence. Much of this, of course, is linked with the supernatural and that creates a difficulty from the point of view of acceptable evidence. At the same time there are so many factual pieces of information and artefacts that have been scientifically verified, as well as observations supported by very large numbers of people, that it is very difficult for any rational person to dispute the reality. All of this information links together, to weave an intricate web of strong positive evidence, that can only be marvelled at. Anybody who looks at this information with an open mind would have to be impressed. There is no shortage of good evidence, therefore, supporting Catholic Church belief, but there is both a lack of knowledge about this evidence and a lack of willingness to examine it.

In many ways belief in the Catholic Church can be compared with belief in God. On the one hand, it is as if God never wants anybody to be able to say, where is the evidence? On the other hand, it is very common to hear, "there is no evidence". We do not need to be reminded, therefore, that for those who believe, no evidence is necessary, and for those who do not believe, no amount of evidence will suffice. Evidence must not only be discovered and presented, but it must also be 'revealed', appreciated and understood.

Many major scientifically and medically supported signs have come to the Catholic Church through phenomena associated with the Eucharist and through visitations of The Virgin Mary. This is significant, as Christianity is divided into two distinct belief systems, based largely on the theological differences, concerning belief in the Eucharist and in the role of The Virgin Mary in salvation. The Catholic and Orthodox Churches believe in the real presence of Christ in the Eucharist, as well as the great significance of The Virgin Mary, who acts as an intercessor between humanity and God. Most other branches of Christianity reject both of these interpretations of Sacred Scripture. For this reason, I will emphasise Eucharistic and Marian signs more than others, but there are many other significant signs described, not under these headings, such as those from the lives of the saints, signs in nature etc. which are also worthy of interest and further study. I will have to leave the great majority of these Catholic miraculous signs to those interested in looking elsewhere, as in this small effort, I could only hope to whet your appetite.

The "Real Presence" in the Eucharist

The conviction that there is a real presence of Christ in the Eucharist is the core and central belief of the Catholic and Orthodox Christian faith. It could be said that the most important division between the two main branches of Christianity, or more specifically between the Catholic and Protestant Churches is due to a difference of belief on this doctrine, described in the Gospel of John, chapter 6. Christianity is divided into those who believe in the real presence of Christ in the Eucharist in the form of bread and wine, and those who do not. It is interesting that the different Churches, who believe in this real presence, are also identical in almost every other aspect of their teaching, such as belief in the authority of the Church which, "is the pillar and foundation of the truth" (1 Timothy 3:14-15) to interpret holy scripture, the seven sacraments, and belief in purgatory. These Churches have also remained few in number, whereas, those branches of Christianity, that do not promote a belief in the real presence of Christ in the Eucharist, have fractured into many thousands of different churches with different doctrines. There is no doubt that the custom of rejecting a teaching authority within the Christian

Church founded by Christ, in favour of individual interpretation of the Bible, which was introduced at the Protestant Reformation, was a major cause for this fracturing of Christianity into the many different groups. When individuals interpret the Bible according to their private ideas, it is understandable how countless opinions, beliefs and sects can be formed over time. The irony of history is that Martin Luther, who began this major split in Christianity with the Protestant Reformation, believed in many aspects of Catholic and Orthodox teaching. This included the authority of ministers from Christ to forgive sin, as well as devotion to The Virgin Mary. These teachings are now very unlikely to be part of most Protestant thinking and belief.

From the standpoint of the way we humans generally think and rationalize the world about us, the idea of God, the Creator of the Universe, taking on the form of bread, so that humanity could have spiritual nourishment, seems to be completely irrational. It is amazing therefore that up to 25% of humanity would claim some allegiance to this belief, accepting that the number who sincerely believe this, would be less than this figure. Can it really be possible for such a large number of people to believe this extraordinary doctrine of Catholic faith, without some more tangible evidence, other than the Church's authority to infallibly interpret the teaching of Christ? Of course, it has been said that, if one can accept that Jesus rose from the dead, then everything else is minor by comparison.

Those who know nothing about the Eucharist will be very surprised, if not astounded or shocked, to find the extent of the evidence available which suggests that the Eucharistic host is certainly not ordinary bread. Many large books have been written on the subject of this 'real presence' in the Eucharist such as, Eucharistic Miracles[18], Moments Divine[19], The Secrets of the Eucharist[20], and others. In these books, very large numbers of miraculous events associated with the Eucharist have been well documented. In this short account all I can do is give a flavour of what is available and encourage readers to investigate more. I will concentrate mostly on events with good biological, scientific and historical support. I will begin with some very short accounts of the lives of three saintly individuals, who lived within the last century and who survived for many years on the Eucharist, as their only source of food and drink.

Alexandrina Da Costa

Alexandrina Da Costa lived in a village about forty miles north from Oporto, Portugal[21]. She was born in 1904 and she died on the anniversary of the great sign of Fatima, on the 13th October, 1955. She is known as the fourth seer of Fatima because of her close association with the Fatima story (see page 125). One hundred years before the birth of Alexandrina, a cross was seen to form on the ground in the village where she was born. This was a perfect image of a cross, a few metres in length, formed naturally in the texture of the grass. There was no natural explanation for it, and the mark of this cross can still be seen in this village. Similar cross images have appeared in a number of other places around the world, associated with mystics (see page 435), but in Alexandrina's case it was unusual in that the cross occurred one hundred years before she was born. Alexandrina had very little schooling and she was employed as a seamstress. One day in 1924 she was attacked by her former employer, who was trying to rape her. In order to escape, she jumped through a window from the first floor. As a result of this jump her back was badly injured in such a way that she became completely paralysed. She was bed ridden for the rest of her life.

She offered herself as a victim soul and from then on had tremendous suffering and pain. She reached high levels of mysticism and this culminated in experiencing the passion of

Christ, which occurred for three hours, every Friday. Witnesses saw that, during her passion, she regained the strength in her paralysed limbs and she would leave the bed and stagger, as if carrying the cross. As soon as the passion was over, she became paralysed again. These ecstasies were filmed and were reported to the Church authorities. In response to a command, which she reportedly received from Jesus in 1939, Alexandrina wrote to Pope Pius XII, asking for the consecration of the world to the Immaculate Heart of Mary, in order to achieve peace in the world. The Pope already knew about Alexandrina from a report, which he had received from her Archbishop in Portugal, and he had already received a similar request for the consecration of the world, from Sr Lucia in Fatima. Pope Pius XII undertook to make this consecration in 1942. This was the first effort by a Pope to fulfil this special request made by The Virgin of Fatima. Alexandrina offered all her suffering for peace in the Second World War and she suffered terribly for this purpose. During these periods of sufferings, she was attacked several times by the Devil. It was common for her friends and priest to see her being hurled against the wall, and suffer all kinds of injuries from these attacks. She was near death on a number of occasions and her bed was sometimes seen to be covered in black smoke, which was accompanied by a terrible stench. There were often some hideous sounds and voices heard saying blasphemies. Her priest, Fr Pinho, was also attacked by the Devil on a number of occasions. During one effort at exorcism he demanded to know the name of the assailant. The response came, "I am Satan, do not doubt it", and the voice cursed the priest.

The final stage of Alexandrina's life came with a phenomenon associated with the Eucharist. For the last thirteen and a half years of her life she neither ate nor drank, living only on the daily Eucharist. This phenomenon is known as Inedia. She was taken into hospital on at least two occasions to have this fast verified.

For forty days and nights she was watched around the clock by impartial teams of medical professionals, including doctors and nurses, who were sceptical or even hostile to her, to ensure that no food or water reached her. One of the Consultants, who was very sceptical in the beginning, employed his own sister who was in charge of a ward, to both keep watch and to organize others for the watch. Her health and weight remained the same throughout these forty days and the medical profession was stunned by this. The doctors eventually decided that it was a prodigy and a statement was issued which said that the fast "was scientifically inexplicable". Alexandrina said that our Lord had told her that, "You are living only by the Eucharist because I want the world to know the power of My Body and Blood and the power of My life for souls". In 1955 Alexandrina's condition suddenly deteriorated and after a long hot summer, she died on the 13th October 1955, on the 38th Anniversary of the great sign of Fatima. Alexandrina Maria da Costa was solemnly beatified (with five others) by Pope Paul II on Sunday 25th April, 2004. She is now being promoted by the Catholic Church for canonization as a saint.

Therese Neumann

Therese was known to her friends as Resl Neumann[22]. She was born on Good Friday, 1898 in the village of Konnersreuth in Bavaria, Germany. She was a great Catholic mystic and stigmatic. She died on September 18th, 1962. In 2005, the Bishop of Regensburg formally opened the process for her beatification.

When Therese was a young girl, she wanted to become a missionary sister in Africa. She was seriously injured when she was twenty years old, while trying to fight a barn fire and this put an end to those plans. Further falls led to paralysis and blindness and she developed pneumonia and abscesses in her ears, which resulted in deafness. Terrible bed sores developed and her health got steadily worse. Therese had great devotion to St Therese of

Lisieux and on the day St Therese was beatified, she regained her vision and began to recover dramatically. Two years later on 17th of May, 1925, on the day when St Therese of Lisieux was canonized, she was suddenly cured of dislocated vertebrae and crippled legs. She stood up completely well and again began to work on the farm.

Her suffering however did not end there. A mysterious voice told her, "You must suffer more and cooperate with priests for the salvation of souls". She mystically received the five wounds of Jesus in her hands, feet and side (the stigmata). In 1926, she received the marks of the Crown of Thorns. In 1929, she received a terrible shoulder wound and marks of scourging on her back. From the years 1922 until her death in 1962 she ate no food except for one consecrated host every day. From 1926 until her death she also drank no fluid. In July 1927 a medical team, consisting of a doctor and four nurses, observed her closely to verify that she was not eating or drinking. Despite the lack of food and drink, she lost no weight and did not get dehydrated.

Therese was also famous for living without sleep, for performing many medical cures, for having the ability to recognize priests and relics despite many disguises used to hide their identity. She also had a great gift of prophecy as well as the gifts of levitation, bilocation (being in two places at the same time), and the ability to understand and speak many foreign languages, despite very little education. She regularly experienced the pain of the Passion of Jesus and there are many disturbing photographs of her bleeding profusely, particularly from her eyes. Many American soldiers visited her during the Second World War, and while speaking to them, she was widely reported to have predicted the downfall of America, at some time in the future, through major natural disasters. She was very opposed to the Nazi movement, and there is some evidence that she warned Hitler of his downfall if he did not change. She ranks among the great Catholic mystics of the twentieth century, and her life serves as outstanding evidence in support of the authenticity of Catholic doctrine and theology.

Martha Robin

Martha Robin was another great lady, who lived in recent times, and who survived only on the Eucharist for many years[23,24] She is a very well known mystic and was physically handicapped, blind and bedridden for most of her long life. She lived a life of prayer and sacrifice and established a movement for the education of lay people, in the Catholic faith, known as the Foyers of Charity – (Foyer meaning houses of charity). One of the principal activities of this movement is the promotion of five day silent retreats. Many hundreds of thousands have now been involved with these retreats and the movement is continuing to spread all over the world.

She was born on the 13th March 1902 in Chateaunuef de Galaure, which is a small village, in the south eastern part of France. She was the youngest of a family of six and she was frequently ill during her younger years. In 1918 Martha got a severe illness and collapsed. Her legs were paralysed and she fell into a semi-coma, which lasted for seventeen months. On the 25th March 1921, she had a vision of The Virgin Mary and her parents thought she was dying. In 1925, when she was 23, she recovered a little and made an act of abandonment to the love of God. By 1928 Martha ceased eating altogether and for the next fifty years, until her death in 1981, she did not consume anything except the Eucharist, which was brought to her once or twice weekly. When she received the Eucharist, it vanished instantaneously without any normal ingestion. Her digestive system had ceased to function completely. In addition, Martha never slept. She had numerous medical examinations and she submitted to all of them. Although she was paralysed, she joined the third order of St Francis and the Legion of Mary. Although her limbs were paralysed, she carried out her duties from her bed, by talking to people, giving instructions and praying for others. In the early part of October 1930 she received the Stigmata. During an apparition, a shaft of flame split into five, and wounded her two legs, her hands and her heart. These wounds continued to bleed and she continued to suffer the pains of the crucifixion, particularly from Thursday to Saturday, sometimes going into Sunday. During her life, she received many messages from St Thérése of Lisieux. She died on the 4th February 1981.

Eucharistic Miracles

Hundreds of Eucharistic miracles have been described and documented down through the centuries. The most extraordinary are those where the bread and wine have been visibly changed into flesh and blood. This phenomenon has also been described recently on a number of occasions. The best known recent examples are those associated with Maria Esperanza, in Venezuela, and those associated with Julia Kim, in Naju, Korea. St Pope John Paul II would have been very much aware of these two individuals and is known to have been present with Julia Kim, when one of these incidents of the host changing into flesh is said to have taken place. Although Maria Esperanza received full approval by Rome, Julia Kim has fallen out of favour with her local Bishop in recent years and at this time is not an officially approved visionary.

Many incidents and Eucharistic prodigies have also been described, often in association with the lives of the saints. Some of the most common are involved with bleeding hosts. In some of these cases the blood from the hosts was identified as human blood, when investigated by scientific laboratories. All of these incidents are distinct and different in many respects. Taken together, however, they become a powerful support for Catholic

Eucharistic theology. These Eucharistic miracles also give great insights into this extraordinary phenomenon of the real presence of Christ in the Eucharist, which is very difficult for our human minds to comprehend.

The Eucharistic Miracle of Lanciano

Probably the best known miracle of the Eucharist is that which occurred in approximately 700 A.D. at Lanciano, Italy. It occurred in a monastery which was dedicated to Saint Longinus, the Roman Centurion, who was reported to have pierced the side of Jesus with a lance. A monk who was celebrating Mass had great doubts about the doctrine of transubstantiation, that is, the power he had as a priest to induce Christ to transform the bread and wine into His body and blood, during the consecration of the Mass. At the consecration, he witnessed the bread and wine being transformed into flesh and blood right before his eyes. The flesh and blood were not consumed but were preserved in a precious ivory container. It was noted at the time, that the blood had separated into five separate clotted particles. In 1713 the particles of flesh and blood were enshrined in a silver monstrance, in which they are preserved to this day, in the Church of St Francis, in Lanciano.

In 1970, Pope St Paul VI authorized a scientific investigation of this event and a team of scientists was assembled to carry this out. A number of laboratories were selected and it was decided that the team should be chaired by Professor Odoardolinoli, who was a Professor of Histopathology. He was assisted by Professor Ruggero Bertilli from the University of Sienna. On examining the container in which the sacred species were contained it was noted that the Lunette containing the flesh was not hermetically sealed (that is, it was exposed to the air). The flesh was described as being yellow brown in colour, irregular and roundish in shape, thicker and wrinkled along the periphery. The five pellets of blood were noted to be finely wrinkled, compact, homogenous and hard in consistency, being a yellow chestnut colour and having the appearance of chalk. A small sample was taken from the central part of one pellet for microscopic examination and scientific study. A small sample of the flesh was also taken for examination in the hospital, in Arezzo, Italy.

Scientific reports from the professors were published, on the 4th March 1971. Previous to the publication of the official reports, Professor Odoardolinoli had sent a letter to the director of the shrine, in which he suggested that at the beginning of the investigation he was very sceptical of the whole matter, but he had since become convinced of the reality of the miraculous event. That letter began as follows: "In the beginning was the Word and the Word was made flesh". The final official report contained the following points:

1. The flesh and blood were real

2. The flesh and blood were of human origin

3. The flesh consisted of heart muscle

4. The flesh and blood had the same blood type, namely blood type AB.

5. In the blood, the proteins were in the same proportion as one would expect in normal human blood.

6. The blood also contained minerals, such as Sodium, Chlorides, Phosphorus, Magnesium, Potassium and Calcium as in human blood.

7. There was no sign of any chemical preservatives, either in the flesh or in the blood. The flesh and blood were in their natural state after thirteen centuries, despite being

exposed to the action of the atmosphere and to biological agents. This could not be explained by scientific means.

A further note of clarification was added by Professor Linolli. He said that, "Although it is alien to my task, strictly speaking, I feel I should insert the following reflection into the study just completed". He then went on to suggest that the evidence seemed to point to the fact that this was not a fraud and that the flesh and blood could not have been taken from a preserved body many years previously. If the blood were from a mummy it would have rapidly decayed through putrefaction. The flesh would likewise have decayed, as there was no evidence of any preservative substances found, which is often seen in bodies preserved by mummification.

Eucharistic Miracles of Siena

The Italian city of Siena is famous in the Catholic world for St Catherine and St Bernardino. Siena is also known for two Eucharistic miracles. The first was in the year 1330, and the second occurred exactly four hundred years later in 1730. The miracle of 1330, concerned a consecrated host, which a priest had placed between the pages of his breviary, while he hurried away to see a man who was very ill, in the community. When the priest opened his breviary he found the page stained with the blood from the host. This sacred host was examined in recent times, by microscopy and photography. It revealed real blood and the clear image of a man. Several examples of similar bleeding hosts have now been recorded throughout the world and this particular relic can now be seen in the basilica at Cascia, where it is stored beside the incorrupt body of St Rita.

The second miracle in Siena occurred after a gold ciborium, full of consecrated hosts, was stolen from the church of St Francis, on the eve of the feast of the Assumption (15th Aug.) 1730. The hosts were later found covered in dust in a poor box. The hosts were not consumed and now almost three hundred years later, these hosts still remain fresh and have not decayed or deteriorated in any way. The hosts are stored in a ciborium which has the Bishops official seal attached to prevent tampering with the lid. The cover is not hermetically sealed (that is, air and microorganisms have access through the container lid), and under these circumstances, hosts would be expected to survive no longer than a few years. A number of scientific investigations have been made over the years and the preservation of these hosts (approximately 230) is now regarded as miraculous.

Maria Esperanza & Betania

A more modern example of a Eucharistic miracle is from Betania, in Venezuela. Maria Esperanza Bianchini was an extraordinary mystic, who died in 2004. Maria was a personal friend of Padre Pio (see below) and had many mystical gifts, but she is best known, outside of religious circles, for her prophecy of 9/11 in New York. Betania is one of the very few sites of major apparitions which were approved officially by the Church, while the events were still going on. Maria was told that mankind was reaching an hour of decision and that there was a great danger of a war in Asia. She was told that Russia would act in a surprising way, when least expected, during this period of decision. She was also told that there is a great day of light coming soon. During this day, the state of the consciences of all people will be revealed, so that they may put their house in order and offer to Jesus the just reparation, for the daily infidelities that are committed, on the parts of sinners (see chapter 12 for more details). The Catholic Church's evaluation of the apparitions, prophecies, mystical lights, beautiful aromas, healings etc., which took place in Betania, was recorded in 1987, and are described in the book, Bridge to Heaven.[25] The local Bishop, Pelo Riccardo, approved the site and his words were as follows:

"After having studied repeatedly the apparitions of the most Holy Virgin of Betania and having begged the Lord earnestly for spiritual discernment, I declare, that in my judgement, the said apparitions are authentic and have a supernatural character. I, therefore, approve officially that the site, where the apparitions have occurred, be considered as sacred".

As if to confirm the Bishop's findings, soon after the approval, on the vigil of the Immaculate Conception (Dec. 8th), a very unusual miracle took place associated with the Eucharist. Fr Otty Ossa described what happened while he was saying Mass in the open chapel, next to the grotto. He said, "I broke the host into four parts. Suddenly, when I looked down at the plate I could not believe my eyes. I saw a red stain forming on the host and from it a red substance was beginning to emanate similar to the way blood spurts out in a puncture. After the Mass I took the host and protected it in the sanctuary. The next day, at 6.00 a.m., I observed the host and I found that the blood had started to dry." A video record of this host has been taken, which clearly shows the blood. When a sample of this was analysed in a laboratory, it was found to be human blood.

Maria Esperanza had many miraculous events associated with her during her long life. She clearly predicted the 9/11 Twin Tower explosions and travelled from Venezuela to be in New York on the day of the famous event. She made great efforts, through her many contacts, to try to prevent America going to war in Iraq. She said that if this happened that it would not end well. She was a personal friend of St Pope John Paul II and took on some of his suffering for him. She died of an unusual form of Parkinson's disease (similar to St Pope John Paul II), in 2004. The Pope seemed to be overcome with sadness at the time of her death. After her death, the Pope's illness got rapidly worse and he died on Divine Mercy Sunday, 2005. There is good evidence that St Pope John

Paul II bilocated to her home, in Venezuela, for discussions during their efforts to prevent America going to war in Iraq. This is described in, Bridge to Heaven.[25]

Julia Kim

Julia's original name was Hong-Sun Yoon. She was born in Naju, Korea, in 1947. Soon after the start of the Korean war, in 1950, her father and grandfather were killed by the communists. Her mother and Julia had to struggle hard to survive. In 1972, she married Julio Kim, a civil servant in the department of Agriculture, in Naju city. They have two sons and two daughters.

Soon after the birth of her last child, Julia got cancer and after several attempts at surgery her doctors finally gave up hope of recovery. Julia's health deteriorated rapidly and she seemed to be close to death. As a last resort her husband, Julio, took her to a Catholic priest, whom he knew, for a blessing. When the priest was blessing her, Julia felt a warm sensation travel through her body. She rapidly regained her complete health in what seemed to be a miraculous cure. After this cure she began a deep prayer life, as a fervent Catholic.

One night at 3.00 a.m. Julia had a vision of Jesus bleeding from His Heart because of the sins of humanity. She offered her whole life in reparation for sins. She began to suffer severe pains and stigmatic wounds of the crucifixion began to appear in her hands and feet for several days at a time. On June 30th, 1985, Julia saw the statue of The Virgin Mary in her room weep tears for the first time. This weeping occurred 700 times until January 14th, 1992. On October 19th, 1986 the clear tears turned to blood. This was shown to be human blood in a medical laboratory. Fragrant oil exuded from the statue for 700 consecutive days between November 24th, 1992 and October 23rd, 1994.

The consecrated host changing into visible flesh and blood on Julia's tongue was recorded on at least twelve occasions, between 1988 and 1996. One of these events was witnessed by St Pope John Paul II, in his private chapel, in the Vatican, on October 31st, 1995. Bishop Danylak from Toronto witnessed a similar miracle in Naju and Bishop Su from Sibu, Malaysia, witnessed the miracle in Sibu. Both of these Bishops have documented their observations. A sample of the blood from Julia's mouth was tested at Seoul National University and confirmed as human. I have not seen any record as yet, of more detailed genetic or antigenic analysis of this blood.

Julia began to receive messages from The Virgin Mary on July 18th, 1985. All the messages she received, confirmed Catholic teaching. She was told to promote the truth of the Real Presence of Jesus, Body, Blood, Soul, and Divinity, in the Eucharist, the need for self denial and sacrifices, and the need to pray fervently for the defeat of evil in the world. She was also told to hurriedly spread the message of love and trust in God and she said that respect for the human life of the weak, sick, elderly and unborn was essential for peace in the world.

As mentioned above, Julia has now fallen out of favour with her local Bishop. Local Bishops sometimes make mistakes, however, and I have been informed that the thinking of some senior Church officials in Rome, does not coincide with the view of the local Bishop. Time as usual, is likely to reveal the truth. I know of three priests who found their vocations from an encounter with Julia Kim.

Miraculous Images

Many books have been written over the centuries, on the subject of miraculous events that have been associated with images of Jesus and The Virgin Mary.[26,27] From the Irish point of view one of the best known of these images is connected with Walter Lynch, Bishop of Clonfert, in the seventeenth century. In 1655 Bishop Lynch fled the Cromwellian persecution to Gyor, a small town in western Hungary, where he was made auxiliary to the local Bishop. An image of The Virgin Mary, which he brought with him from Ireland, began to shed tears of blood on March 17th 1697, which was one of the darkest years in Irish history. This bleeding was witnessed over a long period by large numbers of believers and non-believers alike. The image since then has become a great centre for prayer and intercession. The two hundredth and fiftieth anniversary of the bleeding miracle was 1947. This was a dark hour for Hungary, and was an occasion when the famous Cardinal Mindszenty gave one of his last great sermons, before his imprisonment and torture.

Over the last fifty years, and especially over the last twenty, there has been a great increase in the number of images, weeping tears, particularly those of The Virgin Mary. These tears have turned to blood on several occasions. The tears and blood from many of these weeping images have now been verified scientifically to be of human origin. Many of the images have also been submitted, by sceptical Church authorities, for x-ray examinations, in order to exclude fraud. All this, together with the messages and healings associated with these images, strongly suggests that this is a real supernatural phenomenon. The obvious question then is, why? and what does it mean? Albert Joseph Hebert asks these questions in his book *The Tears of Mary – and Fatima, Why?*[28] This book, (which has sold widely, with at least ten print runs and two editions to date), describes large numbers of these weeping images.

Images of Our Lady of Fatima and Rosa Mystica are the most common images found weeping. These images have wept in many countries of the world, but especially in Italy and in the United

States. In 1972 the Supreme Court in the US ruled in favour of legalizing abortion. Many images wept in the US that year, particularly in New York and New Orleans. In this small effort of mine, it is not possible to go into any detailed analysis of the many events surrounding these weeping images. **I can only suggest that Mary weeps because She knows how bad things are, how many souls are being lost, what lies ahead, and how bad things will get.**

Charisms of Healing and other Spiritual Gifts

There is no difficulty in finding evidence for unexplained, mysterious, and what have been widely accepted as miraculous medical cures. These occur on a regular basis world-wide, in Christian communities, and in some cases these are associated with particular individuals. It has to be regarded as significant that there is almost always a definite and obvious link with prayer of some kind, especially prayer associated with the Eucharist. The most reliable accounts of these healings, which seem to have no natural explanation, and thus suggest a supernatural connection, are obviously those from modern times, where there are living witnesses and where there is access to convincing scientific or medical evidence.

Sr Briege McKenna

There are many examples of individuals with special charisms of healing and other gifts, some of whom I have personal experience. For those who wish to explore a little in this area, I would suggest a study of the life of an Irish born nun, Sr Briege McKenna, in the order of St Clare, as a good subject to start with. Her book, Miracles Do Happen,[29] is a beautiful, simple, well written book, which touches on many different aspects of the spiritual life. She was born in Newry, Co. Down, Ireland in 1946. Her mother died when she was thirteen years old. Two years later, she entered the local Poor Clare convent, as a novice. At the age of twenty four she was a young nun in a wheelchair, crippled with rheumatoid arthritis. She was not only completely cured in an instant at a prayer meeting but was also told that she had the gift of healing for others. This book also shows very clearly that all Christians (Catholics sometimes think that they are the only ones) can get great gifts from the Holy Spirit. The clear message is that the Holy Spirit of God knows no boundaries. Humanity makes the divisions between people, not God.

Some years ago, the priest in my home parish, in county Clare, Ireland, told me of his experiences with Sr Briege. Fr Sean Foy never drank alcohol until he was about twenty five years old, but after his first drink, he rapidly became an alcoholic. He overcame this problem but soon afterwards became an insulin dependent diabetic. His peripheral leg pulses deteriorated rapidly and he developed gangrene in one foot. One weekend he found himself, as a relatively young man, very depressed, in hospital in Galway, in pain, and waiting for an operation on Monday to amputate a portion of his foot. It was then that a priest friend of his brought Sr Briege to visit him and pray with him. Fr Foy had never heard of her before but gladly accepted her prayer with him. He felt nothing at the time and thought no more about her, when she left. After some hours he noticed that the pain had gone but again thought nothing of it, except to be grateful for the moment. The surprise came on Monday, the morning of the operation, when the bandage was removed from the foot. The foot was completely normal and the gangrene, which had been present for weeks, had disappeared and the pulses were normal. Everybody who has any knowledge of this kind of vascular problem will know that this kind of healing just does not happen naturally. There was no medical explanation for it. This Poor Clare Sister has a particular gift for healing priests, both in body and soul. Thousands of clergy attend her retreats in many countries of the world, every year. She foresaw the events in Medjugorje (see page 163) and told a

Franciscan priest from that parish, at a retreat in Rome, some months before the events began. Her life is yet another constant reminder of the occasional, direct, and tangible action of the supernatural into the realm of suffering humanity.

John Bradburne

John Bradburne was a British army officer of Anglican background, who fought in South East Asia during World War II. He was always a spiritual man and after the war he began to travel the world in search of truth and in search of a meaning for life. He became a Roman Catholic after many trials and opposition from his family and friends. His journey to Rome took years and the story of his conversion reads like some other great English conversion stories, over the last two centuries, such as Cardinal Henry Newman. During his search he walked on foot to the Holy Land. After his reception into the Catholic Church, he then tried to enter various religious orders. He was having no success and eventually he arrived in Zimbabwe, Africa. There he continued to pray and to search for his vocation in life.

Eventually John was encouraged to visit a Leper colony in Mutemwa. When he arrived there, he felt certain that this was where God was calling him. After his first trip to the lepers he expressed three wishes to a Jesuit friend. These were that:

> He could work for the lepers.

> He would die a martyr.

> He would be buried in Franciscan Robes.

He spent the rest of his life (nine years) working and caring for these lepers. He had great difficulty with some of the local farmers, who used to use break the perimeter fence of the lepers' land to enable their own cattle to get at whatever meagre crops the lepers had managed to grow. John was horrified at this and used to repair the fences. The farmers got upset and they decided to tell the freedom fighters that he was a government spy, and made many efforts to have him removed. They brought him to a local chief who refused to condemn him as he was well known for helping the lepers and all the local children loved him. All of John's days were spent either working for the lepers, praying, or writing poetry. John used a small mountain nearby as a favourite place where he spent much of the nights in prayer. On the way up the mountain he constructed Stations of the Cross and on the top he made a rosary circle.

The locals knew his life was in danger and kept warning him. He was very upset by all these warnings and because everybody wanted him to leave. The locals described one occasion, when he was very agitated, how he had spent a long time up the mountain praying. When he came down, he was full of peace and from then on, he radiated this peace everywhere he went. He said that he had met the Archangel Michael on the mountain, who told him that it was God's wish for him to stay with the lepers. Eventually the local farmers succeeded in arresting him and bringing him to trial before a group of freedom fighters. By now it was 1979 and the civil war for freedom was at its height in Zimbabwe. The leader of these freedom fighters knew that the locals in the area had a very high regard for John, so he tried to save him by offering to take him to Mozambique. John refused however, knowing that it would cost him his life. On Sunday, 2 September 1979, the guerrillas came for him. Accusing him of being an informer, they kidnapped him and then shot him. He died instantly, on 5th September, at the age of 58.

The local farmers were scared of the authorities finding out about the killing of a white man and so they tried to hide the body. When they approached the body, however, they heard what was described as beautiful singing from Heaven, which scared them away. They also described three shafts of light coming from his head and his two feet and joining together at a point, over the body. Above the three shafts of light, there was a big white bird rising and falling as if to protect the body. John's body was providentially found later that morning, by a catholic priest who happened to be driving by.

During the funeral service, which was held in the Cathedral, three drops of blood fell on the floor from the coffin, to form a small pool. The undertaker was very upset, thinking that the body had not been prepared properly. He ordered that it should be returned immediately to the funeral home. Mysteriously the shroud was found to be perfectly dry with no signs anywhere of blood stains. While the body was there, one of the attending sisters (Sr Margaret) noticed that he was not dressed in his Franciscan Robes, as he had prayed and wished for. These robes happened to be nearby so Sr Margaret immediately set this right. Thus John Bradburne got his three wishes, in life and in death. He was buried in a Franciscan Habit, according to his wishes, at the Chishawasha Mission Cemetery, about 18 kilometres (11 miles) northeast of Salisbury (now Harare).

Many miracles and strange Godly events have been associated with John, since his death. A close Jesuit friend of his, Fr Dove, has described healings, associated with the red head band which he wore. One of the best known strange events told about John since he died, concerns the kidnapping of a twelve year old girl, for a large ransom. This little girl was locked in a tin hut in the bush, in a car dump. She was discovered after many weeks and was returned home safely. She described how a man, with a long beard, came to her every day while she was in captivity and told her wonderful stories, sang for her, prayed the rosary with her, and told her not to worry. He said that everything would be well and that she would get back home. He always seemed to know when her captors were coming, as he used to tie her up again and leave just in time, only to return when her captors were gone. She eventually recognized John as her secret visitor, from a photograph shown to her by her mother. When her mother informed her that the man in the photograph was dead for a number of years, she insisted that she was certain that he was the person who visited her.

I have a priest friend in Zimbabwe, Fr Tim Peacock, who described visiting John's holy mountain. Apparitions of The Virgin Mary and many other visions are now appearing on this mountain. A large cross and a stone altar have now been constructed on top and many thousands of pilgrims are flocking there, from all over Africa. Fr Tim and his group, like many other pilgrims, witnessed a miracle of the sun on top of the mountain. The sun seemed to spin in the sky and give off large shafts of light in many colours, somewhat similar to those seen in other apparition sites of The Virgin Mary, in different parts of the world. The general opinion is that soon the Church will declare John Bradburne to be a saint. He lived life to the full in simplicity. He searched for his vocation in prayer and found it. He loved God and loved those he came in contact with. His life has been rewarded and now stands as a brightly lit signpost for anybody who will lift their eyes to Heaven. In a sense we are all called to be like John Bradburne.

Love

John Bradburne

Love is a short disease, a long desire,
Is strong and lasting healing.
Love is like an angler landing fish,
A hand at lyre,
A road-hog flogging home his motorbike.
Love is a deep unsleeping thing,
Leaps time, and steeps amidst eternity for rest,

And love is like three candles,
Lighting rhyme and metre, I am making for the best.
An alleluiatic sequence,
Shows a little of love's eloquence that lasts.
Love has three lights,
One to another glows, a third proceeds between.
Nought overcasts true love,
Because it knows that it possesses being possessed,
A zest above distresses.

St Padre Pio

Padre Pio was a well-known Capuchin friar, who lived in San Giovanni Rotondo, in the south of Italy.[30,31] He died in 1968 after having the stigmata for exactly fifty years. The stigmata is a phenomenon, whereby some individuals have the wounds and begin to suffer some of the pains that Christ suffered during His passion and death. These sufferings may be visible or invisible. Padre Pio had visible wounds in his hands and legs. Several books have now been written detailing the life of this man and the many miraculous events which surrounded him daily. From his childhood he was in continuous communication with his guardian angel, so much so, that it was a surprise to him to find out, as he got older, that others were not able to communicate with their angels in the same way. Padre Pio had many of the great mystical gifts of The Holy Spirit, which were associated with only very few of the famous saints in the history of Christianity. These included the gifts of miraculous healings, the gift of languages, the gift of prophecy, and the gift of bilocation (being in more than one place at the same time) etc. He had the gift of knowledge to an extraordinary extent and he used this regularly in the sacrament of confession, by reminding penitents on the details of the sins that they had forgotten to confess. In fact, this simple friar seemed to have more charismatic gifts than any other saint recorded in the history of the Church. The life of Padre Pio is a huge study in itself and for those who are interested it will serve as an outstanding support for Catholic theology and teaching. There are large numbers of people still alive who knew him. Those who had miraculous cures as a result of contact with Padre Pio, and many still survive, are legend. Since his death, there are also many reports of his appearances all over the world, with messages of direction, comfort and healing. I am personally acquainted with a man who claims to see Padre Pio on a regular basis and from the evidence of what this man has said and what I know of this individual, I have little difficulty believing him.

One interesting story associated with Padre Pio only came to light recently, soon after the death of St Pope John Paul II.[32] It concerned a very close friend of the Pope, who worked with him in the resistance movement, during World War II. Dr. Wanda Poltawska had survived the concentration camp and at this time was a young mother in Poland. While the Pope was still a Bishop in Krakow, she became very ill with cancer. St Pope John Paul (as Bishop of Krakow) wrote to Padre Pio (in Latin) and asked for his help. The secretary of the Padre later related how when he read this particular request aloud, which was one of about 2,000 letters per week, Padre Pio made the following comment: "We cannot refuse him !" The secretary was left in no doubt that there was something special about this Bishop, but he was not told what. The operation for the tumour was to be on a Friday and when the Bishop of Krakow (now in Rome for the beginning of the Vatican Council) phoned home on the following Saturday to inquire how his friend was getting on, he was told that the doctors could not find the tumour during an operation to remove it. The tumour had apparently mysteriously disappeared without any trace. Bishop Woytila wrote a note of thanks to Padre Pio, who in turn instructed his secretary that he should put this letter away safely, as it would become important in the future. When St Pope John

Paul II visited San Giovanni Rotondo in 1987, to pray at Padre Pio's tomb, his friend, Dr. Wanda Poltawska was with him.

Famous eye cures: There are many other extraordinary cures associated with Padre Pio. One of the best known is the healing of a blind seven year old girl, named Gemma Di Giorgio, from Palermo, Italy.[33] This little girl had been blind from birth and had no pupils in her eyes. Her Grandmother never gave up hope of a miraculous cure and she eventually got the little girl to San Giovanni Rotondo. Gemma visited Padre Pio in June, 1947, and after receiving her first Communion and a blessing from him she also received perfect sight, although her eye deformity remained. Gemma currently lives in Riber in the province of Agrigento. She continues to see perfectly although she has no pupils, which according to Opthalmologists, "is inexplicable".

Another eye healing often quoted is that of the construction worker, Giovanni Savino, who got a very severe injury which completely removed his right eye from the socket and badly damaged his left eye. Two friars and a doctor, who saw him immediately on coming to hospital after the injury, confirmed that his right eye was completely removed from the socket. Other doctors later confirmed that one eye was completely avulsed and beyond repair. A few nights after the accident he exclaimed that Padre Pio was with him because he felt somebody slap him on the right cheek, and he smelled the beautiful aroma associated with Padre Pio. He could not see him as his eyes were both bandaged. There was great amazement a few days later when his bandages were removed. His sight was perfect in both eyes and his face had no sign of injury. This happened in 1949.

Restoring a dead baby to life: Doctor Sanguinetti, who was a close friend of Padre Pio, was a witness to this strange event, in San Giovanni. He saw a woman arrive one morning and join the confessional queue for the Padre. She carried a suitcase and was crying uncontrollably. As she neared the confessional her cries got louder and louder. She eventually opened the suitcase for Padre Pio to reveal a dead six month old baby wrapped in rags. She said that when she began her journey, her baby was very ill but still alive. The baby had died on the way. Padre Pio was very moved and took the baby in his arms and began to pray. After a little time he gave the baby back to the mother saying, "stop weeping, can you not see that your baby is only sleeping?." The baby was indeed breathing and sleeping peacefully.

San Giovanni Rotondo was never bombed during World War II: Allied pilots stationed at Bari, Southern Italy, on many occasions, during the war, saw a monk appear in the sky and prevent them from dropping bombs on San Giovanni. Very few believed the story at first but as the number of pilots of different nationalities and faiths who had witnessed this grew, so did the credibility of the story. An American General eventually decided to check it out by going with a bombing squadron, who had the mission of destroying a German arms depot, near San Giovanni. As they neared the target he recalled that suddenly they saw a friar in front of them with his arms raised. All the bombs from all the planes were released automatically without any direct action from the bombing crews and fell harmlessly on the surrounding woods. Furthermore, he said that the planes automatically were turned back towards their base.

When the Germans later retreated, the same General with some pilots visited the monastery in San Giovanni. The first greeting from Padre Pio was to lay his hand on the shoulder of the General and say, "so you are the one who wanted to blow us all up!" The General only spoke English but nevertheless was able to have a long conversation with Padre Pio, who never spoke English himself. Following the meeting the General converted to Catholicism. He was only one of many converts, who became

Catholics after their first encounter with this friar. The best known converts were the communists and masons, who had previously attacked the church and scoffed at Padre Pio for many years, before personally meeting him.

The Englishman: Many years ago at a conference in Glasgow I had the privilege of hearing many first-hand accounts of encounters with Padre Pio. There were Anglicans as well as Catholics telling their stories. One of the most interesting I heard was from Cecil Humphrey Smith. He had become a Catholic in 1953 and in 1954 he began to work in Italy as a quality control chemist with Heinz Corporation. In 1955 he had a car accident, which resulted in very severe injuries, including a fractured skull and a fractured vertebra. Immediately after his accident he had two strange experiences. One was a near death, out of body, experience and the second one was of being visited by a Franciscan friar, who gave him a very detailed confession with communion afterwards. He found it very odd that, during the confession, this friar seemed to know all his sins before hand, and he even reminded him of certain misdeeds which he had forgotten. Furthermore, nobody in the locality seemed to know who this friar was.

One of Cecil's close friends was Bernardo Patrizi, of Papal nobility, and he helped him after the accident with the assistance of the daughter of Umberto, the last king of Italy. He eventually recovered enough to return to England but soon he began to suffer terrible agony from headaches. This continued for the next seven years, despite visiting all the medical experts in England and Rome. During one of his trips to Rome to see Professor Visintini, his friend Bernardo insisted that he should also go to visit a friend of his. His pain was very bad at this stage and he was not prepared for the long train and car journey which followed. It was winter and in the middle of the night, when he arrived in San Giovanni to attend a Mass to be said by Padre Pio. This was the first time that

Bernardo mentioned his close friendship with this friar. Cecil immediately recognized him, as the friar who came to him after his accident. He met Padre Pio briefly after Mass, in a row with other pilgrims. He got three taps on the head and suddenly his severe pain disappeared completely.

This Englishman later became a very close friend of the Padre. On one occasion when he saw how much Padre Pio was suffering, he asked if he could take some of the suffering from him. Padre was reluctant saying, "You couldn't. When you had pain you could not cope with it". The Englishman insisted as he was leaving. For the next year, Cecil was awakened every night at the time of the consecration of Padre Pio's Mass, with a very severe unbearable headache. He eventually went back and asked Padre Pio to remove the pain as it was overcoming him. The pain immediately disappeared and his personal contacts with the Padre became less frequent. Early in the morning of September 23rd, 1968, when Cecil was back in London, he got this severe headache back, with all its intensity. He rolled around the bedroom floor with his wife trying to comfort him. It lasted about one hour. When the pain ceased, he instinctively phoned Italy to find that Padre Pio had just died. Whenever I read a new book on Padre Pio, I am left with the same thought. How can anybody know the details of the life of this extraordinary friar and not want to be a Catholic? Many may be a bit like the author, Graham Green, who was taken to San Giovanni Rotondo by Cecil's friend, Bernardo. Graham Green refused the opportunity to meet Padre Pio saying, "I didn't want my life to be changed by a saint". Years later, however, he said in an interview with The Tablet, that he always carried a picture of Padre Pio in his wallet.[34] The truth can sometimes be difficult to accept, but only a fool would refuse to be forgiven and cared for by a loving God. Padre Pio is an everlasting reminder to us of the need for and the value of prayer, as well as the supernatural power associated with suffering as a victim soul. In March 2008, it was discovered after the exhumation of Padre Pio's body, that it did not undergo the normal process of decay.

Conclusion

In the light of these brief accounts, it is useful to recall the words of the Gospel of Matthew (11:25) – "I bless you Father, Lord of Heaven and earth, for hiding these things from the learned and the clever and revealing them to mere children." Be certain that intelligence and secular education are no advantage when approaching the Lord in the Eucharist. For anybody having trouble believing in the Real Presence of Christ in the Eucharist therefore, it may be useful to remember that understanding and faith in these mysteries, grows from the humus of humility. This growth is stimulated by watering with prayer, good works, fasting, penance, and also by study of the great number and variety of the miraculous events associated with the Eucharist. We must all continue to ask God in humility, to reveal to us the spiritual enlightenment that we need for eternal life.

5. One Fact that should and will Change the World

I will give you a teacher. Under her guidance you could become wise. Without her, all wisdom is foolishness. I am her son. Ask my mother what my name is?

St John Bosco - from a mystical dream

The evidence that The Virgin Mary has appeared in various places in the world, bringing messages to humanity directly from God, is phenomenal, overwhelming and well beyond reasonable doubt. In fact the evidence is so strong, it is reasonable to say, that those who do not accept the reality of apparitions of The Virgin Mary are either those who do not want to accept them or those who have not looked at the evidence. The eyewitness accounts now number in many millions and these are supported by scientific and medically substantiated facts and signs as well as many audio and video recordings and many detailed prophecies already fulfilled. The honest sceptic, therefore, has no room for manoeuvre. There is no doubt that God is warning humanity of impending disaster, through The Virgin Mary, who was the only faultless human person that ever lived, other than The God-Man Himself, Jesus Christ. Sadly, humanity is deciding to ignore these warnings and the consequences of the failure to recognize this evidence and these warnings will be catastrophic for all of us.

There has been a dramatic increase in the numbers of apparitions of The Virgin Mary especially within the last hundred years. This is very unlikely to be due to better communications, as "significant" messages from The Virgin Mary were always recorded in Church historical records, even if in earlier centuries the information was slower to disseminate outside the local areas. A good estimate for significant Marian apparitions in the eighteenth century was 20, with 100 in the nineteenth century, and approximately 400 in the twentieth century.[35] Very few of the 400 recorded apparitions over the last century have been officially approved by Church authority, as this can happen only after a full and thorough investigation. Even if many are not yet approved, and history shows that not many prove to be false, there can be no doubt that the complexity, urgency, and significance of the messages from the Mother of Jesus have increased dramatically. Cardinal Ratzinger, in the Ratzinger Report,[36] said that "one of the signs of our times is that the announcements of Marian apparitions are multiplying all over the world". The number of Catholics now living, who claim to have experienced private encounters with The Virgin Mary, is large. There is a reason for all this.

As I already mentioned in chapter 1, the year 1517 is associated with the Protestant Reformation, 1717 is associated with the start of the modern Freemason movement, which led to the French Revolution, and 1917 is remembered for the beginning of Communism in Russia. These three dates represent milestones on the road to an erosion of traditional Catholic and Orthodox Christian belief, in favour of more modern secular ideas, which are now in the ascendancy but on the other hand, the apparitions and messages of The Virgin Mary have played a major role in mitigating this erosion of traditional Catholic belief, over the last four centuries. At the time of the beginning of the Protestant Reformation in Europe, millions of Mexican and South American pagans were being converted to Catholicism, mainly through the influence of The Virgin of Guadalupe. The influence of the French Revolution was likewise counteracted by major interventions of The Virgin Mary in Paris, at La Salette, Lourdes, and later at Pontmain, Banneux, and Beauraing. The beginning of Communism in Russia was clearly predicted at the Fatima apparitions, which to date have been the most authenticated series of messages ever given through The Virgin Mary to mankind (see below). The battle goes on, and all the indications are that we are rapidly moving toward a climax. It is thus important to have some understanding of the messages of The Virgin Mary to humanity since the reformation, in order to appreciate some of the complex aspects of the catastrophe now facing humanity. I will concentrate on the apparitions and messages which are relatively well known and considered to be of major significance.

Guadalupe

As mentioned above, it could be said that the great modern revolt against Catholic Church teaching began with the Protestant Reformation in 1517. One of the first major responses by Heaven to this revolt came in the form of an apparition by The Virgin Mary in Guadalupe, Mexico. Although Marian apparitions have been occurring right throughout the history of Christianity, of all of them, The Virgin of Guadalupe is regarded as one of the most famous and best known. Devotion to The Virgin Mary has been steadily gaining influence in Catholic teaching, since this apparition of the early sixteenth century.

The story involves the mysterious appearance of The Virgin Mary to a poor recently baptized Mexican, named Juan Diego, at Tepeyac Hill, near Mexico city, on 9th December 1531. The local Bishop found his story difficult to believe and asked for some convincing sign from The Virgin before he would believe. This sign given was somewhat similar to Lourdes in France, three centuries later, as in both cases some of the evidence provided for an authentic Heavenly messenger was roses blooming in the "wrong" place, out of season. When Juan told The Virgin Mary of the Bishop's request, she asked him to collect up some Castillian roses which had mysteriously appeared out of season on Tepeyac Hill. He gathered them up in his tilma and went off to show them to the Bishop. When he arrived in the presence of the Bishop, Juan opened his tilma to let the roses drop on the ground. This alone would have been enough to convince the Bishop, but there was more. As the tilma unfolded, to the astonishment of everybody present, a beautiful image of The Virgin Mary, now known as *Our Lady of Guadalupe*, had become imprinted in a mysterious way on it. There are many aspects to this image, now recognized as not of natural origin, which remain unexplained. The survival of this cloth through the centuries is also unexplained, as the lifetime of this material, being made of roughly woven plant material, was usually only five to ten years.

The scientific work done on this image over the last forty years has shown, beyond any doubt, that it is not a normal painting of human origin.[37,38] It is an image which cannot be reproduced by science. One of the many extraordinary things about it is the picture seen in the eyes, when the images of the pupils are magnified. One can see a picture of the individuals who were present in the room, when this image of The Virgin Mary first miraculously appeared. At first, three or four individuals could be seen, including the Bishop, when The Virgin's pupils were magnified. Over the last two decades, more and more detail has been identified by modern technology, and it is now believed that there were twelve individuals present in the room, when this image was first exposed. In other words, the reflection from the pupil of this image is like the reflection that would be in a human eye, at a particular moment in time. There is no way that this could ever be introduced naturally and this is one of a number of scientifically supported phenomena, associated with this image, which has led to its acceptance as being of a supernatural origin.

There were lots of hidden messages in this image, which were in keeping with many of the beliefs of Mexicans at the time, including the black belt, which was worn around The Virgin's waist, as an indication of pregnancy. This image is now being promoted worldwide as a pro-life icon, because of this visible relationship with pregnancy. Some of the scientists who have investigated this image over the years have become converts to Catholicism as a result of their investigations. This event took place in Mexico, when the Protestant Reformation was just taking hold in Europe. More converts came into the Catholic Church as a result of this image, than were lost, during the decades that followed the Reformation (see Divine Design page 376 for further details).

The Miraculous Medal

Marian apparitions began to occur far more frequently over the last two centuries, and especially over the last fifty years, when there has been a literal explosion in frequency, significance and complexity of these apparitions and apparition sites. This new era of growth in Marian apparitions began with the now famous Miraculous Medal apparition, in Paris, in 1830.[39] The Virgin Mary gave a design for a medal which has led to the distribution of many hundreds of millions of these medals, all over the world. This design was given to a twenty four year old Vincentian nun, who also received many messages regarding future events, which later took place as she had predicted. Her identity, as the nun who saw The Virgin Mary, was kept secret all her life, except for her Bishop and priest. Her identity was eventually revealed just a few months, before she died.

Most Catholics will be familiar with this medal. It has been called the Miraculous Medal because of the many miracles, especially miracles of grace, which have been acclaimed through wearing it around the neck. There are some very extraordinary stories told about it, which one can write off as coincidence, but the coincidences are so unusual and so numerous that chance has been discounted a long time ago. One of these significant coincidences was that the body of the nun, now known as St Catherine Labouré, never decomposed naturally. Her body was not subjected to any form of artificial preservation, and when it was exhumed fifty years after she died, there was not even the smallest sign of natural decomposition. The limbs were still supple and even the eyes were still described as blue in colour. The body was in a state of perfect preservation. You can still see this body in the Rue De Bac, in Paris, to this day. The doctor who was present at the exhumation of her body, soon afterwards converted to Catholicism from atheism. St Catherine Labouré joins many hundreds of others saints of the Church, whose bodies failed to decompose naturally. Description of some of these can be found in the book, The Incorruptibles.[40]

Another extraordinary story associated with the medal concerned the Jew, Alfonsine Ratisbone, who wore the medal as a result of a bet with a Catholic friend. Through a strange series of events, he was drawn into a Catholic church within days of starting to wear this medal. Like St Catherine, he too had a vision of The Virgin Mary in this church. During the vision, he was supernaturally infused with a profound knowledge of the truths of the Catholic faith, without knowing anything of these doctrines previously. He became a Catholic convert and he was later ordained to the priesthood. After some years as a priest, he started a religious order for the conversion of the Jews.

There are many other incidents described in association with this medal, particularly connected with medical healings. Some of these have been written up in several books. It may also be of interest for some to know that the German Catholic, who designed the flag for the European Union, got the idea of the twelve stars, which are prominent in this flag, from the design of the Miraculous Medal. These twelve stars are mentioned in the bible – Revelation 12 – (see also chapter 16 on sacred astronomy and prophecy).

Conversion on Death Row: Finally a story widely circulated regarding a conversion of a prisoner in the US may be of interest to some. "In 1943, twenty-year old Claude Newman was awaiting execution in a Mississippi prison for shooting Sid Cook, his beloved grandmother's abusive second husband. During his stay in the prison, Claude noticed a medal hanging around the neck of a fellow prisoner and he asked the man what it was. The latter responded by throwing the medal on the ground with a curse, as he said "take that." Unbeknown to him, the pendant was a Miraculous Medal and even though he knew nothing about it or what it represented, Claude picked it up and hung it around his neck. He had no idea how this simple action would change his life.

During that night, Claude was awakened by a glowing vision, which he later described as "the most beautiful woman that God ever created." The lady in the vision calmed the frightened man by saying "If you would like me to be your mother and for you to become my child, send for a priest from the Catholic Church." "A ghost, a ghost, screamed Claude, as the woman disappeared and he called for a priest. The next morning, Fr Robert O Leary (who later recorded the story) was called for. After listening to the extraordinary account and speaking to him, the priest found Claude to be a very simple, illiterate soul who knew very little about God or religion. The priest proceeded to teach the young man about the Catholic Faith and soon the catechism lessons grew to include four other inmates who were deeply impressed by Claude's story. Several weeks later, Father O Leary introduced the Sacrament of Confession and Claude volunteered.

"Oh I know about that! The lady told me that when we go to confession we are kneeling down not before a priest, but before the Cross of her Son. And that when we are truly sorry for our sins, and confess them, the Blood that Jesus shed for us, flows down over us and washes us free from all sins". The others were stunned at this new revelation. But, seeing their surprise, Claude apologized, "Oh don't be angry, don't be angry, I didn't mean to blurt it out."

Assuring him that he was not angry, Fr Robert asked Claude if he had seen the lady again. Taking the priest aside, the young man said "She told me that if you doubted me or showed hesitancy, I was to remind you that while you were lying in a ditch in Holland in 1940, you made a vow to Her which She is still waiting for you to keep." This revelation fully convinced the priest of Claude's claim because during the war Father O'Leary had promised to erect a church in honour of Our Lady's Immaculate Conception if he survived. As he and Father returned to the class on Confession, Claude told his friends, "You should not be afraid of Confession, you're really telling God your sins, not the priest. You know, the Lady said that Confession is something like a telephone. We talk through the priest to God, and God talks back to us through the priest."

Finally, the catechumens were received into the Church, as in the baptismal records of St Mary's Parish, Vicksburg, MS, Claude's baptism is registered on January 16th, 1944, four days before his scheduled execution. As the day for his execution neared, the Sheriff asked Claude if he had a last request. "Well, all my friends are all shook up. The jailer is all shook up. But you don't understand. I'm not going to die: only this body is. I'm going to be with Her. So then, I would like to have a party. "The Sheriff was shocked, but consented and even allowed Claude's fellow inmates to attend.

On the morning of the execution, Claude was full of joy. As he mentally prepared himself with Father O Leary, the Sheriff rushed in shouting that the Governor had granted a two-week reprieve. To everyone's amazement the young man broke down in sobs, inconsolable. "But you don't understand! If you ever saw Her face, and looked into Her eyes, you wouldn't want to live another day! What have I done wrong these past few weeks that God would refuse me my going home? Why Father? Why must I still remain here for another two weeks."

Suddenly Father O Leary had an inspiration. James Hughes, a fellow prisoner on death row, harboured a particular hate for Claude and he also hated all things religious, despite having been raised a Catholic. Father Robert suggested that Claude offer his disappointment for Hughes' conversion. So, Claude spent the final two weeks of his life praying for this man's return to the Faith.

Claude was executed on February 4th 1944. Father O Leary testified: "I've have never seen anyone go to their death as joyful and as happily. Even the official witnesses and the newspaper reporters were amazed. They said that they couldn't understand how anyone could sit in the electric chair beaming with happiness"

When the time came for James Hughes to be executed, he violently refused all spiritual assistance, cursing and blaspheming, even while seated in the electric chair. Suddenly, looking intently towards a corner of the room, a look of surprise came over his face, quickly followed by one of sheer horror. He shouted, "get me a priest." Father O Leary approached him and heard the man's full confession. Father asked him for an explanation for his change of mind. The condemned man said that he had seen Claude Newman and The Blessed Virgin standing behind him with Her hands on Claude's shoulders. At Claude's request Our Lady showed James a glimpse of Hell, which filled him with horror and he immediately called for the priest.

Once again, the simple wearing of the Miraculous Medal called down our Mother's gaze and saved not only one, but many souls in that Mississippi Prison.

Fr O Leary did fulfil his promise to Our Lady and had a church erected in Clarksdale, Mississippi (MS 31684) in honour of Mary's Immaculate Conception in 1947.

Lourdes

Other well recognized apparitions of The Virgin Mary that occurred in Europe during the 19th century were at Lourdes and La Salette in France, Pontmain in Belguim, and Knock in Ireland. Lourdes in France is one the best known and is still one of the most popular places for pilgrimages. The message at Lourdes was given to a young, poorly educated teenager, named Bernadette Soubirous. Like the body of St Catherine Labouré, the body of St Bernadette, even though she died of severe tuberculosis of the bone, is also incorrupt and can still be seen in Nevers, France. Large numbers of miracles of healing have occurred in Lourdes over the years. A number of these have been fully authenticated by medical and scientific experts, who have testified that there was no natural explanation. On average one major miraculous healing event is reported on a weekly basis, but, however, only approximately 1% of these are eventually fully medically and scientifically authenticated, to the extent that they can be accepted as miraculous by the Catholic Church. Some of these are absolutely extraordinary and truly merit the term supernatural. When scars disappear or when patients, who have been ill and paralysed for years from very demonstrable physical diseases, suddenly stand up and are completely healed, it is difficult to find a natural explanation. As an example of an authenticated Lourdes miracle, I will relate briefly one such dramatic healing, connected with Mr John Traynor, from England, in 1923. More details on this healing can be found in the CTS booklet, I met a Miracle,[41] and medical details on this and many other Lourdes miracles can be found in *The Miracle of Lourdes*.[42]

John Traynor: One of the most famous cures recorded in the history of Lourdes is that of a soldier, from the First World War, named John Traynor. He was seriously wounded, at the battle of Gallipoli, in 1915. He was injured in the chest, head and right arm. One bullet entered the side of his right arm and cut the nerves at the axilla, which supply the skin and the arm with sensation and also control the muscles. The result of this injury was a loss of sensation and paralysis of the arm, with resulting muscular atrophy. Doctors told him at that time that there was no hope of receiving any power back in the arm. In other similar situations patients are usually encouraged to have their arm amputated, as a 'dead limb' becomes a nuisance, but he refused amputation during his many trips to hospital. He was sent to five hospitals in all, and there were many futile efforts to relieve his condition. During his last hospitalisation, his skull was opened in the hope of helping his epileptic attacks, which now averaged three per day. He was finally discharged with a full military pension and sent home to Liverpool. Both legs were partially paralysed and there was a loss of control of bladder and rectal function. The following is a personal account by John on how he got to Lourdes:

"When I was a little better, I was discharged in an ambulance and carried to my own bed... I could not walk or stand and I was in a very bad way. I had not moved my right arm for eight years. My wife received "attendance allowance" for helping and looking after me. After several months in bed, the British Red Cross lent me a chair, so that I could get out in the fresh air. My wife or my daughter always carried me from my bed to the chair or from the chair to my bed. I was supplied with an air cushion on account of bed sores at the bottom of my spine. In the month of July, 1923, I was at home, helpless as usual, when a neighbour came to the house and spoke of an announcement that had been made in our parish. A Liverpool diocesan pilgrimage was being organized for Lourdes. It would cost thirteen pounds to go, and a down payment of one pound would engage a place. My wife was out in the yard and I called her in. I told her to go upstairs and get a certain box in which we kept a gold sovereign, which my brother had given me and which we were treasuring for some special emergency. I told her I was going to give it to Mrs. Cunningham, our neighbour, as a first payment on a ticket to Lourdes. My wife was very disturbed, but finally did as I told her, and the neighbour went off and made the booking. Soon one of the priests in charge of the pilgrimage came to see me. "You cannot make the trip", he said, "You will die on the way – please give it up." I said I had made my first payment and that I was going to Lourdes. Then came the matter of a medical certificate. We called in several doctors. – Every one of them said that such a journey would be suicide. The priest came again and begged me to give up the idea. I would not give in and I finally succeeded in going without a medical certificate. To raise the twelve pounds, the balance due on my ticket, we sold some of our belongings and my wife even pawned some of her bits of jewellery".

The day of departure came. There were two trains and in the confusion of getting all the sick aboard, Traynor missed the first train, that is, the one he was supposed to board. Again the priest tried to persuade him to give up and go home but Traynor was determined not to give up. There was another train, and he said that they could put him on that one. By being stubborn he eventually succeeded in getting on the train.

The journey was a nightmare. Three times they tried to take him off the train, as he seemed to be dying. Each time, there was no hospital at the town where they stopped and so they decided that the only thing to do was to keep on going. The pilgrimage reached Lourdes on July 22nd, after days of travel. Traynor by then was in a terrible condition. He was taken to the Asile Hospital and kept under sedatives. On July 24 he was examined by three physicians – Dr. Azurdia , Dr. Marley and Dr. Finn, who issued the following certificate:

"This is to certify that on July 24, 1923, we examined Mr John Traynor, of 121 Grafton Street, Liverpool, and found his condition to be as follows:

1. He was an Epileptic and we saw several attacks during his journey to Lourdes.
2. The nerves of his right arm (radial, median and ulnar) were paralysed and he had wrist drop and muscular atrophy.
3. The shoulder and pectoral muscles were also atrophied.
4. The opening in the right parietal region is about 2 cm. The pulsations of the brain are visible. A metal plate covers the trephine orifice.

5. There is an absence of voluntary movements of the legs, with loss of sensibility.

6. Incontinence of urine and faeces occurs."

On the morning of the second day, when he was due to be brought to the baths, he was seized with a severe epileptic fit. He said that he felt something burst in his chest, and blood flowed freely from his mouth. The doctors in attendance were very alarmed and they did not want him to go into the bath. Being stubborn again, he insisted and eventually they allowed him to go into the baths in the grotto. There was no apparent change when he came out of the water except that, unknown to him at the time, a change had taken place. It marked the end of his epileptic fits, and he never had another fit after that first day in the Lourdes baths.

This again is how events unfolded, in his own words: "The afternoon of July 25 came. I seemed to be as bad as ever. There were many to be bathed and we all wanted to be finished before the afternoon procession, which began at four o'clock. When I was in the bath, my paralysed legs became violently agitated, so much so that I almost emptied the bath. The brancardiers (assistants) and attendants were terribly alarmed, thinking, no doubt, that I was in a fit, though I knew it was not so. I struggled to get to my feet, feeling that I could easily do so and wondered why everything and everybody seemed to be working against me. When I was taken out of the bath, I cried from sheer weakness and exhaustion. The brancardiers threw my clothes on hurriedly, put me back on the stretcher, and rushed me to the square, in front of the Rosary Church, to await the procession. Practically all the other sick were already lined up. I was the third last on the outside, to the right as you face the church. The procession came winding its way back, as usual, to the church and at the end walked the Archbishop of Rheims, carrying the Blessed Sacrament.

He blessed the two ahead of me, came to me, made the sign of the cross with the monstrance and moved on to the next. He had just passed by when I realised that a great change had taken place in me. My right arm, which had been dead since 1915, was violently agitated; I burst its bandages and blessed myself - for the first time in years. I had no sudden pain, that I can recall, and certainly I had no vision. I simply realised that something momentous had happened. I attempted to rise from my stretcher but the brancardiers were watching me. I suppose I had a bad name for my obstinacy! They held me down and immediately after the final Benediction rushed me back to the Asile. I told them that I could walk and proved it by taking seven steps. I was very tired and in pain. They put me back in bed and gave me another hypo (pain injection) after a while."

"At five-thirty", says Traynor, "I heard the bell of the Basilica begin to ring out the Ave. I jumped out of bed and knelt on the floor to finish the Rosary I had been saying before I fell into a short sleep. Then, I dashed for the door, pushed aside the two brancardiers and ran barefoot out of the Asile. I may say here that I had not walked since 1915 and my weight was down to eight stone (112 pounds or 50 Kg). Dr. Marley was outside the door. When he saw me run out of the ward, he fell back in amazement. Out in the open now, I ran towards the Grotto, which is about two or three hundred yards from the Asile. The brancardiers ran after me but they could not catch up with me. When they reached the Grotto, there I was on my knees, still in my night clothes, praying to Our Lady and thanking her. After I had prayed for about twenty minutes, I got up surprised and not pleased, to find a crowd of people gathered round, watching me. They drew aside to let me pass as I walked back towards the Asile". (When he took off his bandages on returning from the Grotto he found that every one of his sores had healed).

"By now the hotels of Lourdes were emptying and an excited crowd had gathered, in front of the Asile hospital. I could not understand what they were doing there, as I went in to dress. I put my clothes on in a hurry but kept away from the bed for fear those doctors and brancardiers would tackle me again and treat me as a sick man. I went to the washroom to wash and shave. Other men were there before me. I bade them all good morning but none of them answered me. They just looked at me in a scared way. I wondered why? It was still pretty early in the morning when a Priest, Fr Gray, who knew nothing about my cure, entered the ward where I was and asked if anybody there could serve Mass. I answered that, I would be glad to do it, and I went off and served his Mass in the chapel of the Asile. It did not seem strange to me that I could do this after being unable to stand or walk for eight years. I went into breakfast in the dining room of the Asile. The other men drew back as if they were afraid of me. I could not grasp the situation nor could I understand why people were staring at me so hard. The next day was a nightmare of excitement and crowds. – Later I was brought to see the priest who had opposed my coming to Lourdes. I saw him in another hotel, and when we met, he broke down and began to cry".

The Pilgrimage left for home on July 27th. Early that morning the three doctors again examined Traynor and found that he could walk perfectly, that he had recovered the use of his right arm, that he had regained sensation in his legs, and finally that the opening in the skull was closing up.

There was great excitement in Liverpool when the pilgrimage was due back from Lourdes. His wife and friend had great difficulty reaching the platform gate. When his wife told the official that she was Mrs. Traynor, he said, "All I can say is that, this Mr Traynor coming cannot be a Catholic, as there are already seventy or eighty Mrs. Traynors on the platform!

An official report was eventually issued by the medical bureau in Lourdes on October 2nd 1926. The report declared that, "this extraordinary cure is beyond and above natural causes". The most amazing part of this cure is probably the instantaneous healing of the right arm. The nerves going through the axilla, which supply the arm, skin and muscles, had been irreparably damaged eight years previously. Four surgical operations had done nothing to alleviate the situation. The instantaneous repairing of these nerves is an impossibility as far as medicine is concerned. Usually, if any repairing is done with surgery, this is minor and rare and very slow. According to the doctor's report, Traynor arrived in Lourdes a veritable wreck, a pathological museum, paralysed in the right arm and in both legs. He went back to London from Lourdes pushing his own wheelchair, arm and legs normal with a complete cessation of the epileptic fits.

"I am in the coal and haulage business now", he states in his conclusion. "I have four lorries (trucks) and about a dozen men working for me. I work with them. I lift sacks of coal weighing around 200 pounds with the best of them and I can do any other work that any able bodied man can do. I go to Lourdes every year and serve as a brancardier there".

Fatima

The Fatima apparition of The Virgin Mary is probably the most famous in the world. It ranks with Our Lady of Guadalupe, in Mexico, and Lourdes in France, in terms of the number of millions of pilgrims visiting each year. The Fatima messages, on their own, stand as a great bastion of support for Catholic Church teaching, and studying these messages in detail should be a great help to those looking for solid evidence supporting the Christian message of salvation. The Fatima messages also mark the beginning of a series of modern dramatic warnings to mankind from The Virgin Mary. These warnings indicate that, unless major changes are made in human behaviour, disaster will overcome the world. This warning has been repeated in different forms in the later messages of Garabandal in Spain, Akita in Japan, and Medjugorje in Yugoslavia. There is no doubt that the messages of The Virgin Mary at Fatima, Portugal, began a new and significant era in Marian messages. Before the events at Fatima, the global impact of Marian messages was much less, but from then on the messages and warnings were to have enormous global significance.

The apparitions at Fatima began in 1916, with an angel appearing to three little shepherd children, named Lucia, Francisco and Jacinta.[43] He presented them with the Eucharistic Host, suspended in the air above a chalice. The children described drops of blood coming from the host and falling into the chalice. The Angel prostrated himself before the host and chalice and said the now famous prayer: –

"Most Holy Trinity, Father, Son and Holy Spirit, I adore you profoundly. I offer you the most precious Body, Blood, Soul and Divinity of Jesus Christ, present in all the tabernacles of the world, in reparation for the outrages, sacrileges, and indifference, by which He is offended. Through the infinite merits of His Most Sacred Heart and the intercession of the Immaculate Heart of Mary, I beg the conversion of poor sinners".

He then gave Lucia the host and he gave the chalice to Francisco and Jacinta. Coincidentally, on this same day, in a parish dedicated to St Michael the Archangel, very close to the village of Fatima, a priest noticed during morning Mass, that one host had disappeared. He also noticed that a few drops of consecrated wine, which he had put in the tabernacle from the previous Mass, had also been dropped on a purification cloth near the chalice as if somebody had been removing some consecrated wine. He was very upset by this and he mentioned it at Mass asking the congregation to pray that he would come to understand what happened. He was worried that the tabernacle, sacred hosts, and consecrated wine had been desecrated. It was some time later that he heard about the details of the apparition of the angel and somebody explained to him that this may have been the answer to both the missing host, and consecrated wine.

The angel was preparing the children for the visitation of The Virgin Mary which began on 13th May 1917. The Virgin told the children that she would come back to them on the 13th of every month until October. A number of secrets were given by The Virgin, to be revealed to the world at a later time. The first secret was concerned with a form of atheism, which was about to be imposed in Russia, and how this would spread rejection of God, as well as war and suffering, throughout the world. Another major aspect of the early secret was concerned with the reality of Hell, the eternal suffering of souls, and the large numbers who go to Hell due to serious sins, and because there was nobody to pray for them. **On the 13th July 1917 the children were shown a vision of Hell. They saw a sea of fire with black glowing images in human form, floating in the fire. There were also frightful demons, in horrific animal like forms, and they heard frightful screaming and groaning, during this brief experience. The Virgin later told Jacinta that, during these times, sins of the flesh were the commonest reason for souls going to Hell.** The second part of the secrets were concerned with a second great war, which would occur during the reign of Pope Pius XI (not yet elected Pope), and how this war could be prevented. The final part of the secrets was concerned with the suffering of the Church and the Pope. This final secret was not revealed until the year 2000. Many other messages were also given to the children at various stages and many believe that Sister Lucia continued to get messages, both from Jesus and The Virgin Mary, for the rest of her long life.

Francisco and Jacinta were told that they would soon be going to Heaven and this, needless to say, was a message which shocked their parents at the time. Both died a few years after the apparitions, towards the end of the Spanish flu pandemic, in 1919. Lucia was told that she would have to live on in the world for a little while, in order to proclaim and spread the messages of Fatima, and spread devotion to the Immaculate Heart of Mary throughout the world. In fact she survived for many years and died on 13th February 2005. The "little while", therefore, turned out to be almost 88 years.

A Prophecy of a Great Sign: In order that humanity would believe that these messages were from God, a great public miraculous sign was predicted several months in advance. This was the first time in history that a major sign was predicted so that humanity would be convinced that a message was coming directly from God. This message was urgent with regard to the atheism about to begin in Russia and the damage it would do to peace and harmony in the world. The predicted time for this great sign was noon on the 13th October, 1917. At that time the Government in Portugal was very anti-Catholic and at one stage, government officials put the three children into prison, for disturbing the peace, so that they could not keep their appointment with The Virgin, on the 13th August. The August apparition occurred a few days later after their release from prison, during which the children were told that because of their arrest, the great sign of October would be reduced in magnitude. The Government Officials then decided that they would use the whole event to scoff at the Church, as they felt convinced that nothing would happen on the predicted date. The suppression of the news in the media was thus stopped, and pilgrims were allowed to freely enter Fatima.

In the morning of the day of the predicted great sign, large numbers of people gathered in Fatima. Estimates were that seventy thousand had travelled through the muddy roads to get there, in order to witness this great sign. The Government forces were there in strength. The predicted time of noon came and nothing happened. A scoffing multitude soon began to laugh at the whole affair. One o'clock in the afternoon came and still nothing happened, while large crowds waited in the pouring rain. At this stage the crowd was getting very restless and fights were breaking out. Suddenly the children gave signs that The Virgin Mary had appeared and what is now known as the Great Sign of Fatima occurred about 1.20 p.m. on the predicted day. The children screamed, "look at the sun" and as everybody began to look towards the sun, the so called "**miracle of the sun**" began to unfold. It took about ten to thirteen minutes to occur. Those present described the sun as spinning in the sky, with tremendous colours radiating outwards all over the sky. Then suddenly the sun seemed to be dropping down towards earth. The sun appeared to get larger and larger and as everybody thought that it was coming down rapidly toward earth, the crowd began to scream with fear. Then, just as suddenly the sun seemed to climb back to its normal position in the sky. This was witnessed by many disbelieving newspaper reporters and scientists, who were also there. These newspaper reporters had been pouring scorn and ridicule on the children and on the Church for weeks before hand. Nobody who was there denied that a spectacular event had occurred. Many very dramatic medical cures were also recorded during the apparent gyrations of the sun, while all noticed the ground was completely dry afterwards, despite the torrential rain during the whole morning. The people there also noticed that their wet clothes, which were also largely covered in mud, had also become perfectly clean and dry during the apparent movement of the sun. The sign of the great miracle of the sun was also seen as far away as 30 kilometres, so the idea of mass hysteria, which was later used by some to try to explain it away, could not be sustained as a valid explanation.

The reason this event did not occur at the predicted time of noon was later explained. At that time the clock was two hours ahead in Portugal, for Summertime, and in fact the time it occurred was actually noon by the sun, and not as measured by Portuguese clocks. The local priest and the other clergy who, up to that point in time had been doubting the story of the children regarding their conversations with The Virgin Mary, were now convinced of the veracity of the events. On the following morning, the newspapers in Portugal were all describing this major sign that was given from God, which had been predicted by the children. The October revolution, which took place very shortly after the great sign, and which was followed by the beginning of Communism in Russia, was only the first of many events which would later confirm the accuracy and authenticity of these Heavenly messages, given to the three young children.

The Second World War: Another part of the message concerned World War I, which was then going on. The Virgin told the children that World War I would end soon, but that a second, even greater war would begin in Europe during the reign of Pope Pius XI, if people did not change their attitude to Church teaching and listen to Her advice. The Virgin made it very clear that war was a punishment allowed by God because of sin. The children were told that before the beginning of this second Great War, another sign would be sent, consisting of a very bright light seen in the sky. This would indicate that a major war was again about to begin in Europe. This sign, which was predicted, occurred on the night of the 25th January, 1938. It is a matter of public record that Lucia wrote to her Cardinal and told him that this was the sign which The Virgin Mary had promised, and that war was about to break out again in Europe. Furthermore, she said that although this sign looked like a normal aurora, when scientists investigated, they would find that it was not normal. The sign did seem like a gigantic aurora all over the northern hemisphere. It was seen right into the Mediterranean countries and all over Canada. Fire brigades were out all over Europe on that night, looking for the fires being reported. The abnormality of the aurora was confirmed by American scientists many years later, when they pointed out that the aurora effect had to come from two light sources rather than one, even though there is only one known source of light, that is, the sun. It so happened that on this night also Hitler was taking over the army and making plans for war. Hitler and his generals saw the blood red sky from their mountain retreat and decided that it was a good omen for war. Within a few weeks the tanks were rolling into Austria (12th March 1938). Technically therefore, World War II began during the reign of Pope Pius XI, as predicted by the children, but it was Pope Pius XII who reigned as Pope during most of World War II.

One of the very important aspects of the message regarding World War II was that The Virgin said this war could have been prevented, by the consecrating of Russia and the world to her Immaculate Heart. This specific request was made known to Sr Lucia at Tuy in Spain in 1929. The major message therefore, which Heaven wanted to convey to humanity, through The Virgin at Fatima, was very clear. Firstly, God wanted to establish in the world devotion to the Immaculate Heart of Mary, and secondly, peace in the world has been entrusted to Mary. Not only is this true, but God wants it to be seen and understood by everybody that it is true. In a very mysterious way, God wants it to be clear to all humanity that this is the only way peace can come into the world. The Virgin said, **"In the end, My Immaculate Heart will Triumph and there will be peace"**. This is a most profound statement with huge implications, not only at the time it was said, but particularly now, and going forward into the future. Unfortunately, when this request for consecration was first made in 1929, the Church authorities did not appreciate either its urgency or its significance. The Virgin Mary also told Sr Lucia, "The consecration will be made, but it will be late".

Consecration of Russia and the World: The first effort made by Catholic Church authorities, at consecrating the world to The Immaculate Heart of Mary, was by Pope Pius XII, at the request of a Portuguese lady, named Alexandrina Da Costa (see page 82). She is often referred to as the fourth seer of Fatima because of her intimate connection with this message. A battle, according to Churchill, which was the turning point of the war, was fought and won by the Allies, three days after this effort by Pope Pius XII. The final effort at consecration to the Immaculate Heart was made by Saint Pope John Paul II, on the feast of the Annunciation, (25th March) 1984. He directed that all the Catholic Bishops in the world should make this consecration of the world including Russia, in union with himself, to the Immaculate Heart of Mary, in order to achieve peace in the world. Some still say this was not done properly or at least not done as well as it should have been. There is little doubt, however, that major changes happened in Russia, almost immediately afterwards. Within a short time after the consecration, the communist system in Russia began to crumble and Gorbachev came into power. Remarkably, there was a peaceful change from the strict communist regime to what we have in Russia today. As if to confirm the role of the Immaculate Heart in the changes brought about in Russia, it was an interesting coincidence that the official declaration of the abolition of State Communism in Russia, took place on the 22nd August, 1991. This was a date in the Catholic calendar, when the feast of the Immaculate Heart of Mary was celebrated and now the *Queenship of Mary* is celebrated.

Fatima connecting France, Russia and the Pope: Sr Lucia had many follow up messages, both from Jesus and The Virgin Mary, until her death in 2005. Many of the details of these messages have not been made known. One of the messages, which has been reported, was a follow up message concerning the delay to the requested consecration, made in 1929. It was from Jesus to Sr Lucia, on August 1931, and said, "Tell my ministers that by delaying the carrying out of My request, for the consecration of Russia and the world, they follow the same path as the King of France. It too will have terrible consequences, and, like the King of France, they too will follow him into misfortune". This was a reference to a request made to King Louis XIV, through St Margaret Mary Alacoque, to consecrate France to the Sacred Heart. This request was made on June 17th, 1689. This request, however, was not complied with and one hundred years later to the day, on June 17th 1789, King Louis XVI was removed from power, at the beginning of the French Revolution. King Louis XVI finally made this consecration, just before he was guillotined four years later. Although the consecration did not save his own life, it led to the saving of the life of his son, through strange circumstances, so that the monarchy has still a direct line now living in France. The survival of the son of King Louis XVI would, however, still be disputed by many historians. In the famous apparition of **La Salette**, in France, 1846 (This message, like Fatima, is also approved by the Catholic Church), it was revealed to one of the visionaries that the son of King Louis XVI did not die in prison, and they were told who the true heir to the throne of France was at that time. The visionary was later taken outside France to meet him. The present heir to the throne in France is said to be living quietly in a monastery, waiting for expected events to take place, which will restore the French monarchy, and place him on the throne. All this is very mysterious, but many Catholic prophecies down through the centuries have spoken about the restoration of the monarchy in France, which will in turn be responsible for the restoration of the Papacy, after a coming conflict, which will dislodge the Papacy from Rome. Time will reveal all (see chapter 11 for more details on this).

Some Fatima Coincidences: There are a lot of interesting coincidences surrounding the shooting of Saint Pope John Paul II, in 1981, which relate to the Fatima message. First of all he was shot on the 13th May, reminding us of the Fatima message, which spoke specifically, of the suffering of the Pope. It was explained above that the 13th of May was the date of the first apparition of The Virgin at Fatima, and it has now been established in the Church as the date for this feast day. It was also an interesting coincidence that the time of the Papal shooting was 19.17 in the evening, Moscow time (that is 17.17 in Italy), bearing in mind that the 1917 Fatima message was concerned, to a significant extent, with Russia. The Pope said afterwards that he felt that it was Our Lady of Fatima who protected him from certain death. Some interesting information came to light after the shooting, regarding the main bullet changing course within the Pope's body so as to avoid vital structures, but this information is difficult to verify or be certain of.

Another interesting event associated with Fatima concerns the bombing of Hiroshima, at the end of World War II. In his book, *Fatima, The Great Sign,*[44] Francis Johnston describes this.

"When the atomic bomb destroyed Hiroshima in 1945, eight men living near the blinding centre of the nuclear flash miraculously survived the searing hurricane of blast and gamma rays, while everyone within a mile radius perished and others residing further afield continue to die from the lethal effects of radiation. For over thirty years, some two hundred scientists have examined these eight men, trying in vain to determine what could have preserved them from incineration. One of the survivors, Fr H. Shiffner, S.J., gave the dramatic answer on TV in America: "In that house, we were living the message of Fatima." The miracle amid the ashes of Hiroshima was but one in a chain of grace released on the world through Fatima ever since the firmament-shaking miracle of the sun in 1917. To cite another of the author's many examples: while no nation on earth seems able to stem the global advance of Communism (which our Lady had foretold with unerring accuracy in 1917, together with the reason for it), nevertheless, in those countries where sufficient people resolutely complied with the Fatima message, the red tide, even at the last moment, was mysteriously halted and routed. Such was the case with Austria (1955), Brazil (1966), Chile and Portugal (1975). And behind the Iron Curtain, the Pilgrim Virgin of Fatima was the direct cause of the first churches to be built in Poland since the end of the Second World War."

The Japanese Government still refused to surrender unconditionally, and so a second atomic bomb was dropped on the city of Nagasaki three days later, on August 9. Nagasaki was the secondary target, but cloud cover over Kokura, which was the primary target, providentially saved it from destruction on the day. Nagasaki was in fact the city where two-thirds of the Catholics in Japan were living, and it seemed that after centuries of persecution, they were asked to make this final sacrifice, which would end the war. There was also a strange parallel incident in Nagasaki to the survival of the Jesuits in Hiroshima described above. A Franciscan friary, established by St Maximilian Kolbe in Nagasaki before the war, was likewise unaffected by the bomb which fell there. St Maximilian had a deep devotion to The Blessed Virgin Mary and when he was building his friary, against the advice he had been given, he decided on another location in the city. The friary, on the day of the bomb, was undamaged as it was protected from the force of the blast by intervening high ground.

13th October: The message of Fatima was a message of peace, with directions from Heaven on how humanity could find peace in the world. History shows that a series of events have occurred over the last century, particularly on the 13th October, which were connected with peace. There are many indications down through Church history, that Heavenly communications place a lot of emphasis on anniversaries and dates. Many experts on the Fatima message believe that there was a very definite connection between the apparitions occurring on the 13th of the various months and the story in the Old Testament book of Esther. Queen Esther interceded with her King, on behalf of the people of Israel, whose destruction was set for the thirteenth day of the month. This view is supported by the single star (Esther meaning star) which appeared near the foot of the apparition of The Virgin and is depicted in the images of Our Lady of Fatima.

The modern drama began when Pope Leo XIII got a weakness during thanksgiving prayers after his daily Mass. When he recovered he was very shaken and he described a vision he had, telling him that Satan was about to be released more freely, to wreak much greater havoc in the world, over the coming century. He immediately composed a prayer to St Michael the Archangel, which from then on was said at the end of each Mass worldwide, right up until the changes introduced at the Second Vatican Council in 1964. The date of the vision, which Pope Leo XIII had, is often quoted as the 13th of October 1884, but there is no definite record of this and it can be taken that this is no more than an approximate date. The witness to these events was regarded as very reliable but could not remember the exact day or date. Some had hoped that the consecration of the world to the Immaculate Heart of Mary in 1984 (100 years later), was the beginning of the end to the extra freedom Satan was allowed on earth. It is also not definite, however, that the period of extra freedom allowed to Satan was exactly a century and the emphasis and hope now is on this period of Satanic freedom ending on the 13th of October 2017, that is, the centenary of the great sign of Fatima, which was on the 13th of October, 1917.

Another significant event which occurred on the 13th October, was the death of Alexandrina Da Costa, (fourth seer of Fatima) - on the 13th October, 1955. The major message of Akita (see page 172), was a subsequent message from Fatima, given on the 13th October, 1973. There is a long list of other events world wide of lesser significance, also associated with peace, which coincidentally are also linked with the 13th of October. Coming from Ireland, I took note that the first peace agreement between opposing political sides in Northern Ireland, was on the 13th of October, 1994, when the Unionists declared a ceasefire. The latest and final agreement for peace and power sharing in the North of Ireland, in 2006, was also signed on the 13th of October. Coincidences are coincidences, however, and we must be careful not to put too much emphasis on them. The action of God directing or permitting these coincidences is unknown. Some saints would say that, as God directs everything, there are no coincidences. Frank Duff, founder of The Legion of Mary (now probably the largest lay Catholic organization in the world, with approximately 10 million active members and 50 million auxiliary or praying members) , used to say that coincidences were one of God's ways of sending humanity messages.

The Significance of Fatima: The messages given to humanity at Fatima in 1917 were of enormous consequence. The events at Fatima lifted Catholic prophecy to a new level of authenticity and accuracy. The Queen of Prophets has made it abundantly clear that She is for real, and that She communicates messages directly from God to humanity. The great *Miracle of the Sun* cannot be doubted as a real event and the messages from Fatima have been confirmed many times since that miraculous event. The *Miracle of* *the Sun* (usually in far less dramatic detail than in Fatima), has become a kind of authenticating sign for Heavenly approval. It has occurred in association with many places and events of Marian significance all over the world, since 1917. This *Miracle of the Sun* was witnessed, for example, when Pope Pius XII was proclaiming the doctrine of the Assumption in Rome in 1950. The messages of Fatima emphasise the truth of Catholic doctrine and theology, and can be summarized in the following four points:

1. The Virgin Mary has been chosen by God to bring messages of advice and warning from God to humanity.

2. War is a punishment for sin. There is a great need for repentance and reparation. There will be catastrophic consequences for humanity if God's laws continue to be rejected.

3. Hell is a real place and a large number of souls go there to suffer eternal damnation and suffering, in the presence of demons.

4. Peace in the world has been entrusted by God to the Immaculate Heart of Mary. There is no other route to world peace and everybody will know this, sooner or later.

The great miracle of Fatima, therefore, was a real event. It was witnessed by large numbers of both Catholic believers and non-believers, up to a distance of thirty kilometres from Fatima, so mass hysteria is not a valid explanation. A valid and reasonable hypothesis is that this was instigated and executed by a supernatural force, and the fact that it was predicted beforehand to occur at an exact time, by The Virgin, indicates that She was in some way involved. Subsequent events confirmed the ability of The Virgin Mary to predict the future. The events at Fatima in 1917 can be ignored but cannot be denied. Fatima is now an unassailable obstacle to those who deny the existence of God, to those who dispute Catholic theology, and to those who deny the reality of Hell.

Garabandal

Garabandal, or more correctly San Sebastian de Garabandal, is a small village of about 80 houses in Cantabria, in the North of Spain, about one hour by car to the south west of Santander. It is in the municipality of Rionansa, and is situated beside the hillside of Pena Sagra (sacred mountain), where legend says that St James spent some time on his way to Santiago De Compostella. The road stops in this village and from there, to travel further south, you will have to walk into the mountains. Between 1961 and 1965 four young girls in the village had apparitions and long detailed talks with The Virgin Mary. During that period over two thousand apparitions occurred. Some of these encounters lasted for hours and over the first two years in particular, The Virgin Mary could be said to have virtually lived in the village.

All the inhabitants of the village at the time had their own personal experiences. The adults often had to accompany the children into the hills, sometimes in the middle of the night, and in the rain and snow of winter. They saw extraordinary events during that period and the old villagers had no doubt whatsoever about the validity of these apparitions. Most were convinced that these extraordinary events had to have a supernatural origin. There were many strange happenings, such as ecstatic marches, with very rapid and unnatural movements over the land, both backwards and forwards. During these marches the children were looking upwards in an ecstatic state all of the time. In spite of these very rapid movements, over very rough and rocky terrain, sometimes in the dark of night, the children were never seen to stumble or fall. There were also extraordinary contortions, and unnatural positions adopted by the visionaries, as for example, when coming downstairs in houses, at a completely unnatural angle. These were seen by large numbers of people, as every house in the village was visited by the girls when they were in their so called, "ecstatic marches". The young girls were able to find people and find objects in the dark, without looking directly at them or for them, but gazing continually at the object of the vision. On some occasions these objects had been lost in the mud of the village streets. It was common for the girls to be given large numbers of rosary beads and other religious objects to have The Virgin bless them. During the ecstasies and after the blessing, the girls always returned the items to the correct owners, while still gazing at the vision. There were many other aspects to these events, which also led to the firm conviction of both the local priest and the people that these children were speaking to The Virgin Mary.

There are usually two main messages quoted from Garabandal, but there were a number of others messages given, which are also of great significance. The two central messages for humanity are recorded as follows:

Firstly, on October 18th 1961:

"We must make many sacrifices, perform much penance, and visit the Blessed Sacrament frequently. But first we must lead good lives. If we do not, a chastisement will befall us. The cup is already filling up, and if we do not change, a very great chastisement will come upon us."

Secondly, on June 18th 1965:

"As my message of October 18th has not been complied with and has not been made known to the world, I am advising you that this is the last one.

Before the cup was filling up, but now it is flowing over. Many Cardinals, many Bishops, and many priests are on the road to perdition and are taking many souls with them. Less and less importance is being given to the Eucharist.

You should turn the wrath of God away from yourselves by your efforts. If you ask His forgiveness with sincere hearts, He will pardon you. I, your mother, through the intercession of Saint Michael the Archangel, ask you to amend your lives.

You are now receiving the last warnings. I love you very much and do not want your condemnation. Pray to us with sincerity and we will grant your requests. You should make more sacrifices. Think about the passion of Jesus."

After getting the second message, the visionary Conchita, inquired how it was that the children in the womb could be killed, without killing the mother. Apparently The Virgin Mary had told her clearly, that this was one of the great growing evils in the world, and that it was one of the main reasons why, "The cup was overflowing". Conchita had never before heard of killing unborn babies.

The Garabandal events are best recognized and promoted by Catholic faithful because of the prediction that a great chastisement will happen for humanity unless there is a turn back to the laws of God. Before this chastisement comes there was also a prediction of a "Great Warning", when every human person will see the state of his or her own soul in the light of God's truth. This Great Warning has been predicted in Catholic prophecy, in many different ways by many saints and saintly individuals, down through the centuries. The messages about this great event have become very frequent over the last hundred years, but none of the previous messages were as detailed as given in Garabandal. The sudden great act of self-awareness will cause many to amend their lives, though sadly, many will quickly fall away again. The visionaries said that nobody should die from this experience, except perhaps a very small number who may die of shock and in terror. This Great Warning is to occur soon and will be a *Unique World Transforming Event*.

The Warning will be followed within a year by a Great Miracle and a Permanent Sign. This Permanent Sign is predicted to be left beside a cluster of nine pine trees on the hill, which overlooks the village of Garabandal. These pine trees were planted by a grandfather of Conchita, one of the visionaries, in memory of a first communion in the village, and also in honour of the nine choirs of angels. The visionaries have said that this sign will be seen by all, as everlasting proof and confirmation of the authenticity of their messages. It will be possible to photograph it but not to touch it. The visionaries have said that this would be a great final act of Mercy from God, to try to convince humanity not to keep rejecting God's laws. Otherwise, The Virgin Mary has said that a great punishment will occur, to such an extent, that the living will envy the dead. After the Warning, the Miracle and the Sign, humanity will have very little time to repent, convert and prepare for the chastisement. The extent of the chastisement will depend on how the people of all nations respond, in humility and repentance, to these "mega" world events. Chapter 12 deals in more detail with the prophesied Warning and Miracle. It is important to note the similarities with these predicted events and similar predictions in Medjugorje (see below, page 164).

After encountering the story of Garabandal for the first time, many have the feeling of reading science fiction. Fact however, is sometimes stranger than fiction and there is a large amount of good factual evidence to support the reality of The Virgin Mary's appearances, and the messages which she gave, in this mountain village, in Spain. The young girls spoke very openly about their meetings with The Virgin Mary, which numbered over two thousand in all. The details of the Garabandal events have been recorded in many books.[45,46] One of the most authentic and detailed books on the subject is, She Went in Haste to the Mountain.[47] This has recently been condensed from a three volume set, to a single volume. Of the many events recorded, I will briefly describe a few, which I hope will help to give substance and credibility to the whole story.

Miraculous Communion: The first event which I will describe is the miraculous communion which was given to Conchita, (one of the visionaries), by St Michael the Archangel. During many previous apparitions, when there was no Mass in the village, the children were seen, as if receiving communion from somebody. The girls explained that it was an angel who gave them communion, but neither the angel nor the communion, was visible to those present. According to the children's account, The Virgin Mary was persuaded to work a small miracle (milagro), so that the people would believe them. Conchita had predicted, some weeks in advance, that this host which the angel was said to be placing on her tongue, would become visible on the 18th July 1962. This was also the day of the local festival to honour Saint Sebastian, who is the patron saint of the village.

On that day, large crowds had gathered in the village, to take part in the festival and in particular to see this predicted miracle. The most interesting aspect of this event for me was that the 18th July came and went and the promised small miracle did not occur. It was very early in the morning of the 19th when Conchita got "the call" to go out into the street. She dropped to her knees and held her tongue out, as if to receive communion. At first, the tongue was bare and then a host was seen to appear on the tongue and enlarge in size. This was photographed by a visitor with a movie camera. The whole event with the extended tongue took about three minutes.

For a number of years I did not understand why the mystical communion did not occur on the 18th as predicted, but occurred very early in the morning of the 19th. The reason was eventually explained to me by an old carpenter, named Pepe, who was beside Conchita when she received this mystical visible communion. Pepe explained that this was the time when Church regulations did not allow the Eucharist to be received more than once each day. Conchita had received the Eucharist at Mass, on the morning of the 18th, as this was a feast day in the village. She was prohibited, therefore, by the Church regulations of that time, from receiving communion again on the same day. The predicted miracle had to wait therefore until the next day, in obedience to Church laws. This was not something that anybody thought of at the time, but it later emerged as a valid explanation for the delay of the predicted event. As with the predicted Great Miracle of Fatima (see page 129), this was also likely to be by sun time, rather than by Spanish clock time. It is likely that the miracle also occurred at the first moments of the 19th, sun time, which was well past midnight by summer "clock" time. This was hardly something that a sixteen year old girl could have invented. There were many witnesses there to corroborate Pepe's account, who also saw the host appear on Conchita's outstretched tongue. The event was later verified by the video photographs taken under the light of a torch.

The Andreu family: The Andreu family was an unusual Catholic Spanish family. There were four Jesuit priests in the family and after the father of the family died the mother entered a convent, and became a Visitation Sister. A number of impressive events in the Garabandal story are connected with this family. The first event is connected with Fr Luis Andreu, who had been investigating the girls during the apparitions. This young Jesuit theologian was allowed to see the future major miracle, which is to occur as a sign for humanity, in Garabandal. The girls found it strange to be able to see Fr Andreu, during the apparition of the 8th August 1961, as they claimed that they never saw anybody, except The Virgin Mary, during these occasions. Fr Luis explained afterwards, that he had actually seen the future miracle in a vision, and he confirmed that everything the girls were saying was true. During the remainder of the evening, he spoke continually about how wonderful the Mother of Jesus was, and how lucky we were to have Her as a mother also. On the road home from Garabandal, in the early morning of the 9th, he continually spoke about the wonderful experience which he had that evening. Suddenly, this young healthy Jesuit priest just lay back on the rear seat of the car and died. It was said at the time, that he died of joy. A few days after the death of Fr Luis, the girls saw him with The Virgin Mary, during an apparition. Fr Luis, was a great linguist, and during the apparition, he taught them how to pray in Latin and in Greek. The girls gave evidence that they not only recognized him clearly but also knew his very distinctive voice. His whole family later developed a great interest in Garabandal, especially his brother, Fr Raymon, who became a life-long promoter of the Garabandal events.

Fr Raymon Andreu became a very significant figure in the Garabandal story. He personally witnessed more than two hundred ecstasies and took many detailed notes. He ranks as one of the most reliable witnesses of the whole story. He was present when Conchita read the first official message from The Virgin Mary. He saw large crowds gather on a day which was very wet and rainy, up on the hill, where Conchita read the message. He heard Conchita, in a very low voice, read a very simple message, saying that we were not giving enough attention to the Eucharist and that we must pray, fast more and generally do more penance. He immediately felt that this was far too simplistic, and that there was no way that this could be a major message from Heaven, as he was led to believe in the months before. He immediately lost faith completely in Garabandal and fell into a very deep depression. Afterwards he spent many hours roaming around the mountain in the rain, very upset because he felt that he had made a major mistake in believing the story of the apparitions, despite the strange events surrounding the death of his brother. He had thoughts of leaving Spain and going to America, away from everything in Garabandal. Eventually he returned to the village, which by then, was in the darkness of late evening.

On his return, he was surprised to discover that the girls had been told by The Virgin, about his sorrow and depression. The following morning Conchita took him on a tour of the mountain and told him exactly where he was the day before, and exactly what was going through his mind. She related to him the thoughts which he had, in great detail, in each particular place. It is generally accepted that there are many different spiritual charisms, which can be given to individuals, but it can sometimes be difficult to decide whether these gifts are from an evil source or from God. In other words, spiritual charisms can sometimes be satanic in nature, which can cause great confusion, if it is assumed that accompanying messages are from God. The one gift that you can always be sure comes from God is when thought processes are read, or in particular, when an individual's thoughts can be repeated back in detail. Conchita told Fr Raymon that The Virgin had said that this was a special gift and sign for him from God, so that at no stage in the future would he ever again need to doubt the authenticity of the message of Garabandal.

This influenced Fr Raymon greatly, and he also had a number of other personal experiences associated with the message. On August 14th, he came back to Garabandal after burying his brother. During an ecstasy that evening, he was able to hear the girls speaking about the funeral details of his brother. They spoke in

146

great detail about what had actually happened and also about the number of items which had been changed from the normal funeral ceremony for priests, which they could not have known about. They also spoke in great detail about his disagreements with his brother and about vows he had taken. He knew that nobody could have known these details except himself and God. This, again, impressed him greatly.

Fr Raymon also had an earlier personal experience, in October of 1961. Coming to the village he was involved in a very bad car accident in which he injured his ankle. Two doctors in the village made the diagnosis that he had fractured his ankle. He was feeling very unwell, sweating, in shock, and had to be carried to bed. That night, Jacinta, who was one of the visionaries, came to the house in ecstasy and requested entry. She came to the bed-side of Fr Raymon and gave him a message from The Virgin, which said that his leg would be cured. When the doctors came back in the morning, they found that there was no swelling, the leg was perfect and he was able to walk normally. One of the doctors said, "What strange things are happening in this village!" Fr Raymon later went to live in California, where he became the spiritual director to Jacinta, and where he died on 11th Nov, 2004.

There are two final points regarding the Andreu family, which are not very well known, but are of interest. Firstly the mother of the four Jesuit priests, who became Sr Maria of the Visitation order after the death of her husband, described an incident when she was getting ready to go to bed one evening. Her room was filled with light. She described that in the middle of this light was, "my son Luis Maria, with two other men who had their backs to me. I could tell that they were priests because they were wearing cassocks. My son looked the same as he did when he was alive. I thought he came to say goodbye since he was not able to do so before he died. The vision then began to pale until it disappeared.

I was left in great peace and internal happiness". Secondly there was a very interesting coincidence regarding the death of the older of the brothers, Fr Aejandro Andreu. He died at the exact same time and exact same date 19 years after Fr Luis, who died on August 9th 1961 at 2 a.m. in the morning. Fr Aejandro died on August 9th, 1980.

The Permanent Sign: There is another interesting event concerning the Garabandal story, worth relating briefly, and which may be connected to the Permanent Sign, which is predicted to be left for all time at the pines on the hill overlooking the village. A few years after the events began, a young herdsman from the neighbouring village of Cosio, was on top of the mountain near the pines and late in the evening he made a fire to keep himself warm. He was unable to extinguish the fire, however, even though it never went out of control. This fire remained on the same spot of ground and burned for many weeks afterwards. During the day it could be seen as smoke, rising from near the pines, and during the night it could be seen as a fire. There was nothing obvious to burn but the fire kept burning. Eventually the soil around the whole area was carted off to a local University to have it studied, as nobody could understand what was keeping the fire going, without any obvious source of fuel. There is a possible connection with this event and the permanent promised sign. The pillar of cloud by day and the pillar of fire by night is described in the Old Testament, as the sign which guided Moses and the people of Israel out of Egypt. If the Permanent Sign was to be recognized as a "Shekinah", it would obviously have a great significance for Jewish believers (see page 650) for more details.

The Popes, St Pio, St Teresa of Calcutta, and Garabandal
One of the most commonly quoted messages from Garabandal, is the message given to Conchita regarding the Popes. She was told

that there would only be three more Popes before "the end of times" (that is after Pope John XXIII). She was also told that there would be a fourth Pope but that, "He would not count". The general view is that this present era of time will end after the prophesied Warning, Miracle, Permanent Sign, Chastisement and renewal of the world to a Christian way of life has begun (see chapter 12 for more details). It is now very significant that the present Pope, Benedict XVI, is number four since Conchita got that message. It is possible that the phrase, "He will not count", could mean that Pope John Paul I did not count because of his very short reign (33 days), or that the present Pope will not count, as the Garabandal events will occur during his reign and that Benedict XVI will witness the predicted Great Warning and Miracle. Most would believe it unlikely that Pope John Paul I did not count as he was a properly elected and valid Pope.

Conchita was also told that St Padre Pio would see the great miracle before he died. Needless to say, the death of St Padre Pio, in 1968, was consequently a great shock for her. This illustrates very well how visionaries, even when completely bona fide and authentic, can have false understandings of their messages, and why the Church must always act with the utmost caution in giving credence and acceptance to them. As it later turned out, one month after the death of St Padre Pio, Conchita got an urgent message to meet a delegation from St Padre Pio's monastery, in Lourdes, France. Conchita travelled to Lourdes with her mother and two friends. They received a personal message from Padre Pio, written before he died, telling Conchita that he had seen the miracle in a vision. He had also instructed that the cloth covering his face after death, should be given to Conchita, and she received this from the delegation. There are many other incidents, well recorded, that confirm beyond any doubt, that this famous stigmatic priest believed and supported the authenticity of the Garabandal messages.[48] Among these is a personal letter sent to

Conchita by St Padre Pio, explaining to her that people would believe in the Garabandal visions when it was too late. Mother Teresa of Calcutta also believed and supported the Garabandal messages. She became close personal friends with the visionaries and asked to see them on a few occasions when she was ill. It is very difficult to believe that these two great spiritual mystics and giants of the Church could have been led astray by a fraud, or worse still by something diabolical. There is also very good anecdotal evidence that both Pope Paul VI and Saint Pope John Paul II were believers in the Garabandal events and messages. In fact every visionary with any significant standing within the Catholic Church, over the last forty years, to my knowledge, have all believed in the authenticity of the Garabandal messages.

A Garabandal Cure: Finally, I would like to relate the experience of a personal acquaintance and friend, Fr George Costigan. Fr George was an American army chaplain, decorated for bravery on a number of occasions. After leaving the army he developed a malignant brain tumour and radiotherapy for the tumour had left him blind in one eye. During a trip to the Catholic Shrine of Lourdes, in France, with an American group, he overheard somebody speak about Garabandal. He agreed to go on a coach trip from Lourdes. As soon as he stepped off the coach in Garabandal, a little child ran up to him and asked in perfect English: "Would you like Jacinta to pray with you?" He responded, "Why would Jacinta want to pray with me?" The child said, "Are you not the priest with the brain tumour?" He was very surprised, as he was not dressed as a priest and he had not told anybody on the trip about his medical problem. When he agreed, the child then led him to Jacinta, who was about to say the rosary in the church. She said nothing to him but blessed him with her rosary at the church door. He then proceeded to say the rosary with those present inside the church. During the last decade of the rosary, the sight completely and instantly returned to his blind eye. He was obviously excited and he related to me how he stayed awake all that night in a prayer of thanksgiving, as he was afraid that the sight would go again in this damaged eye. The sight has remained and now many years later the tumour has not recurred. It was also a surprise at the time that, even though the village is very small, nobody knew or could find out who the little child was, who could speak English. FrGeorge later returned with his niece, Valerie who has Multiple Sclerosis, to live in Garabandal. When he related his story to the local Bishop, he was asked never to speak about it publicly. Over many years he honoured that request. I overheard him truthfully respond to a private question as to how he first became interested in Garabandal. Other medical cures have also been recorded in association with the Garabandal events.

The Significance of Garabandal: There is good evidence to suggest that the events at Garabandal were authentic messages to humanity from God, via The Virgin Mary. Those who reject them as such are usually those who, either do not want to believe, or know nothing about any of the details. **Marian messages have suggested that the 1960s marked a pivotal point in time, for the relationship between God and humanity.** From that time forward, a Divine chastisement became inevitable, and it was then a matter of what form this chastisement would take, and how serious it would be. The Garabandal messages indicated details of specific events which will lead up to the chastisement. The messages of Akita (see page 172) and Medjugorje (see page 164) confirm this chastisement, and indicate how bad it could get. For those interested, therefore, the Marian messages at Garabandal, Akita and Medjugorje should be studied together in some detail. **It would be hard to imagine anything which would be a bigger world changing event than the predicted Garabandal Warning** (see chapter 12 for more detail). As such, it is impossible to overestimate the significance of the events at Garabandal.

Mary in Cairo

One of the least known appearances of The Virgin Mary over the last 50 years was at a Coptic Church in Zeitun, Cairo, (Egypt) between 1968 and 1971. Historically it is interesting that this Church is built beside the route which the Holy Family (Jesus, Mary & Joseph), is believed to have used in the Flight into Egypt. One of the family members, who donated the money for the construction of the Church, had a Heavenly message fifty years previously indicating that this Church would be blessed, in a very special way, sometime in the future, The Coptic Christians have beliefs very similar to Roman Catholics. The history of the Coptic Church goes back to the See of Alexandria, which was started by St Mark. This See separated from other Bishops (as in the See of Antioch, Syria, the See of Jerusalem and the See of Rome etc.), around 451 A.D. due to a misunderstanding on how to express the fact that Jesus was both God and Man. The Patriarch of Alexandria became the Coptic Pope and he continues to hold that title up to the present day. Essential beliefs in the Eucharist, the sacraments, the role of The Virgin Mary and other aspects of teaching remain the same, as in the early Christian Church teaching. The Coptic Church is thus very similar to the Roman Catholic Church. A commission is now working to bring the two Churches together.

The first vision at Zeitun occurred on 2nd April 1968. A Muslim worker saw a lady dressed in white on top of the middle dome of a Coptic Church. He pointed with his bandaged finger, alerted his friends and began to shout, "Lady don't jump, don't jump". The fire and rescue services were called and within minutes there was great commotion. The lady then stood up and revealed herself, as a luminous lady full of light, with a large halo above her head. She floated effortlessly above the domes, while bowing and greeting the people with gestures. This was the first of many appearances over the next three years. Next morning, Farouk Atwa, the man who first saw The Virgin, had an appointment to go to hospital to have his finger amputated because of gangrene. When the bandage was removed from the finger, both he and his doctors were amazed to find his finger completely healed.

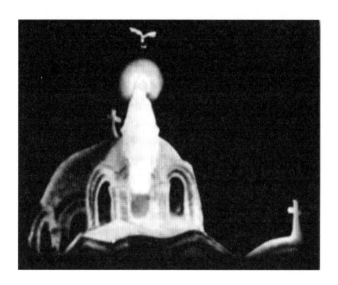

Within a few weeks the crowds reached an estimated 250,000 each evening, composed of Christians, Muslims, Jews and others. Sometimes there were great red and purple clouds rising around the vision, while the smell of incense filled the air. The local Bishop said that it would take millions of censers to produce this amount of incense. Sometimes she appeared with Jesus in her arms and other times with St Joseph and Jesus as a young boy. Muslims were commonly seen praying on their mats and reading from the Koran, verses in praise of Mary. One of the most interesting and unusual aspects of these appearances was the number of people who saw her. Many photographs were taken of the image and this was very unusual as it is not normal to be able to photograph apparitional images of The Virgin Mary so easily. The events have been described in a number of books, as in, Before Our Eyes,[49] and *Our Lady Returns to Egypt.*[50]

The evidence for these appearances of The Virgin Mary was considered overwhelming, and never before was there such unanimity between different churches on this point. The Official Coptic Church, with their Pope as head, approved the apparitions, and officials of the Roman and Greek Catholic Church also agreed with this. Dr. Ibrahim Said, head of the Evangelical Church and spokesperson on behalf of all the Protestant Churches in Egypt, officially announced the certainty of the appearances of The Blessed Virgin Mary at the Coptic Church, in Zeitun. Confirmation of the apparitions also came from the Government of Egypt, who did an investigation because of the major disruption to traffic and life in the area over the three years. The Government report said that the possibility of fraud was investigated and found to be completely without foundation. This was very big news in the Arab press at the time, but it was generally not reported in the mainstream western media.

One of the best eyewitnesses to give detailed accounts of the whole story was an American Lady, named Pearl Zaki, who was visiting her relatives in Egypt at the time. She was so impressed by what she experienced that she wrote a number of books on the subject.[49] Every night there were new appearances and new experiences. One of her descriptions was as follows: "The figure of The Virgin Mother was all in light... Each person present, as I talked with them, felt alone with her, and drawn completely to her. It was an experience that enveloped me and left me completely empty. Being human, I can never justify or explain its beauty in words or actions, but only attempt to utter praises to God, for the rest of my life".

Fr Jerome Palmer, an American Benedictine from Indiana, also visited Cairo at the time and collected eyewitness evidence of the apparitions. Almost everybody in Cairo, to whom he managed to speak to at the time, had seen The Virgin. Mr Wadie Shumbo, a Protestant engineer with Mobil Oil, said, "I have seen The Virgin, I tell you. I have seen her in full body. I have not seen shadows … .I saw Mary in full body, standing before the cross. I cannot describe what I felt. The Muslims all started to cry". Mohammed Hassen, told Fr Palmer, "It was no artefact. It was The Virgin". They met many others including the Egyptian Minister of Labour and an official from the TV Broadcasting Company, who all had seen the vision, some of them on many occasions. One of the leading Muslims in the district claimed that Our Lady had appeared to him and asked him to stop throwing stones at the Christians and told him to put the sign of the cross on his house. Although remaining a practising Muslim, he was now convinced of the authenticity of the visions. In response to the request of The Virgin Mary, he had forty big white crosses painted around the walls of his house.

Miraculous Cures: There were many miraculous cures associated with these apparitions. Shortly after the first reports of healing the Patriarch of the Coptic Church, Pope Kyrillos VI, set up a medical commission, consisting of seven medical experts, to document and verify the cures. The head of this commission was Professor Shafik Abdel-Malek, from the Faculty of Medicine, in Cairo. There were large numbers of medical cures recorded, but the reason why some individuals were selected for cures, was not at all obvious, as cures came to Jews, Muslims, and non-believers as well as Christians. There was a long list of very dramatic and instantaneous cures. Many of these are described in the various published books, some already mentioned. It may be of some interest here to very briefly describe a few of them.

1. Madiha Mohammed Said was a twenty year old, who was blind and dumb since birth. She was brought to the apparition site, by her two brothers, who asked a priest nearby to pray for her. This was June 4th, 1968, and while the priest was praying, Madiha suddenly shouted, "I see the apparition of The Blessed Virgin". In an instant she could see and speak.

2. Dr. William Nashed Zaki was an ex-director of a medical therapy centre. For thirteen years he had suffered regular pain from a recurring hernia despite a number of operations to repair it. One morning while watching The Virgin blessing the people, he prayed for a cure. His pain disappeared, and when he got home he found that the hernia too was gone.

3. Linda Kamal had suffered from a paralysis of the hand for twelve years. She spent the night of June 1st, 1968, at the Church praying for a cure. Her prayers were answered. Three professors who examined her hand afterwards found her hand to be completely normal.

4. Sami Abd-el-Malek was a 40 year old, who suffered from a recurrent malignant tumour of the bladder. When he visited the Church, he had pain resulting from the tumour which had recurred again. The tumour was described to him during his last hospital visit, as the size of a lemon. On the night he saw The Virgin his pain disappeared, and on subsequent medical examination, by a Professor of Urology, in Cairo, it was found that the tumour had also disappeared without medical intervention.

5. Theresa Gadahla Beshai got polio when she was one month old. She was now a young girl unable to walk. She saw The Virgin Mary on the 30th April, 1968, and immediately she seemed to fall into a coma. Helpers carried her into the Church and placed her on the ground, with other sick individuals, who were being blessed by a priest. As soon as the priest blessed her and prayed for her she roused, stood up and walked out of the Church completely cured.

It is interesting that no words were spoken during these public apparitions, (like Knock, Ireland in 1879). As one eyewitness put it, "It was as if God said: SEE - MY MOTHER, – and we did". It was also interesting that The Virgin Mary had previously informed a young girl, to whom she appeared to in Lithuania, on the 13th July, 1962, in order to save her life, that she would soon be coming to Cairo.[49] A very short time before the appearances in the Cairo Church, The Virgin also appeared to the holy priest of the Church and said to him: "Get Ready, I am coming soon, to this Church". He fell off the stairs with the shock, and injured himself, but he kept this incident secret and did not speak about it publicly. The story was later made known by his Bishop, to whom he had revealed it just before he died, in 1984. It is interesting that to this day, people of all beliefs will be found worshipping in this Church, emphasising again that religious divisions are made by man, not by God. We are all children of God, called to love God and love each other.

More Apparitions in Egypt: On the 17th August 2000, exactly one year after the destructive earthquake at Izmit, Turkey, The Virgin Mary began to appear at St Mark's Coptic Church in Assuit, Egypt. There were large luminous doves, strong smells of incense and beams of light, very reminiscent of the apparitions over St Mary's Coptic Church, in Zeitoun, Cairo from 1968 – 1971. This apparition was also later approved as authentic by the Coptic Church. The Catholic Church also accepts the validity of these apparitions which were witnessed by very large numbers of people (including non Christians). There were also two lesser known apparitions of The Virgin Mary over churches in Cairo, in recent years. These were at St Demiana, in the Shoubra district, between 1986 – 1991, and at Warraq in 2009. All these apparition sites were thoroughly investigated by the police, mainly because of traffic problems caused near them due to the great interest. This went as far as turning off all electric power in that area of Zeitoun so as to make sure that the light source was not man-made. Emmet O Regan[205] points out that the Dragon pursuing the woman (adorned with the sun), described in the Bible, Rev 12, so as to devour her child as soon as it is born, reflects on King Herod's attempt to kill the infant Jesus, during the slaughter of the Holy Innocents. It is interesting therefore that both the Zeitoun and Assuit apparitions traditionally mark sites where the Holy Family of Jesus, Mary, and Joseph stayed during their time in Egypt. In trying to further connect these apparitions with historical efforts to sacrifice innocent children, Emmet also points out that the first attempt to curtail the Jewish population was the order by the Egyptian Pharaoh to have all Jewish male infants cast into the Nile river. The famous apparitions in Zeitoun began, not only coincidentally at the time when Pope Paul VI returned relics of St Mark to Egypt (patron of the country), but also when the 1968 abortion act was legalized in the UK (April 1968). This UK law opened the door for other countries to follow suit with laws permitting the slaughter of the innocent.

Mary in the Ukraine

On Sunday, April 26th 1987, twelve months exactly to the day, after the Chernobyl disaster, The Virgin Mary appeared in bright light, over a locked church, in the Ukrainian village of Hrushiv. It was Divine Mercy Sunday (first Sunday after Easter), when twelve year old Marina Kizyn first saw The Virgin Mary. She was on her way to school, at eight in the morning. She went and alerted her mother, whose home was near the church. Marina's mother also saw a beautiful Lady, holding a baby, who smiled and bowed her head in greeting. The Virgin was dressed in black. The details of this apparition have been wonderfully documented in a film and in the book, *Queen of the Ukraine*,[51] by John Bird.

One week later, over 100,000 pilgrims and curious onlookers, from all over the Ukraine, gathered at this church, to give thanks, pray and see The Virgin if possible. Towards evening, as the sun began to sink, beautiful colours of blue, yellow, orange and red covered the area. Suddenly The Virgin Mary appeared. Almost everybody there claimed to have seen her. Some prostrated themselves on the ground while others just prayed. The Virgin took Her rosary, amber and blue in colour, kissed it, and spoke to the people as follows:

"I come to you with tears in my eyes and I implore you to pray and work for good and for the glory of God. Ukraine was the first country to acknowledge me as Queen and I have received her under my care. Work for God, for without this there is no happiness, and no one will gain the kingdom of God".

The authorities tried to stop the people coming, but failed. They tried to block the only road leading to the church, by cutting large 300 year old trees growing on the roadside. A strong wind blew up, however, and the trees fell on top of the police cars rather than on the road. Appearances were at irregular intervals up to the 13th of May. From then on appearances were regular, up to the feast of the Assumption, on the 15th of August. There were also many other sightings of The Virgin, in other shrines in the Ukraine, over the summer period. Many remembered an old prophecy which said, that The Virgin would appear in fourteen Ukrainian shrines, before they would get their freedom. In mid-May, The Virgin Mary gave this message:

"My faithful, how joyful I am to be with you at your shrines. I see your faith and strength and how you have persevered in fidelity to the Church, even when all hope seemed to have gone. This is why I ask you to forgive your enemies. The conversion of Russia will come through you and the blood of the martyrs. The time is coming when this nation will attain its statehood. You are dear and precious to me. If there is not a return of Christianity to Russia, there will be a third world war, and the whole world faces ruin."

Josyp Terelya is one of the most famous lay leaders of the Ukrainian Church. He spent many years in Soviet prisons and suffered terrible hardships. He survived being crucified on a cross for days in a lonely wood, before being discovered. He also survived the famous freeze cells in Siberia, where the Soviets put prisoners, whom they wished to freeze to death. The Virgin Mary appeared to him, and his cell became so warm that he had to take off his shirt. He was investigated by medical institutions for some years afterwards, to try to explain how he survived the extreme cold. He had many other private visitations and messages from The Virgin. He was released from prison by new Glasnost rules under Gorbachev, in February 1987, and he too was a witness to the Hrushiv apparitions. His story is told in the book, *The Witness*.[52] When he left Russia, he visited St Pope John Paul II. He related how the figures, which they regularly sent to Rome, were falsified and did not reflect the true number of believers in the Ukranian Church. By 1985 there were in fact approximately 700 priests, with a large number of seminarians "underground", despite seventy years of persecutions. Josyp said that the Vatican official, who had falsified and obstructed the truth, repented in his presence. Josyp now lives in Canada, in poor health.

1988 was the 1000th anniversary of Christianity in Russia. The authorities decided that the celebrations should be open to Western visitors. The celebrations really belonged to the Ukraine as Christianity began in Kiev, but the Ukrainian Church was still illegal. In April 1988, The Virgin returned to the Holy Trinity church in Hrushiv as if to take part in the celebrations. An army Captain, who was present at one of these apparitions, took out his pistol and shot at the Image of The Virgin, which was surrounded with light. He immediately fell unconscious on the ground. He recovered consciousness after several days in hospital, but could no longer remember any of his former life. He then began to travel from village to village as a beggar, teaching Christianity.

This was not the first time The Virgin Mary had come to Hrushiv. The first recorded appearance was in the middle of the seventeenth century. She also returned in the middle of the nineteenth century to help stop a cholera epidemic. On May 12th – 13th, 1914, two weeks before the outbreak of World War I, she appeared to twenty two farm workers over a twenty four hour period. She warned them that war was about to begin. She was also reported to have said, that Russia would become a Godless country, that the Ukraine would suffer terribly, and would have to endure three major wars, but afterwards would be free. Eventually Gorbachev met St Pope John Paul II, in December 1989, and the Ukrainian Church was given freedom.

Rwanda

A series of well-known apparitions of The Virgin Mary occurred in association with a Roman Catholic school in Kibeho, Rwanda from 1981 to 1988. The messages came to six young girls and a fourteen year old boy. Jesus first appeared to the boy, Emmanuel Segastashya, in a bean field. He was a pagan at first and Jesus taught him the *Lord's Prayer* and instructed him in the ways of God. Emmanuel and the six girls later began to see The Virgin Mary in the school grounds. One of the six girls was a Muslim and soon after the apparitions began, the boy and this girl, with her whole family, converted to the Catholic Church.

1981 was also the year when the great messages began in Medjugorje, and this created great excitement for some Catholic believers. When we heard about the events in Rwanda in 1982, we were wondering was there some connection with events in Yugoslavia. There were very few similarities, however. The young people in Medjugorje were communicating with The Virgin Mary together as a group whereas the young Africans were getting their messages as individuals one after another. The voices were not audible to onlookers, in Medjugorje, although the lips could be seen moving. In Rwanda, when the visionaries were in their conversations with The Virgin Mary their voices could be clearly heard, and these communications were regularly recorded both in audio and video. It was a decade later that at least one connection became obvious. Yugoslavia and Rwanda were to become centres for terrible civil wars, slaughter and genocide in the early nineties. These problems began in Yugoslavia on the tenth anniversary of the first apparition.

On the 28th November, 1988, Alphonsine Mumureke, had two apparitions in the grounds of the school. The first was at noon, and the second, lasting almost two hours, was in the late afternoon. This was on the seventh anniversary of the first message. As she had been told previously by The Virgin when her next apparition would be, the technology was in place to record it on camera. When I watch this recording on video,[53] I cannot help wondering if the sceptics believe that this girl was imagining all of this or who do they think that she was communicating with? If it was all an act, the performance would have merited an Oscar award, as she was obviously very upset and weeping uncontrollably during some periods. Nobody can doubt that the authenticity of the visions of the rivers full of blood and headless corpses, since later unfortunately they became a reality in Rwanda.

In 2008, an extraordinary book was published describing the events surrounding this genocide in Rwanda, in 1994.[54] This book describes how The Virgin Mary gave details and warnings, of what was to happen, to these young visionaries, during the decade before the events took place. Several thousand saw many miraculous events and as they could hear the words of the visionaries, when speaking with The Virgin Mary, they had first-hand accounts of the warnings and descriptions of the atrocities that were soon to happen. Some of these conversations extended for hours, and as mentioned above, were recorded on audio and video tapes. The visionaries were also taken on trips to Heaven, Hell and Purgatory: experiences which they afterwards found difficult to describe in words. Two of the young visionaries who were taken on these trips by The Virgin had forewarned their school superiors that this would happen. "It will seem that I am dead but please, please do not bury me." It did indeed seem as if they were dead, as their breathing stopped and they had no audible heart-beat. Doctors, who were called in, debated on whether to pronounce them dead. On one occasion this death-like trance lasted from Good Friday until early Easter Sunday morning. At that stage the visionary seemed to return to life and awoke, as if from a normal sleep, hopped out of bed and announced that it was time to wash and prepare for Mass.

A flavour of other events described in this book can be had from the following brief extracts:

"There, far above our heads, was an image of Jesus on the cross, with The Blessed Mother standing below Him with Her head bowed in grief." This scene was witnessed by 15,000 people who dropped to their knees, - "as they looked to the sky through tears of love."

"Visionary after visionary received the same images from the weeping Virgin" ... "The fire did indeed come, and there was nowhere to hide for more than a million innocent souls, whose bodies were chopped to pieces during the genocide that engulfed Rwanda in the spring of 1994. Thousands upon thousands of bodies were dumped into the rivers that ran thick with blood. Alphonsine's apocalyptic vision was so horrifically accurate that Mary's messages would eventually be believed and accepted by everyone, from peasants to the Pope. But by that time it was too late."

Medjugorje

One of the latest and greatest communications of The Virgin Mary to humanity is the alleged series of apparitions reported to be occurring in Medjugorje, Yugoslavia. According to the testimony of six young adults, from the parish of St James, in Medjugorje, they were seeing and speaking with The Virgin Mary since the 24th of June, 1981. Mary has asked for conversion and prayers, in order to bring peace to the world. She has introduced herself as the Queen of Peace. The Virgin Mary has been giving daily messages since these apparitions began and continues doing so right up to the present day. These messages confirm again the authentic teaching of Catholic Doctrine and are a continual reminder of the catastrophe facing the world if humanity does not listen, accept, respond and live the messages that she is giving. There are very few church going Catholics who have not heard something about these happenings. In fact, no reported supernatural happening within the Catholic Church has ever attracted such world-wide interest as these alleged apparitions in Medjugorje.

The emphasis of the messages is the urgent need for conversion. The messages describe five methods to be used to attain eternal salvation, namely, prayer, fasting, reading of Scripture, the sacrament of confession and reception of the Eucharist at Mass as well as living good lives. Mary's true message can be summarized in seven words: **God, faith, conversion, prayer, fasting, peace,**

and reconciliation. Prayer should be from the heart and not from habit. The Virgin Mary has said that through fasting and prayer we can stop wars and even suspend the laws of nature. The Mass should be the centre of our lives. "I am your Mother and the Queen of Peace", is the constant message of The Virgin Mary.

Ten Secrets: Three of the visionaries no longer receive daily visits from The Virgin Mary. They continue to see her at various intervals on specific dates. She has given ten secrets to each of these. She continues to appear daily to the remaining three, who have each received nine secrets and will receive one more before the end of their daily apparitions. The visionaries have been told that we are living in a time of grace and conversion. A chastisement is also to come to humanity during this time because of sins in the world. There is therefore an urgent call for all to repent and convert, and go to the sacrament of reconciliation.

Initially, before the chastisements take place, there will be three warnings that will be given to the world. After this a Permanent Sign will be left on the mountain at Medjugorje, similar to that promised in Garabandal. The visionary Mirjana, has been chosen to tell a priest ten days before each of these events or secrets are to happen. The priest, already chosen, is Fr Peter Ljubicic. He will pray and fast for seven days before announcing it to the world. The visionaries were told that the first secret, "will break the power of Satan in the world", and will begin to confirm the truth and reality of these messages. Subsequent secrets and events will follow rapidly. There will be very little time to convert at this stage. The ninth and tenth secrets are reported to be serious and grave matters.

Medical investigations of the visionaries: The visions in Medjugorje are unique. Never before in the history of the Church has a visitation of The Virgin Mary been witnessed with such frequent apparitions, over such an extended period of time, and been so well known. Daily appearances have now been recorded since 1981. Three other apparitions, within the last fifty years, have also been associated with large numbers of appearances, namely, in Garabandal (Spain), in Betania (Venezuela), and in Cairo.

As with most apparitions of The Virgin Mary, those receiving the apparitions, often referred to as seers, normally go in a state of ecstasy, for the duration of the apparition. Many detailed medical investigations have been carried out on these young people in Yugoslavia, while they were in ecstasy. These investigations were carried out mainly in the early years, during the alleged apparitions and with the permission of The Virgin. A follow up investigation was also done by a French medical team, for the twenty fifth anniversary of the visions, in 2006. The official reports of these early medical investigations are now easily available.

One of the most detailed medical investigations was carried out by a French team from Montpellier, led by Professor Henri Joyeux and his colleagues. The details of these medical investigations have been published in a number of books by the internationally famous Marian theologian, Fr Rene Laurentin. The book, *Medjugorje - Facts, Documents, Theology*, by the Irish theologian, Fr Michael O'Carroll CSSp, also gives an account of these medical investigations.[55] Various trips to Medjugorje were made by the French team, in June, October and December, 1984. They performed electro encephalograms (brain wave measurement) before, during and after the ecstasies. They measured ocular movements and reflexes. They also studied the response of the visionaries to sounds of various decibel strengths, before, during and after the ecstasies. The following is a summary of their conclusions:

"There was no sign of hallucination, hysteria or pathological ecstasy. It cannot be a cataleptic state as during the ecstasy the facial muscles are working normally. The movement of the orbs of the eyes, from all the visionaries, move with perfect synchrony. At Medjugorje, the ecstasies are not pathological or a trick. They do not belong to any known denomination and cannot be explained scientifically."

An Italian neurophysiologist, Dr. Marco Margnelli, was among one of the large numbers of medical experts, who examined the visionaries. In 1985, Dr. Margnelli went to Medjugorje out of curiosity. He is a specialist on altered states of consciousness and ecstasy is included in his area of interest and study. Dr. Margnelli said that he had verified a genuine state of ecstasy. He further explained, "There is no lying and the children enter an alpha state of consciousness. We were in the presence of an extraordinary phenomenon". He was also impressed by the fact that the birds, which were usually singing during the evenings, while he was there, all fell into absolute silence as soon as the apparitions began. A lady from Milan who was there with him also related a strange story to him. She was very ill with leukaemia and she went to Medjugorje with the hope that the Madonna could embrace her. She told nobody about this and after one of the ecstasies one of the visionaries singled her out among the hundreds present and gave her a big hug. The visionary said to her, "that is the embrace you wished from the Madonna". Her leukaemia was healed. It is interesting that Dr. Marco Margnelli, who was a convinced atheist, later converted to Catholicism after his Medjugorje experience. Doctor Frigerio, is an Italian neurologist, who also examined the visionaries. He discovered that they had no corneal reaction during the apparitions. He also demonstrated that their eyes did not see objects put before them while the ecstasy lasted. He said that all of this ruled out play acting. In 1985, a team of twelve medical doctors and scientists met in Italy, with Fr Rene Laurentin, to consider the events in Medjugorje. Their report, which was known to be favourable towards the apparitions, was forwarded to the Vatican.

Within the Roman Catholic faithful, we can find a wide range of beliefs and attitudes toward the events in Medjugorje. These beliefs range from those who say that it is a hoax promoted by the Franciscans, to healthy scepticism, to those who are completely convinced of the authenticity of the visions and messages. The great theologian, Father Hans Urs von Balthasar, was very positive towards Medjugorje. He said, "The theology rings true. I am convinced of its truth. Everything about Medjugorje is true in a Catholic sense. What is happening there is so evident, so convincing".[56] Many other theologians and Bishops are also supportive of messages in Medjugorje. There is much anecdotal and hearsay evidence and it is widely accepted that St Pope John Paul II was also supportive.

The Local Bishop: It is odd, that the greatest opposition has come from the local Bishop. There seems a touch here of the prophets not being recognized in their own home. A new local Bishop was appointed on July 24th 1994, but he, like his predecessor, also opposes the authenticity of the apparitions. In 1986, the decisional authority on the matter was removed from the local Bishop and transferred to the Yugoslav Bishop's Conference, by Cardinal Joseph Ratzinger (later Pope Benedict XVI). Cardinal Franjo Kuharic, Archbishop of Zagreb and President of the Bishop's Conference, said on Croatian public television, December 23rd 1990 that the Yugoslav Bishops's Conference, including himself, "has a positive opinion on the Medjugorje events". On the occasion of the twenty fifth anniversary of the first apparition in 2006, the local Bishop again made a very negative statement on the events. Rome was again forced to clarify the situation by giving a press statement saying, that the Medjugorje events were not condemned by the Catholic Church. Most believe that the origin of the opposition from the local Bishop goes back to the long history of antagonism, between the Bishop and the Franciscan order, who have been in the area for many centuries, and who have strong local support. The bone of contention seems to be, who should run the parish? Should the Franciscans be involved, or not?

Medjugorje and other religions: There are some interesting reports of events relating to The Virgin's comments regarding non Catholic religious beliefs. At one stage, She was reported to have said that one of those closest to God, in the village, was an old Muslim woman. Another notable event was recorded (January 1985), as a result of the questions from a Catholic priest, who could not understand how a non-Catholic gypsy child was cured of a serious illness, through the intercession of The Virgin. The report recorded the words of The Virgin as follows: "Tell this priest and tell everyone, that it is you who are divided on earth. The Muslims and the Orthodox, in a similar way to Catholics, are equal before my son and me. You are all my children. **Certainly all religions are not equal, but all men are equal, before God, as St Paul said** (my emphasis). It does not suffice to belong to the Catholic Church to be saved, but it is necessary to respect the commandments of God in following one's conscience. Those who are not Catholics, are no less creatures made in the image of God, and destined to re-join someday, the House of the Father. Salvation is available to everybody without exception. Only those who refuse God deliberately are condemned."

When I first encountered these accounts, I could not help remembering Mother Teresa of Calcutta, who always had the utmost respect for all people, regardless of their religion. Her way was to love them and encourage them towards the true God. The reference to St Paul is from Romans 5:18, "..as one man's trespass led to condemnation to all men, so one man's act of righteousness leads to acquittal and life to all men".

The significance of Medjugorje: The first indication that something was about to happen in Medjugorje, came at the International Retreat for Priests, held in Rome, in 1981. While Sr Briege McKenna (see page 96) was praying with Fr Tomislav Vlasic, a Franciscan from Mostar, she got a vision of the church in Medjugorje packed with young people drinking water, which was flowing from the altar, while Fr Tomislav presided at the service. At the same meeting, Fr Emil, a French Canadian Sacred Heart priest, came toward both of them, from the other side of the room a short time later, and said to Fr Tomislav that he had a word of knowledge for him. He said that The Virgin Mary would soon be visiting his church. Fr Tomislav was not in Medjugorje at the time, but he was transferred there, a short time later. I relate this to make the point that prophecy is a well recognized, valid, and authenticated charism of the Holy Spirit, which is manifested regularly, especially associated with particular individuals – (see chapter 11 for a more detailed discussion on Catholic prophecy).

Medjugorje is big, very big. There are many similarities with Garabandal and it is generally believed by those who support both, that the early secrets/events promised in Medjugorje, are similar to the Great Warning, Miracle, and Permanent Sign of Garabandal. Some spiritual writers suggest that if the recent major Marian apparitions and messages are authentic, then there must be a definite link between them. It is possible that Permanent Signs of God's presence will appear in a number of Marian apparition sites around the world, at the same time. In contrast to Garabandal, many millions of lay Catholics, including at least, up to 50% of clergy would give some support to Medjugorje. Large numbers of lay Catholics have had their own personal mystical or quasi mystical experiences, while visiting this village. The clergy see the spiritual fruits in those who go on pilgrimage and the conversions are numerous. "By their fruits, you will know them", and many are convinced of the truth of Medjugorje, because the fruits are recognized as good rather than bad. By 1990, the year before the war, almost two million pilgrims visited the church. In Austria, 500 Medjugorje prayer groups have been established with more than that number established in other countries, such as the United States. The confidence invested by Catholic believers, therefore, is enormous and the Catholic Church would suffer greatly if the messages of Medjugorje turned out to be a fraud.

To have daily appearances of The Virgin Mary (who Catholics recognize as the Mother of God), since the evening of 24th June, 1981, at a predicted time and in a known place, is a major event by any standards. The visionaries have been told that this is the last time The Virgin Mary will be coming to earth in this way, and this is yet another pointer that a "fullness of time" is approaching. The date of 24th June, when these events began, I am convinced is also significant. It is the feast of the birthday of Saint John the Baptist, who had the job of preparing the way for the Lord. Exactly ten years after the first vision of Mary (evening of 24th June, 1991), Croatia decided to break away from Yugoslavia. This declaration of Independence was publicly announced the following day, on 25th June. War was about to begin.

The real significance of Medjugorje is found in the messages. "I have come to call the world to conversion for the last time. Tell the whole world to convert. Do not delay" and another: "If you knew how much I love you, you would die of joy".

Finally, for those interested in reading more on the events in Medjugorje, I can highly recommend a book on the subject written by one of the visionaries, Mirjana Soldo, published in 2016.[57] I finish this account with two extracts from this book:

171

"I tell them as much as I can. Our Lady is preparing us for everything that's going to take place in the world. She is training us for victory. When the events in the secrets begin, everything will be clear. You will see, for example, why she chose to appear to me on the 18th of March every year, and why I experience the other apparitions on the second day of every month. You will understand the importance of these dates, and you will realize why she's been appearing for so long. Every mother knows that children need constant guidance. Through her messages, Our Lady persistently reminds us to stay on the right path."

"I wish I could divulge more about what will happen in the future, but I can say one thing about how the priesthood relates to the secrets. We have this time that we are living in now, and we have the time of the triumph of Our Lady's heart. Between these two times we have a bridge, and that bridge is our priests. Our Lady continually asks us to pray for our shepherds, as she calls them, because the bridge needs to be strong enough for all of us to cross it to the time of the triumph. In her message of October 2, 2010, she said, *'Only alongside your shepherds, will my heart triumph.'*"

Mary in Akita

The story of Akita concerns a Buddhist convert named Agnes Sasagawa.[58,59] She was born in Japan, in 1931, and from an early age she suffered much illness. She was bedridden for almost ten years, after a medical mishap with a spinal anaesthesia injection which paralysed her lower limbs. During one of her hospital stays in 1958, she was befriended by a Catholic nurse, who gave her some books to read. Among these books was a famous book, written by a Catholic radiologist, who gave his life for the people in Nagasaki injured by radiation after the atomic bomb, called – The Bells of Nagasaki. This book made a big impression on Agnes, and largely as a result of reading it, she became a Catholic convert in 1959.

After recovering somewhat from her illness, she began to work as a catechist at a newly built mission house in Joutsu City. In 1969 Agnes joined a religious order called The Institute of the Handmaids of the Eucharist. In March 1973, she lost her hearing. She was examined and certified as eligible for government relief because she was regarded as suffering from total and incurable deafness. In May 1973 she was transferred to the Mother house of The Handmaids of the Eucharist, in Akita, which is about 200 kilometres north of Tokyo. The local Bishop, Bishop Ito, had given this community of nuns the obligation of adoring the Blessed Eucharist, in the spirit of atonement for sins in the world.

On June 12th 1973, when Sr Agnes was adoring the Blessed Sacrament, she suddenly saw some brilliant rays of light coming from the tabernacle. On June 28th, she saw the bright light again, when it covered the whole altar. She also saw countless angels adoring the Eucharist. That same day, a cross shaped wound about 3cm by 2cm mysteriously developed on the palm of Sr Agnes's left hand, causing her severe pain. On the Friday this wound bled profusely but by Sunday it had disappeared completely. This happened again in each of the following three weeks. Even more mysterious was that at the same time as the bleeding of Sr Agnes' hand, the wooden statue of The *Lady of All Nations* (see page 672 for more details on this image), in the same convent chapel, also began to bleed real human blood from the palm of the right hand. Among the witnesses was Bishop Ito himself, who collected some of the blood to have it examined.

On July 6th 1973 at 3.00 am in the morning Sr Agnes was visited by her guardian angel. After identifying himself, the guardian angel led her to the chapel and then vanished. There in the chapel, the statue of *The Lady of All* Nations came to life and began to speak to Sr Agnes. The Virgin Mary gave her what was to become the first of three messages. The latter two were given on August 3rd and October 13th of the same year, 1973. The earlier messages stressed the importance of the Eucharist, and the importance of adoring Our Lord Jesus, truly present in the Eucharist.

Although the wound in Sr Agnes' hand disappeared on July 29th, 1973, the wound in the palm of the statue remained until September 29th. Fresh blood flowed frequently from the cross shaped wound in the hand of the statue along the palm. After the wound disappeared from the statue, perspiration began to appear on the statue every day, up until October 15th. The Bishop and the nuns wiped the perspiration away many times with gauze and cotton, which became saturated. Tears were shed by the statue for the first time on January 4th 1975. Tears were shed a total of 101 times until September 15th 1981 and there were many hundreds of eye witnesses. Among the eye witnesses were many non-Christians, including the local Buddhist Mayor of Akita. Bishop Ito also witnessed the weeping and he sent the following report to Cardinal Ratzinger, in Rome, on March 13th 1982:

"I, who am Bishop, witnessed the weeping of the statue four times. I observed tears well up and overflow from the eyes of the statue and stream down, just as a human being sheds tears. I watched the tears stream down the statue's cheek, accumulate on the chin, then flow down the statue's garment, reaching the feet and then flow along the globe on which the statue stands. Then the tears reached the pedestal that supports the globe and statue. I wiped away the tears from the statue of the Holy Mother. Twice I tasted the tears, which tasted salty just like human tears."

Another eye witness was Professor Eiji Okuhara from the Biochemistry Department, who was also a former fellow of the

174

Rockefeller foundation. On the 25th January 1975 Professor Okuhara asked his colleague, Professor Kaoru Sagisaka, to analyse the tears and blood, which had been collected from the statue. Dr. Sagisaka issued a medical report confirming that the constituents of the liquid were identical to those of human tears and that the blood was human blood of Group B. Dr. Sagisaka was not a Christian. In 1975 Professor Okuhara testified in a newspaper that, "These series of phenomena were observed by people who can be trusted most deeply, and these specimens (blood and tears) were scientifically identified as containing the ingredients identical to those of a human body".

Bishop Ito then organized a thorough investigation, and on Easter Sunday, April 22nd 1984, he issued a pastoral letter, in which he proclaimed the supernatural character of the apparitions and messages at Akita. In the pastoral letter the Bishop said, "After the investigations conducted up to the present day, I cannot deny the supernatural character of a series of mysterious events concerning the statue of the Holy Mother Mary, which is found in the convent of the Institute of the Handmaids of the Sacred Heart of Jesus in the Holy Eucharist, at Yuzawadai, Soegawa, Akita. I do not find in these events any elements which are contrary to Catholic faith and morals. Consequently, I authorize throughout the entire diocese with which I am charged, the veneration of the Holy Mother of Akita.

During these events Sr Agnes was cured of deafness on a number of occasions. On the 13th October 1974, during adoration of the Blessed Sacrament, Sr Agnes regained her hearing. She lapsed into deafness again, however, on March 10th 1975. Then on the 25th March (feast of the Annunciation) 1982, her guardian angel appeared to her to tell her that her hearing would be restored permanently. On the 30th May 1982, the feast of Pentecost, at the moment of Benediction of the Blessed Sacrament, Sr Agnes' deafness was instantly and completely cured.

Sr Agnes was recognized in the convent for having many spiritual gifts. There are many recorded stories regarding these gifts, but one of the most pleasant concerned the story of two robins who befriended her. These robins, named Peasuku and Peako, visited her room regularly. Very early one morning, Sr Agnes was heard chatting to the robins, who were chirping much louder than usual They had found a special rosary of hers in the garden, which she had received as a gift and had lost many years previously. They brought it up to her second floor room and left it on the window ledge, undamaged but covered with earth. All three were rejoicing. This rosary is now stored in the convent, where it is known as, "Tori no rosario" or "The rosary of the bird". Both of Sr Agnes' parents later converted to Catholicism.

A Warning and message of Finality

The most widely known message of Akita, is the one given on the 13th of October 1973, which was the 56th anniversary of the great sign of Fatima (13th Oct. 1917). The message, given by Mary to Sr Agnes, reads as follows:

"As I told you, if men do not repent and better themselves, the Heavenly Father will inflict a great punishment on all humanity. It will definitely be a punishment greater than the Deluge, such as has never been seen before. Fire will plunge from the sky and a large part of humanity will perish...The good as well as the bad will perish, sparing neither priests nor the faithful. The survivors will find themselves plunged into such terrible hardships that they will envy the dead. The only arms which will remain for you will be the Rosary and the sign left by My Son (The Eucharist).

Each day recite the prayers of the Rosary. With the Rosary, pray for the Bishops and priests. The work of the devil will infiltrate even into the Church. One will see Cardinals opposing other Cardinals and Bishops confronting other Bishops.

The priests who venerate me will be scorned and condemned by their confreres: churches and altars will be sacked: the Church will be full of those who accept compromises and the demon will tempt many priests and religious to leave the service of the Lord.

The demon is trying hard to influence souls consecrated to God. The thought of the perdition of so many souls is the cause of My sadness. If sins continue to be committed further, there will no longer be pardon for them.

With courage, convey these messages to your superior. He will tell each one of you to continue prayers and acts of reparation for sins steadfastly, while ordering all of you to pray fervently. Pray very much the prayers of the Rosary. I alone am able still to help save you from the calamities which are approaching. Those who place their total confidence in Me will be given the necessary help."

A further message was received by Sr Agnes, on September 28th, 1981, thirteen days after the final weeping of the statue, which has some interesting theological significance. The figure thirteen again reflects the connection with Fatima. During adoration of the Eucharist that evening, a large majestic Bible appeared before her eyes. She heard her guardian angel instruct her to read a passage, which was verse 15, chapter 3 of Genesis, and it reads as follows:

"I will place enmity between thee (Satan) and the woman (Mary), between thy seed and hers. She will crush thy head and thou shall lie in wait for her heel". The angel further said to her: "There is a meaning to the figure 101 (This was the number of times the statue wept). This signifies that as sin came into the world through a woman, it is also through a woman that salvation came to the world. The zero signifies The Eternal God, who is from all eternity to eternity. The first 'one' represents Eve, and the last 'one' represents Mary". It was very significant that the message should be explained with the authority of scripture. It appears that the bleeding, the weeping and the particular image of The Virgin, were all chosen by God to emphasise the role of Mary as Coredemptrix. The image of The Lady of All Nations was carved in wood for the sisters, by a Buddhist. He copied the image from a picture received from Holland.

The Significance of Akita

It is important to reflect again that the events in Akita were officially approved by the local Bishop, Bishop Ito, as an authentic communication from The Virgin Mary. At the time, this approval was accepted by Cardinal Ratzinger (later Pope Benedict XVI). The immense and awesome nature of this warning for the world, therefore, is alarming, frightening and almost beyond comprehension yet, there is a fuzz of silence surrounding this warning, which may suggest to some that it has no basis in fact. Nothing could be farther from the truth! I have mentioned already how Church authorities are extremely cautious in promoting any of these events. Unfortunately, this silence also extends to the laity. Ignoring the danger will not remove it. The only hope now is that humanity will repent and change rapidly and dramatically, when the Great Warning announced at Garabandal becomes a reality.

This was not the first time that The Virgin Mary had warned humanity of the threat of purification by fire. On the feast of the

Immaculate Conception 1954, The Virgin gave this message to a young girl in the Ukrainian village of Seredne:[51]

"My daughter, my daughter, you see I hold many graces which I am unable to give, because so many of my sons and daughters have turned away from me, and no longer ask for them. In this jubilee year in My honour, I desire greatly to help poor sinners. A catastrophe is near, just as in the time of Noah. Many will die, not from flood but by fire, because they have so greatly offended God. Never in its history, has humanity fallen so low as at this time. It is the age of the kingdom of Satan."

If this was the situation in 1954, there is little doubt that the rejection of God is far worse now. Little Jacinta from Fatima seemed to indicate that 1972 was the significant year in the spiritual life of the world. Spiritually the world had been on a steady decline during the 1960s and in the early 1970s many sacred images began to weep human tears.[28] There are grounds for believing that things had reached such a low point in 1972, that from then on, severe punishment from God became inevitable. Akita, beginning in 1973, seemed to be a confirmation of this, as was the statement in the second message of Garabandal in 1965 – "the cup is now overflowing.." I have placed the discussion of Akita at the end of this chapter, even though chronologically it occurred before Medjugorje. Eschatologically (end times theology), it would seem that Akita belongs at the end. All the indications suggest that the events prophesied in Akita will mark the end of this era of time, before the era of peace begins.

The image of The Virgin (*The Lady of All Nations*) chosen in Akita, is not without significance. The message of The Lady of all Nations (1945 - 1970)[60] came from Holland, and it is long and detailed. It was approved by the local Bishop in Holland and is associated with a special prayer approved by Rome. This message is closely associated with what is likely to be the next, and probably the final Marian dogma to be declared by the Catholic Church, namely: that Mary the Mother of Jesus, is **"Mediatrix, Coredemptrix, and Advocate",** through the design and wishes of The Most Holy Trinity. See also chapter 16 on sacred astronomy, for a possible explanation on how fire could rain from Heaven, to fulfil the prophecy of Akita.

6. The Good, The Bad, and The Ugly

What a tangled web we weave, when first we practice to deceive.
Sir Walter Scott

There are two great movements in the world today opposing truth. These are the New Age and the One World Order. These two movements are supportive of each other at many different levels and intersect and cross fertilise in various programmes all over the world. They are promoted from the same source. Unlike Charles Lamb's orange, the outside is not a mirror of the inside. These programmes and teachings look good, plausible and wholesome but they are full of deception. Both are rotten at the core. They look like innocent flowers but they hide the serpent. The New Age is the fuzz of error and deception for ordinary individuals. The One World Order is the fuzz of error and deception for politicians, bankers, powerbrokers, organizations and institutions.

The New Age Movement

Astrologers believe that the age of Pisces (the fish), which has been identified with Christianity, is ending, and a new age known as the Age of Aquarius (the water bearer) is beginning. Coincidental with this, a new movement is being promoted world wide, referred to as the 'New Age', which rejects the teaching of Christianity. Over the last twenty years a large number of books have been published, detailing the difference between the New Age and Christianity.[61,62,63] The Catholic Church in turn rejects this new teaching, as not based on truth, and has published a critique of this new movement in , Jesus Christ, The Bearer of the Water of Life. [64]

The New Age is a complex phenomenon of cultural change, which has developed slowly over the last century and more rapidly in recent years. It involves a progressive rejection of a personal God and a rejection of traditional or allopathic (orthodox) medicine, which are regarded as not capable of fulfilling the spiritual and healing needs of modern humanity. The New Age is not regarded as a religious movement but rather as a new kind of spirituality, which promotes a new spiritual dimension. Some of the traditions that flow into the New Age are ancient Egyptian occult practises, Kabbalism (unusual interpretation of Hebrew scripture – sometimes spelled with a 'C'), early Christian gnosticism (a movement believing in intuitive religious knowledge), Islamic mysticism, Druid lore, Celtic Christianity, medieval alchemy, Renaissance hermeticism (occult sciences), Zen Buddhism, Yoga, etc. New Age thinking and teaching has largely been influenced by theosophy (claiming intuitive insight into divine nature), spiritualism and anthroposophy (a system of beliefs and practices based on Rudolph Steiner, 1861 – 1925, who maintained that by correct training and discipline, one can attain new experiences of the spiritual world). The New Age promotes feelings above reason and intuitive thinking above rational thinking. This is sometimes referred to as a left to right brain shift. A good summary of the New Age is that it is a collection of non-Christian beliefs, therapies, and practices, which are freely selected by individuals who like to "do their own thing". Rational analysis, incompatibilities and inconsistencies are ignored.

The New Age movement is described as syncretistic, that is, it is a combination of different ideas, which are both religious and sociological. It is a combination of eastern mysticism, various religious views and beliefs, combined with some western occultism. It is a spirituality which is completely against the teachings of Christianity. For those who believe in the New Age Movement, the Age of Christianity has now been superseded by the New Age of Aquarius. They believe that this New Age is just beginning and it is presented as a new vision of the world, which will create peace, unity, and harmony.

It differs radically from Christianity in that it does not promote belief in a single personal God. It is not a monotheistic belief, therefore, but what is known as a "monistic" belief. The God of the New Age is not a person but an energy that is present in all things. The New Age promotes a oneness, which obliterates any difference between evil and good, which is referred to as dualism. The New Age promotes the belief that we are all part of God and human beings can all become gods. The idea of Christ awareness is not as taught in Christianity. Christ awareness in the New Age teaches that Christ is just another enlightened being, and we all have that power within us to become enlightened as Christ. New Age promoters believe that human activity flows from either illumination or ignorance. As there is no good and evil, there is no need for forgiveness, there is no Hell and there is no spiritual authority higher than the personal inner experience. Decisions are made on situation ethics instead of moral absolutes.

The New Age movement is new, in that it has only come into prominence in the last fifty years or so. It is more of a collection of different movements than a single movement, but it has a number of common themes. The New Age is very much a movement which was put together by various individuals and ideas are knitted together in various different forms. The teachings of these various prominent ideas are promoted by charismatic individuals. Everything comes together in a great vision of the world in harmony, and joy.

Pantheism: A common theme among all New Age followers is that they believe we all have unlimited human potential and we have psychic powers which we need to learn how to develop. Through the development of these powers we can become God. There is great emphasis on the old pantheistic idea that everything is God. All nature is God and all animals are God and we are part of this God. Nothing is new and there is only one personality in the whole universe. There is no you or I, and there are not millions of different entities. There is only one, and we are all part of this oneness. These ideas are now being promoted in all levels of society, such as in health seminars, business seminars, industrial seminars, and educational seminars. Individuals are being drawn towards these ideas because of what they seem to offer. Sadly these programmes offer a lot more than they deliver.

Hinduism and Buddhism in the New Age: The New Age movement draws heavily on the belief systems of Hinduism and Buddhism. Hinduism is a religion which is polytheistic in that it promotes belief in many gods. Hindus also believe that the true self is God and that all of creation is one and this oneness is God. Hindus, like Buddhists, do not believe in the concept of good and evil, as promoted in Christianity. For them, good and evil are subjective and not separate, but part of the same concept. What is good for one may be evil for another. The search therefore must be to find the true self, which is God. This discovery is made through "the path", which is found through the practice of Yoga. Yoga is a very important aspect of New Age teaching. Hinduism promotes the belief that one should lose one's personal ego consciousness, and drift towards God. Everybody is encouraged to say, 'I am Brahman' i.e. "I am God" and for the Hindu this is moving towards spiritual enlightenment. The purpose of Yoga is to alter the consciousness from a lower to a higher state, and thus encourage this spiritual enlightenment.

Yoga: There are many different forms and practices of Yoga. Some of the common ones are as follows:

1. Japa Yoga promotes the mechanical path to salvation and it involves the repetition of a mantra or sacred word, which is usually the name of a Hindu spirit or god. By emptying the mind of all thoughts and repeating this mantra, the individual becomes unaware of what is going on around them. This is referred to as pure consciousness or transcendental consciousness.

2. Patha Yoga is reaching salvation through the physical manipulation of the body in order to create an altered state of consciousness. This occurs through the effort put into the exercise, to control the central nervous system.

3. Kundalini Yoga is often promoted in New Age programmes. It teaches that salvation comes through the serpent. Hinduism teaches that there is a triangle at the base of the spine, where lies the "Kundalini" or the serpent power. The belief is that this power is usually dormant but when it awakens it travels up the spine to the top of the head, from where it travels out through six centres, called "Chakras". These are psychic centres and as the power passes through these centres the individual can get psychic experiences and extra new power. When it reaches the top Chakra, a feeling of liberation occurs with an accompanying new power to perform miracles.

4. Tantra Yoga promotes achieving salvation through stimulation of pleasure centres and thus, pleasure and indulgence is believed to be the key to enlightenment in this form of Yoga.

Spirit Guides: To move towards enlightenment, the Hindus and New Age students are usually encouraged to have guide masters or spiritual Gurus. In the Hindu belief, these are referred to as "Avatars" or Hindu gods, who have become incarnated on the earth in times of great need. Another type of Guru is a "Sad-guru" or a perfect master, but unlike the Avatar, who comes from

Heaven, the Sad-guru is said to ascend into the divine while he is still on earth. The Guru's function is to lead each student in their discipline, which is called Seadhane. Even with encouragement and effort, to follow this spiritual discipline, sometimes the Hindu student does not reach full realization of God. This is said to be due to "Karma", which interferes or inhibits this. Karma is the law of retribution, which is said to result from some past action in a former life. Both Hindu and New Age teachings promote a belief of re-incarnation.

Buddhism: The New Age movement also promotes many ideas developed from Buddhism. Buddhist belief was started by the Hindu, Siddhartha Gautama, who lived in or near 500 BC. This man was known as the great enlightened one, or Buddha, and he was said to have developed this enlightenment through many hours of deep Hindu meditation. He eventually developed what are known as, "The Paths". Buddhists are directed to live their lives along these paths or ways of life, which generally promote goodness and coincide with what Christians would regard as a virtuous way of life. These paths are listed as follows:

1. Knowing the truth
2. Having the intention to resist evil
3. Saying nothing to hurt others
4. Respecting life, property and morality,
5. Doing work which does not do any harm to others.
6. Making an effort always to keep one's mind away from evil thoughts
7. Controlling one's thoughts and feelings
8. Practising proper forms of meditation

Buddha believed that there was a continuous cycle of death and rebirth and that there can never be freedom from pain and suffering within this cycle. The only way to be released from this suffering is to reach "Nirvana", which is a state of total happiness and peace. This can only be attained by completely freeing oneself from all desires. His teachings were known as "Dharma" and there are now several different schools promoting variations on this teaching.

Zen Buddhism is promoted widely in the New Age movement. Zen is a Japanese word meaning meditation. The emphasis on this form of Buddhism is to use concentration and meditation to empty the mind. This is achieved by using a technique which is involved with a contradictory riddle called a "Koan". This Koan helps to increase pressure on the mind until the structures of ordinary reason collapses and individuals are thus left only with an intuition or an emptying of the mind, where they realise that all is one and opposites are equal. The Zen idea is that all is one, one is none, and none is all. This is the so-called true monistic experience, which gets rid of the dualism idea of good and evil. Monism teaches the validity of all values and identifies very much with Zen Buddhism. This concept is also promoted by the Chinese symbol of Yin and Yan, where opposites are identical.

The values promoted in Buddhism are essentially good but the teaching is inward looking and self-centred. Buddhists try to find the God within themselves, whereas, Christians are outward looking and try to know the God, who is continually being revealed to humanity.

The Human Potential Movement: New Age thinking promotes the belief that we are all gods, or at least, that we have the potential to become gods, and that we must all try to realise this. The view is that our problems do not come from our sin, but rather from the ignorance of our divinity. The belief is that mankind can be saved by this new way of thinking, but there is a need to develop a new mind and a new consciousness. We are told that humanity needs to throw off the old idea of God controlling man, and accept the idea that we are all gods, but we must be *self-realised or self-actualised*. This idea has developed into what is known as "the human potential movement".

Abraham Maslow was one of the principle promoters of the human potential movement. He became a great force in modern psychology, in the U.S.A, from the 1950's. He invented the theory of "self-actualization". Carl Rodgers, who is considered the father of "non-directive therapy", worked closely with Maslow. The non-directive approach in education is used widely in many programmes, such as, self-esteem, sex education, drug education, skills for adolescents, growing healthy, and many others. Dr. W. R. Coulson worked closely with Carl Rodgers and later, when he realized the errors of their teaching, he made a number of international tours to education institutions warning them of the dangers of American psychological ideas in education. I heard him on two occasions, in Ireland, admitting his own errors for having listened to Maslow and Rodgers. Dr. Coulson maintained that every major study on the non-directive method in education has shown that it produces the opposite effect to what it was supposed to do. Nothing is called wrong because of non judgementalism. Children are always looking for objective standards and thus they become completely confused when they are told that nothing is wrong. Good children turn bad. In comparison with the rest of the world, American students became over confident while they knew very little. According to Dr. Coulson, there are a number of major destructive aspects of this "humanistic education" still widely operating in class rooms today. The most important of these, he said, were:

> **(a) Abraham Maslow's work, with self-actualization and hierarchy of needs.**
> **(b) Carl Rodgers's work based on non-directive teaching.**
> **(c) Lewis Rath's work on values clarification.**

All of these ideas were developed initially from humanism, which was promoted by John Dewey. Dewey was the main author of the first Humanist Manifesto, in 1933.[65] Humanists regard the universe as self-existing and not created. They believe that there are no moral absolutes. There is a fundamental incompatibility, therefore, between all these programmes and Christianity, as they each have different views concerning both God and man.

Maslow's book on motivation and personality also promoted the idea of a "third force" in humanistic psychology. In this he promoted the idea of individuals self-realizing themselves by integrating their lower animal instincts with their higher God like self. All through his life Maslow promoted the attributes of God in man, although he publicly claimed to be an atheist, as he did not believe in a single personal God. In the 1960's and 1970's a force called the "fourth force" of transpersonal psychology was developed, and this was also promoted by Maslow. In contrast to the third force of humanistic psychology, which is associated with the promotion of human potential and goals, transpersonal psychology, or the fourth force, emphasised transcendental experiences such as, out of body experiences, space and time travel, telepathy, clairvoyance, re-birthing, and self-healing. These ideas are now also widely promoted in New Age programmes. Although humanistic and transpersonal psychological theories seem to have a great seduction and many people get interested in them, they eventually lead nowhere, except to trouble. The individuals go on a search for the deity of self, which cannot be found. These psychological theories appeal only to the basic flaw of humanity. Many apparently find the idea that, "You can be gods", appealing. The final outcome is often confusion and depression. Maslow's ideas are still popular among modern psychologists.

Reiki

Reiki is the epitome of everything that is bad and dangerous about New Age programmes. Yet we find that of all the new age practices, Reiki is being promoted more than any other. Large numbers of good people are being drawn into spiritualism without any idea of what they are getting involved in. The subtlety runs very deep. It is being presented as a harmless and beneficial technique of healing. Many Catholic religious also regard Reiki as harmless and are giving this advice in the community. Many Christian religious institutions are in fact actively promoting Reiki all over the world. Although the critique of the New Age published by the Roman Catholic Church deals with the problems of the enneagram and other aspects of the New Age, it unfortunately does not deal with Reiki, which is a lot more dangerous. This is probably because Reiki was not very popular when this critique was written. There is a great lack of good Christian education generally therefore, on the New Age, among religious and laity alike, and in particular there is a lack of good information on Reiki. Reiki is in fact deeply rooted in the occult.

Reiki is a Japanese word meaning "energetic spirit" or "universal or spiritual guided life force". Reiki is a term used for supernatural knowledge or "spiritual consciousness". This spiritual consciousness is the wisdom that comes from what is regarded as the god of "higher self". KI is a term used to describe an all-encompassing cosmic energy or life spirit. KI is the same as CHI in Chinese or PRANA in Sanskrit (classical Indian language). KI is used in meditative breathing exercises and by the Shamans (spirit healers) of all cultures, for divination, psychic awareness, manifestation and healing. Reiki is therefore a spiritualist channelling technique.

Reiki was developed by a Japanese Buddhist named Mikao Usui.[66] Mikao sought the key to miraculous healings of Buddha and Jesus. In the early 1900's after a long fast he believed that he was suddenly struck with light, and the Reiki symbols were revealed to him. He had knowledge of medicine and psychology and he was a member of a spiritualist group which was trying to develop psychic abilities. Reiki was further developed by a retired Japanese naval officer, who was trained by Mikao Usui. He in turn passed it on to a Hawaiian lady who practised this over a period of forty years. In 1970 she began to train other masters and before she died, in 1980, she initiated 22 masters to promote Reiki healing. Today there are a number of different schools of Reiki including Raku Reiki, Angelic Reiki, Tibetan Reiki and Traditional Ucusui Reiki, named after its founder.

Reiki practitioners would claim to be a channel for "life force to flow through them". This life force is directed through the hands of the practitioner to the subject's body. It is not uncommon now to find nurses and other medical personnel doing Reiki treatments in hospital and indeed to have Reiki as training in some basic nursing courses. Reiki teams of healing have discovered that it is best not to talk about Reiki at first, but rather to refer to healing energy. Likewise the terms riaura, chakras, and other technical terms are not used in the beginning as they tend to cause mistrust. Some Reiki practitioners claim the power to achieve distance healing.

Sometimes those who come for Reiki healing are in great need of proper medical care. They are often not aware of the risks that they run by Reiki healing. Most experienced Reiki practitioners are well aware of these dangers. Those who receive Reiki healing leave themselves open to great emotional stress and sometimes to the danger of spiritual possession. Reiki students are warned not to proceed too quickly with their master training, as to do it quickly can be associated with symptoms of what is referred to as "clearing". This "releasing" or "clearing" of the Karma (law of retribution from a former life) can have a disastrous effect emotionally. If subjects carry this Karma, which needs to be released, and they are not ready to release it, then there can be dangerous effects. It is described to the students as like raising the "Kundalini" without a Guru watching over the person. It is more simply explained by the great emotional trauma that can result from having direct contact with spirits and spiritual powers, especially for those who may not be aware or even believe in spirits, occult or otherwise. This, in the extreme situations, can result in serious psychiatric illness. To a lesser extent this can also happen during the training process when patients are having Reiki treatment. Experts in Reiki and those who practice Reiki at the second and third levels, recognise that the source of Reiki energy comes from "the higher power". This higher power is believed to be mediated through the healing Buddha and the master spirits of Reiki. This power is not from the Christian God but rather from occult spirits. There is no doubt that the vast majority of those involved with Reiki would prefer to think of this healing energy as coming from some mysterious self-healing force of nature which they have found a way to tap into.

Students of Reiki are obliged to go through a process of initiation. The first part of this is concerned with the physical dimension, the second with the emotional dimension and the third with the spiritual dimension. Attunement energies are said to flow from the Reiki Master to the student. These special energies are generally regarded as being guided by "the higher power". From this attunement, some students will feel warmth in the hands or they can see various colours. Others have visions of spiritual beings and this experience seems to be relatively common in Reiki, even among those who are just beginners. In my very limited contact with those who practice Reiki, I would be aware of a number of situations where these spirits became visible, to the alarm and astonishment of the beginners. These spiritual beings, that are seen, are occult spirits. The final stage in Reiki training involves being appointed as a Reiki Master. Those reaching this stage are introduced to their own Reiki "spirit guide". Reiki therefore is without doubt a form of spiritualism. Reiki Masters are usually told that when they reach this final stage that nothing can be reversed. "When the energy transmission is activated it remains for life".

Reiki practitioners are taught to use secret symbols. These symbols invoke Reiki power and they are instructed that they should be kept secret. The first Reiki symbol is referred to as the power symbol, the second symbol is referred to as the Buddha mind symbol, the third symbol is related to right consciousness, and the fourth symbol is often referred to as Usui Master symbol, named after the founder of Reiki. The fourth symbol is also known as the great shining light symbol and is said to be a Zen expression of one's own true nature or Buddha nature. This final symbol, therefore, is a power symbol from Zen Buddhism. Reiki symbols are regarded as sacred symbols because they interact with the higher levels of Buddhas or gods. Many practitioners believe that the main aim of Reiki is to build bridges to former lives. It is not surprising therefore, that Reiki practitioners generally believe in re-incarnation. Reiki training also involves re-awakening what they call the "third eye". This allows a person to see the god within everybody and everything. Treatment focuses on this "third eye" as well as the throat, the heart, chakras, and the energy centres, which are in charge of re-incarnation.

It is difficult to find someone who is involved with Reiki who does not feel some effects and the commonest is a feeling of being healed. It is precisely because of these feelings that Reiki is so popular. There is a general feeling that, "it works". Healings may occur but at what cost? The cost is spiritual bondage. **It is important, therefore, to understand that, those who practice Reiki, run the risk of spiritual bondage, whereas the whole purpose of Christianity is to deliver people from spiritual bondage.** Most people who get involved in Reiki have no idea of this danger. Ultimately, Reiki Masters knowingly or unknowingly, act as channels for occult spirits, both for themselves and for others.

I have said that healings can apparently occur due the practice of Reiki but Satan can appear as an angel of light and appear to heal. In reality, however, he can do nothing good, so these apparent healings are temporary and in fact often leave the patient worse than they were before. If Reki is using occult power, then no real healing can be offered by it. This is especially true for spiritual healing, as Reki will have the opposite effect.

New Religions of the Nineteenth Century

In many ways the New Age movement could be said to have origins in the religious movements of the nineteenth century, which was a time of great activity for new religious beliefs. The Mormon religion began in 1820. The Mormon book, Pearl of Great Price, states that Jesus was a spirit brother of Lucifer before he entered the world. Spiritualism, which became a recognised religion around 1850, promoted the practice of contacting the dead or demonic spirits posing as spirits of the dead. Around 1860, Mary Baker Eddy began to promote her new religion, Christian Scientology, claiming it to be the only true religion, based on her own understanding of the Bible. The Jehovah's Witness religion, which denies the divinity of Jesus, was founded in 1879.

In 1875 the Russian satanist, Helen Petrovna Blavatsky, founded the Theosophical Society. She claimed that the Tibetan holy men in the Himalayas, whom she referred to as the masters of wisdom, communicated with her in London by telepathy. She said that Christians have it all backwards, and that Satan is good and that the God of the Bible is evil. She further said that, Christians and scientists must be made to respect their betters, who could be found and understood through the wisdom of the "Ascended Masters", and that this philosophy should be made known in Europe and America. Madame Blavatsky was heavily involved in the occult and her ideas have formed the basis for much of the New Age thinking. She claimed that her main book, *The Secret Doctrine*, was dictated to her by the "The Ascended Masters of Wisdom", who were guiding mankind. This so called, "automatic writing" is well recognised and popular in New Age present day thinking.

Adolf Hitler was a well-known follower of Blavatsky. He studied her Secret Doctrine in great detail. Nazi beliefs and teachings were based, to a significant extent, on the teaching and writing of Blavatsky. The Nazis and Theosophists both believed that humanity was guided by supermen (uebermenschen), who live in remote regions of the world. Blavatsky was followed by Dr. Annie Besant and later by Alice Bailey, as heads of the Theosophical society. Alice Bailey founded the *"Lucifer Publishing Company"*, in 1920. This later became the *Lucis Trust*, in order to conceal the satanic origins from the general public. Some of the best known world financial and political leaders became members of this organization. These same individuals controlled the Council on Foreign Relations, which in turn formed the United Nations organization. The *Lucis Trust*, was initially run from an office in the United Nations Plaza, New York. It actively promotes the New Age movement.

Alice Bailey wrote over twenty books, which, according to her, were all dictated by her spirit guide, Djwahl Khul, a Tibetan master spirit. Like Blavatsky, her writings were anti-Jewish and anti-Christian. She justified the Jewish Holocaust of World War II as a necessary development, in order to prepare the way for the coming New Age. She said that the World Wars were good and that this great energy of purification (shamballa force) was necessary for regenerating humanity. She said that the failure of Christianity could be traced to its Jewish background which was full of hate and blood sacrifice rather than loving service. She said that the coming New Age would set all this straight and make it clear to all that there is no angry God, no Hell and no punishment. She said that it was not necessary to be a Christian in order to be affiliated to Christ, but the Christ she promoted was a New Age invention, and not the Christ of Christians or the Christ of The Holy Trinity.

The New World Order

In the early 1980's, Gary H. Kah was a very successful young man in a US government career. He travelled around the world dealing with the American embassies, foreign government officials, International business leaders and sometimes press media. He had already received many awards for academic achievements, including a Wall Street Journal award for Outstanding Economic Achievement. Through his travels around the world, he became aware of plans being laid worldwide for the establishment of a one world government, often referred to by those involved as the New World Order. He was sceptical at first but gradually became convinced of the reality of this from the many circumstances and experiences he was having and also from the calibre of the people who were giving him information. Eventually he became completely fascinated by these plans and decided to do his own investigations. **He then spent many years of research on this subject and finally came to the extraordinary conclusion that humanity would soon have a one world government, imposed by powerful Luciferic forces and organised by secret societies.** He discovered that these plans were being made all over the world, from Taiwan to Israel, from the Soviet Union to the United States. To some extent, he had an insider's view of the plans being made to create this One World Government, by being involved in some of the organizations participating in the effort.

The Conspiracy: It is very difficult for the average citizen to believe that there is this enormous conspiracy being hatched and planned by secret societies. Many can easily accept that there is a lot of political intrigue, or that large international financial institutions and multinationals have a lot more influence than they should, at the political and economic level, but that is as far as it goes. The reality of a great conspiracy, which aims to put world-wide political, economic, and religious control, into the hands of a small number of select individuals, would seem to most people to be utter nonsense and make believe. World news, for the majority, comes from the traditional mainstream media, especially TV, newspapers, internet and popular magazines. Although these often promote the New Age in one form or another, there is never a suggestion of any secret world conspiracy. Is this conspiracy real, therefore? What is the evidence?

One of the organizations, in which Kah was involved with, was the World Constitution and Parliament Association (WCPA). This is not very well known as yet but this will change, as some of the most powerful people in the world are involved in the WCPA. Gary Kah has written two books on the subject of the One World Order conspiracy plan. The first, *En route to Global Occupation*,[67] outlines the plans for setting up of this world wide government, and the second book, *The Demonic Roots of Globalism*,[68] traces the links between the plans to set up a one world government and the satanic forces behind it. Two other good books, among many, now published on this subject are, *Conspiracy Against Life*,[69] and *Hope of The Wicked*.[70] These books also outline the details of plans, from various sources, to promote this One World Government. This New World Order plan is linked with New Age programmes and with organizations associated with, and promoting the United Nations as a legitimate world government in the making. The general consensus of these books is that the key organization, coordinating the New Age with the One World Order plan and with the economic, political, military, and spiritual aspects of the United Nations, is the Masonic Order, also known as the Freemasons.

While writing to various magazines for advertising rates, Gary Kah accidentally discovered that the New Age magazine was owned and controlled by the "Mother Supreme Council of The World" Freemasons in Washington D.C. On further research he found that the leaders of illuminised Freemasons had earlier decided that the main preparations and promotions for the New Age, should be handled by the leaders of the Theosophical Society (all female), that is, Blavatsky, Besant and Bailey. As Freemasonry membership is almost exclusively male, that would give the impression that Freemasons were not connected with New Age promotion. In 1985 Kah first recognised that the Theosophical Society, with sister organizations such as The *Lucis Trust* (formerly known as the *Lucifer Publishing Company*, started by Alice Bailey), were laying the ground work for the New Age. The Freemasons were then co-ordinating the New Age programmes with other aspects of the one world government plan.[70]

Freemasons

Many books have been published on the structure and activities of Freemasons over the last twenty five years, mostly by former members.[71,72] The Freemasons are believed to be among the key planners and driving force behind the One World Order. Generally, Freemasonry is regarded as a secret society but masons themselves often like to describe it more benignly as, "a society with secrets". Either way, there is a meshwork of secret societies, which have been spawned from masonry, which have definite and key roles in the planning and promotion of this New World Order. Albert Pike, (famous former Freemason leader in the US) in his book, Morals and Dogma, said that Freemasonry had its origins in Kabbalism, Gnosticism, and the Knights Templars. This view is supported by Kah.

Kabbala is the highest point of mysticism in Judaism's mystical tradition. Kabbalism is an occult explanation of the "Torah" or Old Testament, which was law for the Israelites. These occult teachings were handed down through generations by secret societies. Kabbala was distorted beyond recognition by Italian humanists who mixed it with Egyptian occultism and symbols such as the pyramid. These "Kabbalistic humanists", as they became known, spread strange interpretations of the Old Testament, which later became popular in many European dissident and occult societies, such as the Morovians, Unitarians, and the Neo-arians during the 15th century.

Gnosticism developed as a similar occult counter offensive against traditional New Testament teaching, and in particular promoted the teaching that Lucifer was more powerful than Christ. Gnosticism developed from Kaballism. Gnosticism also flourished in secret societies through the centuries. The Bogomils, for example, in the 9th century promoted the belief that God the Father had two sons. They believed that Satan was the eldest and that he created the world. Jesus was said to be less powerful than Satan and thus Satan is the one who should be adored. These teachings were eventually passed on to the Knights Templars and from them to the Freemasons.

The Knights Templars were established as a religious and military order, in Jerusalem in 1118 A.D., to protect pilgrims going to the Holy Land. By the 14th century they had embraced Gnosticism as their religion and later became worshippers of Lucifer. The Knights Templars were eventually condemned by Pope Clement V in 1312. They then found some refuge in Portugal under King Denis II, who became their protector. At this stage they had major "lodges" established in Edinburgh, Stockholm, Naples, and Paris. Other secret and occult societies, antagonistic to the Roman Church, were also active in Europe up to the beginning of the 16th century. This revolt eventually spilled over into the Protestant Reformation in 1517. It is claimed in the book, *Conspiracy Against Life*[69] that the chief architects of this reformation, belonged to these occult societies. The remnants of the Knights Templars were later blended into a new secret order called the Rosicrucians. This new order, which was promoted as a charitable society, only became public around the year 1600 AD although it had already existed for at least 200 years at that stage.

During the 17th century, the Rosicrucians combined with remnants of a society of stone masons. These were no longer active masons, but through the centuries had become "accepted masons" and "speculative masons". This older order of masons was also influenced by the Kabbalistic humanists and the members were also Gnostics, meeting in secret groups, referred to as "lodges". This eventually led to the formation of the first "Grand Lodge of Freemasons" in London in 1717 AD. The connection of Freemasonry with the Templars and Rosicrucians is still easily recognizable, as the "Knight Templar" and the "Knight of the Red Cross" are degrees in modern masonic membership.

The Illuminati were formed in 1776 AD and joined with the Freemasons in 1782 AD (see below). With the financial backing of the Rothschilds, the Illuminati were able to regain the banking and political influence which, the Knights Templars originally had many centuries earlier. George Washington, unaware of the hidden agenda in the Freemasons, joined the organization and this led the Masonic order to gain great popularity and influence in the US. Rutherford, Russel and Smith, who were involved in founding the religions of the Mormons and Jehovah's Witnesses, were high ranking masons.

Albert Pike was an attorney, a 33rd degree mason, considered a genius, and author of the authoritative book on masonry, Morals and Dogma. He was investigated regarding the assassination of Abraham Lincoln and later pardoned for his role by President Andrew Johnson. Pike as well as Weishaupt (the leader of the Illuminati), both believed that Lucifer was the true God, and that the biblical God was the God of evil. While Pike ran the Masonic organization in the US, Giuseppi Mazzini ran it in Europe. Mazzini was the founder of a Sicilian terrorist organization, which was named around 1860 AD as 'Mazzini autorizza furti, incendi, avvelenamenti' (Mazzini authorises thefts, arson and poisoning), known today, in abbreviated form, as the Mafia.

Mazzini (1805 – 72) joined a secret organization known as the Carbonari while he was at university in Genoa. The aim of the Carbonari was the elimination of Christianity especially Roman Catholicism. He was forced into exile in 1831 and he moved to England in 1837, where he founded the "Young Societies", such as "Young Italy", "Young England", "Young Russia" and "Young Bosnia", etc. He later returned to Italy in 1848 to lead the revolution against the Austrians. He was generally regarded as an Italian nationalist and patriot who, with Garibaldi and others were the leaders of the Italian Risorgimento. He became known as "The Evil Genius of Italy". He carried out the activities of the Illuminati through the Alta Vendita Lodge, which was the highest lodge of the Carbonari. This lodge controlled a group known as the Haute Vente Romaine, which led the activities of most of the secret societies in Europe during the first half of the 19th century.

In January 1870, Albert Pike, a Grand Commander of the Scottish rite of freemasonry, announced the establishment of a secret society within a secret society. He said, "We must create a 'super rite', which will remain unknown, to which we will call those masons of high degree of whom we shall select. With regard to our brothers in masonry, these men must be pledged to the strictest secrecy". He went on to say that this supreme rite would govern all freemasonry and become all the more powerful because its direction would be unknown. For this reason, up to the present day, the vast majority of those involved in masonry have no idea of what lies behind the organization at the highest level. Pike established the ultra-secret super rite for Universal

Freemasonry, which he named the "New and Reformed Palladium Rite", with the main centres in Rome, Berlin and Charleston, US. Pike and Mazzini, both signed the constitution forming the Palladium Rite on September 20th 1870. Pike became "The Sovereign Pontiff of Lucifer". In 1889 Albert Pike issued instructions to the twenty three supreme councils of world freemasonry. He said, "To you Sovereign Grand Instructors General, we say this, that you may repeat it to the brethren of the 30th, 31st and 32nd degrees. The Masonic religion should be by all of us initiates of the high degrees, maintained in the purity of the Luciferian doctrine".[67]

Freemasons world-wide, are divided into a number of Rites, of which there are at least ten. They are all bonded together under the Palladium Rite, represented by the 'all seeing eye' of the pyramid. The three best known Rites below the Palladium Rite are the Scottish with 33 degrees, the York with 13 degrees, and the Memphis with 79 degrees. The first thirty degrees of the Scottish Rite are regarded as preparation for the masons entry into the Palladium Rite. Having reached the highest degrees, the final step is to get, "immortality and god like wisdom", which involves initiation into the Palladium Rite.[69]

Freemasonry at the highest level, therefore, is a religion in which Lucifer is regarded as the good God of Light. As explained above, this is in keeping with the origins of masonry from secret European societies, which occurred over the last two thousand years. At the lower levels members are accepted from all religions but freemasonry always teaches that all other religions are subject to its authority. Many who join are well intentioned Christians, who have no idea of its antichristian significance. It is important to emphasise, therefore, that the ordinary members of the Freemasons are good citizens, who happen to belong to a private club, and who help and support each other with the problems of everyday life. There is also no doubt that many lodges do charitable works, especially in the US. The Luciferian worship in masonry, in common with some other secret societies, very often is revealed only at the very highest level of the leadership.

Catholicism and Freemasonry: In 1819 a few years after the Congress of Vienna, when the great European powers decided to wipe Poland off the geopolitical map, a major instruction was issued by the Chief Masons of France, Austria, Germany and Italy.[69] This called for the total annihilation of Catholicism. It said "What we must wait for is a Pope suitable for our purposes ...because with such a Pope, we could effectively crush the rock on which God built his Church... Seek a Pope fitting our description". This was done by encouraging young clergy to join the masons in the hope that one of these could later be elected Pope. This threat almost became a reality when the Cardinal elected to succeed Pope Leo XIII in 1903 was almost certainly a mason. He was not able to take up the position of Pope, however, due to an objection by the Austria-Hungarian Emperor who had a veto at the time. The Emperor had been warned by a French priest about the Masonic involvement of this particular Cardinal.[73] The assassination of the heir to this Austria-Hungarian throne, in 1914, by the "Black Hand" Serbian movement, was later to lead to the First World War.

In a series of messages from The Virgin Mary to Fr Gobbi, Freemasonry is specifically mentioned. Message number 405 and 406, in particular,[3] refers to the book of revelations, in the Bible, where Fr Gobbi was told that the red dragon represented Marxist atheism. The black beast represented masonry and the beast with two horns like a lamb, represented masonry which has entered into the heart of the Church, or Ecclesiastical Masonry.

Some confusion arose with the publication of a new code of Canon Law in 1983, as Freemason membership was not specifically mentioned as forbidden, as in the 1917 code. The confusion was cleared up by a declaration from Cardinal Ratzinger (later Pope Benedict XVI), on Nov. 26th 1983, with the support of St Pope John Paul II. This stated clearly that membership of Masonic associations was still strictly forbidden for Catholics, as Masonic teaching was irreconcilable with the Catholic Church. It further stated that Catholics who belong to Freemasonry are living in grave sin, and may not receive Holy Communion.

A Brief History of the
Planned New One World Order

In 1773 Mayer Rotchschild assembled twelve friends and convinced them that if they all pooled their resources together, that they could rule the world. This meeting took place in Frankfurt Germany. Rotchschild told his friends that he had found a perfect candidate to lead this new organization. This individual was Adam Weishaupt, who was a former professor of canon law, at the University of Ingolstadt. On May 1st 1776 Adam Weishaupt, often called Sparticus, established a secret society called **"The Order of the Illuminati"**. The Illuminati would try, as explained in chapter 1, to establish a New World Order, with the following objectives:

a. Abolition of all ordered governments
b. Abolition of private property
c. Abolition of inheritance
d. Abolition of patriotism
e. Abolition of the family
f. Abolition of religion
g. Creation of a world government.

On July 16th 1782, the Order of the Illuminati joined forces with freemasonry at the congress of Wilhelmsbad. It was also decided at the congress that the headquarters of Illuminised Freemasonry should be moved to Frankfurt from Bavaria. At that time, Frankfurt was a great financial centre from which the Rothschilds operated. In 1785 an Illuminati courier was struck by lightening, while travelling through the town of Ratisbon, in Bavaria. When officials examined the contents of his bags, they discovered the existence of the Illuminati as an organization, but they also found plans detailing a coming revolution in France. The Bavarian Government attempted to alert the government in France concerning this impending problem, but the French Government did not take heed of the warning. Most of the Officials in the Illuminati were arrested but Weishaupt and others escaped.

In 1796, Freemasonry became a major factor in the presidential elections in the United States. John Adams who won the election said "I do conscientiously believe that the Order of Freemasonry, if not the greatest, is one of the greatest moral and political evils under which the Union is now labouring". In 1797 John Robinson, who was Professor of natural history at Edinburgh University, published a book called, "Proof of a Conspiracy" in which he revealed attempts by Adam Weishaupt to recruit him into the Illuminati.

Since joining with the Freemason movement, in 1782, the Illuminati, as illuminised Freemasonry, have promoted and supported various national revolutions, especially the French Revolution. In 1821, George W. Hegel put together what has been called the 'Hegelian Dialectic', which outlined the process by which the Illuminati objectives could be achieved. The plan was firstly, to start a crisis. Then there would be an enormous public outcry that something should be done about this particular problem. A solution is then offered that would bring about the changes wanted in the first place, but which the people would have been unwilling to accept initially.

In 1848 Karl Marx (Moses Mordecai Marx Levy) wrote the communist manifesto with the help of Engels. Marx was a member of a front organization for the Illuminati, called the 'League of the Just'. He believed that the family should be abolished and that all children should be raised by a central authority. He also said, "We must war against all prevailing ideas of religion, of state, of country, and of patriotism. The idea of God is the keynote of a perverted civilisation. It must be destroyed." When Marx and Engels wrote the communist manifesto, Rotchschilds were recognised as the outstanding capitalists in Europe, yet there was no criticism of them. There is evidence that Marx was more interested in doing the bidding of secret societies rather than helping the common people. He wrote the drama, *Oulanem*, which convinced many that he was a Satanist.[70] His poem, *The Player*, seems to confirm this:

> The Hellish vapours rise and fill the brain,
> Till I go mad and my heart is utterly changed.
> See the sword?
> The prince of darkness sold it to me.
> For me he beats the time and gives the signs.
> Ever more boldly I play the dance of death.

Mazzini and his International masons would use Marx to subvert the socialist labour movement. So obvious was the connection between Marx and the Illuminati that, during the early days of the Russian Revolution, the revolutionaries called themselves Spartacusts (Spartacus was a name used by Adam Weishaupt – founder of the Illuminati), before being known as Bolsheviks and later Communists.[74] In 1922, Winston Churchill recognised the connection between the Illuminati and the Bolshevik revolution in Russia, when he said that, "From the days of Spartacus - Weishaupt, to those of Karl Marx, to those of Trotsky, Bela Kun,

Rosa Luxemburg and Emma Goldman, this world wide conspiracy for the overthrow of civilisation and for the reconstitution of society, on the basis of arrested development, of envious malevolence and impossible equality, has been steadily growing. It played a definite recognizable role in the tragedy of the French Revolution. It has been the mainspring of every subversive movement during the 19th century, and now at last this band of extraordinary personalities, from the underworld of the great cities of Europe and America, have gripped the Russian people by the hair of their heads and have become practically the undisputed masters of that enormous empire".[75]

The Committee of 300

This was modelled on the British East India Company's Council of 300 which began in 1727. The committee of 300 also known as the "Olympians" began in 1838, composed of managers, from banks, insurance companies, large foundations, and communication networks. According to one often quoted book, *Conspiration Hierarchy, The Story of the Committee of 300,* by Dr. John Coleman,[76] this is one of the most powerful of the secret societies and controls many other secret movements and societies. They work through the Royal Institute of International Affairs (RIIA), which in turn created the Tavistock Institute, a "superbody" with influence in military and education institutions worldwide. According to Dr. John Coleman (a former British intelligence agent for MI6, who has written what seems to be the only authoritative book on the Committee of 300), all Tavistock Institute and American foundation techniques have the single goal of breaking down the psychological strength of the individual and thus render him helpless to oppose the dictators of the World Order. This is done by methods of Freudian psychotherapy, which induce permanent mental illness in those who undergo this treatment by destabilising their character.

The main objective of the Committee of 300 is to establish a New World Order with a One World Church and a world unified monetary system under their direction. Other more detailed objectives are in line with the Global 2000 Report. This was a report published in 1982, by a number of US agencies, especially the Council on Environmental Quality and the Department of State. It outlined, "the probable changes in the world's population, natural resources, and environment, through the end of the century". It suggested that there would be enormous problems of starvation, social upheaval and chaos, if drastic action was not taken, such as reducing the world's population by three billion. The Global 2000 report was accepted and approved by President Carter on behalf of the US Government.

Some of the objectives of the Committee of 300 described in Dr. John Coleman's book in 1992, are as follows:

1 Destruction of the Christian religion on the premise that it is the principle obstacle to change.
2 Erosion of National identity and pride.
3 Infiltration with influence on all governments.
4 Control of educational systems.
5 Control of world economics so that it can be collapsed at will.
6 Reduction of the world population by three billion – considered useless eaters.

The *One World Order* is also to be promoted by bringing international institutions, such as the International Monetary Fund (IMF), World Bank (WB), and the Bank of International Settlement (BIS), under the United Nations.

The Federal Reserve

There is little doubt that the real control over the United States and its people, by a powerful banking cartel, began with the formation of The Federal Reserve Bank. This happened on December 23rd 1913, when a Presidential Act transferred the power to create money from the American Government to a private group of Bankers. The Federal Reserve Act was hastily passed, just before the Christmas break, in the Congress. Congressman, Charles A Lindbergh Senior (father of the famous aviator) warned at the time, "This act establishes the most gigantic trust on earth. When the President signs this bill, the invisible government of the Monetary Power will be legalised ...the worst legislative crime of the ages is perpetrated by this banking and currency bill". Three years afterwards, President Woodrow Wilson said, "I am a most unhappy man. I have unwittingly ruined my country. A great industrial nation is controlled by its system of credit. Our system of credit is concentrated. The growth of the nation, therefore, and all our activities, are in the hands of a few men. We have come to be one of the worst ruled, one of the most completely controlled and dominated governments in the civilised world. No longer a government by free opinion, no longer a government by conviction and the vote of the majority, but a government by the opinion and duress of a small group of dominant men".

The monetary system in the US is not operated, therefore, by the US Government, but by a private corporation, now generally referred to as the 'Fed'. The Federal Reserve is owned and controlled by Rothschild Banks of London and Berlin, Lazard Banks of Paris, Israel Moses Seif Banks of Italy, Warburg Banks of Hamburg and Amsterdam, and Lehman, Kuhn–Loeb, Chase Manhattan, and Goldman Sachs banks of New York.[70] Several congressmen, over the last century, have tried to expose this and do something about it, without success. One of the best known was Larry P McDonald. In 1976 he wrote the introduction to The Rockefeller File, which described how the *One World Government* was being created by super–Capitalism and Communism working together. He said that there was a group who were "carefully following a plan to use their economic power to gain political control, firstly of America, and then the rest of the world... I am convinced that there is such a plot, International in scope, generations old in planning, and incredibly evil in intent". He died in 1983, in a mysterious Korean Airline incident when a large passenger aircraft, "accidentally" strayed into Russian air space and was "accidentally" shot down. Senator John Heinz and John Towers were two others who tried to expose some Fed secrets. Both died in mysterious aircraft accidents, one day apart, on the 4th and 5th of April, 1991.

Louis T. McFadden was the chairman of the committee on Banking and Currency in the United States between 1920 and 1931. Concerning the Federal Reserve, he stated that, "When the Federal Reserve Act was passed the people of the United States did not perceive that a world banking system was being set up here. A Super-State, controlled by International Bankers and International Industrialists, acting together to enslave the world for their own pleasure. Every effort has been made by the Fed to conceal its powers but the truth is, the Fed has usurped the Government. It controls everything here, and it controls all our foreign relations. It makes and breaks government at will". Concerning the Great Depression in the US, he said, "It was no accident. It was a carefully contrived occurrence. The International Bankers sought to bring about a condition of despair here, so that they might emerge as rulers of us all".

The Council on Foreign Relations

In July 1921 Edward M. House reorganised the Institute of International Affairs into the Council on Foreign Relations (CFR). Colonel House was a close adviser to President Wilson and in 1913 had convinced him to sign the Federal Reserve Act. Ever since the CFR was founded, 80% of the top positions of every administration in the US, whether Democratic or Republican, have been occupied by members of this organisation. The term "New World Order", has been used by the CFR since the beginning, to describe the planned World Government. On December 15th, 1922 the CFR endorsed the idea and necessity of a World Government in its magazine, 'Foreign Affairs'.

In 1928 H. G. Wells (who was a Fabian socialist), wrote a book called, *The Open Conspiracy*. In this book he stated that, "The open conspiracy is the natural inheritor of socialist and communist enthusiasms. It may be in control in Moscow before it is in control in New York. The character of the open conspiracy will now be plainly displayed. It will be a world religion". In 1933 in another book called, *The Shape of Things to Come*, H. G. Wells predicted a second world war around 1940, originating from a German Polish dispute. He also said that after 1945 that a "World State" would succeed after the third attempt and that it would come about from events that would occur in Iraq. It was also in 1933 that the insignia of the order of the Illuminati appeared on the reverse side of the U.S. one dollar bills. The year 1776, in roman numerals (MDCCLXXVI), can be seen at the base of a thirteen storey pyramid.

At the top of the pyramid is the all spying eye, radiating in all directions, and symbolizing the controlling body. Below the pyramid, is written in Latin, "Novus Ordo Seclorum" (New Secular Order). In 1950 an International financier named James Warburg, a member of the Council on Foreign Relations (CFR), told a Senate Foreign Relations subcommittee, "We will have world government whether you like it or not, by conquest or consent."

The Bilderbergers

In 1954 Prince Bernhard of the Netherlands established the Bilderbergers at the Bilderberg Hotel in Oosterbeek, Holland. This is an International Group of Bankers and Politicians who meet secretly on an annual basis. It is the group responsible for the integration of European countries and was responsible for promoting and encouraging the Treaty of Rome, which led to the European Common Market and later the European Union. Prominent American Bilderbergers have included David and Nelson Rockefeller, Henry Kissinger, Robert McNamara (former president of the World Bank), Donald Rumsfeld and President

Gerald Ford. The leadership is closely connected with the CFR and is thus regarded as a sister organisation.

Daniel Estulin, in his book, *The True Story of The Bilderberg Group,*[7] outlines in great detail how this group, together with others, such as the Trilaterals and the CFR promotes, what he terms, sophisticated subversion, with the ultimate aim of creating a New World Order, which will eventually allow a small elite group of people to control and enslave the rest of the world. These groups select and control the American Presidents and have enormous power and influence in Governments all over the world. The Trilateral/Bilderberg/CFR model is composed of top financial managers and Establishment insiders. Estulin believes that the main objective of these groups is to find a way to convince ordinary citizens to surrender their liberties, in the name of some common threat or crisis, which may be real or imaginary. The global warming problem is one of a number of issues being used to this end at the moment.

The Club of Rome

A significant percentage of the members of this group are from the CFR. The Club of Rome (COR) is composed of teachers, industrialists, business people, and international civil servants. The COR was created by the Committee of 300 in 1968, with the task of unification of the entire world under governable regions, for the purpose of promoting the One World Order. The organization claims to have the solution for world peace but this is at the expense of national sovereignty and at the expense of lots more which we are not told about. The Club has already divided the world into ten different political − economic regions, originally referred to as kingdoms, as follows:

1. North America
2. Western Europe
3. Japan
4. Australia and South Africa
5. Eastern Europe and Russia
6. Central and South America
7. Middle East and North Africa
8. Central Africa
9. India
10. China

One has to wonder if there is a connection between these proposed ten kingdoms and the biblical references of Daniel 7:23-25 and Revelation 13. It is Christian belief that Antichrist will come when the world is ruled by ten kings and he will come as the chief king over them. According to Kah, the most disturbing thing about the COR is that it is driven by an occult spiritualism. The New Age connection with the COR is also confirmed by its American membership, which includes leading promoters of the New Age. American membership also includes: four congressmen, representatives from Planned Parenthood, officials of the UN, and members of the Carnegie and Rockefeller foundations.

The Trilaterals

In 1973 the International Banker, David Rockefeller, started a new organization called the Trilateral Commission. The official aim of this commission was to harmonise political, economic and social relations between three major economic regions of the world. These areas were North America, Europe and the Far East. He invited future President Jimmy Carter, to become one of the first founding members. The idea was to eventually form these into three Super States, which could be ruled under a One World Government. The movement towards a Super State is already happening rapidly in Europe and over the next few years will move significantly in North America. Barry Goldwater (retired Republican Senator from Arizona) described this organization in his autobiography as follows: "In my view the Trilateral Commission represents a skilful, coordinated effort to seize control and consolidate the four centres of power: political, monetary, intellectual and ecclesiastical. All this is done in the interest of creating a more peaceful, more productive world community. What the Trilateralists truly intend is the creation of a worldwide economic power, superior to the political governments of the nation-states involved... As managers and creators of the system, they will rule the future."

The Federal Emergency Management Agency

In 1979 the Federal Emergency Management Agency (FEMA), was given enormous power in the US. In a "National Emergency" laws can be suspended and anybody can be arrested without a reason. Property, supplies, transportation systems etc., can be seized in the name of the common good. In May 1994, President Bill Clinton, signed the Presidential Decision Directive number 25. This directive, later issued to members of Congress, authorised the President, to turn over control of the US military units to the UN command. All these Presidential directives may be very benign and represent precautions only, but they could also be used to work against the common good.

The United Nations

This was started in 1945 by a committee composed largely of members from the American Council on Foreign Relations (CFR). In order to make certain that the United States would not back out of joining the United Nations (UN), as happened with the League of Nations, John D. Rockefeller donated the land in New York for the UN building, thus ensuring that it would be on US soil.

The UN is supposed to be the moral watchdog for the nations of the world but in many countries there is now a decreasing respect developing for the UN. We have only to remember the UN peace keepers in the "safe haven" of Srebrenica (1995), who permitted Serbian soldiers to round up and slaughter thousands of Muslims, or worse still was the behaviour of the UN, in Rwanda, in 1994. The UN commander on the ground, in Rwanda, knew for a long time of the impending disaster and was continually sending advice on the action that needed to be taken. The UN leadership did nothing to support him or prevent the slaughter of almost one million Rwandan citizens in a bloody civil war. One of the worst indictments of the UN, however, is the failure of any of the UN human rights commissioners to utter a single word in defence of unborn life. The sad fact is, that any individual who opposed widespread abortion, would not be approved as a UN human rights commissioner. We must also acknowledge, however, the good in the UN and the great contribution UN peace-keepers make in many troubled areas around the world. The UN has the potential to make an enormous contribution to world peace and to the relief of poverty and disease in many poor nations.

More than any other organization, the UN serves as the great International body which represents a world government in the making. World nations contribute financially and politically to varying degrees, but in theory at least, it is a very useful worldwide forum for nations to develop a unified approach for solving world problems. The UN, therefore, has great potential for good or evil, depending on how it is organised and what International laws are agreed to be implemented worldwide. Those with the greatest influence and control in the UN will also be those with the greatest influence and control over International law and over International UN projects and programmes.

In the first chapter of this book, I mentioned the polarization of views in the world on questions of morality, and the global chaos and conflict which now seems inevitable, because of this. I suggested that the most important reason for this conflict will be spiritual rather than political. At this time the UN has opted for a secular value system as a basis for international law.

The important question at this time, therefore, is, can agreed international laws, based on secularism, be a foundation for peace and stability in the world, or will laws permitting the killing of the unborn, have dramatic and dire consequences for humanity, as Roman Catholic theology (in particular) suggests?

The UN International Conference is the forum, at the moment, where the two opposing value systems are being vigorously debated. The two views are mutually incompatible. The Vatican, since 1964, has had permanent observer status in the UN as a non-governmental organization. A very dramatic confrontation between Catholic views and secular views, on the right to life of the unborn, occurred at the UN International Conference on Population and Development, in Cairo, 1994. St Pope John Paul was very outspoken in his condemnation of the UN programme to endorse abortion and redefine the family. He said that the Cairo UN Conference was designed to destroy the family and that it was a snare of the devil. The role of Vatican delegates at this conference is described in, *Global Bondage – The UN Plan to Rule the World.*[77]

The Pope's concern went far beyond abortion and UN hypocrisy. A Vatican statement said, "The Holy See is very much aware that the future of humanity is under discussion." Alfonso Cardinal Lopez Trujillo said at the time that, if the UN endorsed abortion as an international "right", then the Cairo conference could lead to "the most disastrous massacre in history." Some saw apocalyptic overtones in the Pope's comments and were convinced that he believed it would lead to a Divine intervention. Newsweek wrote that, "The Pope is driven by his foreboding that the world is heading towards a moral apocalypse." Time magazine named St Pope John Paul II, man of the year in 1994, for opposing the UN. For nine days the Vatican delegates, under the Pope's direction, lobbied and filibustered. They kept the Latin American nations in line and made alliances with Islamic nations opposed to abortion. In the end, the Pope won.

Saint Teresa of Calcutta, when she was suggesting that abortion represented the greatest danger to peace in the world, also reminded us of the words of Jesus Christ, - "Whatever you do to the least of these – you do to me." She also said, "If we can accept that a mother can kill even her own child, how can we tell others not to kill each other?" The implication is that nations, who kill their unborn at the rate many nations are now doing, will drift into civil war and do not deserve to survive.

There is little doubt that the views of the secret societies are very much in the majority within the UN leadership. All former American Presidents since World War II, with the possible exception of Ronald Reagan and Kennedy, were either masons, Trilateralists, or members of the CFR. President George Bush senior and Bill Clinton both promoted the New Age and the One World Order, even to the extent of using occult terms (according to Kah[67]), such as "a thousand points of light" as used by the *Lucis Trust*. The *Lucis Trust* has an active role in the UN Economic and Social Council. Robert Muller, who was Assistant Secretary to the UN for 36 years, was a devoted student and promoter of Alice Bailey, who started the *Lucis Trust*. Alice was head of the Theosophical Society and guided by a Tibetan master spirit, who dictated many books to her. In one of her dictated books,

Externalization of the Hierarchy (1939), she said that the Jewish and Christian religions were causing major problems for humanity.

When the UN promotes secularism and rejects the possibility of God and God's love for humanity, then it also rejects the dignity of every human person and the dignity of human life itself. A secular UN will do more harm than good for humanity.

One World Religion

The One World Religion, which is now over a decade old, has all the signs of a One World Order plan for religious control. It was formed by bringing senior delegates of different major world religions together, and trying to work out a system of beliefs that would incorporate all of them. Holy waters from all the different holy shrines and different religions all over the world were combined together in a large container, in this great effort to produce this New Age, One World Religion. It is very difficult to be judgemental about any of the particular individuals involved, who may be completely sincere in their efforts to create harmony. Superficially, it is a collective human effort to produce a man made religion, which could be accepted by everybody and lead to harmony and peace. This effort is not realistic, however, and there must be a strong suspicion that the ultimate aim, of those in charge is not world harmony, but world control. Is the plan to have this One World Religion enforced in the future by a One World Government? The Catholic Church was one of the few religions not to take part officially in this plan.

If the leaders of the One World Religion are serious about uniting religious views in the world for the good of all, then a number of essentials need to be recognised. Firstly, it must be recognised that a One World Religion cannot be imposed. The best that could be hoped for is a Charter of Religious Principles, with wide agreement across all the major religious beliefs. After all, there is good in all religions and the "Paths" in Buddhism have a lot in common with the Ten Commandments. If this could be achieved, it would open up new avenues and create new opportunities for promoting peace and harmony in the world. There is a great need for the various religions and nations to move forward, in mutual respect, in search of truth. An agreed world Charter of Religious Principles would be a good stimulus for this.

Secondly, the principles on which any religious charter could be constructed would have to be based on an interpretation of natural law, rather than on secular humanist values. Natural law would not necessarily exclude the views of humanists and atheists, whereas secularism likes to exclude God.

Thirdly, for a charter of religious principles to have any value and a hope of being accepted, it would have to:

a) Recognise the personhood of the unborn.
b) Recognise the natural, intrinsic, or inalienable rights of each person, with every state having the obligation to support these rights in opposition to any other man made law.
c) In keeping with the intrinsic rights of each human person, everybody should have the right to practice the religion of their choice, provided that this religion is based on love and respect for all peoples in all nations.
d) Reject religious views promoting war, hatred, or failing to recognise the rights of individuals.
e) Allow a freedom to promote and share information on all religious views, with the aim of promoting harmony and establishing truth as the ultimate goal.

It would be nice to believe that the different views on morality, between secularism and monotheism, could be sorted out by peaceful debating and democratic voting. Sadly, this will not happen. God's law, or natural law, is not based on a democratic decision and natural law has already been rejected as a basis for international law. The stakes, therefore, are much higher. Natural law dictates that when the bomb is dropped, it will fall, and no amount of democratic voting will change this. Natural law also dictates that evil acts, such as the killing of the unborn, will have consequences, which also cannot be changed by democratic voting.

The evidence seems to suggest that many of those, especially in the leadership of the secret societies, who promote secular values, far from being mere secularists or atheists, believe that Lucifer is the true God. This, therefore, is rapidly developing as a fight to the death. It is a fight between the forces of The Virgin Mary, on behalf of Christ, against the forces of Lucifer. Most of humanity may die before it is finished. You will have to choose who to fight with and who to fight against. If you have not already chosen, choose wisely.

National Security Study Memorandum 200

This document was put together in the US in the last years of the Nixon administration. It is also known as the Kissinger Report as it was produced when Henry Kissinger was US Secretary of State. It was declassified in 1988. This document identified the rapid population growth in the "Third World" as the greatest security threat to the US as a world power. The solution offered was massive population control, through financial incentives and aid. The countries identified particularly for this depopulation effort were the Philippines, Thailand, Indonesia, India, Pakistan, Ethiopia and Bangladesh. This programme has been implemented over the last thirty years, mainly through the machine of International Planned Parenthood Foundation (IPPF), which promotes contraception and abortion world-wide, with UN and US support. Abortion is now killing more than 150,000 unborn every day world-wide, which makes all previous human holocausts fade into insignificance, compared with this modern holocaust of the unborn. IPPF is one of the main driving forces for abortion. IPPF was founded by Margaret Sanger who was a eugenicist and spoke of populations in Asia, Africa and Latin America as "unfit to live". It is very sad to see such a great nation as the US, stoop so low and act so arrogantly against poorer nations. President George Bush, to his credit, began to redeem the situation somewhat by withdrawing some US funds from IPPF. The IPPF hit the headlines in 2016, when its business of selling body parts from aborted babies was exposed. President Donald Trump has now stopped US financial aid for IPPF but, unfortunately, there is no shortage of billionaires and world governments who have announced that they will make up the financial loss due to Donald Trump's action.

Seeds of Destruction

Population control in third world countries became a national security priority for the US, after the publication of NSSM-200.The information for this security report came from a Presidential Commission on, "Population and the American Future", in 1972, chaired by John D. Rockefeller III. A plan was hatched, in association with One World Order planners, to reduce the world population by three billion, who were regarded as "useless eaters". Documents were circulated thirty years ago which suggested that global chaos with mass starvation would result, if drastic action was not taken to reduce the world population. This plan was initially implemented by promoting birth control and abortion, mainly through US funds, as explained above, given to International Planned Parenthood (IPP). Another wing to the plan was control of world food. Now there remains the worry for all of us that a deliberate instigation of social disorder and war may be the final part of the solution to reduce the world population to one billion. This plan, I accept, is difficult to believe. Let us not forget, however, that just as Alice Bailey, former leader of the Theosophical Society, justified the Jewish Holocaust and World War II, as a necessary development in order to prepare the world for the coming New Age, so we can expect that some who are now in positions of influence in the UN and world governments, have similar views.

The progress with world-wide food control has been detailed in 2007, in the very interesting book, Seeds of Destruction,[6] written by William Engdahl. The Rockefeller Foundation, the Ford Foundation and the World Bank control the Consultative Group on International Agricultural Research (CGIAR). World Bank aid is dependent on accepting population control policies. The International Service for the Acquisition of Agri-biotech Applications (ISAAA) promotes GM crops world-wide and is controlled by a few multinationals such as Monsanto, Syngenta, Bayer AG, Dow Agri-sciences, DuPont, as well as the Rockefeller Foundation.

In 1998 Monsanto paid 1.8 billion to acquire what was known as Terminator Technology. This allows a "suicide gene" to be put into plants, so that the plants will not reproduce and be for one season only. This has been given the fancy name of Genetic Use Restriction Technology (GURT). After years of promoting GM seeds in the third world, under the guise of better yields (which was false), and promises never to use the GURT technology, this has all now changed. GURT technology GM seeds are now promoted widely in the third world countries and the poor farmers are often blackmailed into buying them. The result has been many thousands of poor farmers in the Third World committing suicide over the last few years, because they no longer can afford to renew enough seeds to plant food for their families. This is nothing less than enforced starvation of millions, in the poor countries by western multinationals, with the support of western governments and One World Order interests. It is well appreciated that independent small farmers could be a great obstacle to a One World control plan, simply because they are self-sufficient and independent.

The World Health Organization (WHO) is also assisting with population control in the Third World countries, by promoting contraception and abortion. The Mexican Catholic pro-life movement has exposed and condemned the WHO for promoting a particular tetanus vaccine, in Third World countries, for women (not men, or children) aged 15 to 45 years. One reason for this promotion was not the prevention of tetanus, but in order to make the girls infertile, as the vaccine also contained Human Chorionic Gonadotrophin (HCG). This normal human hormone is needed in females to maintain pregnancy. By combining HCG with tetanus toxoid, the women make antibodies to HCG, which inactivate the hormone and prevent a stable pregnancy. The trial of this vaccine was documented in the medical magazine, The Lancet, June 11, 1988. This vaccine has been promoted in poorer countries, especially in the Philippines and Nicaragua.

St Pope John Paul II strongly criticised the hypocrisy of the US and the UN after the UN Development Conference in Brazil in 1992, when he said in Evangelium Vitae: "Today not a few of the powerful of the earth act in the same way (like the Pharoah's murder of male babies in Ex 1:7-22). They too are haunted by the current demographic growth, and fear that the most prolific and poorest peoples represent a threat to the well-being and peace of their own countries. Consequently, rather than face and solve these serious problems with respect for the dignity of individuals and families and for every person's inviolable right to life, they prefer to promote and impose with whatever means, a massive programme of birth control. Even the economic help which they would be ready to give is unjustly made conditional on the acceptance of an anti-birth policy."[78]

Conclusion

In the previous chapters I have mentioned the inevitability of major world conflict because of the clash between two opposing supernatural forces competing for the allegiance of humanity. If we are to believe a number of Roman Catholic revelations and mystics, a battle is now raging in the spiritual world and it will soon be raging in wars between world nations. This clash will eventually spill over into world chaos, major religious wars, severe persecutions, especially of the Roman Catholic Church, and eventually the possible death of a significant portion of the world population. Chapters 11 and 12 discuss how this battle is likely to unfold in the near future. According to John Bird,[79] who echoes the belief of Bartholomew Holzhauser (died 1658),[80] this battle will bring to an end the fifth era of human history. The sixth era is predicted to be an era of peace and prosperity, when the Christian gospel is preached world-wide. This was promised by The Virgin Mary at Fatima (see chapter 5): – "In the end My Immaculate Heart will triumph and there will be peace". The final or seventh era will come with the manifestation of the Antichrist (see the last chapter for a detailed discussion on the coming of the Antichrist).

For those not familiar with some of the modern Roman Catholic revelations, detailed in chapter five, or the goings on of secret societies, which I have outlined in this chapter, I can understand that what you have read so far may be surprising for you, or even shocking for some, and difficult to believe. Yet in all of this we must remember that God is in control and that there is goodness in every human person, which can be promoted and developed at any time. At the moment, for example, it is impossible to believe that the leaders of all the powerful nations are secret worshippers of Satan. On the contrary, some are committed Christians. Donald Trump and Vladamir Putin are both openly promoting Christianity. Mikhail Gorbachev was a key figure in bringing about the great peaceful change to Russia in the 1980s, from the strictly closed Communist regimen of the previous seventy years. In doing so, he became a close associate of St Pope John Paul II, and he visited the Vatican to see the Pope several times, in the years afterwards. We also know that the Catholic Church has many demons active within it and a number of these are now being exposed. We can also be sure that when the major problems begin some of those now apparently living good lives will turn bad and in turn those who now appear evil will become good. In the end it is well to remember the words of Benjamin Franklin, who said, "There is so much good in the worst of us and bad in the best of us that it belittles any of us to speak ill of the rest of us". It is important that we do not judge or label individuals as we have no way of knowing what their secret motives are or how well-meaning or otherwise they may be. In the words of Christ, "Judge not and you will not be judged". Our task is to recognise the evidence suggesting that humanity is on the threshold of a calamity. We must prepare as much as we can for what is coming, so that the outcome will be a little less painful than it might otherwise be. We must pray, prepare, hope and not worry.

7. Exploring the Castle

When evening comes, you will be examined in love. Learn to love...
A soul enkindled with love is a gentle, meek, humble and patient
soul...A soul that is hard because of self-love grows harder.
St John of the Cross

In this chapter I discuss different levels of spirituality. This ranges from a brief mention of the lives of saints who have soared to the heights of holiness, to souls condemned to the depths of Hell. The purpose of life is to get to know and love God and to love, help, and support others. Good spirituality is therefore measured in love, and after death we will be judged by love. The more we love, the closer we get to God and the more fulfilled and happy our life will be. There is great confusion and there are major problems in modern society, because of a lack of love and a lack of good spirituality. As a consequence there is a great need for healing and change in society. It is some comfort to recognize strong indications of Christian unity moving ahead and gathering momentum. Divided Christians are now putting a lot more emphasis on studying the history of Christianity in the first four centuries and in particular, the study of the ancient Fathers of the Church. Prayer and suffering are also discussed briefly in this chapter.

I deal with demons and Hell in more detail than the other aspects of spirituality, as I believe that in the present situation **one of the greatest gifts one can give another human person is to help them understand the reality of Hell.** The Christian belief is that in the end each of us will finish up either in Heaven or in Hell. One of the reasons for writing this book is to emphasise, highlight, and confirm this reality, in so far as I can. Support for the belief that eternity exists was put succinctly, but with some flippancy, by a car sticker which said, "Tickets for eternity, choose smoking or non-smoking". By enabling others to appreciate that Hell is real, I hope to help not only myself, but as many others as possible to avoid this horrific place, where suffering is eternal.

The Saints: One of the first religious books which I read as an adult was the autobiography of Saint Therese of Lisieux, *A Story of a Soul.*[81] This is a beautiful, uplifting book, which points to the spirituality of, *"The Little Way"*. This book promotes the idea that the simple, humble, mundane, seemingly irrelevant events of the day can have great spiritual value, and therefore we should try to do the little things well, for the glory of God. Saint Therese lived and died in a French Carmelite monastery as a complete unknown, but her spiritual influence on countless millions is now legendary and continues to grow. I went on to read the lives of many other saints and the more I read the more I lost interest in reading fiction. The truth in the lives of the saints was far more challenging, interesting and rewarding. I enjoyed particularly reading a number of the many books on the life of the Italian stigmatist, Padre Pio, now a saint. As mentioned in chapter 4, anybody who seriously studies the life of this saint will find a wealth of support for Catholic theology, which is difficult to dispute. The power of his witness is all the more convincing because many are still alive who knew him intimately and many of his miraculous cures have been medically verified.

St Teresa of Ávila was responsible for writing two of the great masterpieces of Christian spirituality. *The Interior Castle*[82] and The *Way of Perfection*,[83] serve as a blueprint guide to holiness and leave no doubt that the purpose of life is to get as close as possible to a loving God. St John of the Cross was the second great

Spanish mystic of the sixteenth century. Among contemplatives, St John is an acknowledged master in mystical theology. He was a close friend of St Teresa who was born in 1515 and twenty seven years older than St John. Together they reformed the Carmelite Order and founded the Discalced branch, which is devoted to the service of The Blessed Virgin Mary through prayer and penance. The writings of St John of the Cross are difficult. His spirituality is definitely only for those who already have a good understanding of the spiritual life. His writings are especially for those with spiritual vows and can probably only be fully appreciated by those separated from the world. He has been described as a spiritual masochist, encouraging us to choose pain over pleasure, what is more difficult over what is more pleasant, and life after death over life after birth. The profundity of his spirituality is illustrated in the following from *The Ascent of Mount Carmel*, Book1, chapter 13:[84]

"To reach satisfaction in all desire its possession in nothing.
To come to possess all desire the possession of nothing.
To arrive at being all desire to be nothing.
To come to the knowledge of all desire the knowledge of nothing.
To come to the pleasure you have not you must go by a way in which you enjoy not.
To come to the knowledge you have not you must go by a way in which you know not.
To come to the possession you have not you must go by a way in which you possess not.
To come to be what you are not you must go by a way in which you are not.
When you turn towards something you cease to cast yourself upon the all.
For to go from all to all you must deny yourself of all in all.
And when you come to the possession of the all you must possess it without wanting anything.

Because if you desire to have something in all, your treasure in God is not purely your all.

In this nakedness the spirit finds its quietude and rest.

For in coveting nothing, nothing raises it up and nothing weighs it down, because it is in the centre of its humility.

When it covets something in this very desire it is wearied."

It can be very rewarding to read some of St John's words of wisdom, which can be found in books such as, The Little Book of John of the Cross.[85] I include the following examples:

"Suffering for God is better than working miracles.

For the intellect, faith is like a dark night. God is also a dark night to the soul in this life.

Strive to be incessant in prayer.

Remember always that you came here for no other reason than to be a saint: thus let nothing reign in your soul that does not lead you to sanctity.

Where there is no love, put love, and you will draw out love...

Endeavour to remain always in the presence of God."

The significance of the writings of St Teresa of Avila and St John of the Cross, to Catholic spirituality, are like the writings of Shakespeare, to English literature. You will not be educated in Catholic spirituality until you have studied these saints.

Everybody can benefit from reading *The Interior Castle*. For St Teresa, *The Interior Castle* is the soul, in the centre of which dwells the Trinity. In this book St Teresa gives a practical and challenging description of the soul's journey home to God. Growth in prayer allows the individual to enter deeper into intimacy with God, and to travel into the many apartments, or mansions, of the Castle. Each apartment is characterized by a new stage in the evolution of prayer and progress towards God. The ultimate aim of the soul is to journey within itself, where eventually it can reach God in an ecstatic union of love. *The Interior Castle* guides us, in great detail through seven dwellings, or levels of spirituality in the soul. Unfortunately, most of us never leave the first level. These seven levels can be seen depicted as a stairway picture, over the altar in the church of the Carmelite monastery, in Coimbra, Spain. It is noteworthy that in this monastery, Sister Lucia from Fatima spent most of her long life.

St Teresa outlines different stages in the life of prayer, in a metaphorical manner, like trying to secure water for the irrigation of soil. The first water is from a well carried with a bucket. There is fatigue and aridity from time to time, but it is the beginning of the prayer of meditation, which leads on to "acquired contemplation". The second water is got with a pump and a bucket and this represents "the prayer of quiet", which is a gift from God. The third water, or method of irrigation, is achieved using a stream or river flowing through the garden. This represents an intensification of "the prayer of quiet", leading on to the "sleep of the faculties". The fourth water of irrigation is directly from God, that is, the rain. The soul becomes passive and there is a state of union with God in prayer. Anybody who reads St Teresa will be left in no doubt that the garden of their soul needs watering with prayer.

Prayer: Many books have been written on prayer. I include here only a few points which readers may find helpful. Prayer to the soul is like breathing to the body. Without prayer the soul will die.

Prayer is communication with God and it is only by opening our minds and hearts to God that we can become more holy. Only God is truly holy and our first call is a call to holiness. Our first vocation is a vocation to pray.

Two things are necessary for prayer, - thinking and loving. You will know that you are praying enough if you are growing in virtue, especially growing in the love of God and love of others. If you are not growing in love then this means that you need to put more time and effort into prayer. Distraction is to be expected in prayer. St Thomas Aquinas said that twenty seconds was about the measure of duration of normal attention. Distractions can be a blessing as they indicate the parts of life not yet integrated with God. If something or somebody is a cause of distraction, it must be recognized and prayed about.

I heard the mnemonic ALTAR suggested once for the qualities which we should have in prayer:

>Adoration
>Love
>Thanking / Gratitude
>Asking / Petition
>Repentance and Reparation.

One of the most useful books I have come across on prayer was, *Prayer – The Breath of Life*.[86] From this little book, I learned how St Thomas Aquinas said that, the most important attention we need in prayer is, not so much thinking of the words we are saying, but rather thinking of the one to whom prayer is addressed. It further explained that when attention is directed to the Divine Person, the impersonal rote recitation disappears, and warmth, light, love, and a majestic dominating presence begins to be appreciated. St Teresa of Avila explained this in a similar way, when she spoke to her nuns in the following manner: "I want you to understand that if you are to recite the Lord's Prayer well, one thing is needed. You must not leave the side of the Master, Who taught it to you....All I want is that we should know and abide with the Person with whom we are speaking... I am not asking you to think of Him, or to form numerous conceptions of Him, or to make long and subtle meditations with your understanding. **I am asking you only to look at Him"**. St Teresa further explained that she got this method of prayer directly from God. She said, "For my part I must confess that, until the Lord taught me this method, I never knew what it was to get satisfaction and comfort out of prayer. The practice of Prayer by Looking must be continued with perseverance, until the habit has been formed and has become second nature. This may take six months, or a year, but that is a short time to acquire so great a benefit. It is an inestimable benefit that changes life profoundly. St Teresa said that, "The difficulty found in prayer comes from, "not looking". Real prayer, such as prayer by looking, has a quality of infinity, because it reaches God.

To contemplate means, "To look at steadily".[87] Christian contemplation is looking at Jesus with love. To know and love somebody is very different from merely knowing about them. Sometimes when we cannot choose the right words in order to pray properly, the Holy Spirit expresses our thoughts in a far better way than we can with words. This can be by speaking, "in tongues" or in silence, and God can read our hearts. Eucharistic Adoration is the best and easiest way to look at and contemplate Jesus.

We should try to pray as much as we can. The Catholic Church especially recommends a number of specific forms of prayer. The Mass is recognized as the best prayer and for Catholics it is a serious sin not to attend Mass on Sundays and holydays of obligation, without a valid reason. The Church also recommends the official Divine Office of psalms and readings, especially morning, evening and night prayer, which unites the Church in a standard form of prayer throughout the whole world. This will be standard for each day, each feast day, and in the seasons of Advent, Christmas, Easter, and Normal time of the Church year. The rosary, the Stations of the Cross (while meditating on the passion of Jesus), and more recently, the chaplet of Divine Mercy are also highly recommended. The most important quality of prayer is that it should be from the heart. When we wish to pray spontaneously or informally, then we can use any form of words. We should use the form of prayer that helps us to come close to God and this will vary with individuals, and in different situations. We must remember that it is the one to whom the prayers are addressed, who must be pleased.

The Key to Powerful Prayer: This is the title of a book by John Gillespie.[88] John is an Irishman who suffered for many years with excruciating pain from arthritis. He prayed for healing for many hours every day for many years but to no avail. Eventually he had a dramatic healing and was led, in a mysterious way, towards a particular form of prayer which is more likely to yield results. Firstly, John says that all prayers are heard, but God finds it difficult to act on prayers if those praying are not living and obeying God's Laws. The most important aspect of our prayer should be to pray with faith. "When we pray, we should ask and believe that we have received. That's FAITH." John says that we need to change our way of thinking about prayer. What moves God is faith, and he describes faith and patience as the "power twins" of prayer. John was not only healed himself but received the gift of a great prayer ministry. Many miraculous healings have now been associated with John's prayers. He also has the gift of discernment, especially on how evil spirits can influence illness and other aspects of peoples' lives. He strongly encourages us to use Sacred Scripture in our prayer. As well as the book mentioned above, there is also another book associated with the story of John called, *The Miracle Ship.*[89] Both books are very popular and very educational. Frances Hogan also describes the same approach of praying with power in her book, *A Path to Healing A Nation.*[90]

Christianity Divided: Soon Uniting?

Christianity is united and divided by the Bible. The Bible is recognized by all Christians as the inspired and revealed word of God. There is a problem, however, with individual Christian believers, who accept the Bible as the infallible Word of God, but who have a myriad of different ideas and nuances, when they come to interpret various scripture passages. When the various interpretations contradict, how can a sincere Christian decide which, if any, are correct? Roman Catholics believe that the Roman Church interprets the Word of God in the Bible, in an infallible way, which is not prone to error, and thus they believe that Roman Catholicism is the only Church with the "fullness of the truth". Catholics are assured by the Bible passage (1 Timothy 3: 14-15), which somewhat ironically states, that the pillar and foundation of the truth is **not the Bible**, or any individual interpretation of Sacred Scripture, but rather, **The Church founded by Jesus Christ.** The great dichotomy, therefore, between the Catholic and Protestant view of Sacred Scripture is that, whereas Catholics believe that their Church interprets the Word of God infallibly from the Bible, with only one valid interpretation, Protestants believe that the Bible is infallible, but allow individual private interpretations of the Scripture. There is now no escaping the fact that, when the Protestant reformers rejected the authority of the Roman Church to validly interpret scripture, and promoted other views on various scripture texts, a mechanism of perpetual division was introduced into Christianity. After 500 years, this has led to a significant degree of doctrinal chaos, among Churches of the Reformation **tradition.**

The claim to infallibility by the Church of Rome is often misunderstood. It is not generally appreciated that the number of doctrines defined infallibly are very few in number, - only five. Infallibility, however, does represent a last court of appeal to the sovereign Pontiff, when there is dispute over a serious matter, on a particular Christian doctrinal interpretation. It is also argued that infallibility is very logical, if the promise of Jesus Christ to always guide and protect His Church from error, is accepted. In this context, it is important to recognize that the claim to infallibility rests with the Church as a teaching body with the Pope as the head (as Jesus promised to protect His Church), rather than with any single individual. The Pope is a sinner like all humans and goes to confession on a regular basis (St Pope John Paul II confessed daily). The Pope is prone to error like everybody, **except** when he teaches doctrines of faith, in union with the Church as a teaching body. On the other hand, a Christian Church which does not claim to be infallible must accept that error in doctrine becomes inevitable, because of human fallibility and the myriad of possible interpretations on the various sections of Bible scripture. The immediate question then becomes, where are they wrong?

The Protestant Reformation must now be regarded as a great failure. Instead of reforming the Christian Church, it has led to the formation of many thousands of different sects, groups, as well as larger established Congregations, all with different shades of opinions on the meaning of different biblical texts. The history of Protestantism since the Reformation, seems to indicate that when a new denomination was formed, one of the earliest items on the agenda was division. The success of the new denominations was also as much dependent on the scholarship and leadership qualities, as on the sanctity, of the founders. The final result now is great disarray, division and confusion among Protestant Churches. This division was inevitable, when private interpretation of scripture was allowed. Protestant teaching is now very diverse and in many cases has strayed a long way from the views of Martin Luther.

Another very significant factor promoting disunity among the Protestant reformers, which is not often recognized, was the denial of the "Real Presence" of Christ in the Eucharist and the consequent loss of the Mass as the most powerful prayer maintaining Church unity. In this regard, it is interesting that the Christian divisions before the Protestant Reformation, remain relatively few and by retaining a valid Mass, these divided Churches also retained a belief in the other sacraments, and still believe and teach doctrines identical to the modern Catholic Church. Apart from the question as to whether or not the Pope is the head, and the "Progression of the Holy Spirit", there is little else that separates the Coptic and Orthodox Churches from Rome. For these pre-Reformation divisions in Christianity, therefore, unity can be as much a political and managerial problem as a doctrinal problem. With the prayer and goodwill that is now evident among most of these Churches, progress towards complete union should be rapid.

The "Good News" is that there is now a great general movement towards Christian Unity. This movement is not only coming from the efforts of the major Christian Churches to reach understanding, but even more so, through believers sharing the scholarship of Bible study and the study of Christian history. The writings of the Ancient Fathers of Christianity in the early centuries of the Church, have had a great impact on those who have studied them. Recent improvements in the standards of biblical scholarship, as well as the wide availability of the fruits of this scholarship, through modern means of communication, is helping to move serious Christian believers together, into a unified Church, with the Pope as head.

Unfortunately, however, we must also recognize that there is now no shortage of renegades, with all flavours of Christian beliefs in all Christian churches. There are signs of many new fractures, not just within Protestant denominations, but also within the Catholic Church. Female ministers, female priests, female Bishops and ordination of openly practicing homosexual clergy, is putting great strains on unity, within some denominations. So called "a la carte" Catholics, now appear to be more numerous than those who respect the rules, and try to live by them. Being a faithful Catholic is not easy and there are many members that practice various degrees of doctrinal rejection. St Pope John Paul II said that, there are rules to this club (Roman Catholic Church), and if you want to belong, you must keep the rules. It is very obvious that many millions of former Catholics now no longer wish to keep these rules. At what stage one ceases to become a Catholic, has never been precisely defined. In particular artificial birth control and regular confession are obstacles to many, and these are now greatly swelling the numbers, of the nominal or "pretend Catholics". On the other hand, many sincere Christians in Protestant denominations are now making their way back to Rome. The Catholic Church of the near future, therefore, is likely to be smaller, leaner and with a lot of sincere Protestant converts.

Marcus Grodi was a former Protestant pastor who converted to Catholicism. He is now the presenter of The Journey Home programme on EWTN (Eternal Word Television Network), in the US. He helps run an organization to assist fellow Protestant pastors, who through finding new truths in the Bible, are contemplating that which for most of their lives was unthinkable, namely, becoming Catholics. Over 1,000 pastors from 80 different denominations in the US have now come into the Catholic Church within the last two decades, and the number is steadily growing. Converts like Marcus himself, Scott Hahn, Peter Kreeft, and many others have made enormous contributions to the Catholic Church since joining. Anybody who wants to be a serious student of sacred scripture will find the work of Scott Hahn on the Bible, second to none.[91,92,93] His wife Kimberly also became a convert to Catholicism, specifically due to Catholic Church teaching on birth control, which she had researched.[94]

Marcus Grodi has described his own journey into the Catholic Church from being a Presbyterian Pastor for nine years, in his book, *Journey Home*[95] and also in the book, *Surprised by Truth,*[96] where he joins ten other Catholic converts describing the story of their return to Rome. In explaining his conversion, he selected readings from the Bible that had a major influence on this change of direction in his life, and which highlight some of the problems associated with new biblical interpretations, which emerged from the Protestant Reformation. Although he has selected a small number of biblical texts, he suggested that there were many more which he could have chosen. He had used some of these readings many times in his Presbyterian ministry, but he never noticed the significance of them, until he began to question the basis for the truth of his belief. Although he had read some of the readings many times, he claims that he never "saw" them, until their significance was pointed out to him by his colleague, Professor Scott Hahn, who had previously converted to Catholicism.

Marcus had worries for a number of years, concerning his understanding of various readings in the Bible. If the Bible was so clear, how was it that many of his colleagues had different ideas from himself on many basic teachings? He eventually decided that he would have to give up his post as pastor, so that his uncertainty would not lead others astray. Soon after this, he met his old friend Scott Hahn, who posed the question: what is the pillar and foundation of truth? The reply Marcus gave was, "the Bible", as all good Protestants would give. He was then directed to 1 Timothy 3 14-15, which says that, **The Church is the pillar and foundation of**

truth, not, the bible. This was a big shock for Marcus, and the question then became, which Church?

On the question of, which Church? Marcus went to Matthew 16, 13-19, to read again the establishment of the Church by Jesus. Protestant teaching for centuries has disputed Peter as the rock, and spoke on the word used in the Greek translation which referred to Peter as a little pebble, not as the rock on which Jesus was building His Church. Marcus now realised that Jesus did not speak Greek, which has two words for rock, male and female (petros and petra). The male version which was applied to Peter means pebble. In Aramaic or Hebrew, however, there is only one word for rock and Peter was and is the rock. This is now recognized in some modern Protestant translations of the Bible.

Protestant interpretation of the Bible generally places no value on tradition, as opposed to scripture, as a basis for teaching the truths of the faith. At the Protestant Reformation, tradition was not just demoted, but rejected completely. The second shock for Marcus was from 2 Thessalonians 2:15, which says: "Hold on to the traditions which were told by us, - either by word of mouth or by letter". In fact most of the teaching in the early Christian Church of the first centuries A.D. was oral and based on tradition. The Protestant concept of "sola scriptura" therefore, rejects any role for tradition as a basis for Christian teaching.

Salvation by faith alone is one of the pillars of Protestant teaching. This was now a problem also for Marcus as Revelation 14:13 says, referring to the dead, that, "Their deeds follow them" and Revelation 2 says, "I will give to each of you as your works deserve".

Romans 10:14-15 says, "How can men preach unless they are sent?" The word "apostle" comes from the Greek word meaning "to send". Preachers, therefore, must be sent from the Church and their teaching must carry the authority of the Church, not their own private ideas on the interpretation of the Bible. Individuals starting their own version of Christianity and teaching their own ideas are thus invalid and carry no authority. We must trust in the Lord and the authority given to Peter as head of the Christian Church. Proverbs 3:5 tells us not to rely on our own understanding.

John 15:4 and also John 6:56 indicate that it is necessary to, "abide in Christ". John 6 is the part of the Bible that divides Christian believers into two camps, that is, into those who believe in the "Real Presence" of Christ in the Eucharist and those who do not. It is also the part which is generally ignored in Protestant teaching. In order to abide in Jesus, you must eat His Body and drink His Blood. When Jesus was giving this teaching, many left him, because they could not understand it or accept it. Not only did He not call them back but, he continued to insist several times the need to eat His Body and drink His Blood. Scott Hahn has some wonderful books and tapes explaining John 6.[97,98] **He compares the Last Supper with the Jewish Passover feast. The Fourth cup which is the last in the Passover feast is taken by Jesus on the cross. Then, "it is finished", and the sacrifice must be eaten as is the Jewish custom. In the Mass, which is a continuation of Calvary, the Lamb of God, who takes away the sin of the world, is consumed** - (see chapter 4 for more information on the "Real Presence" of Christ in the Eucharist). In Luke 24-35 the story of the disciples on the road to Emmaus indicates how the disciples of Jesus did not recognize him when he explained the scriptures to them. They needed the Eucharist to recognize Him.

Then there was the question of devotion to Mary, the mother of Jesus. Luke 1 says, referring to Mary, "All generations will call me blessed". Protestants do not call Mary blessed. They look on her as just another woman, who happened to become the mother of Christ and generally speaking, Protestants do not have a devotion to Mary. Consider what Frank Duff, the founder of The Legion of Mary (a lay Catholic organization numbering many millions), said in the Legion of Mary handbook:

"**No true Christianity without Mary**: In return for this infinite gift, all generations must henceforth call that maiden blessed. She who brought Christianity on earth cannot be denied a place in Christian worship. But what of the many people in this world who hold her cheaply, the many who slight her, the many who do worse? Does it ever occur to those people to think that every grace they have they owe to her? Do they ever reason that if they were excluded from her words of acceptance that night, then Redemption has never come on earth for them? In that supposition they would stand outside its scope. In other words, they would not be Christians at all, even though they may cry: "Lord! Lord!" all the day and every day. (Mt 7:21) And on the other hand, if they are indeed Christians, and if the gift of life has come to them, then it has only come because she gained it for them, because they were included in her acceptance. In a word, the baptism that makes a person a child of God makes one simultaneously a child of Mary. Gratitude, therefore – a practical gratitude – to Mary must be the mark of every Christian. Redemption is the joint gift of the Father and of Mary. Therefore, with the words of thanks to the Father must go up the word of thanks to Mary."

Confession: One of the most important, rewarding, and at the same time difficult and controversial aspects of Catholic teaching concerns the sacrament of reconciliation or confession. There can be no doubt that Jesus gave authority to his apostles to forgive sins in His name (John 20:23). From the beginning, the Catholic Church, through its ordained priests and Bishops, have exercised that ministry to forgive sin in the name of Jesus. Martin Luther originally held on to a belief in this teaching, and in some Lutheran and other reformed Churches the practice of confession can still be found. Forgiveness of sins is one of the key requirements for healing individuals and society. It is sad therefore that most Protestant Churches have rejected this sacrament. The usual excuse is that the scripture reference is regarded as superfluous and not necessary. More realistically, however, the rejection of this sacrament is due to the difficulty of admitting personal evil thoughts, words and actions to another human person, rather than rejecting it over a dispute on the Biblical basis for this authority, given by Jesus to His Church.

Suffering: Finally, with respect to the very important subject of suffering, in Colossians 1:24, Paul says, "I rejoice in my suffering for your sake, and in my flesh, I complete what is lacking in Christ's afflictions, for the sake of His body, that is, the Church". This is the basis for Catholic theological teaching on suffering, which is explained by St Pope John Paul II, in *Salvifici Doloris*.[99] Protestant teaching generally lacks a proper theology on the value of suffering, which Reformed Churches usually regard as evil, meaningless, and with no redemptive value. In contrast, the Catholic understanding is that suffering, when united with the suffering of Christ, can have immense value for conversion and for the salvation of souls. What is needed more than anything else in the world at the moment are victim souls prepared to suffer for the sake of Christ and others. Padre Pio (see page 102), who suffered more than anybody on a daily basis, was very jealous of his suffering. St Faustina (see page 450) said that the angels in Heaven envy humanity two things. These are the Eucharist and the ability to suffer. Martin Luther failed to appreciate the significance of these two gifts. Suffering is discussed in more detail below (page 247), especially in relation to Purgatory.

The Papacy: The papacy is the longest lasting line of succession authority in the world at the moment. There is no doubt that Jesus intended to appoint Peter as head of the new Church, which He established, with the words, "You are Peter and upon this rock, I will build my Church". In Old Testament times, God always had a Chief Shepherd of his people, as in Abraham, Isaac, Jacob, Joseph, Moses etc. It would be no different in New Testament times. The appointment of Eliakim by King Hezekiah as head of the House of Judah in the Old Testament account and giving him the keys of the House of David, has many similarities with the appointment of Peter by Jesus (as the new King of the Jews), to the head of His Church. "I will place on his shoulder the key of the house of David: he shall open, and none shall shut: and he shall shut, and none shall open" (Isaiah 22: 22). "I will give you the keys of the Kingdom of Heaven: whatever you bind on earth shall be bound in Heaven and whatever you loose on earth shall be loosed in Heaven" (Matthew 16. 19). Peter's main task as leader of the infant Catholic Church was to look after the people of God. "Feed my lambs.. feed my sheep" (John 21: 15 – 17). As history unfolded the successors of Peter came to be known as Popes. Pope Francis is the current successor of Peter.

The Early Church Fathers: Marcus Grodi has also explained how the study of the early Church Fathers influenced his understanding of the teaching of Christ. He has described the significance of many different aspects of the history of early Christianity in his writing and in his television programme, *Journey Home*, as explained above. It may be useful to consider briefly some of the points that he has highlighted.

For the first three centuries of the Christian Church, it was largely traditional accounts and teachings, handed down through the authority of the Bishops, rather than accepted written accounts that guided the Church. It became very clear to Marcus, from studying the Early Church Fathers that, the structure and teaching of the Church, in those early centuries, was in the form of the modern Catholic Church. There was no sign of the traditional Protestant approach.

St Clement of Rome was the fourth Bishop of Rome. While still a young man he was ordained a priest by St Peter. He conversed regularly with the apostles, and died towards the end of the first century. He wrote a letter to the Christians of Corinth, indicating the importance of selecting the proper candidates as Bishops, so that there could be proper apostolic succession in the Church. He stated in the letter that the apostles foresaw the difficulties that would arise in the selection of Bishops as their successors, and emphasised that only approved individuals would be valid Bishops.

St Ignatius of Antioch was born in Syria, around the year 50 A.D. and he was martyred in Rome, in the early part of the second century. He said, "You must follow the Bishop as Jesus follows the Father... Let it be considered a valid Eucharist, that which is celebrated by the Bishop or by one whom he appoints. Where the Bishop appears, let the people be. Just as where Jesus Christ is, there is the Church. This is, the Catholic Church." This may have been the first reference to the Catholic Church.

St Ignatius of Antioch, writing in 107 A.D., said that heretics did not celebrate the Eucharist, "Because they do not confess that the Eucharist is the flesh of our Saviour, Jesus Christ." St Justin Martyr was born in 100 A.D. He converted from paganism, at the age of thirty and was martyred in Rome, at the age of 65. He wrote that, "The Eucharist .. is both the flesh and blood of the incarnate Jesus, made so by the Eucharistic prayer. Nobody is permitted to take part who does not believe this."

St Irenaeus, Bishop of Leon, France, lived at the end of the second century. He wrote a book against heresies. He said that in the Church there should be one heart and one mouth, and that the authority and the tradition must be the same. Referring to the Church in Rome, founded by the glorious apostles Peter and Paul, he said, "With this Church, because of its superior origin, all Churches must agree, that is all the faithful in the whole world. ..It is in her that all the faithful have maintained, everywhere, the apostolic tradition."

The importance of Rome, in the early Church is easily detected in the early writings. St Clement (fourth Pope) wrote with authority, giving direction to the Church in Corinth. When writing to Rome, St Ignatius of Antioch began by saying, "To the Church in Rome, which holds the Presidency". In 251 A.D. St Cyprian of Carthage, said that the Church was founded on a single chair with primacy given to Peter, and that to be confident of being in the Church, one had to recognize Peter. He quoted Matthew 16, to defend the authority of the Pope. St Ambrose of Milan (340 – 397), also wrote on the importance of the succession of Peter, for the authority of forgiving sin. St Ignatius of Antioch in 110 A.D. said, "Do not support anybody who causes schism, as your own salvation will be in danger." St Augustine, around 400 A.D., said that there was nothing more serious than the sacrilege of schism, as there is never a justifiable reason for breaking the unity of the Church.

Suffering

Suffering is a mystery. Christians believe that Jesus Christ, the second person of the Blessed Trinity (only one true God), became man and suffered terribly by crucifixion, to atone for all sins and reconcile humanity to God the Father and thus free repentant sinners from the punishment we all deserve. The first clear message from this, therefore, is that suffering is the fruit of sin.

This has been the teaching of the Church through the centuries, which has been confirmed by many mystics and saints and by The Virgin Mary at Fatima, when she explained that war and suffering were the results of evil in human hearts. The task of reconciling God's justice and human suffering is not always easy to understand in some of the accounts in the Old Testament. Many of the terrible events described in these stories seem to contradict what we have learned in the later years of the New Testament, regarding God's merciful dealings with humanity. It is generally felt, however, that the Hebrew writers used a lot of traditional ideas and mythological themes when recording these Old Testament stories. Christians cannot, therefore, be bound to their accuracy and the true qualities of God are more reliably learned from the New Testament and in particular the words and life of Jesus. The Catholic Church uses the whole of the New Testament as a foundation for its teaching.

We cannot fail to recognize, however, that the Jews committed many atrocities in early history, even if these may have been greatly exaggerated in Old Testament accounts. The Old Testament is really an account of how a loving God, gradually revealed himself to a chosen people. Initially the Jews were a pagan people, living like everybody else in the ways of the world at that time. Gradually, God enlightened them about their responsibility to do good, and about the suffering in this life and in the next, which results from doing evil. Sometimes God enlightened them by giving them serious punishment when they behaved very badly. For example he banished them from their homeland, when they began to worship false gods. Typically the remnant would repent and God would allow them to regain their homeland. After sometime they would return to their old pagan ways and the cycle of punishment and suffering would begin again. By the time Jesus came, only the Sadducees and their followers refused to believe in the next life. Christ admonished the

Jews because of their hardness of heart, and he taught them a higher law. Instead of thinking of an eye for an eye, He told them to love their enemies and to do good to those who persecuted them.

In considering suffering it is important to understand that, for the full effects of the crucifixion and atonement of Jesus to be realised, each person must recognize their evil, repent of it, and ask for forgiveness. Free will means that everybody can choose evil or good. Choosing evil will lead to suffering. The Catholic doctrines of "The Mystical Body" and the "Communion of Saints" help us to understand the mystery of suffering, and in particular why some "good" people sometimes suffer greatly. These doctrines teach us that, in a mysterious way, we are all part of the Mystical Body of Christ, with Christ as the head. Any evil or good deed done by any individual reflects on all, and every person, to some extent, will reap the fruits of this deed. This balance of good and evil was, to some extent, summarized by the old catechism explanation, on the need for a General Judgement at the end of time, in the words: "A General Judgement is required, in order that the providence of God, which sometimes permits the good to suffer and the wicked to prosper, may appear just before all men." It is God's wish, therefore, that everybody should have eternal happiness, but unfortunately many choose otherwise and offend an infinite goodness (God), to the extent that justice merits an infinite suffering.

Purgatory: It may be useful to give a brief explanation for those not familiar with Catholic teaching on Purgatory. It is a Roman Catholic belief that after death, each soul goes to one of three destinations. Many, unfortunately, go to eternal suffering (Hell), few go directly to eternal joy (Heaven - that is, only those who die in perfect love), and finally many go to Purgatory (those who need some purification or perfecting before getting to Heaven). The word "Purgatory" comes from the word to purge and this is a place where souls go after death, to have their evil purged before getting into Heaven. The souls who go to Hell are lost forever, whereas those who go to Purgatory are guaranteed to get to Heaven eventually. The extent and type of suffering in Purgatory depends on the state of the soul at death. The doctrine of the "Communion of Saints" tells us, that we can also atone for the sins of those who are in Purgatory, and thus speed their movement towards Heaven. The souls in Purgatory cannot merit graces for themselves by prayer, but they can and do pray for those who are still alive. Prayer for the "Holy Souls" has always been recommended strongly by the Catholic Church and by all the saints. The souls in Purgatory are apparently very much aware of the problems and difficulties of those who remain on earth, and continually intercede for them by prayer.

Purgatory is full of love, whereas Hell is full of hate. Every soul in Purgatory knows that they are on the way to eternal bliss, and everybody helps one another, whereas every soul in Hell, knows that they are there for eternity. The recent well known Catholic prophet, Anne, was allowed to mystically visit Purgatory, as many saints and visionaries have done in the past. Anne (an American lady now living in Ireland) is unusual among modern Catholic prophets and visionaries, in that she has the complete support of Church authorities. Anne has described different levels in Purgatory. Those who are nearing Heaven, come out of a thick mist into a beautiful clear area, with very little suffering. Some move slowly and others move rapidly from lower to higher levels. She found it particularly interesting to see individuals who lived in different centuries communicating as they met travelling through the various levels of purification. She has referred to Purgatory as, *The Mist of Mercy*.[100] Finally, it should be said that Purgatory makes sense. Very few die with an attitude of perfect love and their souls need to learn this perfect love, through gaining Divine grace, before entering Heaven.

Many good books have been written on the subject of Purgatory.[101,102] I was particularly impressed by the book of Maria Simma,[103] who was in constant contact with departed souls. She illustrated many times how we can never judge the state of a dying soul. This was particularly illustrated by an incident described in one of her books, when a mother died, soon after an abortion, but she went rapidly to Heaven. Another man from the same parish, who was a daily Mass goer, in contrast, had to spend many years in Purgatory. It later came to light that the mother who had the abortion, died very repentant after a sincere Confession. The priest, who attended her before she died, was heard to remark afterwards that, "My wish is that I could die as repentant as that woman". In the case of the man, it was also known that he opposed the burial of this mother in the Catholic cemetery, because he felt that she was not worthy, as she was such a serious sinner. Maria also said that the souls of most of those who die of suicide are not condemned to Hell, as there are many other factors involved. This is not, however, to condone suicide or fail to recognize it as a serious sin. Hell, in contrast to Purgatory, is full of hate as everybody there recognizes the hopelessness of their situation, which is everlasting, and everybody is blamed and everybody is hated for their loss. Most of those who go to Hell are those who refused to believe the reality of its existence while they were alive. - (see chapter 8 for further discussion on evidence for life after death).

St Pope John Paul II explained in his Apostolic Letter, Salvifici Doloris [99], why suffering should be recognized as a sublime gift and a privilege. Uniting suffering with the suffering of Christ especially at Mass, can give personal suffering an infinite value. This is because when we offer our sufferings back to Christ, we are thereby offering them for our sins and the sins of others. This is a source of grace for us and it will help us have an increase in happiness in the next life. Since the next life is infinitely long, the merits brought on by uniting our suffering with that of Christ, will also have an infinite quality. Redemptive suffering, according to St Pope John Paul II, is suffering that loves unconditionally and holds nothing back. I mentioned above how the ability to suffer was one of the two gifts given to humanity that angels crave. Understanding this concept can be a great help to those in hospital, to the handicapped and to those in prison or suffering in any other way. This understanding can also prevent hopelessness or despair and give a purpose to those struggling or suffering, with great difficulties in life. When this suffering is channelled in the right direction, it can have a great salvific value in the spiritual realm.

We can learn many lessons about suffering from the saints.[104] St John of the Cross said, "O you who want to walk in security and in consolation. If only you knew how pleasing suffering is to God, and how helpful it is in acquiring other benefits, you would never seek consolations in anything, but rather would deem it a great joy to carry the cross in the footsteps of Jesus." St Gertrude related as follows, what God had said to her regarding suffering: "My daughter, you will never do Me a greater service than that of patiently bearing, in memory of My passion, whatever tribulation befalls you, whether internal or external, and of always trying to do those things which are most contrary to your desires." Finally some of the words of Jesus to St Teresa of Avila, were as follows: "The souls most pleasing to My Heavenly Father are those who suffer the greatest afflictions and tribulations." From then on, St Teresa had a great love of suffering and she was unhappy when she was not suffering.

Fr Edgardo M. Arellano in his book, Victimhood – Hope of the present Crises,[105] explains how only the reparation of victim souls who pledge themselves to be victims of love, can now save the world from catastrophe. Victimhood gives true meaning and importance to reparation and it repairs the sins of arrogance and pride. Christ knew for certain that even after His death, many millions would still reject His act of reparation and would consider His sufferings useless. Many millions still refuse to acknowledge evil and reject it. Many millions still refuse to repent and therefore many millions still go to eternal suffering. This is the great sadness of humanity. Remember that The Virgin Mary said in 1917, in Fatima, that many souls are going to Hell. Hell is real.

Demonic Activity

There is a story often told in relation to Pope Leo XIII, who on the 13th of October 1884 was attending a Mass of thanksgiving as usual, after his own Mass, when he had a vision of Satan antagonizing Jesus. The Pope heard that Satan would be given extra freedom over the next century and then his freedom would be rapidly curtailed. Pope Leo was very upset by this and immediately afterwards he composed the now famous prayer to St Michael, the Archangel, for the defeat of demons in the world. This prayer was said after every Mass up to the Second Vatican Council, in the 1960's. Pope Leo XIII also personally wrote a prayer of exorcism, which is included in the Roman Ritual (1954 edition). He recommended that Bishops and priests read these exorcisms often in their dioceses and parishes. Pope Leo was known to recite exorcism prayers often through the day.

Pope Paul VI spoke publicly on at least three occasions about Satan and demonic activity. On November 15th 1972 he said, "Whoever refuses to recognize the existence of the demonic reality, denies biblical and ecclesiastic teaching". Pope John Paul II spoke publicly on at least eighteen occasions on the reality of Satan. On April 24th 1988, he also beatified a Spanish Carmelite, Fr Francisco Palau, who devoted the last years of his life, ministering to those possessed by demons.

Like all subjects, the best and easiest way to get good information is to read, study, and ask the experts. Demonology is no different, and the experts are those who have studied, written and worked as official exorcists under Church authority for a significant part of their lives. Father Edgardo M. Arellano, spiritual director of The Alliance of the Holy Family International (AHFI), in his book, How to Win your Spiritual Warfare,[106] describes diabolical infestation in some detail. In it he describes infestation by the devil under the two headings of, ordinary and extraordinary. Extraordinary infestation is rare but ordinary infestation is common.

Ordinary Infestation

Temptation: Ordinary infestation occurs as a result of temptation. Temptation is the solicitation of Satan to entice a person to commit evil. Only Satan tempts. Temptation, if successfully resisted, can be an instrument of purification and spiritual growth. The three stages of temptation are: suggestions to commit an evil act, allurement, and consent. Consent may be imperfect or perfect and imperfect consent is associated with less serious sin. Temptation is conquered by, first of all, recognising where Satan attacks you and then overcoming this. Fasting, mortification, and vigilance help to overcome temptation.

Fasting: Fasting helps to build up discipline in one's personal life and also in the community. Fasting is a most powerful means to reject the evil one from a soul and from the community. There are particular evil spirits which can only be cast out by fasting. The devil fears fasting. Many Catholics no longer tend to fast, and even the fast days of Good Friday or Ash Wednesday are no longer adhered to, by most Catholics.

Mortification: Mortification is defined as the struggle against our evil inclinations, in order to subject them to our will, and then to subject our will to the Will of God. Mortification helps us to live a higher spiritual life and it helps us to strengthen our will. To persevere in good works and to keep free from sin requires mortification. Mortification must be practised with prudence and discretion. What should we mortify? We must try to mortify our tongues, our ears, our eyes and our interior senses, especially memory and imagination. Disciplining the intellect is also important and this can be aided by faith and reason. Efforts should be made to correct problems coming from pride, ignorance, curiosity, haste, and obstinacy. Our will should always obey God's Will in all things, and it should be strong enough to control our appetites. In order to achieve this we must be able to overcome a number of interior and exterior obstacles. Some of these interior obstacles would be lack of reflection, over-eagerness, indifference and fear of failure. External obstacles can be either positive or negative. Negative ones could be too much respect for the opinions of certain people or being too much influenced by the bad examples of others. External positive obstacles could be concerned with our ability to make decisions, and our ability to be firm and constant in our decisions, without losing our calm.

Vigilance: Vigilance demands self denial, and the spirit of sacrifice. The Bible says, "Watch and pray that you may not enter into temptation". Vigilance may be positive or negative. Positive vigilance is staying awake and watching while negative vigilance is avoiding evil. We must avoid proud presumptions which could make us rush into danger. We should avoid dangers and shun daydreaming and idleness. We should check and assess our soul's weak points by regularly making an examination of conscience and resolving to overcome every inclination to evil.

Extraordinary Infestation

Fr Gabriele Amorth in his book, An Exorcist Tells His Story,[107] lists four ways we can fall prey to extraordinary satanic activity. These are:

(1) with God's permission.
(2) as innocent victims of an evil spell.
(3) due to a grave and hardened sinful condition.
(4) through association with evil people or places.

He also says that sorcery is the most frequent cause he has come across in those who are struck by possession or other evil influences. World events normally occur in line with the laws of nature or natural law. That which is outside natural law, such as prodigies, miracles and preternatural phenomena are referred to as "extraordinary". There are three kinds of extraordinary diabolical phenomena, namely, local, personal and diabolical.

Local Infestation: This is associated with unusual happenings over a period of time in a specific place or locality or attached to particular objects. These happenings can be strange or frightening sounds, footsteps, groans, screams, loud laughter, strange smells, cold air, and sometimes the appearances of ghostly figures. Black creatures and objects such as crows, cats, dogs, clothes and ornaments seem to be favourite instruments used by Satan.

Personal Infestation: This is when the devil focuses attention on a particular individual. The infestation remains external, unlike complete possession, and the victim's free will and reason are not interfered with. Anybody can be a victim. Those dabbling with satanic curiosity in the form of games, such as ouija boards, and those who try to contact spirits in other ways, can be at special risk. On the other hand, and somewhat paradoxically, the most common victims are those who lead holy lives. Many saints were the victim of diabolical attacks on a regular basis, as for example St Theresa of Avila, St Catherine of Sienna, St Rose of Lima, St John Vianney, St John Bosco, St Gemma Galgani, St Padre Pio and many others. Exorcists and theologians who confront the devil, or expose evil activities in other ways, can disturb evil spirits and also be singled out for attack.

The attacks can take many forms. There can be words, songs, noises, nauseating smells, or severe physical beatings. St John Bosco experienced the devil in the form of many wild animals, such as, a giant frog, a bear, an elephant, a lion, or a snake. More dramatic forms of personal infestation are levitation or telekinesis (movements of the body through space, with no obvious natural explanation).

Diabolical Possession: This involves the presence of the devil in the body of a particular individual with the satanic power taking complete control over that person. The possessed person is usually not aware of his or her actions, while under the direct control of the devil, although the exercise of the diabolical power is not continuous. The individual, therefore, cannot necessarily be blamed for any misdeeds. There is no recognised physical or psychological predisposition to diabolical possession. If there is any predisposition to involuntary diabolical possession, it is goodness, as it is believed that the devil does not direct any of his activity to the impious, or to those who are already in his power.

Only God can permit the devil to take possession of a person. This may seem odd, but the theological position is that God permits this for good reasons. In fact, there can be several reasons why God permits possessions. Ars Exorcistica, published in 1606, lists fourteen of these reasons. The first reason why God may permit diabolical possession is in order to prove the truth and power of the Christian religion, which is the only religion with power over evil spirits. The Fathers of the Church used exorcisms for this purpose. God may also permit possession for the spiritual good of the victim, who can grow in humility, patience and love of God. Non-Christians, who are suffering from diabolical possession, can also be motivated to convert to Christianity in their efforts to get rid of the demons. A final example is that diabolical possession can be a punishment for sins, in this world rather than in the next. We should not be too quick, therefore, to judge the eternal destination of those who are possessed by Satan. Nevertheless, many who are possessed have become so voluntary, either through a life of evil ways or through contact with satanic organizations, in an effort to get power, wealth, or to attack Christianity. Hitler and Stalin are sometimes quoted as examples of voluntary possession.

Disguises of Satan

Despite the devil's great power to influence the free will of people towards evil, his activities and presence are always in some way discernible. In general, evil influences are in the negative such as, 'unclean', 'unfaithful', 'untrue', 'disobedient', 'discontent' etc. as the influence is the negative of what is good. The devil's disguises are listed under the six headings of: conversational temptation, seduction, oppression, obsession, channelling and lordship.

1.Conversational Temptation: Temptations of this kind are said to be ordered by the least or weakest of evil spirits. Overcoming temptation can bring great graces and the best way to overcome temptation, through conversation, is by interior and exterior silence. Interior silence is when our intellect and will are attuned to God. Exterior silence is when we also turn our external senses toward God. Sometimes silence is described under the four headings of, intelligent, creative, generous and charitable. Intelligent silence is knowing when to be silent. Creative silence is when we occupy ourselves with doing something good rather than talking. Generous silence is when we remain silent, even when it hurts, for a higher motive. In other words, offering it up for the love of God. Finally, charitable silence is when we speak only when we have something good to say. The rule would be to think well, to speak well, and to do good to all. Appropriate silence can bring powerful graces for conversion.

2.Seduction: This is the second and more intense form of disguise which the devil uses. This is done by skilful imagery, somewhat like modern advertising. The victim falls into addiction, unregulated passions, and intemperance. Pornography is a favourite channel of seduction. The first fruits are adultery, fornication, gambling, alcohol and other drug addictions. Addiction alters the entire character of the person, and this is a recognizable fundamental change in all victims of addiction. The second fruits follow, such as broken marriages, poverty, illness of all kinds, including HIV infection, etc. and ultimately death of body and soul. Seduction can also lead directly to spiritualism and occult practices.

3.Oppression: Unlike number 1 and 2 where the victim is encouraged towards something that they think appealing, oppression uses force and fear, which leads to the recognition that an evil influence is at work. Evil spirits who act as oppressors, work against faith, hope and charity. The ultimate aim is always the extinction of faith. Just as holy angels widen our perception from within and lead us towards charity, holiness, and happiness, so oppressor demons crush us from the outside with restlessness, perplexity, and scepticism. Oppression is often accompanied by mysterious physical pain, moral doubts and sometimes psychological mental disorders. The antidote to oppression influences is the strengthening of faith, hope, and charity, fostering a good community life and doing some good works, so that attention is on the problems of others rather than on self.

4.Obsession: This is the fourth form of disguise, which represents a more intense degree of oppression. A number of demons from the fourth dominion (the destroyers) are involved. In itself, obsession does not cause death, as evil spirits do not have the power to kill, but the victim can be driven to suicide by torture. There are uncontrollable evil thoughts that torment, especially at night, but sometimes continually. The victim may be physically beaten up, burnt or terrorized. There are usually some external signs such as smells, a feeling of great fear in the room, or animals may run away whining in fear. Many cases of obsession have been recorded with the saints. Padre Pio (see page 102), Marthe Robin (see page 86) and Alexandrina Da Costa (see page 82) were all attacked violently by demons. St John Bosco used to be attacked by large strange animals and there are many records of other saints and saintly people being attacked. Prayer, fasting, penance, the Sacrament of Penance, and patience are the antidote to obsession. When a victim is freed from obsession by exorcism and other spiritual activities, it is wise for them to move to another place to live, as spirits often come back to the same rooms after obsessions. The experience is that, if they find the room blessed and changed and the victim not there, although they often make noises of rattling, whistling and howling for a short time, they then disappear.

Demons tend to attack five main areas, namely, health, business, affectations, enjoyment of life, and bringing about the desire for death. Demons have the power to cause physical and mental illness. Fr Amorth has had experience of ovarian cysts and brain tumours, being caused by demons, which disappeared after exorcisms. Having said that, however, it is important that everybody should recognize that this must be a very, very rare cause of these medical problems. Individuals with demonic obsession, may also find it impossible to find work or keep a job, after getting employed. Life can be bleak, with complete lack of hope. The final goal of the demon is to bring his victim to despair with a longing for death.

5.Channelling: This is the last stage before the victim decides, as an act of free will, to give their soul to the devil. The devil selects particular individuals for channelling and anybody with the gift of free will can be a victim. Lonely people or those who are prone to self-pity, tantrums or rage are more likely to be selected. Demons particularly attack the lower appetites of the flesh. The victim is first isolated and then made dependent on the evil spirit. Dependence can be related to success in a career or other aspects of normal living. The victim will eventually feel so dependent that if the demon should leave them, they feel that they would loose everything of value in life. At the stage of dependence, therefore, the victim will find it very difficult to break away. At this stage the spirit begins to appear and be friendly and helpful. Any efforts to reject the evil spirit, however, will result in a vicious attack. Exorcism is the only answer at this stage.

The following is a brief summary of a real case of channelling described in How to win your Spiritual Warfare.[105] The story concerned a young man (call him Dermot – not his real name) who was born in New York in the early 1960's. His father died of alcoholism in the 70's. His mother began to work as a prostitute and left Dermot to care for himself. From his early years Dermot noticed that, when his parents looked at him, he often saw strange peculiar faces replace the faces of his parents. Although this scared him a lot at first, he gradually got used to it. When he was alone, he would always feel a spiritual presence near him.

When Dermot was 18 years old, he parted from his mother and began working in various jobs. It was at this stage that his mysterious presence became visible and introduced himself as Ponto. He was approximately four and a half feet in height, 'with two bulbous eyes, a contorted mouth, pointed ears, pointed chin, a big forehead and a pointed head. His hands were like a three pronged fork. He had the feet of a duck, the body of a cat, with one leg shorter than the other'.

Dermot got a job as a radio announcer and Ponto helped him a lot with news information, figures, statistics and other very useful information, which he was able to use on air. Dermot's fame quickly spread, and he became one of the most popular radio announcers in the US. It was at this stage that Ponto proposed marriage to Dermot. At first Dermot was just shocked and ignored the suggestion, but he knew he was in trouble when Ponto kept bringing the subject up. He was then introduced to an exorcist by a friend, but he decided to see a psychiatrist instead. Months later he felt things were getting worse, so he asked for the help of the exorcist. The exorcist was accompanied by another priest and three assistants. It took five days in total, before Dermot was finally free of his demonic attachment. The most difficult step was for Dermot to renounce the evil spirit as he knew that in doing so he would lose his status on radio. During the exorcism, it was discovered that Ponto was controlled by a more superior spirit. The spirits were eventually driven away in the name of Jesus. As they were going, the cords binding Dermot to a bed were broken and severe howling in the room scared all the exorcist's assistants away. When it was over the exorcist fell exhausted and Dermot fell into a deep sleep. Dermot awoke from this sleep feeling peace, joy and tranquillity for the first time in many years.

6.Lordship: This is also known as The Master and it occurs when, by consent, the victims surrender themselves to the devil and become a possession of Lucifer. The victim is completely controlled and becomes part of a plan to rule the world with evil. To choose the devil is to get the devil's reward, that is, despair. The antidote against the devil acting as Master, is faith in Jesus Christ, and obedience to the Church.

Curses

A curse is a generic word, normally understood as causing harm to others through the power of demons. Fr Amorth distinguishes four forms of curses. These are regular curses, magic, the evil eye, and spells. The commonest form of regular curses that are encountered, are those involving parents or grandparents, who call down evil on their children or grandchildren. There is a great evil associated with these and they often result in severe family illness. The evil eye involves casting a spell with a will to harm somebody through the power of demons by just looking at them. Although this is real, it is rare.

Witchcraft and Magic

Magic, witchcraft, and other satanic rites, invoke demons in order to obtain a curse and harm against particular individuals, without the use of objects. The worst form of satanic rite is the so called "black mass", where consecrated hosts (stolen from Catholic churches) are sacrilegiously used. Alternatively, human sacrifices are sometimes used in these masses. White witches are often mistakenly promoted, since they are claimed to have the power to lift curses, but Fr Amorth advises that no distinction should be made between witches, since all use demons as the source of their power. Norm number eight of the Roman exorcism ritual also warns against seeking the help of sorcerers, warlocks, or witches, to lift or neutralize curses. Usually what happens is that the symptoms disappear and return more severely, after a while. The financial cost usually goes up on each return visit. In most countries, however, there is no shortage of sorcerers and witches, whereas exorcists are much more difficult to find.

Spells

A spell is also known as a malefice (from the Latin, male factus – to do something bad), or hex, and in the experience of exorcists, spells are by far the most common means used to do evil to somebody. As sacraments in the Catholic Church use matter, so spells use matter, that is, some kind of material or object. A spell or hex, can be applied to an individual either directly or indirectly. The direct way for example, may consist of mixing material with food. The indirect way is to use objects that belong to an individual, such as photographs, clothes etc. The evil effect is not in the material, but in the will to harm through demons. A doll is often used and sticking needles, for example, into the head can be associated with severe headaches. Hexes take different forms, depending on the harm that is desired. An "illness" curse is a common one and the illness is often made more specific to different organs by a "binding" hex. A binding hex usually is associated with cloths of different colours for different body parts. The commonest of these hexes is on mental development. A "death" curse is often referred to as a "destruction" hex. The ultimate aim of the demon in this case is to drive the subject to suicide. The most difficult spells to lift in the experience of Fr Amorth are those from African witch doctors, Haitian voodoo, and in particular a Brazilian spell, called "macumbe"

The Exorcism Ritual

The Roman Catholic ritual for exorcism lists 21 norms which must be followed by the exorcist. These were written in 1641 but are still valid today. These directives are full of wisdom and come from centuries of Church experience, often handed down from one exorcist generation to the next. There is much practical advice on how to recognize the presence of demons and a guide on how the exorcist should behave. Exorcists often use euphemistic language and when speaking of demonic influences refer to it as "negativity". There are a very large number of records of exorcisms that give great details regarding the interrogation of demons, which leave no doubt about the reality of demonic possession. The extent of this evidence is now so large that any reasonable investigation would find it difficult to dispute. Unfortunately, knowledge of demons and of their power to influence humanity towards evil is not well known, and this information is not easily available. Those who do not believe in demons would benefit from studying the evidence.

There are four paragraphs in the Catechism of the Catholic Church dedicated to exorcism. These are number 517, 550, 1237, and 1673. These paragraphs deal specifically with the exorcisms done by Jesus. One of the great signs that the kingdom of God has come to earth is that demons can now be cast out by the power of God. We are reminded that baptism is a release from the slavery of Satan. There is a renouncement of Satan, by the recipient or candidate for baptism, who is also exorcised. Canon Law makes exorcisms applicable, not only to demonic possession, but also to demonic influences. The liberation is not limited to people, but can also apply to animals, houses, other places and objects. When considering exorcism, it is important for all Catholics to realise that Satan is far more enraged when souls are taken away from him, through the Sacrament of Confession, than when a human body is taken away from him, through exorcism. The Sacrament of Reconciliation or Confession, therefore, is a very important means of preventing demonic possession.

Making a diagnosis of the need for exorcism: Complete demonic possession is rare but there is a definite belief, within the Roman Church and among Catholic exorcists, that the frequency is increasing at this time. Bearing in mind that Christianity is the only religion that claims to have power over demons, it is not surprising that there is an inverse relationship between the frequency of demonic activity and the practice of Christianity and Christian virtues in the community. In Ireland, where there is still a relatively good level of practice of the Christian way of life, demonic possession is rare. This is not the case in many other parts of the world. It is interesting that there seems to be a definite increase in satanic activity in Italy, in the US and in other countries where Christian standards and beliefs are not practised with the same fervour as previously.

The impression of exorcists is that the young are the most vulnerable to demons, and demonic attacks, especially if they are not well formed or established in their Christian faith. Many exorcisms that take place involve possessions from a very early age. Most exorcists will also say that they exorcise more women than men but Fr Amorth has also said that, as an exorcist, he has asked more men than women to change their lives and they have refused. Demons are not sexual beings and so they have no preference for either sex.

Fr Amorth tells us that it can be very difficult at times to diagnose diabolical possession. It can be especially difficult to identify demonic influences in those who have psychological or psychiatric problems, as well as demonic influences. It is generally very rare, however, for psychiatric problems to be confused with demonic possession, and the Catholic Church has always been very aware of confusing medical illness with demonic influences. This is recorded among the decrees of the Synod of Reims in 1583, long before psychiatry was established as a branch of medicine. Fr Candido Amantini (who trained the current expert, Fr Amorth), was a very well known exorcist in Italy, and he always worked closely with Professor Mariani, a Professor of Psychiatry in Rome, when he came across difficult cases. In some cases it was Professor Mariani, who would invite Fr Amantini to help him when he suspected demonic possession, rather than a medical condition, and both would work together to make a final diagnosis.

When trying to decide if a case of demonic possession is present, an initial examination is made of the symptoms and signs, in a similar manner to making any medical diagnosis. The failure of traditional medicine and drugs to have any impact on the symptoms is a useful start. Likewise, the failure of very high doses of sedatives to calm victims can lead to suspicion. If an illness has a demonic origin, the experience is that medicinal drugs will have no effect on it. Visions, locutions, false mysticism, or the claim to be a visionary are frequent signs of evil influence. Blessed oil, blessed salt, or holy water, can be used to demonstrate signs. Victims will often tear off clothes that were blessed in secret, or are unable to eat or may get very ill after eating food, cooked with blessed salt. Physical symptoms, such as an aversion to the sacred, even blessed candles, are not uncommon. There may be a history of contact with witches, sorcerers, séances or card readers. There is almost always evidence of bizarre social behaviour. In very rare cases, there can be extraordinary signs such as levitation but these are exceptionally rare as demons like to remain hidden. The Ritual recognizes three specific signs that indicate demonic possession. These are listed as:

(1) Talking in languages not known by the victim.
(2) Exhibiting superhuman strength to the extent of breaking strong binding.
(3) Knowing secrets which the victim could not know.

It is not possible or wise to wait for all these signs before doing an exorcism, as in Fr Amorth's experience, and in the experience of the other exorcists he has known, these signs often only become manifest during the exorcism prayers. Pets, such as dogs and cats can sense an evil presence in a room, and may scurry out quickly, or stare all the time at a particular spot in the room.

If there are no signs of improvement several days after the exorcism and there were no signs of 'negativities' during the exorcism, then the problem is unlikely to be due to a demonic influence. On the other hand, if in the end there is dramatic healing from an illness, which was labelled previously as incurable, it is good evidence that the illness was demonic in origin. The cooperation of the individual is essential for the success of the exorcism. In other words, he or she must have the wish and give permission to be exorcised, otherwise the exorcism, if it proceeds, will fail.

Charisms, Seers and Sensitives

Some lay Christians get the charism of the power to liberate individuals from evil spirits. This charism should be tested with the following questions:

Are they good practising Catholics?
Do they get financial reward?
Are they using approved methods of praying?
Are the fruits good?

I am aware of one well known lay individual in Ireland who has this charism. Other individuals have the gift of seeing and or feeling an evil presence in places and associated with people. They can often locate the source of the problem, and sometimes they have the gift of understanding the circumstances of how the problem began. Fr Amorth recognizes the great assistance that these individuals can be to an exorcist. I am familiar with a well-known carpenter in Ireland who has this gift, and I have witnessed him making use of this gift on a number of occasions.

Interrogation of Demons

Norm 20 of the ritual suggests that the exorcist should ask the demon the reason for his presence, and especially if it is due to something the subject ate or drank, or if it is due to a foreign object which may be hidden. The ritual does not encourage interrogating the demons just for the sake of curiosity. The demon can be commanded by the exorcist to speak and reveal secrets, such as the name of the demon (or demons) and the reason for his (their) presence, or commanded to reveal the location of hidden objects. One good example of demon interrogation is the story related by Fr Amorth, about an exorcism performed by Fr Candido Amantini for a hex that was causing an abdominal illness in a young girl. The demon was forced to reveal the location of a box which contained material related to the hex. They found a small box, as the demon had said, located near a particular tree buried three metres deep. The exorcists made the mistake, however, of burning the contents of the box, but not doing it properly according to the ritual. The result was that the hex fell on Fr Amantini, who spent many months afterwards confined to bed, suffering from a similar abdominal illness.

Much information can be gleaned from the interrogation of the demons. At a recent conference in Rome (June 08), I heard Fr Giancarlo Gramollazo (who has now replaced Fr Amorth as the chief exorcist in Rome), reply to the question: "Is Latin a better language to use when interrogating demons?" His reply was: "In my opinion, no. During exorcisms, I often use my own Italian dialect, which even most Italians would not understand, much less those from other countries. (The implication was that many of the exorcisms performed by this were on people outside of Italy, and they would not understand his dialect) The demons, however, never have any problem understanding me. The devil is a polyglot (understands several languages)." The implication was that many of the exorcisms performed by Fr Giancarlo were on people outside of Italy, and they would not understand his dialect but the demons had no problem understanding him.

When the interrogation of demons is done properly, there is never any doubt that it is the demons who are responding, rather than the possessed individual. Fr Amantini, in particular, liked to interrogate demons in children, who were far too young to understand the details, complexity and theology of the subjects discussed. In a question about Hell to such a demon he got the following reply: "How stupid you are! Down there everybody lives folded within themselves, in the most profound solitude, and desperately weeping for the evil which they have committed. It is like a cemetery".

Fr Amantini asked an eleven year old possessed boy about scientists and those with fine intellects, who did not believe in either God and his angels, or Satan and his demons. The immediate reply came, - "Those are not very fine intellects! They are fine mediocrities". In answer to the question, "What do you call those who knowingly deny God?", the young boy jumped up in fury and said, "Be careful, remember that we wanted to reclaim our freedom, even before Him".

The Behaviour of Demons: Demons keep the same rank as they had as angels before their fall. Consequently they have various grades of authority and can be found fighting and disputing, especially when there is more than one in possession of a human body. Demons will try everything to remain hidden and consequently are very reluctant to speak. They can be forced eventually to reveal information under the command of the exorcist. Very few are violent. Demons suffer terribly during the prayers of exorcism. Fr Amorth has said that demons have told him on many occasions that they suffer more from the exorcism than they do in Hell. They say that the pain of exorcism for them is unimaginable. Pressing the exorcist's stole against the ailing body parts is particularly painful to the demon. Only high ranking demons are able to utter the name of God or Mary and this is always followed by extreme blasphemies. The lower ranks of demons refer to God, Jesus and Mary as, 'Him' or 'Her'.

The exorcist is always able to find a weak point with the demon, that causes him so much pain, that he will opt to go back to Hell, which is usually where they go after an exorcism. Demons will often be very defiant towards the exorcist in the beginning, but toward the end will howl and cry out in pain saying, 'You are killing me' etc. When demons have well-known names from sacred scripture, such as, Satan, Beelzebub, Lucifer, Asmodeus etc. then the exorcist will know that they are dealing with "heavyweights", who are more difficult to defeat. Much faith, prayer and fasting is needed to get rid of some demons.

Examples of some famous Demonic Possessions

The possession of Annelise Michel: This story concerns a twenty four year old student, from Klingenberg, Germany, who died in the summer of 1986, following a long series of exorcisms. This was publicized widely by the world press, as the two priests involved with the exorcisms were charged with causing the girl's death. It emerged later that the priests had behaved properly at all time, and had the approval of the subject, her parents, and their Bishop. Nevertheless, the case had such wide publicity, that it has dis-encouraged priests from getting involved with exorcisms. An American movie was released and distributed world-wide, in 2005, based on the story.[108] The story in the movie is Americanized, but nevertheless, it is largely based on fact. The main message was that this girl was not possessed because she was evil, but that her possession had a powerful salvific value for her own soul, and for the souls of countless others, who would learn the details of her demonic possession. This girl suffered terribly over the five year period of her possession and some believe that Annelise Michel will become a canonized saint at some stage in the future.

The possession of Antoine Gay: This man was born in France in 1790. When he was young, he was very religious and wanted to become a monk. He was possessed by three demons when he was about thirty years old and the story of this possession is one of the most extraordinary ever recorded. It seems that the principal demon was there under God's command and was there to do God's work .[109]

The early evidence for his possession was from the great detailed and secret knowledge he had of people's lives. When he was interrogated in Latin, Mr Gay was able to respond appropriately in French, although he had no knowledge of Latin. It was usual to hear him speaking in his own gentle way and then suddenly be interrupted by a new voice, with an insulting personality. He was seen many times to be weeping when he was forced to admit the truth of the Christian religion and to give proofs of possession. One demon used to say that, "The greatest suffering I have is to be forced by God to undo my own work. A local priest, Fr Marie Joseph Chiron, had a great interest in helping those with demons and he became convinced that Mr Gay was possessed. Fr Chiron eventually was able to converse regularly with the chief demon in Mr Gay. He was helping two other ladies, who were also possessed by demons, at the time. One of these was recorded as seen by the whole parish on a number of occasions, moving rapidly without touching the ground. The other lady had a demon named Madeste, who was very violent, and argued continually with a demon in Mr Gay, who was named Isacaron. The argument was over which of them was the more senior.

Fr Chiron brought Mr Gay to Ars, so that the famous Cure d'Ars could exorcise him. The Cure said that it would be best to wait a while and have it done publicly in the Cathedral. Meanwhile, Mr Gay was growing in holiness, because of his struggle against the demon. At the same time he was making many converts, because of the witness he was forced to give, on behalf of the Catholic Church. Many other efforts were made to organize an exorcism, but somehow all attempts came to nothing, and no exorcism was ever done. While in Ars, one of the demons in Mr Gay, led him to fall on his knees before the statue of The Virgin Mary and proclaim her Immaculate Conception, years before it was made known to Bernadette, in Lourdes in 1858.

There is no doubt that the chief demon in Mr Gay wanted to be relieved of his duty and in that sense it is the only case recorded where a demon wanted an exorcism. The demon was forced to praise God and he used to complain, "Must I serve as an instrument for man's instruction when my chief delight is in their destruction". The demon was compelled to compose beautiful prayers to The Virgin Mary, and give eloquent sermons supporting Catholic teaching. In one of his sermons he said, "The world believes that humility is weakness and incapacity and I say that humility is power and grandeur. If you knew the misery of the reprobate, you would all be saints. There is no language to describe the torments of the damned and there is no human mind able to comprehend them...Hunger, thirst, death, are nothing: only sin is to be feared...It was pride, ingratitude, and disobedience that led to my rebellion and damnation". Mr Gay eventually died on the 13th June 1871 without an exorcism. There is little doubt that Antoine Gay was a saintly man.

A possession in Iowa, U.S.A. in 1928: This is described in the book, *Begone Satan*, which was written solely to describe this event.[110] It concerns a woman who was cursed by her own father and who was possessed by several demons, from the age of sixteen. These demons included her aunt Mina, who was a witch, her father and his mistress and another demon claiming to be Judas. The exorcism took place in a convent and lasted for twenty three days. All through the exorcism, the woman had terrible visions of large numbers of angels fighting demons. Theresa Neumann (see page 67), half way across the world in Germany, at the exact same time, also saw this terrible battle between the angels and demons. Theresa later said that it was the most frightening vision which she had ever experienced. The woman also later related how The Little Flower of the Child Jesus (St Thérése) appeared to her during the exorcism and encouraged her to be strong. During the visitation by St Thérése, those in the room saw white flowers appear on the ceiling of the room. Satan himself appeared before the exorcist for approximately 30 minutes during the exorcism. He was full of fire with a crown on his head and a fiery sword. Beelzebub stood beside him as he cursed and blasphemed and spoke to the exorcist in a terrible rage. At the end, the exorcist spent the last three days and nights praying, without a moment rest, before he was successful. On one occasion when only the senior demons remained and the exorcist insisted that they should return to Hell, one devil replied in a growling tone, "How can you banish me to Hell? I must be free to prepare the way for the Antichrist". Eventually there was a piercing sound in the room with a terrible stench. All in the room were terrified and began to tremble. Voices were heard saying, "Beelzebub, Judas, Jacob, Mina". To this was added the words, "Hell, Hell, Hell". This was repeated over and over until it eventually faded. The woman who had broken free of her bonds eventually fell back on the bed, opened her eyes for the first time during the exorcism and began to smile, pray, and praise God. Some of those present (mostly nuns) gave written accounts of the details of the exorcism.

International Association of Exorcists: This was approved officially by Rome on 13th June, 2014. The clear message is that the demonic possessions are no longer rare, but on the other hand the Roman Catholic Church is putting a lot more effort into training exorcists. At a conference of this Association, in Rome, Oct. 20th-25th 2014,[234] Don Ermes Macchioni reminded everybody that:

"Pope Francis insistently reminds us that the Devil is not a metaphor, but that he is an insidious enemy who steals hope, instils bitterness, leads to discouragement, and is not a product of socio-psychological literature but rather he has a name and a precise face: the Devil does not belong to ideas that are on the decline."

Don Ermes, who is an exorcist in Italy, also gave some personal experiences of infestations and possessions. He gave an example of a farm with demonic infestation, where the animals were ill, but recovered dramatically when sold to another farm. His help was called for by the Veterinary surgeon involved. Another example was of a young girl with insomnia. He managed to break a spell put on her and during his preparatory investigations he discovered nails without heads that were hidden in her pillow. He also described other spells with objects hidden in pillows. Among a number of other examples he gave was a case where two death spells were put on a young woman, who had very bad health. One of the spells was hidden in a forest in another country and the other was buried at sea. He discovered this during an exorcism, when the demon revealed his name as Lucifer and told him about the death spells. He commanded the demon, in the name of Jesus, to send his satellites to find and destroy these spells. The woman began to improve and now she is happily married.

Fr Cliff Ermatinger, at the same conference, recounted some of his experiences as an exorcist for the Archdiocese of Milwaukee, US. He was the first exorcist for 35 years in that diocese. He had appointed a group of auxiliaries to assist him during exorcisms. His auxiliaries had four important tasks:

1. To act as witnesses.
2. To help with physical restraint during manifestations of evil.
3. To silently pray for liberation of the person.
4. To pray for him so that he could understand the particular problems of the possessed.

He uses English speaking auxiliaries when the possessed is Hispanic and Spanish speakers when the possessed is English speaking to avoid embarrassment to those possessed. He recognises the names of different demonic spirits associated with different problems. These are: Belial for pornography, Lusuriae for lust, Geomantiae for séances (Ouija Board), Veneficii for witchcraft, Prestigiae for tarot cards, Divinationis for mediumship and psychics, Fornicationis for fornication, and Effeminatiae for disordered sexual behaviour. If he recognizes or suspects any of these spirits he always names them, while following the Pope Leo XIII exorcism ritual.

In the case of difficult possessions, caused by witchcraft and Satanism, including a formal consecration to Satan, he uses the Latin exorcism of St Cyprian. Sometimes in these situations there can be a number of demons "knotted" together and they cannot be sent away individually until the "knot" has been broken or dissolved. Knotted demons tend to be located in the same part of the body and the commonest location that he has experienced is the back. Immobility of the demons is one of the ways of recognizing knots and finding the weakest demon is often a help. In one particular case the key to breaking the knot was given by the weakest demon who advised using prayers of the precious blood of Jesus over a satanic pentagram disc which was used in a blood pact, made by the woman possessed, during a satanic ritual. Such objects can also be the sources of curses present in houses. He noted on one occasion during an exorcism of a woman, a small metal object given to her by a Satanist was discovered in her house. When her husband went to retrieve the object, it scalded his hand.

Other random observations noted by Fr Cliff were: Using the novena to "Mary, the Untier of knots" promoted by Pope Francis is very powerful. The renewal of baptismal promises is often the time you experience the first manifestation of Evil One. Sometimes the demons that are in the highest hierarchy in Hell are not always the ones that possess the person in the strongest way. He gets most of his new cases in the period before 31st October and in Lent.

Some unusual cases of possession experienced by Fr Cliff were as follows:
1. He had two cases involved with Eastern practices. Both had a similar manifestation called the "third eye". The phenomenon seems to relate to the search for hidden knowledge and manifests as a bump in the forehead that appears during the exorcism.
2. He experienced a twenty five year old lad who was possessed by seven demons since he was seven years old. Although he had a very religious father, his mother was very involved with New Age practices, which she introduced to her daughter. When his older sister was a teenager, she wanted to be a witch. She was instructed by a mature witch to offer an innocent soul to Satan. She,

consequently, made her little brother eat cursed sage in a salad and that was the time the demons entered him. The demons even told Fr Cliff the exact date it happened.

3. Another of his subjects was a man possessed for 24 years. It turned out to be the result drinking cursed Coca Cola which a lady he had rejected gave him many years before and insisted that he drink it all at once.

4. He has experienced many cases of possession through pornography. Often he questions the demons in a language which the subject does not understand. In the case on one man, possessed through pornography, he asked the demon in Italian, how he had entered this man. The demon replied in perfect Italian, which the young man could not speak, "through my best invention: internet pornography". His manifestations were classic, with "white eyes, his face turned, hypersensitive to the sacramental and sacred images, ability to speak foreign languages that were unknown to him, plus the 'third eye'" as explained above. The man was released after three months of weekly exorcisms. Less than a year later his girlfriend told Fr Cliff that she felt very agitated near him. This made him worry for two reasons. He worried that she had a demon as well and that her boyfriend was repossessed. He later confirmed that this was true and he eventually managed to free both of them from the demons. Demons, he said, are like dogs and when you put them close to each other, one of them has to assert its superiority. The weaker one then becomes nervous and agitated.

5. Finally, another extraordinary case described by Fr Cliff was a lady who became possessed, while she was still a foetus in her mother's womb (that is, before she was born). Her mother had a row with a lady, in her native city of Mexico, who cursed her before she was born. During the exorcism, neither she nor her sisters recognized the name of the

person that the demons claimed was responsible. When they called their mother in Mexico, however, she remembered the lady named very well and was able to give them a full account of the dispute, thirty years before.

HELL

There is a story told about the famous preacher, Dr Ian Paisley (RIP), from the North of Ireland, who was preaching about Hell to his congregation one evening. He was quoting from the gospel of Matthew (8:12) regarding the weeping and gnashing of teeth. An old lady suddenly inquired what would happen to those who had no teeth. Dr Paisley looked at her sternly and said, "Teeth will be provided".

Eternal punishment is mentioned in the Bible several times, as for example, "eternal fire" Mk 9:43, "the fire is never extinguished" Mk 9:48, "the smoke of their torment will go up forever and ever" Rev 14:11, and "their torture will not stop, day and night, for ever and ever" Rev 20:10. Peter 5:8 says, "Be calm but vigilant, because your enemy the devil is prowling around like a roaring lion, looking for someone to eat. Stand up to him strong in faith". Eph. 6:12 says, "Our battle is not against human forces, but against Principalities and Powers, the rulers of the world of darkness". I appreciate of course, that those who are not Christians will need a bit more convincing about Hell than biblical quotations, but there is a lot of good quality evidence for the reality of Hell.

The doctrine of Hell is a core teaching of Christianity and anybody who does not believe in Hell can hardly claim to be a Christian, as it was the clear teaching of Jesus. Taken together, Heaven and Hell form the framework around our moral choices. Cases where deceased individuals have given very good evidence that they were condemned to Hell are very numerous and the statement that, "Nobody has ever come back from death to tell us about Hell", is absolutely false. Much of the Catholic writings on Hell indicate that it is impossible for the human mind to comprehend either the suffering or the eternity of Hell. Neither can we comprehend the infinite evil of serious sin, which merits Hell. Theologians try to explain it, not so much in terms of anyone doing an infinite evil, but in terms of a serious offence against the infinite goodness of God, which merits an infinite punishment.

It is traditional Catholic teaching that there are certain sins which are so serious that those who die refusing to repent, are likely to go to Hell. Examples of these sins are serious pride, murder, abortion, homosexual acts, fornication, adultery, artificial birth control and in some situations, even the rejection of solemn laws instituted by the Roman Church. There are two important considerations to remember with respect to the terrible reality of eternal suffering. These are, firstly, that God's mercy is also infinite and it is never too late in this life to repent. Secondly, we can never presume on this mercy of God (presumption), unless we repent, and most people die as they live. We must also remember that death bed repentance is not common, but on the other hand, sudden deaths are not uncommon.

There is a great trend in modern society and in modern religious teaching to ignore Hell or pretend that it does not exist. This does not change the reality. Hell has never been denied by the Jewish religion, by the Muslim religion or the many large numbers of break-away Christian groups and sects. From what I have read of Hell, and I have read many books and descriptions of this place, **I would encourage everybody to read at least one book on Hell, before committing their eternal happiness to the very foolish assumption that Hell does not exist.**[111,112] Where is the evidence that Hell does not exist? On the contrary, there are large volumes of evidence, not just from sacred scripture, but also from saints, seers, prophets and mystics who have visited Hell. There are also volumes of evidence from ordinary individuals, who have recorded details of friends or relations who have returned to them after death, to inform them of their eternal damnation in Hell. A proper study of demons, as briefly described above, should help convince many that Hell is a possible destination after death. Finally there are the authenticated messages of The Virgin Mary, which leave no doubt about the reality of Purgatory and Hell (see Fatima, page 125).

Apparitions of the Damned: Accounts of damned souls returning to communicate with the living, are numerous and varied. This can happen for many reasons or even apparently for no known reason. Some of the noted reasons are pacts made to friends while alive, in response to continual prayer by relatives for damned souls, as a special grace given to saints, or in order to cause demonic possession as described above. It is a good time to mention again, that it can be dangerous to try to contact the dead, through mediums, ouija boards, séances or any other spiritualism techniques. This is very unlikely to lead to the truth, as it deals with "the father of lies", and it can lead to serious demonic activity and even possession.

One detailed and well documented return of a damned soul, was recorded by the grandson of the military governor of Moscow, during the 1812 Napoleonic campaign.[107] One of the Army Generals, who was a disciple of Voltaire, made a pact with General Count Orloff, just before one of the major battles of the war. They agreed that which ever one died first, would if at all possible, return to the other from the dead, to confirm what they both believed, that there was no Hell. Count Oroloff was shocked when his friend came to him one night shortly afterwards, and said, "There is a Hell and I am there. What do we do now?" Twelve days later, the news officially came from the battle front to Count

Orloff, telling him of the death of his friend, precisely at the time he saw him in his bedroom.

There is evidence that the fire of Hell is real. St Augustine said that, "It is the same fire that tortures the damned (in Hell) and purifies the elect (in Purgatory)". There are a number of well documented stories of souls coming back from Purgatory seeking prayers and leaving imprints of scorched limbs on wood, as proof of their return (see chapter 8).

Many of the saints had direct communications from souls after death. St Margaret Mary said that the sight of a soul falling into Hell is of itself, an incomparable pain. St Padre Pio (see page 102) had departed souls call to him all the time, especially to thank him for his prayers, for their release from Purgatory, on their way to Heaven. **This great mystic said that, most of those who go to Hell, were those who did not believe it existed while they were alive.** He is also often quoted for a reply which he gave to an Italian communist, who said to him that he did not believe in Hell. **His stark reply was, - "You will believe in it when you get there".**

St Faustina's description of Hell: St Faustina visited Hell and wrote of it in her diary. She is the saint of Divine Mercy, with dramatic miracles attributed to her (see page 450). She was canonized by St Pope John Paul II. She is also one of the chosen saints for these "End Times" and gave us dramatic prophecies on the major problems that lie ahead. She was not just asked but **commanded by God**, to tell people that they cannot avoid Hell by claiming that they did not know it existed. Some of the words of St Faustina regarding her description of Hell, are as follows:

"Today, I was led by an Angel to the chasms of Hell. It is a place of great suffering, awesomely large and extensive. The first kind of suffering I saw, and the main suffering that constitutes Hell, is the loss of God. The second is perpetual remorse of conscience. The third is that one's condition will never change. The fourth, is the fire that will penetrate the soul, without destroying it. It is a terrible suffering, since it is a spiritual fire lit by God's anger. The fifth suffering is continual darkness and a terrible suffocating smell. Despite the darkness, the devils and the souls of the damned see each other and all the evil, both of others and their own. The sixth suffering is the constant company of Satan. The seventh suffering is horrible despair, hatred of God, vile words, curses and blasphemies. These are the sufferings suffered by all the damned together, but that is not the end of the sufferings.

There are special sufferings destined for particular souls. These are the torments of the senses. Each soul undergoes terrible and indescribable sufferings, related to the manner in which it has sinned.

There are caverns and pits of suffering where one form of agony differs from another. I would have died at the very sight of these sufferings if the omnipotence of God had not supported me.

Let the sinners know that he will be suffering throughout all eternity, in those senses which he made use of, to sin.

I am writing this at the command of God, so that no soul may find an excuse by saying there is no Hell, or that nobody has ever been there, and so that everybody will know what it is like. I, Sister Faustina by the order of God, have visited the abysses of Hell, so that I might tell souls about it, and testify to its existence.

I cannot speak about it now: but I have received a command from God to leave it in writing. The devils were full of hatred for me, but they had to obey me at the command of God. What I have written is but a pale shadow of things I saw. I noticed that most of the souls who were there, were those who disbelieved that Hell existed, while on this earth."

Sr Josefa Menendez' description of Hell: Sr Josefa was a Spanish nun who died in 1923 at the age of 33 and wrote revelations, like Sr Faustina above, by the direct command of God. These revelations have been published in the well known spiritual book, *The Way of Divine Love*.[113] She wrote extensively on Hell. She repeatedly wrote on the greatest torture of Hell, namely, the inability of a soul to love. The damned souls continuously cry, "This is my torture. I want to love and cannot. All that is left for me is hatred and despair". Sr Josefa wrote as follows:

"Every day now, when I am dragged down to Hell and the devil orders them to torture me, they answer: "We cannot, for her members have undergone torture for Him..." (then they blasphemously name Our Blessed Lord)....then he orders them to give me a draught of sulphur ....and again the reply is: "She has voluntarily deprived herself of drink..." Try to find some part of her body to which she has given satisfaction and pleasure." When they shackle me to take me down to Hell, they never can bind me where I have worn instruments of penance. I write all this simply out of obedience." (April 1, 1922).

She also records the accusations made against themselves by these unhappy souls as follows: "Some yell because of the martyrdom of their hands. Perhaps they were thieves, for they say: "Where is our loot now?.... Cursed hands.... Why did I want to possess what did not belong to me... and what in any case I could keep only for a few days...? "Others curse their tongues, their eyes... whatever was the occasion of their sin... Now, O body, you are paying the price of the delights you granted yourself!... and you did it of your own free will..." (that is, illegitimate delights - April 2, 1922).

"It seems to me that the majority accused themselves of sins of impurity, of stealing, of unjust trading: and that most of the damned are in Hell for these sins." (April 6, 1922).

"I saw many worldly people fall into Hell, and no words can render their horrible and terrifying cries: "Damned forever … I deceived myself: I am lost… I am here forever … There is no remedy possible … A curse on me…"

"I saw several souls fall into Hell, and among them was a child of fifteen, cursing her parents for not having taught her to fear God nor that there was a Hell. Her life had been a short one, she said, but full of sin, for she had given in to all that her body and passions demanded. Especially she had read bad books." (March 22, 1923).

"On one occasion when I was in Hell, I saw a great many priests, religious and nuns, cursing their vows, their order, their Superiors and everything that could have given them the light and the grace they had lost….

One priest said: "I ate poison, as I used money that was not my own… the money given me for Masses, which I did not offer."

Another said that he belonged to a secret society which had betrayed the Church and religion, and he had been bribed to connive at terrible profanations and sacrileges".

Josefa noted that the greater number of religious plunged into Hell-fire were there for abominable sins against Chastity … and for sins against the vow of poverty.

"It is impossible to describe the confusion and shame a soul feels at that moment, when it realises: - 'All is lost, and I am damned forever'. I saw Hell with the long dark corridors, the cavities, the flames. Not a finger-nail escapes terrifying torments and all the time, one cannot move even a finger to gain some relief, nor change posture, for the body seems flattened out and [yet] doubled in two. Sounds of confusion and blasphemy cease not for an instant. A sickening stench asphyxiates and corrupts everything. It is like the burning of putrefied flesh, mingled with tar and sulphur."

"All I have written," she concluded, "is but a shadow of what the soul suffers, for no words can express such dire torments".

Others: A number of other saints have also visited Hell. Saint Veronica Guiliani (1660 – 1727) was allowed to go to Hell on particular days, during her life, so that on those days nobody went to Hell because of her suffering.[114] St Catherine Emmerich went to Hell many times to repair for the mortal sins of many souls who would otherwise have been doomed to go to Hell.[115]

Marian Visionaries and Hell: Like the saints, many of the modern Marian visionaries have also mystically visited Heaven, Purgatory and Hell and these visits have been described in detail by them. In Medjugorje (see page 164), Mirjana was told that after death, most go to Purgatory first, before getting to Heaven. The next greatest number go to Hell and very few go directly to Heaven. Being a Catholic is no guarantee of salvation. In fact many accounts suggest that Catholics suffer more for their sins, because they were offered more help and graces to avoid sin. Part of the message of Garabandal (see page 139) was that, "Many Cardinals, Bishops and priests are on the road to perdition and leading many astray". The Message of Fatima (see page 125) is very strong and convincing evidence for the reality of Hell. The children were shown a vast sea of fire. In this fire they saw demons and the souls of the damned, like transparent burning embers, blackened or bronze, with human forms. You can see a very good depiction of this in the wax museum in Fatima.

The Catechism of the Catholic Church says that, "Hell is the state of definitive self-exclusion from communion with God and the blessed." Let us finish by quoting the words of Pope Benedict XVI. He described Hell as, "a state of existential abandonment and loneliness into which love can no longer reach". In March 2007, he said that, "God's mercy and love are great but those who reject Him, should know that Hell exists and is eternal".

A Society in Crisis

In modern society, the majority do not believe that Hell exists, or that even if it does exist, they believe that there is not the remotest possibility of going there. How foolish they are! How can anybody study the great sign of Fatima and not believe that Hell exists? St Augustine told us that we are made for God and we cannot be happy until we rest with God.

Philosophers throughout the ages have identified four levels of happiness. These four levels can be seen in the ideas of Plato, Aristotle, St Augustine, and St Thomas Aquinas, as well as in many writings from Judaism, Hinduism, Buddhism, and Islam. The first two levels are regarded as lower levels and happiness is immediate and easily apparent. Levels three and four are regarded as higher forms of happiness, which are more enduring and deeply satisfying. The first level comes from an external stimulus, like a new car, or a sweet for a child. The second level comes from ego gratification, like winning football matches or other games. The third level is when we try to make a contribution with our lives to the world outside ourselves, as in working for a good cause. This still does not exhaust the depths of human desire, which is found in the fourth level. This is the desire in the human person for unconditional and perfect love, perfect goodness, perfect truth and perfect beauty.

The problem we have in our modern society is that there are very few who seek happiness above level two. We live in a 'take' world rather than in a 'give' world. This results in a lack of love. There is a lack of love for others and a lack of love for God. Robert J. Spitzer S.J., in his book, *Healing the Culture*,[116] describes this problem as, **loss of intangibles, through grounding our culture and public policies in "metaphysical materialism"**. Everything that is not visible or tangible is regarded as not real. In this environment, love, commitment, truth, justice and other intangibles are devalued. Personhood and inalienable rights of the human person are also devalued. The personhood and right to life of a human embryo, is no longer considered by many to be a legitimate question. We end up with a radically incomplete view of human community, human dignity, and human destiny. The result is moral chaos and the direct intentional killing of between fifty to one hundred million unborn humans every year, at various stages of gestation. In the case of partial birth abortion, some of these babies are full term and partially born. More than anything else, this reflects the moral depravity and moral chaos to which humanity has now descended.

Fr Spitzer gives the objective definition of a 'person' as, "A being, possessing an intrinsic guiding force toward fulfilment (whether this be merely genetic, a soul, or both), through unconditional, perfect and even infinite Truth, Love, Goodness, Justice, Beauty and Being". He considers this to be an objective definition because it relies on publicly accessible data and not private subjective data. The view of society, on what a person is, directly influences views on "human rights". Human rights are also obligations of states and individuals towards all other individual persons. These may be natural human rights (inalienable), or established by law (extrinsic rights). Inalienable rights belong to persons (all beings of human origin) and do not belong to a court or a state. The state cannot usurp the inalienable rights of the unborn, as the state must acknowledge (not declare) the personhood of every human embryo. Any state that does not do this is making corrupt laws and opening the door to denying personhood to all manner of human beings. No court or state can deny that humans are persons, regardless of their size, age, dependency or state of health.

It is Roman Catholic teaching that the soul is infused into the embryo at conception. This view was supported by the appearance of The Virgin Mary to St Bernadette in Lourdes, France, in 1858 when The Virgin said, "I am The Immaculate Conception". From the scientific point of view there is no more appropriate moment than conception, to ascribe personhood to an embryo. At this time the new embryo already has the full genetic and biological information of a new human being. To choose any other time would be false and subjective, like choosing the age that an embryo can be legally killed.

Rights, therefore, prohibit society from removing qualities necessary for individuals to survive as a human being. Views on rights will in turn influence views on "the common good". If the view of the common good is totalitarian, then it can be used to justify killing a significant portion of the human population, as happened under Hitler, Stalin, Chinese Communism etc. Views on what constitutes "the common good", therefore, can be dangerous if not controlled by the concept of inalienable rights. An inalienable right cannot come into conflict with the common good. No state has the right to deny even one person inalienable rights, in order to give a new extrinsic right to others. Any decision, democratic or otherwise, to remove inalienable rights is by its nature corrupt, and will be a corrupt law.

The killing of innocent individuals world-wide, at this time, is probably far worse than it ever was under Hitler, Stalin, or in China, Cambodia, Rwanda etc. all put together. Very few nations or international bodies are speaking out against abortion, or defending the right to life of the unborn. The Catholic Church stands almost alone, against this great evil. Mother Teresa of Calcutta told us that the greatest risk to world peace would come from the killing of the unborn. Peter Kreeft[117,118] has said that, "not to be nice", is now considered to be the great new evil. It is amazing, however, how "nice" people (even some American Presidents) think nothing of promoting the right to choose killing unborn babies, as something acceptable and even good for society. Sin against God is hardly recognized. This loss of the real sense of sin and the sense of God, which is promoted by humanism, liberalism, and the New Age, is the root cause of this moral crisis in society.

The mind-set of humanity is now very remote from the Ten Commandments. This mind-set will not be set right without a lot of suffering. This suffering will come first from the evil in human hearts, encouraged by legions of demons. Suffering will later come directly from God through demands of Divine justice and truth and probably to prevent humanity from self-destruction. Before the direct action of God, there will be the greatest act of God's Mercy, in the form of a World Wide Warning. This Warning will be the last chance given by God, to humanity for change (see chapter 12 for details). Unfortunately, it looks as if we may already be on course for the destruction of the majority of humanity, due to pride, stupidity, obstinacy and evil ways. There is always the hope that we can step back from the abyss. We can hope, but we have to be realistic, and at this time, being realistic, I cannot be confident.

8. Some Evidence for Life after Death

Níl sa bhás ach múchadh na coinnle, toisc go bhfuil an oiche thart agus an maidin tagtha. (Death is only putting out the candle because night has gone and morning has arrived).

Old Irish proverb

Most people regard a discussion on death as morbid and depressing. Is death the end or can we expect to survive in some form after death? This must be a question that every adult confronts at some stage of their lives and would like to have definite evidence, one way or another.

Belief in life after death was a firmly held view by the vast majority in all cultures all through history and it is only relatively recently, that is, within the last two centuries, that some world cultures have begun to seriously question this commonly held belief. A significant majority of people still believe in life after death, but as an atheistic and secular value system continues to gain ground world-wide, so belief in life after death continues to lose ground. Nobody escapes death so establishing the truth should be important. Maybe death should be approached with joyful anticipation!

The new atheists of today are sometimes referred to as reductive materialists. They believe that material reality is the only reality and although they can accept immaterial experiences and entities, they believe that these immaterial entities are a result of material forces, not yet fully understood, such as chemical, electrochemical, magnetic forces, etc. The best form of evidence to present in this kind of secular, atheistic, materialistic culture, therefore, has to be evidence based on science and reason. For a start, however, it is well to remember that atheists generally base their lack of belief in God and life after death on lack of evidence, that is, "evidence not found", from their perspective and this is very different from, "evidence found not to exist". To put it another way, believers have faith based on God and how they perceive God interacting with them personally as a result of answered prayer or some other Divine communication, but the atheist has no similar basis for lack of belief in a God, except a perceived lack of evidence.

It has been said that it is wrong, always, and everywhere for anyone, to believe anything upon insufficient evidence. This also, of course, is an argument that can be used for not believing in God, but there is a difference. The evidence for God is overwhelming and positive but it needs to be recognised and assimilated, whereas the evidence for the non-existence of God is negative and based on invalid conclusions. The philosopher, Bertrand Russell is well known for suggesting that we cannot believe in a teapot which may be circulating in the solar system because our scientific instruments cannot detect it, but here we have to ask, which is the most reasonable: - to believe in God and life after death or to believe in Russell's teapot? I would suggest that belief in God and life after death is reasonable whereas belief in Russell's teapot is not, even if we cannot prove either.

Atheists sometimes argue from the point of view of a philosophical approach called "logical positivism". This proposes that there are only two ways to prove that something is true. The first is by definition and the second is by empirical verification. Even scientific laws, however, cannot be definitively proven to be true in all circumstances. The best we can do is to say is that this is very likely to be true based on previous experiments and results. It can be readily agreed that such an approach **cannot** be used to prove the existence of God and life after death but then neither can it be used to prove the opposite proposition. The bottom line is that atheists may like to promote the view that science and reason convinces them to believe that there is no God and no after life but the truth is that they have no basis for this conclusion. As Dinesh D'Souza[119] puts it, "in the classroom and in culture they pose as apostles of science and rationality, but in truth they sell their product on the basis of smoke and mirrors". Either way, I hope that it is a useful way to begin a discussion on life after death, by realising that proving either proposition is difficult. All we can do is gather some evidence and let those who read and examine this evidence decide how convincing it is for them. The effort in this chapter is to present some of this evidence, through information gleaned from individual experiences, focusing particularly on those who had near-death experiences. Other chapters will give other aspects of evidence which is also supportive of the reality of God and life after death.

Peter Kreeft

In his book, *Because God is Real*,[120] the philosopher Peter Kreeft says that there are dozens of arguments for the existence of God. He details ten of them under the headings:

1. The existence of the universe.
2. The order of the universe.
3. Your mind.
4. Your desire for happiness.
5. Morality.
6. Miracles.
7. The Jews.
8. Saints.
9. Jesus.
10. Pascal's Wager.

The first nine are real because God is real and number 10 is an effort to prove that, regardless of other arguments and evidence, it is always reasonable to believe in God.

Pascal's Wager: Pascal was a French philosopher, scientist and mathematician, from the seventeenth century. He invented the vacuum cleaner and the first known workable computer. He had a great interest in the meaning of life. As atheists cannot be certain that God does not exist he suggested that they should put on a wager, or bet, **for or against God**. He then pointed out that the only reasonable thing for atheists to do was to bet for the existence of God, as betting that God does not exist is very foolish, for the following reason. The bet **for God** is the only bet that will pay dividends. If God exists, then you win God and all that goes with it. If you bet **against God** and God exists you win nothing, and you may finish up in some very uncomfortable place like Hell for all eternity. God offered you eternal life in happiness and you turned it down. If God does **not** exist, then there is nothing to win and nothing to lose. The only possible way to win, therefore, is to bet on the existence of God and the only way to lose is to bet against God. Believing in God is the best bet in the world.

Near-Death Experience

Many books have now been published on the subject of "Near Death Experiences" (NDE). One of the most impressive books which I have read on this subject is based on a large study done by a radiation oncologist, Jeffrey Long, who collected and analysed NDE accounts from many hundreds of individuals from all over the world.[121] He used a validated research method (asking sixteen specific questions) to distinguish experiences that were near-death from those that were not. He pondered how he could make certain that the stories he was collecting were valid. For this he used a well established technique of redundancy questions. This involved asking the same questions in slightly different ways. He became impressed with how consistent the responses were. Although no two of the near-death experiences were identical, there were easily identifiable themes running through them. He listed these under twelve headings, as follows:

1. **Out of body experience:** The spirit left the body and could hear and see events and objects, outside the room where the body was. These events and objects were often later verified by others. 75.4% of his study group had this experience.

2. **Heightened senses:** There was a great feeling of going home at last. A feeling of belonging and completeness with a higher level of consciousness and alertness than in normal every-day life. 74.4% had this experience.

3. **Intense emotions:** Usually these were positive. "All I felt was love, joy, happiness, and every wonderful emotion you could feel all at once. − Total peace, total calm." Unfortunately some of the experiences at this level were frightening. These are not discussed in the book but are discussed in an accompanying web site (http://www.ndeFrorg/evidence). 76.2% admitted to the feeling of incredible peace or pleasantness.

4. **Passing through a tunnel**: Some were aware of passing through a tunnel, very well lit with different colours and the dimensions decreasing as they moved rapidly towards a single bright light. 33.8% described this experience.

5. **Encountering a mystical brilliant light:** The light was described as "like a million suns", but not hurtful. There was a great desire to approach or merge with the light. 64.6% had this experience.

6. **Encountering other beings, mystical or deceased relatives or friends:** "I heard my mother's and my daughter's voices. ....my daughter was grown up (she was only two years when she died)." 57.3% had this experience.

7. **Alteration of time or space:** "I experienced so much in a small length of earthly time." "Both time and space on earth stopped completely". 60.5% had this perception.
8. **Life review:** Some describe seeing every second of their lives come before them. "You will see how you have treated others ... and you will be harder on yourself than anyone, to judge you." 22.2% had this experience.
9. **Encountering unworldly (Heavenly) realms:** The colour, the music and the beauty were "out of this world" and were said to be impossible to describe. 52.2% had this experience.
10. **Encountering special knowledge:** "The whole was the collective knowledge of all. ...When I looked into his eyes all the secrets of the universe were revealed to me. "31.5% had this experience.
11. **Encountering a boundary or barrier:** Some describe reaching a point where a decision has to be made, that is, go back to life or forward into death. One described meeting a friend who had died from cancer two years previously. This friend told her, "This is as far as you can go, - now go back and live your life fully and fearlessly". 31.0 % had this experience.
12. **A decision for voluntary or involuntary return of the spirit to the body:** 58.5% experienced an awareness of a decision for the spirit to rejoin the body. For some this was voluntary, for others it was a command with no option. "Under protest I was sent back. ... Pure love is the best way to describe the being and place that I would be leaving." "She must live. ..she has a son to raise."

He listed his final conclusions under nine headings as follows:

1. The elements in NDE are **consistent and logical**. Although patients are clinically unconscious or dead, the level of

consciousness and alertness during NDE is usually greater than during everyday life.

2. What individuals with NDE hear and see are **realistic and are later verified.**

3. **Normal or supernormal vision** is experienced with NDE by those who were **legally blind or blind from birth.**

4. Typical NDE can occur **during general anaesthesia** when conscious experience should be impossible.

5. Life reviews in NDE include **real experiences** during that particular individual's life, even when events were forgotten.

6. When those with NDE **encounter beings** they were virtually always deceased, **usually deceased relatives.**

7. The NDEs of young **children were similar to adult** experiences.

8. The characteristics of NDE were **remarkably consistent** around the world.

9. It is common for NDE to **lead to long lasting and consistent changes in life** patterns afterwards.

Proof of Heaven

Another book of great interest on the subject of NDE is, *Proof of Heaven – A Neurosurgeon's Journey into the Afterlife,*[122] written in 2012. This is a very personal account written by a well-known neurosurgeon from Duke and Harvard Medical centres in the US. He was on the fence of death secondary to E. coli meningitis, when he had this experience. The life-long researcher on NDE, Dr. Raymond A. Moody, Jr., said of this book, "Dr Eben Alexander's near-death experience is the most astounding I have ever heard in more than four decades of studying this phenomenon.... The extraordinary circumstances of his illness, and his impeccable credentials, make it very hard to formulate a mundane explanation for his case."

Dr Eben had many strange experiences. When he posed questions, he had them answered immediately through a strange thought process. In his words, "these thoughts were solid and immediate – hotter than fire and wetter than water – and as I received them I was able to instantly and effortlessly understand concepts that would have taken me years to fully grasp in my earthly life." He came to understand that there are many universes but that love is at the centre of them all. In his words again, "Evil was present in all the other universes as well, but only in tiniest trace amounts. Evil was necessary because without it free will was impossible, and without free will there could be no growth – no forward movement, no chance to become what God longed for us to be. Horrible and all-powerful as evil sometimes seemed to be in a world like ours, in the larger picture love was overwhelmingly dominant, and it would ultimately be triumphant." Intelligence and knowledge in some of these universes was far more advanced than with humanity on earth. Although he referred to other universes, he presented no evidence to contradict the view that what he may have encountered was just different forms of intelligent life on other planets rather than universes.

Other Books

There are also many other recent books such as, *An Army in Heaven*, written in the US by an intensive care nurse, Kelley Jankowski, based on detailed notes which she recorded from her patients who described details of their NDEs to her. There is a book, *Going Home*, written by a journalist, Colm Keane, on various collected NDE stories from Ireland and there is a book, *My Descent into Death,* written by an atheistic professor of art, Howard Storm, describing a personal NDE which he had in Paris, while waiting many hours for surgery to repair a perforated duodenum.

Both sexes from all ages and all religious backgrounds, as well as atheists, experience NDEs. Colm Keane, in his book, *Going Home*,[123] gives an account of a Gallup poll in the US which suggested that one in every twenty Americans experience an NDE with double that number estimated as having, what is described as, an "out-of-body" experience. Although the majority of these experiences were overwhelmingly positive, a small percentage, (less than 10% in most studies), were very unpleasant. Colm Keane also describes a number of NDE which many famous media personalities had. Among the film stars he noted who had recorded a NDE were, Peter Sellers, Sharon Stone, and Jane Seymour. Elizabeth Taylor also had a NDE during surgery in the 1950's, when she met her former husband Mike Todd, who had previously died in a plane crash. There are also recorded, much rarer experiences, when those who have just died can appear to friends still living. Such an incident was recorded in 1924 by Dan Breen, a guerrilla Irish freedom fighter, when his friend Seán Treacy appeared to him very shortly after his death, which was ten days before he had the official account of his shooting.

In his book, *After Life*,[124] Michael Brown quotes a Gallup survey in the 1980's, which showed that as many as eight million Americans, claimed to have some kind of otherworldly experience associated with a near death event. This book also mentions a study by the American Sociological Association which indicated that more than 80% of the American public believe in life after death.

Marija Pavlovic, a well-known visionary from Medjugorje, (see page 164) once explained that God gives everyone the grace to see and review their own life at the time of death. In the Divine Light, each individual then chooses for themselves what they personally deserve for all eternity. The same visionary described Hell as a big sea of fire where she saw a beautiful young girl being transformed into a horrible animal creature, no longer human.

This was very similar to the vision seen by the children at Fatima, 1917 (see page 125). Michael Brown further quotes some statements of The Virgin Mary in Medjugorje, regarding Hell, such as, "Those who say, 'I do not believe in God' how difficult it will be for them when they approach the Throne of God and hear the voice: 'Enter into Hell,'" and "...Those who are in Hell, no longer have a chance to know a better lot." St Thomas Aquinas said that the reason Jesus spoke so much about Hell, was that to the sinner, talk of Hell is more compelling than talk of Heaven.

Ned Dougherty

One of the best known NDE individual stories "on-line" is that of Ned Dougherty. He was a child of an alcoholic and broken home but by his thirties, he had become a very successful business man. He had his NDE in 1984 after a heart attack, following a fist fight. At the time he was a non-practising Roman Catholic. During the NDE, he met an old friend who had died many years previously in the Vietnam War. They communicated telepathically with thoughts, feelings and emotions. His friend communicated to him that he would not die but that he was being given a special mission for the rest of his life on earth. For this purpose, he was being spiritually rescued from a negative event taking place in his life. He also met many relatives and friends who had died, including a girl from high school, who he did not know was dead. Suddenly he was surrounded by a brilliant light, and he felt suspended before a magnificent presence which radiated love for him beyond description. He believed that he was in the presence of God who began to imbue him with universal knowledge. He then experienced a life review in which he found himself being the sole judge of his own actions, measured against the light of truth and knowledge. Afterwards he found himself with a "being" that he referred to as "The Lady of Light". She revealed to him his own personal future together with general prophecies for the world.

In his book, *Fast Lane to Heaven: Celestial Encounters that Changed my Life*, published in March 2001, he detailed his NDE and the prophecies he got. This was six months before 9/11 and in page 253 of this book is noted, "A major terrorist attack may befall New York or Washington, DC, severely impacting the way we live in the United States." The Lady of Light showed him flash points in the Middle-East and in Italy. He was informed that fanatical religious groups would perform acts of aggression and terrorism and cause major incidents in Middle-East, in Europe, and all over the world. He was also informed that a chain reaction of man-made catastrophic events would start in the Middle-East, spread to Africa and Europe, and later to Russia and China. He was told that China will become a threat to global peace, and that the US government will collapse, due to financial problems and the destruction of military bases secondary to natural disasters. This will leave the country vulnerable to attack by China. He was shown that the axis of the earth's rotation would shift leading to major continental changes, earthquakes and volcanoes and a great darkness secondary to dust and ash in the atmosphere. In another scene, depicted like a black and white movie, he saw large tidal waves and large walls of water hit the east coast of the US. Off Miami beach, he saw a new land mass rise above the ocean.

The Lady of Light finally showed him how beautiful it will be on earth for everybody after these dramatic and traumatic events take place. He was told that the world can now be saved from disasters by prayer only, and not by political leaders. After this life changing event, Ned Dougherty founded a spiritual centre, called *Mission of Angels Foundation (www.fastlanetoHeaven.com)* and he publishes private locutions on a monthly basis since 2005.

Heaven is for Real

One of the best known NDE stories is told in the New York Times Bestseller, *Heaven is for Real,*[125] which was later the subject of a major motion movie of the same name. It concerns the events surrounding a young boy, Colton Burpo, a few months short of four years, who had a perforated appendix with multiple abdominal abscesses. He was operated on in Nebraska, US, in March 2003. He almost died during surgery and, after his eventual complete recovery, he related to his parents how he had left his body during surgery and went on a trip to Heaven. He was able to describe exactly what his parents were doing in separate rooms of the hospital while he was being operated on.

During his trip to Heaven, he met Jesus, John the Baptist, and many relations who were dead. He said that Jesus was the only one in Heaven who wore purple and he had a gold circle on his head. His relations told him many stories about events that had happened long before he was born. He met his great grandfather who had died in a car accident in 1976, that is, twenty three years before he was born. What really convinced his parents that he was telling the truth was when he announced that he met a little girl, without a name, in Heaven who said that she was his sister and could not stop hugging him. His mom had lost a baby in early pregnancy before he was born, and there was no way that he could have known about this. His parents did not know that this baby was female. One of the many interesting comments this young boy said to his dad was in 2006, when he was then seven years old: - "Dad, did you know that there's going to be a war? ... And dad, I watched you. You have to fight too."

Tenderly Loved

One of the most interesting books, that I have read in recent years, had the title *Tenderly – Loved*.[126] It concerned a revelation to a nuclear physicist, from South America, regarding what those of us who are lucky enough to get to Heaven, can expect. This revelation came to him after many years of prayer, with the special request of getting some understanding of Heaven. A manifestation, to this elderly gentleman, took the form of being visited by a female acquaintance from his youth, while he was relaxing, having coffee and smoking a cigarette. She was then in Heaven and described herself as a very inferior blessed. She was sent to him by God as an answer to his persistent prayer. A comment made on the book, by Oscar A. Romero, Archbishop of San Salvador, El Salvador, may be an appropriate way to begin a brief account of the story:

"This work takes on a special interest, because it invites everyone to walk the road of the Kingdom, with the consequential vision of the consummation. This is equivalent to living life, with the hope which impresses transcendental value on all our acts."

He described the lady who came to visit as about twenty years old, of exquisite beauty, dressed in the accustomed garb of the middle class, with no jewellery. She spoke as if she knew him well, and announced that she was from the city of San Luis Potosi. She reminded him that she sang a particular song for him which he liked very much a long time ago when he was only eight years old. All this puzzled him very much and even more so, when she said that the incident was so many years ago.

It is impossible in this very short account to cover the many extraordinary insights of existence in Heaven which this book tries to convey. Of necessity therefore, I restrict accounts to a few brief points which may be of particular interest. The author asked his Heavenly visitor the following questions:

Why is the love of charity of such value? A paraphrase of the answer was that, giving alms out of compassion, fear, humanism, or philanthropy is not as good as doing it with the motive of pleasing God and showing God love, which is true charity. When human love is bound with Divine love, it is no longer man who acts, but God. It is then God who gives man the fervour, the efficacy and the triumph.

Another question was: It is said that true love is reciprocal. Describe God's love for us? The answer was: "The Creator is – and listen well – profoundly in Love with each of his adopted human children. He does not love globally, the entire human race, as a farmer cares for his crop. No, He loves each one of us with a Supreme Love which infinitely surpasses the greatest created love. Our Lord Loves you singularly, with vehemence and energy, and with ineffable loving need, with immense affection, with indescribable tenderness and with thousands of other qualities, which are explicable neither on the earth nor in Heaven."

The immediate question that comes to mind after reading this account of God's love for us is, why would a God, who loves each person so much ever send a soul to a Hell of suffering for eternity? The explanation given for this is that, God does not want it, but His justice demands it. God is infinitely good and therefore an offence against God carries with it an infinite quality of evil. The sacrifice of Jesus (who is infinite) was required to expiate this infinite evil as well as demonstrating the infinite love God has for us. If a soul persists in rejecting God's love and persists in seriously offending God without repenting (having sorrow for their sins – see Pascal's Wager above), then the consequences for the soul after death can be horrific.

A further question was: Are humans ever actually alone? The answer was: No mortal is ever completely alone. In the first place, God is always there beside them. Then there are angels, and blessed or glorified humans also present. The more humble and charitable the human person is, then the greater the number of the blessed who will be observing them, so that they can give praise and glory to God when these individuals do good deeds. "You can't imagine how quickly news travels in Heaven. The most insignificant traveller, who is a faithful Christian, begins to be famous in the glory."

The Heavenly visitor said that creation is infinite and she described a fifth dimension, which she called *"created eternity"*. Created eternity allows us all to participate in absolute eternity which is of God alone. Created eternity starts with us on earth and does not begin after death. "You don't exactly remember, she added, what you did ten years ago today. Nonetheless, it has not only been registered as a recording but it remains alive in the prodigious archive of created eternity." History, therefore, lives endlessly in created eternity. Created eternity is not significant for the natural sciences. It is very important in religion, however, as it shows us the decisive importance of every act and circumstance of how we live our lives on earth. Every act of existence is transcendental and all acts continue in the fifth dimension. Moral evil is the only thing that can be annihilated from creation. The redemptive power of Jesus is very great. Individual human nature is restored physically, morally, and spiritually. Forgiven sin will, therefore, be completely deleted or annihilated from created eternity. Afterwards, in Heaven, these annihilated space times will be missed, which should have been filled with love of charity, which is necessary in order to better enjoy *accidental glory*. In eternity, we will be able to re-visit each act of kindness that we did at any time, during our earthly life. Avoidance of serious sin, repenting of sin and getting forgiveness is, therefore, of crucial importance for the after-life.

Finally, the Heavenly visitor described herself as a very inferior blessed, who had her home near one of the very distant stars. Travel was no problem, but she could only be in four places at the same time. The superior blessed, she said, could be in many, many places at the same time. This was only one of extra special powers and graces that they were allowed. This, of course, would make perfect sense, for the teaching of Catholic theology and the power of prayerful intercession to the saints. If one billion people pray to The Virgin Mary, she can be there beside each single one of them, to listen to their requests and intercede to God for help for them. It should, perhaps, also encourage us not only to pray for the souls of our own deceased relatives but also to ask them for their prayers of intercession for us. If they are in Heaven (or in Purgatory), and even if they can only be in a few places at the same time, it is unlikely that large numbers of people will be praying to them for requests.

Purgatory is for real also

Purgatory is a well-established Christian doctrine. Various Church Councils formulated the Catholic doctrine of purgatory and the Council of Trent (1545–1562) dogmatised what had been believed for a long time. The new Catechism of the Catholic Church confirms this doctrine. The Reformers such as Luther and Calvin, rejected the doctrine of purgatory. Those who die without any imperfections are very few and thus the vast majority of souls, who are lucky enough not to be condemned to Hell, need purification before entering Heaven. Like Heaven and Hell, Purgatory is also known to have several levels. According to the teachings and descriptions from many saints, who visited Hell and purgatory, while still alive, they explain that at the particular judgment, immediately after death, the soul becomes clearly aware of its imperfections and gravitates to the *appropriate place or sate for purgation and purification.*

It has also been explained to us through several saints and seers that the lower levels of Purgatory are close to Hell and souls can spend many years there, being purified, before eventually getting to Heaven. Sr Lucia, one of the seers in Fatima (see page 125), asked The Virgin Mary, during her apparitions in 1917, about two young friends who had died. She was told that one was in Heaven and that the other would be in Purgatory until the end of the world. The fires of Purgatory and Hell are said to be the same. The essential difference is that the soul in Purgatory, despite its great suffering, is also filled with a joy beyond words as it experiences the love of God and knows that it will soon be united with God.

There are numerous accounts of individuals who have died and have come back and appeared to the living, pleading for prayers, so that they could be released from the suffering of Purgatory. Fr Joseph Pius Martin who was a personal caretaker of the Capuchin, St Padre Pio, (1887 – 1968, - see page 102), related how this famous friar had told him that more souls of the dead came up the road to their monastery, seeking help, than souls of the living and that amounted to very large numbers. Padre Pio was known to have regularly communicated with the dead, who were allowed to come and ask for his help. In contrast souls coming back from Hell, although well described, are much less common. Souls from Hell usually manifest to instruct their friends to stop praying for them as they have now no hope. One often quoted example of a soul coming back from Hell, both in audio and written accounts, concerns a young lady from Munich, who died in a car accident. She told her former friend to stop praying for her. She described how she had trampled many graces underfoot from her childhood up to her final NO to God on the morning of her accident. She then described her soul going down like a sulphuric yellow shadow to the abode of eternal torment.

There is a small museum of Purgatory attached to the church of The Sacred Heart of Suffrage, in Rome, where there are ten specimens of relics exhibited, illustrating various burn marks imprinted on paper, cloth and wood, by souls appearing from Purgatory, requesting prayer to relieve their torment. These exhibits are described in some detail in the book, *Hungry Souls*,[127] and are listed as follows:

1. Image of the face of an anguished soul on the wall behind the altar.
2. A prayer book with three burned finger marks made on March 5th 1871 by a lady called Palmira who died December 28th 1870. She was asking for Masses to be said by her brother, who was a priest, for her.
3. Burn marks of five fingers on a nightcap of Louis Sénéchal, left by the ghost of his wife Louise, who had died two years previously, requesting Masses.
4. Copy of burn marks left by a Benedictine choir sister on an apron and on a piece of linen, in a German monastery, in 1696. She had died of the plague in 1637 and, therefore, had been in purgatory at that stage for 59 years.
5. Copy of a burned-in hand print on the sleeve of the nightshirt of Joseph Leleux, by his mother who had died 27 years previously, requesting Masses. As a result, Joseph converted and started a congregation for pious lay people.
6. A burned imprint of a forefinger on the pillow of a Poor Clare sister, in Bastia, Italy, June 5th, 1894. The imprint was from Sister Maria of the convent, who had died that morning. She had suffered terribly from tuberculosis for two years before her death and although she was very good and pious, she was known to be very impatient. She informed her friend that she was in Purgatory because of her impatience and not accepting God's will.
7. Four burn marks left by the ghost of Father Panzini, an abbot from Mantua, Italy, on the eve of All Soul's Day, November 1st, 1731. He came to Mother Isabella, a Poor Clare nun and left an imprint of his left hand and the sign of the cross, deeply burned into the wood on top of her work table. The left hand imprint was also

seen on paper, as well as on the sleeve of sister's clothes. The imprint burned her clothes completely through and the inner garment was blood stained.

8. Burned–in hand impression on a copy of the book, *The Imitation of Christ,* left by the mother-in-law of Marguérite Demmerlé, from Metz, France, in 1815. She had died 30 years previously and was requesting Masses. It is of interest that the visiting soul did not speak until asked what she wanted. Typically, apparently souls from Purgatory, wait in humility, hoping that their host will ask for their request and usually will not speak until this request is made. After two Masses she came back to inform her daughter-in-law that she was being released from Purgatory.

9. Burned finger marks on pages of the prayer book of Georg Schitz, made by the ghost of his brother, Joseph, on December 21st, 1838, in Lorraine, France. He was requesting prayers and the burn marks, on the various pages of the prayer book, seem to specifically indicate prayers for the dead.

10. Copy of a ten lire bank note. 30 of these notes were left in a monastery in Montefalco, Italy, between August and November, 1919, by the ghost of a priest, who requested that these notes be used as stipends for Masses.

There are many other examples of burned imprints of hands recorded, in different parts of the world, produced by the ghosts of souls seeking prayers so that they could be released from Purgatory. One of the best known examples is from a Franciscan nun, at Foligno, Italy, on November 3rd, 1859. A deceased sister returned after death to appeal for prayers and left a famous burned hand imprint on the door of the linen room. It so happened that this sister had a very unusual hand and the bishop gave permission to have her body exhumed, as she had only recently died. Her hand was found to fit exactly the burned imprint on the door, which helped confirm the validity of the story. The fact that many of these burned hand images (above average) are associated with priests and religious sisters may be due to the fact that these souls are particularly permitted to come back and seek help, or that the records and specimens are better stored and preserved.

Howard Storm's Descent into Death: This is now one of the best publicised accounts of a near death experience, from somebody who felt that he was on the way to Hell. The story has been detailed in a movie and in a book.[128] Howard Storm was an American professor of art for twenty years at Northern Kentucky University. He was an atheist but after his NDE, he studied Christianity, changed his life and became a Protestant pastor in The United Church of Christ.

Before his NDE, Howard had only contempt for religious people who he thought believed in fairy tales because "they couldn't cope with the harsh reality of life." He did not believe in life after death. This was all to change very rapidly, while on tour with his wife, Beverly, and some art students, in Paris.

He had a sudden very severe pain in his abdomen which was diagnosed as a perforated duodenum. He was rushed to hospital but later collapsed unconscious on a hospital bed, while waiting for an operation. He next found himself standing between two beds, "more alert, more aware, and more alive than I had ever felt in my entire life." He tried to communicate with those around but nobody responded. This filled him with anger, fear and confusion.

He heard voices in the corridor calling him, in English, which was odd as nobody in the hospital spoke English. They offered to help, so he went with them along a dark corridor even though he could not see them clearly. They walked a long way but as they went they got more and more aggressive towards him, especially when he asked questions or tried to stop moving. It was completely dark now, but he knew that there was a large number of male and females pushing him onwards. They next began to swarm over him, to bite him and tear at his skin. He described them as being "stripped of every impulse of compassion". He suddenly heard a voice three times saying, "Pray to God". He resisted at first, but then noticed as he began to make efforts to pray that it had two effects. Firstly, they became more furious and secondly they began to retreat. He remembered a song from his childhood days and began to shout at the top of his voice, "Jesus save me, Jesus save me."

He then noticed a pin point light in the distance which was moving towards him. Eventually a loving brilliant luminous figure appeared before him, embraced him and healed his torn flesh. The ecstasy swept away the agony. He became aware of indescribable wonderful goodness, power, knowledge and love. He said, "I cried the tears of a lifetime", tears of hopelessness, shame and joy. "I felt like garbage, filthy rags, before the Holy One". Jesus then called angels and saints to him who answered every question he could think of. He asked why God does not write "Love God" on the sky to get peoples' attention. He was told that God does not demand or compel us to love. That defeats the very nature of love. Love must be a choice. He was taken through a complete review of his life and then told that he must return to the world.

He recovered somewhat and went back to the US. He spent many more weeks in hospital, on the critical list most of the time. During that time he was visited, when he was wide awake, by an angel who informed him that he would recover and that God was looking after him. He eventually did recover completely and changed his life.

Alfred Nobel: Alfred Nobel, of Nobel-prize fame, had a life changing NDE with a difference. He read his own obituary which had been printed prematurely in a newspaper. He was upset that he would be remembered only as the "Dynamite King" for having discovered this explosive. His main aim in life had been to help and unite people for the betterment of humanity, rather than be a destructive force or invent ways of blowing up parts of the world. He was upset that his efforts at promoting goodwill and peace were not recognized in his premature obituary. It was at that stage that he decided to try to correct the view others had of him. He eventually left most of his large fortune, in trust, for perpetual awards to be given after his death, for outstanding achievements in physics, chemistry, medicine, literature, and peace. Seeing ourselves as other see us, no doubt, could be a blessing for many of us. Seeing ourselves as God sees us is invariably life changing.

A word of Caution on NDE: It can be difficult to discern in some situations between experiences that are a product of nature, from a body that is on the brink of death, from those that are truly a spiritual experience of an existence beyond the grave. So called "out of body experiences" can be naturally induced. So called, "Astral Travel", when the spirit leaves the body, can also be practised by individuals while alive and healthy, but there are many dangers associated with this, particularly and especially demonic attachments. A man, who practised astral travel is described in Colm Keane's book,[123] but he sensibly gave it up when he began to appreciate the great dangers. Astral travel is, however, some evidence for a spirit life, outside of the body. In the case of near death experiences, knowledge of articles, events, and discussions outside of a dying person's immediate environment is also good evidence for the spirit (soul) leaving the body.

The experience reported in the majority of near death experiences is positive with only approximately 15% reporting a "Hell" experience. These impressions from NDE should be compared to messages given by The Virgin Mary and recorded by a number of visionaries in recent years, which say that, after death, the majority of souls go to Purgatory, the next largest number go directly to Hell, and only very few go straight to Heaven. These figures are supported, to some extent, by a recent account from a regular US visionary (with some approval from the local Bishop), under the title, "Message of Merciful Love". This recent message said that approximately 85% of those who are now dying are in a state of disgrace, rather than in a state of grace, and are not fit to meet God.

The Final Word

Everybody should read some of the many good books now being published on NDE. Not alone will your reading confirm the need to act justly, love tenderly and walk humbly with your God but it will also take away the fear of death. The more we can all prepare properly for death, then the more it should become a joyful expectation. It is appropriate that the last word on NDE should go to St Thomas Aquinas. This lumbering, overweight, gentle, shy man, who was dubbed by his classmates, "the dumb ox" and whose genius, as G. K. Chesterton said, has bellowed down through the centuries, seems to have had some form of NDE late in his life. He said, "I can write no more. I have seen things which make all my writings like straw."

9. Reality, Relativity and Absolute Simplicity

I cannot believe that God would choose to play dice with the Universe.
Albert Einstein

No discussion on the subject matter of this book would be complete without some consideration of the great contribution made by science and mathematics to our understanding of truth and reality. When deciding to include this chapter, however, I had to recognize that the subjects of science and mathematics can be a complete turn off for some. This was one of the principal reasons for not locating this chapter earlier in the book. If you find some aspects of this chapter boring, unrewarding, or difficult, therefore, I suggest that you skip those bits and move on. For those who are not already familiar with some of the information described below, however, I hope that it will provide a new exciting appreciation and understanding of reality.

It is sometimes suggested that science and religion have no common ground. While I agree that the study of many aspects of science and religion are completely separate, nevertheless, science and religion can mutually contribute to our understanding of some observations and events. This should already be obvious from previous chapters. There is a lot to be gained from building links across the boundaries of all branches of knowledge, which after all are no more than artificial divisions of reality made by our small minds. For this reason, a small amount of philosophy and metaphysics have also been included in this chapter as a way of identifying some common areas of interest, and as a way of trying to help bridge the gap between science and religion.

Reality must be independent of ourselves and of our ability to perceive it. Reality is discovered in truth. Having the knowledge of well established scientific facts is a good basis for appreciating truth and reality. It is important to realise, however, that scientific fact is not the only basis for truth. A truth promoted in science can never be opposed to a truth promoted in religion. If this does happen then we can be certain that at least one side is in error. In the end the beliefs of religion and science must all meet in the splendour of truth (Veritatis Splendor).

The Complexity of it All

The more science investigates and discovers the world around us and the Heavens above us, the more we are led to an understanding of the complexity of it all. Mathematics is a noble subject and mathematicians have contributed greatly to our understanding of this complexity. Numbers can be confusing, as we all know. When we start talking about billions it can be very hard to conceptualize. When I first started to do sums, a billion was one million, million. This was an English billion. Now we all refer to billions as a measly one thousand million or the American billion. Bacteria can divide and produce two from one in about twenty to thirty minutes in a favourable growth environment. Billions of bacteria can be produced from one single organism in less than twenty four hours. When we hear of disinfectants killing 99% or 99.99% of germs in dirty toilets or floors, it becomes rather meaningless in terms of dealing with small particles of dirt or faeces, which can have more than ten billion bacteria per gram. This will still leave well in excess of one million bacteria per gram, after disinfection, if we apply the rules of the advertising. This is also the reason why the maths can tell us that toilets and floors need proper cleaning, rather than disinfecting. This is why soap and water, in most situations, is the first and best disinfectant.

When in college, I used to visit the roulette tables on occasions. I had a system for making money. I used to wait for three reds or three blacks and then start betting on the opposite colour. I doubled the bet if I lost, until I won and then started all over again. I had, of course, to put a limit to my doubling. At the time I was not aware of breaking any rules and nobody seemed to notice my method. I learned some patience and made roughly two pounds per hour profit, when there was no minimum wage and the average hourly rate was a lot lower. Looking back, the idea of waiting for three of the one colour was simplistic and made no mathematical sense. On the other hand, the more I think about this the more it fascinates me. One of my long term dreams now is to have a mathematician prove that nothing is random, or in other words that three blacks in a row, may have some influence on the next throw of the dice. To what extent are "random" events influenced, if at all, by other events in time or by what has gone before? The difficulty mathematicians have producing truly random numbers seems to suggest that maybe nothing is random. In those early college years, I was also not aware of the significance of God playing dice with the universe. I was later to discover this, when I read a little about the quantum theory (see below).

Molecules and Atoms

Avogadro's number, 6×10^{23} (six with twenty three zeros after it), is well known in basic chemistry. It is the number of molecules in one mole (atomic weight in grams: hydrogen = 1, carbon = 12 etc.) of any substance. It is difficult to get a concept of the fact that just 12 grams of carbon contains this astronomical number of molecules. As 22.4 litres of any gas also represents a mole, this volume of the gases, in the air we breathe, will also have the Avogadro number of molecules. In order to get some idea of how small molecules are it was suggested to me once that if small round sweets (smarties, m&m etc.) represented molecules, then the Avogadro number would cover the whole of western Europe up to approximately one kilometre high, with these sweets.

Molecules are made up of atoms, with one or more types, depending on whether the molecule is made of a single element or a mixture of elements. Where there is more than one element involved then the ratio and total number of atoms in each molecule will determine the chemical structure and characteristics of that substance. The structure of atoms has gradually been discovered over the last century. The centre is composed of protons with a positive charge and neutrons with no charge. In orbit around this centre are electrons with a negative charge equal to the proton positive charge. Electrons have a mass of approximately 1/2000 fraction of protons or neutrons. These electrons orbit the nucleus in various levels or "sHells" in a complex system of orbit shapes and spins, the basics of which can be studied from simple chemistry or physics textbooks.

In the early 1970's it was recognized that **protons and neutrons can decay into smaller particles known as quarks** (a name which came from James Joyces' book, Finnegan's Wake). There are six recognized flavours" of quarks and each flavour comes in one of three "colours" namely, red, green or blue. The colours are not real colours, of course, and are used as labels. The six flavours are referred to as **up, down, bottom, top, charmed**, and **strange**. A proton contains two **up** quarks and one **down**, and a neutron contains two **down** and one **up**.

When high energy particles collide, some of the energy can be converted into mass in the form of a wide variety of particles. These particles were eventually classified into two families known as **Leptons and Hadrons**. Leptons are considered to be elementary particles, that is, not composed of smaller particles. Six different leptons with their anti-particles have been described. **Hadrons are divided into Baryons and Mesons.** Mesons have masses between electrons and protons while baryons are heavier particles. Mesons are composed of a quark and an anti-quark while baryons consist of either three quarks or three anti-quarks. Over one hundred different types of baryons and mesons have been described.

Relativity and Quantum mechanics

The simplest view of the universe is that it is composed of mass-energy and space-time. The interaction of this mass-energy with space-time is carefully regulated by cosmological constants, which are precise numerical values, controlling the physical forces which operate within the universe. Einstein's now famous equation $E = mc^2$ illustrates the relation between mass and energy, where E is energy, m is mass and c is the speed of light (300,000 km / second). The quantity of energy contained in a small amount of mass is therefore extremely large and this is the basis of nuclear power. Finding a completely safe way to release and harness this energy from mass must therefore be one of the great dreams for future humanity as it would solve all our energy problems.

When I was a young student I read a book on Relativity by Albert Einstein.[129] He described dropping a stone from the window of a moving train and posed the question: does it drop straight down or in a curve? The answer was that it dropped both ways. Relative to the train it was straight down and relative to an observer on the embankment it dropped in a curve shaped fall. That was my first lesson on relativity. It was not long before I realised that appreciating, both the maths and the implications of the theory of relativity, were completely beyond me. I had to be satisfied with understanding some of the basics, which were fascinating enough.

Einstein was one of the greatest and best known among a number of great physicists who created a revolution in the subject of theoretical physics in the 20th century. Einstein changed our perception of reality with his theory of special relativity in 1905 and his theory of general relativity in 1915.

Special relativity is a theory on the structure of space-time. Some of the implications are:

    1) Two events which look simultaneous to two observers will not appear simultaneous if the observers are moving with respect to each other.

    2) There is a relation between mass and energy - ($E = mc^2$).

General relativity is a theory of gravitation. Some of the implications are:

    1) Orbits behave in a way not expected by Newton's theory of gravity.

    2) The universe is expanding.

Isaac Newton was the principal scientist of the 17th century, who was responsible for working out the laws of motion. These laws are based on the forces, acceleration, and momentum that control the way physical bodies move and form the basis of what is called classical mechanics. These laws helped with the development of machines in the 18th and 19th century and with space exploration in the 20th century. Towards the end of the 19th century, however, physicists began to recognize that Newton's laws of motion would not work when it came to the motion of very small particles at the atomic and sub atomic levels. If the rules of classical mechanics were applied to atoms, the electrons would spiral rapidly towards the nucleus and all matter would end up in a very dense mass - or mess.

This created a lot of confusion, especially when trying to understand the nature of light. Newton had said that light was composed of particles. In the 19th century Thomas Young did a famous experiment by shining light through a sheet with two slits (double slit experiment) and he was able to show an "interference" pattern with light, which was typical of waves, as one might see from water pouring through two outlets in a dam. In 1900 Max Planck suggested that light, Xrays, and other waves could only be emitted in small packets which he called "quanta". Furthermore, he suggested that each quantum had energy which varied with the frequency of the waves. A few years later, Einstein explained how ultra violet light shining on a negatively charged metal sheet could cause it to lose its charge, whereas visible light would not. The explanation given was that packets of light (referred to as photons), would dislodge electrons from the metal sheets. Visible light has less energy, due to a longer wavelength than UV light, and this was not sufficient to dislodge the electrons

In 1906 J. J. Thomson won the Nobel Prize for demonstrating that the electron was an elementary particle and thirty years later his son G. Thomson (with others) was awarded the same prize for showing that electrons behaved as a wave.

The solution to the confusion eventually came with **the theory of quantum mechanics** which was proposed by physicists such as Heisenberg, Dirac, Schrodinger, and a French prince, Louis de Broglie. The final conclusion was to recognize that quantum objects sometimes behave like a wave and sometimes like a particle. This theory simply describes how nature works, but it does not explain why nature works in this way, which for now is a great physical and mathematical mystery. Erwin Schrodinger, who was an Austrian physicist working in Germany, had decided to leave physics and become a philosopher after World War I. Events, fortunately, kept him in physics and he later discovered the famous equation (now named after him) which describes how quantum probability waves move. When Hitler came to power, Schrodinger left Germany and became professor of physics in Dublin, Ireland. Nobody can really understand quantum mechanics but it is now generally agreed that this theory is very successful in making predictions, with great diversity, and with major implications for the development of technology in the future. The development of the modern electronic industry, which is based on semiconductors, transistors, and integrated circuits, has all been due to the use of quantum mechanics. Quantum mechanics differs from classical mechanics in that it does not predict a definite result or outcome, but rather **the probability of a certain outcome.** The physicist Paul Davies has said, "The 19th century was known as the machine age, the 20th century will go down in history as the information age. **I believe the 21st century will be the quantum age.**"

Force Particles

Quantum mechanics indicates that sub-atomic particles move as waves. The shorter the wave length, the more energy in the particle. This energy is measured in electron volts (eV), that is, the energy that an electron gets from an electric field of one volt. Every force in the universe, including gravity, can now be looked at in terms of particles. These various particles are described as having a "spin" value, depending on how much they need to be rotated before the shape looks the same again. A spin of 0 shape will always look the same, a spin of 1 will need 360 degrees (like an arrow head), a spin of two will need 180 degree turn (like a double arrow head) etc. Some particles are described as having a spin of ½ , in other words two 360 degree turns are required before returning to their original appearance.

All particles are divided into two major classes. These are, matter particles (those with spin ½), and other particles with other spins values. The non-matter particles account for the forces that arise between matter particles. The matter particles obey what is called Pauli's exclusion principle. This says that two similar particles can never exist in the same state, that is, both cannot be together in the same position with the same velocity at the same time. Physicists believe that if the world had been created without this exclusion principle, then all matter would collapse in on itself, into a very dense mass. The electron spin of ½ was explained by Paul Dirac (a mathematician from Cambridge, UK.), in 1928, when he predicted the need for an anti-electron, now known as a positron (discovered 1932). It is now understood that all particles have antiparticles.

Force particles are referred to as virtual particles, as they are very difficult to detect. They are grouped into four different categories depending on the force that they carry.

(i) The first category is the gravitational force. This is by far the weakest of all the forces. It is universal in that every particle feels the force of gravity. It works over very long distances and it is always attractive. It operates through a particle known as a graviton with spin 2. The exchange of gravitons between the earth and the sun makes the earth orbit the sun.

(ii) The second category is the electromagnetic force. This acts between electrically charged particles like electrons but not with non-charged particles such as gravitons. The strength of this force between electrons is about 1040 times the gravity force between them. The electromagnetic attraction between the negatively charged electrons and the positive protons causes the electrons to orbit the nucleus of the atoms.

(iii) The third category is the weak nuclear force responsible for radioactivity and acting on all matter particles, with spin ½. In addition to the photon, there are three other particles, known as massive vector bosons called W+, W-, and Z0, that carry this force. Boson particles are believed to be exchanged when forces occur.

(iv) The final category is the strong nuclear force, which binds the quarks in the protons and neutrons together. The particle carrying this force is called a gluon.

The Higgs Boson

Peter Higgs is well known for a theory which he developed while walking in the Scottish Highlands, during the 1960s. He proposed that particles get mass from interacting with empty space, which (contrary to what was expected), he suggested, contains a very low energy field, now referred to as the "Higgs Field". Coincidentally, others concurred with his mathematical deductions, and efforts to demonstrate this Higgs field had been in the planning stages for a long time. This was best done indirectly, by detecting the particle associated with this field, known as the "Higgs Boson" (quantum theory suggests that all energy fields must have a particle associated with them). The Higgs Boson is sometimes referred to as "The God Particle", a name given it by the physicist, Leon Lederman, in 1993, perhaps to identify it as the key particle linking energy to mass.

The Higgs Boson is difficult to detect due to its massive size compared to the other particles, with the result that enormous amounts of energy are required to produce it. The CERN European particle accelerator, known as the Large Hadron Collider (LHC), constructed at enormous expense, was eventually switched on for the first time in September 2008, to begin long awaited experiments for the detection of this illusive Higgs Boson. On March 14th 2013, the scientists at CERN confirmed that they had found the Higgs Boson. The existence of the Higgs Field was the last unverified part of the Standard Model in particle physics and thus has been a major breakthrough for the subject of particle physics.

A fifth force: Recently a new subatomic particle has been described which may represent the discovery of a new fundamental force of nature after many decades of recognizing only the four forces described above. If confirmed, it represents another major step towards the unification of forces and a better understanding of dark matter. It is estimated that dark matter makes up about 85% of the mass of the universe. In 2015 a team of physicists from the Hungarian Academy of Sciences were searching for "dark photons" and noticed a radioactive decay anomaly, which pointed towards the existence of a particle approximately 30 times heavier than an electron. A group of workers from the University of California, Irvine (UCI) have followed up on this work and have suggested that, instead of being a dark photon, this particle may be what they called a "protophobic X boson." Normal electric forces act on electrons and protons but this new particle only interacts with electrons and neutrons. Further experiments will hopefully confirm this particle.

Heisenberg Uncertainty

One of the most significant elements to arise from the quantum theory is referred to as the **Heisenberg Uncertainty Principle**, for which Werner Heisenberg was awarded the Nobel Prize in 1932. Heisenberg showed that the uncertainty in the position of particles, multiplied by the uncertainty of the velocity, multiplied by the mass of the particle can never be smaller than a certain quantity, which is known as Planck's constant. Albert Einstein was not happy with this uncertainty and neither were those who believed in fate or determinism, as they saw this theory as a threat. The physical universe no longer existed in a way that could be determined exactly but rather as a collection of probabilities or potentials. It was about this that Einstein made his famous statement: "I cannot believe that God would choose to play dice with the universe". Niels Bohr (the physicist, who was the director of the Institute in Copenhagen, where Heisenberg worked) was said to have responded: "Einstein, don't tell God what to do." This uncertainty principle has profound implications for the way we view reality, not just in physics and mathematics, but also in philosophy and theology. The present position is that many famous theoretical physicists now believe that, whereas many philosophical ideas may be logically consistent with quantum mechanics, pure materialism is not. This is epitomized in the statement of the late Sir Rudolf Peierls (a great theoretical physicist), who said that you cannot describe the whole function of the human person, such as knowledge and consciousness, in terms of physics as there is still something missing.[130] Quantum theory made physicists realise that even complete knowledge of a physical system was still not enough to predict everything about its future behaviour. The great physical argument therefore in favour of scientific determinism (a theory which said that as science could measure accurately the position and velocity of particles, that it could predict how bodies could behave in the future) and against free will, was becoming obsolete. This was appreciated as one of the implications of quantum theory from very early on. Quantum theory and in particular the Heisenberg Uncertainty Principle began to lead theoretical physics towards philosophy and theology and help bridge the gap between science and religion.

Quantum Gravity

The universe can now only be described by scientists in terms of two theories, known to be inconsistent, namely the theory of general relativity, and the theory of quantum mechanics. The great search at the moment is in trying to find an explanation for the inconsistency of these two theories or to unify them into one theory. As it stands, both cannot be correct in all situations. Einstein spent the last thirty years of his life trying to find a theory that would unify electromagnetism and gravity. He had already described gravity in terms of general relativity and had shown that there was no such thing as absolute space and time but quantum mechanics posed a problem for him. Physicists now realise that to succeed in unifying the four forces of nature, they must combine general relativity with quantum mechanics. Both of these theories agree with Newton's physics within the usual everyday scale of measurement. They do not agree with Newtonian physics, at the extremes as in subatomic distances, where quantum mechanics rules, or at very large distances or large objects, where general relativity rules. The search for a theory to unify all four natural forces, often referred to as a quantum gravity theory, is now pursued by physicists from the two different aspects or starting points of quantum mechanics and general relativity. Of the two, the quantum approach is by far the most popular. Just as matter is made up of very small elementary particles, so quantum gravity workers now believe that space and time are also composed of irreducible lumps. The scale of measurement of these irreducible lumps of space, distance, energy, etc. is known as the Planck scale.

The size of the smallest space (quantum volume) and smallest time (quantum time unit) has been described by Jim Al-Khalili, in his excellent book, Quantum.[131] Firstly, there are more atoms in a single glass of water than there are glasses of water in all the oceans of the world. Secondly, many billions of atomic nuclei can fit into a single atom (that is, most of the atom is taken up by the space between the nucleus and the circulating electrons). Finally, an atomic nucleus can accommodate more quantum volumes than there are cubic metres in our galaxy (10^{62}), which is eighty thousand light years across. The smallest space therefore is, as they say in Ireland, fierce small altogether! Similarly the quantum unit of time is very, very short. There are a lot more quanta of time in a single second (10^{43}) than there are seconds, since the universe began – over 14 billion years ago.

The physicists, who are trying to unify the four forces of the universe, building on quantum mechanics, only need to incorporate gravity into their quantum theory. The first major effort made was to suggest that the fundamental particles are tiny vibrating strings with different frequencies. By 1990, the string theory had been altered and was then referred to as the superstring theory. There were five different versions of this superstring theory. The mathematics of the theory was so complex, that some believed that the mathematical methods needed to solve the equations, had not been invented. In 1995 a new theory was proposed known as the membrane or M theory. This proposed a method for unifying the different superstring theories and suggested that the fundamental entities of our universe are composed of two dimensional membranes, with occasional three dimensional blobs. Nobody knows the mathematical equations for this theory and thus some refer to it as the Mystery theory. The M theory predicts that we live in an eleven dimensional space-time universe. Six or seven dimensions of the space are curled up very small within the strings and membranes.

A smaller group of workers are trying to unite the four forces of nature by starting with general relativity. The theory that has emerged from this group is referred to as the "loop quantum theory", but this seems at the moment to be making little progress. Only time will tell if the M theory holds the solution to the problem of uniting these forces of nature.

Science and Religion

When I was a young secondary school student, I remember, on one occasion reading in my apologetics book (these have now gone out of fashion), that we can get to know God from, "The existence, order, complexity, and beauty of creation". This seemed, at the time, to be a simple enough statement and it was years later that I began to understand, that I could spend the rest of my life trying to plumb the depths of these words. The first part of this chapter has attempted to look at some of the complexity and order of matter. Beauty is subjective to a large extent and, like other intangibles, it is not usually subjected to a scientific method of measurement. The rest of this chapter will look at "how and why we exist" and the religious implications of this. This will be done especially with respect to what scientific and mathematical evidence suggests regarding the need for God or a creator.

There is a common myth, that science and religion are in a contest to the death and eventually only one will survive. This is a false view and it is important to recognize that the scientific method cannot be used to either prove or disprove the existence of God. In the first place, a creator would not be limited to the laws of nature.

There is also another myth, which says that if something cannot be proven by the scientific method, then it cannot be accepted as true. The famous scientist, Anthony Flew, who relatively recently became a believer in God, identified three "proofs" that convinced him of the reality of a creator. These were the existence of the universe, the laws of nature, and the singular organization and complexity of life. These are obviously not proofs, in the mathematical or scientific sense, but they were enough to convince Anthony Flew of the need for a creator, as the most reasonable option to explain the complexity which has been observed in the universe.

Before I try to explain how intricately balanced the physical laws that keep the universe in existence are, I would first like to discuss two particular areas of apparent conflict between science and religion, which have given rise to a lot of misunderstandings. The first is the famous historical conflict between Galileo and the Roman Catholic Church in the early 17th century. The second is the more modern and ongoing difference of opinion between some religions beliefs and Darwinian evolution. It is useful to consider both of these in the light of the contribution scientific evidence can make to an understanding of reality and truth.

Galileo

Some false impressions have arisen from historical inaccuracies on this subject, but these have now been corrected by some good books which have been written on the facts of the case, which are now generally accepted.[132] Like many disagreements, the problem was due to misunderstandings and a lack of respect for factual information when it was presented.

Galileo's views were first developed by Copernicus, who was a Polish canon and astronomer of the 16th century. Copernicus had his book, On the Revolution of the Heavenly Spheres, saying that the earth encircled the sun (rather than the reverse, which was the common idea at the time), published in 1534, the year he died. This book was in fact dedicated to Pope Paul III and had the endorsement of his local Cardinal. It could be considered odd, therefore, that Galileo should come into conflict with Catholic Church teaching, by supporting the view of Copernicus eighty years later.

Galileo was convicted in 1633 of disobeying an injunction placed on him in 1616, not to promulgate the Copernican idea that the earth circulates the sun. At that time the Church was following Aristotle as he was regarded as master of all: except for theology, where Thomas Aquinas was regarded as master. During the earlier Middle Ages the Church had still not agreed to the ideas of Aristotle. After the Middle-Ages, interpretation of Bible teaching on scientific matters was gradually changed to fit the ideas of Aristotle. This was probably influenced by the publication of Aristotle's work in Latin and after the Protestant Reformation, the scientific views became more entrenched in favour of Aristotle. Despite this, in 1616, Cardinal Bellarmine, who was head of the Roman Inquisition at the time, warned the Catholic authorities of the danger for the Church, of resisting solid evidence produced by using the newly discovered telescope. At this time, Galileo's work had also been accepted by some Jesuit astronomers. Unfortunately, after Cardinal Bellarmine died, those in charge of the Inquisition, during Galileo's second encounter with the Church authorities, had different views. Many of these were from the Dominican Order, advised by scientists following the ideas of Aristotle. Galileo was therefore very much in opposition to the scientific establishment of the day, which was supported financially and otherwise by the Catholic Church.

Accepting Galileo's ideas would have meant rejecting a literal interpretation of the Bible, but this was never a problem for the Catholic Church. St Augustine was opposed to rigid literal interpretations of scripture. His view, which was later supported by St Thomas Aquinas in his Summa Theologiae, was that when convincing evidence and arguments became available to suggest that a particular interpretation of scripture was in error, then those views should be listened to. The rejection of Galileo, therefore, was more of a scientific rejection rather than a matter of faith. Down through the centuries, the Roman Church has always encouraged scientific investigation and supported it financially, resulting in many religious becoming well known scientists. The Galileo case was probably unique therefore. The traditional Catholic position was, and is, that good scientific evidence should never be in conflict with Christian theology.

The punishment Galileo received was to be confined to his villa in Florence, but he was allowed to go outside to visit his daughters. Galileo remained a devout Catholic and probably understood Church politics better than anybody. Those Christians, who today insist on their view of a literal interpretation of the bible, should learn from the experience with Galileo, especially when scientific evidence points in another direction. The story reached a final conclusion when in 1992 another Polish priest (Copernicus was a Polish canon), in the form of Pope John Paul II, apologised on behalf of the Catholic Church for the mistakes made and the injustice done to Galileo.

Evolution

As a Roman Catholic, this is a subject that has never caused me much concern. I see no contradiction between evolution and a belief in God. If anything, I would have to say that the respect and awe I have for God, would increase rather than decrease if the final conclusion is that life has evolved slowly over millions of years. I recognize it as a very important subject to discuss, however, because many of my colleagues, past and present, who I regard as reasonable people, often use their positive attitude to evolution, as a bedrock for their atheistic views.

Evolution is a term generally used to describe the development of life from simple molecules, through various stages of complexity, from single cells, to multi-cellular organisms, to the vast array of the different species of life forms that we now know. Darwinism is a theory put forward to explain how this may have taken place through a process of pure chance by random mutation of the DNA code, followed by natural selection, with the survival of the fittest. Evolution and Darwinism are emotional terms and are sometimes associated with confusion and misuse. Both terms have been strongly linked with a materialist view of the world, which rejects a belief in God. The view that God the creator was no longer necessary became popular in the nineteenth century, after Darwinism became well known. This was promoted by scientists, secular humanists, and Marxists, among others. Neither evolution or Darwinism, however, preclude the existence of God, although an understanding of the origin of life is one of the most important aspects of the debate on the need for God, and how God may continue to interact with our world.

Christianity and Evolution

There are three general approaches or views on the subject of evolution. The first is the traditional scientific materialistic view that life in all its complexity developed and evolved from the basic elements, over millions of years, by a natural process of chance and natural selection, without any assistance from a God. The second approach to understanding the development of life is promoted mainly by Christians who believe in a private and often literal interpretation of the Bible, and who have no time for the materialist view. This is often referred to as a creationist approach or sometimes "Young Earth Creationism". A common belief among those who promote it is, that all the different forms of life were created by God, about ten thousand years ago, and that humanity is only approximately 6,000 years old. The final approach to understanding how life developed is a mixed view or a more middle of the road attitude, which assesses the evidence for and against the first two views, and reserves judgement on the many issues which are not clear. This approach proposes a creation and an evolutionary process which could be in keeping with the existence of a God. It is sometimes referred to as Theistic Evolution. The traditional Roman Catholic view on evolution follows this last approach, which can be summarized simply as looking at the various facts and evidence and making a judgement on what these indicate. Having said that, there are many Roman Catholics who are completely opposed to the view that life slowly evolved, from simple to complex forms. The general view from Rome, however, is that this is a matter for science rather than for theology, provided the existence of the human soul is accepted.

From the Roman Catholic point of view therefore, which would be supported by many in other Christian denominations, recognizing a relationship between the development of different life forms, at biochemical and genetic level does not conflict with, either a belief in God, or in the existence of a human soul. Pope Pius XII said that, "If the origin of the human body comes through living matter which existed previously, the spiritual soul is created directly by God." The search for the truth about the origin and complexity in life forms must go on with honesty and integrity, in the knowledge that the truth in science can never oppose the truth about God.

Darwinism

The theory of Darwinism was first published in 1859 and it could be said to have had a golden century between 1870 and 1970 when it was very widely accepted in the biological sciences as a scientific basis for the origin of life. A strong atheistic view of the universe had piggy backed on this. Darwinian evolution is now beginning to look more and more overcooked and it is coming under strong attack. From around 1970 onwards, the wheels of Darwinism began to get more and more stuck in the mud and the list of unexplained and unanswered questions is now getting longer all the time. In 1986, Wallace Johnson published a long list of these problems in his book, now published with the title, The Death of Evolution.[132] He included two quotations in particular, which pointed to the uncertainty which was developing in the scientific community, against Darwinism. In 1967 the Nobel prize winner, Sir Peter Medawar said that, "Science knows of no genetic process that could produce variations required for evolution" and in 1978 the famous Australian geneticist, Professor Jerome Lejune, said that, "Genetic science has put neo Darwinism into the museum of obsolete ideas". In particular as the complexity of systems become more understood the idea of an intelligent design as a necessity for the development of complexity in biological systems, began to gain some favour, at the expense of Darwinism.

Fossils and Evolution: Christian fundamentalists say that the rocks are dated by the fossils found in them and that the fossils are in turn dated by the rocks in which they are found. Darwinists would reject this completely, but there is no doubt that fossil records are far from ideal in supporting a continuous slowly evolving new species of life, with increased complexity, as suggested by Darwinism. In fact the fossil records are proving hostile in many ways to the theory of Darwinism. Every time a new form of life appears in fossils it seems to have appeared rapidly and there is a great lack of intermediate fossil forms which Darwin expected to find. Every kind of living creature appears in fossils as they are today. Flowering plants were thought to have been the last to evolve as they are regarded as far more complex than marine plants, but angiosperm pollen grains (from flowering plants) were found in the Precambrian shale of the Grand Canyon according to Wallace Johnson, where only primitive algae should be found, going by classical Darwinism. All the Major categories of animal and plant life are found in the Cambrian period (600 million years ago). Polystrate fossils (fossils extending through many different rock layers), are a major problem for the theory that sedimentary rocks were formed slowly over millions of years. Fossilized trees have been found that protrude up through many layers of rock, which suggests that these sedimentary rocks were laid down rapidly, probably during an ancient flood.

While reporting on an international conference on evolution from Chicago, Newsweek (11/3/1980) noted that, "Evidence from the fossil record now points overwhelmingly away from the classical Darwinism, which most Americans learned in high school". At the same time, leading evolutionists at the conference demoted natural selection to the task of conserving species rather than upgrading them into more complex species. Darwin had regarded natural selection as the key to evolution and the development of new species.

Radioactive Dating of Rocks: Radioactive dating of rocks is associated with some problems which can undermine confidence in the scientific dating systems of some fossils. A chemical element is defined by the specific number of protons in the nucleus. Different *isotopes* of the same element can have slight variations in the number of neutrons in the nucleus and thus have different atomic weights. Radioactive decay is a spontaneous process by which an isotope of one element (parent) can be transformed into a new element (daughter) by losing particles (protons in particular) from the nucleus. The rate of this transformation or decay is expressed in terms of an isotope's half-life, which is the time taken for half of the parent isotope to be changed into the new element (daughter element). These half lives can range from minutes to billions of years. By measuring the relative quantity of parent and daughter elements in substances, the age of these substances can be estimated. A number of these decaying isotopes have been used to estimate the ages of rocks, - sometimes referred to as the clocks in the rocks. The most commonly used isotopes in geology are as follows:

Parent Isotope	Daughter product	½ Life
Uranium 235	Lead 207	704 million years
Uranium 238	Lead 206	4.5 billion years
Thorium 232	Lead 208	14.0 billion years
Potassium 40	Argon 40	1.25 billion years
Rubidium 87	Strontium 87	50 billion years

There are a lot of practical problems associated with the use of radioactive dating methods for rocks. This was well illustrated with the rocks brought back from the moon which were dated to have ages between two million and 28 billion years. Some of these difficulties can be described for argon. Argon 40 is said to be radiogenic, that is, derived from potassium, whereas argon 36 is non radiogenic. Only about 1% of argon found in rocks is radiogenic but the ratio can vary. Potassium 40 can also decay to calcium 40 as well as argon. There are similar problems associated with the other isotope systems and rocks generally do not represent a completely closed system. Gases and minerals in rocks can leak or be subject to contamination. It is also often assumed that the decay products, such as the element lead, coming from the element thorium, are not present in the rocks at the beginning and this may not be true. It is no wonder, therefore, that radioactive dating of rocks can be very inaccurate and lead to a lot of confusion. New rocks formed by volcanoes in particular are very often wrongly dated and those only a few hundred years old, can be dated to many billions of years. I am not suggesting that the whole radio dating system of rocks is nonsense but for somebody like me, with no knowledge of geology, this just adds to the uncertainty and confusion surrounding the age of fossils.

Is Evolution Dead? Far from it. *The Death of Evolution,*[133] which is the title of a book by Wallace Johnson, is unfortunate. This book is useful in that it points out some of the flaws and problems, associated with some aspects of the evidence for evolution. Not all of the criticisms are valid, however, and the book certainly does not sound the death knell of evolution. Neither does it point to the demise of Darwinism, although it does make the point strongly, that Darwinism with simple natural selection is not sufficient to explain the development of all the complexities in biological systems.

The best and strongest evidence for evolution does not come from the age of sedimentary rocks and the fossils found in them, where there are a lot of gaps, a lot of confusion and a lot of unanswered questions. The best evidence, rather, comes at the genetic and biochemical level, where there is an obvious relationship between all forms of living cells. The evidence for this relationship at the genetic and protein structural levels gets stronger between related species. Even the order of the functioning genes on the chromosomes compels any reasonable biologist to recognize similarities. Francis S. Collins[134] (who is a well known convert from atheism to Christianity and was the leader of the Human Genome Project) quotes the leading Russian Eastern Orthodox Christian and biologist, Dobzhansky saying, "Nothing in biology makes sense except in the light of evolution."

DNA: There is some irony in the fact that deoxyribonucleic acid (DNA), which was used for the last 50 years to explain how Darwinism and natural selection could work, is now becoming evidence in favour of a complex purposeful design plan in biological systems. The extraordinary complexity of the coded language found in DNA, is posing a problem for materialistic Darwinism. Bill Gates, the founder of Microsoft, is often quoted as saying that, "DNA is like a software programme, only much more complex than anything we've ever designed." Information theory suggests that information cannot be put in the same category as energy and matter. DNA contains the information of a complex language made up of three billion letters. This has been estimated to be equivalent to books covering fifty feet of library shelves. The opinion is now growing that it is not reasonable to assume that this vast amount of complex meaningful and precise information has come about by natural selection as we understand it. Certainly Richard Dawkins, or no other scientist has explained how natural selection could lead to the formation of and the encoding of the complex language found in the nucleic acid molecules. Francis Crick (who discovered DNA with James Watson) was among some scientists who went so far as to suggest, that nucleic acid and life forms are so complex, that they must have come from outer space. I hasten to add that this view of Crick is not a common view.

Intelligent Design and Evolution

In 1999 the Wethersfield Institute in the US, invited three leading proponents of intelligent design to present their views at a conference in New York. These were Dr. William A. Dembski, a mathematician from Chicago, Stephen C. Meyer, a philosopher of science from Cambridge University (US), and Michael J. Behe, who is a biochemist and professor of Biological Sciences, from Leigh University, in Pennsylvania. Their collected views can be read in the proceedings of this conference.[135]

A Mathematical – Physical View of Evolution

William A. Dembski, has written a small book called, The Design Inference: Eliminating Chance Through Small Probabilities, in which he outlines his evidence for design in the universe. In everyday life he writes that we have three modes of explanation, namely: necessity, chance and design. Modern science has struggled trying to distinguish between these three. In the seventeenth century Newton believed that, although the planets in the solar system are held in place by the laws of gravity, their origin could only have come from "the counsel and dominion of an intelligent and powerful being", in other words by the design of God. By the nineteenth century design fell out of favour and chance and necessity began to be accepted to account for every aspect of the universe. In the history of scientific philosophical thought, most philosophers and scientists had rejected design by the beginning of the twentieth century. This rejection may now be coming to an end after one century, and design could soon be rehabilitated. This rehabilitation is due to rigorous criteria, which have been developed for discriminating intelligently caused objects from others. These can be seen in forensic science, cryptography, archaeology, artificial intelligence and in the programmes searching for extraterrestrial intelligence etc. According to Dembski, when intelligent agents act they leave behind certain signs, which he calls **"specified complexity"** and he names the criterion for detecting this as the **"complexity specification criterion".** When we infer design he believes that we must establish three things, namely: **contingency, complexity and specification.**

Contingency: By contingency is meant that an event must be one of several possibilities. This has a general application, as for example, the position of scrabble pieces on a scrabble board cannot be reduced to natural laws governing the motion of scrabble pieces. Likewise the sequence of bases in DNA, coding for a protein, cannot be reduced to the bonding affinities between the different bases. The sequence is therefore regarded as contingent.

Complexity: It must be complex enough to eliminate chance. Complexity (improbability) of itself is not sufficient to eliminate chance and guarantee design. A coin tossed 1000 times will generate a unique sequence, with a probability of repeating in the order of one in a trillion, trillion, trillion, but it is still not enough to accept design.

Specification: The specification must exhibit patterns characteristic of intelligence. Complex patterns are divided into two types. These are the patterns, despite the complexity that do not warrant a design inference, described as "fabrications" and the patterns that do warrant a design inference, described as "specifications". The key factor is "independence". A specification is a match between an event and an independently given pattern.

The universal probability limit that Dembski proposes for The Design Inference is 1 in 10^{150}. One suggestion sometimes made is that so called evolutionary algorithms can generate specified complexity apart from design. **Dembski uses the widely promoted and accepted evolutionary algorithm of Richard Dawkins in his book, The Blind Watchmaker,[136] to illustrate basic mathematical errors by Dawkins.**

A Biochemical View of Evolution

There are two opposing views of life in the universe. The first is epitomized by the views of the Oxford biologist, Professor Richard Dawkins who said that, "The universe we observe has precisely the properties we should expect, if there is no design, no purpose, no evil, no good, nothing but pointless indifference." The second view is that promoted by the former Cardinal Joseph Ratzinger, now Pope Benedict XVI. The Cardinal's view was that, "We can say today with a new certitude and joyousness that the human being is indeed a divine project, - not a mistake but something willed".[137]

Michael J. Behe was impressed by the fact that Ratzinger reached his conclusion by looking at the "great products of the living creation", and in particular from the evidence from the molecular structure of life. In his book Darwin's Black Box,[138] Behe proposes the idea of "Irreducible Complexity" in some biological systems, which make it impossible for them to have evolved in single step changes, as proposed by the Darwinian evolution theory. He explains irreducible complexity as, "A single system, which is composed of several well matched, interacting parts that contribute to the basic function, and where the removal of any one of the parts causes the system to effectively cease functioning". There are several examples of these irreducible complex systems in biology that challenge Darwinism, according to Behe. He quotes, as examples, the complexity of the eye with the mechanism of sight, the blood clotting cascade system, organs of motion such as cilia and the bacterial flagellum etc. Behe, however, has not yet convinced evolution biologists of the downfall of Darwinism with these arguments.

Christian philosophers and biologists, who often support evolution, have pointed out the difficulty of using irreducible complexity as an argument for God. This argument runs the risk of being undermined, when some of these gaps in our knowledge are finally discovered and explained. The term, "God of Gaps", is sometimes used in these discussions. At this time, this argument is not regarded as a convincing one on the need for God, but that could change as the complexity in biological systems is more and more appreciated.

A Philosophical – Physical View of Evolution

In the 1960s, physicists discovered that the existence of life in the universe was the result of a very precise and very highly improbable balance of physical factors. Even a very slight alteration in the values of the rate of the universe expansion, the strength of gravity, the electromagnetic attraction, or the value of Planck's constant, would render life impossible. The convergence of all these complicated coincidences was referred to as the fine tuning of the universe. The impression of design was overwhelming.

Mathematical Constants

Martin Rees in his book Just Six Numbers,[139] has highlighted six numerical constants as key values controlling the universe. Two of these are values for basic forces, two fix the size and texture of the universe and the final two fix the properties of space.

> **N:** This is the strength of the electrical forces holding atoms together divided by the force of gravity between them.
>
> **E:** This value defines how firmly all atomic nuclei bind together and how all the atoms on earth were made.
>
> **Ω:** This relates gravity with the expansion speed of the universe. The value of this figure controls the material (density) in the universe, as in the form of galaxies, dark matter, and diffuse gas.
>
> **λ:** This is an antigravity force, which controls the expansion of the universe. This new force was described in 1998.
>
> **Q:** This has a value of approximately 1/100,000 and is said to control the fabric of the universe. The value is derived by dividing the force of gravity by the total rest mass-energy ($E = mc^2$).
>
> **D:** This has a value of 3 for the spatial dimensions of the universe. Time is a fourth dimension but it is distinctively different from the others.

The laws of physics, therefore, give the impression of being the result of an ingenious design. The gravitational constant needs to be exactly at 6.67 by 10^{-11} Newton-metres^2 per kilogram^2 and has been estimated to need fine tuning to the order of one part in 10^{40}. Likewise Coulombs law has a value of 8.85 by 10^{-12}

Coulombs^2 per Newton-meter^2, the electron charge to mass ratio is 1.76 by 10^{11} Coulombs per kilogram, Planck's constant is 6.63 by 10^{-34} Joules-seconds and the expansion rate of the universe must be tuned to an accuracy of one part in 10^{60} etc. Physicists have discovered more than thirty physical and cosmological parameters that require precise calibration in order to produce a life sustaining universe. There are also many other parameters in chemistry, biology, and geology etc., that also need a very high degree of tuning to sustain life. Brandon Carter showed in 1970 that if the strong force was 2% less it would prevent elements larger than hydrogen from forming and if the force was 2% greater than all the hydrogen would have been converted to helium from the beginning. **Oxford physicist Roger Penrose has said that the big bang required such fine tuning that the creator must have been precise to the order of 1 in 10 billion multiplied by itself 123 times and that this was the precision needed to get the universe into motion. That number is impossible to write, as it has more zeros than there are elementary particles in the entire universe.**[140]

A Catholic Philosophical – Metaphysical view of Evolution

St Pope John Paul II made a number of interesting statements on evolution. At a general audience in July 10, 1985 he said, "To speak of chance for a universe, which presents such a complex organization of its elements and such a marvellous finality in its life, would be equivalent to giving up the search for an explanation of the world as it appears to us. In fact this would be equivalent to admitting effects without a cause." The well known statement of St Pope John Paul II, in 1996, that, "evolution is more than a hypothesis", is usually taken to mean that he at least accepted some aspects of evolution. In this talk entitled "Truth cannot contradict Truth",[141] it is well to note that he also said that theories on evolution, which suggest that the spirit emerges from the forces of living matter, are incompatible with the truth about man and are unable to ground the dignity of the person. The spiritual is not something that can be measured by science. He goes on to say that, "The experience of metaphysical knowledge, of self-awareness and self reflection, of moral conscience, freedom, or again of aesthetic and religious experience, falls within the competence of philosophical analysis and reflection, while theology brings out its ultimate meaning according to the Creator's plans".

Emeritus Pope Benedict XVI, has spoken and written on a number of occasions on the subject of evolution. He does not promote a literal interpretation of Genesis in the Bible. He sees the evolution debate as largely something for scientists to resolve and he believes that is not the function of the Catholic Church to adjudicate on the merits of scientific theories on evolution. He sees very important limits, however, in that the science of evolution has no competence to decide against God as a creator or to deny that each human person has an immortal soul. This area of study belongs to philosophy and theology. In his book, *In the Beginning: A Catholic Understanding of the Story of Creation and Fall*,[137] he points out that it is not valid to talk about, "creation or evolution", as these are complementary, rather than mutually exclusive realities. The theory of evolution tries to understand and describe biological developments but cannot explain where the "project" of human persons comes from. In his book Truth and Tolerance,[142] published a few years before he became Pope, Benedict XVI suggested that the scientific evidence for microevolution (change within species) is such that nobody can seriously doubt it. The research done by evolutionary biologists has demonstrated the adaptive capacity of living systems, which seems marvellous. The problem comes with macroevolution (change from one species to another) where the Pope believes that the evidence is less persuasive. Here he quotes the two scientists, Szathmáry and Maynard Smith, both supporters of evolution, who nevertheless state that, "There is no theoretical basis for believing that evolutionary lines become more complex with time and there is also no empirical evidence that this happens." Emeritus Pope Benedict believes that the greatest danger with Darwinism is that it promotes the idea that only empirical science can produce certainty. He believes that Christianity relies on truths deeper than empirical observations, in particular that life has a definite purpose. In the end, the message from what Emeritus Pope Benedict XVI has said must be, that we should never worry about the discovery of natural science, as the search must always be for truth, which ultimately is one.

Quantum, Godel, and the Human Mind: The quantum theory supports the view that the human mind cannot be reduced to simple physics. The quantum theory, now almost one hundred years old, is regarded as one of the most profound discoveries ever made in physics. Quantum theory was originally developed to solve problems in atomic physics and in the theory of electromagnetic radiation. **The problem with the quantum theory for materialists is not the mathematics or the mathematical predictions, but with the philosophical implications.**

The quantum theory has changed the whole basis of classical physics in two fundamental ways that are relevant to our understanding of how the human mind works. Firstly, quantum theory gives predictions, based on probabilities, rather than definite outcomes. This has implications for free will. Secondly, the real world is based on definite events, rather than hypothetical events. Only the "human observer" doing the measurement can say what the definite outcome was. Quantum physics, therefore, forces physicists to take the "observer" into account, examining how mind and matter are related. The observer relates the hypothetical to the fact. The human mind can discern what is true and what is not true. It is now generally accepted by leading physicists that the quantum theory indicates that the mind of the human person cannot be described by mathematics.

Kurt Godel was an Austrian logician who is famous for a theorem he proved in 1931. Simply stated, this theorem says that any non-trivial mathematical theory will be either incomplete or inconsistent. Another way of stating it is that: in any consistent formal mathematical system, in which one can do mathematical and simple logic, there are arithmetic statements, which can neither be proved nor disproved, using the rules (axioms and rules of inference) of that system. In 1961, John Lucas, a philosopher at Oxford, proposed that on the basis of Godel's theorem, the human mind cannot be like a computer program. In 1989, Roger Penrose, (a well-known physicist and mathematician, also from Oxford) supported this view, and on the basis of Godel's theorem, he believed that the human mind could not be explained entirely in material terms.[143]

Professor Stanley L. Jaki is a well-respected Catholic Benedictine priest, philosopher, scientist and a member of the Pontifical Academy of Sciences. He believes that Christians should be all-out evolutionists. He says that only those who are inclined to resist facts or sane philosophy or both, reject evolution. He was among the first to point to the significance of Godel's mathematical theorem for those trying to find a theory to explain everything. Until recently, physicists had assumed that it was possible to discover an ultimate theory which would explain the universe in a finite number of ways. In a lecture given by Professor Stephen Hawking with the title, "Godel and The End of Physics",[144] he said that he too used to believe in the ultimate theory but he has now changed his mind. Just as the Heisenberg uncertainty was the first major blow to scientific determinism (see page 324), so Godel's theorem adds to this uncertainty and now it should be acknowledged that it is not possible to explain everything at the physical and mathematical level. As well as posing a major problem for materialistic evolution, this also has obviously broader religious implications.

The Dawkins Delusion

I had most of this book planned when I came across *The God Delusion*, by Richard Dawkins.[1] In many ways I was delighted to get this book, as it distilled the case for atheism into one book, and by critically examining the points the author made, it would make it easier for me to put the case for God. Richard Dawkins is a well known atheist with attitude, some might even say aggressive. He is a biology Professor from Oxford, England, and he has written a number of well known books, such as *The Selfish Gene*[145] and The *Blind Watchmaker*,[136] promoting evolution and Darwinian natural selection. He is untiring in his efforts to convince his readers that a belief in evolution demands atheism. The God Delusion is his latest effort, with the stated objective of converting as many as possible to atheism. He decries supernaturalism in all its forms and he claims that no intelligent person now believes in miracles. These are extreme views.

I was well on the way to writing a section for this chapter, opposing these extreme views, which I had headed *The Dawkins Delusion*, when I came across a book with this exact title by Alister & Joanna McGrath.[146] I was glad to discover this new book, as these authors have done a far more scholarly critique of The God Delusion than I could ever do. Those interested should find and read these well written counter arguments against Dawkins. These authors are also coincidently from Oxford. The opinions of Dawkins on God and religion are in conflict with many of the views expressed in this effort of mine. For this reason and also because

347

he directs a lot of his anti-religious venom towards the Catholic Church, I feel obliged to challenge some of these particular aspects of The God Delusion.

The first thing to appreciate about Dawkins is that he knows very little about religion. Most would consider it odd, therefore, that he should be putting himself forward as an expert on the existence of God. He gives the impression that theology is not a real subject at all and he also seems to have no knowledge of metaphysics. He says that he has restricted his comments on religion mostly to Christianity, as this is the religion he is most familiar with. Yet it is very obvious that he knows very little about Catholicism, so he must know practically nothing about other religions. He believes that religion is not rational and this has prompted me to think that some of his strange ideas about God and religion may come from his experience in Anglicanism, even though this experience has also been limited. Of all the branches of Christianity, Anglicanism is the most varied and difficult to understand, in terms of beliefs and teachings. In trying to be all things to all people this teaching has now finished up with a fair degree of confusion. An example of this confusion is the use of *The Thirty Nine Articles of Faith,* on which the religion is supposed to be based. Most Anglicans either do not believe, or just ignore, at least some of these articles and there is a great absence of unity and authority in Anglican teaching.

Dawkins has some other ideas on religion and God, however, which cannot be blamed on Anglicanism. He reads and interprets the Bible either like a history book or a textbook in biology. He says that a particular Anglican theologian is beyond satire for trying to justify the value of suffering, but in my opinion, this theologian should in fact be praised, as one of the weaknesses of "reformed" Christianity is the lack of a good theology on suffering. Later he castigates the same theologian for regarding God as simple. He is obviously confusing the term "simple" as used in metaphysics with the normal use of the word in English. One gets the impression very quickly from *The God Delusion* that, as the author believes natural selection explains everything we need to know about life then, simply, there is no God, as there is no need of God.

Is it reasonable to believe in God?

Robert J Spitzer S J in his essays on *Finding God through Faith and Reason*,[147] says that as God is the source of both faith and reason, there cannot be a conflict between them. He deals briefly with St Thomas Aquinas and his proofs for God. St Thomas argues that there must be one uncaused cause for anything else to exist, or in other words, that nothing could exist without something causing it to exist. A large number (even an infinite number) of caused causes amounts to nothing without one uncaused cause (something that can exist of itself without a cause). St Thomas goes on to explain that this something that needs nothing to exist is an unimaginable pure being or pure power with no boundaries and no finite restrictions on action. There can only be one pure acting power, as if there were more, then something would have to distinguish them. Any difference would restrict their existence and thus would not be compatible with all existence. In summary, therefore, for anything to exist, there must be one uncaused cause satisfying the following conditions:

1. It must be a pure unrestricted acting power
2. It must be compatible with everything that exists
3. It must be one and only one.

Modern philosophy has a similar approach to the existence of God. The one uncaused cause of St Thomas is referred to as one unconditioned reality, which is something that does not need any conditions fulfilled for it to exist. There is no location in space time needed, no structures, no electric fields, etc., just no restrictions. This unconditioned reality must have no boundaries if it is to be compatible with everything that exists. **This is referred to in metaphysics, as "absolute simplicity".** At least one unconditioned reality must exist in all reality.

Dawkins is very scathing about what he calls the "infinite regress", in these arguments. He dismisses St Thomas Aquinas in a few lines, which is some achievement, considering that Aquinas is respected as one of the greatest philosophers in the history of humanity. There is nothing unreasonable about suggesting that there must be at least one entity which can exist of itself (dependant on nothing) for everything else to exist. Dawkins asks the question, who created God? This is missing the point as expressed in philosophy, where this circular argument does not work. If it is agreed that nothing can exist without a cause then this creates a closed circle of one entity causing another. You can only get out of this circle by proposing an entity which can exist of itself without the need to be created. If one travels the circle an infinite number of times, it amounts to nothing, as infinity cannot be achieved. If one travels the circle a finite number of times you finish up with the need for something to exist without a cause or without a condition. There simply needs to be an initial, single unconditioned reality. The argument for God, therefore, is that there is a need for an entity, which does not need to be created, but can exist of itself, and therefore can function as the one necessary unconditional reality, so that everything else can exist. The position taken by Dawkins, that there is no need for any unconditioned reality, and that if God exists, then this God also needs to be created, implies that he believes everything needs a cause. If nothing can exist without a cause, then nothing will ever exist unless something starts it off by existing of itself. An infinite number of caused causes is zero. The position, therefore, that there is no need for any unconditioned reality, is in fact far more unreasonable than the position taken by St Thomas Aquinas.

What is the probability of God existing?

I heard a talk on evolution some time ago, which began with a slide of Mount Rushmore, in the US, with the images of the former presidents carved into the rocks. The speaker asked the question, what is the probability that these images came about by chance? He followed with another question: - what is the probability that these presidents in person developed from rocks over a very long period of time by chance? A somewhat similar argument made against evolution, having come about completely by chance, is the comparison sometimes made between New York or London, with the single animal or human living cell. The bricks building the structures of the city can be compared with the molecules of a cell (I have calculated this to be roughly the same number). Is it reasonable to consider the city of London developing a system which would lead it to reproduce itself exactly, using just the material resources of the bricks and the environment, by chance, or by a process of natural selection, which in turn was developed by chance? Would it require some other ingredient other than just a very long time? The argument goes therefore that if one cannot accept that humanity developed from rocks, or that London or New York could self reproduce another identical city if given enough time, then there should be some reasonable doubts developing about the validity of materialistic evolution.

It is not possible to prove the existence of God by mathematics, physics or astronomy in the same way that it is attempted when using philosophy and metaphysics, as in the example of St Thomas Aquinas, explained briefly above. As the existence of God cannot be proved or disproved, therefore, the fundamental question becomes, which view is the most credible, based on the facts which we can establish? Almost all physicists and mathematicians would agree that on the basis of the very finely tuned universe force constants, described above (see pages 321 & 341), that the anthropic (life supporting) properties of our world and universe could not have come about by chance. That is, unless our universe is one in many billion and we are just the lucky ones. Richard Dawkins wonders why more physicists than biologists believe in God. It could be that when biologists understand the details of how nucleic acid information is translated into the exact amino acid sequence needed for the many proteins in the cell, they feel that they have cracked the code of life and there is nothing more they need to know. Physicists, on the other hand, usually recognize more the complexity of the universe and how much we still have to learn. It could also be that physicists are often better mathematicians than biologists and mathematicians find it easier to accept the existence of God, at least as a possibility, and in many cases as a probability.

Richard Dawkins says that on the grounds of probability, there is almost certainly no God. Probability theory is obviously not his forte. As suggested by the mathematician William A Dembski (see page 338), Dawkins makes a mathematical error in suggesting that evolutionary algorithms can generate complexity apart from design. This latest suggestion in The God Delusion that mathematically the existence of God is extremely improbable is another similar error of mathematical confusion. Dawkins believes that the existence of a God, who could design something as complex as the universal force constants, must be even more improbable simply on the grounds that this God must be even more complex than these constants. He is confusing complexity with probability.

To get around the idea of accepting a Creator in the midst of all these vast improbabilities of the universal force constants, some scientists have postulated the existence of a very large number of parallel universes. This "many worlds" hypothesis is now the most popular naturalistic explanation for the anthropic fine tuning of our universe. In other words, of the many billions of other universes (proposed to exist) we are the lucky ones with conditions for life. In this sense it could be said that, **the theory of multiple universes (multiverse or megaverse) is the last refuge of the atheist**. There are major problems with this theory, however, in that there is practically no evidence for other universes, or for any universe generating mechanism. Even if such a mechanism existed, it would also likely need very accurate physical constants to operate. More and more mathematicians and physicists, therefore, are beginning to accept that belief in a Creator is a much more realistic and reasonable option. To illustrate this, the philosopher Robin Collins asks us to compare the idea of a palaeontologist who proposes the existence of an electromagnetic "dinosaur bone producing field", as opposed to actual dinosaurs, as an explanation for fossilized dinosaur bones.[148] Both are possible explanations, but we must ask, which is the most reasonable for us to accept? It has been suggested by Clifford Longley that the use of the many worlds hypothesis (many universes), to avoid the theistic design argument, betrays a kind of metaphysical desperation.[149] Longley also is well known for suggesting that: not to accept the anthropic design hypothesis, is equivalent to suggesting that Shakespeare may have been written by a billion monkeys typing at a billion keyboards for a billion years. Francis S Collins[134] in discussing the multiverse theory says, "This near infinite number of universes strains credulity. It certainly fails *Occam's Razor*. Those categorically unwilling to accept an intelligent Creator will argue that the option (of a Creator) is not simpler, as it requires the intercession of a supernatural being. It could be argued, however, that the Big Bang itself seems to point strongly towards a Creator." Collins goes on to mention the words of Stephen Hawking on the Big Bang as follows: "The odds against a universe like our emerging out of something like the Big Bang are enormous. I think there are clearly religious implications". Hawking in, A Brief History of Time[150] says: "It would be very difficult to explain why the universe should have begun in just this way, except as the act of a God who intended to create beings like us." Finally, Collins makes the point that, "There are good reasons to believe in God, including the existence of mathematical principles and the order of creation. They are positive reasons, based on knowledge, rather than default assumptions based on (a temporary) lack of knowledge."

Past time cannot be Infinite

For those who still cling to the no God – multiverse hypothesis, there is also another obstacle, which is the suggestion that past time cannot be infinite. The "Big Bang", which is thought to have been the starting whistle for everything to begin (about 14 billion years ago), is in keeping with this. In other words, even if there are many billions of universes, they too would have to have a prime cause and a moment in time when they came into existence. Fr Robert Spitzer continues his arguments for the existence of God by describing three approaches to show that past time can only be finite in any possible universe.[147] This contradicts the belief of the old Newtonian understanding, that past time was infinite.

The first approach to prove that past time is finite is the philosophical *via negative* approach. Infinity can never be achieved as it lacks at least one terminus. Past time has been achieved and therefore it cannot be infinite, as infinity is always unachievable. If past time has not been achieved then it is no different from present or future time and thus it is meaningless and your neighbour's pussy cat could be alive and dead at the same time. An achieved unachievable is a contradiction, so past time cannot be infinite.

The second approach is to consider the constituent parts of past time. Constituent parts have a measurable magnitude, as in the length of seconds for example, and constituent parts make a difference to the whole value. Non constituent parts as points on a line have no size and if you take one away, or add one, it makes no difference to the whole. You can have an infinite number of non-constituent parts, but you can only have a finite number of constituent parts. Taking away, or adding constituent parts to infinity makes no difference, as you still are left with infinity.

The third approach Fr Robert Spitzer mentions is the so called, Hilbertian prohibition, named after the famous mathematician, David Hilbert. Hilbert showed that any time you try to apply infinity to an algorithmically finite structure, you get so many contradictions that the whole of mathematics is undermined. Hilbert said that infinity does not exist in nature. It cannot therefore be applied to past time. Of the three points made by Spitzer, this one is the most likely to be accepted, as the best.

If past time is not infinite then, it must have had a beginning. If past time existed before the "Big Bang", there is an argument suggesting that this time would also need a starting point. The second law of thermodynamics indicates that in the overall picture, energy gets degraded and disorganization (entropy) increases. This is also evidence suggesting the need for a beginning. The weight of evidence and thus the most reasonable thing to believe is that time, and certainly our universe, had a beginning. Past time could not have been created by itself, or by anything conditioned by past time, such as any universe. There is, therefore, a need for a Creator of past time, who must transcend time.

Can God's communications with humanity be scientifically investigated?

Dawkins claims that if God really does communicate with humans, then that fact should emphatically not be outside the realm of science to investigate it. For some reason, which I cannot understand, he then assumes that science can have no role in investigating this kind of communication. A good portion of chapters 4 and 5 in this book has been concerned with situations where science can play a very definite role in establishing facts, in relation to the many events which have been claimed to be the result of direct influences and communications from God. In mentioning the apparitions at Fatima, in 1917, he admits that it is difficult to understand them, but then dismisses them completely, on the grounds that he just does not believe in the supernatural. He says that, "No testimony is sufficient to establish a miracle, unless the testimony be such a kind, that its falsehood would be more miraculous than the fact which it endeavours to establish." He then says, "That is really all that needs to be said about personal 'experiences' of gods or other religious phenomena." How can anybody take his views on God and religion seriously after those comments? He goes further by making some silly and flippant comments on various apparitions of The Virgin Mary, as if it were different people appearing in different places, and he refers to the various apparitions of The Virgin Mary as a kind of polytheism. He obviously knows nothing about this subject and much less on the many and complex scientific investigations done, both on the witnesses and on those cured. A number of these Marian apparitions were described in chapter 5 of this book.

Dawkins speaks about "the conscious raising experience" of Darwinism. Any atheist who wants a real conscious raising experience should spend some time investigating the evidence for the supernatural. Those who find it difficult to accept the supernatural may find it useful to spend some time with an authentic Christian exorcist, or with those who can authentically discern spirits, and who often help the exorcists. A more detailed explanation of exorcism is found in chapter 7. To investigate the reality of evil spirits is to investigate the evidence for Hell. This is not a pleasant place to spend eternity, because of a failure to investigate the evidence for its existence. For those who are scientifically inclined, they could also look at the scientific evidence in support of the miraculous (see below). In particular, they may like to begin with the scientific evidence for the miraculous image of The Virgin of Guadalupe in Mexico (see chapter 5, page 111 and page 376 below).

The Great Prayer Experiment: A famous Irish show-biz personality once described how, as a young man, he had fallen deeply in love, and began to pray non-stop for the success of his relationship with a girl, who did not want to know him. Many years later he encountered the same lady as he entered a crowded bar in his home town. His first thought was, "thank God for unanswered prayers". Richard Dawkins has a lot to learn about prayer. He describes a great prayer experiment which was carried out in some churches in the US, where some ill parishioners were prayed for, so that they would regain full health. The only detectable effect was that some of those prayed for got worse and this for him was positive proof that prayer is nonsense. I could quote many prayer experiments, where the results were a resounding success. These can be checked from historical records, particularly if one looks under the heading – "Rosary Crusades". Particular note should be taken of Austria, in 1955, when the Russian troops, who had occupied this country since the end of World War II, mysteriously left without an explanation, after the conclusion of a major rosary crusade that was organized by the Austrian Bishops. Likewise in Brazil, in 1966, the communist president fled the country after a large rosary crusade. Then there was the

Philippines, on the 8th of Dec, 1989, when the army was prevented from taking over the government, by a large apparition of The Virgin Mary appearing before the tanks, while the troops were facing the people on the streets of Manila. The troops mysteriously and quietly returned to their barracks. This too, happened after a large rosary crusade organized by Cardinal Sin.

The power of prayer is in fact one of the greatest proofs for the existence of God. It is more private than public, however, as it is very much a personal communication between God and the individual and only rarely are public signs manifested through private prayer. If you want to get to know God you must talk to God, and one of the great results of prayer is what is referred to as "signal graces". God interacts with each person who prays, in a very personal way. Each individual, including Richard Dawkins, can do their own private experiment on prayer. For prayer to bear fruit, it must be humble, persistent and with faith. Each person can be the judge of how successful their communications with God has been. God, however, will only grant our wishes when it is good for us or good for others. Demanding your rights from God is as unlikely to get results, as praying to a false god. All the lives of holy people, and in particular the saints, in their own individual ways, have been great prayer experiments. St Pio (see page 102) is a wonderful modern example of this. Here was an individual who had miracles on tap. He left nobody in any doubt that prayer, suffering and the love of God were the source of his power. He prayed the rosary continually and referred to it as his weapon against evil.

The Science of Miracles

The science of miracles is something one does not hear discussed. Some scientists have a philosophy which completely rejects the supernatural, and for those, miracles can never be a consideration. At the other extreme, there are many who ascribe many mundane events to the miraculous. The reality is that there are rare events, which have been carefully and scientifically documented and supported and which cannot be explained within the realm of natural laws as we now understand them. There is a "natural" reluctance among scientists to face the reality of the miraculous, but not to accept this possibility is to deny a lot of valid observations, by a very large number of sane, well balanced individuals.

It is a general belief from the earliest days of Christianity that Jesus Christ revealed himself to be God, by the miracles which he worked, especially by raising Himself from the dead. That was a long time ago, however, and concrete evidence for miracles 2,000 years ago is virtually impossible to find. This kind of evidence is available, however, from the miracles of modern times, for those who care to investigate. One of the first fundamental steps in a scientific investigation of the unknown is to make valid authentic observations. After making the observations, a hypothesis is then proposed to explain the observations, in the light of what is already understood. The hypothesis is then tested by making valid deductions and testing these deductions, in so far as possible, with demonstrable facts gleaned from repeat observations. The evidence which can be collected from "miraculous events" is complex and varied.

When the uniqueness, the similarities, connections, and the tremendous variety of the "miraculous" are taken together with the medical and scientific support, they tend to weave a web of undeniable evidence, for the direct action of God in our personal lives, that we can only marvel at. It is as if God is saying: "What more proof could you need? What more evidence could I give that I have not given, and still preserve your free will, to say yes or no?" This in essence is why the study of the miraculous is so important and significant. To ignore miracles is to ignore the possibility of God. To ignore scientific and medical evidence is unscientific. The God hypothesis and the Hell hypothesis cannot be investigated by those who will not accept, or continue to ignore, evidence.

Einstein and God

Richard Dawkins quotes Einstein at length to convince us that he was an atheist, and he may well have been, but Einstein did say a lot of interesting things about God. Of great interest is what he said in Letters to Maurice Solovine 1956, where he marvelled at the organization of the universe. He said:

"You find it strange that I consider the comprehensibility of the world - as a miracle or an eternal mystery... a priori one should expect a chaotic world... The kind of order created, for example by Newton's theory of gravity, is of quite a different kind. Even if the axioms of the theory are posited by a human being, the success of such a human enterprise presupposes an order in the objective world of a high degree, which one has no a priori right to expect. That is the 'miracle' which grows increasingly persuasive with the increasing development of knowledge".

That was written over fifty years ago, and the major growth in our understanding of the mathematical constants controlling the universe since Einstein, as explained above, has been truly phenomenal. If Einstein was alive today, I believe that he would be a lot more convinced that the case for God is intellectually very strong at the physical mathematical level, before ever considering philosophy, metaphysics and theology.

Prejudice is stronger than Intelligence and Evidence

Hilaire Belloc describes two types of sceptics.[151] The first, is the intelligent sceptic who uses reason and to whom you can reason with and give evidence in one direction or another. The other type of sceptic works at the emotional level only and reason and evidence will have no impact. I like to think that most of us work on various mixtures of emotion and reason and few fit into the two pure categories described by Belloc. We all get stuck in ruts of thinking, with deeply held beliefs, and the older we get the more difficult it is to change. We all have prejudices and suffer from prejudice programming. There is also a sense in which we try to make the evidence fit our prejudice, especially when it comes to topics we feel strongly about. Discussions on evolution and the existence of God are topics very good at exposing prejudice. This prejudice of course, works in both directions and in particular, is easily recognizable among those Christians that are strongly opposed to evolution.

Forty years after Einstein's general relativity and thirty years after Edwin Hubble did his famous experiments on receding galaxies, two thirds of the leading astronomers and physicists in the US still believed that the universe had no beginning. Was this a case of old ideas die hard, or was there a philosophical prejudice towards materialism and against God, who would be suggested as responsible for kicking off the existence of the universe, if it was agreed to have a beginning? Since then, lots of other physical evidence has accumulated in favour of the Big Bang, which suggests that the universe began approximately 14 billion years ago. At this stage, just as any honest biologist should find it difficult to dispute that there is evidence in favour of evolution at the biochemical level, so any honest physicist or astronomer should find it difficult to disagree that there is good evidence for the Big Bang.

Of the thousand or more Protestant pastors, from many different denominations in the US, who have joined the Roman Church in recent years, they invariably mention one great obstacle, which is described as "thinking the unthinkable".[96] They all found it almost impossible to consider that Roman Catholicism could have the correct interpretation of the Bible, due to prejudice in Protestant communities against Catholicism. Likewise, there are some Christians who, in their efforts to make science fit their interpretation of the Bible, become prejudiced against scientific evidence. In this context, it is worrying that so many Christians still believe in Young Earth Creationism (that life is only 10,000 years old). This has to be one of the greatest examples of prejudice programming against scientific evidence – (see chapter 17 for further discussion on this). Many Christians have also rejected the Big Bang theory, even though it is based on a lot of solid scientific evidence, simply because it does not agree with their opinion on what the Bible says about the age of the earth. For any group who are promoting belief in the existence of God, the rejection of the Big Bang would seem to be self defeating, as it is good support evidence on the need for a Creator.

The prejudice of Richard Dawkins is not hard to identify. It is worrying that there is such wide acceptance of his promotion of Darwinian natural selection as the complete explanation for the origin of complexity in life. This interpretation of Darwin's theory is based on unsound mathematics, as pointed out by the mathematician William Dembski. The acclaim Dawkin's book, *The God Delusion*, has received is equally worrying, for the same reason. His argument that on the grounds of probability God almost certainly does not exist is based on equally unsound and confused mathematics, and a number of his readers will likely be confused with him. He is, in fact, promoting a falsehood based on confused mathematics. More than that, it could be said that, in

The God Delusion, an intelligent man is becoming irrational, because of his prejudice against God and religion.

Dawkins is not only prejudiced against religion but also against all forms of supernaturalism. He starts out with the philosophical presumption that miracles are impossible, so therefore he can never accept any evidence to suggest a miracle, and he believes that no intelligent person should ever express a belief in miracles. The famous philosopher Bertrand Russell, who did not believe in God, is reported to have replied to the question, "what would you say if you were confronted by God after death?" – "I would say, Sir, you did not give sufficient evidence". Evidence for miracles, like evidence for God, must be sought and recognized before it can be accepted or rejected. This book presents evidence for God, Satan, Hell, and miracles, but it is up to the reader to accept this, reject it, or do more investigations. The problem is not lack of evidence for God but a shortage of a willingness to seek it out, investigate it and assess this evidence. Peter Kreeft, in a talk given to Lighthouse Media,[152] explains that God does not give us too much proof of His existence as that would compel us to believe. God gives us just enough evidence with the promise that those who continually seek God will find Him.

The evidence in favour of a grand design in the universe is gathering momentum, but attitudes are slow to change. It will still take some time for the limitations of Darwinism to be accepted widely and still longer before Darwinism stops appearing in children's textbooks, as the complete guide to the origin of life. The great physicist Max Planck is quoted as having said, "A new scientific truth does not triumph by convincing its opponents and making them see the light, but rather because its opponents eventually die, and a new generation grows up that is familiar with it."

Finally, I must say that I was impressed with one statement Dawkins made in *The Blind Watch Maker*.[136] He said, "I may not always be right, but I care passionately about what is true". Everybody who seeks the truth must be respected, and those of us who have different opinions must move towards each other with this respect. My wish for Richard Dawkins (as it is with all those I know, who are atheists), is that some day he will see the light and have his Damascus moment, by being knocked off his hobby horse. I am sure that my atheist friends have a similar interest in my welfare.

Aggression against God

The final question I would like to address from The God Delusion is, why is Dawkins so aggressive against God? He admits that he cannot be certain that there is no God but he is obviously willing to take the chance and take the consequences if he is wrong. He must equally believe that there is no Hell of damnation, but he also cannot be certain of this, and he is prepared to take the risk. It is a pity that he did not study the message of Fatima a little more carefully, before he dismissed it as nonsense.

In my experience, in talking about God to large numbers of people over the years, I find that the commonest attitude to God is an individualistic or "a la carte" approach. Many nominal Catholics, for example, would reject certain aspects of Catholic teaching, and the same is true for members of other religions, who also often refuse to accept all the teachings of their chosen religion. Aggression against God, however, is not common and is much less than 5%. Some years ago, when I was studying microbiology in Oxford, England, I had the occasion to do some home visitation on behalf of the Catholic Church. On one occasion, we met an individual who was very aggressive against belief in God, religion, and in particular the Catholic Church. We were later surprised to hear from the parish priest that, in his experience, those who are aggressively anti-God are in fact much more likely to be believers, and to return to their faith, than those who have no interest in discussing religion whatsoever.

In trying to understand this aggression against God, I find it useful to consider three categories. In the first group are usually those who were believers at one stage and who, for one reason or another, feel hurt and let down by organized religion. The reason may be an illness, break up of marriage, death of a young relative etc. These individuals tend to be fighting with God, and in many cases still keeping talking to God, even if it is in an aggressive way. This is the commonest category. In the second group, there are those who, through upbringing and various experiences in life, become convinced that religion and God are evil influences in society, which we must get rid of for the common good. These represent a small percentage of those who are agnostics or atheists. In the third group are those who are much less common, but far from being atheists, are firm believers in the reality of God, but have opted to work for evil instead. This group although small, is growing. Many are Satanists and some fast and do penances for evil, as Catholics do for the sake of what they believe to be good causes. Figures quoted for satanic groups are, approximately 10,000 in the US with roughly half that number in various European countries.[153]

Richard Dawkins, if we are to take him at his word, fits neatly into the second group as he believes that religion and belief in God are evil influences. The fact that he completely rejects all forms of the supernatural is a good indication of this. He does, however, talk a lot about fairies at the bottom of the garden, which makes me wonder if he, or somebody he trusts, had some ghostly experience. Richard should honestly open his mind and heart to the reality of the supernatural and investigate. He should begin to pray and if he does and he can overcome his prejudices, he is likely to become a great Roman Catholic.

A Summary of Evolution

There are two fundamental questions raised by evolution. The first is, how has life developed? This is largely a scientific question. The second question is, did the development of life occur by a random process "naturally" or through a decision or plan of God? Science may be able to help with this second question but it can never give the final answer. If life did originate by a natural process, this would not exclude God, but neither would it be evidence in favour of the existence of God. On the other hand, if it could be shown that there was a need for some other mysterious driving force, due to the fact that life was very unlikely to have developed by a process of chance based on natural selection, as suggested by Darwinism, then this would be evidence for an outside influence and would be indirect evidence for God.

The biological and genetic evidence that life has evolved is very strong. There is no doubt about the evidence for a pattern of molecular structural relationship between the different forms of life. It is not just nucleic acid, and the order of genes in the various species that is common. There are also a myriad of other organic molecules and biochemical pathways, for creating energy, structural proteins and carbohydrates, common among the different forms of life. This evidence can never be absolute as it will never be possible to re-run the evolution experiment, but the weight of evidence is such that most biochemists, biologists and geneticists are generally happy to agree that it indicates that life has evolved.

If it is accepted that life is likely to have evolved from the simple to the complex, the next question becomes, whether it has occurred as a plan of God, which is what is suggested by theists and the promoters of Intelligent Design (ID). ID is a term that has drawn some opposition, not just from Darwinian materialists, but also from scientists who believe in God, and even from some Catholic philosophers and theologians. The Benedictine priest, Fr Stanley Jaki, who is well known as a Catholic physicist and philosopher, claims that science cannot discover purpose in life, as this belongs to philosophy and metaphysics. For the same reason, he worries about the Intelligent Design (ID) movement invading metaphysics and being incompatible with it. This may be doing some injustice to those promoting ID, who are merely suggesting that the scientific complexity observed in physical, chemical and biological systems, indicates that life as we know it, in all its complexity, could not have occurred by chance or by the mechanism of natural selection, as described by Darwin. There are no pretensions among the mathematicians and biologists promoting ID, to define the purpose of life, of being, or the nature of God. This can be left to the philosophers and theologians.

At this stage, however, it must be said that just as natural selection does not explain all the complexity of life, so too Intelligent Design has some way to go before it is proven. Recently, I asked a mathematical friend to review Dembski's ideas on complexity and design.[154] His comments were interesting. The problem he saw with Dembski's ideas on design was that: "He assumes that design is on a par with chance and necessity. This precludes the idea that one or both of necessity and chance, may be aspects of design, a notion that some might consider fundamental to any proper understanding of God's creation." Looking at Dembski's criterion in practice, he further commented as follows:

> "In practice, we cannot take into account natural laws of which we are unaware. So any application of Dembski's scheme will inevitably involve using a weaker notion of

contingency and a weaker notion of complexity than those stated. They are weaker in the sense that more events will be deemed contingent and, correspondingly, more events will be deemed complex than in the theoretical scheme. These facts in turn mean that the practical version of Dembski's criterion is this: the event matches an independently formed pattern and, taking into account all known natural laws, has an extremely low probability of occurring. Because it eliminates ignorance of natural laws from its structure, this criterion has the advantage over the theoretical one that, for some events, it may be possible to calculate the level of their complexity with accuracy. The whole process then can be made precise by fixing a figure for the probability of occurrence below which an event is deemed to be complex.

But the criterion will no longer detect only the intelligent intervention that Dembski calls design. It will detect also the existence of hitherto unknown natural laws, without necessarily being able to state them with any exactness. Moreover, it will not be able to distinguish between intelligent intervention and new natural laws. In such a case, scientists will invariably assume the existence of some hitherto unknown law rather than herald an intervention. Who can blame them? Is this not precisely what experimental science has been doing all along? And surely most scientists, whether they are theists or not, stand in awe and wonder at the discovery of natural laws and at their operation. In the natural laws they find the most intricate and delicate patterns and the most compelling evidence of intent and design in the Universe. That Dawkins and others choose not to regard it as such, does not diminish its import one whit."

The Blind Watchmaker: In theology, ID is described as a teleological argument for the existence of God. Teleology is a study of purpose or directive principles in nature. Darwin's evolution theory, with natural selection, is supposed to be devoid of teleological or directive forces. Yet the evolutionary algorithm promoted for years by Richard Dawkins, in his book, The Blind Watchmaker, as a proof of how natural selection can produce complexity, is deeply teleological, as pointed out by Dembski.

In the example Dawkins gives, he starts off with twenty eight characters including letters and spaces. He then proceeds to change these at random using a computer programme (which in real life is supposed to represent random mutations in nucleic acid or amino acid changes in a protein structure). The purpose of the exercise is to reach the final sentence:

"METHINKS.IT.IS.LIKE.A.WEASEL"

(from Hamlet), which is known before hand, and which in turn represents a protein or piece of nucleic acid which is needed for the next step in order to increase the complexity of a living cell. The probability of getting it right on the first go, by complete chance, is estimated to be approximately 1×10^{40}. This is reduced dramatically by the computer program, which leaves unchanged a letter when it occurs in the right order (this is supposed to represent natural selection). There are many problems with this, however, as nobody has explained why each step is naturally selected and who revealed the destination in the first place? Thus, instead of 10^{40} tries on average, for pure chance to generate Dawkins' target sequence, it now takes only approximately 50 tries to generate it via this evolutionary algorithm. This algorithm preserves the correct position of the letters as they appear, so that they can be passed on to the next try (generation), as follows:

Try (0) WDLMNLT DTJBKWWIRZREZLMQCO P
Try (10) MDLDMNLS.ITJISWHRZREZ.MECS.P
Try (30) METHINGS.IT.ISWLIKE.B.WECSEL
Try (43) METHINKS.IT.IS.LIKE.A.WEASEL

There is no doubt that so called, point mutations (change in nucleic acid base pairs at one point), can have survival value for micro-organisms in hostile environments. Most point mutations, however, do more harm than good. To suggest that complex protein molecules can develop, through inheriting a sequence of these point mutations, is many steps too far, for our present understanding of genetics. If natural selection were to work in this super-efficient way, it would suggest a level of complexity, based on possibly layers of natural laws, still to be discovered, so complex that no scientist would be likely to ever understand. For a start, it would mean that individual nucleic acid base pairs or individual amino acid changes in the structure of proteins (which may lead to complex three dimensional structural changes), on the way to making new metabolic molecules, would have some kind of survival value, so that having this mutation, an organism would be naturally selected to survive. This level of extraordinary complexity could be used as a powerful argument for purposeful design.

Evolutionary algorithms, however, are supposed to be devoid of teleology. The algorithm described above could be compared with going through a very complex maze, in order to find the secret of how complexity has developed in life. The example given by Dawkins is like going through this maze with signs pointing to the way out at every junction. The question is, who put the signs up, and who built the maze in the first place? Dawkins is at pains to point out that natural selection is not random and not chance, but it has never been explained how natural selection could generate life from chemical molecules, or how the complexity of the DNA molecule originated. Dawkins describes faith as a great "cop-out" for those who want to believe in God. It could be said, with a lot more conviction, that to suggest that natural selection explains everything we need to know about the development of life, is wishful thinking in the extreme. The conclusion must be that in the natural order, there are no blind watchmakers, unless every move they make, and every step they take, is carefully guided by something or somebody.

Can we conclude therefore that Darwinism and natural selection can create complexity, if and only if, there is a teleological principal built into it? It could be that there are many new natural laws, still to be discovered, which will eventually explain the origin of life, but that still leaves the question of the source of these laws. It would be ironic if this evolutionary algorithm promoted by Dawkins, as a reason why God is not needed in evolution, turned out to be good evidence in favour of the need for God. It would even be a greater irony if Darwinism, which has been promoted for over a century, as a reason why God is not real, could turn out to be only the opening of a door to biological complexity, which will eventually reveal an inherent design system, as suggested by Behe, with no other reasonable explanation for life except a plan of God. As explained above, this complexity has now become apparent, at the physical mathematical level, in the anthropic coincidences maintaining life in the universe.

In trying to understand the totality of evolution, the first great marvel is how the mathematical values of the universal forces should be so finely tuned to allow the various chemical elements to be formed from the various subatomic particles, eventually leading to planets, stars and galaxies. This is the complexity of cosmic, chemical and stellar evolution. The next great marvel is how these elements should apparently have properties inherent in them to allow the complexity and the huge variety of molecular compounds to be formed, especially carbon based organic compounds, which would become the building blocks of living organisms. Then comes the mysterious appearance of the molecules, with the codes for life, in the form of the nucleic acids. The complexity of the information code in DNA, which controls metabolism and cell division, is now recognized as an extremely complex language system, which has not been explained by natural selection.

Finally comes the complexification of life structures into conscious humanity. This is the second great milestone, and by far the most significant one, in trying to understand evolution from a religious viewpoint. If we accept that the human body is likely to have evolved and come into existence like other forms of life, then there came the great moment in history when a human body was infused with a "soul" and the first parents of the human race were formed. Christian theology is clear that the beginning of the human race required a direct intervention by God in creating the "person/s", male and female, who were to be the first parents of the human race, and not only had a body, but also a spiritual soul, created directly by God. How humanity began is very much a mystery, both in science and in religion and for now, this should be accepted as such.

No longer was life just a mixture of molecules organized in such a way that it could reproduce itself. Now there was a life form that could reflect on itself, which was now a "person" with knowledge of good and evil, right and wrong. The soul is believed to be created by God, as each human person comes into existence. Christians also believe that souls do not die, but exist for ever and are judged by God, when the body is separated from the soul, at the death of each individual. A number of chapters in this book present the evidence and implications of this life after death for each individual human person. Many other religions have various beliefs and understandings of these individual souls (or spirits) which would not be in accord with Christian belief. Science has no competence in deciding for or against the existence of these spiritual souls.

In having a soul and body, humans, therefore, have two aspects to their nature. One has a biological origin and the other in the words of Emeritus Pope Benedict XVI in his book, *God and The World*,[155] "is a personal conception of God". In the same book the Pope comments on the great mystery of brutality in nature. The Catholic Church sometimes relates this to the "Fall of Adam and Eve". By rejecting God's rules, Adam and Eve, as the first human couple, changed the whole of creation, so that it no longer reflected the will of God. Creation afterwards became distorted towards an inclination to evil and violence in humanity, which was also reflected in the lower forms of life. Christians believe that man was created perfect and made in the image and likeness of God at the beginning of the human race, but this perfection was lost by rebellion against God's will. Many who would reject the concept of "Original Sin" can hardly doubt the inclination to evil which is an easily recognizable human weakness. See chapter 17 for further discussion on the origins of humanity.

A Summary of the Evidence for Evolution

In trying to summarize the evidence on evolution, I am left with the following conclusions:

> a) There is good biochemical and genetic evidence to link different species of life, strongly suggesting that life has evolved.
>
> b) Darwinism, with natural selection, is not sufficient to explain how the various species have increased in complexity. There is a great lack of evidence, clarity, and

understanding in explaining how the great variety and complexity of the various species of multicellular living organisms could develop from simpler unicellular life.

c) At this time in the history, evolution of life from simple inanimate matter to conscious humanity is by no means a fully explained scientific fact. If this evolution of life has occurred, the big question must be, what is responsible for the hidden force in nature and biology which has driven inanimate chemical matter and life towards complexity?

d) If life has evolved from the simple to the complex, therefore, we must firstly recognize that we do not fully understand how this process came about and secondly that there are at least two particular milestones which mark very major events in this process of evolution. These are the development of self perpetuating life forms from inanimate matter and the development of conscious humanity. Both of these are still very much in the realm of mystery.

e) There is strong evidence at the physical and mathematical level that the life supporting properties of our universe could not have come about by chance. This is evidence which cries out for a Creator.

In the end what we a looking for in the totality of evolution, is an explanation of how subatomic particles formed hydrogen gas and other elements, which evolved with increasing complexity to eventually reach conscious humanity. This is a pathway of astounding complexity, with such awesome unimaginable potential complexity hidden within the hydrogen atom that no human mind could or will ever completely understand. What we are looking at, is the Majesty of God.

Divine Design

I have presented some support evidence for the supernatural, and for the validity of Roman Catholic teaching, in chapters four, five and seven of this book. I have also emphasised the importance of further investigation and study for those who wish more evidence of this kind. In chapter five, I discussed briefly, the image of The Virgin of Guadalupe. Not only has scientific investigation indicated that this is not a normal painting, but there are reflections of persons in the enlarged eye of this image, similar to what can be seen in a human eye at a particular moment in time (see page 112). Further investigation of this image has revealed many other fascinating details which give an overwhelming impression, not just of a miraculous image, but also an image with an intricate, intelligent, and possibly "Divine Design".

The Aztecs communicated through written pictures and symbols, rather than a written language. Experts believe that the profound effect which this image had on the Aztec natives, leading them into the Catholic Church, can be explained by the extraordinary design detail of this image. Firstly the woman standing in front of the sun indicated that she was greater than their sun god, Huitzlipochtli. She stood on the moon, which also made her greater than the moon god, Tezcatlipoca. The angel holding her indicated to them that she was a Heavenly being. The blue green colour of her cloak indicated that she was connected with the divine and the sash at her waist, indicated that she was pregnant (with a divine child). Her posture of prayer and looking down, however, indicted that she was not a goddess herself, and that there was somebody greater than her. The white fur at the neck and sleeves marked royalty for the Aztecs. The broach at her throat was the same black cross worn by the Spanish Friars.

For the Aztecs, flowers also represented the divine. The four-petalled flower over her womb was an Aztec symbol pointing to "Ometeotl", the God who created all things. This flower,"nahui ollin" had more than eighty associations with divine attributes, which made it the perfect symbol of the Divine Presence, in the womb. Nine larger triangular flowers on the image are Mexican magnolia, which symbolized the beating heart of human sacrificial victims. Because there are nine, the nine levels of the Aztec underworld were perceived to be full, with no more need for human sacrifices. The pregnant woman wearing them indicated that her child would become the final complete victim.

The image was first seen when Juan Diego opened his tilma, to show the roses which The Virgin had collected for him, to the Bishop. It was estimated that this was the date of the winter solstice and it may have been at the exact moment of the solstice (10.36 a.m.), on 12th Dec. 1531 (the old Spanish calendar at that time was 10 days behind). The stellar sky map for the time of the solstice, in Mexico City, 1531, is also imprinted on The Virgin's mantle. The main constellations of the Northern sky can be seen on the right side of the cloak, with the Southern constellations on the left. The constellation of the Corona Boreans (Boreal Crown) rests upon The Virgin's head. Virgo (The Virgin) is on Her chest near her hands. Leo is on Her womb (where lies the Lion of Judah). The main star in Leo is Regulus, indicating king. There are many other details described in recent books on the symbolism in this image. These especially relate to The Holy Trinity, The Eucharist, and The Book of Revelation. Divine timing and Divine design seem unmistakable.

It is important to recognize that the symbolism of the stars, on The Virgin's Cloak, has nothing to do with astrology. The ancient cultures in Egypt, Persia, Greece, China, and Rome all recognized in the stars, the same constellations and the twelve signs of the

Zodiac. This came from a proper study of the stellar patterns throughout the year. Astrology only distorts the meaning of measurements made in astronomy. As with other miraculous signs and events described in this book, if you want more "proof", you will need to do your own further investigations.

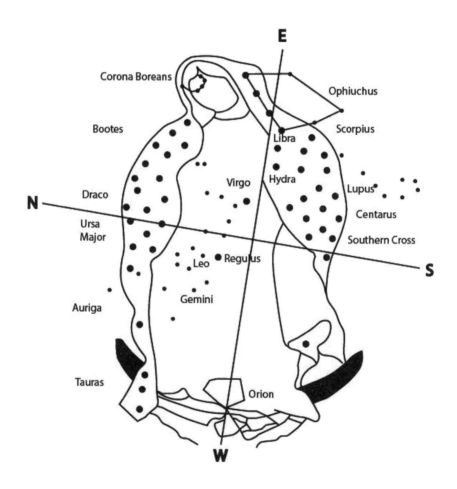

Conclusion

The complexity of our physical world is so far beyond what our small minds could conceive of, that it is truly a humbling experience to study and contemplate it. As explained above mathematics has already made an enormous contribution to our understanding of the universe. Mathematicians and physicists will eventually decide if it is possible to unite general relativity and quantum theory into a single theory. The mathematical complexity associated with the M theory is not an encouraging sign for early success, but the beauty and constant drive of mathematics, is not just describing precise relationships, but also in simplifying the complex. This was illustrated to me recently by a friend who introduced me to the equation:

$$e^{i\pi} = -1$$

"e" is an irrational number = 2.718, associated with natural logarithms. "i" is the square root of -1, discovered by the Irish mathematician, William Rowan Hamilton (associated with Hamilton Bridge in Dublin). "π" (pie) is the relation between the diameter and circumference of the circle. This equation helped me to appreciate more, the comment on mathematics made by Francis S. Collins, leader of the Human Genome Project in his book, The Language of God.[134] When referring to the beautiful universal equations that describe the reality of the natural world he said, "Are these mathematical descriptions of reality signposts to some greater intelligence? Is mathematics, along with DNA, another language of God? Certainly, mathematics has led scientists right to the doorstep of some of the most profound questions of all. First among them: how did it all begin?"

We must recognize that the truths of science and religion should not conflict but rather should complement one another in our efforts to understand our universe. From the study of chemistry, physics, and mathematics, particularly over the last 50 years, it now seems that the existence of God is becoming a strong rational probability as a way of explaining the fine tuning of the universe for conditions enabling life forms to develop. To more and more scientists the existence of what they would regard as a very complex design system makes the existence of God likely as a creator and first cause. When all of this is put together with the evidence for the miraculous and the supernatural described in other chapters of this book, as well as the evidence from metaphysics and philosophy, then the case for God becomes overwhelming.

It may be that quantum theory is the beginning of the road towards some understanding of how our complicated existence came about. This seems to exclude just simple materialism as an explanation. Einstein's theory of general relativity was accepted in favour of Newton's theory of gravity because Einstein's theory more accurately predicted the reality of the motion of the planet Mercury. In the same way any comprehensive theory which can explain the natural and supernatural observations which can be made in our world must lead to an acceptance of God as a reasonable hypothesis. Darwinism was proposed as an explanation for the way life has evolved through a process of natural selection, but it falls short as an explanation for the development of biological complexity. It also falls short as an explanation of how life began, how consciousness, morality, truth, love, goodness, appreciation of music, beauty and the many other intangibles developed. These deficiencies of Darwinism are the questions biologists need to honestly face and try to move beyond Darwinism. It is certain that the more we discover in biology the more we will continue to expand our understanding and appreciation that nature is majestic, beautiful and awe inspiring. As our understanding of the complexity increases so the evidence for a design plan is gaining favour, even if it is not yet proven. Gradually, it would seem science is moving us towards the realization that the world is truly, in the words of the poet, Gerard Manly Hopkins, "Charged with the grandeur of God".

It is a great myth, therefore, to believe that science is making God obsolete. The contrary is what is happening. The more science discovers the complexity of the universe, so also, the more science is pointing towards the need for a creator, to explain this complexity. Let us not forget that light travels at a speed of 300,000 kilometres every second. Travelling at that speed, it would take light at least 15 billion years to travel across our universe. As a way around the God hypothesis, materialists have proposed the existence of an almost infinite number of other universes, to explain why our universe is so finely tuned, so that it can support life as we know it. It may be that in the future we will be able to recognize that there is more than one universe, but for now, these other proposed enormous number of universes are not observable, not demonstrable, and are not detectable. Why then do so many continue to reject the God hypothesis as a realistic option? The vast majority, of course, of those, who do not believe in God, have never heard of the multi universe theory. The reason why some people are atheists and some are theists is complex, and probably has little to do with evidence, intelligence, logic, or reason. It is likely to have more to do with prejudices, inherited value systems, as well as some emotional experiences and other environmental influences. All of this is then shrouded in the mystery of iniquity combined with the final act of free will, to accept or reject God. I have to conclude that, those who cannot accept the possibility of the supernatural, suffer from some kind of mental or spiritual blindness, and they are cocooned in a false reality. Albert Einstein emphatically rejected, as false thinking, the conviction that only this which is cognizable to our senses exists.

Much positive evidence has been quoted in the earlier chapters of this book, in favour of the reality of God. On the other hand, evidence for atheism can only be negative and requires a lot more "blind faith". Most significantly of all, the God hypothesis can be tested. It is best tested by prayer as explained in chapter 7. I should warn those atheists, who sincerely investigate the God hypothesis by prayer and study that they need to be careful. Faith is very near, and they may be surprised or even shocked by the truth which they will undoubtedly discover. As a reward, however, they are also likely to be surprised by joy. As pointed out by Francis S. Collins,[134] however, it is rare for non-believers to look at the evidence for the existence of God. He says, "Some who have, and a rather distinguished list it is, have unexpectedly converted themselves to a belief in God."

To exclude the reality of God is also to exclude the reality of Hell. The great significance and tragedy of all of this is that many who reject the supernatural and reject God run the risk of being surprised by Hell. Some of my friends and acquaintances, who I respect and care about, fit into this category. Evidence for the existence of Hell was also described in the chapters 7 and 8.

10. Unidentified Flying Objects
Knowledge Increases Unreality
William Butler Yeats

Unidentified Flying Objects (UFOs) are of many and varied types. Some prefer to use the term UAP (Unidentified Aerial Phenomena) to separate more serious investigations, or for other reasons, as the term UFO can be over emotional or used to describe flippant observations of little interest. In general, however, UFO and UAP are interchangeable terms. The interest in this topic has grown steadily over the last hundred years. Some interest, no doubt, has been driven by the increase in the number and variety of flying objects now seen in the sky which are easily identified, so the odd one out, not so easily identified, becomes a curiosity and of interest. The growth in number and variety of main-stream media outlets have, no doubt, also contributed, with reporters world-wide always searching for a good story, which will catch the interest of the public and of course, in very recent years, the availability of social media outlets. There is also evidence, however, that UFO sightings are grossly under-reported. The reason for this may range from fear of ridicule, to assuming that there is a normal rational explanation, to not knowing where the report should be made, to just lack of concern and interest. There is also the encouragement to pilots from some airlines not to file UFO reports and a very strong message from some governments that they do not wish to hear about such reports being made public.

Most of the sightings of UFOs over the years usually finish up with good explanations when the facts are examined and the various experts consulted. A small percentage, 5% or less are not, however, explained and the 'facts' as they emerge point towards, mystery, intrigue, obfuscation of the truth and sometimes military 'cover-ups' and 'classification' of information. These efforts to hide information, especially by government military and secret service authorities, only add to the intrigue and interest. The effort in this chapter is try to extract some truth from the tangled webs often woven around the facts, particularly by some world governments in an effort to conceal the truth, for whatever reason. Although at this stage there are several thousands of detailed reports of UFO sightings, in this short account we have to restrict interest to the following categories:

1. Objects in the sky observed with solid radar evidence.
2. Objects reported by significant numbers of well qualified observers.
3. Where the objects credibly reported possessed extraordinary physical characteristics or movement capabilities, well beyond known technology.

The big question of course, for all who have an interest in UFOs is: are Alien life forms for real and are we being visited by other world creatures?

We must be grateful to the French who made public the first comprehensive official government report on the subject of UFOs, in 1999. This was the COMETA report, which was produced by thirteen retired generals, as well as aviation scientists and aero-space experts, who spent three years investigating official French military records, which also included data from other countries, on reports of UFO sightings. Of the conclusions reached, the first was that the evidence for UFOs pointed to a real phenomenon, with grave national security implications, warranting immediate international attention. They also said that, of the approximately 5% of UFO sightings that **cannot** be attributed to known natural explanations or secret military operations, they seem to comprise of, "completely unknown flying machines with exceptional performances that are guided by a natural or artificial intelligence." They finally said that, the most logical explanation for these sightings is, "the extraterrestrial hypothesis."

We must be grateful also to the good investigative journalists, such as Leslie Kean, who have helped to promote the above COMETA report in the public domain as well as helping to open many hitherto secret government files, through freedom of information legislation. Leslie Kean's book, *UFOs – Generals, Pilots, and Government Officials go on the Record*,[158] has made a major contribution, documenting factual details of UFO sightings worldwide and is a "must read" for all those interested in a serious study of UFOs. This book documents evidence of experts from nine different countries and summarizes conclusions as follows:

1. "There exists in our skies, worldwide, a solid, physical phenomenon that appears to be under intelligent control and is capable of speeds, manoeuvrability, and luminosity beyond current known technology.
2. UFO incursions, often in restricted airspace, can cause aviation safety hazards and raise national security concerns, even though the objects have not demonstrated overtly hostile acts.
3. The U.S. government routinely ignores UFOs and when pressed, issues false explanations. This indifference and/or dismissals are irresponsible, disrespectful to credible expert witnesses, and are potentially dangerous.
4. The hypothesis that UFOs are of extraterrestrial or inter-dimensional origin is a rational one and must be taken into account, given the data we have. However, the actual origin and nature of UFOs have not yet been determined by scientists, and remain unknown.

5.   Given its potential implications, the evidence calls for systematic scientific investigation involving U.S. government support and international cooperation."

The Belgian Wave

Leslie Kean begins her book with an account of the best ever documented localized cases of UFO sightings. These were a "wave" of UFO sightings in Belgium, over a two year period, beginning on November 29th 1989. The details of the events were given to her by the Belgium Major General Wilfried De Brouwer, who was asked at the time, to investigate the problem, by the Belgium Minister for Defence. General De Brouwer was noted for his meticulous attention to detail and factual accuracy and was described as never being prone to exaggeration or embellishment. De Brouwer described that, "hundreds of people saw majestic triangular crafts with a span of approximately one hundred and twenty feet and powerful beaming spotlights, moving very slowly without making any significant noise but, in several cases, accelerating to very high speeds."

During the two year period these silent, gliding or hovering objects, usually triangular in shape, were seen by thousands of people, including many police officers, and investigated by government officials and university scientists. Secret military aircraft, such as American stealth fighters and American or other "black ops" were eliminated early on. The general opinion of highly qualified expert witnesses was that they were not dealing with conventional technology. Despite the great number of witnesses and the frequency of observations, only a few photographs were taken. These events, however, were before the wide availability of cell phone cameras. Some unusual phenomena were also noted with the photographs which were taken. Very bright spotlights on the UFOs were hardly visible in photographs and it was also difficult to detect the triangular shape of the UFOs in the photographs, which was easily visible to the naked eye. It was suggested by experiments that these aberrations were due to infrared light around the UFO, which apparently can cause objects to disappear in photographs. Other photographs analysed by NASA and French experts from French National Space Research revealed a halo around the UFO. Special optical processing inside the halo showed the light particles forming a pattern like snowflakes in turbulence around the craft similar to iron filings in a magnetic field. Professor Marion from the Department of Nuclear Physics, at the University of Paris-Sud and the National Space Centre said that this could suggest that the UFO was moving by using a magnteoplasmadynamic propulsion system as suggested by Professor Auguste Meessen in one of his studies.

On the first night of November 29th 1989, it was estimated that more than 1,500 individuals saw the flying objects from over seventy locations. Other nights of interest were December 11, 1989, April 22nd, 26th and July 28th 1990, and 11th and 15th March 1991. On July 28th 1990, a husband and wife couple decided to flash their car lights at one of the crafts flying 60 to 100 metres above the car. The craft responded by tilting towards the car and the lights from the craft were flashed three times. Overall there were approximately 2000 reported cases registered by government authorities. In the end the origin of the flying objects, witnessed by thousands of people over Belgium between 1989 and 1991 could not be determined. The Belgian government were honest in admitting this publicly.

A summary of some of the conclusions from official government investigations were as follows:

(a) Not one aggressive hostile act was noted.
(b) No electromagnetic effects, such as radio interference was noted.

(c) Most but not all of the flying objects were triangular in shape.

(d) The flying objects did not try to hide but came close to the observers and responded to signals such as turning on and off lights.

(e) The technology exhibited was much more advanced than known human technology even to this day. Examples were: Stationary or hovering vertical or at 45 degree angles, accelerating faster than any known aircraft while being silent. Experts were convinced that the spotlights were of a very advanced technology. The ground could be completely illuminated from approximately 100 metres. On occasions red balls of light were seen to leave the crafts and later seen to return.

UFOs and many odd unexplained incidents

There is historical evidence of UFOs being around for millennia. In 1663 and 1892 there were descriptions of UFOs over Moscow. Leslie Kean, in her book[158], describes an interview which she had with Dr. Richard Haines, a retired senior research scientist from NASA Ames Research Centre. He had constructed a database of over 3400 first hand UFO sightings by commercial, military, and private pilots. The descriptions were many and varied, "ranging from silver discs to green fireballs, flying loops around passenger aircraft, pacing alongside despite pilots' evasive attempts, or flooding cockpits with blinding light." There was never any attempt to attack or damage the aircrafts and the principal safety concerns were judged to be from the pilots' response to these experiences. Evidence from many accounts of sightings, especially by pilots, seem to suggest that some UFOs have the ability to disappear, possibly using some kind of shield and it has been suggested that UFOs may also have some kind of Force Field

Generators to repel laser weapons and protect against missiles. There were many shapes described for UFOs. The most common shapes noted were, saucer, cigar, round orbs, and triangular or boomerang.

High Speed Movement: There are many descriptions of UFOs moving at incredible speeds and then doing a sharp right or left hand turn. No biological system could survive the enormous gravitation (G) forces generated by these speeds, so it is surmised that UFOs must have some form of inertia/drag cancelling technology. The limit of the G force which a human can survive is less than 10G, before loss of consciousness, and it was estimated that UFOs flying at high speeds, with the sharp turns observed, would be generating G forces in the hundreds if not thousands.

Mexico, 6th Dec. 1952: Four objects approached an Air Force fighter jet at a speed of several thousand kilometres per hour. As they flew by, one broke away and began to track the plane for a short period. Next all four reformed and joined what looked like a much larger "mother ship" which then flew away at speeds exceeding 9,000 miles per hour.

UFO over Tehran: On 18th September 1976 a large bright UFO began to circle over Tehran, about 6,000 feet up, seen by large numbers of witnesses. The Air Force sent two F-4 fighter planes up to investigate. General Parviz Jafari, who was one of the pilots and the flight commander at the time, described the incident in Leslie Kean's book. There was an intense red, green, orange and blue light coming from the craft. As he moved up close about 25 miles distant, suddenly in an instant, the UFO jumped back to 27 miles. Then a round bright orb, like a bright moon came out of the craft and moved towards him at great speed. He decided to launch a missile because at this stage he got very scared and surmised that he was being attacked. Suddenly nothing was working. All instruments were out of action, including his radio. He thought that he would have to eject before the impact, but the approaching object stopped suddenly about four miles away, then circled around him and went back to join the main craft. Another bright moon like object came out of the main craft and headed rapidly towards the ground. It landed gently on the ground radiating a powerful light, so bright that he could see all the sands from about fifteen miles away. An emergency squaking noise was heard from this area where the small craft landed. After landing at his own base, he flew with a helicopter, over the area and landed where the squaking noise was heard but he could see nothing disturbed or any object which could explain the source of the on-going noise. This noise went on for days and was also heard by commercial aircraft flying overhead.

This event got great publicity in Tehran at the time. The Shah of Iran was still in power at the time and he took a great personal interest in it, including talking personally to the air crew. An American Lieutenant Colonel from the American Air Force, who was an adviser in Tehran at the time, said that the pilot was lucky that his equipment did not work and that he was unable to fire the missile. Later the American Air Force issued a statement saying that, "This case is a classic which meets all the criteria necessary for a valid study of the UFO phenomenon." There were multiple highly credible witnesses from different locations, there was radar evidence of the objects, the loss of instruments happened to three aircraft (a commercial flight in the vicinity also had instrument loss for a period), as well as an inordinate amount of manoeuvrability displayed by the UFOs. The information was also said to be "confirmed by other sources."

The Roswell Incident: This incident is famous and at the same time infamous. It concerns a crash of some kind of UFO near Roswell, New Mexico in July, 1947. It happened at a time when interest in UFOs was growing, due to many reports published in the 1940s, especially during WWII. There were a number of witnesses and some described unusual materials and the bodies of aliens at the site, which were described as having been taken away by the military. It has become famous because of the wide publicity at the time and it has become infamous because it marked the start of an aggressive campaign by the US government and military to suppress, debunk, and misinform the public about this and other UFO sightings. The government began at the time by suggesting that it was a weather balloon which crashed. The story was later changed to imply that it was a device used for spying on Russia. The final status of this incident remains shrouded in deep confusion and remains buried under many layers of government mis-information, lies, and what reads like Byzanthine intrigue.

In her book, Leslie Kean traces the roots of UFO debunking in the US. In 1947, Lieutenant General Nathan Twining sent a secret memo concerning "Flying Discs" to the Commander of the Army and Air Forces at the Pentagon. Based on numerous reports furnished by various branches of the Air Forces he said, "the phenomenon reported is something real and not visionary or fictitious." He further commented on the extraordinary manoeuvrability of these crafts which must be controlled, either manually, automatically, or remotely. He described the crafts as metallic or light reflecting, normally silent, circular or elliptical with flat bottoms and domed tops. Following this, a security study group was set up with the code name "Sign". A report from *Project Sign* later concluded that the UFOs were most likely extraterrestrial. The study group was later named *Project Grudge* which then became the well known *Project Blue Book* in 1951. In 1952 the CIA became aware of, "sightings of unexplained objects at great altitudes and travelling at high speeds in the vicinity of major defence installations ...not attributable to natural phenomena or known types of aerial vehicles."

The CIA began working on a national policy in 1953. It was decided that as UFOs did not show any threat to national security, the sole objective should be to reduce the public interest so as to prevent alarm. *Project Blue Book* ran from 1951 to 1970 with the job of investigating reported sightings of UFOs but with the sole intention of misleading the public on the details and significance of the data collected. It was common to have ridiculous explanations accepted for the incidents reported. In 1966, for example, during a two day period, in Dexter and Hillsdale, Michigan, over one hundred witnesses saw UFOs at low altitudes. These were later explained by an Air Force spokesperson as due to swamp gas. The ridicule by the media in the aftermath apparently became legendary and made everybody realize that the debunking had gone too ridiculous and too far. The official line now is that the US government is not officially investigating UFO reports and has no specific interest in the subject, but nobody with any knowledge of UFOs believes that.

Canada's Roswell: On 4th October 1967 there were dozens of witnesses who saw four unusual orange lights flashing in formation, over Shag Harbour, a small fishing village in Nova Scotia, Canada. The lights were later seen to go into the water, a few hundred metres off-shore, by members of the Royal Canadian police, accompanied by 16 other witnesses. In the beginning, this was assumed to be a plane crash and rescue services were contacted. Fishing boats over the crash area, however, could find no debris. The only material found was a 300 foot slick of sulphurous smelling yellow foam which they were unable to collect. Divers sent by the Canadian Navy also failed to find any evidence of a crash after a three day search according to official reports. By the 8th of October it had become a national story, and there was talk of a UFO and of a government cover-up. The media then began to play down the idea of a UFO and a Jesuit priest, Fr Michael B. Gaffney, who was an astronomer in St Mary's

University in Halifax and a great sceptic of UFOs, was given significant publicity.

Christopher Styles witnessed the event when he was a young boy from nearby Dartmouth. The event made a deep impression on him and as an adult he collected information on all the details he could get on the story. When official government documents became declassified 25 years later, he was able to acquire access to them for study. His discoveries from the released documents were unexpected and revealing. There were many reports of UFO-like activity from all over Nova Scotia on that night of October 4th, including some from airline pilots. Sightings were recorded all along the coast of Nova Scotia in the hours before the Shag Harbour sighting. These sightings included a solid image on a Decca radar system for two hours, in a large fishing vessel off Sambro.

Christopher Styles also discovered that the Navy had also concentrated a major search and diving investigation at Shelburne, which was 25 miles up the coast from Shag Harbour. This was recognized as a centre for oceanography, which was closed to the public, but it was also used as a monitoring station for foreign submarines. Two crafts were discovered on the ocean floor and non-human creatures were described, with one craft apparently assisting the other. A number of ships kept vigil for about six days but were then called away unexpectedly to confront an intruding submarine. When the ships disappeared, both submerged crafts surfaced and flew away. This also coincided with multiple separate eyewitness accounts of two UFOs seen in the sky over the area from Shag Harbour to Yarmouth, at approximately 10 p.m. on 11th October. Generally there was an impressive amount of detail in the government documents released after 25 years and one report described the paper trail for these events, from the various government and military agencies, as being a mile wide. In common with the US government investigations of UFO incidents, the Canadian authorities decided that this information should be suppressed at the time of the events and were it not for a few enthusiasts, would have remained hidden. We must be grateful to Christopher Styles and those who helped him for breaking the barriers of the "free" press and spilling the beans.

British UFO Incidents

The British government has generally been much more open about UFO documentation than the US government. Prime Minister, Winston Churchill was known to have developed an interest in UFOs from investigations into some reported RAF sightings, during WWII. He did suggest, however, that this information should be classified for at least fifty years, in order to avoid causing panic and / or undermining Christian faith. Nick Pope was appointed official in charge of UK government UFO investigations, between 1991 and 1994. His early sceptic attitude was quickly overcome by the power of the evidence which he encountered during his enforced period of interest. He subsequently became one of the most prominent and outspoken former government officials, on the solid evidence for the reality of UFOs. Of the large number of sightings recorded, three short accounts are chosen just to give a flavour of the evidence and the variety.

Rendlesham Forest UFO Event: This occurred near Ipswich, late on Christmas night, 1980. The main witnesses were US Air Force personnel stationed at the RAF bases at Bentwaters and Woodbridge, in Suffolk. A three man patrol from the 81st Security Police Squadron saw a small metallic craft moving through the trees and landing in a small clearing. They approached and saw strange hieroglyphs on the side of the craft. They estimated the size to be about three metres tall and about three metres wide at the base and the fabric on the shell was described as "like a smooth opaque black glass." The base commander, Lieutenant Colonel Charles Halt, was very sceptical but two nights later, when the UFO returned, he was able to see for himself. As his team tracked the clearly visible returned UFO, they noticed that their radio equipment and lights began to malfunction. Commander Halt described what he saw as like a large eye winking at you, which irritated or burned the eyes of the on-lookers. Light beams were coming from the craft down beside commander Halt and his men.

Commander Halt later wrote an official report on this UFO incident and became one of the most senior military officers ever to go on record regarding a UFO sighting. He described the craft as metallic in appearance and triangular in shape. There was a pulsating red light on top and a bank of blue lights underneath. The animals in a nearby farm were noted to be making a lot of noise. Radiation measured at the landing site was discovered afterwards to be about seven times what would be expected for that area.

There was also a report of even more extraordinary events in Rendlesham Forest on the night of December 28th as witnessed by Sgt. Adrian Bustinza and private Larry Warren, who were out on patrol around 11pm. They witnessed a small red ball of light move in from the coast at great speed and hover about 20 feet above the ground. It was the size of an American basketball. This red light suddenly exploded and a craft appeared on the forest floor. They also claimed to have witnessed an alien being and later observed the craft take off at a forty five degree angle at great speed. All this happened without noise.

When Nick Pope took over responsibility for UFO investigations in the UK in 1991, he reviewed all these records of this case in detail. He discovered that it was not properly investigated at the time of occurrence, most likely due to an inadvertent date error in the Halt report. When the preliminary investigations looked for radar support the wrong dates were being looked at. Nick Pope was able to confirm radar evidence for a UFO when the correct dates were used. In summary therefore, not only was there radar confirmation but the UFO in this event actually landed and was seen close up, by many military witnesses and thus there was strong corroborating physical evidence. Witnesses were described as being in great awe at the advanced technology.

Cosford UFO Incident: This was on March 30th and 31st 1993. It was a coincidence that on the same date exactly, three years previously, there was a major UFO occurrence during the Belgian *wave* (see above, page 386). There were a series of sightings over two nights, with hundreds of witnesses, including RAF, military and police officers, who saw UFOs over the RAF base in Shropshire. A report from Staffordshire detailed a UFO estimated at 200 meters in diameter. Another report described a UFO moving slowly at 40 mph over the countryside before it suddenly moved away at a speed many times the fastest military plane known. When the UK government made inquiries through the US embassy, to out-rule any secret US operations, they discovered that the US were also experiencing similar sightings themselves at the time, but information on these was being suppressed.

Gigantic UFO's over the English Channel: A commercial pilot, Ray Bowyer with his passengers witnessed two enormous UFOs on April 23rd, 2007, off the coast of Normandy. Both were emitting light and were of a brilliant yellow cigar shape with a dark band two thirds of the way from one end. On reporting this observation to Jersey air traffic control, they were able to confirm that they had two reflections from primary radar fitting this observation, both to the southwest of Alderney. He later determined, with assistance from air traffic control, that he was approximately fifty miles away from the UFOs and from his years of experience judging size at distance, he compared these UFOs with a small town, and judged them to be approximately a mile long. Ray Bowyer was also later informed by Jersey air traffic control that another pilot had made a report of a sighting of one of these UFOs matching the description which he had reported and within the same time frame, twenty miles south of the tiny island of Sark, while inbound to Jersey from the Isle of Man.

Many other reports of UFO incidents have been described by Neil Arnold in his book, *Shadows in the Sky – The Haunted Airways of Britain.*[160]

UFOs in Russia

Stalin, like Churchill, had a great interest in UFOs and this interest continued after WWII. There are a number of incidents recorded, and now in the public arena, which involved the shooting down of UFO crafts by the Soviet air force. There are also available a number of accounts made public of some UFOs crash landing. In all situations these crafts were taken away by KGB agents for detailed examination.

In 1948 there was an encounter between a Soviet MiG pilot and a silver cigar shaped UFO. The Soviet pilot was ordered to engage. It is believed that the UFO fired a particle beam weapon at the Soviet pilot, who reported that he was being blinded by some kind of rays. At the same time a lucky shot with a Soviet missile damaged the anti-gravity / force field of the UFO, or caught it off guard, with the result that both crafts crashed to the ground. Soviet teams quickly salvaged the wreckage and transported it to Kapustin Yar. This was the location for a secret military air base in Russia for many years. It is located 500 miles south of Moscow and 60 miles east of Volgograd.

In 1969 there was a report of a UFO crash in the state of Sverdlovsky. A video account was broadcast on a TV show, where video evidence was presented of the recovery. This show also included video evidence of an alien in the cockpit. It was also noted that three coroners who did an autopsy on this creature all died on the same day, 24th March, 1969, one week after the autopsy. The cause of death was unknown.

There was also a report of a UFO being shot down near the city of Prohlandnyi on August 10th, 1989. The craft was small (20 feet long) and cigar shaped. Two dead alien bodies and one barely alive were reported to be in the craft. It was reported that efforts to keep the injured alien alive failed. The UFO was taken to Kapustin Yar. The aliens were between three and four feet tall. They were described as having a grey outer layer covering a blue green reptilian like skin. They had no hair, large black eyes with a covering protective lid, and long slender arms with webbed fingers. The aliens are said to be preserved in large specimen jars, which would be good physical corroborating evidence for this story, when and if these specimens are made available to public scrutiny.

A Melbourne event with safety implications

There is a general impression of a non-aggressive attitude from the many thousands of UFO incidents now recorded world-wide. There is also, however, the impression of great curiosity on behalf of the UFOs and this combined with the very rapid speeds and the very high manoeuvrability which these mysterious crafts seem to have, can together create major safety problems. There can be near misses and pilots over reacting to a perceived danger can make the situation more dangerous. Sometimes UFOs can interfere with flight radio communications and navigation guidance equipment and this will also have obvious safety implications.

A particular unexplained event took place near Melbourne, Australia, on October 21st, 1978. It involved twenty year old Frederick Valentich, while flying a single engine propeller plane, at an altitude of 4,500 feet, over Bass Strait. Just after 9pm he radioed air traffic control at Tullamarine airport in Melbourne. For six to seven minutes he described a UFO with a green light which kept orbiting his plane at great speed and chasing him. He described the structure as long, metallic and shiny but not an aircraft. At the end of his recorded communication there was a period of seventeen seconds of a metallic sound, before all went silent. There were twenty eyewitnesses from the ground who saw this event take place in the early stages, before the small plane and the orbiting erratic green light went out of sight. This young man was never seen after this event and no sign of the plane was ever discovered. The news of this strange event was reported at the time in the mainstream media world-wide.

Extraterrestrials & Alien Abductions

John E. Mack was a well known Harvard Professor, who worked as a psychiatrist at Harvard University's Cambridge Hospital. He shocked the academic community in 1990, when he said publicly that individuals he had examined and who had claimed that they were abducted by Aliens, were not crazy but that their experiences were genuine. He began his first contact with these patients by trying to define their mental disorder. He quickly found that he was unable to define any recognizable psychiatric or delusional illness and developed a great interest in their stories. He studied over 200 of these individuals in some detail, including business people, students, writers, psychologists and other professionals. Over many years, he developed a great respect, sympathy, rapport and friendship with them. He said that dreams do not behave like that and there is a "compelling powerful phenomenon here which I cannot account for."

Those who get abducted, sometimes referred as an "experiencer", explain that the encounters can happen at any time, but most commonly in their homes at night. They describe being very hot, unable to move and sometimes floating through solid objects. They are accompanied by a number of humanoid beings who bring them onto some kind of space ship. Instruments are then used to penetrate many organs.

When Professor Mack went public by publishing a book on the subject, *Abduction: Human Encounters with Aliens*, he received a letter from the university informing him that his work was to be investigated. He was accused of harming his patients rather than curing them by confirming them in their delusional states. The inquiry continued for over one year and it became very public. Eventually after evidence from many supporters, Harvard dropped the accusations and issued a statement, reaffirming his academic freedom to study what he wished and that he "remains a member in good standing of the Harvard Faculty of Medicine". In 2004 Professor Mack died after being knocked over by a drunk driver in the north of London, UK. He was visiting the city to give a lecture on a subject for which he had previously received a Pulitzer prize in 1977.

Cattle Mutilations and Crop Circles

There is a lot of circumstantial evidence collected over the years, linking UFO sightings with these two mystifying global puzzles. Bret Lueder, in his excellent book, *A UFO Hunter's Guide*[159], discusses these two mysterious occurrences as well as many other unusual phenomena which have been linked to UFO sightings.

Cattle Mutilations: In the case of cattle mutilations there are no signs of other animal scavengers and the mutilations have all the signs of intelligent design. Some of the theories put forward to explain them are, secret mad cow disease monitoring, secret weapons testing, Satanic cults, and extraterrestrial/UFO related testing. Some of the very odd occurrences noted by Bret Lueder in his book were, increased radiation levels around some of the mutilated animals, metal objects of 90% platinum located within some animals, cows whose brains were missing with no break in the cranium, spines that were excised in impossible ways, and carcasses which did not decay even in heated rooms. All this and more, surrounding these mutilations, seems very strange indeed and we have to begin to question how reliable all these reports are, but there are a lot of them. If we accept that the UFO phenomena have a physical realness then an association with cattle mutilation is a possibility but this needs a lot more solid investigation. UFOs have been sighted on the days before and in the vicinity of farms, where mutilated animals were later found.

Crop Circles: These have been with us for centuries. They are mysterious mathematically very precise designs carved into crops in fields, with no definite known cause. In the 1970s a variety of these appeared over the South of England and although the circles have been noted in over twenty countries, the great majority have occurred in England, especially in Wiltshire and Hampshire. These countries have very large deposits of chalk and this has led to the suggestion that this may be related to the cause. Some believe that the crop circles are caused by some kind of electromagnetic beam technology and one investigator, Freddy Silva, has reported photographs of beams of light associated with Crop Circles. The Australian, Brian Sullen, has associated a high pitched sound with these beams in the range 6 kHz. The UFO Magazine 24, number 2, March 2011, discusses a video shot by John Whaley on August 11, 1996, known as *The Oliver's Castle Video*, which shows two orbs creating a crop circle. The film maker Patty Greer, who was the author of the article, explained how when this video was played backwards slowly, a direct line of communication became visible, between the two balls of light, just before the circle was laid down. Many books have now been written on the mystery of Crop Circles, but the mystery remains. The connection with UFOs, is a common theme, in most of the books published on the possible cause of crop circles. The Nexus magazine is a very good source for regular informative articles on UFO news as well as Crop Circles. See Nexus Vol. 23 No. 6, 2016 (and others) for some beautiful extraordinary pictures of Crop Circles.

What do we conclude?

The evidence presented above is suggestive that there is much more to the UFO story than imagination, hallucinations or realistic dreams of one kind or another. The problem is that we make judgments based on prejudice as much as we make judgments based on evidence. Many like to think that everything they believe is based on evidence, even on scientific evidence as much as possible, but on close investigation we find that beliefs are based on feelings and "hunches" as much as on evidence. For most of my life, I would have rejected the idea of UFOs and extraterrestrial forms of life as nonsense, with no substantial evidence. Over the last decade, I have changed my mind, mainly due to the good quality books which I have encountered on the subject and the evidence presented.

Two of the contributors to Leslie Kean's book made some comments on why in the "elite" culture, discussing UFOs is taboo. The individuals involved were Raymond Duvall, Professor and Chair of the Department of Political Science at the University of Minnesota and Alexander Wendt, Professor of International Security at the Ohio State University. Although in popular culture interest in UFOs is very common, the "elite" culture dictated by governments, the scientific community and mainstream media have the official view that UFOs are "not real." The current official view is that UFOs result from overactive imaginations and serious thinkers do not discuss this subject. The problem is the **evidence**, which points in another direction. Why the resistance? At least we should have an open mind on the question and admit that as UFOs are unidentified and that we just don't know the origin of these objects. Furthermore, why the need to cover-up and falsify facts relating to UFOs? Is it the fear that extra-terrestrials may engender?

Professor Wendt and Professor Duvall noted some arguments offered by sceptics as a reason why UFOs cannot be real. One of the arguments often used is the physical constraints of interstellar travel. The nearest star system that might support life is suggested to be too far away for Aliens to travel to earth, that is, 4,500 years travelling at 70,000 miles per hour. Another argument used is that because of our advanced surveillance technology we would definitely know if aliens were visiting earth but the problem here is that the mountain of evidence that is there, is denied, undermined, altered and generally debunked as a national policy by some governments.

The Cometa 1999 report produced on behalf of the French government was the first sign that at last world governments were beginning to take well substantiated UFO sightings seriously. The French government is generally acclaimed for maintaining the most productive, systematic scientific investigation of UFO sightings. It seemed that the French prompted more openness by other countries and since 2004, as pointed out by Leslie Kean, Australia, Brazil, Canada, Chile, France, Ireland, Mexico, Peru, Russia, Uruguay, and the United Kingdom have released secret files. In 2009, Denmark and Sweden followed by each releasing 15,000 files. Alas some governments, especially the US have continued to promote cover-ups and misinformation on the subject.

Accepting that there is substantial evidence for UFOs does immediately pose the question, where do they come from? The technology in UFOs seems to be very superior to ours and it is possible that our present perceived knowledge of the limitations of time travel may also be very inferior. Einstein explained the bending of space and Einstein's equations are said to be littered with *wormholes.* A good way to describe how much faster it would be to travel by wormholes in space travel is to imagine a big sheet folded over with a small hole in the middle from one side to the other. Going through the hole is a much faster way of getting from one side to another rather than travelling on the surface down to the edge and then back to the middle from the other side. It is also possible that there may be parallel universes which we still do not understand and appreciate.

In this short discourse it was possible only to give a very small flavour, of the very large number of observed occurrences of UFO incidents now recorded, with the descriptions readily available in various forms of printed and on-line media. Opinions and theories should be based on evidence in so far as possible. Based on the many detailed data sets collected by and from what seems to be very reliable sources, one is forced to conclude, that the evidence for UFOs in the form of physical flying crafts or machines, with technology far superior to anything which could be manufactured on earth by human efforts, is substantial.

There is also evidence for alien beings on board and controlling some of these crafts but this evidence is less compelling. Although there are numerous accounts of UFO crashes and of aliens been seen, alive and dead, associated with UFOs, as well as reports of autopsies done on some of the aliens (see section above on UFOs in Russia), there is still a lack of good physical verification evidence for alien bodies. The final proof for alien life associated with UFOs can only come when the bodies of these creatures are presented as evidence by those governments that have been reported to have captured and stored alien bodies, following UFO crashes. By the 1980s it was estimated that there were at least 150 global reports of UFO crashes. There were sixty more reported in the 1990s.[159] The alternative news magazine, *Nexus*, reports occasional articles on UFO related phenomena. In the February/March 2017 edition of Nexus, the author, Linda Moulton Howe, presented a detailed report on the life of a US special agent, who had a secret undercover job of retrieving bodies of aliens from crashed UFOs. A number of different types of aliens were described. These included "Greys" from the Roswell crash (see page 390 above), that were smaller than humans. Other types were described, such as the Reptilians, with green scaly and leathery skin and these were much taller than humans.

The assumption is that those countries, where alien bodies are reputed to be preserved, are not willing to make this physical evidence available for public verification. There may be an International understanding, among the select elite, that general humanity is not mature enough to accept this shock and thus, that it would do more harm than good. The doubt about the existence of preserved alien bodies, therefore, remains.

Evidence should always be the compass needle that points us towards truth. As well as the pointed end of compass needles, however, there is also the blunt end pointing in the opposite direction. The fuzz of prejudice can sometimes conceal the direction indicated by the evidence and lead to the wrong conclusion. This was wonderfully summarized by G K Chesterton, when he commented on the validity of miraculous events. **He said that those who believe in miracles do so because of the evidence, whereas those who refuse to believe in miracles do so because of faith.** That is, the faith that "knowing" there is no rational explanation for miracles, they conclude that they cannot be real, and essentially ignore the evidence. In the case of UFOs, this was also illustrated by the differing opinion of two scientists.

The nuclear physicist and author, Stanton T. Friedman, is regarded as an International icon for UFO researchers. He has written widely on the subject. In the US he presented evidence at the UN and provided written testimony to congressional hearings. He also challenged all Air Force personnel to refute what he called, irrefutable evidence, for the existence of flying saucers and the fact that some of them are from outer space. Carl Sagan (1934 – 1996), on the other hand, who was a well-known physicist, astronomer, and television host, completely rejected evidence for UFOs. He was a supporter of the US government *Project Blue Book*, which had the reputation, not for investigating evidence for UFO incidents but for stalling or debunking these investigations. At the same time, somewhat ironically, Carl Sagan was a supporter of the US government funded project, Search for Extraterrestrial Intelligence (SETI) which listened for and beamed radio waves into outer space. Many UFO enthusiasts cannot understand why at least some of these funds spent on SETI, were not put into UFO research which would be much more likely to lead positive results as well as produce physical evidence. Stanton Friedman dubbed SETI as "silly effort to investigate."

UFOs, Extraterrestrials, Padre Pio, and The Virgin Mary

Some years ago, I was given two references to two occasions when the famous Capuchin Friar, St Padre Pio of Pietrelcina, Italy, was asked about intelligent life on other planets. I valued his comments because of his extraordinary supernatural gifts including his gift of knowledge, which was confirmed by many specific detailed events (see page 102). One of his comments was, **"The Lord certainly did not limit His glory to this small Earth. On other planets other beings exist who did not sin and fall as we did."** –from a book by Don Nello Castello, *Cosi Parlo Padre Pio (Thus spoke Padre Pio),* Vicenza 1974. On another occasion in response to the remark, "Padre, some claim that there are creatures of God on other planets as well." His response was,

"What else? Do you think that there are no other beings that love The Lord?" This dialogue was said to be officially published by the Capuchin Order, but I have been unable to find a specific reference.

The Virgin Mary is reported to have given two different replies to a question asked by visionaries in Garabandal (page 139) and Medjugorje (page 164) concerning intelligent life in other planets. Firstly, the reply to Conchita in Garabandal in the 1960s was, "yes" but The Virgin did not elaborate.[161] The reply to Marija in Medjugorje in the 1980s was, "That is not for you to know at this time". This latter suggests that the answer was yes also, but now is not the time to think about it or worry about it.

My big problem with accepting intelligent life on other planets was that, if free will and the evil that inevitably seems to go with it existed in other planets, then The Lord would have to suffer again to redeem those *"other world"* creatures. On making this comment to Fr Joseph Ianuzzi (well known theologian and author of a doctoral thesis on Luisa Piceretta – see chpt. 15), in Spain, some years ago, he gave me the following reply. "When the Lord died on this earth, it is my belief that he died to redeem all creatures, humans as well as those on other planets. What upset Satan so much was that he should take on the form of the creature with free will but with the lowest intelligence."

In one of the near death experiences mentioned (see page 297) Dr Eben Alexander also became aware of intelligent life forms on other planets with intelligence far superior to ours. What Dr Alexander also noted was that although these creatures did have free will, evil among them was miniscule. He became aware that the potential for evil was necessary in order to permit free will. Without free will there could be no growth and development in love in the way God wished each creature to develop. He also became aware that the extent of evil on Earth was vast, but among other intelligent creatures on other planets, love was tangible and overwhelming. If aliens present on other planets, are aware, therefore, that they too have been redeemed from whatever evil they possess, no matter how small, by the sacrifice of Jesus at Calvary, we can understand how they may have developed a great curiosity about humanity, evident from the extent of global UFO activity described above. If aliens are present on other planets it should also help emphasize to each of us, how insignificant we are in the larger universal scheme of creation. Our infinite significance is conferred on each of us, solely, by the infinite love which God has for each individual person.

11. Catholic Prophecy & the Future

In all ages there have been persons possessed of the spirit of prophecy, not for the purpose of announcing new doctrines but to direct human actions.

Summa: St Thomas Aquinas

You will be right to depend on prophecy and take it as a lamp for lighting a way through the dark until the dawn comes and the morning star rises in your mind.

2 Peter 1:19

Qué será, será. Whatever will be, will be. The future is not ours' to see. To know what the future holds does not seem to be in the general design plan. Our concept of looking into the future is limited to the odd trend analysis of markets or other aspects of human behaviour. By combining current trends with historical changes we can sometimes get an idea of what certain aspects of the near future might be like. The prospect, however, of predicting detailed specific events in the future, unrelated to current trends is completely alien to us and simply goes against our nature. Einstein has explained to us that, if we could move at the speed of light, then time would have a different meaning for us. Our feet and minds unfortunately move at a much slower pace, so we are stuck in the here and now, with a time vector going in one direction only and growing old. The concept of time in a multidimensional universe is beyond us.

Catholic prophecy, nevertheless, is an officially recognized gift and charism of the Holy Spirit of God and Catholic writings abound with authentic and verified prophetic statements foretelling specific future events. These are especially associated with the lives of the saints. One of the best known examples of a major authenticated Catholic prophecy in modern times, is *The Message of Fatima*. In 1917 The Blessed Virgin Mary appeared to three children in Portugal and predicted a number of major world events clearly and in some detail. The rise of Russian Communism and the Second World War were clearly predicted. In order to verify these prophecies a great public miracle was promised to take place months in advance at noon on the 13th October 1917. This was the first time in recorded history that such a major sign was predicted in order to emphasise the seriousness of the message, and to verify that it was coming directly from God to humanity. The so called Great Sign of Fatima (see page 128), and all the events that subsequently occurred, makes it very difficult for anybody who studies the detail of this to doubt the reality and validity of at least some Catholic prophecy, which foretell future events. Those who regard the events at Fatima as imagination, or mass hysteria, are invariably those who either know practically nothing about it, or those whose minds are closed and refuse to accept the possibility of a supernatural event.

St Thomas Aquinas describes the charism of prophecy for future events under two headings. The first is the prophecy of predestination, when God reveals what He alone will do. In this case the events are unavoidable. The second is the prophecy of foreknowledge, when God reveals future events that depend on the action of created free will. All **conditional prophecy** fits into this second category, but prophecy of foreknowledge is not all conditional, as some proceeds from God's Justice and Mercy. One of the non conditional prophecies of foreknowledge to come from Fatima for example is, "**In the end My Immaculate Heart will triumph and a period of peace will be granted to the world**". This prophecy of The Virgin Mary is not conditional and has still to be fulfilled.

Catholic prophecy is very complex, sometimes nebulous and subject to human frailty. Nevertheless, there is a strong chain of accuracy running through it, which makes it a compelling subject for some, and arguably one of the most important subjects to know something about, at this time in the history of humanity. The knowledge base is low and the subject is complex. It is not a matter of reading one book from one author, or from one prophet, and getting a clear idea of what the future holds for us. Firstly, there are different levels of reliability, that can be attributed to different prophets, and even the best of prophets, who may have a good track record of accurate and definite predictions for some events, can get it wrong in respect to others. Secondly, there are examples of authentic prophets who suddenly, for various reasons such as pride etc. get completely misguided and lose all credibility. Thirdly, as explained above, according to St Thomas, some prophecies are, as if written on stone, while others are conditional and depend on the response of humanity to Divine messages. Finally, especially at the present time, there is no shortage of false Catholic prophets.

There are many good books on Catholic prophecy. One of the best I have come across is Trial, Tribulation & Triumph.[162] Others include: The Prophets and Our Times,[163] Catholic Prophecy,[164] Tears of Mary - and Fatima, Why?,[28] Prophecies – The Chastisement and Purification,[165] The Three Days Darkness,[166] What once was, and What is to come,[79] A Storm Unleashed from the Water of the Abyss,[167] and books from Michael Brown especially, The Final Hour,[168] The Trumpet of Gabriel,[169] and The Tower of Light.[170] Any serious study will leave no doubt that authentic Catholic prophecy predicts a number of definite events in the future, which are regarded as unavoidable. The more one searches for the detail of these events, however, or especially a detailed time frame for their occurrence, the more difficult and less clear the prophetic insight becomes. Many recognized saints and venerable individuals with the gift of prophecy, have usually agreed on the general events, but have emphasised different aspects of the minor details accompanying these events. These minor details are often related to the countries, cities, or the religious orders, where these prophets came from. It is only by reading and studying a number of these historically accepted prophets, therefore, that some of the overall details will emerge.

In order to appreciate the particular significance and urgency of Catholic prophecy at this time in history, the following background summary or points of clarification are useful to remember.

a) Firstly there is a general and well accepted prophetic view that we are now living in "end times". This does not mean the end of the world but the end of this era of time which is described by some as the fifth era or by others as "The Age of Mary".

b) Secondly, a theme in Catholic prophecy suggests that two more eras of time are to come, namely the sixth era, which will be a time of great peace and prosperity for the world, which will be followed by "the time of the end" leading on to the end of the world for humanity.

c) Thirdly, despite many recent confusing messages to the contrary, this is NOT the time of THE Antichrist. THE Antichrist (or final Antichrist) will manifest after the era of peace, during the seventh era, before the end of the world.

d) Fourthly, before the sixth era, (the era of peace) there will be great world transforming events, which will eventually lead to one religion being accepted as the truth world-wide, or, as the Bible puts it, "one fold and one shepherd". This will lead into a great period of prosperity and world peace like nothing ever experienced in the world before.

Most of what I discuss in this chapter on Catholic Prophecy is related to these world transforming events. If we believe in Catholic prophecy, then we can have no doubt, as already mentioned in chapter 1, that we are now living in the most extraordinary time in the history of humanity. We are about to see the majesty of God interact in a direct and tangible way with each living person, in order to renew creation. This is the clear implication from much of Catholic prophecy, from many different sources. One can accept or reject this. Future generations will know the truth.

World Transforming Events

A broad summary of these predicted world transforming events includes the following:

1) Peace on earth has been entrusted to the Immaculate Heart of The Virgin Mary. In the end "My Immaculate Heart will triumph" as explained above.

2) A major chastisement for humanity is now inevitable. This will take two forms. The first will be man-made and it will likely involve a third great war with severe persecution of the Catholic Church. During a period of terrible strife in Italy, the Pope will have to flee Rome. A civil war in France will be one of the early events in this world strife. When strife and persecution are at their worst God will intervene directly. This is likely to prevent humanity from destroying itself and/or to prevent destruction of Catholicism.

3) The Divine intervention will occur in a number of ways including:
    (i) A World-wide Warning, involving a personal experience by every living person, who will see the state of

their souls in terms of good and evil, as God sees it. – (see chapter 12 for more details)

(ii) Clearly predicted world events will be announced by visionaries some days in advance, to leave no doubt that God is directly involved.

(iii) Permanent supernatural signs will be left in different places in the world, again to convince the incredulous of the reality of God, the truth of the Catholic Church and the dire state of the world.

(iv) A Divine orchestrated chastisement of humanity will occur after The Warning. The severity of The Chastisement will depend on the response of humanity to The Warning and signs.

4) During the chastisement the whole of nature will be disturbed. The weather conditions will get steadily worse. There will be severe storms, twisters, floods, earthquakes and terrible tidal waves that will cover large areas with water. There will be terrible famines and great pandemics of infectious diseases. If humanity does not respond appropriately by loving God and one another, by repentance and conversion, then eventually fire will fall on the earth from the sky (which will probably be related to a comet) and a large portion of humanity will be destroyed.

5) The conversion of Russia will be a key event on the way to world peace.

6) It is likely that the restoration of a great Catholic King in France will be an unexpected event, in these times. This King will eventually restore peace in Europe and in the whole world.

7) This restored King of France will become the Emperor of a new Roman Empire which will rule the whole world. At the same time the Papacy will be restored in Rome. This Emperor with the

assistance of an exceptionally holy Pope will rule the world in great peace and prosperity for a period of time in the near future.

BRIEF SUMMARY OF WHAT THE PROPHETS SAY

St. Jacinta and Lucia of Fatima: We must accept that the Fatima seers were among the most reliable of prophets. Little Jacinta from Fatima made the following prediction from her deathbed:[182]

"If men will repent, God will pardon them, but if they do not amend their lives, there will come upon the earth the most terrible chastisement ever known". This message was reported from Sr Lucia of Fatima in 1961:[182]

"Tell everyone that our Lady has, frequently, announced to me that many nations will disappear off the face of the earth. Russia is the scourge chosen by God to punish mankind, if we, through prayer and the sacraments, do not obtain the grace of their conversion. Tell them, Father, tell them that the devil has begun a decisive battle against *Our Lady*, because what most afflicts the *Immaculate Heart of Mary* and the *Sacred Heart of Jesus* is the fall of the souls of religious and priests. The devil knows that when religious and priests fail in their beautiful vocations, they carry along with them many souls into Hell."

In 1983 the Spanish Seer, Amparo, was told by our Lord, "The Father is sending two chastisements to the world. One is in the form of wars, revolutions and dangers of harm from revolutionaries, and the second will be directly from Heaven".

France, the French and the Future

France has had more attention from Catholic prophets than any other nation, especially in regard to the coming world crisis, or minor chastisement, as it is sometimes referred to. Many prophecies have recorded that a terrible civil war in France will be one of the earliest events in this coming crisis. It is important to appreciate that the French Revolution instigated by Freemasons in 1789, was a major antichristian movement, leading to the execution and martyrdom of many Catholics. Some would claim that, whereas the Protestant Reformation was the great movement that began the fracturing of Christianity on the basis of private biblical interpretation, the French Revolution was the movement that began the real war of Secularism against Christianity. This is the war which is now raging world-wide, with great ferocity, and, it is about to reach a climax. As it began in France, so the final battle will be ignited in France and according to Catholic prophecy, by the design of God, the victory for Christianity will also begin in France.

The French Monarchs had a great Catholic tradition from the time when King Clovis and thousands of his followers were first baptized, in 496 A.D. St Remigius, Archbishop of Rheims, who baptized Clovis, made the following prophecy at the time:

"Take notice that the Kingdom of France is predestined by God for the defence of the Roman Church, which is the only true Church of Christ. This kingdom shall someday be great among the kingdoms of the earth, and shall embrace all the limits of the Roman Empire, and shall submit all other kingdoms to its own sceptre."

King Louis XVI consecrated France to the Sacred Heart of Jesus just before he was killed by guillotine during the Revolution. It was revealed by The Blessed Virgin Mary to Maxim Giraud, who was one of the seers in La Salette (1846),[171] that the son of King Louis XVI did not die in prison as is usually believed, and that a descendent of his would eventually be restored to the throne in France.[172] There are many other Catholic prophecies which also say that the King will be restored in France and that this King will save Europe. His name will be Henry of the Cross and he will be a direct descendent of King Louis XVI. This future King is prophesied to be the key individual who will bring peace to Europe and the World after a period of terrible devastation. He will also be responsible for restoring the Papacy after the Catholic Church goes through a period of great persecution, when the Pope will have to flee Rome and probably die in exile.

Marie Julie Jahenny: Marie Julie Jahenny was a famous stigmatist from a small town called La Fraudais in Brittany, France.[173] She was born in 1850 and died in 1941. She had many supernatural gifts, particularly that of prophecy. Although she was one of the most extraordinary mystics who ever lived, and she is still within living memory, she remains almost unknown outside of Brittany. She suffered a great deal during her life, especially for the redemption of souls. She was deaf, blind, dumb, and paralyzed for many years. She was also stigmatized and suffered greatly from these wounds. For 68 years she suffered the pains of the crucifixion every Friday. On Tuesdays and Thursdays she had apparitions and ecstasies. It has been claimed that nobody else in history had a more complete stigmatic example of the wounds suffered by Christ at the crucifixion. Like some other mystics she also survived on the Eucharist for many years, taking neither food nor drink during that time. During that period her doctor testified that she neither excreted water or solids from her body. Towards the end of her life she regained all her faculties and became relatively well. After her death Padre Pio said that, "This humble violet has now reached the summit of her glory. Her principal work will be posthumous".

Her gift of Prophecy: Marie-Julie had many great insights into future events which were proven right over and over again. She gave a clear prediction of World War I and II. She also foretold of Bismarck's war in Germany against Catholics and the religious persecutions in France by Freemasons and Republicans. She foresaw the French war in Algeria and predicted the Transvaal war twenty years before it happened. In 1881 she outlined in detail the circumstances of the death of Melanie Calvat who was one of the seers in La Salette. Melanie died over twenty years later, in 1904, exactly as Marie-Julie had foreseen.[171]

Marie Julie Jahenny announced that three quarters of the population of the earth would disappear in a major crisis towards the end of a future Chastisement. There would be terrible earthquakes, epidemics of unknown diseases, whose ravages would be frightful. She described terrible famines, inclement weather, cyclones, and rising seas, which would cause terrifying tidal waves. She said the earth would become like a vast cemetery. The bodies of both the wicked and the just would cover the ground. A famine would be great and everything would be thrown into confusion. The crisis would explode suddenly. The punishments would be shared by all and would succeed one another without interruption.

In describing a great tribulation that is to come, and now seems very near, Marie-Julie said, "The time of crimes has begun… Many mothers will be heartless for their own fruits (abortion)… The Devil will appear in the form of living apparitions…Woe to those who dare to make pacts with these personages who appear in diabolical visions…The world will be mad with fear and in this madness, the Devil, who is everywhere on earth, will make them deny their baptism and the cross…"

Marie Julie claimed to have received the following message from the Holy Spirit: "The earth has to perish, not the whole of it, but more than half of it. The earth will turn into a desert. But God, in peace and tranquillity, will populate it all over again."

It was revealed to Marie Julie that three plants would have great medicinal properties against unusual and unknown diseases that would ravage humanity at the time of the chastisement. These are, Ground Ivy, Hawthorn, and Violets. The Virgin Mary is reported to have said to Marie Julie:

"For fits, chest troubles and headaches caused by an unbearable plague which will attack both people and animals, you should use an infusion of Ground Ivy." Ground Ivy (Glechoma hederacea), sometimes referred as creeping Charlie or Gill, is a perennial creeping plant with a flower that blooms from March to June on small tubes. Large blue violet flowers grow in groups of two to four in loose whorls at the base of the leaves. It is quite different from true ivy (Hedera helix). The word Glechoma comes from the Greek name for the grey green colour of the leaf. This herb has long been used medicinally for fevers, coughs and sore eyes. The distinctive and faintly mint scented leaves have also been used in brewing to sharpen the taste of beers. The flowering stems contain the bitter compound glechomine, as well as tannins, saponin and potassium salts. All these components give Ground Ivy astringent, anti-inflammatory, and tonic properties. The fresh shoots and leaves can be added to salads and soups or prepared and eaten like spinach. Jesus is reported to have said to Marie Julie, "I bless this plant... Many will look for it later and will not be able to find it. It will be a cure for a future major widespread plague which will come to people and cattle." This message was given on 24th May 1880. There is no definite time reference for the time of this plague.

Marie Julie Jahenny also confirmed the view, in many of her messages, that the monarchy would be restored in France. She said, however, before the King came back to the throne in France that:

"Half the population of France will be destroyed. After the punishments there will be villages left without a soul. Four towns of France will disappear."

The so called Great Monarch or Henry of the Cross will also be known by a number of titles such as The Man of God, The Chosen of the Eternal, The Peace and Salvation of his People, The Miracle King, and The Saviour of France. It was Marie Julie's impression that this King would make his appearance led by a small group of people at the time when Paris burns. On the 4th February 1882 Jesus appeared to Marie Julie and said the following:

"You will see from Heaven, the triumph of the Church gleaming over the forehead of my real servant, Henry of the Cross." Turning himself towards the King, (who also appeared in the vision), Jesus said: "Do you hear My voice, oh beloved son? You who walked in a foreign land, for so long. Do you not see the road where I will send to meet you, the Princes of the Heavenly armies, my Seraphims, my Cherubims, with their wings, so that the triumph equals in beauty one fit for a King of predilection and blessing? My beloved son, dry your tears. The Lily will be your brother (the Holy Pope) and my Mother will be your Mother (the great monarch will be an orphan) and it is on your forehead that the Lily will always bloom. Then from your forehead it will bloom on your throne. From your throne in France, the Kingdom reserved for you and from there to beyond the French frontiers to the Eternal City." It is believed that the Holy Pope and the great Monarch are both descendents of the martyred King Louis XVI.

Father Constant Louis Marie Pel (1876–1966): He was a personal friend of St Padre Pio who said of him to some French pilgrims, "Why do you come to see me when you have so great a Saint in France?" He was a founder of a convent for women and of a seminary for men, with a great devotion to the *Sacred Heart of*

Jesus and to the *Immaculate Heart of Mary*. He died in a car accident just after Vatican II. Fr Pel would spend nights on his feet in church with his forehead leaning against the Tabernacle, conversing with God in a permanent ecstasy. One of his pupils in the seminary recorded a prophecy which he made in 1945, concerning a chastisement which is to come to France. He said:

"France being guilty of apostasy and denying its vocation will be severely chastised. East of a line stretching from Bordeaux in the south-west to Lille in the north-east, everything will be laid waste and set on fire by peoples invading from the east, and also by great flaming meteorites falling in a rain of fire upon all the earth and upon these regions especially. Revolution, war, epidemics, plagues, chemical poison gases, violent earthquakes and the re-awakening of France's extinct volcanoes will destroy everything... To the west of that line will be less affected . . . because of the faith rooted in the Vendée and in Brittany . . . but any of God's worst enemies seeking refuge there from the worldwide cataclysm will be found out, wherever they hide, and put to death by devils, because the Wrath of the Lord is just and holy. Thick darkness caused by the war, gigantic fires and fragments of burning stars falling for three days and nights will cause the sun to disappear, and only candles blessed on Candlemas (February 2) will give light in the hands of believers, but the godless will not see this miraculous light because they have darkness in their souls..

In this way, my son, three quarters of mankind will be destroyed, and in certain parts of France survivors will have to go 60 miles to find another live human being . . . . Several nations will disappear off the face of the map . . . . A France thus purified will become the renewed "Eldest Daughter of the Church," because all the Cains and Judases will have disappeared in this 'Judgment upon the Nations." Note that this prophecy was made before the now

420

approved prophecy of Akita which has many similarities with it (see page 172).

St Hildegard (12ᵗʰ Century): This German saint had Heavenly visions from the age of three. She is one of the most famous of European Catholic prophets. At the age of five she went into a Benedictine convent on the banks of the Rhine. She was ordered by her Heavenly visitors to write all her prophecies and she claimed that miraculously she was given the gift to write in Latin. Her authenticity as a prophet was supported by St Bernard and Pope Eugenius III at the time. Almost 800 years ago she described these present times and the coming turmoil. She also foresaw the return of a King to France, as can be understood from the following passage:

"Peace will return to the world when the white Flower again takes possession of the throne of France. During this period of peace, people will be forbidden to carry weapons, and iron will be used only for making agricultural implements and tools. Also during this period, the land will be very productive, and many Jews, heathens, and heretics will join the Church".

She also spoke of a "last Roman Catholic Empire". Like Marie Julie Jahenny she too was given to understand that the final Antichrist will come after the era of peace, which will end almost immediately after the death of this King of France.

St Francis of Paula (15ᵗʰ Century): This saint was from Cambria, Italy. He was very famous particularly for his many miracles and for the gift of prophecy. He was canonized fourteen years after his death because of the great evidence for his sanctity and miracles worked through him. There are records of him raising at least seven people from the dead. As with St Teresa of Avila he also claimed to have the gift of prophecy. Concerning the "Great

Monarch", "Great King", or "Emperor" referred to above who will take over France he said:

"He shall be the founder of a new religious order different from all others. He will divide it into three strata, namely military knights, solitary priests, and most pious hospitalliers. This shall be the last religious order in the Church, and it will do more good for our holy religion than all other religious institutions... He shall be the great leader of the Holy Militia of the Holy Spirit which shall overcome the world, and shall possess the earth so completely that no King or Lord shall be able to exist, unless he belongs to the Sacred Host of the Holy Ghost. These devout men shall wear on their breasts, and much more within their hearts, the sign of the living God, namely the cross." It is clear from other prophesies also that it is from this that they will receive their popular name of "The cross-bearers."

St John Vianney (Curé of Ars 19th Century): The Curé is one of the most respected saints from France and he is patron of parish priests. He was believed by his Bishop to be a priest of poor intelligence and for this reason he was sent to the small quiet village of Ars. His sanctity grew rapidly and before long he became a world famous confessor with the gift of "reading souls", that is, the ability to see the past sins of the penitents as soon as they came before him. The message of his life is that we are all called to become holy wherever God has placed us, no matter how lowly that position is. The following detailed prophecy of future events in France was given to him in 1859:

"The enemy will allow the burning of Paris, and they will rejoice at it, but they shall be beaten: they shall be driven entirely from France. Our enemies shall return, and will destroy everything in their march. They shall arrive near Poitiers without meeting any serious resistance, but there they shall be crushed by the defenders of the West, who shall pursue them. From other directions their provisions shall be cut off, and they shall suffer very serious losses. They will attempt to retire towards their country, but very few of them shall ever reach it. The Communists of Paris, (after their defeat), shall spread themselves through all France, and will be greatly multiplied. They shall seize arms: they shall oppress the people of order. Lastly, a civil war shall break out everywhere. These wicked people shall become masters in the North, East and Southwest of France. They will imprison very many persons, and will be guilty of more massacres. They will attempt to kill all the priests and all the religious, but this shall not last long. People will imagine that all is lost: but the good God shall save all. It will be like a sign of the last judgment.....God shall come to help. The good shall triumph when the return of the King shall be announced. This shall re-establish a peace and prosperity without example. Religion shall flourish again better than ever before".

Blessed Anna Maria Taigi: She was an Italian lady with a tremendous gift of prophecy. She saw the entire world past, present and future through a mystical golden globe. This gift lasted for 47 years. Her prophecies were proved accurate over and over again. She was a confidant of a number of Popes. She was a special adviser to Pope Pius XI. Regarding France in the coming times she said:

"France shall fall into a frightful anarchy. The French shall have a desperate civil war, in the course of which old men themselves will take up arms. The political parties, having exhausted their rage without being able to arrive at any satisfactory understanding, shall at the last extremity agree by common consent to have recourse to the Church." It is after this that the King will be restored to the French Throne.

According to Bartholomew Holzhauser[162] we are now living in the fifth period of the history of the Church. This period will end with the arrival of a Holy Pope and a powerful Monarch, who will restore the world to peace. He said that this period of peace will last until the revelation of Antichrist. In general the prophecies agree that the north east and the south of France would be hit hardest in the great trials that are coming. Marie Julie Jahenny was also told that the Brittany area of France would be saved from the worst disasters. The saintly French priest, Pére Lamy,[174] spoke of the destruction of Paris, which he said will be almost completely destroyed by fire. Marie Julie Jahenny also spoke of fire from Heaven uniting with fire from earth destroying Paris.

Sister Marie of Christ The King (Marie du Christ Roi): It would not be proper to leave this section on prophecy without a brief account of this other great French Lady. She was born Olive Danze' in a Breton village in 1906 into a poor family. At the age of five years, the boy Jesus visited her to play with her and became her constant companion during her childhood. The well known Irish Marian theologian, Fr Michael O Carroll C.S.Sp., was a personal friend of this lady later in life and he published privately a short story of her life, a few years before he died.[175] John Bird also tells her story in the last of his films made on the history of the Catholic Church in France.[172] I am grateful to these two sources for the information I have on her life. The following is a description she wrote of her first encounter with Jesus in bodily form at the age of five:

"I said to my doll, if we had a friend to come everyday with us, we would really be happy. I had scarcely finished speaking when I saw a little child of my age who came up to me and said, "Come and play". "Yes" I said at once. "I am only too happy to find a little friend to play with me". He put me in my go-car with my doll. He brought me to the oratory where Mama said her Office. There was

a statue of The Blessed Virgin there, a crucifix and picture. I looked at all this instead of looking at my little Friend. Afterward He left me quite alone, but as Mama had locked the door, she was quite astonished when she returned to find me in the oratory. She seemed to be in ecstasy before me and my doll. She said, "But who gave you entry here, little one?" "A little child, Mama". She asked, "Who is this little child?" I did not know what to say to Mama, I did not know him at all. "But how was He dressed?", Mama asked me. And I said to her, "He was all in white: His little feet were bare, His little hair curled and a ring of gold on His head."

"It's all well", said Mama, "I know Him. It is not surprising that He could open a locked door." "Come" said Mama to me, "you are more His, than mine."

All Olive's life was full of supernatural visitations and communications. At the age of fourteen she was visited by The Virgin Mary, who suggested to her that she should join a Benedictine convent in Paris. Her name in religion was Sister Marie du Christ Roi. The Mother Superior recognized her sanctity from the beginning. This was the reason she accepted her story that Jesus had conveyed a message to her of His wish to have a Basilica constructed on the grounds of the monastery. This Basilica was to honour His titles as King, Prince of Peace, and Master of the Nations. This church was built rapidly as it had the approval of the Cardinal in Paris and approval from Rome. On the 27th Oct. 1940, feast of Christ the King, the first solemn Mass was celebrated by Cardinal Verdier.

Sister Marie suffered all through her life, especially from those in her Benedictine Order, who did not believe her. The greatest suffering was to be banished from her convent with two companions. She visited President De Valera, in Ireland, on two occasions. He received her as a special guest and promoter of love for Christ the King. The President was well aware of all her troubles and with his wife had previously presented one of the large bells to her church, on behalf of the Irish people. Recently I learned that De Valera, who had bad eye sight, was almost completely cured at his first meeting with this nun. She eventually died in very poor circumstances on 2nd May 1968, in her Breton village, where the parish priest had found simple accommodation for her and her companions. The new superiors of the Benedictine convent in Paris, had the church sold to property developers, in 1977. At 16 rue Tournefort, where this church was, there is now a block of flats, called Le Pantheon. In his book, Fr Michael O Carroll, said that a special revelation from Jesus had informed her that her body would one day be found incorrupt. He also said that it was his belief, and those of her devotees, that in the future she would become a "new Joan of Arc," for France. Further it was revealed that when the King is restored to France (Henry V), he will rebuild the Basilica in this exact location (where Le Pantheon now stands), in honour of Christ the King, as the Lord had requested.

Sr Marie also spoke of a terrible destruction in France before the return of Henry V (Henry of the Cross) to the Throne. She foresaw a Russian invasion of France. She was also told that as the sanctuary of Christ the King was destroyed, so Paris would be destroyed. She wrote to Pope Paul VI, concerning the Vatican Council. She said: "Most Holy Father, the Council will not bear fruits. First chase the 'Lodge' from your Church. It is not my little voice, but that of Mary, my Mother, who has told me to say this to you, Mary Mediatrix."

It is difficult for French people at this time to contemplate the return of a King to the Throne in France. It is more difficult for them to contemplate a French King who will restore peace in Europe and the world. Nevertheless, this King has been mentioned in many hundreds of Catholic prophecies extending back almost

15 centuries. No other individual has been spoken more about in Catholic prophecy, than this great monarch.

England

An old English prophecy found on a tombstone at the Kirby cemetery in Essex says:

"When pictures look alive, with movements free, When ships like fish swim beneath the sea, When men outstripping birds can soar the sky, Then half the world deep drenched in blood shall die. In Germany begins a dance, Which passeth through Italy, Spain and France, But England shall pay the piper. When Our Lady shall lie on Our Lord's lap Then England will meet with a strange mishap."

The Irish saint, Malachy of Armagh, from the 11th century, is most famous for his prophecies on all the Popes down through the centuries. He is also well known for his prophecies on Ireland and England. He said that, "Ireland will suffer English oppression for a week of centuries (seven), but will preserve her faith in God and His Church. At the end of that time she will be delivered, and the English will afterwards suffer severe chastisement. Ireland however (with the help of France), will be instrumental in bringing back the English to the unity of the faith".

St Malachy's prophecy of England separating from the Catholic faith was confirmed by the English saint, St Edward the Confessor, who gave the following prophecy in 1066, just before he died.

"The extreme corruption and wickedness of the English nation has provoked the just anger of God. When malice has reached the fullness of its measure, God will, in His wrath, send to the English people wicked spirits who will punish and afflict them with severity, by separating the green tree from its parent stem....but at last without any national government assistance this same tree shall return to its root, flourish again and bear abundant fruit".

St Edward claimed to have received this information from two holy monks from Normandy, who he had known in his youth, and who had appeared to him just before he died. It is generally felt that the separating of the tree referred to Henry VIII separating from Rome and it is interesting that his prophecy is that the return to Rome will be without government help.

A number of prophecies have spoken about England suffering from severe flooding, earthquakes and tidal waves which would eventually leave a large portion of the nation under water. A priest of the 17th century, Fr Balthassar, is credited with the following prophecy:

"I saw a land swallowed up by the sea and covered with water. But afterwards, I saw that the sea receded little by little and the land could be seen again. The tops of the towers in the city rose again above the water and appeared more beautiful than before, and I was told that this land was England".

The famous German prophet, St Hildegard, (see above) made this similar prophecy about England:

"Before the comet comes, many nations, the good excepted, will be scourged by want and famine. The great nation in the ocean that is inhabited by people of different tribes and descent will be devastated by earthquake, storm and tidal wave. It will be divided and, in great part, submerged. That nation will also have many misfortunes at sea and lose its colonies."

Italy

Sister Elena Aiello was an Italian stigmatic who suffered terribly, especially on Fridays. She was famous for the many locutions which she received. The Virgin Mary said to Mother Elena at Rome on July 18th 1973 "A world revolution is on the verge of exploding, and no human can stop it." In 1975 in a vision with Padre Pio, Mother Elena was shown many floods, many caved in houses and a revolution with many bombs exploding and causing great destruction. On April 2nd 1976 Mary came again with Padre Pio to Sister Elena and said "A terrible anarchy will break lose and because of what will happen, Italy will be purified in blood. A great revolution will break out and the streets will be streaming with blood...Listen to me and be attentive to what I tell you. A world revolution will soon explode. Russia will trample over all the nations of Europe, especially over Italy and will raise her flag over St Peters Dome". Sister Elena later said, "Italy will be severely tried by a great revolution, and Rome will be purified in blood for its many sins. The flock will be scattered and the Pope will suffer greatly."

Other prophecies also speaking of Italy say, "There shall be great confusion with people against people and nations against nations. The Russians shall come to Italy. Some Bishops shall fall from the faith, but others will remain steadfast and suffer much for the Church. Priests and religious shall be martyred, and the earth, especially in Italy shall be soaked with their blood."

A Capuchin Friar from the 18th century famous for his prophecy is credited with the following prediction:

"During these calamities the Pope shall die. Through the death of the Supreme Pontiff the Church will be reduced to the most painful anarchy. Through the influence of three hostile powers, three popes will be contemporaneously elected. One will be Italian, another German, and the third Greek. The Greek pope shall be placed on the throne by force of arms." These will be false popes.

Pope St Pius X said: "I saw one of my successors taking to flight over the bodies of his brethren. He will take refuge in disguise somewhere and after a short retirement he will die a cruel death".

Brother John of the Cleft Rock made the following prophecy about the times we live in: "At that time, the Pope, with the Cardinals will have to flee Rome in trying circumstances, to a place where he will be unknown. He will die a cruel death in this exile. The sufferings of the Church will be much greater than at any previous time in her history".

Russia and the European Conflict

There is a general feeling that a world economic collapse will be the first event in the next major conflict. The so called "Ecstatic of Tours" gave the following prophecy:

"Before the war breaks out again, food will be scarce and expensive. There will be little work for the workers, and fathers will hear their children crying for food. There will be earthquakes and signs in the sun. Towards the end darkness will cover the earth"

On the 22nd August 1960 Mother Elena Aiello received the following message: "If people do not return to God with truly Christian living another terrible war will come from East to West. Russia with her secret armies will battle America and will over run Europe. The river Rhine will be running over with bodies and blood. Italy will be harassed by a great revolution".

430

Many of the prophecies state that this Chastisement (which is prophesied to precede Antichrist by a significant period of time, ? 30 years) will be like a little general judgment. It appears to be a foretaste of the Major Chastisement foretold for the end of the world. It will contain many of the same elements but to a lesser degree. For instance, this and other prophecies confirm that there will be "earthquakes and signs in the sun" during this Chastisement. The big-big question for us now is, will the message of Akita and/or the tipping of the earth occur within the next few years or around the time of the Antichrist in about 30 years into the future? See chapter 16 and the last chapter.

A Divine message to four children at Heede, Onasbruch, Germany in 1937 got Church approval. Part of the message concerning these times was as follows:

"This generation deserves to be annihilated, but I desire to show myself as merciful. Great and terrible things are being prepared. That which is about to happen will be terrible, like nothing ever since the beginning of the world"

The following prophecy is also attributed to the so called Ecstatic of Tours: "When everyone believes that peace is assured, when everyone least expects it, the great happenings will begin. Revolution will break out in Italy almost at the same time as in France. For a while the Church will be without a Pope. England, too, will have much to suffer."

In 1820 Venerable Anna Katerina Emmerick gave the following message from a vision which she had:

"I see more martyrs, not now but in the future... I saw the secret sect relentlessly undermining the great Church. All over the world, good and devout people, especially the clergy, were harassed, oppressed, and put into prison. I had the feeling that they would become martyrs one day... Then, I saw an apparition of the Mother of God, and she said that the tribulation would be very great."

A number of old prophecies say that a third world war will occur after problems in the Balkans, not very different from the situation which led to the start of World War I. Other prophecies say that a third world war will begin in late July early August, a few days after the murder of a leader in the region of Yugoslavia – Hungary.

Bernhardt Rembordt (18th century) is credited with the following prophecy:[162]

"Cologne will be the site of a terrible battle. Many foreigners will be slaughtered there. Both men and women will fight for their faith. It will be impossible to prevent this horrible devastation. People will wade up to their ankles in blood. At last a foreign king will appear and win a victory for the cause of the righteous. The remaining enemy will retreat to the Birch tree country (Westphalia – central Germany). There, the last battle will be fought for the just cause. At that time France will be divided. The German Empire will choose a simple man as the Emperor, who will rule for a short time. His successor will be the man for whom the world has longed. He will be called a Roman Emperor,"

An old German prophecy says:[162] "A terrible war will find the North fighting and South. The South will be led by a Prince wearing a white coat with a cross on the front: he will be lame afoot. He will gather his forces at Bremen for Mass. Then he will lead them into battle beyond Woerl near the Birch-tree country. After a terrible battle at a brook running eastwards near Berdberg and Sondern, the South will be victorious."

It is interesting that a number of other prophecies also describe the Great Monarch as being lame.

Fr Nectou gives the following prophecy: "Two parties will be formed in France, which will fight unto death. The party of evil will at first be stronger, and the good side will be weaker. **At that time there will be such a terrible crisis that people will believe that the end of the world has come.** Blood will flow in many large cities. The very elements will be confused. It will be like a general judgement."

There are also other prophecies that predict a Russian invasion of Europe. Alois Irimaier, a well reputed prophet of Bavaria, had a clear vision in 1947 of a three pronged attack by Russian armies descending in a line. This will begin in Prague and moved north. There were many other prophets who have also made these prophecies through the centuries.

Aloisia Klettener, from Eisenberg in Austria in 1982, received a message from The Virgin Mary saying that communists would invade the free nations of Europe and start a world catastrophe. Aloisia was a famous lady who got many prophecies. In 1956 an extraordinary grass cross appeared in the ground near where she lived. This was similar to the grass cross that appeared in a village in Portugal where Alexandrina Da Costa was born (see page 82).

In the 13th Century the abbot of a monastery in Otranto, Southern Italy said: "The Great Monarch and the Great Pope will precede the Antichrist. The nations will be at war for four years and a great part of the world will be destroyed.

Sister Jeanne le Royer (18th century): She was from Brittany, France. She was in the order of St Clare and was totally illiterate.

She foretold the French Revolution many years before it happened. She predicted a future Church Council in the following manner:

"The storm began in France, and France shall be the first theatre of its ravages after having been its forge. But the Church in Council assembled shall one day strike with anathemas, pull down and destroy the evil principles of that criminal constitution. What a consolation! What consolation, what joy for all the truly faithful."

It has been said that the triumph of the Immaculate Heart of Mary will not be complete until the dogma of "Mary, Mediatrix, Coredemptrix and Advocate" has been proclaimed, as foretold by The Lady of All Nations.[60] This may not be done until this next Council.

As the forecast of the great tribulation, plagues, and chastisement, go back for centuries so do the predictions of the final victory of the Church. Prophecies say "whole nations will join the church shortly before the reign of the Antichrist. These conversions will be amazing and edifying. The nations of Russia, England and China will come into the Church. The Catholic religion will triumph everywhere and will create peace and happiness in mankind.

St Louis Marie Grignion De Montfort (18th Century) is well known for his writing on The Virgin Mary.[176] The following is one of his prophecies: "The power of Mary over all devils will be particularly outstanding in the last period of time. She will extend the Kingdom of Christ over the idolaters and Muslims, and there will come a glorious era when Mary is the Ruler and Queen of Hearts"

Pope Pius IX spoke about a great sign from God, which will come to humanity. He said, "There will come a great sign, which will fill the world with awe. This will occur only after the triumph of a great revolution during which the Church will undergo ordeals which are beyond description."

Three Days of Darkness

Marie Julie Jahenny predicted three days of complete darkness which would cover the whole world. These three days of darkness are well known, and have been mentioned in many ancient and modern Catholic prophecies. Marie Julie said that the three days of darkness would be on a Thursday, Friday and Saturday. "The earth will be covered in darkness and Hell will be let loose on the earth." The thunder and lightening will cause some of those who have no faith and trust in God to die of fear. During these three days of terrifying darkness no windows should be opened, in order to have the best chance of survival. The sky will be on fire, the earth will split and nobody outside a shelter will survive. The earth will be shaking as at the judgement and fear will be great. "During these three days of darkness let a blessed candle be lighting everywhere, as nothing else will give light." Everything will shake except the piece of furniture on which the blessed candle is burning. Everybody should gather around the crucifix and the picture of the Blessed Mother. This will keep away terror. During this darkness the devils and the wicked will take on most hideous shapes. Red clouds like blood will move across the sky and the crash of the thunder will shake the earth and lightning will streak the Heavens out of season. The sea will rise, and rolling waves will spread over the continent. The wicked will commit all kinds of horrors. The holy host will be dispersed on the roads. They will be discovered in the mud and the Priests as well as the faithful will pick them up and carry them on their breasts. Marie Julie also said, "I understood that the angels would carry away many tabernacles from the churches and shield the Holy Sacrament from the outrages".

Marie Julie further said: "Those who have served the Lord well and invoked his name and have a blessed picture in their homes and who carry the rosary on them and say it often will be kept intact and all who belong to them. The heat from Heaven will be unbearably hot, even for those in the closed homes. The whole sky will be on fire, but the lightning will not penetrate into the houses where there will be the light of the blessed candle. This light is the only thing that will protect you."

Blessed Anna-Maria Taigi (see above) gave the following prophecy: "God will send two punishments: one will be in the form of wars, revolutions and dangers originating on earth, the other will be sent from Heaven. There shall come over the whole earth an inner darkness that will last three days and three nights. Nothing will be visible, and the air will be pestilent and foul and will harm, though not exclusively, the enemies of religion... During those three days of darkness artificial light will fail, only blessed candles will burn. During those days of darkness, the faithful should remain in their houses, praying the Holy Rosary and asking God for mercy... All the enemies of the Church, whether known or unknown, will perish over the whole earth during that universal darkness, with the exception of a few who will be converted. St Peter and St Paul will intervene in the election of a new Pope."

Sister Elena Aiello (see above) received the following prophecy from The Virgin Mary on Good Friday 1954: "Clouds with lightning rays of fire and a tempest of fire will pass over the whole world and the punishment will be the most terrible known in the history of mankind. It will last 70 hours (three days). The wicked will be crushed and eliminated. Many will be lost because they will have stubbornly remained in their sins. Then they will feel the force of light over darkness. The hours of darkness are near. ... Some nations will be purified while others will disappear entirely."

Relating Catholic Prophecy to the Bible

All Catholic prophecy for future events, dealing with "end times", should be measured against the eschatological texts (dealing with the end of time), in the Bible, especially from Matthew 24 and Mark 13. To interpret prophecy in the Bible and also to relate it to a particular time in history can be difficult. Over the centuries, some biblical prophecies can relate to more than one period of time. Non biblical prophecy also tends to be more specific in relating to individuals, places, and countries, whereas biblical prophecy, of necessity, is written in a much briefer style and usually refers to Christianity in a world context. Although non biblical prophecy is more detailed and easier to place in time, it can never be considered more reliable than biblical prophecy, which is understood to record the words of God.

Two future events are described in Matthew 24 and Mark 13. The first is the destruction of the Jewish Temple, in Jerusalem. The Lord said that it would happen, "before this generation passes away.. and there will not be left one stone upon another". The Temple was completely destroyed, within forty years of these words being spoken. The second event described was the end of time and the return of Jesus. This was to be away in the future. A number of pointers are given in the Bible texts to indicate when the end of time is approaching. One of these is apostasy. In the Bible, Luke 18:8 says, "When the Son of man comes, will He find faith on earth?" Christian apostasy is now world-wide. In Matthew 24 and Mark 13, a great tribulation is described, "that no human flesh could survive, if that time is not shortened, for the sake of the elect". Immediately after the tribulation, "the sun will show no light".

What we are expecting in the very near future, is not the end of the world (or the end of time), but rather, the beginning of the end. The non-biblical prophecy, described above, seems to indicate that the return of Jesus will begin in a more Eucharistic sense, with the visible sign of God appearing in a number of locations around the world. The end of the world with the final judgement and all that has been described in the Bible, to go with that, will not occur until after the time of great peace. The biblical reference to the great tribulation and the sun showing no light, correlates very well with the tribulation described above, by the Catholic prophets, as well as the three dark days (see above). There is every indication that the coming tribulation will be severe, but hopefully not as severe, as the tribulation described for the time of the end of the world. – See the final chapter for a more detailed discussion on this.

When will the turmoil begin?

We can never be sure when these major events will begin. Some would say that they have already begun and that the world problems and natural disasters will gradually grow in intensity. The authenticity of any prophecy, Catholic or otherwise, is easy to test when a particular unusual event is predicted at an exact future time. This rarely happens, except for Fatima (see page 125) and Garabandal (see page 138), which are examples of where this has happened. We have been told by the visionaries in Medjugorje that certain world events destined for the future will be announced publicly some days in advance to confirm the authenticity of these visions and messages that have occurred over the years. This does not help us in the short term however with the broad time-table for the coming turmoil. For this we have to rely on the many messages received with less precise time details. These, however, can give some indication of time when checked against each other.

Very few prophets get exact time frames with their messages and impressions of time picked up by them are often mistaken. Timing of prophesied events, as explained above, seems to be controlled by two factors and both of these can work together in some instances. The first is the decision by God to have an event happen, at a particular moment in time. This can be to convince doubting humanity or to emphasise something significant. The great sign of Fatima was an example of this. The great sign prophesied for Garabandal, for example, also seems to definitely indicate the significance of the Eucharist, as it is to happen on a Thursday at 8.30 on the feast of a saint martyred for the Eucharist. The second factor is that the timing of other events will often depend on the response of the free will of humanity. This could happen in the case of a major chastisement, when deaths might result. It seems that everything will be timed to perfection by God the Father, so that the maximum number will attain eternal salvation, and thus this kind of timing is said to be "hidden in the bosom of the Father".

Over the last two decades many of the prophets who have made predictions as to when future events were to occur have got it wrong. Most notable has been Fr Gobbi who, directed by locutions, founded the Marian Movement of Priests (approximately 100,000) to prepare the world for these coming transforming world events. He felt that everything would begin around the start of the new millennium. It is of course possible that he was right and we may think that he was wrong only because we have failed to see the signs (see the opening of the sixth seal in 1999, Chapter 16). In Ireland, Christina Gallagher, had the impression around 1990 that everything would be over by the year 2000 but she was also careful to say that no precise timetable was given to her. The world famous prophet from Venezuela, Maria Esperanza, who clearly foresaw and had the timing right for the 9/11 explosion in New York, always felt over the years that

2004 was a significant year. It turned out that it was for her, as she died in that year.

Bruno Cornacchiola was an Italian who saw The Virgin Mary in a field north of Rome, near Tre Fontane, where St Paul was beheaded. This apparition, later approved by the Church as, "Our Lady of Revelation", caused Bruno to return to Catholicism and stopped him from assassinating Pope Pius XII, as he had planned. This happened in 1947 and Our Lady came to him annually every year afterwards. He announced in 1995 that 1996 would be a special year of great light and understanding in the world. Many at the time felt that he was describing the Great Warning, although none of the other signs of the warning were present. Like Maria Esperanza, what he was foreseeing also was his own death.

It is easy to get false impressions on the significance of particular world events and the role that these events may have in ushering in world turmoil. In 1999, for example, when the whole Catholic world should have been celebrating the 2000th anniversary of the Incarnation on the 25th March, the only world event of significance which I could note on that day, was the beginning of American bombs falling on Kosovo. The bombs began to drop as darkness fell on the evening before the 25th of March, which is the traditional time for the beginning of the feast. I felt at the time that this was a very bad omen, but nearly two decades later the world is still in relative normality and Kosovo, at least for now, is peaceful.

St Malachy, the Irish saint of the 12th century, as already mentioned, is best known for his prophecy of the various Popes through the centuries. These predictions appeared vague and cryptic for the most part, but looking back most would agree that there was a good accuracy about his descriptions. Many years ago I read that his prophecy of the present Pope pointed definitely to

St Benedict as his short account was headed, "De Gloria Oliviae" and the Benedictines are known as the Olivians. This was also said to be in keeping with a prophecy of St Benedict, which said that a Pope with devotion to himself would lead the Church when it was enduring a period of the greatest trials in history. This prediction was mistakenly discounted, however, after the death of St Pope John Paul II as there was no Benedictine Cardinal at that time. After many centuries of Papal predictions, it is interesting that St Malachy stopped at Pope Benedict XVI and declared a break. He gave no indication of the significance of this break. His only comment after the break was that, "The last Pope will be Peter the Roman". It is also interesting that St Pope John Paul II died at the beginning of the feast of Mercy (2005), which occurs on the first Sunday after Easter Sunday. Knowing what St Faustina (see below, page 449) has told us (The time of Justice will follow the Time of Mercy) we have to wonder if this means that the time of Divine Mercy is coming to an end and that the time of Justice and Tribulation is near. Pope Francis declared a special year of Mercy for the world, fixed to end on Nov 20th, Feast of Christ the King, 2016. For more information on this see chapter 16.

The prophecy of Conchita in Garabandal (see page 149) also strongly implies that Pope Benedict XVI was "the last Pope of these times" (normal times). All this is in keeping with many prophecies that say that we have now reached a period of history marking an end of an era or a "fullness of time", when there will be world chaos and the Church will undergo severe persecution. The end of the world will not follow these events, however, and we still can look forward to a period of great world peace and human fulfilment, the like of which the world has never known.

Everything, therefore, seems to fit with our present time being a great time of confusion, both for the Roman Catholic Church and the world. Pope Pius X said that he foresaw one of his successors, with the same name as himself, having to flee Rome. Pope Pius X had the name "Joseph" as does Pope Benedict XVI (Joseph Ratzinger). When Pope Francis replaced Pope Benedict, the validity or some of these prophecies had to be seriously questioned. It is well to bear in mind, however, that there is often a twist in the tale and this is in no way trying to avoid the clear prediction of these two prophecies. It is much easier to see the validity in prophecies after the event and Emeritus Pope Benedict may still have to flee Rome. A typical example of when prophecies are difficult to interpret is the case of Nostradamus, who was an authentic prophet but his writings are much too difficult to interpret before-hand. The Great Sign at Fatima was predicted to occur at noon on the 13th Oct. but it did not occur at noon but between one and two p.m. This was because the noon in the prophecy was sun time, rather than clock time. Likewise the miracle in Garabandal did not occur on the 18th July, as predicted, but very early on the 19th (sun time), because Conchita had already received communion on the 18th and Church law did not permit Holy communion more than once daily at that time. On the other hand, the suggested connection of Pope Benedict with Saint Benedict, according to St Malachy's prophecies, was thought to be an error until he had chosen the name Benedict. Those familiar with Garabandal will have heard that, "Something will happen which will stop everybody believing in Garabandal but at that stage the Bishop will have a private experience which will convince him of the truth and he will begin to promote the authenticity of the visions". To some extent, therefore, in prophecy we must be aware that human thinking does not always coincide with the Divine Plan and we must expect the unexpected.

The following is attributed to Sr Lucia of Fatima (died 13th February 2005). She is reported to have said on 7th April 1990 that, "The events taking place in Europe are a deception. Russia will be the scourge of all nations, because it was not converted.

Russia attacks the west, and China invades Asia". My feeling on this is, if Sr Lucia of Fatima said it, then it will happen, as she was the most trustworthy of all the recent prophets. I have not, however, been able to get good evidence to confirm that Sr Lucia said this and it is also worth noting that major moves have occurred in Russia since 1990, under Putin, towards the revival of Christianity as the official State religion (see pages 50 and 671). The statement does, however, fit in with three separate statements from the visionaries in Garabandal, who said at various stages "when Communism comes back". Bearing in mind that the Garabandal messages were given in the 1960's before there was any sign of the Soviet Union breaking up and Communism at that stage had not, "gone away".

We must not forget that the turmoil will be worldwide, even though most of the prophecies mentioned have been concerned with Europe. Maria Esperanza suggested that major problems in her own country – Venezuela – would be one of the first manifestations of the coming major world disorder. In December 2004 I was given a hand written note from a friend who described a talk given by a son in law of Maria, shortly after she died (Aug. 2004). In it Maria is reported to have warned her family to expect the major world events to begin between 2005 and 2009 and to start preparing.

Messages from The Lady of All Nations to Ida Peerdeman[60] have also suggested many problems in other parts of the world. The growing instability in the Middle East and in the stock market could lead to chaos overnight. There are a number of prophecies which suggest that the world will go from relative normality to chaos very quickly. The major power cuts in three centres in the US followed by London, Scandinavia, and Italy all within a few months of each other, in 2003, is enough to warn us how quickly chaos can come, if not make us suspicious as to the cause. On the other hand there is no immediate sign of civil strife in France, although this country seems a lot more unstable now than it was a few years ago. Conchita from Garabandal is reported to have said to a German author, "When the Pope comes back from Russia almost immediately Europe will drift into chaos." I have not been able to confirm this although it is widely reported. Many feel, therefore, that if the Pope visits Russia, that this will be an ominous sign and the purpose of his visit could be a final attempt to prevent a European catastrophe.

There are a few points of view which could suggest that we may still have a few years of normality. Natural disturbances, such as the predicted rise in water levels, the worsening weather and increased severity of earthquakes, tend to occur gradually over years rather than over months. We can also expect that God will give us every chance to convert and change. Many feel that it is Mary who is now preparing the way for Jesus to be proclaimed as King of All Nations. Days, dates and numbers of years seem to be important in Heavenly communications with humanity. The final conclusion must be that these world transforming events seem to be overdue and can begin at any moment. The chances of them happening within the next few years now seem very likely.

Garabandal is the Key

This village is always very quiet by comparison with other Marian Apparition centres but July is usually a busy season. Recently official Church authorities have become much more positive in their comments about the claimed apparitions and messages in the 1960's. Those who take the trouble to collect and examine the data on the Garabandal events will find the evidence strong, as explained in chapter 5. Seeing the village with virtually no pilgrim/tourists in 2017, one cannot help reflecting on the Biblical passage which says that the stone rejected by the builders may soon become a corner stone.

It is interesting how some of the few Catholics interested in Garabandal do not believe in the authenticity of Medjugorje. Far more common, however, is the reverse, and many pilgrims going to Medjugorje will not even be aware of Garabandal. Most Catholics in Europe will certainly not be aware of Akita (see page 173), which has received a substantial degree of official Church approval, unlike either Garabandal or Medjugorje. When we hear good Catholics criticize various well known Marian apparition sites as not authentic, we can have a number of different reactions. We can listen carefully, as they may know more than we do, and we may learn from them. The safest position is always to remain faithful to official Church authority. We must also be cautious and pray for wisdom and discernment, but at the same time not obstruct the working of the Holy Spirit, or condemn Marian apparitions without evidence. When the Church officially decides against an apparition then it should be avoided. It is important to keep up to date with the official Church position, however, as false rumours always circulate freely. In the case of Medjugorje, at the moment, the authority of deciding the authenticity has been removed from the local Bishop. This is a very unusual step taken by Rome, which indicates the significance placed on these events. In the case of Garabandal, the Archbishop of Oviedo, in charge up to 2007, has spoken very favourably about the events and the present parish priest, like the parish priest present in the village during the apparitions, seems to be convinced of the truth of the visions and messages. Both the priest and Bishop, as one would expect, will always act and behave subject to a final decision by Rome.

The comparisons between Garabandal and Medjugorje are obvious although not often mentioned or discussed. First of all, the frequency of the appearances of The Virgin Mary was unusual, with over two thousand in Garabandal and many more now in Medjugorje. There were the very rapid movements by visionaries over the ground in both places, a unity of movement during the apparitions, large numbers of eyewitnesses, the warnings, the promised signs and the teaching being completely in line with Catholic theology. Of great interest is the fact recorded in Michael Brown's new book, Tower of Light,[170] that Mirjana in Medjugorje knows the date and the hour of a great prophesied sign. Conchita from Garabandal also knows the date and the time of a great miracle to occur at the pines in Garabandal. Both are to announce these events some days before hand. It is easy to believe that there may be similar events which will take place, at the same time, in different parts of the world where Marian apparitions have occurred. Permanent supernatural signs have also been prophesied to be left in both places, so that humanity will forever remember these respective events.

I say that Garabandal is the Key, not because I believe that it is more important than Medjugorje, but, if and when the Great World Warning (see chapter 12) comes, interest will immediately switch to the messages of Garabandal, which have predicted The Great Warning and The Great Miraculous Sign in more detail than any other Marian message. Furthermore, the approximate time of the great predicted miracle in Garabandal will then also be known. This is to occur between the 8th and 16th of the month of March, April or May on a Thursday at 8.30 pm on the feast day of a little known saint martyred for the Eucharist. There are various opinions on how easy or difficult it will be to travel to Garabandal at this time, as a significant degree of world chaos is expected before and after The Great Warning. Those who know the village will know that the surrounds are like a huge open air theatre, where millions of people can gather and watch the unfolding events from the nearby hills.

The messages in Garabandal and Medjugorje are not in opposition. Neither are the messages from Fatima, Bethania, Akita or any of the other authentic places of Marian appearances. It is the same messenger emphasizing different aspects of the same warnings and the same teachings. Repent and believe the teaching of the Gospel if you are to avoid suffering and merit Heaven.

Hogar De La Madre: This is a new Catholic religious order of priests, brothers and consecrated sisters, which has developed within the last three decades, near Santander in the North of Spain a short distance from Garabandal. This new order is beginning to flourish and spread to other countries. They now have houses in Italy, Ecuador and in the US as well as in many parts of Spain. They are soon to open a house in Ireland. They do not openly promote the message of Garabandal preferring to remain quietly in the background developing the vocations and charisms of their order. This order has three charisms. These are:

1) The protection and promotion of love for the Eucharist.
2) Promotion of the virtues of The Blessed Virgin Mary, especially her virginity.
3) Winning young souls for Christ.

Those who know the origin of this religious order will know the connection with Garabandal. It is not for us to reveal this story which will surface in God's good time. For now the progress of this order is just another sign for the authenticity of this urgent message from God given to humanity by The Virgin Mary.

Final words from Marie-Julie

Finally, in this section I would like to reflect briefly on two other prophetic statements made by Marie Julie Jahenny, concerning the times we are now living in. The first is concerned with the reason why God feels chastisement is now the only option to change humanity. ("Chastisement" implies punishment from a parent (God), out of a motive of love and concern, as opposed to "tribulation" which is the suffering which will result from evil deeds.) God the Father said to Marie Julie on 16th Sept. 1904:

"If My Divine Son and I were to work miracles greater than all the ones in Judea, than all the miracles of the past, all these marvels would still be scorned. They would continue to insult My Divine Son and His Holy Mother…It is a blindness. It is an infernal veil woven by the enemy, jealous of the marvels and power of My Divine Son. In place of marvels, blows will be necessary. Decimation, yes a terrible decimation…… Half the population of France will be destroyed. After the punishments, there will be villages left without a soul. Four towns in France will disappear".

This is hard to hear. The status of Marie Julie and other prophets who have said this, however, makes it impossible to ignore. Sadly, the French people, like the rest of the world, have no idea of the troubled times ahead, so it is unlikely that anything will be done to mitigate the suffering. Another statement from Marie Julie which may be of particular interest concerns a message which she got on 14th Dec. 1881:

"Many souls will be possessed (by evil spirits) a few months before (the major world crisis). The whole world will be mad with fear… . In all corners of the world there will be Antichrists, as at the time of the Last Judgement, who will travel through the world to pervert".

Reflecting on this statement is now prompting some immediate concern for us. This is due to a request, which came from the Vatican to chosen people, to immediately begin the training of

448

exorcists around the world, **"as they will be greatly needed in the near future"**. We were informed of this by one of those charged with the responsibility of organizing some of these courses that are now taking place. Let us not forget that reports on all the Catholic prophets and mystics (authentic and otherwise) are going into the Vatican on a regular basis. It is likely that those with responsibility for analysing these reports will have the best view of the pictures emerging from these prophetic antennas world wide. If this is the source of the belief that exorcists will soon be needed in the world, then this prophecy of Marie Julie takes on a new significance over the near future.

Divine Mercy and a Polish Trio

We are now living in the time of Divine Mercy. Divine Mercy is infinite, deserved by nobody but accessible to everybody. Three saints in Poland have been intimately connected with this message. These were St Faustina Kowalska, St Maximilian Kolbe, and St Pope John Paul II. Although these three individuals lived at the same time, no more than fifteen miles apart at one time, they never met. In the Spring of 1938 while St Faustina, a 33 yr old nun, lay dying from tuberculosis, in her Krakow convent near Warsaw, Karol Wojtyla, the future St Pope John Paul, was graduating from his school in Wadowice. At the same time a 44 yr old Franciscan priest, St Maximilian Kolbe, was guiding 700 clergy in his monastery in Krakow. Three years later St Maximilian would die a martyr's death, when he offered his life as a replacement for another prisoner of the Nazis, in Auschwitz, less than 30 miles from Krakow.

St Faustina Kowalska: She was born in 1905. During her early years Jesus began to appear to her regularly and he gave her a special Divine mission to tell the world about His Divine Mercy. At the age of twenty she joined the convent of the Sisters of Our Lady of Mercy and began her secluded life as a nun. The many messages that she received, she recorded in her now famous Diary of Divine Mercy.[177] She got many messages about God's unfathomable Divine Mercy. Jesus said to her, "It is on My Divine Mercy that the future of the world will depend...It is a sign for the end-times. Afterwards will come the Time of Justice... Let them first have recourse to My Mercy". Jesus also said to her that faith alone was not enough and that people must practice daily acts of mercy by deed, work and prayer. On February 22nd 1931 Jesus gave her the now famous picture of Divine Mercy with the caption, **Jesus I Trust in Thee.** She died on October 5th 1938.

St Faustina was almost unknown outside Poland until St Pope John Paul II was elected. He had studied her writings for many years, and he was a great promoter of her messages and her sanctity. He eventually was responsible for her beatification and later her canonization. One of the great miraculous events which led to her beatification was the cure of the American young lady named Maureen Digan.[178] Maureen suffered from an incurable disease of the lymphatic system called Milroy's disease. She had her left leg amputated at the age of 17 and in her twenties she was told that her other leg would also have to be amputated. At this stage she was also a mental and spiritual wreck and was getting regular seizures. She was on regular medication for severe pain and was addicted to antidepressants. It was at this time that a Catholic priest suggested that she go on a pilgrimage to Krakow in Poland. On the 28th of March 1981 she found herself at St Faustina's convent saying the chaplet of Divine Mercy. She thought that she heard an interior voice say to her, "If you want something you have to ask for it". She responded by saying, "Faustina, you got me here, so if you are going to do something for me, do it now." Instantly all her severe pain, which she had suffered for eighteen years, disappeared, and her swollen leg came down to normal size so rapidly that her shoe was falling off. There was no longer any need for her to take medication. When she returned to the US her astonished doctor had her thoroughly investigated by cardiologists and vascular surgeons. There was no explanation for this cure. Eleven years later her sudden cure was declared a miracle by the Catholic Church through the intercession of St Faustina Kowalska.

St Maximilian Kolbe: He was born Raymond Kolbe. When he was ten years old The Virgin Mary appeared to him, while he was praying at a side altar in his local church, and offered him two crowns to choose from. One was white in colour for purity and the second was red for martyrdom. He asked, "Can I not have both?" Mary apparently agreed to this request. His mother firmly believed this story as she said that his whole attitude to life changed completely after this experience. At the age of sixteen he joined the Franciscans and was later ordained a priest with a doctorate degree in philosophy and theology. He believed like St Pope John Paul II later that the best and easiest way to achieve sanctity was to be consecrated to God through The Virgin Mary. In 1917, he started an organization in Rome call the Militia Immaculatae (MI) and they began printing a magazine, which is still published as a periodical, called the Knight of the Immaculate. He organized the building of several Franciscan monasteries. The largest of these was in Poland with over 700 priests, making it the largest monastery in the world at that time.

In 1930 he joined a small group of Franciscans going to Japan. They established a monastery in Nagasaki and within one month they were publishing their magazine in Japanese. This monastery later became famous for not being damaged by the atom bomb on August 9th 1945 despite the building being near the explosion (see page 135). He returned to Poland and was there for the beginning of World War II. At that time it was common for the monastery to be feeding 3,000 Jews. The magazine which he established had a wide circulation and published many articles critical of the Nazi party. The inevitable happened and he was imprisoned in Auschwitz in 1941. Here he was told that Jews survived an average of two weeks and priests an average of one month.

St Maximilian's martyrdom came when he volunteered to replace a fellow prisoner, named Francis Gajowniczek, who was selected to be put to death with nine others. This was as a reprisal for one prisoner who had escaped and death was to be by deprivation of food and drink, in an underground bunker. The usual moans, groans and blasphemies that could be usually heard from these death cells were not heard from the cell containing St Maxmilian. Instead, what was heard was prayers and hymns. On the evening of the 14th August, 1941, after a number of days without food or water, only four prisoners remained alive. Those alive included St Maxmilian, and these remaining prisoners were killed by lethal injections of carbolic acid. Francis Gajowniczek had a number of mysterious escapes from death, in the years that followed, including one occasion where the camp doctor hid him under a pile of dead bodies. After the war, he spent his whole life telling his story of how he survived a Nazi concentration camp. He was present in Rome for the canonization of St Maximilian Kolbe in 1982. His last talk was given in the US in January 1995. He died six weeks later aged 93.

St Pope John Paul II: He was the great promoter of Divine Mercy as revealed to St Faustina. His mother died when he was eight years old. His older brother, who was a doctor, died from a streptococcal infection, which he got from one of his patients, when the future Pope was eleven. St Faustina and St Pope John Paul II were the two key people in proclaiming to the world the message of Divine Mercy. St Faustina was the link between God and humanity and St Pope John Paul II was the link between St Faustina and the rest of the world. The Pope had studied and proclaimed this message from his early years in the priesthood.

From the beginning of his papacy he felt it that it was his Divine mission to proclaim this message to the world and his first encyclical was "Dives in Misericordiae" (Rich in Mercy – 1980). Speaking about Poland, Jesus said to St Faustina, "From Her (Poland) will come forth the spark that will prepare the world for My final coming," (Diary 1732). It is widely now believed that St Pope John Paul II was that spark.

One of the requests from Jesus to St Faustina was that the Church should proclaim the Sunday after Easter as "Divine Mercy Sunday". St Pope John Paul II fulfilled this request and on the first Divine Mercy Sunday in 2000 he canonized St Faustina as the first saint of the new millennium. The Pope said on the same day, "This is the happiest day of my life". St Pope John Paul died at the beginning of this feast of Divine Mercy, five years later, in 2005.

In 1976 St Pope John Paul, as a Cardinal, said, "We are now standing at the greatest confrontation humanity has ever experienced. We are now facing the final confrontation between the Church and the anti-church, between the Gospel and the anti-gospel, between Christ and the Antichrist". A few years later, as Pope he said, "We must prepare ourselves to suffer great trials before long, such as will demand a disposition to give up even life, with a total dedication to Christ and for Christ. With our prayers it is possible to mitigate the coming tribulation but it is no longer possible to avert it..." (See chapter 16 for what Pope John Paul II said about the third secret of Fatima). Have no doubt that St Pope John Paul II was well aware of what is coming and how serious it will get.

The Lay Apostle, Anne

One of the most recent Catholic prophets to become popular is the prophet "Anne". Anne is a middle aged American lady who has been receiving locutions from Heaven since 2003. She was directed to move from the US and live in the midlands of Ireland. She gets many messages and directions from God the Father, Jesus, The Virgin Mary and many saints. These are recorded in a series of books which explain the changes which are soon to take place on earth and how humanity should prepare and understand that these changes are now a necessity. As a relatively recent prophet she is unusual in that she has had the support of her Bishop in the US and now she has the support of her Bishop in Ireland. We understand that she had a number of private messages for St Pope John Paul II, which were given to him in the last few years of his life. The messages which she receives are generally very positive. For this reason and others I thought it appropriate that I should introduce her to those who may be interested and in particular to those who may be disturbed by some of the events described in this book. I have selected the following brief examples from her books to illustrate the kind of messages she receives and promotes, (Quoted here with permission).

Message from St Therese, the Little Flower, given July 5th, 2004:
"Dear holy souls, you are approaching difficult days. You know this, of course, if the Spirit is active within you. Your world is in darkness and must be cleansed. All of this has been said. What Our Lord wills at this time is that we, your Heavenly brothers and sisters, provide you with specific information and guidelines. Pray for discernment and you will see that there is no other path than the path that leads to Heaven and to Jesus Christ. The time of darkness nears. The world has not converted, despite the efforts of many, both in Heaven and on earth. Souls cling rebelliously to sinful ways and do not even fear God's justice. They have embraced evil.

The world is going to go even further in the direction of anti-God and you will stand out even more starkly against the Godless landscape. This will not be comfortable for you but you will have complete Heavenly assistance and support. Brothers and sisters, I, Therese, am only one of countless saints who has been commissioned to assist you. You will find us always near and always willing to instruct and console. We will petition the Spirit and obtain the most sublime gifts of wisdom and discernment for you. My dear fellow servants, we are entering the storm, but not without Jesus, our rudder. Children of God should not fear God's intervention. Given my Heavenly knowledge, I assure you that the only fearful thing for this world would be a decision by God to leave it to itself. Welcome, brothers and sisters, to the legion of Heavenly soldiers who fight for Christ. You will earn your place in Heaven."

Message from St Anthony, given July 9th, 2004: "My dear friends in the world, all is well in Heaven, where you will eventually dwell. All is tranquil and graces flow freely from one soul to another, after originating in the Godhead. Truly, we are at peace. With this said, we are also at the alert because we are, like you, awaiting the sweeping changes that will alter the way of life in your world... Can you imagine how this makes us feel? If there were not changes coming, we would feel helpless. But changes are coming so we feel invigorated and optimistic. We are all committed to working alongside you to bring about changes on the ground.

"I am Anthony. I love you dearly and consider you my closest friends. I want only to help you and I continue to thank Jesus for allowing me to communicate with all of you on earth. I am your friend. Talk to me. Allow me to help you. There are many of us and if you have friends in Heaven, you must ask them for help now because they have been given enhanced intercessory powers during this time. We are all going to work together to see you through this transition, and the earth will be remarkably beautiful afterwards. All that need concern you is service on each day. Everything else will be cared for by Heaven. Never become discouraged because truly there is no need to be."

Message from St Julie, given July 21st, 2004: "There will come a time when the world will seem very dark. You will have little hope that God is going to turn it around and allow His grace to take the earth back. My friends, during this time you will use us. God does everything for the good of His people and it will be important to remember that during the times to come. I do not seek to frighten you but in the eyes of non-faithful souls it will seem as though God wreaks vengeance. In your eyes it will seem that God has forgotten you. In the eyes of Heaven, the Truth will be that God is preparing to return. The darkest hour truly can come before the dawn, and it will be that way during the time of transition. We, Heaven's saints, will be active and aggressive for our kindred spirits on the earth. You will ask us for help. You will get it. We will secure great courage for you. We will help you maintain your faith and your hope. We will even help you with practical matters on occasion."

Anne has produced three large books. *Climbing the Mountain*[179] deals with Anne's journey on the Mountain of Holiness and her experience of Heaven where she was allowed to visit and The Mist of Mercy,[100] describes in detail her experiences during time she was allowed to spend with the holy souls in purgatory. Her latest large book, *Serving in Clarity – A Guide for Lay Apostles of Jesus Christ the Returning King*,[180] is another spiritual gem, giving instructions on how to move from self-will to Divine Will. Approximately twenty smaller booklets have also been published from her messages. Half of these books give directions to humanity for the coming times and the other half deal with specific advice to those with particular problems such as advice to prisoners, soldiers, those with depression, addictions, after divorce, after clerical abuse, after abortion, those considering suicide, those away from the Church, those who have rejected God, those in financial need, those who have experienced tragedy, and those preparing for death. The overall message from Anne is clear and unambiguous. The world is about to be transformed and renewed completely, root and branch, − BUT, be not afraid. God is in control, − BUT, you must acknowledge this and respond accordingly. This clear message, with the support of more than one Bishop is yet another confirmation of how much senior Catholic Church clerics are aware of impending world changes.

Saint Faustina Kowalska appeared to Anne on the 27th September, 2005. She said, "Anne, our missions are destined to be joined. Your mission is an extension of my mission, in that it is all part of the Divine Mercy". We still live in the Time of Mercy. Soon we will live in the Time of Justice. REPENT & PREPARE.

For further discussion on Catholic prophecy, especially on the question of the nearness of Antichrist and how modern prophetic messages can be compared and integrated with prophecies in the Apocalypse of the New Testament, please read the final chapter of this book.

12. The Warning and the Miracle

This stupendous pillar, at one time of cloud and at another of fire, was a figure of Mary and of the various offices which she performs on our behalf.

St Alphonsus Ligouri

It has already been explained, that four visionaries from Garabandal, a small village near Santander, in the north of Spain, were told that "These Times" would end with two major events of global significance, which would mark the beginning of a major change in the history of humanity. The first of these events is to be a direct warning from God, to each living person. Everybody will see themselves as God sees them, at that particular moment in time, in order to encourage them to repent and live good lives. This warning will be followed within a year with a major miraculous event, which will end with a permanent supernatural sign, which will be visible to the end of the world. Conchita, one of the visionaries, was also told that before the end of "These Times", there would only be three more Popes after Pope John XXIII. There would be a fourth Pope, "but he would not count". Emeritus Pope Benedict XVI, was the fourth Pope so, if her revelation is true, the end of "These Times" is at hand.

What is The Warning?

Many visionaries have been given information on different aspects of "The Warning". The most detailed information, however, has come from the Garabandal visionaries. All four were given general information. Maria Loli was told the year of The Warning. Conchita was told the date of a great public miracle, which is to occur within a year of the Warning and Jacinta, was given details of the state of the world when the Warning would occur. She has said that, "It will occur when things are at their worst."

Conchita wrote the following note, dated 2nd June, 1964: "The Blessed Virgin Mary told me on the 1st of January, that a warning would be given before the Miracle, so that the world may amend itself. This warning is a very fearful thing for the good as well as the bad. It will draw the good closer to God, and it will warn the wicked that the end of time is coming and that these are the last warnings... Yes, the warning will be like a revelation of our sins and it will be seen and experienced equally by believers and non believers alike."

Various other descriptions of the Warning given by the Garabandal visionaries are as follows: "It comes directly from God and will be visible throughout the entire world to every human person at the same time. The Warning will be a revelation of our sins and it will be experienced by Catholic believers, those with other religions and those with no religion....We would prefer to be dead than to experience The Warning.... The Warning is like a purification for the Great Miracle ... It is supernatural, it will be seen and felt and will not be explained by science...The Warning will be a correction of the conscience of the world....We will find ourselves alone with our conscience before God.... We will all feel it differently.... It will take only a few minutes. It will bring no physical harm except for those who die of shock or heart attacks.... One way, I sometimes describe what I saw in The Warning, is that it will be like two stars that crash together and make a lot of noise and a lot of light, but they don't fall down... It is not going to hurt us". One of the first recorded private revelations, giving us some knowledge of this major world changing event and act of Divine Mercy, was from the "Pearl of England", St Edmund Campion S.J. Martyr. (1581). He is quoted as saying, "I pronounce a great day, not wherein any potentate should minister, but wherein the terrible Judge should reveal all men's consciences and try every man of each kind of religion. This is the day of change: this is the day which I threatened." Some other references by saints and visionaries which have been noted and collected by other writers are as follows:

Ann Marie Taigi: Italy, 1769: "A great purification of the world shall be preceded by an illumination of conscience in which everyone will see themselves as God sees them. Many souls shall be saved by this warning, this miracle of self illumination."

Marie-Julie Jahenny, French Stigmatist, 1878: (see chpt 11 and below for more details). "One more judgment shall take place before the last one, a judgment of justice, altogether with a judgment of glorious resurrection in peace and hope for the friends of God".

Teresa Neumann, German stigmatist, seer, prophet, 1898: "This time of warnings, our Lord himself called it a minor judgment."

Julka, Victim, seer, visionary, Yugoslavia, 1921: "Jesus said, a small judgment is approaching".

Four Visionaries, Heede, Germany, 1937: Jesus said to them, "With a few faithful, I will build up my kingdom. As a flash of lightning, this kingdom will come much faster than mankind will realise. I will give them a special light. For some, this light will be a special blessing, for others darkness. The light will come like the star that showed the way to the wise men. Mankind will experience my love and my power. My beloved children, the hour comes closer and closer. Pray without ceasing."

Maria Valtorta, French mystic, seer, 1943: Jesus spoke to her as follows: "My fire will descend on this world quicker than you expect it to come, so that those without sight of their sins may suddenly see their guilt. It is in my power to bring this day forward, or to shorten it, for this hour will bring so much distress, that many will curse the hour of their birth, but no one shall escape from this hour. Those who truly love me shall be cleansed. Many will continue to live unholy lives. When I break the sixth seal... they will take to the mountains and hide in the caves, but who can escape the great day of purification?"

Amparo Cuevas, Spain, Jan 14th, 1983: The Virgin Mary told Amparo that, "each one will see what they have done during his whole life."

Vassula Ryden., Greek Orthodox, Victim soul, seer: On Sept. 15th 1991, she received the following description of The Warning: "Turn your eyes to the East and to the West, to the North and to the South and I am there. I tell you truly that once more my Spirit will be poured on you and my image will spread across the face of the world. What I have planned shall happen and what I have told you shall be fulfilled... It will be sooner than you think. You are heading for your ruin. Rise from the dead. The end of times is nearer than you think... A breath shall slide over your face...suddenly... I will allow your soul to perceive the events of your lifetime. I will unfold them one after the other. To the great dismay of your soul you will realise how much innocent blood your sins shed from victim souls. I will then make your soul aware to see how you have never been a follower of the Law. The eyes of your soul shall behold a dazzling light...so pure and so bright...that your souls will see what they had once seen in that fraction of a second, at the very moment of your creation...He who held you first in his hands, the eyes that saw you first... he who shaped you and blest you... the most tender Father, your creator... Shrivelled with your awakening, your eyes will be transfixed in mine...your heart will look back on your sins and will be seized with remorse...When that day comes, the scales of your eyes will fall so that you may see how naked you are...Your laments and your wailing will be heard only by you then. I am sending my servants, the prophets, to cry out in this wilderness, that you should fear me and praise me, because the time has come for me to sit in judgment."

On March 3rd1992, Jesus said to Vassula: "The great day of my purification is soon to come upon you. Everyone on this earth will have to be purified. This will be given to everyone like a secret revelation, to reveal the obscurity of your soul. All races and religions shall see me in their interior darkness. Some of you today are sad because the world is passing premature judgment on my Sacred Heart and the Immaculate Heart of your Mother, but soon Our Two Hearts will show the world how wrong it was about judging, because I will reveal my holy face in them." This is a reference to the Bible scripture passage (Jn.16.8): "When he comes, he will convince the world of wrong judgment because, the Prince of this world has been judged".

Veronica Garcia, Denver, Colorado: On July 28th 1992, Jesus told her, "I have come to you my littlest soul. Soon will be the time when all my children will see me. They will be asked to make their choice. They will be shown the depths of their souls and will be frightened by what they see. The proud will be uprooted, the rich will be left with nothing. Only my meek and humble lambs will survive the great test. I come to you now so that you may warn them."

Matthew Kelly: An Australian who received locutions and was asked to promote these messages around the world. In 1993, he was told by Jesus that, "The mini–judgment is a reality. People no longer realise they are offending me. Out of my infinite mercy I will provide a mini-judgment. It will be painful, very painful but very short. You will see your sins: you will see how much you offend me every day. Unfortunately, this will not bring the whole world into my love. Some people will turn even further away from my love. You will see your own personal darkness contrasted against the pure light of my love. Those who repent will be given an unquenchable thirst for this light. Their love for me will be so strong that united with Mary's Immaculate Heart and the Sacred Heart of Jesus, the head of Satan shall be crushed and he will be detained in Hell forever".

Philip Bebie on the Warning

In order to get another view of The Warning, it is worth briefly recording some of the points made in a book written on the subject in 1982, by Fr Philip Bebie.[181] These points can be summarized as follows:

a) It will be like the conversion of St Paul. In a glorious vision it was revealed to him what he was doing wrong and the blinding light of the risen Christ convicted him of his sin. We too will hear the words, "Why have you persecuted me?" Paul heeded the warning and left his former life behind.

b) It will make everybody, believer and unbeliever, aware of God. We will all be aware of God's existence, immeasurable power, mercy, love and concern for our salvation.

c) It will show us our sins. Our consciences will be thoroughly illuminated, exposing self-deception, lies, compromises, stubborn and unkind decisions, neglects, refusals, undone deeds, and unfulfilled plans etc.

d) It will be a taste of eternity. Time will stop and we will all be aware of timeless existence.

e) It will be a Mercy from God. Mercy allows us to sample the pain that sin bequeaths to us. God wants us to be happy and to become perfect. We must decide.

f) It is a sign of the future. It will be the major turning point in world history. It will be the major event leading to conversion for the whole world. It will be a direct intervention from God. Never before has God acted so directly and universally. All the deception which has obscured the light of the Gospel (the fuzz) will be swept away.

g) It will call us to choose. From now on we must choose for God or against God. We are all free to choose our eternal path, Heaven to Hell. To delay will be to choose against God.

h) It will prepare the world for the Great Miracle, predicted to occur within one year of The Warning. This will be associated with a permanent new and visible sign, given by God to humanity, to mark these majestic and world shattering events.

i) We will understand our eternal state and destiny, should we have died at that time. We will momentarily suffer the pain of our sin, the pain of separation from God, the pain of Purgatory or Hell. God will let us see it all.

John Bird and the Warning

John Bird is an Englishman, who spent many years as a movie maker in the USA. About twenty five years ago, he returned to England to visit and help his ill father. During his stay he went on pilgrimage to the Marian shrine in Lourdes, France, which he had visited once before as a boy. He got the shock of his life while praying at the grotto, when The Virgin Mary appeared to him, showed him the state of his soul, and encouraged him to give up what he was doing and to start making films for God. He returned to England and after many months of soul searching, he eventually decided to give up all the possessions he owned, and begin by making a movie on Medjugorje (see page 164). He knew very little about this event at the time, apart from a brief story which he read in The Sunday Times. Since then he has made many top quality documentaries and written several books on these so called "End Times". His books and documentaries give a good overview of the problems that the world is now facing.

In particular John Bird has collected a lot of information on The Warning. He has become an expert on the famous French mystic, Marie Julie Jahenny (see page 416). In his book *A Storm Unleashed from the Waters of the Abyss,*[167] he gives details of Marie Julie's comments on The Warning. She was told that The Warning would occur near the beginning of the 21st Century. A message given to her on 15th June, 1882 said:

"I forewarn you, a day will come when, in the early hours of the morning, there will be little light from the sun, or from the stars: it will be in the early month of the year. There will be insufficient light for people to leave their houses. It will not be in mid-summer, during the longest days, nor during the shortest ones. It will not be at the end of the year in December, but rather when the spring wheat will not quite have reached its third notch of growth" (March).

"It will be a day of continuous thunder and lightning and terrible upheavals in the atmosphere. The sun will be almost completely darkened. This will start mid-day (in France) lasting till 4.00 p.m. It will signal the commencement of the Chastisement of the earth… If governments and political leaders continue then, to ignore and reject the sovereignty of God, there will be a severe Chastisement which will change the face of the whole earth. The few who survive, will be charged with the responsibility to rebuild a world renewed in Christ."

John Bird in the same book also gives an account of a Spanish visionary, Amparo Cuevas, whom he believes to be authentic. She was told in 1982, that an asteroid, called Eros, would be involved in The Warning. It was interesting that this name was revealed years before any asteroid had this name. On the other hand, Eros is in a stable orbit and should never come near the earth. As usual, only time will reveal how accurate this revelation will be. A summary of the message is as follows:

"The asteroid Eros, will illuminate the earth causing it to appear to be surrounded by flames. During a period of some twenty minutes, an event will spread panic everywhere... Many people will wish to die at that moment in that shower of fire, which will strike fear in everyone... All those who believe in God and the Holy Virgin will remain in a kind of ecstasy during this period. This will occur in the near future."

Fr Gobbi and the Warning

Fr Gobbi, as explained in the introduction, got locutions from The Virgin Mary from 1973 up to the last day of the last century, in order to instruct the Catholic priesthood and to prepare them for these coming major transforming events in the world.[3] These are recorded under numbers and dates in the now famous, Blue Book, which forms the basis for the world wide cenacle prayer group meetings, held regularly (monthly or weekly), under the banner of "The Marian Movement of Priests". I quote here (with permission) some of these messages which seem to me and to others to specifically refer to The Warning.

No: 383 Feast of Pentecost, May 22nd, 1988: "The time of the second Pentecost has arrived. The Holy Spirit will come, like the Heavenly dew of grace and fire, which will renew the whole world. Beneath His irresistible action of love, the Church will open up to live the new era of her greatest holiness, and will shine out with a light so powerful as to attract to herself all the nations of the earth. The Holy Spirit will come, so that the Will of the Heavenly Father may be fulfilled, and the created universe can come back to reflecting His great glory. The Holy Spirit will come to establish the glorious reign of Christ, and it will be a reign of grace, holiness, love, justice and peace. With His divine Love He will open the doors of hearts and He will enlighten all consciences. Every man will see himself in the blazing fire of divine Truth. It will be like a judgement in miniature. Then Jesus Christ will bring His glorious Reign into the world. The Holy Spirit will come through the triumph of my Immaculate Heart. For this reason, I invite you all to enter into the Cenacle of my Heart. In this way, you will be prepared to receive the gift of the Holy Spirit, Who will transform you and make you into instruments with which Jesus will establish His Reign."

No: 426 Feast of Pentecost, June 3rd, 1990: "You are approaching the moment in which the great prodigy of the second Pentecost will come about. Only the Spirit of Love is able to renew the world. Only the Spirit of Love is able to form the new Heavens and new Earth. Only the Spirit of Love is able to prepare hearts, souls, the Church and the whole of humanity to receive Jesus, Who will come back to you in glory. For this you are entering into the times in which the divine action of the Holy Spirit will become increasingly powerful."

No: 478 Feast of Guardian Angels, Oct 2nd 1992: "This final period of the purification and of the great tribulation corresponds to a particular and powerful manifestation of the Angels of the Lord. You have entered into the most painful and most difficult phase of the battle between the Spirits of good and the Spirits of evil, between the Angels and the demons. It is a terrible struggle, which is going on around you and above you. You, poor earthly creatures, are involved in it... What comes about will be something so great, such as has never been from the beginning of the world. It will be like a judgement in miniature and everyone will see his own life and all his works in the very Light of God."

No: 529 Oct 13th 1994: "My times have arrived...I foretold to you the great chastisement, which was to strike this poor humanity, which has gone back to being pagan, which has built up a new civilisation without God, and which is threatened by violence, hatred and war and is in danger of destroying itself with its own hands. My extraordinary interventions, which I performed in order to lead it onto the road of conversion and of its return to the Lord, were neither accepted nor believed. And so it is that now you find yourselves on the eve of the great trial, which I foretold to you: it will be the supreme manifestation of the divine justice and of mercy."

No: 546 Feast of Pentecost June 4th 1995: "Tongues of Divine fire will come down upon all of you, my poor children, so deceived and seduced by Satan and by all the evil spirits, which in these years have obtained their great triumph. So it is that you will be enlightened by this Divine Light and you will see yourselves in the mirror of the truth and holiness of God."

Marino Restrepo and Others

One of the best known individuals who has experienced this illumination of consciousness is the Columbian, Marino Restrepo (marinorestrepo.com). He was kidnapped by rebels in his native Columbia, South America when he was visiting his family from Hollywood, USA. He was born a Catholic but he had lapsed and was a follower of New Age practices, when he was captured. In a dark cave, where he was imprisoned, he experienced his whole life come before him one night. He had the extraordinary experience of seeing all his good and bad actions during his life appear before him, as if in a film, over a short period of time. He saw his actions and thoughts reflected against the light, justice and love of God. He was filled with remorse and wanted nothing more than to go to the Sacrament of Confession. He also was infused with knowledge about many aspects of Church teaching. He was released after six months and he now spends his life travelling the world evangelising. He speaks Spanish, English and German.

Two others: I know of two other individuals who seem to have experienced a similar illumination of consciousness. The first is an American priest who appeared before God in judgement after a very bad car accident. He was destined for Hell but through the intercession of The Virgin Mary he did not die, but was sent back for a second chance. I heard him tell his own story. He remembered it all clearly and he said that his problem was that as a priest, he was telling his flock what they wanted to hear, rather than the truth of the gospel. His fellow priests had encouraged him to behave in this way for a quiet life and so that the collections would not decrease. While lying on his hospital bed, suddenly it was as if a great light surrounded him, and he saw his whole life pass before him, with all the evil and good he had done. During the judgement he felt that, - "I was being judged by truth". He could not deny anything because he knew that it was true. He was shown the place in Hell which was prepared for him. He then saw The Virgin Mary in the background and she pleaded to Jesus to give him another chance, pointing out that this was because he had some devotion to Her. Jesus said to His' mother, "Take him, he is yours". He then felt life flow back into his body. He completely changed his life afterwards and has travelled widely speaking of his experience.

The second story I heard told by an Irish American couple, Kevin and Patrice McCarthy, from Indianapolis, during one of their tours of Ireland, in 1998. They described the story of an Anglican friend of theirs who started to pray the rosary and do Eucharistic adoration. He had the 'illumination' experience during adoration one day. He described that he felt he would die, if he did not go to a Catholic priest for confession. He was also infused with a complete knowledge of the Catholic faith. This is interesting for a number of reasons. Firstly, the Great Warning of Garabandal is predicted to be for all people and afterwards, everybody will know the truth about God, through infused knowledge. Secondly, it was similar to the experience of the Jew, Alphonsine Ratisbone, when he began to wear the Miraculous Medal (see page 113).

An Aurora: The final description of The Warning, with which I would like to leave you, is from the Garabandal visionaries, recorded in earlier historical notes. Three points are mentioned:

1. It will be associated with a phenomenon beginning with the word "A" in Spanish.
2. It will be like a fire but will not burn you.
3. All engines will stop.

There is little doubt that this describes a huge world-wide aurora, probably related to a nearby comet. Remember that the sign announcing World War II, which was promised at Fatima, was also an aurora (see page 130, chapter 5). It was discovered in 1966, (after the US hydrogen bomb test – Teak explosion) that one of the effects of an aurora, secondary to electromagnetic radiation, was to cause electrical systems to fail. This would explain the statement, "All the engines will stop." This is also very unlikely to be an invention of four poor Spanish teenagers in the early 1960's. The important thing to emphasize, however, is that the Warning will only be **associated with** these physical signs, but the Warning itself will be spiritual rather than physical. It will be a direct intervention by God on the conscience of each living person.

When will the warning come?

A Spanish book published in Mexico, El Gran Aviso De Dios[182], gives some interesting pointers in time, according to some prophets and visionaries, as to when we should expect The Warning to occur. In particular a number of these describe the scene in Rome at the time.

Serafin (the older brother of Conchita, Garabandal visionary), said that he heard Conchita say, "The Warning will occur after a very sorrowful event in the Church – something like a schism."

Maria Loli (Garabandal visionary – now deceased) said: "The Pope will not be able to appear openly in Rome and he will have to go into hiding, a short time before The Warning."

Blessed Anna Maria Taigi (see page 423) said that, "Religion will be persecuted and priests will be massacred. The Holy Father will be obliged to leave Rome."

On Sept. 14th 1976 a well know American seer (**Veronica**) said, "When there is a revolution in Rome and when The Holy Father has to flee Rome to seek refuge in another country, then the time of The Warning has arrived"

On August 1989, **Jacinta Gonzalez** (Garabandal visionary) said that, "The Warning is connected with an invasion of Rome in which Communism will play a very important part. The Warning will take place shortly after these events, when things are at their worst."

On August 1998, The Virgin Mary is reported to have given a message to an American visionary (**Sadie Jaramillo**), which said that, "The Warning will occur at a time of great chaos and confusion."

The Miracle.

Conchita, from Garabandal, knows the date of the Miracle. She will reveal it to the world eight days before it is due to occur. The Blessed Virgin told the visionaries in Garabandal that "nothing bad would happen on the day". Father Luis Andreu saw the miracle in a vision and was said to have died of joy on the same day (see page 144).

Father Philip Bebie,[181] records some of the characteristics of The Miracle as follows:

a) Millions will be able to see it on the day.
b) It will be a revelation especially of God's mercy.
c) It will be Eucharistic
d) It will be ecclesial
e) It will be Marian
f) It will be for the conversion of the whole world
g) It will be sacramental
h) It will serve as another warning
i) It will be for the Glory of God.

Garabandal Journal

The Garabandal Journal is published every two months and outlines the many details associated with the Garabandal events[48]. In March/April, 2004, edition this Journal listed a summary of the events that have been predicted regarding the Great Miracle.

Before the Miracle: There will be many reported "apparitions" throughout the world. (This prophecy made in December, 1962, has already been fulfilled) A Bishop of Santander will come along who will not believe at first, but will receive a sign and allow priests to go up to Garabandal for the Miracle. Shortly before the Miracle something will happen that will cause people to stop believing in Garabandal. A period of 12 months or less will elapse from the time of the Warning to the Miracle. Conchita will announce it eight days in advance.

Day of the Miracle: It will occur on a Thursday at 8:30 in the evening, between the eighth and sixteenth (inclusive) of March, April or May. It will coincide with a great ecclesiastical event in the Church (not unique, but rare, like the declaration of a Dogma). It will be on the feast day of a young martyr for the Eucharist (not very well known). It will last approximately fifteen minutes. It will be seen in the sky. All those either in the village or on the surrounding mountains will see it. The sick who are present will be cured, sinners converted and the incredulous will believe. It will be the greatest miracle that Jesus has ever performed for the world. The Pope will see it from wherever he is at the time. It is of interest that St Padre Pio was given the privilege of seeing the Miracle before he died and the Garabandal visionaries had predicted that this would happen, consequently everybody then wrongly assumed that St Padre Pio would be alive at the time.

After the Miracle: A permanent, visible supernatural sign will remain at the Pines, until the end of time. It will be possible to televise, film and photograph this wonder but not touch it. It has been likened to a column of smoke or a ray of sunlight but is not either one. As a result of the Miracle, Russia and other countries will be converted. On the day after the Miracle, the body of Father Luis Andreu will be removed from his grave and found incorrupt.

There is some evidence that the Permanent Sign, predicted for the hill in Garabandal, may be related to the pillar of fire and cloud that helped Moses lead the Jews out of captivity in Egypt, (see chapter 5 and chapter 19). There is also a promise of a Permanent Sign on the hill at Medjugorje and there are suggestions from other visionaries that similar signs will be left in other parts of the world, at some of the other sites, where there have been Marian apparitions.

The Miracle of Garabandal, therefore, will have three main aspects. The first is the permanent sign of the presence of God that will probably be left in different parts of the world, including Garabandal. The second is the conversion of many people and nations to the Roman Catholic Church. The third is the healing of the sick, which will probably be localized only.

Which Saint?

As explained above, The Miracle is predicted to occur on the feast of a little known saint, martyred for love of the Eucharist, within the dates described above. The names of a number of saints in particular, are often mentioned in connection with this, but we cannot be sure of any of those suggested, especially as it is believed by many that it will be a male saint and a saint who was not Spanish.

Blessed Imelda Lambertini: She is described as having died in ecstasy, while receiving her First Communion, aged eleven years, in 1333 A.D. She would be regarded as a martyr of the Eucharist but there is the strong impression, gleaned from what the Garabandal visionaries have said, that the saint martyr will be male rather than female. Her feast day is on the 13th May. This falls on a Thursday approximately every seven years. I have suggested above and elsewhere (see page 148), that I suspect that the Permanent Sign to be left at the pines in Garabandal, in Medjugorje and perhaps in other places around the world, is likely to be some form of, "the visible presence of God with us", as the

Shekinah was for the Jews, as described in the Old Testament. Ascension Thursday might be a suitable day for this to happen as it may be appropriate that Jesus should return in a new way on the day when His Church remembers His departure.

St Hermenegild, Martyr – 586 AD At the moment some are supporting this man as the saint of the Garabandal miracle. His feast day is on the 13th April which will be on Holy Thursday, in 2017 but again the strong impression, based on what the visionaries have said, is that the Miracle will not occur during Holy Week. April is the favoured month, according to some experts on the events. Hermenegild was the eldest son of Levigild, King of Spain. His father raised him in the Arian heresy. He converted to Catholicism after instruction from his wife and St Leander, Bishop of Seville. His father later put him into prison, in the tower of Seville, in 586 AD He was martyred for refusing to receive the Eucharist from an Arian Bishop. St Gregory the Great attributes the conversion of his brother, King Recared, and the conversion of the whole kingdom of the Visigoths in Spain, to the merits of Hermenegild's martyrdom.

St Pancras of Rome: This saint is a patron for children. He was beheaded for his Catholic belief, in Rome at the age of fourteen, in 304 A.D. His feast day is on the 12th of May. The name of this saint is sometimes also mentioned in association with the Garabandal Miracle.

St Tarcisius: A number of reports have suggested that when Conchita was describing the Miracle, she said that it would occur on the feast-day of a young martyr of the Eucharist. She then went on to describe a boy who was carrying Communion to persecuted Christians, who was stoned by other young people on his way because he refused to take part in their games and refused to let them see what he was carrying. This described St Tarcisius exactly and how he died in Rome during the third century. He is the patron saint of altar servers. A large statue of St Tarcisius, presented by altar servers to Emeritus Pope Benedict XVI, August 4th, 2010, is now in the Catacombs of St Calixtus where he is buried. His original feast-day was August 15th but this is now given over to the Assumption of The Virgin Mary. He must now also be considered as a candidate for the martyr associated with the Garabandal Miracle but there is no known date, as yet, for a new feast day.

Conclusion

The locutions of Fr Gobbi, together with the many messages to a large number of widely acclaimed visionaries and saintly individuals over the centuries, clearly indicate that we are now on the threshold of the most incredible world events. Nothing like these events have ever been previously experienced, in the history of humanity. The Holy Spirit of God is about to reclaim the world from major satanic influences, which have been working on the mind of man, especially over the last one hundred years. In chapter 7, chapter 11, and other sections of this book, you can read about some of the events associated with this coming awesome world transformation, as described by the visionaries of Garabandal and many other visionaries. A good source of information on Garabandal is the web site of Des Monaghan, Armagh, Ireland – garabandaluk.com

The most astounding thing about the events at Garabandal is, why are they so much ignored? I already mentioned in chapter 5 and elsewhere how Garabandal links with many other Catholic prophecies. I have mentioned also that the events were supported by St Padre Pio, St Teresa of Calcutta, and recent Popes, to mention but a few. Yet the events at Garabandal, like the events at Akita (chapter 5) are almost unknown. I will conclude with statements from two Popes, which relate to the Garabandal story. The first is a letter from Pope John Paul II to Albrecht Weber the author of the book, Garabandal – Der Zeigefinger Gottes (Finger of God) in 1993:

"May God reward you for everything, especially for the deep love with which you are making the events connected with Garabandal more widely known. May the message of The Mother of God find an entrance into hearts, before it is too late."

The second quotation is from Pope Pius IX,[162] who said:

"There will come a great sign which will fill the world with awe. This will occur only after the triumph of a revolution, during which the Church will undergo ordeals which are beyond description."

13. Islam

Muslims frequently say that we, the critics of Islam "know nothing about Islam". They are correct. The truth is that no one truly understands Islam, neither Muslim scholars nor Muslims in general. Even the best of its critics don't understand it...

Walid Shoebat.

When I wrote the first edition of this book the 'Arab Spring' had not yet started. At the time, I suggested that the Middle East countries were heading for a time of great suffering. In 2011, the 'Arab Spring' all started with a protest movement in Tunisia and quickly spread like a virus to other Arab nations. The popular sentiment was that the existing political systems, which were mostly based on oppressive and corrupt dictatorships, would give way under pressure from the masses to a more humane and even democratic way of governance. Unfortunately, what started as a dream of achieving a peaceful emancipation has turned into a nightmare.

Over the next five years leaders were toppled in four countries and there are still civil wars raging in Libya, Syria and Yemen. In many Arab nations, the economic and social structures have deteriorated dramatically, resulting in increased debt, unemployment, corruption and poverty. In some of these nations human tragedy and suffering is almost as bad as in a major war situation and the refugee crisis is out of control. It is as if Islam is beginning to implode, whilst it goes on relentlessly pursuing a policy of self-destruction. In order to get an understanding of how this internecine conflict has erupted, it is necessary to have some understanding of the faith of Islam.

The Faith of Islam

The word *Islam* is derived from the Arabic word *salaam* or the equivalent Hebrew word *shalom* meaning peace. The word Islam as now used in Arabic translates more as "submission to the will of God" rather than peace. Islam is not a religion of peace, although it is often promoted as such, but this is a deception. The growth of this religion has been dramatic ever since it's foundation by Muhammad (570 – 632 A. D.) who Muslims (followers of Islam) revere as the last and greatest prophet of God. In Islam, God is usually referred to as *Allah*, which is the Arabic word for God. Islam is the fastest growing religion world-wide with approximately 1.5 billion nominal members. This growth is mainly because believers have larger families, but also through new converts. Every year tens of thousands of Americans convert to Islam and after Sept 11, 2001, there was evidence of a dramatic increase in converts rather than a decrease as might have been expected.[183] The growth in numbers of Muslims in Europe is also increasing rapidly due the influx of refugees.

The Islamic religion is similar to the Christian and the Jewish religion in that all three are monotheistic, that is, they promote the worship of one God. Muslims misunderstand the Holy Trinity, however, and think that Christians worship three Gods. Muhammad spoke of the Trinity in a derogatory way, saying: - "Allah has been given some companions, but he has never authorised such a thing." Islam is more like Judaism than Christianity in that it places more emphasis on practices than beliefs. It is said that Christianity puts emphasis on orthodoxy or right belief, whereas Islam emphasises orthopraxis or unity of religious practice. There are five main central practices, often referred to as the five Pillars of Islam. These are, Confession of Faith, Prayer, Fasting, Almsgiving, and Pilgrimage (Hajj).

The Koran is the holy book of Islam. It contains 114 chapters called surah or sura. It claims to record the literal words of Allah as dictated to Mohammad. Concerning the treatment of Muslims on the one hand and non-Muslims (infidels) on the other hand, it promotes two very different sets of guidelines. There is also another source of written teaching for Muslims which is generally regarded as of equal importance to the **Koran**. This is the **Sunna**, meaning a clear or well-worn path. Muslims regard Mohammad as the perfect example for all humans and the Sunna records the life of Mohammad in two separate collections of literature, namely the **Hadith** and the **Sirat**. The Hadith records what he said, whereas, the Sirat is more of a biography.

The Hadith: This is a collection of Islamic traditions including sayings and deeds of Muhammad as recorded by those who knew him, handed down first, second, and third hand. As well as dictating the Koran, which he claimed to have received directly from Allah through the angel Gabriel, Mohammad also gave personal instructions as to how Muslims should live their lives. Although these instructions or traditions in the Hadith have less force than the *surahs* of the Koran, they are nevertheless regarded as authentic teaching and are binding on Muslims.

The Fracture of Islam

Immediately after Muhammad's death a dispute arose as to who should succeed him as leader. Those who favoured an inherited right to lead, chose Muhammad's cousin, Ali and later Ali's two sons, Hasan and Husain. The majority, however, rejected the view of inherited leadership and selected a leader who would lead them in the true path, forming the *Sunni* branch of Islam. This led to the great schism and feud between *Sunni* and *Shiite* which still exists and is very evident in wars developing between Muslim nations at this time. Sunni is from the word Sunna or "tradition" and they follow the teachings of tradition or how scholars have understood the teaching of the Prophet down through the centuries in the *Hadith*. Approximately 85% of Muslims are Sunni.

The Shiites are the largest non-Sunni group. They follow the teaching of Ali, who was Muhammad's cousin and husband of his daughter Fatima. They believe that the leaders or Imams, who followed Ali, also had Muhammad's prophetic spirit. They believe that there were twelve Imams. The last one mysteriously disappeared from earth and he will return as the Muslim leader, known as the Mahdi in the very near future, to conquer the world for Islam.

Islam has also fractured into a number of smaller break-away groups with many variations in religious practice and teaching. The Wahhabis are a Sunni sect which began in Saudi Arabia, in the eighteenth century, and is still mainly active there, where it has significant political influence. They emphasize a literal reading of the Koran and the Hadith and as a result, tend to be aggressive and violent in their efforts to promote Islam. Some of the best known of the other groups are the Ismailis, the Sufis, the Druze, the Bahais, the Alawites of Syria (Shiite sect with a special devotion to Ali), and the Kharijites of Oman. The Aga Khan is the leader of the Ismailis. The Ismalis believe in seven cosmic ages, guided by the seven prophets, Adam, Noah, Abraham, Moses, Jesus, Muhammad and Ismaili. The Sufis are a mystical sect in Islam and their ideas have infiltrated into Christian books especially through the promotion of the enneagram or nine personality types. The Druze have developed beliefs accepting reincarnation and the transmigration of souls.

Bahais: The Bahais started in Iran in the eighteenth century and is now well known world-wide. They were originally seen as apostates (breakaways) from Islam but now are more seen as a separate religion. They take teaching from all religions as well as Islam, including teachings from Krishna and Budda. In that sense this religion is sometimes described as syncretic but it would also be reasonable to say that this religion is admirable in that it promotes goodness. Their teaching is for peace, justice, honesty and unity for humanity, with no class distinction, with a need to pray to a one true God in order to save our souls.

Learning Arabic is regarded as mandatory for any Muslim who takes their faith seriously. It is claimed that the teaching of Islam cannot be understood clearly in any other language. This is in stark contrast, for example, to the Roman Catholic Church which embraces all cultures. Surely Divine truths should be global and cannot be bound by any particular race, language or man-made culture.

Islamic Law & Non Muslims under Sharia Law

There are four Islamic schools of jurisprudence, namely, the Hanifites, the Malikites, the Shafiites, and lastly the Hanbilites, which is the strictest and most fundamental of the four. These schools differ in their interpretation of Islamic law. Islamic law is also derived from four sources, namely, the Koran, the Hadith, Al-Qiyas or precedent legal decisions already made, and Ijma or consensus decisions made by reputed scholars. The door, to some extent therefore, is open for various Fatwa (legal opinions) to be given by legal scholars.

There are two categories of infidels: Dar-ul-Harb (household of war), whose blood and property are not bound by a peace treaty and not protected by law, and Dar-us-Salam (household of peace) who have the protection of the law. Dar-us-Salam infidels, in turn, are classed under the following three headings:

1. **Zimmis (dhimmí or those in custody):** Those who agree to pay a Jizya (tax), in exchange for protection and safety. Often these may be born natives of the country but are not classed as citizens.

2. **Hudna (truce):** Those who sign a peace treaty after defeat in war and are like the zimmis, but can live in their own place or country.
3. **Mustamin (protected one):** Those who come to Islamic countries as messengers, merchants, visitors, or as students wanting to learn about Islam. There is no obligation to pay a Jizya.

In areas controlled by Islamic teaching, that is, where Sharia law operates, infidels are treated differently from Muslims. An Islamic state, therefore, intentionally discriminates against non Muslims. Zimmis, such as Christians and Jews are not allowed to build new churches, temples or synagogues, or to promote their religion in any way publicly. On the other hand, Islamic law requires Muslims **NOT** to force Zimmis to accept Islam. Zimmis also have the right to practice their religion at home and in their places of worship. Zimmis are largely subject to the same civil laws as Muslims. Zimmis cannot testify against Muslims, however, as their oaths are not considered valid in an Islamic court. A Muslim male can marry a Zimmi female but a Zimmi male cannot marry a female Muslim. If one parent is a Muslim, the children must be raised as Muslims. Zimmis cannot join the army, except in an emergency, and they do not get permission to carry weapons. Once an individual becomes a Muslim they cannot recant. The punishment for the crime of apostasy is death and this is accepted by all four schools of jurisprudence. Contrast this with Christianity. The only reason we are asked to believe in Christianity is because it is true. It is still a free choice.

Extreme Islamic Groups

The recent emergence of a number of extremely aggressive Islamic groups especially ISIS (Islamic State of Iraq and Syria) and Boko Haram (founded in Northern Nigeria), have caused many to reassess the teachings of Islam. ISIS is a militant group which follows an extreme interpretation of an Islamic Wahhabi doctrine of Sunni Islam. It has recently become notorious for promoting persecution, torture and public beheadings of non Muslims. ISIS promotes slavery, as well as rape, other atrocities, and finally execution of all infidels. These outrageous atrocities are not only encouraged by ISIS against all infidels, including young children, but are often considered blessed actions.

The reassessment of Islamic teaching has resulted in a torrent of news articles in main-stream media world-wide, as well as many new books exposing the satanic deceptions promoted by some sects whereby evil actions are promoted as the will of God. The great Christian historian, Hilaire Belloc, described Islam as the greatest of all heresies. If Christianity is true, then Islam must be false as Islam completely contradicts Christianity and refuses to accept the Divinity of Jesus and denies the crucifixion. Satan always pretends to be God. Lust and debasement of sexuality is exalted in some Islam sects, whereas, purity is promoted in Christian teaching. Jesus told His disciples to make disciples of all nations by teaching, giving good example, by loving God, and loving one another. Islam tends to declare war, in one way or another, on those who will not accept Islam.

Islam promotes Violence

There are many verses in the Koran as well as sections of the Hadith narrative promoting violence:

Koran (2:216) says: "Fighting is prescribed for you, and you do not like it, but it is possible that you dislike something which is good for you and that you like something which is bad for you. Allah knows and you do not know."

Koran (8:12) says: "I will cast terror into the hearts of those who disbelieve. Therefore cut off their heads and every finger tip of them."

Koran (8:67) says: "It is not for a prophet that he should have prisoners of war until he has made a great slaughter in the land."

Koran (9:30) says: "The Jews say , Ezra is the son of Allah and the Christians say, The Messiah is the son of Allah. These are the words of their mouths. They imitate the saying of those who disbelieved before. May Allah destroy them."

Koran (48:29) says: "Muhammad is the messenger of Allah. Those with him are ruthless against the disbelievers and merciful among themselves."

Imam Bukhari (800 – 870 AD) and **Tabari** (839 – 923 AD) were early Muslim scholars and collectors of Hadith writings. Both were renowned scholars and had memorised the Koran at an early age. Two of the most revered books of the Hadith are the *Sahih Bukhari* and the *Sahih Muslim*. From these books and writings we have the following:

Bukhari (52:177): Allah's apostle said, "The Hour will not be established until you fight the Jews and the stone behind which a Jew will be hiding will say, "O Muslim! there is a Jew hiding behind me, so kill him."

Bukhari (52:65): The Prophet said, "He who fights so that Allah's Word, Islam, should be superior, fights in Allah's cause."

Bukhari (52:220): Allah's apostle said. "I have been made victorious with terror."

Bukhari (11:626): Muhammad said, "I decided to order a man to lead the prayer and then take a flame to burn all those who had not left their houses for the prayer, burning them alive inside their homes."

Tabari (7:97): The Prophet declared, "Kill any Jew who falls under your power."

Tabari (9:69): The Prophet declared, "Killing unbelievers is a small matter to us."

Also from **Muslim Book 20:4645:** Muhammad said, "There is another act which elevates the position of a man in Paradise to a grade one hundred fold higher and the elevation between one grade to the other is equal to the height of the Heaven from the earth." He was asked, what is that act? And he replied, "Jihad in the way of Allah!"

Women in Islam

In pre-Islamic Arabia, female infants were sometimes buried alive. The ancient Arabs considered women as property with no inheritance rights. Mohammad condemned this attitude to women. On the other hand, it is very clear that the Koran regards women as inferior to men and they are treated as second class citizens in traditional Muslim countries. Muslim men are permitted to marry up to four wives. It seems that, in Islam, this superiority of men over women also continues into Paradise. In Islamic teaching, men who reach Paradise are promised many virgins as well as beardless boys, who will be at their disposal. In Islamic courts of Sharia law, the evidence from one man is as good, or better, than the evidence of two women. It is also virtually impossible for women to prove that they had been raped. If testimony concerns rape, fornication or sodomy, four male witnesses are required. Four male witnesses are virtually impossible to produce, so an accusation of rape by a woman then becomes an admission of adultery. This is why, according to *Inside Islam,* [184] many of the women in prison in Pakistan are there for the crime of being a rape victim.

Rape: The atrocities promoted by ISIS have recently focused attention on the Islamic teaching promoting slavery and rape. There is one particular phrase which is used frequently in the Koran and which is important to understand in relation to how the Islamic religion, firstly, promotes slavery and secondly, dictates what is lawful and sometimes even a blessed way of treating slaves and captives. The phrase 'whom their right hand possesses' is used many times in relation to slaves and prisoners.[185] The Koran teaches that men are free to have sex with their slaves and prisoners – (whom their right hand possesses), if they wish, without any blame attached. The **Koran 4:24** forbids sex with married women, unless they are slaves or captives. Rape is not mentioned but there is no question of getting consent. Mohammad claimed that Allah gave him special privileges regarding the number of women which he could take as a wife but, in doing so, we must recognize that he was not the only male spiritual leader to claim special sexual privileges. The idea of a loving God giving a blessing on forced sexual activity with slaves and captives or with children is unthinkable at any stage in history. The essence of the God worshipped by Muslims, therefore, is beyond doubt, different from the God of Jews or Christians.

Islamic Eschatology

Eschatology is the branch of theology that deals with the end of the world. Two books written by Joel Richardson, namely, *The Islamic Antichrist*[185] and *The Mid-East Beast*[186] serve as a great source of information on how Muslims view the end-times and how significant the near future is for the Islamic ambition of total world domination.

The Koran records five beliefs which a Muslim must have in order to be considered a Muslim (Surah 2:177). These five beliefs in order are:

1. Belief in Allah
2. Belief in the Last Day
3. Belief in Angels
4. Belief in the Scripture
5. Belief in the Prophets

Knowledge of the last day and of the end times are high on the agenda of every religious Muslim. Muslims believe that towards the end of time, three individuals will come into prominence on the world stage. They will have an enormous impact on events and on the future of humanity. The events will eventually lead to the establishment of the Islamic religion as the only religion remaining after the other false religions are deserted or destroyed. These individuals expected are:

1. The coming of the Muslim Messiah or Saviour (Al-Mahdi)
2. The coming of the Muslim Antichrist.
3. The return of the Muslim Jesus.

The Mahdi: The arrival of this individual or the "Awaited Saviour" is the first of the major signs expected by Muslims to indicate the arrival of the end-times. He is not regarded as a Messiah by Sunni but as a Caliph or great ruler. The arrival of this man is now eagerly awaited by Muslims. A list of some of his characteristics are as follows:[185]

It is believed that the Mahdi's name will be Mohammad.

He will be a devout Muslim

He will be a universal leader for all Muslims.

He will be an unparalleled spiritual, political, and military world ruler.

He will come after a period of great turmoil and suffering in the world.

His ascendancy to power will be preceded by an army from the East carrying black flags or banners.

He will conquer Israel.

He will invade many countries and establish a new world order.

He will have miraculous powers and will be able to control wind and rain and crops.

He will distribute large amounts of wealth.

He will establish Islam as the only religion on earth.

He will discover new biblical manuscripts which will lead the Jews to convert to Islam.

He will rediscover the Ark of the Covenant from the Sea of Galilee, which he will bring to Jerusalem.

All inhabitants of the world will love him.

It is of interest that at this time, when Muslims are expecting the arrival of their Mahdi, that Jews are expecting their Messiah and Christians are expecting major events as a prelude to a coming of Christ, especially the manifestation of a Christian Antichrist – (see the final chapter for a discussion on the three comings of Christ). There are some reasons for believing that this Muslim Mahdi will be the same individual as the expected Christian Antichrist. The Bible points out that the Antichrist will be a leader, with authority all over the world. The Christian Antichrist and the Muslim Mahdi are both expected to be spiritual, political and military world leaders.

The two groups who will be specifically targeted by the Antichrist are the Jews and Christians. Some Muslims believe that the Mahdi will "eradicate those pigs and dogs" that is, those Christians and Jews who refuse to convert to Islam.[185]

The Christian Antichrist and the Mahdi are both identified with a rider on a white horse. The Islamic tradition and Christian biblical scholarship ironically both identify with this section of the Bible (Revelation 6: 1-2). After this individual (rider) appears the world drifts rapidly into chaos. The opening of subsequent seals in Revelation 6, brings war, famine, plagues, persecution, martyrdom and a great earthquake. It is a little surreal, therefore, that Muslim scholars use Biblical references to the Antichrist to describe their coming Mahdi, or saviour.

The Return of Jesus: Muslims also believe that Jesus is about to return at this time. They are expecting Jesus to come back as a devout, radical Muslim, who will fight and defeat the Muslim Antichrist, known as the Dajjal. Some Muslims believe that Jesus will be subordinate to their Mahdi. He will also oblige them by declaring Islam to be the only true religion, outlawing Christianity, destroying all crucifixes, and giving the Christians and Jews the option of accepting Islam or suffering death. This Muslim Jesus figure is identified in the Bible as the second beast or the false prophet (Revelation 13: 11). He will not be the gentle, self-sacrificing Jesus of the gospels, but rather the wolf in sheep's clothing. The Muslim Jesus will be an executioner, being an assistant and doing the will of the Mahdi or Antichrist.

The Muslim Antichrist: The third great figure expected by Muslims at this time is known as the Dajjal or 'false Jesus' who they believe will be accepted by the Jews as their Divine Messiah. The real Jesus, in Muslim tradition, will be recognised by the fact that he hates Jews and he will kill the 'false Jesus' or Jewish Messiah, who will be defending the Jews. According to some Sunni opinions there may be two Dajjals. The first will trigger the coming of the Mahdi and the second will trigger the coming of (the Muslim) Jesus.

Lies in Islam

According to the book, *The Islamic Antichrist*,[185] lying is not only permitted but sometimes promoted and even commanded in Islam. Efforts to convert non-Muslims to belief in Islam is regarded as part of jihad, that is: it is war. One of Mohammad's famous sayings was "War is Deception". There are two doctrines in Islam promoting lies and deception, namely, kithman and taqiya. Kithman is a command to deliberately conceal beliefs and taqiya is similar as it promotes concealing or disguising the truth.[186] It is permitted to lie regarding a belief in Islam when you do it for protection or promoting the Islamic cause. Deception is also permitted in Islam to help gain wealth, prosperity and achieve new goals especially for the good of Islam. Sunni Muslims may claim that these doctrines are only used by Shi'a Muslims.

After 9/11 in the US many "moderate Muslims" made speeches promoting Islam as a religion of peace. This peaceful view of Islam is widely accepted in the West for a number of reasons. Some of these reasons are: clever Islamic propaganda, lack of knowledge of Islamic teaching, failure of other religious leaders to expose Islam due fear of conflict, over emphasis on secularism, political correctness, moral relativity at the expense of truth and a failure of main stream media, with a few exceptions, to expose the true beliefs and teachings of Islam. The author of *The Islamic Antichrist*, puts it like this:[185]

"I understand that to call anyone a liar is quite an insult. That is why I felt it important to demonstrate thoroughly the fact that Muhammad, the Qur'an, and hadiths, as well as Islam's most respected scholars, allow lying as a means to achieve any number of goals. I have documented this fact quite plainly. This is not an unfounded accusation made by the "people of falsehood" (a name that the Qur'an ironically applies to non-Muslims) but is indeed an established doctrine and practice within Islam."

This author did not write this book or his later one, *Mideast Beast*,[186] for the purpose of insulting Muslims but rather to encourage them to confront the truth. There is an inherent goodness in all people, which springs from an awareness of good and evil implanted in our conscience. Our individual decisions of what is good and evil must be based on an informed conscience and on good solid evidence, wherever possible. The intellect must rule the heart and we must always strive for what is true and what is good. We must never fear the truth as (to repeat again), in the words of the philosopher, Peter Kreeft, "Truth trumps everything". There are many aspects of Islam that are good, such as, prayer, fasting and almsgiving and the vast majority of Muslims are good and truthful. The problem is that there are aspects of teaching in some interpretations of Islam that are evil. The demonic aspects of, at least some of, Muhammad's revelations in the Cave of Hira must be recognised. The surahs promoting these evil acts must be abrogated as has been done with other "unreliable" surahs. It is an accepted fact in Islamic tradition, that some surahs had to be "abrogated" (cancelled) because, while Muhammad was said to be waiting to hear the inner voice, Satan would seize the opportunity to deceive him with an *ayah* of his own.[187] Muslims are our brothers and sisters as children of the same fatherhood in God. We must treat them with love and respect but we must also warn them of the deception of Islam. Muslims must also begin to treat those of us who have other faiths, or no faith, as they would like to be treated by us, and understand that lies and deception can never be acceptable as a way to succeed or a way to build confidence, respect and friendship.

Are there Historical mistakes in the Koran?

The answer is yes, although Muslims would find this difficult to understand. It is believed and well accepted in Islam, as explained above, that Allah can change his mind and cancel some verses of the Koran that have "been inspired by Satan". An error on a matter of fact according to Islamic teaching, however, is believed to be impossible. The Koran says, "This is a mighty scripture. Falsehood cannot reach it from before or from behind" – (Sura 41:41-2). There are, however, several examples of historical inaccuracies described in the Koran. The denial of the crucifixion of Jesus is only one of them. Others are listed in, *Inside Islam – A Guide for Catholics*[184]. The crucifixion of Jesus is supported by many secular historical sources, such as, *The Annals of Imperial Rome-Book XV*, by Tacitus, *Life of the Emperor Claudius,* by Suetonius, and in *Jewish Antiquities*, by the great Jewish historian, Josephus, as well as others.

Sins Allah will not forgive

The Koran teaches that there are three sins which Allah will not forgive and merit Hell forever, (Sura 4:116, 4:93 and 3:90). These are:

1. Attributing partners to Allah (which Muslims believe Christians do).
2. The killing of a believer in Islam.
3. Apostasy from Islam.

Item number 1 would seem to imply that the Koran teaches that all Christians are damned. Item number 2 should also mean that those who die during war between Muslim nations and suicide bombers who kill other Muslims are also damned. The Koran also preaches predestination as a doctrine, rather than free will. Although some Koranic verses seem to be in favour of free will, there are over forty Koranic passages that deny free will.[188] An extreme view of this could be that God has created (for whatever reason) many defective individuals destined for Hell.

Contrast between Christianity and Islamic Extremists

The Koran gives a clear directive encouraging Muslims to kill Jews. In contrast, Christians are told to love the Jews and pray for their conversion so that they can soon accept Jesus as their Messiah. During the second World-War, it is now well established that Pope Pius XII was responsible for saving the lives of large numbers of Jews, despite many efforts to label and malign him as Hitler's Pope. The chief Rabbi in Rome during the war, Rabbi Israel Zolli, paid many tributes to this Pope and later converted to Catholicism, with his wife and daughter, many say because of his experiences in Rome during the war years. He took the name of Eugenio Maria Zolli, at baptism, in honour of Pope Pius XII, who was also named Eugenio Maria. Some days before his death, he accurately predicted to a nun where he was hospitalized, that he would die on the first Friday of the month at 3 p.m. He died on that very day and at that exact hour on March 2nd 1956.

Contrast this with the Grand Mufti of Jerusalem during the same war. Muhammad Amin al-Husseini was strongly anti-Semitic. He built up a close friendship with Hitler and wanted Hitler to help him eliminate the Jews from Palestine. He made propaganda radio broadcasts against the Jews for the Nazi party. Although he was originally appointed to his Jerusalem position by the British in 1921, he became strongly anti-British in 1936 and fled to Lebanon. He also recruited many Bosnian Muslims to fight with German SS troops.

This is a time when all of us must be prepared to confront and get rid of our demons. The Islamic faith must also confront the demons in their teaching. No modern society should accept (and will soon reject outright) a religious belief that encourages the torture and execution of non-believers (infidels – for Muslims). Likewise no society can accept a religion that encourages lying as a means of promoting the interests of this religion. These teachings of Islam have largely remained hidden from non-Muslims down through the centuries. However, with the advent of extreme groups such as ISIS and Boko Haram, Islamic teaching is now being circulated widely in the exposé of global media coverage, particularly through the internet. If the Islamic faith, therefore, is to survive into the future, it will have to abrogate (cancel) these sections of the Koran and other Islamic texts, that promote violence and hatred, otherwise this religion will inevitably self-destruct in the very near future, as good begins to overcome evil in the world. There are already signs of this, in that the failure of many Muslim leaders to condemn **the teachings** that promote violence is becoming very obvious. It is no longer enough to condemn the violence associated with suicide bombing. It is now necessary for the sake of everybody, for the sake of peace in the world, and especially for the sake of the vast majority of good peaceful decent Muslims, who want nothing to do with violence, to abrogate those sections of the Koran, that are promoting physical violence. How can Muslims expect us to take them seriously when they tell us that Islam is a religion of peace, and when there are several verses (for some examples see pages 484/5/6 above) in the Koran, that call Muslims to war with nonbelievers, for the sake of Islamic rule? Some of these verses are very graphic indeed. The only way Islam could be peace loving is if these verses in the Koran are ignored. If they are meant to be ignored then these verses should be abrogated so that extreme elements will not use them to encourage violence.

Many Islamic refugees are beginning to convert to Christianity, not only in Germany (Sunday Times – May 15th 2016) but also in Iraq and other traditional Muslim states. This is all despite the severe penalty associated with Islamic apostasy. On the other hand, the many noble aspects of Islam, already mentioned must be encouraged, so that humanity with all its creeds can work together in peace, to create a free, just, and caring global society.

It is wrong to compare the violence of the Koran with the violence of the Old Testament of the Bible when comparing Islam with Christianity. The Old Testament reveals the early history of the people of God, the Jews, up to the time of Christ. Their knowledge of God was very imperfect, but as time went on it gradually developed, thanks to the teaching of the various prophets. Moving on to the New Testament we see the central figure is Christ. With Christ came the revelation of The Holy Trinity as well as a clear understanding of the infinite humility, infinite love and infinite mercy of God. The message of Christ is to love your enemies, not to hate them, and after death we will be judged by the law of love, that is, by how much we have loved God and loved others. Christianity and Christian teaching, therefore, is based on the New rather than the Old Testament of the Bible. The coming of Christ thus marked a revolution and a renewal of humanity. The Christian message promotes a completely new way of living our lives, with a particular emphasis on unselfish, self-sacrificing love.

I will end this comparison with some points made by Mark Mallett in his blog of December 26th 2014. Mark is a well-known Canadian singer, songwriter and gifted Catholic apologist, who I have mentioned in the foreword to this edition. Mark notes:

Islamic religious extremists (IRE) force others into their creed: Christian martyrs invite others to live theirs.

IRE kill others in service to their faith: Christian martyrs give their lives for the faith of others.

IRE blow up others for the glory of God: Christian martyrs serve others to the point of death for God's glory.

IRE demand allegiance, taxes, or one's head: Christian martyrs renounce their possessions and very lives.

IRE denounce others infidels as they slaughter: Christian martyrs pronounce forgiveness of their executioners.

IRE arm and train children for war: Christian martyrs become like little children.

IRE often take many wives as concubines: Christian martyrs often take a vow of chastity.

IRE burn churches, hospitals and schools: Christian martyrs give their lives building them.

IRE fast and pray to bring about the victory of war: Christian martyrs fast and pray to end wars.

IRE cover their faces like cowards: Christian martyrs boldly show the face of Christ.

IRE commit suicide for the pleasures of paradise: Christian martyrs give their lives so that others may enter Heaven.

IRE hate their enemies as a sign of their fidelity: Christian martyrs love their enemies as a sign of their faith.

Conclusion

The consequences, therefore, of free and almost total information sharing in the modern world means that the sections of the Koran promoting hatred and violence can no longer remain hidden. Of the 1.5 billion Muslims at the moment, it is estimated that only approximately 250,000 are "radicalized", that is, are prepared to carry out all sorts of atrocities, in the name of Allah, as they believe is directed by the Koran. There are unfortunately many millions more, of devout Muslims, who are asking themselves how they will react when the *"jihad"* begins, and a significant number of these would also probably react with terrible violence, given the opportunity and the right circumstances. The remainder of Muslims, who fortunately represent the biggest section by far, want nothing to do with violence, hatred, or extreme Sharia law. These, like the rest of us, have natural law written in their hearts and minds and know the difference between good and evil. They are decent people who want to live decent lives of love, live and let live, but it does not serve them well to keep telling us that the Islamic faith is a religion of peace. They, more than us, need to recognise that the Koran teaches unacceptable violence and ironically it is the peace loving Muslims who are often at the receiving end of this violence and suffer the most. Government leaders and some religious leaders are often heard promoting Islam as a religion of peace. It is hard to believe that these leaders have been fooled by Islamic propaganda and it is far more likely that truth is being sacrificed for political "correctness". Ultimately, telling lies in order "to be nice" creates more problems than it solves.

Walid Shoebat: He had a Muslim Arab father and a Christian American mother. He was born in Bethlehem and raised as a Muslim. His paternal grandfather was a close friend of Haj-Ameen Al-Husseni, the Grand Mufti of Jerusalem who was a friend of Adolph Hitler (see above). His maternal great grandfather was Mayor of Eureka, California, and a close friend of Winston Churchill. He grew up as a terrorist, but when he married a Christian lady he began to examine the Bible and compare it with the Koran. The following is a quote from his book, *The Case for Islamophobia*,[188] which he co-authored with the Ben Barrack:

> **"Only Biblical truth has transformed my way of thinking from being a follower of Mohammed and idolizing Adolph Hitler to believing in Jesus Christ. From believing lies to**

knowing the truth, from being spiritually sick to being healed, from living in darkness to seeing the light, from being damned to being saved, from doubt to faith, from Hate to Love, and from evil works to God's grace through Christ. The wonderful thing about God is that when someone sincerely and humbly cries out to Him for help and to find the truth, He always answers that prayer. Today I am a Christian."

The future of the Islamic faith, therefore, is clear. The Arab Spring has turned out to be an Arab Autumn and the leaves are already falling off the Islamic tree. The decay has begun and it will be rapid. No house divided against itself can survive, unless the warring factions learn to forgive. The good Muslims, who know how to love, will hopefully survive. Those who want *jihad* will get it and self-destruct in the process. If the Antichrist is to be a Muslim, as suggested by Joel Richardson,[185,186] and others, then this religion is unlikely to disappear completely until after the defeat of the Antichrist.

Those who love and survive will eventually unite with Christianity and other world religions under a single leadership which will promote truth and love for all. Secular humanist morality will be rejected and the world will again be renewed completely. This time it will be with a peace and joy that humanity has never before experienced.

14. Homosexuality

"One of us has to go"

(On his death bed, while looking at dreadful wallpaper) **Oscar Wilde.**

I have positioned this chapter near the end of this book as I think it important to assess and weigh private views and opinions on this very controversial and divisive subject against information and evidence presented in the earlier chapters. This particularly concerns evidence for God and natural law, life after death, and the reality of Heaven and Hell. It also concerns the obligation on all of us at all times to promote truth and goodness, as well as respect for the dignity of humanity generally, and more particularly, for those individuals who we interact with on a daily basis. Establishing what is true and good is the first and the greatest challenge.

The term homosexual is used to refer to individuals who prefer sexual relations with members of the same sex as opposed to heterosexuals who are attracted to members of the opposite sex. Most of the good research work on homosexuality has come from the US, but evidence from other studies outside the US is broadly supportive of US data.

In 1948, the well-known Kinsey study in the US, suggested that 10% of the population was homosexual. This figure is still quoted although it is now well discredited, mainly due to the fact that a significant portion of those studied were volunteers, prisoners, ex-convicts and sex offenders, and thus not representative of the general population. Many studies since then have put the figure for male homosexuality as between 2% and 3% of the population with female homosexuality at between 1% and 2%. The National Health and Social life survey across the US in 1994 found that 8% of 16-year olds thought they were gay but by the age of 25 only 2% thought they were gay.

The Cause of Homosexuality

The cause of homosexuality or homosexual preference is not known at this time, although there are many theories. There is no homosexual gene and we can be definite that it is not purely genetic. In sets of identical twins, one can be a homosexual and the other not. The rules of genetics are also very well stacked against homosexual inheritance as homosexuals tend not to pass on their genes, so even if a homosexual gene existed, it would not be expected to survive in the gene pool. This does not mean that certain gene types, yet to be described, cannot make individuals more prone to homosexuality. It is well known, for example, that when individuals with certain antigenic tissue types, react with environmental factors, they become more prone to developing various types of malignant tumours, arthritis or other medical problems. It would be expected, however, that if this genetic predisposition to homosexuality exists, it would have to be a weak link, as if it was strong, then it is likely that the general lack of offspring from homosexuals would also eliminate these genes over a number of generations. In the case of male homosexuality, inheritance could possibly be explained if a particular associated gene or genes were carried on the X (female) chromosome but this has not been confirmed by genetic analysis.

Another more likely possibility for a biological cause or influence for homosexuality is the complex area of hormone levels. This could be related to abnormal hormone levels during gestation, in-utero, or during later development after birth. The normal hormone levels either in the pregnant mother or the baby may be interfered with in some way which could have effects lasting into adult development. These effects are also not restricted to abnormal sexual gland activity, as other hormones, such as those in the adrenal glands, can indirectly alter sexual hormone levels. Oestrogen and progesterone levels are known to be altered in adrenal deficiency and, on the other hand, girls with chronic adrenal hyperplasia, can have high levels of testosterone. Unknowingly some drug therapies during pregnancy could also interfere with normal hormone levels.

Finally, there is the contribution, if any, which can be made by epigenetics. Epigenetics is a relatively new and very complex area of study in genetics. It relates to the study of how normally inactive genes can sometimes be expressed or "turned on". Epigenetic change is a natural occurrence but it can also be influenced by environmental factors as well as life style, diet and disease. At this time there are no epigenetic factors known which contribute to a cause for homosexuality.

Some Scientific Studies: Jeffrey Keefe, O.F.M. has outlined and discussed a number of scientific studies done on efforts made to discover a possible genetic or biological cause for homosexuality.[189]

a) Simon LeVay studied the size of the interstitial nuclei of the anterior hypothalamus (INAH) which are located in the brain, just behind the attachment of the two cerebral hemispheres. He found that the third INAH was twice as large in heterosexual males, when compared to male homosexuals. This observation has not been confirmed by others, and if it is ever confirmed, one of the questions which must also be answered is: does the change in the INAH size cause the homosexuality or result from it?

b) Other reports have suggested that homosexuality is related to changes in other INAH (there are four), but these have likewise not been confirmed in further studies.

c) Bailey and Pillard did a study on male homosexual twins and brothers. If one was homosexual there was a 52% chance of both identical twins being homosexual. This figure dropped to 22% for fraternal co-twins. The figure for adopted brothers was 11% which was higher than the 9.2% for non-twin natural brothers. This work recruited twins by advertising in homosexual newspapers and magazines rather than from material used by the general public so it is possible that there was a bias towards gay twins. In the year 2000, Bailey et al. repeated the experiment, but with twins recruited from the Australian Twin Registry. In this study only 20% of the identical twins shared the same homosexual orientation, rather than the previously reported 52%. These figures suggest that while genetic factors may influence male homosexuality, biological, psychological and / or social environmental factors have a stronger influence.

d) In 1992, Allen and Gorski found that the anterior commissure (a nerve fibre tract joining the temporal lobes of the brain) was larger in homosexual males when compared to heterosexuals. The AIDS virus has an affinity for brain tissue and some have suggested that infection with this virus may be responsible for this observation. This is still not confirmed one way or the other.

e) One study showed a linkage between male homosexuality and a region (Xq28 region) of the female (X) chromosome (the male is an XY pair as opposed to XX in females), but this study was not properly scientifically controlled and subsequent studies have failed to confirm this.

f) Finally in 1995, H. Meyer-Bahlburg reported a study on the synthetic female hormone, diethylstilbestrol (DES), which used to be given to prevent miscarriages, before it was banned due to an association with vaginal cancer. This hormone had a defeminizing effect by interfering with oestrogen and there was evidence of a small increase in bisexual and homosexual attraction at a psychological level as a result of exposure to this hormone in utero.

Sexual Development.

Normal human sexual development has both physical and psychological characteristics.

Physical: There are three different phases of physical sexual development before birth, that is, genetic or cytological sex, gonadal or anatomical sex, and sexual differentiation in the brain. Genetic sex depends on the normal complement of X and Y chromosomes decided at conception. The second phase of anatomical organ development begins at the seventh week of gestation, and the final phase starts in the second trimester of gestation. At the final phase the hormones, now being produced by the recently formed foetal sex organs, transform brain cells in the hypothalamus, thalamus and limbic systems of the developing brain, through a neuro-hormonal programming process, necessary for later development into mature males and females.

Psychological: Psychological or conscious sexual development occurs after birth. Normal sexual psychological development also has three aspects or components. The first is the basic conviction of being male or female, referred to as core gender identity. The second is the development of behaviour and attitudes culturally associated with being male or female, referred to as gender role identity. The third is the preference for male or female partners, referred to as psychosexual orientation. This final psychosexual orientation is what defines and separates homosexuals from heterosexuals.

Orientation: Sexual orientation in humans is a mental condition which encourages relationship behaviour towards the same or opposite sex. There is some evidence from animal experiments that sex hormone manipulation after sex organ differentiation in utero can lead to behaviour changes. This is far more marked in the lower animals such as rats, however, and is more difficult to detect in the higher animals, such as monkeys. John Bancroft, M. D. who has researched and written widely on human sexuality concludes that, "the uniquely human phenomenon of sexual orientations is a consequence of a multifactorial developmental process in which biological factors play a part but in which psychosocial factors remain crucially important."[190] Another research worker on human sexuality, John Money, also concludes that antenatal antecedents may facilitate a homosexual orientation, "provided the postnatal determinants in the social and communicational history are also facilitative."[191] Dr. A. Dean Byrd of the US National Association for Research and Therapy on Homosexuality (NARTH), has said, "There is no animal model that accurately reflects human sexuality, - Pigs don't date, ducks don't go to church, and mice don't fall in love."

Attractions & Behaviours: The origins of homosexual attractions and behaviours are described by Richard P. Fitgibbons, M.D. in the book, *The Truth About Homosexuality*,[189] as follows:

"The most common conflicts at different life stages that predispose individuals to homosexual attraction and behaviour are loneliness and sadness, mistrust and fear, profound feelings of inadequacy and a lack of self-acceptance, narcissism (exceptional interest or admiration for oneself), excessive anger, sexual abuse in childhood, and a lack of balance in one's life, coupled with overwhelming feelings of responsibility. During times of stress, these inner difficulties are activated. In an attempt to seek relief or to escape from this unconscious emotional pain, strong sexual temptation and behaviour can occur. This dynamic of inner emotional suffering leading to homosexual desires and activity rarely can begin during childhood, but usually it develops in early adolescence. However, adult life may be the first time for the emergence of this disorder."

The most frequent cause of sadness and loneliness, among teenagers, is living apart from parents and also rejection by peers because of low ability at sports etc. Strong feelings of insecurity can also result from rejection by parents and friends. There may be a fear of being inadequate in having a relation with the opposite sex, due to experiences in the home or among teenage groups. The sexually compulsive, highly dangerous and life threatening behaviour of a significant percentage of homosexuals may suggest a form of sexual addiction which is now becoming more recognised. An extreme form of selfishness (narcissism) and grandiose ideas can be associated with this. The most significant type of anger which can contribute to homosexuality is anger with oneself because of perceived poor physique or some other reason. Finally there may be the desire to escape the responsibility of a wife, or husband, and raising a family with children. This may be associated with a lack of balance in life, along with perfectionist thinking, leading to a feeling of excessive responsibility.

Father John Harvey, the founder of **Courage**, a US support group for people with same-sex attraction who are striving to live chaste lives, published a book especially for parents entitled, *Same-Sex Attraction: A Parent's Guide.* His opinion is that prevention of same-sex attraction remains largely with parents, because the roots of this condition are laid early in life.

The Gender Problem: There is now a list of somewhere between 50 and 100 different genders. Two have now become 50+. Some of the more common terms are: Lesbian, Gay, Bisexual, Pansexual, Transgender, Transsexual, Queer, Questioning, Intersex, Intergender, Asexual, Ally etc. A few years ago there were just over twenty. In this "golden age of new genders", it seems that a new gender is appearing on *facebook* every few months. Social science now has a branch completely devoted to gender study. This is strongly suggestive that gender is a psychological-social construct and is evidence that homosexuality in its different forms, falls into the same category.

Homosexual Marriage

In countries where homosexual marriage is legalized, there is also the legal right to adopt and raise children. Homosexual marriage, therefore, creates not just one, but two new demographic family structures. Some children will now be raised by two men and some by two women. This will create three classes of children, who will likely have different profiles of social, behavioural, psychological and health problems.

Social evidence clearly shows that there are measurable effects when children lack either a mother or a father and these effects are emotional, social and intellectual. The evidence from many decades of study is overwhelming and shows that development of children is best in a stable family environment, where there is a mother and a father living in harmony with love. There are also the extra concerns of less stability within homosexual unions when compared to heterosexual, as well as more health problems, more violence, and much younger death rates among homosexuals. Homosexual marriage, therefore, raises great concerns for society generally and for the welfare of children in particular. We have to recognize that many of those who have pushed for the legislation of homosexual marriage did so out of genuine compassion, but their sentiments are sadly misguided. What are seen as "rights" demanded for adults are denied for children, who have a right to a father and a mother. Many may also not appreciate that by supporting homosexual marriage they implicitly accept the morality of homosexual acts, and thus reject traditional Christian teaching.

Homosexuality and Paedophilia

The Family Research Institute in Washington, DC, USA has produced the results of a number of studies on homosexuality.[192] They reported that three kinds of evidence were used to estimate the extent of the problem of childhood molestation by homosexuals. These were:

(a) Survey of reports of molestation in the general population.
(b) Survey of those convicted of molestation.
(c) Survey of what Homosexuals have reported.

Their evidence suggested that adult homosexuals were responsible for between 20% and 40% of all child molestation. In 1983-4, a random survey of 3,132 adults in Los Angeles, USA, found that about 35% of childhood sexual assaults were homosexual.[193] Another report was published soon afterwards, in 1985,[194] which concluded that homosexual acts were involved in 25% to 40 % of the cases of child molestation recorded in the scientific and forensic literature. The Family Research Institute claimed that study after study had confirmed these figures. These figures are very contentious, however, and a number of further studies did not support these observations. The confusion may come from the way figures are interpreted and how one defines the terms paedophilia and homosexuality. It is well established that while about 3% of men are homosexuals, 25 to 40 % of paedophiles have homosexual preferences. Paedophiles, with a homosexual preference, also abuse more children than heterosexual paedophiles. This does **NOT** mean, however, that homosexuals are more likely than heterosexuals to be paedophiles. In other words, just because 25 to 40% of paedophiles have a homosexual preference, this does not necessarily mean that homosexuals are more likely than heterosexuals to be paedophiles.

Sexual abuse of minors by Catholic Clergy

In recent decades the Catholic Church has been vilified for one particular item more than any other, that is, the sexual abuse of minors by Catholic clergy. Many well publicised abuse cases in many parts of the Catholic world have been painful for many Catholic faithful and very damaging to the reputation of this Church. Efforts by some senior clergy to hide and suppress some information did nothing to ease this pain and upset.

The US Catholic Bishops commissioned a study on the problem of sexual abuse of minors by Catholic priests covering the period 1950 -2010. The first section of this study is referred to as the Nature and Scope study and this was followed by the Causes and Context study.[195] Other studies have also been done on this problem. Two national studies in the US compared sexual abuse of minors in the decade between 1992 and 2002. The National Incidence Study (NIS) was a congressionally mandated study done by the Department of Health. The other source of figures is from the National Child Abuse & Neglect Data System (NCANDS) but it is recognised that all data sources have limitations. In 1992, the average sexual abuse figure per study centre or state was 246 per 100,000, with Alaska being the highest at 688 per 100,000 and New Jersey being the lowest at 87. In 1992 the figure for sexual abuse of minors by Catholic priests was 15 per 100,000. The 100,000 figure for priests was not based on the total population but on the number 'exposed' to priests and this was estimated on the basis of the number of children getting the Catholic sacrament of confirmation during that year. The figure would obviously be much lower if the priest abuse was taken from the whole population. In 2001 the average figure per state had dropped to 134, with Arizona being the lowest at 23 and Alaska again being the highest at 788. In the same year the abuse figure by Catholic priests had also dropped to 5 per 100,000.

As for homosexuals, some of these studies described above have also been used to suggest that the problem of sexual molestation of minors by, Catholic clergy is also likely to be linked to homosexuality. This again has not been established and it may be a false extrapolation of the figures. Although there is little doubt that the prevalence of homosexuality is higher among Catholic clergy than the normal male population, the figures if anything, suggest that paedophilia among Catholic clergy is relatively low when compared to other male groups and thus, like homosexuals in this respect, Catholic clergy may also be falsely maligned.

The SAVI Study: One of the most revealing and best studies done on sexual abuse in society was the SAVI Report (Sexual Abuse and Violence in Ireland), done by the Department of Psychology, Royal College of Surgeons in Ireland, in 2002. This study was based on 3120 respondents which represented 71% of those requested to take part. A staggering 20.4% of females and 16.2% of males claimed to have been sexually abused as children. This does not mean that this abuse is much higher in Ireland compared to other countries, as these figures included detailed classification of the various types of abuse ranging from minor to more serious types and not just those where legal action was taken as in some other studies. It does, however, indicate the extent of a very serious problem which must be recognized and rooted out of society, going forward. Men alone represented 89% of perpetrators, women alone represented 7%, and in 4% there was more than one abuser. In the case of girls, one quarter of abusers were family members, one quarter were strangers, and half were non family members known to them. In the case of boys, 14% of abusers were family members, 20% were strangers, and 66% were non family members, known to them. Overall only a small percentage fitted the current stereotype of abusers of children. Fathers represented 2.5% of abusers, clerical/religious ministers or clerical/religious teachers were 3.2%, whereas uncles were 6.2%, with 88% others.

Homosexuality and the Catholic Church

The teaching of the Church, as stated in the Catechism of the Catholic Church (CCC), is that homosexual persons, including priests, must be accepted with respect, compassion, and sensitivity and that every sign of unjust discrimination in their regard should be avoided. The Church expresses the belief that people with same-sex attraction do not choose that condition and for many of them it is a trial. These persons are called to fulfil God's will in their lives and, if they are Christians, to unite to the sacrifice of the Lord's cross, the difficulties they may encounter from their condition" (CCC2358). The struggle to live chastely is one in which all Christians share, whether they are homosexual or heterosexual.

Regarding gay sexual activity, the catechism states that homosexual acts are intrinsically disordered and that under no circumstances can they be approved. For those who have problems with the term "intrinsically disordered", it should be made clear that this term can equally be applied to heterosexual activity which is against natural law. These prohibitions apply especially to the clergy who make vows of celibacy at their ordination. The Canon law of the Catholic Church requires that Catholic clergy observe perfect and perpetual sexual continence for the sake of the kingdom of Heaven. A distinction is made between "homosexual attractions", which are not considered sinful, and "homosexual acts", which are considered sinful. The Catholic Church, therefore, recognizes heterosexuals with a homosexual problem rather than homosexuals per se, in the same way that it recognizes men and women with gender problems.

Clerical Homosexuality: In the US, the John Jay Report suggested that homosexual oriented men entered the Catholic seminaries in large numbers from the late 1970's onwards.[195] Only 3% of priests who were in training in the US during the early 1970's were aware of a homosexual subculture in their seminary. This figure jumped to 40% for those who were in seminary during 1980's and 1990's. In a national US survey of priests ordained between 1980 and 2000, 50% were aware of a homosexual subculture in seminary. There is little doubt that the rise of the gay liberation movement during the 1970's and later, contributed to this. A survey by the Kansas City Star during the 1980's reported that the AIDS-related death rate among priests was more than six times the general population, in the 14 states surveyed.

This problem is now recognised, to a greater or lesser extent, in various countries all over the world. Studies find it difficult to quantify the exact percentages of Roman Catholic priests who have a homosexual orientation. Several studies, however, suggest that the incidence of homosexuality in the priesthood is much higher than in the general population. A 2002 *Los Angeles Times* nationwide poll with 1,854 priests responding found that 9 percent of priests identified themselves as homosexual. On August 1st 1995, a journalist of the Corriera della Sera (Italian daily newspaper) published an article suggesting that 25% of Austrian Bishops were practising homosexuals. A survey on the attitude towards homosexuality among parish priests in Holland in 1983 indicated that 86% of those who responded (350) did not agree with Church teaching. A later survey in 1987, of 375 priests in the archdiocese of Utrecht, indicated that 84% had a positive view of homosexuality and 28% admitted to being homosexual.[196] In the UK the situation is no different and homosexuality is also known to be common among Anglican Church clergy. In 1994, the homosexual organization, *OutRage,* revealed that ten Anglican Bishops were homosexuals[197] and openly homosexual men and women have been ordained into the Anglican Communion. A further problem for the Catholic Church is that efforts by Rome to eliminate the problem of active homosexuals from Catholic seminaries, is proving very difficult. It may be that senior clergy and teachers in these seminaries are compromised, are not willing to accept that there is still a problem, or still do not wish to confront or are unable to confront the issue.

Implications of Roman Catholic teaching on Homosexuality.

The Roman Catholic Church, as well as the Orthodox Christian Churches (that is the Christian Churches who believe in the doctrine of transubstantiation or the real presence of Christ in the Eucharist) are now the only remaining major international force which is contradicting a secular global interpretation of sexual morality. There is a widespread and growing opinion within many influential groups in society, such as, the main-stream media, educational authorities, social and health care professionals, and many political and religious leaders, that homosexuality is not a disorder. American psychiatric and psychological associations agree with this attitude. By condemning homosexual activity, therefore, the Catholic Church teaching is now becoming more and more isolated, while at the same time, it is well recognised that many ordained Catholic clergy are known to be practising homosexuals.

Homosexuality and abortion represent the two principle spear-head attacks by secularism on Roman Catholic teaching. Catholic teaching says clearly that homosexual acts, like abortion, are always morally wrong, contrary to natural law and thus contrary to God's law. The Bible, as well as Papal and Church teaching, down through the centuries, is crystal clear on these issues. Catholic clergy who say otherwise and preach doctrine contrary to this view, are seriously misrepresenting the Roman Church. The Jesuit,

Fr John McNeill, wrote a book, *The Church and the Homosexual*, in 1976, in which he made an effort to defend the practice of homosexuality from a theological aspect. This book was condemned by the Vatican and became an embarrassment for the Jesuit order, until Fr Mc Neill was finally dismissed from the Jesuits in 1986.[198] Likewise "Catholic" organizations who directly or indirectly promote the morality of homosexual acts are not being true to Church teaching and ultimately are doing an injustice to homosexuals, by leading them astray. Other religions, including many Protestant branches of Christianity, already accept the morality of homosexuality and abortion, in certain circumstances, and will have little difficulty supporting the *"One World Church"* already established by secularists. The sections of the Bible often quoted to support Catholic Christian teaching are: Romans 1:26 – 27, 1 Corinthians 6:9 – 10, 1Timothy 1:9 – 10, and Jude 1:7.

The Great Evils of Sexual Immorality and Abortion.

Roman Catholic teaching suggests that these represent two great evils of modern society.

1. Human sexuality is a Divine gift to a married couple, which allows them to cooperate with God in an act of creation, by being co-responsible for the creation of **a new eternal soul**, at the conception of each human person. Corruption of human sexuality is thus a great offense against God.

2. Abortion is a renewal of the old pagan practice of parents sacrificing their children. This too is a great offense against the fatherhood of God, who has displayed infinite love for each human person and has adopted them as children of God. Sacrificing children to the evil spirit of Molech is referred to in the Bible, Old Testament, Leviticus 18:21, "You must not hand over

any of your children to have them passed to Molech". This referred to the Canaanite and pagan practice of child sacrifice.

International secular humanism is promoting a morality devoid of God and which is no longer based on natural law, but rather on a subjective relativism which rejects natural law. This view of morality is now being funded by most governments throughout the world, as well as the UN, WHO, IMF, Amnesty International, many other NGOs as well as a host of multinational companies. The pressure being exerted by International companies is now evidenced by the blackmailing of state Governors in the US to remove the freedom of religion clause in state legislation, as a price for these companies to remain operating within those particular states. There are two inevitable consequences to this drive to secular morality, if it is allowed to continue:

1. The growth and spread of secular morality will now progress rapidly throughout the world, as it is funded and supported by world governments and International finance institutions.

2. The persecution, destruction and eventual complete annihilation of Roman Catholicism and believers of other faiths, who reject subjective or relative morality.

In *The Ratzinger Report*, 1984, Cardinal Ratzinger, later Pope Benedict XVI, said, "What we are living through in our day is the result of an ideology that has completely severed body and soul, and that's the very definition of death. Barring a Divine intervention, we must now endure the full consequences of the uprooting of the human person in the depth of his nature – an uprooting that stems from the fact that sex has remained without a locus and has lost its point of reference since the cultural embrace of contraception. By detaching sex from procreation, the essential meaning and natural orientation of the gender distinction is lost and one's sex is eventually viewed as a simple role, interchangeable at one's pleasure."

Either Secular Humanist morality or Roman Catholic and Orthodox Christian teaching on morality will prevail. Both can no longer coexist and this is now a fight to the death. The reason simply is that although secular morality is supposed to be based on tolerance, this morality is prepared to tolerate everything except disagreement. Secular morality is now being imposed more and more by legislation. In contrast, Roman Catholic morality can only be proposed or suggested and free will must be allowed to operate. G. K. Chesterton famously said that, when all other virtues are gone, all that remains is tolerance. Those who do evil deeds must also be prepared to tolerate evil deeds done by others. He also said that morality is always a very complex issue for those who have no morals.

Implications for Homosexual Christians

There is a great danger in the current climate of secular ascendancy that homosexuals, who at one stage may have been Christian believers, could now see the Christian message as anti-homosexual or "homophobic", which is an unfortunate term. Christians, if they follow the teaching of Christ, should neither fear nor hate homosexuals, but should treat them with self-sacrificing Christian charity, as they should every human person, without distinction

For Catholics, the message of Fatima, however (see page 125), confirmed by Church teaching down through the centuries, warns of the dangers of eternal damnation of souls who sin against the virtue of chastity, without repentance. This applies equally to heterosexuals as well as homosexuals. To appreciate the reality of life after death and Hell, it is safer to look at the evidence, some of which is presented in earlier chapters of this book, rather than accept a one sided and false secular view. Those who do look at this evidence will learn to appreciate that those who most love and care about the welfare of homosexuals are those who want to give them truth, rather than those who tell them that they can behave as they wish. In the end, however, each individual will have to take responsibility for their own decisions and actions and we must respect that free choice.

Aggressive Homosexuality: This is another side to homosexuality. There are groups in all countries aggressively promoting a gay agenda, as if they hate the rest of humanity and, therefore, ironically, could legitimately be labelled "homophobic". These are homosexual "activists" who want unlimited promiscuity. They want to completely undermine and destroy Judeo-Christian morality. I am convinced that most homosexuals want nothing to do with these groups, but there is a danger for them to be sucked into this agenda, in order to achieve what they perceive as extra "rights" or for some other reason. Some of these activists are influential in promoting sex education and "life skills" courses in schools and are supported financially by rich individuals and large Marxist oriented International organizations. Most of these programmes are dishonest, unjust and evil. Legislators and teachers bear a high responsibility for allowing these programmes in schools, the origin of many, which can be traced to "Cultural Marxism" as described in chapter 2.

Oscar Wilde: He was a famous 19th century author and playwright and a well-known homosexual. He was born in Dublin in 1854 into an Anglican family. At the age of 23 he had a meeting with Pope Pius IX that left him "speechless". He later began to study the writing of Cardinal Newman and expressed an interest in becoming a Catholic. His father threatened to cut off his hands if he converted and at the last minute Oscar decided against conversion. In 1900, he developed cerebral meningitis. As he lay on his death bed, his homosexual friend, Robbie Ross, brought a Catholic priest to him, who received him into the Catholic Church as his friend knelt by the bedside. He died on the following day.

Book of Gomorrha: I will conclude with some comments on the writings of St Peter Damian (1007–1072) on the subject of homosexuality. The following is an extract from his book, Liber Gomorrha (Book of Gomorrha), which was given to Pope Saint Leo IX (1002 – 1054) as a help to reform customs in the clergy at that time. St Peter Damian said: "This vice produces the death of bodies and the destruction of souls. It pollutes the flesh, extinguishes the light of reason, expels the Holy Spirit from His temple in man's heart and introduces into it the devil, who is the instigator of lust."

Traditional Roman Catholic teaching on homosexuality has not changed in the last 1,000 years. It is still taking into account the plan of God for every man and woman and the transience of this life followed by eternity in Heaven or Hell. The practice of homosexuality is still a problem, however, within the clergy as well as among the laity. The difference now is that homosexual activity is promoted world-wide as "normal" and harmless, with major financial resources behind this promotion. There is also a strong liberal group within the Roman Catholic Church, (sometimes referred to as "Rainbow Catholics") with many influential lay people, such as the former President of Ireland, Mary McAleese, which is also promoting this view. Emeritus Pope Benedict XVI, since he retired, has referred to a "gay lobby", within the Vatican, that were making efforts to influence decisions.

In a letter from the Vatican in March 2013, Saint Pope John Paul II with Cardinal Ratzinger at the time (later Pope Benedict XVI), left no doubt about Roman Catholic teaching. The following extract on homosexual unions confirms this:

"Legal recognition of homosexual unions or placing them on the same level as marriage would mean not only the approval of deviant behaviour with the consequence of making it a model in present-day society, but would also obscure basic values which belong to the common inheritance of humanity."

The Catholic teaching on homosexuality was also emphasised by Fr Paul Check (head of Courage International – dedicated to the pastoral care of homosexuals) in Rome, Oct. 3rd, 2016, just before the Synod on the family. He said:

"In the Gospel Jesus does not only bestow his compassion, but he also calls us to conversion, because he knows that we will be truly joyful and fully realized as persons only when we live in the way that God wanted us to live when he created us. Many of today's approaches to homosexuality do not include this fuller perspective of the human person. They rather seem to limit themselves to an acceptance without recognizing the call of Jesus to conversion. They defend a "right" to sexual intimacy but they do not acknowledge the plan of God with respect to marriage to which Jesus refers to in Matthew 19."

Catholic homosexuals may feel that the Church is being very hard on them but they must appreciate that the Church has no authority to change natural law or God's law. Life after death is a certainty, not some vague religious notion, and thus all our efforts in this life must be to reach Heaven, and all the efforts of the Catholic Church must be to love us and lead us in that direction. We all have crosses in this life of one kind or another and many are a lot more difficult than homosexuality. The great majority of homosexuals who "come out" and declare themselves publicly to be homosexuals, do so in order to promote the "normality" of homosexuality or else for what they perceive as "rights" which in the end will not contribute to their happiness or fulfilment as persons. It is not clear what causes the homosexual inclination but the practice of homosexuality is always a free choice. It is not for us to judge, to be unkind, or to isolate in any way, other individuals, but in justice to those who have suffered in silence with this problem over the centuries, let us not pretend that it is "normal" or normative.

15. The Ultimate God

*- God presents us with infinite humility and infinite love for humanity- :
Why else would He humble Himself, to take on the form of bread and
wine, so that He could nourish us and so that we can become part of His
body?*

jc

The more one delves into and begins to understand the teaching of Roman Catholicism, the more one becomes astonished and astounded by two aspects of this teaching. The first is the astounding love, mercy, and humility of the God that is being promoted in this religion. The second is the enormous amount of tangible evidence that is more and more being made available to humanity to support the reality and the truth of this Roman Catholic God. Various aspects of this evidence have been noted in earlier chapters of this book, with particular emphasis on The Virgin Mary, as described in chapter five and elsewhere, - *"One fact that should and will change the world."* The Virgin Mary was the only perfect (sinless) human person ever to live outside of the God-Man Himself, Jesus Christ. As such she has a very special place in the relationship between God and humanity. All the very major signs that are now being manifested through Her gives a very clear indication, it will be through this Majestic Queen and Mother, daughter of The Father, mother of The Son, and spouse of The Holy Spirit, that all humanity will come to know and love, the one true God in the Holy Trinity. She is a mere human creature but has been specially chosen by God to be the new **Ark of the Covenant** and all communication between God and humanity comes and goes through her, whether we are aware of it and appreciate it or not.

Unfortunately, humanity has a long way to travel before The Holy Trinity is accepted generally as the one true God. Evidence was presented in chapters 11 and 12 suggesting that humanity is to be dragged kicking and screaming to this realization, through major world events, in the very near future. This new realization of The Holy Trinity will be heralded by man-made disasters and war, by natural disasters, by Divine interventions and signs, and finally by a Divine chastisement, which will result in the death of many. The final number who will survive will depend on the extent to which humanity is prepared to recognize the difference between good and evil, repent of evil, and submit to God as a merciful and loving Father, who only wants to lead all His children to everlasting joy in Heaven.

The relationship between humanity and the creator has already been completely purified and renewed on two previous historical occasions. The first purification was by water at the time of Noah's flood, approximately 4,000 years ago, and the second purification was by the blood of Christ at the crucifixion, approximately 2000 years ago. We now anticipate a third purification and indications are that at this time, it will be mainly by fire. In the message of The Virgin Mary at Akita, Japan, on Oct. 13th 1973, (approved – see page172) it was stated clearly that if humanity did not change and begin to obey the laws of God, fire would come from the Heavens and up to two thirds of the population of humanity would die. This message has been largely ignored so we now seem to be on a downward slope to this catastrophe. One way or another, it seems to be in God's plan at this time to again completely renew and purify His relationship with humanity for a third time. The renewal, on this occasion seems to be in order to prepare humanity for the reception of the supreme gift of the

"Divine Will". Humanity was slowly being prepared for this gift over the centuries and this preparation reached its final stages with the birth of a special soul who was chosen by God to communicate the details of this gift, which has been printed in 36 volumes and which has now received the first stages of approval from the Roman Catholic Church.

Luisa Piccarreta

The special chosen soul was an Italian lady who was born in Corato, southern Italy, on the Sunday after Easter Sunday (now known as Divine Mercy Sunday), on 23rd April, 1865. She was a mystic, an author, and notable for having survived on nothing but consecrated Communion hosts for sixty years. **Luisa Piccarreta**, is also known as the "Little Daughter of the Divine Will". She died on 4th March, 1947, aged 82. Less than one year after her death, Luisa was declared to be a *"Servant of God"*, which is the first step towards canonization.

Her cause for beatification and canonization was opened in November 1994. By the end of 2005, the process of inquiry and documentation within the Italian Archdiocese of Trani-Barletta-Bisceglie was complete. Her cause was then passed on to the Congregation for the *Causes of Saints*, in Rome which opened its examination March 7, 2006 and was completed in 2010 with a positive judgement. The Congregation for the *Causes of Saints* appointed a Roman lawyer, Silvia Monica Correale, as the postulator of Luisa's Cause for Canonization. The very famous Saint Padre Pio of Pietrelcina, Italy, referred to Luisa as, "that angel in Carato". He said that in the future, she would be seen as one of the greatest saints of all time.

From the time of her first Holy Communion at aged nine, she was able to dialogue with Jesus, sometimes for a number of hours each day. On one occasion, during her teenage years, she saw Jesus carrying His cross, and looking at her, He said, "Soul, help Me". From then on, she had a very strong desire to suffer for the salvation of souls. In her very early 20's her appetite for food diminished and she began to survive on the Eucharist only, a situation which lasted for the rest of her life, sixty years later. During all of these sixty years, she was confined to bed in a sitting position.

The Messages and Teachings of Luisa Piccarreta

I have been watching with interest the very slow and gradual progress of the messages and teachings of Luisa Piccarreta, coming into mainstream Roman Catholic spirituality, for the last three decades. At this stage, it is my belief that one of the greatest contributions made by the Roman Catholic Church to humanity generally, in my lifetime, apart from safeguarding the truths of gospel teachings and administering the sacraments, has been the positive support for the writings of this Italian mystic in 2010. This positive attitude of the Roman Catholic Church for her writings has opened a highway to a stratosphere of sanctity, which seems destined to lead to the development of some of the greatest saints in the history of humanity. Fr Edward D. O Connor explains in his book, *Living in The Divine Will*,[199] what Luisa's unique role was in making known the doctrine of The Divine Will. On April, 20th 1923, Jesus said to Luisa:

"It is established that two Virgins must come to humanity's aid – (that is The Blessed Virgin Mary and Luisa). One was for the salvation of man, and the other to make My Will reign upon earth. To give man his terrestrial happiness, to unite two wills, the Divine and the human, and make them one, so that the purpose for which man was created may have its complete fulfilment. I will take care of making my way, to make known everything I want. What I most care about is to have the first creature in whom to centralize my Volition, and My Will, and to have life in her on earth as in Heaven: the rest will come by itself."

Luisa was called, therefore, to bring about the reign of God's Will on earth. This brings to the world the third Fiat, that is, the Fiat of Sanctification. The first two Fiats were: the Fiat of Creation and the Fiat of Redemption.

On the Oct 6th 1922, when Luisa asked Jesus why he had waited so long and chosen the most unable, ignorant and "bad little one" (herself) to convey this gift to humanity, Jesus replied:

"First I had to form the Saints who were to resemble Me and copy my Humanity in a more perfect way, as much as is possible for them: and this I have already done. Now my goodness wants to go beyond, and wants to give to greater excesses of love: and therefore I want them to enter into my Humanity and copy what the soul of my humanity did in the Divine Will...

Besides, it is so true that I have called you as the first, since no other soul, though dear to Me, have I manifested the way to live in my Will, the effects of It, and the wonders and goods which the creature operating in the Supreme Volition receives. Check as many lives of Saints as you want, or books of doctrines: in none of them will you find the prodigies of my Volition operating in the creature and of the creature operating in It. At the most, you will find resignation, union of wills: but in not one of them will you find the Divine Will operating in her and she in It."[199]

The growth in knowledge and understanding of the internal life of Jesus has grown and developed within the Church through the centuries from the time of the apostles. This has happened through the Divine action of The Holy Spirit influencing the study and contemplation of believers who, like Mary, pondered all these things in their hearts (Luke 2:19). As the centuries go by, the faithful Christian believers advance towards the fullness of Divine truth, under the guidance of official teaching authority of the Roman Catholic Church. This official authority is invested in the Bishops, who teach, instruct and give guidance in union with the Pope.

In his book, *New and Divine – The Holiness of the Third Christian Millennium,*[200] Hugh Owen describes **a new and deeper participation in the interior life of Jesus Christ, through the action of the Holy Spirit and The Virgin Mary, which is now opening up for those who wish to live in The Divine Will.** In the same book, John M. Haffert lists four steps involved in our efforts to abandon ourselves and live in The Divine will. These are:

1. **Total abandonment to The Holy Spirit and The Blessed Virgin Mary, His Spouse.**
2. **Intimate identification with the Hearts of Jesus and Mary.**
3. **An appreciation of the unique role of the Pope and the clergy in union with him in mediating the "New and Divine" holiness to the Church and the world.**
4. **The full recognition of one's responsibility for the participation in the imminent *Triumph of The Immaculate Heart of Mary* and the *Reign of The Sacred Heart of Jesus* in the world.**

In 1997, in a letter for the centenary celebration of the founding of Rogationist Fathers, by Saint Hannibal Di Francia, Saint Pope John Paul II wrote of **a New and Divine holiness,** with which The Holy Spirit wishes to enrich Christians, at the dawn of the third millennium, in order to make Christ the heart of the world. This sharing in the interior life of Jesus has been experienced and described in a new way, by many servants of God, venerables , blesseds, and saints, especially over the last century. The long list includes especially and particularly Luisa Piccarreta, who had thirty six volumes of instruction dictated to her by Jesus, with others such as, Sr Faustina, Maximilian Kolbe, Padre Pio, Elizabeth of the Trinity, Dina Belanger, Conception Cabrera de Armida, Martha Robin, Hannibal Di Francia (who was the spiritual director of Luisa Piccaretta), and others. Saint Hannibal also referred to three fiats (be it done), or Divine interventions in the history of the universe. These are: **the fiat of Creation, the fiat of Redemption, and the fiat of Sanctification, epitomized particularly by the spirit of a New and Divine holiness now dawning in the world.** These three great works of God are also noted in the new Catholic Catechism of St Pope John Paul II (CCC, 1352).

It appears, therefore, that a reservoir of this **"New and Divine holiness"**, which has been filling up in the Church especially over the last century is now flowing over into the valleys and glens of the not so blessed, ordinary humanity, with the official Church support for the writings and teachings of Luisa Piccerreta. Is the new Pentecost, prayed for by St Pope John XXIII, at the opening of the Second Vatican Council, at last, beginning to flower? Will this approval of *The Divine Will* teaching, as given to Luisa Piccerreta, mark a watershed moment for the Roman Catholic Church and for all humanity?

St Louis Marie De Montfort, in his book, *True Devotion to Mary*, predicted that toward the end of time, Almighty God and His Holy Mother would raise up great saints who would surpass in holiness most other saints as much as the cedars of Lebanon tower above little shrubs. The writings of St Louis had a great influence on the spirituality of later saints such as St Maximilian Kolbe and St Pope John Paul II, who took as his motto, *"Totus Tuus"*(I am all yours), from his consecration to Jesus through Mary. In Ireland, this book on *True Devotion to Mary* also had a powerful influence on Matt Talbot, the apostle for alcoholic addiction, and Frank Duff, who founded the Legion of Mary, on the vigil of Our Lady's birthday, 7th

September, 1921.The Legion of Mary is an organization for lay Catholics now numbering many millions and has spread world-wide, to become the leading lay Roman Catholic organization for evangelization and other catholic action. It is now of great interest that most of those who are making an effort to develop this new spirituality of *Living in The Divine Will*, are those who were already practising the *True Devotion to Mary*.

The French servant of God, Marthe Robin was a life-long member of the Legion of Mary, despite her great incapacity (see page 86). She encouraged Catholics to take on this spirituality of *True Devotion to Mary* and live in communities of prayer, sharing and Christian charity, known as *Foyers of Charity*, which continues to grow and develop in various countries. Martha referred to members of the Foyers as "Apostles of the Last Days". It is also of some interest, therefore, that Saint Hannibal Di Francia (1851 – 1927, spiritual director of Luisa) believed that Melanie Calvat, approved seer of La Salette, France (1846), had entrusted him with a rule that she had received from The Blessed Virgin Mary for a religious community of "Apostles of the Last Days", although he had not been called to begin this community.

Hugh Owen points out[200] that, in the writings of Blessed Dina Belanger, Venerable Conchita de Armida, and the Servant of God, Archbishop Martinez, and others, Jesus invites us to participate with Him in all the activities of the Holy Spirit. Jesus also points out that the person, who lived this identification with His interior life to the fullest extent possible for a human being, was The Blessed Virgin Mary, His mother and our mother.

It has been pointed out from the teaching of St Paul and the Catechism of the Catholic Church (CCC), that, the Church and its individual members must progress and be perfected in holiness. Quoting St Gregory of Nazianzus the Catechism says (CCC 684), "The Old Testament proclaimed the Father.....The New Testament revealed the Son. ..Now the Spirit dwells among us and grants us a clear vision of Himself. ...By advancing and progressing "from glory to glory", the light of The Trinity will shine in ever more brilliant rays." St Paul's letter to the Ephesians (4: 11 – 13) says: "And to some his gift was that they should be apostles: to some prophets: to some evangelists: to some pastors and teachers: to knit God's holy people together for the work of service, to build up the Body of Christ, until we all reach unity in faith and knowledge of the Son of God, and form the perfect man, fully mature, with the fullness of Christ himself." All this requires an eventual moving towards unity with The Divine Will of The Holy Trinity.

When the Holy Spirit reigns in souls completely, through the gift of the *Mystical Incarnation or Divine Substitution,* The Holy Spirit reproduces the human experience of Jesus in the soul of the receiver. Thus He reproduced in Conchita de Armida, the interior sufferings of Jesus, many of which had been hidden from the saints, with the exception of The Blessed Virgin Mary.[200]

The writings of St Maria Faustina, Blessed Dina Belanger, and Venerable Conchita de Armida all indicate that the "Real Presence" of Jesus in them, was inextricably linked to their participation in His interior sufferings. Jesus told Venerable Conchita de Armida:

"I only remained on the Cross of Calvary for three hours, but on the interior cross of my heart for my whole life....I wish, above all, that the interior sufferings of my heart be honoured, sufferings undergone from my Incarnation to the Cross and which are mystically prolonged in my Eucharist. These sufferings are still unsuspected by the world. Nonetheless, I declare to you, from the first moment of my Incarnation, the Cross already planted in my heart overburdened me and the thorns penetrated it."

Making the Rounds

According to the revelations given to Luisa, everything in God's creation is an "I love you" from God to us, His children. Every drop of water, every blade of grass, every snowflake, every planet, every star and every wavelength of light etc is an "I love you" from the Creator to us. We must try to return this love by saying from our hearts from everything we encounter during the day, "I love you too". Three different headings are identified for making the rounds, which are in line with the three great works of God, namely, **Creation, Redemption and Sanctification.**

In the **Creation** rounds we tell God the Father that "I love You too" in every and all created things, such as, galaxies, stars , planets, rivers, lands, lakes, hail, rain and snow, all varieties of plants and animals etc.

In the **Redemption** rounds we say to Jesus "I love You too" for our Redemption in all its aspects. I thank you and love you Jesus for every day of Your life, Your prayers, Your healings and especially Your suffering on the cross, Your death and resurrection, Your gift of the Church and the gift of Your mother as our mother, the gift of the seven sacraments, and the clergy to forgive us our sins and provide us with the Eucharist etc.

In the **Sanctification** rounds we tell The Holy Spirit "I love You too" for all the graces mediated to us through the birth and life of Jesus, through the intercession of Mary, St Joseph and all the saints and especially now for opening up a door for humanity to return to the gift of the Divine Will, which Adam and Eve lost at the fall into original sin, so that we can return to the place and to the purpose for which we were created, namely to live in the Divine Will and return appropriate love and glory to the Triune God.

The rounds, therefore, are an exchange of life, which is nourished and amplified by the Life of the Supreme Fiat. The purpose is to give back to God the Glory which is due to him. The rounds are made up of acts of love, of reparation, of praise, and of gratitude. The rounds connect us more intimately with the immensity of God and with the creative and preserving power of The Divine Will. The rounds encourage a life of peace and serenity with an amplification and expansion of the soul in God and of God in the soul.

Living and Praying in the Kingdom of the Divine Will

Jesus gave the following instructions to Luisa: To pray in the Divine Will we must learn to forget self. We begin by saying, "Jesus wants to pray so I pray with Him". On 9th February 1908, Jesus instructed: First you must,

Enter into Me

Make yourself one with Me

Take what you find in Me

Everything is achieved by the *"Golden Rule"* which is: **We desire it, and Jesus does all the work.** It is therefore the desire of the heart which ensures living in the Divine Will.

St Paul said, "Put on Christ," so we do everything as another Christ as He is doing everything within us. This includes all our thoughts, our words and our actions. It includes all the movements and work we do, even every breath we take and every beat of our heart – everything except sin. Jesus told Luisa (14th August 1912) that while on earth, during the first 30 years (His Hidden life), He took unto himself all the thoughts, words and actions of every person from Adam to the last person He created, and He redid everyone's life in His Divine Will. In this extraordinary way, there is a Divine version of every person's life.

We can also pray, work, speak, walk, eat, sleep, and enjoy ourselves etc., in the name of everyone (The Kingdom of The Divine Will, Volume 1). Jesus said to Luisa: "In My glances I took all the creatures' eyes, in My voice their words, in my movements theirs', in My hands their works, in My heart their affections and desires, in My feet their steps and making them like Mine, My humanity satisfied The Father. ... Now why cannot you also do it? **FOR HE WHO LOVES, ALL IS POSSIBLE UNITED TO ME.** In My will, pray and bring before the Divine Majesty in your thoughts, the thoughts of everyone, in your eyes the glances of everyone: in your words, movements, affections and desires of those of your brothers, to make reparation for them: to obtain light, graces, and love for them. In my Will you will find yourself in Me and in everyone. You do my Life. You will pray with me: and the Divine Father will be content with it, and all Heaven will say, "Who calls us upon the earth? Who is it that wants to embrace this Holy Will in herself, enclosing all of us together? And how much good you can obtain for the earth by making Heaven descend upon the earth."

If the whole of humanity prayed together in a human way, even this volume of prayer would not compare with just one prayer in the Divine Will because a Divine prayer has infinite value, or merit, since it possesses the very dispositions and qualities of Jesus Himself because it is He who is doing all the work in His Divine Will. We can therefore, pray the Rosary or adore Jesus in the Blessed Sacrament in the name of everyone, so that God can receive a perfect return of love and glory from everyone simultaneously in everything we do. **The first requirement to achieve this gift is that we must desire it.**

A Final Summary

In this short chapter, I can do no more than introduce the reader to *The Gift of The Divine Will*. It is then up to each individual to respond to this free gift in their own personal and unique way. The gift of the Divine Will is now available to anyone living without serious (mortal) sin. There are two conditions only. Firstly, we must desire it and ask Jesus for the Gift of His Divine Will. Secondly, we must resolve to no longer live by our own will.

Prevenient Act: When you wake in the morning tell Jesus, "I no longer wish to give life to my human will and so, setting my will in yours, by this *Prevenient Act*, I set all the acts of the day in order in Your Divine Will." **Actual Acts:** In doing particular actions, such as walking, working, eating etc., you should say, "Jesus wants to... and so, I do it together with Him".

"Both acts are necessary. The *Prevenient Act* assists and creates the disposition and makes room for the actual act. The actual act preserves and enlarges the disposition of the prevenient act", (Book 11, 18/8/1912).

Luisa said, July 1942: "Oh, how I wish that all would understand what it means to live in the Divine Will! It is the greatest miracle that Jesus can do for creatures: it is the greatest glory He can receive...If all would understand this, to live in It, would become our predominant passion and all evils would flee from us!"[1]

Luisa explained to a little boy, "Tell Jesus that you give him your will and ask Jesus to give you His Divine Will." Jesus said: "The most beautiful act, and the one that pleases me most is abandonment in My Will". Jesus promised, "...the great event is coming – the New Era in which the Will of God will be done on earth as it is in Heaven – everyone is waiting for this New Era" (Book of Heaven, Vol. XV, July 24th 1923). This is the fulfilment of the prayer and prophecy of Jesus when he taught us the *Our*

Father, **"Thy Kingdom come, Thy Will be done on earth as it is in Heaven".** Jesus told Luisa that, "It will spread everywhere by acceptance in mercy or by justice, in chastisements. Humanity must now choose, which way?"

The more one reads and studies this new form of spirituality, the more one begins to appreciate the magnitude of the transformation facing humanity at this time. This is now a time when only 20% of Europeans believe in God and other parts of the world are only marginally better or worse. What kind of transformation will leave only those who are sincerely trying to live in the Divine Will of the Most Holy Trinity? It is likely to be a very painful time for all of us, but, *God's Will be Done.*

Other books of great value for further study into the revelations on *The Divine Will* include the following: One of the biggest and best is the Doctoral thesis of Fr Joseph Iannuzzi, *The Gift of Living in the Divine Will in the Writings of Luisa Piccarreta.*[201] Next, *The Kingdom of The Divine Will*, incorporates three volumes in one, containing: The Hours of the Passion of Our Lord Jesus Christ, The Virgin Mary in the Kingdom of the Divine Will, and The Rounds of the Soul in The Divine Will.[202] The life of Luisa is told in the book, *The Sun of My Will,*[203] and finally the book, Saints in the Divine Will, contains lots of interesting excerpts from the writings of Luisa.[204]

16. Sacred Astronomy and Prophecy.

We are all in the gutter, but some of us are looking at the stars.
Oscar Wilde.

And a great sign appeared in Heaven: A woman clothed with the sun and the moon under her feet and on her head a crown of twelve stars.
Revelation: 12

There is a difference between astronomy and astrology. Astronomy is a scientific study of the stars and planets and the milieu in which they exist. Astrology, on the other hand, is a study of the alleged influence of the stars and planets on individual lives and on human affairs generally. Astrology is regarded as a form of fortune telling and it is rejected as a valid subject in Christian and some other religions. Sacred astronomy is a study of how religious events or events with some religious implications coincide with various positions of the stars, planets and other "Heavenly" bodies. In the centuries gone by, especially before astronomy was established as a proper mathematical observational or scientific subject, the boundary between astrology and astronomy was less defined than it is now.

Jesus described many signs in the Heavens which would be related to the end-time events of the Book of Revelation (see the final chapter). Given that astronomical and celestial omens were held in such high regard, at the beginning of Christianity, in the first century and before, and that the Bible records them as key events to watch out for in trying to interpret the signs of the times, a brief perusal of this subject is warranted.

The Sign of Jonah

In the Bible a number of "signs" were associated with the prophet Jonah. The best known sign, referred to in Matt 12:39, was the symbolic association of Jonah in the belly of a large fish for three days with the body of Jesus in the tomb for three days. According to St Augustine, because Jesus spoke of this sign at the time when he was speaking about the binding of a strong man (Matthew 12.29), this relates to the crucifixion which bound Satan, and is also related to the unbinding of Satan in Rev 20: In his book, *Unveiling the Apocalypse*,[205] Emmet O Regan also discusses the significance of solar eclipses over the ancient city of Nineveh, which is now the site of the city of Mosul, in Northern Iraq. This was the city associated with the biblical story of Jonah.

When Jonah called for repentance to prevent the city from being destroyed, the King and all the inhabitants of Nineveh declared a fast, put on sackcloth and sat in ashes. It is believed that the reason the Ninevites responded so well to Jonah's warning was that his entry into the city and his preaching was perfectly timed to coincide with an eclipse of the sun, which was seen as a warning sign from God. This solar eclipse is one of the most famous eclipses recorded in ancient history and the details were discovered during the 19th century in a series of cuneiform tablets of Assyrian historical texts. This is known as the Bur-Sagle solar eclipse, and it occurred on 15th June 763 BC. A plague had occurred in the same geographical region a short time before the eclipse and this had led to a revolt in the city, so the inhabitants of Nineveh, at that time, were suitably open to listen to some direction from God, through one of His prophets.

Two more recent solar eclipses have also occurred over the modern city of Mosul. The first was near the time of the beginning of the First World War, now referred to as the *World War One*

Eclipse. Emmet O Regan pointed out that this was on the 35th anniversary of the apparition of Our Lady of Knock, 21st August, 1914. This Marian apparition in Ireland has been associated with the Lamb of God in the Book of Revelation and some, therefore, have associated this eclipse with the release of the Four horsemen of the Apocalypse, that announce war in Revelation:6. This could also be an important signpost to the unbinding of Satan and for the beginning of the period of increased satanic power, as foreseen and predicted by Pope Leo XIII in the 1880's (see page 136). The second total eclipse of the sun in recent years over Mosul was in 1999. This coincided with the possible opening of the sixth seal in the Book of Revelation, as the four signs marking the opening of this seal were observed at that time (see the last chapter). It is apparently extremely unusual for a total eclipse of the sun to occur twice in the same place in the same century and it is also of great interest that the 1999 solar eclipse occurred on the exact day that a rare "Grand Cross Alignment" was formed by the planets of the solar system, forming a cross in the sky, which is the great symbol of Satanic defeat. This cross of planets can be linked to the observation of Miguel Antonio Fiol, who has discovered that the planets arranged themselves in a crucifixion scene on April 3rd, 33 AD, that is the most likely date of the crucifixion. At that time the rings of Saturn could be viewed as a halo or a crown of thorns over the head of Christ.

The Star of Bethlehem

From the Christian point of view, the *Star of Bethlehem*, is the great astronomical sign that most will have heard about as marking the birth of **Jesus Christ** and the beginning of Christianity. A number of possible suggestions have been put forward to explain the exact sign in the sky that was taken as very symbolic by the Magi or so called, three wise men or three Zoroastrian kings from the east, who in the Christmas story, followed "the Star" to

Bethlehem, in order to find the new-born King of the Jews. One suggestion was a triple conjunction between Jupiter and Saturn, when the two planets came together on three occasions, within a very short period of time. These kinds of conjunction are very rare and would have been seen as significant, although more than one triple conjunction seemed to have occurred, around the time of the birth of Jesus. Other suggestions have been that the Star of Bethlehem was the planet Uranus or that the light was from the birth of a new star or nova. The most popular explanation, however, is a triple conjunction between the star, Regulus and the planet, Jupiter and then a conjunction between Jupiter and Venus. This rare conjunction took place between Regulus, the king star, and Jupiter the king planet, in the Jewish season of Hanukkah, or Jewish New Year, between 2 and 3 BC. This was within the constellation Leo, the lion, a symbol of the tribe of Judah. Right behind Leo was the constellation Virgo. Jupiter continued westward and then came into conjunction with the planet Venus, which is associated with motherhood. The two planets were so close that they seemed to be only one and together formed the brightest object in the sky. At this point, the movement of Jupiter seemed to stop as it began to make a retrograde (reverse in relation to the earth) motion. From Jerusalem this position was south, directly over Bethlehem. It is claimed that modern computer programmes, which can re-create the night sky for any date, can confirm that this was near the time of the shortest day, on December 25th, 2 BC. This would all fit with nine qualities identified for the Star of Bethlehem described by the Attorney, Frederick Larson, from his studies of the gospel of Matthew (see www.bethlehemstar.net). These nine qualities were: it signified birth, it signified kingship, it was related to the Jewish nation, it rose in the east, King Herod did not know about it, it came at an exact time, it endured over time, it was in front of the Magi when they travelled south from Jerusalem, and it stopped over Bethlehem.

It does appear therefore that the story of the Star of Bethlehem was not only based on the historical fact of the birth of Jesus Christ, but was also based on definite astronomical observations. This may surprise many, but even more will be surprised to discover that recent astronomical observations suggests that the Star of Bethlehem is now returning in 2016 and 2017 in a new and very significant way.

November 20th, 2016

On this day three events were of interest to Roman Catholics. The first was the Catholic feast day of *Christ The King.* The second was the official closing of The Year of Mercy, proclaimed by Pope Francis, as a year of great grace, when sinners should have repented and lost sheep should have tried to find their way back to the Church. The third and final event was a more complex astronomical event but nevertheless, likely to be of great significance.

On November 20th 2016, the King planet, Jupiter entered into the constellation Virgo (The Virgin) and was astronomically predicted to remain there for a little more than nine months corresponding to the time for human gestation. Jupiter emerges from Virgo on the 23rd of September, 2017. At that stage the sun will be rising just behind Virgo and the moon will be underneath this constellation (I write this toward the end of 2016). This corresponds with Christian sacred scripture, Revelation.12. To complete the scriptural reference to this unique astronomical event, the constellation Virgo will also be "crowned by twelve stars". This crown of "twelve stars" will consist of the nine stars in the constellation Leo, with the three additional planets, Mercury, Venus, and Mars. It is also of great interest, as Emmet O Regan has noted,[205] that on the 21st August 2017 (feast of Our Lady of

Knock), another total solar eclipse will take place (see the Sign of Jonah above). This may have great significance as the "Woman clothed with the sun" who is to crush the head of Satan will be visible in the sky at that time. Many Catholics believe that these signs, so near the centenary of the great sign of Fatima, which will be celebrated on the 13th October 2017, could mark the end of Satan's extra freedom. This solar eclipse will not be seen over Mosul (ancient Nineveh), as at the beginning of the first World War, but over the centre of the United States, which now may represent the new Babylon.

Emmet O Regan further points out the fact that this eclipse takes place again, during the Feast of Our Lady of Knock, may further suggest that the events of 2017 have something to do with the opening of the seventh seal by the Lamb of Revelation. Emmet also notes some interesting parallels between the opening of the seventh seal and the vision of the angel in the Third Secret of Fatima, who threatens to strike the earth with his flaming sword.

After the appearance of the woman clothed with the sun (Rev.12), Michael the Archangel defeats Satan and casts him with his angels down to earth. Satan then becomes furious with the woman and goes off to make war on the rest of her offspring, that is, on those who keep the commandments of God. (Rev 12:17). If this is the point we are now at in the Book of Revelation, then we can expect the great disasters for the world to begin with the blowing of the seven trumpets: - see discussion on the Book of Revelation in the final chapter.

I have already mentioned in chapter five, and elsewhere in this book, that messages coming to humanity from God through the mediation of The Virgin Mary are factual and believable, simply because of the enormous quantity and quality of the evidence supporting them. This is particularly true of those messages that have had some degree of official Church approval, such as the messages of Fatima and Akita. These events cannot, therefore, be regarded as imaginations, or hallucinations, or theories of one kind or another. I appreciate that some non-Catholic Christians may regard these interventions of The Virgin Mary as demonic, so the reader will have to judge whether these messages from Mary are promoting, goodness, truth, and love or something evil. They are factual events, open to historical scrutiny, with many different kinds of evidence supporting the factual basis of the occurrences. Despite this, many will reject these supernatural messages, mainly because they do not want to believe them and consequently refuse, or are psychologically, or spiritually blocked from investigating the evidence.

A very significant aspect of the messages from The Virgin Mary, as explained in previous chapters, has been to give some details of a mystical warning to be given to humanity as well as some details on the chastisement, which will follow, if humanity still does not repent and convert to goodness. This is of particular relevance to the discussion in this chapter as these events in Catholic prophecy could best be explained in association with a cosmic event, which some astronomers now think is imminent. Two major aspects of the chastisement have been detailed. The first was in the Fatima message and the second was in the message of Akita. Although a core part of the Fatima message was about the spread of Communism, the persecution of the Church, the reality of Hell, and the annihilation of nations, one of the most significant aspects of this message was a private supernatural enlightenment, associated with the third secret, given to Sr Lucia, who was the last surviving seer of Fatima. This remained hidden until very recently, that is, an event which will interfere with the axis of the earth and which will likely cause some degree of tipping of the angle of the earth's rotation, with all the destruction that that implies. The fire raining from the Heavens was the significant aspect of the Akita message on the 13th October 1973 (see page 172), given on the 56th anniversary of the great sign of Fatima. In the end we were told that one half to two thirds of humanity will die in these events, if humanity continues to refuse to respect the laws of God. Both of these predicted events could be caused and explained by the arrival of a large planet or possibly brown dwarf star near the orbit of the earth.

The Tipping of the Earth

In May 2015, a new book – *A Pathway under the gaze of Mary,*[206] was published, written by the sisters where Sr Lucia, of Fatima, lived for most of her long life. Of particular interest was a section dealing with the third secret of Fatima.

While Sr Lucia was a Dorothean Sister in Tuy, Spain, in 1943, she became very ill. The Bishop of Leiria came to Tuy and they spoke at length. The book relates the story of the communication between the Bishop and Sr Lucia, as follows:

"Considering the possibility that she could die, the Bishop ordered her to write the third part of the Secret (often referred to as the third secret). Opposing this, as was her usual custom, she resisted, saying: -Reverend Bishop, I cannot do it!

-But then, did not Our Lady tell you to follow the path that I indicated to you? –Yes. -So now this is it. I ask for the glory of God and Our Lady? She does not get angry. If she is disappointed it will be me. She will bless your humility and obedience."

Sr Lucia then became very ill and was advised to have an operation to try to get some pus drained from a bone infection in her leg. She resisted initially as she was worried that she might say something while under general anaesthesia. Eventually she agreed and began to recover.

The book continues, "The order by the Bishop to write the "secret" was not forgotten and it was still a burden on her heart. She said: "If only my strength allowed me to, I wanted to write what the Bishop had ordered me but I cannot explain what was happening to me as my hand shook and I could not form the words. This may have been caused by my impression that I had to write something against the orders of Our Lady, but still by obedience...I attempted several times without getting any results. Because of this conflict, I wrote to the Bishop of Leiria, telling him what was happening to me. His Excellency replied by renewing the order he had already given me, perhaps in more expressive terms. .. This order made me shudder. The Good Lord gave me orders not to tell anyone...

In December, I wrote to the Archbishop of Valladolid to consult him about this problem. I opened my tormented soul to him, telling him about my doubts and my desire to act with perfection. The Bishop of Valladolid advised her to write again to the Bishop of Leiria, which she did on the 19th December".

She later wrote: "While I was waiting for an answer, on January 3, 1944, I knelt beside the bed which sometimes served as a writing table, and again I experienced the same without success. What most impressed me was that at the same moment I could write anything else without difficulty. I then asked Our Lady to let me know, if it was the Will of God. I went to the chapel at 4p.m. in the afternoon, the hour that I always made a visit to the Blessed Sacrament because I was ordinarily alone. I do not know why, but I liked being alone with Jesus in the Tabernacle.

Then I knelt in the middle, next to the rung of the Communion rail and asked Jesus to make known to me what was His will. Accustomed as I was to believe that the order of the Superiors was the expression of the Will of God, I couldn't believe that this wasn't. Feeling puzzled and half absorbed under the weight of a dark cloud that seemed to hang over me, with my face between my hands, I hoped without knowing how, for a response. I then felt a friendly, affectionate and motherly hand touch me on the shoulder and I looked up and saw the beloved Mother from Heaven. "Do not be afraid, God wanted to prove your obedience, faith and humility. Be at peace and write what they order you, **but do not give your opinion of its meaning.** After writing it, place it in an envelope, close and seal it and write on the outside that this can only be opened in 1960, by the Cardinal Patriarch of Lisbon or by the Bishop of Leiria."

"I felt my spirit flooded by a mystery of light that is God and in him saw and heard:

The tip of the spear, as a flame, unlatches and touches the axis of the earth. It shudders. Mountains, cities, towns and villages with their inhabitants are buried. The sea, the rivers and the clouds emerge from their limits, overflowing and bringing with them in a whirlwind houses and people in numbers that are not possible to count. It is the purification of the world by sin as it plunges. Hatred and ambition cause the destructive war!"

In this context it is interesting what St Pope John Paul II said at a meeting with lay Catholics in Fulda, Germany, in 1980, when asked about the Third secret of Fatima. St Pope John Paul II answered, "If there is a message in which it is written that the oceans will flood whole areas of the earth and that from one moment to the next millions of people will perish, truly the publication of such a message is no longer something to be so much desired. Many wish to know simply from curiosity and a taste for the sensational, but they forget that knowledge also implies responsibility. They only seek the satisfaction of their curiosity and it is dangerous, if at the same time they are not disposed to do something, and if they are convinced that it is impossible to do anything against evil." At this point the Pope grasped a Rosary and said, "Here is the remedy against evil. Pray, pray and ask for nothing more. Leave everything else to the Mother of God."

Finally in these times we must consider the message of Akita, given on Oct. 13th 1973 (see page 172), approved at the time by the local Bishop, in association with Cardinal Ratzinger (later Pope Benedict XVI) at the time.

"As I told you, if men do not repent and better themselves, the Heavenly Father will inflict a great punishment on all humanity. It will definitely be a punishment greater than, the deluge, such as has never been seen before." "Fire will plunge from the sky and a large part of humanity will perish... The good as well as the bad will perish, sparing neither priests nor the faithful. The survivors will find themselves plunged into such terrible hardships that they will envy the dead. The only arms which will remain for you will be the Rosary and the sign left by My Son (Eucharist)".

All these statements are in line with authentic Catholic prophecy and are worthy of very serious consideration for that reason. The connection of the Akita message with Fatima (and Garabandal) is beyond doubt. This would seem to have particularly serious implications for the centenary of the great sign of Fatima on the 13th Oct. 2017.

Planet X or Planet-7X or Nibiru

The discovery of new planets in our solar system has often been preceded by astronomers noticing erratic unexplained movements in the planets already described. Such was the case with Neptune (discovered in 1846), the existence of which was suggested for many years on the basis of unexplained movements of Uranus (discovered in 1781). Pluto (discovered in 1930) with its moon were later used to explain strange movements in the orbits of Neptune and Uranus. On the basis of these gravitational forces, and still unexplained erratic orbits of existing planets, it is theorized that a number of other planets are still waiting to be discovered in our solar system.

Zecharia Sitchin wrote a well known book, *The 12th Planet,* in 1976. He was a scholar of Summerian scripts and this book was based on his interpretation of scripts on texts found on clay tablets from this ancient civilization, which described a planet coming near earth in its orbit path of 3,600 year duration. The Summerians are regarded as a very early human civilization, from the region of present day Iraq, often quoted as 6,000 years ago. They had developed a script as well as mathematics and advanced astronomical observations. This planet, described in the book, is often referred to as Planet X and is one of three planets said to orbit a brown dwarf star called Nemesis, which in turn is considered as a twin star for our sun. Nemesis is largely invisible, even with infrared detection systems, due to thick clouds of iron oxide dust surrounding it. The other two planets that orbit Nemesis are known as Helion and Arboda. There are also some moons attached to these planets.

Over the last two decades, there has been an explosive interest in the subject of Planet X. This growth of interest has come mainly from the "rumour" that this planet is heading towards us and it will have drastic consequences when it gets near us, although there is no suggestion that it will actually hit the earth. It is also rumoured that NASA and world governments are aware of this disaster waiting to happen, but are keeping it off the news, because of a fear of panic. Associated with this interest is an enormous amount of confusion and like a lot of other quasi political subjects in this age of the world-wide-web (www), and despite the enormous quantities of information available, the truth can be difficult to find and to discern. If world governments are actually aware of a large potentially dangerous planet approaching and are trying to keep this information hidden, then we can be sure that the www will be used to the maximum to create a web and fuzz of confusion and "false flags", in order to counter the amateur and not so amateur astronomers who are turning on the red lights.

The first source of confusion is the number of different names associated with Planet X. Some of these names are obviously not describing the same Heavenly body and we are then left wondering, how many planets, if any, are actually coming towards us, at this time, that could be a potential problem for us? Some of the names associated with and confused with Planet X are, Planet X as the Tenth Planet (Robert S. Harrington, NASA astronomer, 1993), Planet 7X, P-7X (John Anderson, astronomer, Science Digest, Nov. 1982), Tenth Planet (X Roman numeral for ten), Nibiru, Hercolubus, Tyche, Wormwood, Blue Kachina, Fiery Red Dragon of Old, The Winged Planet, The Destroyer, as well as various star names such as, Chinese Guest Star (with a previous date of 1054 AD), Red Star, and Nemesis, which as explained above is not a planet but rather a brown dwarf star and a twin of our sun.

Gill Broussard: Gill is an amateur astronomer and is one of the best known authors on the subject of Planet X. Although a sceptic in his early time investigating this subject, he later became convinced of the reality of Planet X and has now spent several years working on the details of this illusive subject. His website (www.planet7x.net) gives a number of free videos as well as a free download of a 50 page booklet, with many colour timeline charts, dealing especially with biblical historical events. Gill claims that Planet X (or Planet 7X as he usually calls it) system intersects with the orbit of the earth every few hundred years, rather than every 3,600 which is the usually quoted orbital time. He relates the nearness of Planet 7X to earth, as a reason for various events described in the Bible, such as, Noah's Flood (2349 BC), the destruction of Sodom & Gomorrah (2016 BC), Joseph's seven year famine in Egypt (1793 BC), Joshua's Long Day (1466 BC), King Hezekiah's backward sundial (687 BC), and the extended eclipse of the sun at the crucifixion of Jesus. **He believes that at least four of these previous events were associated with a tipping of the earth's axis, on some occasions, by an additional 26 to 28 degrees** (the earth axis is already tipped from the perpendicular).

The story or the problem of Planet 7X (or Nibiru, Nemesis, etc.) may not be of immediate interest to you now, but it could be some day very soon. For now those of us with some interest in this subject are having great difficulty trying to sort fact from fiction, honest information from fabrication, and conspiracy theories from truth. If you have already read the previous chapter on UFOs or when you read the section on the mainstream media in the last chapter, you will appreciate how many governments go to great lengths to cover up, confuse, and fabricate facts, in order to conceal the truth and spread lies. The US government is particularly good at this. We could be charitable, and suggest that the motivation is good and to prevent panic. We know, however, that the motivation is not always good and sadly, we must remind ourselves of the motto of the mushroom farmers to explain how some governments treat citizens, that is, - keep them in the dark and feed them manure. The many unexplained events surrounding the 9/11 catastrophe in New York should be enough to convince us that much of the truth is often not what we read or hear in the mainstream media. On that occasion, in particular, we were asked to believe that the third building, which collapsed like an inside demolition job and, which was a "football field" away from the other two buildings hit by aircraft, collapsed because of heat radiation, fire balls, or for some other ridiculous reason. Is it any wonder that the people of the great American nation seem to be in revolt and are beginning to "Trump" the old order? In the meantime we are left wondering why, and for what purpose, are all the enormous secret underground facilities being built by the rich developed nations?

What facts can we glean regarding the nearness to the earth's orbit and the dangers associated with this planetary system described above? It is my impression that the tipping of the earth is a very real event to be expected in the near future. The reality of the Fatima message for me, because of the enormous evidence to support it, is beyond doubt. I accept what Sr Lucia and St Pope Saint John Paul II said regarding the oceans covering the land and the disturbance of the earth axis. Many other modern day prophets also had visions of a disturbance in the axis of the earth, that were recorded before the revelation to Sr Lucia, described above, was made public in 2015. Among these were Ned Dougherty, who foresaw the 9/11 disaster in New York, and Howard Storm, both of whom had famous near death experiences – see chapter 8.

I am impressed with Gill Broussard who seems to have truth at heart. He has good information and he is happy to provide it free of charge. His suggestion that some of the major historical floods, extra long days, and unusually long eclipses of the sun, described in the Bible as well as in some ancient historical records, could be explained by "natural" astronomical events seems very plausible. The severe earthquakes, severe volcanic activity, major tsunamis and general severe natural disturbances, described by modern prophets as well as in the Book of Revelation, could all be explained by a very strong gravitational pull on the earth by a large planet or brown dwarf star, causing the axis to tip. The extra chastisement of humanity, by fire falling from the Heavens, as described in the message of Akita, could also be explained by the earth travelling through cosmic debris from the tail of a large comet, an event estimated by Gill Broussard to occur approximately 150 days after the tipping event.

The messages of Fatima, Garabandal, and Akita have given humanity a very clear warning of the catastrophe that awaits us if we do not repent, pray, do penance, and generally begin to respect the laws of God. It has been made clear that it is already too late to completely avert these events but the severity of the death and destruction can be dramatically reduced if humanity responds appropriately. The message of Fatima, in particular, also makes it clear that the Holy Trinity has appointed The Virgin Mary as the humble maid who will crush the power of Satan in the world at this time. It is important, therefore, that as many as possible should recognize this power and influence which has been invested in the Immaculate Heart of Mary and respond accordingly. Remember again Her statement in Medjugorje, "If you knew how much I love you, you would die of joy." The final chapter will discuss a possible time line for these events, particularly as they may relate to the Book of Revelation.

17. Mysteries wrapped in Conundrums

No one loves us more than Christ. But no one spoke of Hell more.
Msgr. Charles Pope.

Introduction: Like many, I enjoy mysteries. The world, and indeed life in general, is full of mysteries. Mysteries are good for us. They not only keep us fascinated but should also keep us humble by reminding us how much we do not know. In this chapter, I will try to discuss a few mysteries with special emphasis on the age of humanity.

I was fascinated a few years ago when I first stumbled across the pyramids in Bosnia. It was not just that they had been hidden in plain sight for millennia, but also the largest was twice the size of the largest in Giza, Egypt. A number of radioactive dating tests also indicated that they were constructed between 30,000 and 35,000 years ago, that is, possibly five to six times the age of the famous Egyptian variety. They were built of a hardened stone material made from local gravel. This concrete-like material has been laboratory tested and found to be artificial rather than natural in nature, with a hardness and water resistance, as good as the best concretes available in the 21st century. Neanderthal man is regarded as having become extinct about 40,000 years ago,[207] therefore, these pyramids, which may be the oldest known man-made structure in the world, were constructed approximately 7,000 years later. One of the first questions must be: who built them?

The Bosnian pyramids were discovered in 2005 by an Anthropology professor, Dr. Sam Semir Osmanagich, near the town of Visoko, in Bosnia-Herzegovina, about 30 kilometres northwest of the capital, Sarajevo. Dr Ali Basrakat, from the

Egyptian Mineral Resource Authority, led a group to study these structures and later said, "Everything that we have seen so far tells us that human hands built these structures a long time ago".[208]

There are five pyramids with the three largest located 2.18 kilometres from each other, forming an equilateral triangle. There are also a number of other structures with a system of connecting tunnels. The largest pyramid is named the Pyramid of the Sun and reaches 220 metres above ground level, whilst below ground level, it reaches a depth of approximately 120 metres. Below ground, the structure is covered by several layers of major flood deposits. The Pyramid of the Moon is the second largest and has a height of 190 metres. This puts the great Egyptian pyramid in Giza into third place as the largest in the world.

The discovery and dating of these pyramids gives a new stimulus to the investigation of the amount of ingenuity and technology which was available to the builders of these massive structures. Even a more compelling question is, how did these builders relate to modern humans, Neanderthal man, or other human like species and how old actually is modern humanity (Homo-sapiens-sapiens)?

The Origin and Age of Humanity

For those who are interested, the origin and age of humanity is one of the most divisive topics that can be discussed. Firstly this is, par excellence, the subject of experts, all of whom are certain of the facts. But they have many different opinions as to what the facts indicate and what the truth is. Having been regarded as an expert on one particular subject for much of my life, I developed a healthy lack of respect for experts, because, over the years I learned to appreciate very much the limitations of human knowledge and ultimately, how little each individual can know and understand. Let's face it, experts get it wrong many times, but that does not mean that experts are not useful.

From the Christian point of view, there are experts with many and various opinions on the origin and age of humanity. Some experts (often known as 'fundamentalists', since they take a literal meaning of the Bible) believe that the world was created in six days (as we now understand a day in time), about 6,000 years ago, and that humanity was created on the last day, as stated clearly in the book of Genesis, the first book of the Old Testament of the Bible. Other experts believe that creation took place over a much longer time scale but they also believe humanity did begin with the creation by God of a perfect man and woman (Adam & Eve) 6,000 ago. There are many other experts (usually referred to as evolutionists) who believe that human life has evolved from lower forms of animal life. In turn all other forms of life, including plants, evolved from even lower form of life. These experts on evolution may be found among Christians, Muslims, and among those with other religions or with those who have no religion at all. What we can say with certainty, therefore, is that experts have dramatically different views on the age and origins of modern humanity.

I have never had more than a vague interest in trying to find out the age of humanity, or in investigating more the details of a time that is sometimes described as pre-history. I never had any difficulty believing that the human race was initiated by, and descended from, one single couple and the genetic evidence that I have read, would not oppose that view. I never seriously considered, however, that Adam and Eve, as the first parents of the human race, were only created a mere six thousand years ago, as proclaimed loudly by many Christian believers from all denominations, including many of my friends, who are Roman Catholics. It just never made sense to me, since the evidence is very strong that human forms have existed on the earth, long before that. I have always regarded the idea of Adam and Eve being created only six thousand years ago as an over literal interpretation of the Bible, and St Pope John Paul II and Emeritus Pope Benedict XVI often warned about this problem. Recently, however, I came across a few new pieces of information which jolted me to such an extent that I began to question my long held views on the time scale of Adam and Eve.

Firstly, there was the revelation of the Divine Will, (see chpt. 15) and those who are experts on this revelation assured me that it implied that approximately 6,000 years ago, Adam and Eve were created. Here I include a copy of a revelation by Jesus to Luisa Piccarreta from her writings on the Divine Will:[204]

"I am such a king. In Creation, My ideal was to form the kingdom of My Will in My creature's soul. My primary purpose was to make each man the image of the Divine Trinity by virtue of the fulfilment of My Will in him. But by man's withdrawal from My Will, **I lost My kingdom in him, and for 6,000 long years I have had to battle.** But no matter how long it has been, I have never given up My ideal nor My primary purpose: nor will I ever give it up. And, when I came to earth in the Redemption, I came to realize My ideal and My primary purpose, which is the Kingdom of My Will in souls. This is so true that, before coming, I formed the first Kingdom of My Will in the Heart of My Immaculate Mother. I would never have come upon the earth outside of My Kingdom. I suffered hardship and pain: I was wounded: and, in the end, I was put to death. But the Kingdom of My Will was not achieved. I laid down the foundations and I made the preparations for It, but the bloody battle between the human will and the Divine Will still continued.

Now, My little daughter, when I see you at work in the Kingdom of My Will – and as you work the kingdom establishes Itself more and more in you – I sense victory in My long battle, and everything around Me takes on an air of triumph and delight. My pains, My hardships My wounds, they all smile at Me, and My own death gives Me back the life of My Will in you. That is why I feel victorious in Creation and in Redemption. Indeed, they are necessary for the Newborn of My Will to form the lengthy rounds, the rapid flights, and constant walks in the Kingdom of My Will. That is why I delight in My victory, and in seeing all the steps that My little daughter takes, and the acts that she performs."

Secondly, I got the opinion of one the foremost experts I know on Sacred Scripture, who also believed that Adam and Eve were created approximately 6,000 years ago but they were also convinced that human "forms" were on earth long before that. These are sometimes referred to as *"preadamites"*. Finally the 6,000 years ago figure fitted with a number of revelations which say that humanity was first purified and renewed approximately 2,000 years after Adam and Eve, at the time of Noah, by the flood. Humanity was purified and renewed again approximately 2,000 later by blood, with the suffering, crucifixion, and death of Jesus Christ, and is now about to be purified again, probably by Fire from Heaven, (see Akita – Oct. 13th 1973, page 172). Could my original views on the age and historicity of Adam and Eve be wrong?

Follow the evidence: If there is one theme that I would like to highlight in this book, it is the obligation that we all have to seek the truth, and in so far as we can to live by the truth. As I have said previously, quoting the philosopher, Peter Kreeft, "Truth trumps everything". We must never be afraid of the truth but at the same time we must have the utmost respect for others, with different opinions, who are sincere searchers for truth, but who reach a different conclusion from ours on where the truth lies. **To find the truth we should follow the evidence**, but we are all aware how good people are at marshalling the evidence, and beating it into submission, so that their evidence will confirm their own prejudices. This is a snare that we all can fall into. Not alone must we love the truth, therefore, but we must be as honest and as objective as we can in discerning the evidence and sharing this honestly, openly, and respectfully with others.

Archaeology, Anthropology, and Palaeontology

The subjects of archaeology, anthropology (study of human origins), and palaeontology (study of fossils and past geological periods) are not exact sciences or at least not as exact as, chemistry, physics, or mathematics. Archaeological digs give one chance only and once the work scene is changed you can never get the original back. In other words these experiments cannot be repeated and in order to verify any new discovery in science it is always desirable to repeat the experiment. Nevertheless, these are very well established sciences and we cannot reject the very large library of information which is now available, from these subjects, on the origins of the human species. Faking of results, however, can be easily done, and for this reason results are often considered suspect when new finds do not fit with the popular modern theory. One of the most famous forgeries of human skeletal remains was the *Piltdown man*, in Southern England 1908 – 1911. This skeleton had a human skull and an ape-like jaw and was promoted at the time as "a missing link". It was scientists at the British Museum, in London, who eventually exposed the fraud in 1950.

The Palaeoanthropology of Man: In the book, *Hidden Archaeology, The Hidden History of the Human Race,*[209] a detailed account is given on the evolution of humanity. The first hominids (primates, which includes apes and humans), or human-like primates, walking erect, appeared in the fossil records, in the Pliocene period, about 4 million years ago. Australopithecus (the "southern ape") is the earliest recognized hominid, 4 to 5 feet tall with a cranial capacity of 300 to 600 cubic centimetres (cc). After about 2 million years Homo habilis appeared, very similar to Australopithecus but with a larger cranial capacity, up to 750 cc. Homo habilis is thought to have developed to Homo-erectus (includes Java Man and Peking Man) about 1.5 million years ago. Homo erectus was 5 to 6 feet tall and had a cranial capacity of between 700 and 1,300 cc. They lived in Africa, Asia and Europe up to about 200,000 years ago. It is believed that Homo erectus developed into early Homo sapiens between 400,000 and 200,000 years ago. Early Homo-sapiens then developed, according to a popular view, to either Neanderthal man or to modern man (Homo sapiens-sapiens). Some Neanderthals had brains larger than modern humans who have a brain capacity of 1,000 to 2,000 cc. Brain capacity is not a direct indication of intelligence, however, as there are very intelligent humans with a brain size of 1,000 cc., whereas, there are some of low intelligence with brain sizes of 2,000 cc. Opinions vary, but it is now believed that modern man, Homo-sapiens-sapiens first appeared about 150,000 years ago. Several skulls were discovered over the period 200,000 to 100,000 years ago, which seem to chart this change from early to modern Homo sapiens. Almost all of these were found in Ethiopia with some in Tanzania. In England the oldest skull of fully human origin that has been discovered was dated to about 100,000 years old. This poses some problems, as the current anthropological view is that modern Homo sapiens migrated from Africa into Europe about 30,000 years ago. The first fossils of modern humans to be identified in Europe were found in 1868 at the 23,000 to 27,000 year old **Cro-Magnon** rock shelter site in south-western France. Modern Homo sapiens is thought to have spread to Israel and Asia from Africa about 100,000 years ago.

According to a popular anthropological view also, humans first entered North America from Siberia about 12,000 years ago but Thomas E. Lee of the National Museum of Canada discovered advanced stone tools in glacial deposits on Manitoulin Island, which were 100,000 years old. Finally, in 1879, modern human skeletal remains were found at Castenedolo, in Italy, from the Pliocene period, that is, over 2 million years ago. This is completely unexplained although there is little doubt that this was due to some major error. There is a great lot of uncertainty, therefore, on the time scale of the arrival of modern humanity in Africa, in Europe, in Asia, and in the Americas. The discovery of very old tools in these continents must, however, indicate some very ancient form of intelligent life.

A good number of examples are quoted of the use of tools many millions of years ago. In the 1960's, sophisticated stone tools were discovered 75 miles southeast of Mexico City. The US Geological Survey gave them an age of 250,000 years. This understanding as to when tools were first made in the North American continent was extended a lot farther back when a stone mortar and pestle was discovered, under Table Mountain in California, dated at 33 to 55 million years old. In Thenay, North Central France, stone scrapers, borers and blades were discovered, estimated at 15 to 20 million years old. Finally the Royal Museum of Natural History, in Brussels, discovered tools near the Ardennes region of Belgium which were estimated to be between 25 and 38 million years old.

Another Historical Timetable: In the book, *Before Atlantis: 20 Million years of Human and Pre-Human Cultures,*[210] the author, Frank Joseph gives a detailed discourse on his view of the paleoanthropological evidence for a historical timetable on the development of Homo sapiens. A brief selected summary of his timetable is as follows:

20 million years ago: Human ancestors working with quartzite tools at Monte Hermosa, Argentina.

9 million years ago: At Table Mountain, California, evidence has been discovered of manufactured, well crafted, mortars and

pestles. (note: another date above of greater than 33 million years ago is claimed for these tools).

3 million years ago: Stone tool users at Miramar, Argentine coast.

1.7 million years ago: Evidence for Homo erectus found in Indonesia.

750,000 years ago: Evidence for stone tool users near Frederick, Oklahoma.

400,000 years ago: Evidence for Homo sapiens in East Africa.

125,000 years ago: Evidence for an urban centre, founded in Alaska, above the Arctic Circle, during an extended warm period in the Northern Hemisphere (secondary to the Abbassia Pluvial, that is, a very wet period in North Africa).

100,000 years ago: Evidence for stone tool makers in Manitoulin Island, near Calgary, Canada.

75,000 years ago: It is believed that one of the greatest cataclysmic events in the evolution of the human species was the eruption of Mount Toba's super volcano in Sumatra, Indonesia, 75,000 years ago. This event left a surface depression over sixty miles across, the largest of this kind on earth. It is believed that the profound atmospheric and temperature changes that resulted from this catastrophe reduced humanity from over two million to little more than two thousand.

55,000 years ago: The owners of bone and stone tools enter Brazil's Toca de Esperenza cave.

15,000 years ago: The Keg Mountain Oscillation inundates coastal Western Europe and most of the Afro-Atlantean Peninsula, stranding human populations on islands high enough to be spared.

9600 BC: Construction of the first permanent building structure at Góbekli Tepe, in Turkey.

8000 BC: The disintegration and collision of the comet Kronos with the earth brought the last ice age to a catastrophic end. There was a major meteoric bombardment of the earth with a consequent major environmental upheaval. Later the melting of the polar ice caps led to sea levels rising and flooding in many parts of the world. Góbekli Tepe was abandoned.

7500 BC: The British Army Colonel, James Churchward, while helping with famine relief in India, in 1870, helped translate ancient Hindu tablets which described an ancient paradise island kingdom in the Pacific, known as Mu or Lemuria. He later published the details of this story as a book, in 1926, with the title, *The last Continent of Mu*. Mu is now regarded as one of the first cities, to have been built anywhere in the world. In fact it appears to have been a thriving urban centre. The story was thought to be a fantasy until the Indian Minister of Science and Technology organized an investigation. This led to the discovery of a city which is now buried under the sea, with streets organised in a grid formation, measuring five miles by two miles. India's National oceanographers later dredged up large numbers of cultural artefacts, in 2001, from the Gulf of Cambay, off the coast of Gijarat. This was 120 feet below the surface of the water and radioactive dating consistently gave the age of these artefacts at 9,500 years old. Geological tables also confirm that, 9,500 years ago, water tables in this area, when compared with water levels today, were 120 feet lower.

Cave Paintings

One of the best pieces of evidence for intelligent beings surviving over 40,000 years ago, are the cave paintings. The earliest known European cave paintings date to approximately 40,000 years ago.

Altamira Cave in Spain marked the first of hundreds of examples of cave art now discovered in Europe, which is a quantity way above any other part of the world.

Altamira Cave: Of this cave Picasso famously said, "After Altamira, all is decadence". The caves of Altamira are located near Santilliana del Mar, Northern Spain, near Santander. They were discovered in 1868. The paintings were of such astounding quality and so well preserved that specialists doubted their authenticity at first and sadly the discoverer had already died before they were officially acknowledged as genuine. They were finally accepted as authentic after other artefacts from the stone-age were discovered in the area. The cave paintings of Altamira are approximately 15,000 years old and remain the most exceptional evidence of Magdalénian culture in southern Europe. A visitor centre allows easy access.

El Castillo Cave: This is another example of at least ten examples of cave art that have been discovered in Cantabria, Northern Spain. The prehistoric dots and crimson hand stencils (Panel of Hands), located in this cave have been dated to at least 40,000 years old. They were dated by a team from the University of Bristol, UK, led by the archaeologist, Alistair Pike. For the dating procedure, they used the decay rate of uranium from the calcium deposits that had formed over the paint. The paint may have been there many years before the calcium and consequently, the paintings may be still older. This age has led to the suggestion that these paintings may have been made by Neanderthals, rather than Homo sapiens. Other cave paintings were recently discovered near Malaga, Spain, in a Neanderthal cave. These were dated to 42,000 years ago but this date was based only on the remains of a charcoal fire on the floor, rather than the paintings, so the date is controversial.

The Chauvet Cave: Located in the Ardèche, southern France. In 1994, it became well-known for the Palaeolithic art work that is found on the walls and the fossilized remains of many animals. On the floor can be seen, the preserved footprints of animals and humans. The cave is uncharacteristically large and the quality, quantity, and condition of the artwork found on its walls is such, that it is now regarded as one of the most significant pre-historic art sites in the world. Most of the artwork dates to the Aurignacian era, that is, 30,000 to 32,000 years ago.

Lascaux Cave: Sometimes referred to as the prehistoric Sistine Chapel. It is located in south western France. This cave was discovered in 1940 by four teenagers. It contains some of the most remarkable Palaeolithic cave paintings in the world, dated to at least 15,000 years old.

The Cosquer cave: It is located in the Calanque de Morgiou near Marseille, France. The entrance is now underwater and was discovered in 1991. Today the cave can be accessed through a 175-meter long tunnel, the entrance of which is located 37 meters under sea level. It was first decorated around 27,000 years ago, that is, during the last ice age, when sea levels were 120 metres lower than they are today. When the polar ice melted, and the water level rose, many of the paintings got destroyed.

The Magura cave: This is located in the Northwest of Bulgaria. The cave is unique for paintings on stone, done in bat guano. They are multi layered and come from different eras (early Palaeolithic to Neolithic). The paintings in the Magura cave represent dancing women, dancing and hunting men, disguised men, as well as a large variety of animals, suns, stars, instruments of labour, and plants. Information can be gleaned through the pictures about religious events and feasts as well as many symbols. Some of the images are very complex compositions and hint about the diversity of ideas in a world rich in the intellectual and spiritual spheres. The drawings suggest there was a temple that was in use for a long period of time - from The Neolith to the Iron-age. The overall length of the cave is approximately 2.5 kilometres. In the cave there is one remarkable giant column, 20 metres high on a 4 metre base.

Prehistoric and Mysterious Maps

In his great tome, *Fingerprints of the Gods-The Quest Continues,*[211] Graham Hancock discusses at length many mysterious maps that predate modern human technology. These maps, as well as the great mysteries surrounding their origin, are yet another great indicator of previously unknown civilizations.

Admiral Piri Reis Map: This was made in Istanbul (Constantinople) in AD 1513. It was discovered in 1929 in the old Imperial Palace at Istanbul, painted on a gazelle skin. It covered the Western coast of Africa, the Eastern coast of South America and the Northern coast of Antarctica. Antarctica, however, was not discovered until 1818. The coast of Queen Maud Land shown in the map is, therefore, a great mystery as the detail of the land beneath the ice, now about one mile thick, corresponded exactly with the seismic survey done in 1949, by a joint British-Swedish scientific team. The Falkland Islands were also described at their correct latitude, although they were not officially discovered, until 1592. Admiral Rees said that his map was taken from a number of source copies, some as old as 400 BC and these older maps in turn were probably copied from still older maps. The mystery is, however, that the latest date that Antarctica could have been surveyed in an ice free condition was approximately 4000 BC.

Professor Charles Hapgood , from Kene College, New Hampshire, in the US, published a book in 1953, suggesting that Antarctica could have been ice free before 4000 BC, which is before it was subject to "earth crust displacement", whereby the outer earth crust in that region moved 2,000 miles southward and thus got much colder. Albert Einstein was very impressed with Hapgood's work and wrote a foreword to this book. Hapgood also said that there was irrefutable evidence that the earth had been comprehensively mapped before 4000 BC by a hitherto unknown and undiscovered civilization.

Oronteus Finaeus Map: In Christmas of 1959, Hapgood discovered another old map of Antarctica in the Library of Congress, Washington DC. This was drawn by Oronteus Finaeus in 1531. He also must have had access to very early source maps. It again confirmed non glacial conditions in Antarctica, with mountains and rivers in the coastal regions and matched closely the seismic survey maps of Queen Maud Land, Enderby Land, Wilkes Land, Victoria Land, and Marie Byrd Land. The Byrd Antarctic Expeditions of 1949, using geological coring tubes, confirmed that rivers were flowing into an ice free Ross sea until about 6,000 years ago. The sediments washed into the sea by rivers were dated using three different radioactive elements, leaving little room for doubt.

Philippe Bauche Map: The famous cartographer, Gerard Kremer (known for the Mercator projection) included the map of Oronteus Finaeus in his atlas of 1569. He also further extended the details of the map of Antarctica from sources other than those used by Oronteus Finaeus. In 1737, the French geologist, Philippe Bauche, also published an amazing map representing Antarctica, when it was completely ice free. The implications of the Bauche map is that he must have been using source maps much older (?thousands of years older), than those described above. The details of this map were confirmed in 1958 by a more detailed seismic survey, done for the International Geophysical year. According to Professor Hapgood's theory, Antarctica may have been completely ice free 15,000 years ago.

The final implications, therefore, of the prehistoric source maps described above is that Antarctica was surveyed over a period of thousands of years, ranging from approximately 15,000 to 6,000 years ago, by some unknown civilization.

Evolution of Humanity

We must now ask the question: did modern humanity evolve over many millions of years from earlier forms of life or not? As explained in chapter 9, there are two **extreme views** on the origin of life generally and this would include the origin of modern humanity. The first is the **purely materialistic, atheistic** view, which is, that life has evolved from inanimate matter, by chance, and in a hit and miss meaningless way. The second extreme view is the **creationist** view that the world was created in seven days, with humanity being created on the seventh day (as it literally says in the *Book of Genesis*), and all this happened about 6,000 to 10,000 years ago. For those who believe in God, there are also many other variations on how life has come about, but in our quest for truth we must ask, **what does the evidence indicate?**

The evidence against life having evolved by chance, from inanimate matter, was already discussed in some detail in chapter 9. The evidence, which has been briefly presented above, indicates clearly that the activity of intelligent human forms of life extends back many thousands of years beyond the six thousand. Therefore, for anybody who can attribute any kind of validity to the scientific process, it becomes impossible to accept that life is only 6,000 to 10,000 years old. Accepting a 6,000 year figure for the age of humanity is, therefore, impossible for anthropologists in particular, as well as for virtually every other scientist who can put some confidence in radioactive dating systems. It is well known that there are problems associated with radioactive dating (discussed in chapter 9) but, nevertheless, there is an acceptable accuracy, when sampling error is not a factor, and when the dates are confirmed using repeat experiments with different radioactive isotopes and different specimens.

The view of anthropology, therefore, is that human life has evolved from earlier forms of life and the scientific support evidence for this is increasing all the time. For an anthropologist, "Homo" is the name given to the human genus, which also includes Neanderthals and many other extinct species of hominid (erect walking human-like primates). Homo sapiens is the only surviving species of the genus Homo. Modern humans are sometimes referred to as the subspecies Homo-sapiens-sapiens to distinguish them from earlier forms of Homo sapiens, who it is now believed were contemporaries of Neanderthals and who probably had a common ancestor with Neanderthals. Modern humans, however, are still very commonly referred to as Homo sapiens.

I understand that it would be a great horror and a great shock to many of my friends to suggest to them that one of their forefathers (even if it was a very, very long time ago) was a monkey. I don't know what they have against monkeys and the resemblance with my friends is uncanny, especially when there is a troop of them together. Every morning I can also see one in the mirror staring back at me while shaving. We must remember that what makes modern Homo sapiens unique is not that we do not resemble monkeys (because we do), but that we have a unique spiritual endowment that helps us to know and love God, with an attached conscience that enables us to discern and appreciate the difference between good and evil.

The historicity of Adam and Eve
As explained above, while discussing the palaeoanthropology of humanity, the common view now is that modern Homo sapiens

originated in Africa and migrated from there to other parts of the world approximately 150,000 years ago.

The genetics of mitochondrial and Y chromosomal DNA: The DNA known to be present in the mitochondria is different from the DNA in the nucleus of cells. New embryos inherit half their nuclear DNA from each parent in what appears to be a random series of recombination or cross-over events. Mitochondrial DNA, on the other hand, is acquired from the ovum or female cell and there is no recombination with male DNA. Genetic comparison of mitochondrial or maternal DNA, therefore, is one ideal way of constructing inheritance or evolutionary trees, as it represents a pure female line. There is another way of looking at a pure male line, which is also commonly used for constructing inheritance trees. The male approach uses the Y chromosome, which is passed on from father to son, with no female involvement.

The construction of these inheritance or evolutionary relatedness trees is complex, and a serious study this area of population genetics (sometimes now referred to as *population genomics*) is no more than a few decades old. We are likely to learn a lot more concrete facts, therefore, as the experience and the experiments get better in the coming years. Mathematical and in particular statistical analysis of the genetic studies is the key to drawing reasonable and accurate conclusions. The larger the portions of DNA and the number of individuals from different races that can be compared, the more reliable will be the conclusions. The number of mutations in different DNA segments is the key to comparing relatedness within a particular time scale. The so called "D-loop" of mitochondrial DNA was selected in early experiments because of a rapid mutation rate in that area. Now, however, we are already at the stage when the complete strands of human mitochondrial DNA have been sequenced into the constituent base pairs and thus can be compared in detail, between different individuals, for different mutation sites. Similarly, complete base pair sequences from various Y chromosomes can now also be compared in detail.

A number of genetic teams have recently compared the genes in Y chromosomes and the genes in mitochondrial DNA from males and females in different parts of the world. On the basis of these studies, genetic predictions were made on the age of a "most recent common ancestor" (MRCA). One view at the moment suggests that genetic diversity among the human population is very restricted due to some recent "bottle neck event" which reduced the human population to very low numbers. The common reason for this bottle neck which has been suggested is Noah's flood. It is important to point out, however, that this kind of genetic molecular clock dating is a very new and as yet an unreliable science.

The Genes of the Family of Noah: It has been suggested that if the biblical account of Noah's flood is true, then DNA genetics should indicate that the whole human race, from about 4,000 years ago, should have come from one Y chromosome only. This is on the basis that males always inherit their complete Y chromosome from their fathers only since females have no Y chromosome, as explained above. The female genetic line, on the other hand, can be traced through the mitochondrial DNA as this is inherited directly, from the mothers only, through the mitochondrial DNA of the ovum. According to the Bible (Genesis 9:18-19), the whole population of the earth was renewed from the three sons of Noah, that is, Shem, Ham, and Japheth, with their wives. This then would also mean that all human mitochondrial DNA should be descended from the three wives of Noah's sons.

According to some investigators, this apparently does fit the evidence. No "ancient" or highly divergent Y chromosomes have been found[212] and there are three main mitochondrial DNA types

568

found across the world, referred to as M, N, and R types.[213] N type is very closely related to R type and both are more distantly related (that is, they have more distinct mutation sites) to M type. On this basis it has been suggested that two of the wives of Noah's sons may have been sisters, but this cannot be proven.

What about the giants mentioned in the Bible?

This is a question often asked but rarely answered. The Bible has several references to giants. These are referred to with different names, such as Nephilim, as the best known, and others such as Rephaim, Anakim, Amorites, and Zuzim. After the Flood, the Bible traces all humanity from the sons of Noah, namely, Shem, Ham and Japheth. The genealogy of the giants after the Flood, in the area approximating the Holy Land, is definitely linked to Ham, that is, they had a natural origin. Goliath, who is the best known giant of the Old Testament, was a Philistine. The Philistines trace their origin back to Ham who was the father of Egypt who was the father of Casluhim from whom, came the Philistines. Goliath was six cubits and one span tall, that is approximately nine feet and nine inches – almost 3.0 metres. (One male cubit is the distance between the elbow and the tip of the extended hand and is approximately 18 inches. One span is one half of a cubit, approximately nine inches – measured as the distance between the tip of the thumb and the tip of the small finger of an open extended hand). Og the King of Bashan (Ps: 135 & 136) was also a giant. He was estimated to be about 12 feet (3.7 metres) tall from the size of his bed (Deut, 3:11), which was nine cubits long and four cubits wide (13.5 ft. by 6 ft.). He was an Amorite who descended from Sidon, who was the son of Canaan, who was the son of Ham. Og was regarded as the last of the Rephaim (a Hebrew word for giant). The pre-Israelite inhabitants of Canaan are identified with the Nephilim in the Bible (Num, 13:33). Although there are some different opinions, most seem to suggest that the word Nephilim comes from the Hebrew word for "fallen".

American Giants: There is strong evidence that Indian tribes populated America between 10,000 and 15,000 years ago. In 10,000 BC, that is, 12,000 years ago, native Americans were mining for mica and using hardened copper to make tools and jewellery. There are numerous reports that many of these ancient Indians were giants. These reports are detailed in a book by Richard J. Dewhurst, *The Giants Who Ruled America*.[214]

In the early sixteenth century, when the Spanish began to explore America, it was common to have reports of many giants among the natives inhabiting some of the villages that they had discovered. Sir Francis Drake also reported seeing taller than average natives during his expeditions. In 1602, the Californian Channel Islands were discovered, and these islands later became a location of great interest because of the discovery of giant skeletons in the early twentieth century. Some were reported to be between eight and nine feet tall.[215]

All this suggests that some pre-historic ancestors of modern humanity were giants. How these evolved is not clear and it may simply be due to some mutation/s in the pituitary gland associated with the production of above average quantities of growth hormone. This tendency to large stature could have been normally inherited over generations until the disadvantages outweighed the advantages. How the American giants were related, if at all, to the sons of Noah is not known.

The Roman Catholic Church and Human Evolution

For the purpose of reducing confusion, it may be useful to discuss briefly here again (already discussed in chapter 9), the attitude and teaching of the Church of Rome towards evolution of life, with particularly emphasis here on the evolution of humanity or Homo sapiens. This Church has wisely never opposed the theory that life generally has evolved, and to do so now would be opposed to a mountain of scientific evidence, which continues to grow. At this stage for a Christian Church to oppose the evidence that life has evolved would essentially be locking out from this Church, for no good reason, honest truth seeking scientists and other reasonable people, who are aware of the strong evidence supporting evolution.

Pope St John Paul II is famous for his statement in 1996, that, "Evolution is more than a hypothesis", although he did not elaborate much on that statement. Emeritus Pope Benedict XVI has shown a great interest in the subject of Darwinism and evolution and he has written and spoken many times over the years on the subject. His views would, therefore, represent a current opinion on official Church teaching on this subject, but they have never been proclaimed as an infallible doctrine.

Emeritus Pope Benedict is not a "creationist" and does not believe in a strict literal reading of the Book of Genesis. He has some sympathy with the "Intelligent Design" view but he does not support it completely as he has difficulty understanding how any of the known biological mechanisms could explain transition from one species to another.

Moral Aspects: At a moral level, Emeritus Pope Benedict XVI believes that widespread acceptance of evolution as a first philosophy (evolutionism) is dangerous for a number of reasons. Evolutionism promotes a meaningless view to life, and this has bad consequences for how people live their lives. This promotes a view supporting such things as: - struggle for survival, survival of the fittest, and a blood thirsty approach to life, with no requirement to have consideration for the welfare of others.

Scientific Aspects: The discoveries of Natural sciences should not and cannot be in conflict with Christian faith (belief) as ultimately truth is one and Christianity and Science both profess to promote and seek truth. At a scientific level, the evidence for "micro-evolution" seems beyond doubt. The case for "macro-evolution" (change from one species to another) is less persuasive and as yet has not been clarified. In his writings, Emeritus Pope Benedict XVI further notes, "Within the teaching about evolution itself, the problem emerges at the point of transition from micro to macro evolution, on which point Szathmáry and Maynard Smith, both convinced supporters of an all embracing theory of evolution, nonetheless declare that: "There is no theoretical basis for believing that evolutionary lines become more complex with time, and there is also no empirical evidence that this happens.""

Spiritual Aspects: In his book, *In the Beginning*,[137] Ratzinger, before becoming Pope said, "The great products of the living creation point to a creating Reason and show us a creating intelligence, and they do so more luminously and radiantly today than ever before." The Italian atheist mathematician, Piergiorgio Odifreddi, published a book, in 2011, in which he critiqued the theological writings of Emeritus Pope Benedict XVI. Like the famous atheistic biologist, Richard Dawkins, he did not accept the value of theology, and referred repeatedly to it as "science fiction". Emeritus Pope Benedict's response to this book was published in a letter to the Italian daily newspaper, La Repubblica. He suggested that science fiction belongs to science rather than theology. He said:

"Science fiction exists, on the other hand, in the ambit of many sciences. That which you explain about theories concerning the beginning and end of the world in Heisenberg, Schrodinger, etc., I would designate as science fiction in the good sense of that phrase: they are visions and anticipations, in order to reach a true knowledge, but they are also, precisely, only imaginations with which we seek to come close to reality. There indeed exists science fiction in a grand style, for instance, within the theory of evolution, the "selfish gene" of Richard Dawkins, is a classic example of science fiction." In saying this, however, he was not opposing evolution, towards which he has a consistently positive view as an explanatory model.

What Emeritus Pope Benedict is pointing out is the distinction between what is imagined by the senses from what is conceived by the intellect. A spiritual statement must be examined by the intellect rather than by the imagination. Theology, like mathematics, is the work of the intellect, that is, conceptual reasoning beyond the material realm. It is not correct, therefore, to regard theology as science fiction, which is merely imagination.

Monogenism or Polygenism? There is a popular scientific and genetic view now that humanity probably descended from more than one set of original parents. This is referred to as polygenism as opposed to the view that all humanity came from one single set of first parents, referred to as monogenism. In this context, it is of interest that, between 1% to 4% of DNA from individuals who are not of African origin, is described as Neanderthal DNA. At the same time, 3% to 5% of DNA from Melanesians and Aboriginal Australians is described as Denisovan DNA.

In the papal encyclical, *Humani Generis*, produced by Pope Pius XII in 1950, polygenism was ruled out as incompatible with Roman Catholic teaching. Pope Pius XII could not reconcile the doctrine of "original sin" with more than one set of first couples. Significantly, the Genesis text on Adam and Eve was not mentioned in the encyclical. This is as if to underline the fact that interpretation of Sacred Scripture is based on reason as well as faith, which considers scientific as well as theological truth, knowing that all truth comes from God and thus truth cannot be divided.

In 2004, an International Theological Commission on evolution, chaired by the now Emeritus Pope Benedict XVI, published the document, *Communion and Stewardship: Human Persons Created in the Image of God.* This document gives some acknowledgement to scientific evidence for a polygenic origin to our species. It says, "While the story of human origins is complex and subject to revision, physical anthropology and molecular biology combine to make a convincing case for the origin of the human species in Africa about 150,000 years ago in a humanoid population of common genetic lineage... Catholic theology affirms that the emergence of the first members of the human species (whether as individuals or in populations) represents an event that is not susceptible of a purely natural explanation and which can be appropriately be attributed to a divine intervention."

Divine Intervention: Christian theology teaches that in the beginning, the Triune God wished to share his life with other creatures and these creatures were thus created from nothing that pre-existed. Angels, who are pure spirits, were created immediately. The angels were given free will and were tested so that they could choose good or evil. The angels, who rebelled against God because of pride, were sent to a place of suffering called Hell and are now referred to as demons.

The second stage of creation was the "Heavens and the earth" and all matter and all living creatures. If the theory that life evolved slowly over 3.5 billion years is true, and now there is a mountain of evidence to support it, the level of complexity required in the structure of matter for life to evolve in this way approaches the infinite, and thus gives great glory to God. This complexity has been discussed in chapter 9.

In totality, therefore, as already pointed out, the evidence strongly suggests that although life has developed through some evolutionary process, this could not have happened by chance. A Divine intervention is required and this contradicts the classical atheistic theory of evolution, which has no mathematical, genetic, or biochemical basis in fact. How exactly our first parents were given a soul has not been revealed. It is only important for us to appreciate that each human person now has a spirit attached, which is separated from the biological body at death. Acceptance of this spiritual reality as part of our personhood, is crucial if we are to have the hope of finding eternal happiness. Evidence for the reality of life after death and our final destination, was presented in chapters 7 and 8.

Roman Catholic theologians believe that our first parents would have received a state of *"original justice"* at the first moment of their existence. This state of original justice was accompanied by sanctifying grace that justified them and made them righteous and friends with God. According to St Thomas Aquinas, at the same time they were also given other gifts, called the preternatural gifts, in order to perfect them by remedying their natural weaknesses.

Firstly, there is nothing inherent to spirit and to matter that would keep them together forever, because by nature humanity is corruptible. The **gift of immortality**, therefore, was given with the state of original justice to overcome this inherent corruptibility, so that they would live forever.

Secondly, human beings are also prone to interior confusion because what we know, what we choose, and what we desire often do not coincide. The **gift of integrity** was given to our first parents to overcome this interior disorder. This preternatural gift orders individuals so that their reason is subject to God, their desires are subject to their reason, and their bodies are subject to their souls.

Thirdly, human beings are limited in our knowledge because we know by learning. In St Thomas's view, the **gift of infused**

knowledge was given to our first parents to remedy this weakness.

Finally, **St Thomas said that because of the gifts of immortality, integrity, and infused knowledge, our first parents were also impassable, that is, incapable of experiencing bodily or spiritual suffering. St Thomas Aquinas also said that God intended our first parents to give their descendants the blessings of original justice.**

With the gift of free will, our first parents would be given the opportunity to choose in favour of God or reject Him, as the angels before them had been given the same opportunity. The Bible tells us that our first parents were put to a test, a test that they failed through an act of disobedience. This was what we now call the **'Original Sin'**. Sadly for us, because they rejected God, they gave up the right to the preternatural gifts, not only for themselves but also for us, their progeny.

In 2011, Fr Brendan Purcell wrote a major philosophical work on the origins of humanity in the light of creation and evolution.[216] He suggests there is no scientific doubt that human origins are partly to be found in the hominid evolutionary sequence. He also says that "If the Big Bang poses a boundary or threshold question about the coming into existence of the Universe, then the conception of each new unique human being is the Big Mystery." He quotes Aleksandr Solzhenitsyn who wrote that, "The Universe has as many different centres as there are living beings in it. Each of us is a centre of the Universe". Then Fr Purcell goes on to say that, "each human being is a world of his or her own, far outweighing in value and mystery the existence of the entire astrophysical universe, up to and including the last of the pre-human hominids. The answer to the question of human origins, then, is that each human being is constituted into existence as a you for You in one cooperative act: creation by an unlimited transcendent and personal source and of co-creation by the child's parents. Each human being outweighs the Big Bang: each human being is a new beginning of a new personal universe. Nothing less would be a sufficient answer." Fr Purcell also quotes Dostoevsky, when criticising the attempt to manufacture a common *liberté, égalité, fraternité* by force he says:

"The Western man speaks of brotherhood as of a great moving force of humanity, and does not realise that brotherhood cannot come about if it does not exist in fact.. One should in fact become an individual to a degree far higher than has occurred in the West. A voluntary absolutely conscious and completely unforced sacrifice of oneself for the sake of all, is, I consider, a sign of the highest development of individual personality.. How is this to be done? – what is needed.. is the principle of brotherhood and love – we must love. Man must instinctively and of his own accord be drawn towards brotherhood, fellowship and concord."

Fr Purcell expands on the act of parents pro-creating and cooperating with an act of Divine love by which each human person is created. Here he quotes Giuseppe Zanghí who says:

"When God enters into relationship with humanity, precisely because he is Love, he can only do it by giving himself completely, by 'not being' in order to make the other equal to himself (as Aristotle said, there can't be true love without equality). This is a kenotic discussion: God is present in the world but as one who has given himself completely... When God creates, he does so by loving. What does 'by loving' mean? By giving everything. When he causes me to be, he causes me to be like himself, that is, he makes me, like himself, 'absolute', complete."

The kenotic discussion refers to the biblical passage of Philippians 2:7, describing where Jesus emptied himself taking on the nature of a servant, made in human likeness.

Fr Purcell further explains that: "In procreating, the parents' co-creation participates in the one act of divine love by which each and every human person is created. My parents were the parents of me in time, and God created me from eternity. T. S. Eliot's famous phrase, 'the intersection of the timeless with time', paraphrased as the intersection of created with uncreated love, is one way of expressing what happened. God respects his creatures as others, who he allows to participate in the miracle of bringing a new human infant who'll live for eternity, into existence. And it's this miracle that father after father and mother after mother is confronted with in their amazement at seeing their child for the first time."

Conclusion

The Official attitude of the Roman Catholic Church, therefore, is not opposed to the theory of evolution. In general, for those who claim to be Roman Catholics, the service of the truth is best served by exploring and being directed by the teaching authority of this Church. This teaching is usually very solidly based on an understanding of biology and the other natural sciences, as well as philosophy, theology and an authoritative interpretation of Sacred Scripture. Individual Catholics have a right and even a duty to express their views, if they are solidly based. But what if their private views clash with the official Church view? Promoting private beliefs, on the evolution of life, publicly as Catholics, which are contrary to official Church teaching, no matter how well intentioned, without stating clearly that they are not in line with the official Church view, is disingenuous and can lead others (especially honest scientists who are searching for truth) astray, cause them to leave the Church, or prevent them from becoming members of this Church.

The Roman Catholic Church teaches that the human person is the pinnacle of the creation of life. The human person alone was designed to be made in the image and likeness of God, destined to share eternal bliss with God in Heaven. As explained already in Chapter 9, in the context of life having evolved slowly over a very long period of time (if one accepts that), there were two momentous events in the evolution of life as we now have it. The first was the creation of a living self-reproducing biological entity from inanimate matter. The second was the creation and welding or infusing of a spiritual entity to a human biological body. How these events happened is a mystery and because of its complexity will always likely remain a mystery to the human mind. We do not know the place or at what point in history, either of these two events were initiated.

The revelation to Luisa Piccarreta (see chapter 15) gives an indication that Adam and Eve existed approximately 6,000 years ago and this can serve as a useful working hypothesis. Further revelations in future years may help to clarify this more. As the creation of each individual human person, however, marks a linking of time with the timeless (each person being created in eternity), the **when** and **where** are not issues that should be of great significance for us or worry us much.

For us humans, many aspects of life are still all a big mystery, wrapped in a conundrum, and will remain so until we die. This is why it is important for all of us to have our lives grounded on facts and in truth, which in turn should be based on solid evidence. Otherwise, we can go in all crazy directions, with crazy ideas that can lead to great sadness. This chapter has indicated that there are many aspects of "pre-history" that are hidden from us now, and humanity must hope that future generations can glean a clearer picture of the truth. For now we must concentrate on what philosophy, science, reason, and revelation indicates to be true. We have a God who loves us infinitely. Eternity and Heaven await us after death, but there is also a Hell. If you are having problems accepting that Jesus Christ is truth, and it is He who points out what your true path in life should be, please, I urge you again, to study the messages of The Virgin Mary, His mother. These messages are factual and She is like a great signpost, always pointing the way to Her Son and to truth. This way leads to joy and to Heaven and tells us that: "If you knew how much you are loved, you would die of joy." For the sake of you and yours, make sure you follow the direction indicated by this signpost.

18. The Money Problem

History doesn't repeat itself but it does rhyme

Mark Twain

I had a great Glaswegian friend many years ago, who used to say, "Money is no damn good, but it is handy for doing the messages." Money is a human invention for the facilitation of exchange of goods and wealth. Usually it is of no value of itself, rather it has an agreed value based on various designs on paper or coins and of course, it is much more convenient than exchanging objects of barter. It is valuable because we feel completely confident that others will accept it in exchange for goods of a particular value or price.

In China some form of currency has been used for 3,000 years and some form of paper money for 1,000 years. In 600 B.C. the King of Lydia in Asia Minor, had coins made from electrum (a natural mixture of silver and gold), which dramatically increased internal and external trade and made him very rich. The first paper money issued by European governments was issued for North American colonies in order to facilitate trade.

Were tulips responsible for the first financial bubble? The first tulips came to Europe from Turkey via Vienna in 1554. In Holland in particular, tulips rapidly became an expensive luxury item at a time when commercial international trade was booming. It normally takes 6 to 12 years to grow a flowering bulb from seed and each bulb only produces a few buds (offsets), so producing large numbers can be slow. By the mid 1630's the rare bulbs became extremely expensive – some single bulbs reaching a price equivalent of 25,000 euro in the currency of today. A futures market was also developed and contracts were agreed to buy particular tulip bulbs, months in advance. The whole tulip fiasco at the time illustrated how insane people can get when putting value on certain items. These events were described in 1841, by Charles MacKay, a British journalist, in a book called, *Extraordinary Popular Delusions and the Madness of Crowds.* Among many stories related about this time of tulip mania, there were many about the impoverished becoming rich and the rich becoming poor overnight. There was one sad story about an unfortunate sailor who saw a chance to grab a measly breakfast and ate what he thought was an onion. Later he discovered his error and found himself in jail for eating a tulip bulb. The cost of his breakfast would apparently have paid for a whole ship's crew for one year,

As a microbiologist, I was interested to discover that the unusual colour stripes which made some bulbs very expensive were due to an infection by a plant mosaic virus, referred to as a tulip breaking virus. This virus also made them more difficult to cultivate. In February of 1637, prices for tulip bulbs collapsed abruptly. It was said that this was due to a failure of buyers to turn up at a sale in Harlem, which was in turn due to a rumour of an outbreak of bubonic plague. It was interesting therefore that, to some extent at least, the cause of the tulip financial bubble was a virus and the bursting of that bubble was caused by a bacterium. Very small things can have big effects.

The Financial World

Understanding the complexity of world finance at the moment is not easy and it is made more difficult by the wide range of different complicated financial schemes designed over the years in order to encourage investors. The world of finance is also complicated by the wide range of financial and economic terms used, and by the enormous volumes of financial commentary printed on a daily basis. This commentary generally gives the impression to the general public that economists are in control and that any current problems will ultimately be sorted without too much pain. It should be helpful, firstly, to look at the origin of some of the problems, and then to look at where we are now, and where we are likely to be going.

Historical

When the value of money was linked to gold, credit was limited and restricted to individuals and countries which could show evidence of ability to repay. Interest rates were also stabilised for many decades through this linkage of currency with gold as neither governments or central banks manipulated interest rates.

All countries, with the notable exception of the US, went off the Gold standard in 1914. This caused chaos in markets and rapid price increases, but it was not until the roaring 1920's that the debt to Gross Domestic Product (GDP) ratio rose rapidly and this had doubled by the early 30's. In 1920 the only currency which could be exchanged for gold was the US dollar and the resistance of European banks to limit debt or return to a proper gold standard led to rapid inflation in European countries, with the exception of France. In 1922, in Genoa, a new gold exchange monetary system was established, solely for the purpose of international money exchange, in an effort to at least bring some stability to international monetary markets. In the 20's stock prices also rose by a factor of almost six until 1929, when stock values crashed by a factor of almost nine. In this crash, GDP also fell much more rapidly than debt, many businesses failed and there was massive unemployment.

The inevitable collapse of the gold exchange monetary system, set up in 1922, came in 1931. This happened when France, worried about inflation in the UK, requested gold in exchange for sterling reserves. The UK could not comply and so the whole system collapsed. This collapse was well expected as no country can operate with fixed exchange rates, open capital accounts and interest rates under national control, which in turn would result in wide variation in inflation rates, - the so called **Impossible Trinity**. The imbalances grew between, gold holdings, credit, and trade until all credence in the gold standard was lost.

In 1944, Bretton Woods developed the next monetary system by giving governments and central banks complete control of money supplies. The plan was that government interventions could reduce unemployment and keep it low. The International Monetary Fund (IMF) and the International Bank for Reconstruction and Development (IBRD), later to become the World Bank, were also set up to assist governments with stabilizing exchange rates. This period, after WWII up to the 1960s, was a time of great growth rates in Europe and North America.

The dollar was to be the reserve currency until a proper gold standard could be reintroduced but this meant that price stability generally depended on US price stability. Inflation rates rose rapidly in the US between 1965 and 1970 and this put great inflationary pressure on other countries. Milton Friedman suggested that the only way to maintain price stability, and prevent US inflation rates being exported to other countries, was to have flexible exchange rates. This resulted in President Nixon breaking completely all links to a gold standard reference on August 15th 1971.

The stability that the gold reference had imposed was now gone and global capital moved towards the countries with high interest rates. Furthermore some countries, either by using closed capital accounts or manipulating the exchange rate of their currencies, or both of these, began to increase exports more and more and to amass great profits. In contrast other countries became borrowers and spenders. By 2007 the borrowing and spending had reached a limit which resulted in the beginning of the recession which is still progressing.

It has been said that the depression of 1920-1921, which followed World War I and the flu pandemic, was short because all bad debts were cancelled and the banks were quickly recapitalised. It has also been said that government intervention in the 1929 financial crash in the US made things worse and because of lack of government intervention in Europe things were not as bad. The message is that markets can correct economic imbalances and government interventions in an effort to prevent deflation often can make the problem worse.

Some Common Financial Terms

In order to get an understanding of the complexities and major problems that now exist in the global financial system, it may be helpful for some, to firstly get a simple understanding of some of the common terms used.

Derivatives: This is a complicated contract that derives its value from an underlying asset. It is an agreement between a buyer and a seller on how much the price of a particular asset will change over a period of time. The assets can be many and varied. It is estimated that derivative trading is now worth at least $600 trillion or ten times the total global economic output. The great majority of large companies use derivatives to lower risks of trading and even to protect themselves against change in interest rates or currency exchange rates. Derivative markets have created a mythical money synthetic banking system which has assets about 15 times the quantity of total global real money. This synthetic system takes over the real money banking system and mistakes with the synthetic or mythical system can cause a collapse of the real system as happened with Lehman Brothers and the collapse of the insurance giant, American International Group (AIG).

Deleveraging: This refers to the reduction of the percentage debt and is the opposite of *leveraging* which is the practice of borrowing money to acquire assets. Thus leveraging allows the acquiring of assets with increase in profits in good times but can lead to major losses in bad times due to the obligation to service high levels of debt. Deleveraging of an economy refers to the reduction of debts in multiple sections of the economy at the same time. When it follows a financial crisis it usually leads to recession.

Collateralized Debt Obligations (CDOs): These are complicated financial bundles of repackaged loans sold on, by banks, to investors on the secondary market. They are referred to as "collateralized" because these loans are expected to be repaid. The bundles consist of all kinds of mixtures of home loans, credit card debts, car loans etc. The advantages for the banks are:
   a. CDOs represent a profitable product to sell.
   b. The funds they receive, provides cash for more loans.
   c. The risk of loan defaults moves from the bank to the investors.
CDOs can contribute to an economy by providing liquidity (more resources freed up to invest or loan) and jobs. Computer programmes need to be written to help quantify the value of CDO bundles and sales people need to be employed to sell them.

The problems arise when firstly the CDOs get so complex that nobody knows the real value of them, as the computer models would value on the basis of prices increasing or staying the same. The extra liquidity created, with the easing of borrowing, can also create a financial bubble and items get over-valued. People take easy loans to buy and sell rapidly at a profit. All is well when prices are steady or rising but when the prices of houses begin to fall, for example, as happened in the US in 2006, the confidence in the banks to value CDOs disappears rapidly and the value of CDOs also drops. In the US the subprime housing mortgages were the first to default. So called subprime mortgages were those given to borrowers who were "subprime", that is, not good candidates for a loan and many of these were interest only loans. This was a badly needed adjustment to house prices at the time, but the major problems arose because of the multiplier effect that derivatives have (in this case the CDOs were the derivatives) on financial bubbles. CDOs are a special kind of derivative, that is, they derive their value from their underlying collateralized loans. Banks refused to lend to each other because they no longer wanted unpredictable CDOs on their balance sheets. The result was the 2007 Banking Liquidity Crisis. The housing slump spread to the stock market via hedge fund investments. All this led to the 2008 financial crisis and global recession.

Credit Default Swaps (CDSs): These were designed to transfer credit exposure from one party to another. The buyer of the CDS makes payments to the seller until the maturity date of the contract. In return the seller agrees that, in the event of a default by the debt issuer, to pay the security's premium as well as interest payments between that time and the date of the security's maturation. A CDS is the most common form of credit derivative and is referred to as a credit derivative contract. It is good to remember, therefore, for the sake of clarification, that selling a CDS on a CDO, for example, means running the same financial risk as owning the CDO. A CDS is insurance against non-payment. CDS trading can get very complex and the fact that they are unregulated means that they are prone to a lot of speculation.

Put & Call Options: A "put" option is a contract giving the owner the right but not the obligation to sell a specified amount of shares at a specified price within a specified time. A "call" option is the opposite, giving the owner the right but not the obligation to buy shares within similar agreed time and price parameters. There are a number of variations on these options but all are essentially a way of gambling on how share prices can go up or down without actually buying the shares. The options cost some money but if there is a big movement in share prices in the right direction a big profit can be made. On the other hand if the price movement is stationary or in the wrong direction then the only loss is the price of the option.

Shorts & Shorting: Short selling (also known as going short or shorting) is a sale of shares (or a security of some kind) NOT OWNED by the seller. The seller borrows the shares to sell and this is motivated by the belief that the price of these shares will fall. When the sale is made the seller is said to be "short" these shares. When the price drops the seller buys back the shares at a lower price and returns the shares to the original owner. The seller makes a profit on the difference between the selling price and the buy-back price, but he also will have to pay some commission for borrowing which will reduce the profit margin a little. Should the price increase the seller will lose as he will have to buy the shares back at a higher price. In contrast to the traditional salesman, therefore, who likes to "buy low and sell high", the short-seller likes to "sell high and buy (back) low".

Shorting, therefore, is based on the belief that the price of particular shares will decline. If you hear of a smart trader going short on some shares, therefore, expect the value of these shares to drop. Going "short" is considered the opposite of going "long". In terms of stocks therefore, long positions are those that are OWNED and short positions are those that are OWED. When an investor uses "put" or "call" option contracts, long and short positions have slightly different meanings. One can also combine long and short with different securities in order to create leverage and hedge against losses. It obviously can get very complicated.

The morality of short selling is sometimes questioned and rumour spreading in order to drive a stock lower is illegal. Short selling, however, can contribute liquidity to the markets and prevent stocks from being overpriced by "the madness of crowds".

Ponzi Schemes: These are fraudulent systems of investment whereby profits are paid to investors from new investors coming into the schemes. The schemes inevitably collapse when investments slow down or when the instigator or promoter can no longer be found. They have a similar structure to a pyramid scheme. An economic bubble is also similar to a ponzi scheme as one investor gets paid by a subsequent investor, with ever increasing unrealistic prices, until there is a collapse. Unlike the typical ponzi scheme, however, the economic bubble cannot be blamed on single individuals.

Hedge Funds

These are privately owned companies that pool investors' money and re-invest it in sophisticated financial systems with a view to outperforming the average market returns. Hedge funds are not publicly or otherwise well regulated as they are privately owned and thus carry more risk. On the other hand they are also able to take more risks in the way money is invested and it is this freedom that attracts investors. Hedge fund managers get rewarded with a percentage of the profits and they tend to be very good at using all kinds of derivatives, futures contracts and CDO's etc. in order to make profits. Managers still get their basic salary even when they lose or do not make profits so they have a continual incentive to take risks.

Hedge funds contributed significantly to the financial crisis in 2008. They owned lots of mortgage backed securities which they thought were protected by a derivative insurance system known as *credit default swaps* (CDS). The owners of the CDS were overwhelmed, however, because of the huge number of mortgage defaults in the US so the market for CDS collapsed. (example AIG). Many banks also had hedge fund subdivisions in an effort to make more profits. This ultimately was the cause of the collapse of Lehman Brothers in 2008, causing global stocks to drop sharply.

Long-Term Capital Management Hedge Fund (LTCM): In the 1990s, this was a very large and famous hedge fund with assets greater than $100 billion and described as "above suspicion". Among the principal share holders were two Nobel Prize winning economists. Like all hedge funds, however, the high risks that are taken, means that they cannot guard against unforeseen serious, major or sometimes even moderately unusual financial events. When Russia devalued its' currency and defaulted on its' bonds, in 1998, US stocks dropped 20% and European stocks dropped 35%. LTCM rapidly lost 50% of its value and the large numbers of pension funds and banks who had invested in LTCM were threatened with bankruptcy. Bear Stearns Bank, who managed all of LTCM derivatives, got worried that they would lose everything and called in a $500 million payment which was impossible for LTCM. The entire banking and financial system was in danger of collapse when the Federal Reserve decided to intervene. Once the large financial firms realized that the Fed would bail them out, when and if they got into serious trouble, then they became even more inclined to take risks. The LTCM crisis was an early warning and it was the precedent to the need for Fed bank bailouts of 2008.

Hedge funds employ a wide range of complicated investment strategies that are continually changing and evolving. Even though they are not sold to the general public or retail investors, the global funds had risen to an estimated $2.4 trillion by 2013. When the high level of risk taking is measured with the complicated inter connections with other investment and banking systems, it has to be asked, are hedge funds building a disaster waiting to happen?

Fractional Reserve Banking

This is the common way by which banks operate and has existed for many centuries. Banks only hold a fraction of the money that has been deposited, based on the premise (and the hope) that not all depositors will want to withdraw their money at the same time. This allows these banks to make loans, both long-term and short-term, as well as providing immediate liquidity for depositors. The interest earned on the loans is then passed on to the depositors at a lower interest rate, while taking a percentage profit for the bank. If depositors wish to withdraw more money than the banks have in reserve, this is generally referred to as a **bank run** and governments, through their central banks, usually act to provide funds of last resort to these banks. It is in the interest of governments, therefore, to regulate and oversee the practice of commercial banks so that sufficient funds are held in reserve. Fractional reserve banking also allows the money supply to grow beyond the amount of money created by the government. For the maintenance of financial stability, therefore, governments should regulate limits for credit creation by imposing reserve requirements and capital adequacy ratios.

Glass-Steagall

The Glass-Steagall Act refers to a US Banking Act of 1932 and 1933 limiting affiliations between commercial banks securities firms. The restrictions of this act were gradually lifted by the Federal Reserve until it became no longer appropriate. In 1998, the merger of Citigroup with Travelers Insurance was the final reason to repeal the Glass-Steagall Act. In 2013, Bryan Marsal, who was the banker responsible for administering the bankruptcy of Lehman Brothers in 2008, said that he had supported the repeal of Glass-Steagall until he saw what happened to Lehman (14th Sept., German press). Others now also see the separation of big banks into deposit and investment banks as the only way of saving deposits from an impending global financial eruption. It seems to be a race against time and time may already have run out. Bail-in legislation is now accepted widely and bank deposits, from now on, will be confiscated to save failing bank investments.

Credit Cycles

In 1974, Hyman Minsky identified three forms of debt financing in the evolution of credit cycles.[217]

1. Hedge - Principal and interest can be paid from income.
2. Speculative - Interest can be paid from income but there is a need for liquid financial markets to pay the principal.
3. Ponzi - Neither interest nor principal can be paid from the income. The price of the asset needs to rise for payments to be possible.

Defaults are rare with 1 but common with 3.

Ominous Signs

The approach of governments to the present global financial crisis is to prevent deflation by taking big international loans and by printing more money where possible, but this is only increasing the debt dramatically. Government efforts to solve the problems of excessive debt by borrowing have created a Ponzi debt for many countries. Many banks, even the larger ones, are too weak to survive a Ponzi scheme collapse. Debt write-offs and bank recapitalisation would cause collapse followed by dramatic deflation.

A report in July 2016, by the McKinsey Global Institute, indicated that the economies of two thirds of households in 25 advanced economies have not risen or are below the levels for 2005. Italy was the worst with 97% not risen, US was 81%, UK and Netherlands were 70%, and Sweden was 20%.

In its annual report the UN conference on trade and development (Sept. 22nd 2016), noted that: "There remains a risk of deflationary spirals in which capital flight, currency devaluations and collapsing asset prices would stymie growth and shrink government revenues. As capital begins to flow out, there is now a real danger of entering a third phase of the financial crisis." Jim Rickards, the CIA's financial threat and asymmetric warfare adviser and author of the best seller, *The Death of Money*, believes that the US economy has reached what he calls, a "super critical state." He believes that smart investors, like Warren Buffett are taking emergency measures now before a historic economic meltdown strikes, which he and his colleagues fear is now inevitable and he believes that an economic crash is now imminent.

The Deutsche Bank was listed by the IMF in June 2016 (Country Report No. 16/189) as the highest contributor to systemic risks, among the Globally Systemically Important Banks (GSIBs). This was followed in order by, HSBC, Credit Suisse, JP Morgan, Goldman Sachs, Bank of America, BNPP aribas, Santander, Bank of NY Mellon, Morgan Stanley, Soc Gen, Credit Agricole, Wells Fargo, Citigroup, and Nordea.

Since January 2016, the EU Bank Recovery and Resolution Directive (BRRD) is now preventing EU governments from bailing out banks without first taking large contributions from shareholders and bondholders. Between 15% and 20% of Italian bank loans are now classed as "non performing" (NPLs) which amounts to approximately 360 billion euros. The equivalent in France is less than 5%, 3% in Germany, and less than 2% in the UK. One of the oldest banks in the world, and one of the largest in Italy, Banca Monte dei Paschi di Siena (BMPS) now has an NPL rate of 30%, equivalent to 50 billion euro. The credit rating of this bank from Moody is now one notch above default. The exposure of French banks to Italian debt, at least 250 billion euro, is the highest in Europe so problems in Italy could also mean immediate problems in France.

German banks are suffering badly from negative interest rates. The two largest banks, Deutsche and Commerzbank have experienced very sharp drops in their share value in 2016. Deutsche also has the largest derivative holdings of any bank in the world (approximately 42 trillion euro compared to a German GDP of 3 trillion) and confidence in this bank seemed to be losing ground rapidly (end of September – early October 2016). This bank is so highly interlinked to other major global banks that a failure of this bank would likely lead to a global financial catastrophe.

Need for Investment Return & Interest Rate Balance

For capitalism to function, it is necessary to have saving and investment. For these two activities to function properly there needs to be a proper balance between interest rates and returns on investment. Some will opt for saving with good interest, while others will opt for investment with good prospects of return with minimal risks. Natural rates of interest reward savers and debtors. **Low profits** lead to less borrowing and thus interest rates fall in an effort by the banks to encourage borrowing. The lower interest rates also give less incentive to save. **High profits** have the opposite consequences.

The problem at the moment is that bank interest rates are hovering around 0% in an effort to stimulate economies. This is not an incentive to save. Some banks are giving a negative interest rate which is giving even a stronger incentive to remove money from the bank as leaving it there is a way of reducing the deposit. Despite this, global economies are still very sluggish. The object generally seems to be to bring everything back in balance with a magic inflation figure of 2% but the big world economies, despite years of effort are still not succeeding.

These near 0% interest rates are also producing a number of new problems. First among these is the loss of large amounts of badly needed revenue to banks, which either have no money to lend, or are lending at very low interest rates. Secondly many borrowers at the moment could be described as "sub-prime", to borrow a phrase from the recent mortgage financial debacle. Many are borrowing relatively small sums because of the low interest, which for the moment is keeping the wheels of commerce turning, but many of these loans are for spending on goods and not for good productive investment and thus many may not be repaid. Small sums can add up and the global debt of 200 trillion dollars continues to increase. David Smith, the economics editor of The Sunday Times summed it up well when he said (7/2/16) that negative interest rates were "a good way of persuading people and businesses that something is badly wrong."

Leigh Skene and Melissa Kidd[217] have listed seven unintended consequences of excessive low interest rates, which I summarize as follows:

1. Proliferation of zombie companies taking markets away from productive companies.
2. Instilling false confidence in governments.
3. Encouraging commercial and shadow banks to lend to unqualified borrowers.
4. Overly pervasive central bank activity, making it difficult to establish true market pricing and thus making economic and financial analysis superfluous.
5. A double whammy hit on pension plans and life insurance companies by lowering assumed receipts and raising assumed liabilities.
6. Printing money which increases income inequality and gives political power to those who redistribute wealth, from poor to rich, such as too big to fail bankers. This is the opposite to the trickledown effect of wealth which monetary stimulus is supposed to create.
7. The credit created by very low interest rates in excess of saving in any given period, creates bad debt.

Why Global Collapse Looks Inevitable.

The following is a short list of observation that together point towards an inevitable global financial collapse:

a) Banking is based on the bedrock of confidence. Greed is a driving force. If goodwill and confidence decline, then greed becomes a driving force for collapse.
b) Banks should work within the legal regulations, but experience has shown that banks can sometimes work outside the law, especially:
1) When the risk of being caught is low, and the opportunities for large profits are high.
2) When the banks are "too big to fail" or executives are "too big to jail" and bail-outs or bail-ins are guaranteed.
c) There is a major Inter-linkage between the larger globally systemically important financial institutions.
d) It is likely that there are still some fraudulent transactions to be made known.
e) Many large banks are in a bad place because of over commitment to derivatives and/or non performing loans.
f) The current very low interest rates combined with high debt represent a high risk. If and when interest rates increase, it has been said that the global ponzi system of insolvent banks supporting insolvent governments will collapse.
g) The "too big to fail" financial institutions that had to be bailed out in 2008/9 are now said to be at least 25% bigger and more dangerous than ever.

Some other worrying indicators are as follows:

Imports and exports from China are also falling dramatically and the monetary easing (printing of money) is also failing to turn this economy around. This is very significant as the increased demand from China and dropping the interest rates were quoted as the great reasons for the "recovery" from the 2008 financial crisis.

The situation in the US is also bad. It has often been quoted that it took 200 years for the US debt to reach 8.5 trillion dollars but this has doubled under Obama. In the US money supply has increased 400% since 2006, all created from nothing by the Federal controlled printing-press. 75% of Americans now have no savings and are living paycheque to paycheque. Figures from the Census Bureau indicate that 52% of workers make less than $30,000 /year and 49% are receiving some form of government benefit every month. Nevertheless, Obama still claims, that anybody who says that the US economy is doing poorly is "peddling fiction".

Alan Greenspan, the former head of the Federal Reserve, the IMF, and the World Bank have all warned about a coming global financial crisis. A recent report on a consensus view from all 16 branches of US intelligence, which includes the army, navy, CIA and FBI, has come to the attention of the public. Impact planning is being put in place for the fall of the dollar as the global reserve currency and the loss of the US superpower status. The scenario includes a worldwide economic crash and a period of global anarchy.

The Japanese Prime Minister, Shinzó Abe, also believes that we are on the brink of a massive global financial collapse. At a G7 meeting in May, 2016, he suggested that a public warning should be issued so that people can prepare for this eventuality. His suggestion was ignored, however, and his comments went virtually unreported by the politically controlled global mainstream media.

The global financial system at the moment is like a badly damaged and entangled piece of string. It is entangled in its own complexities and there are no lose ends in sight, which could help unravel it. It is very complex but at the same time the eventual outcome is now becoming obvious. It cannot survive as it is.

Collapse seems inevitable. The complexities have introduced not one but a number of layers of **Catch 22** into the system which now makes recovery very difficult. There is always the hope that the global economy can recover very slowly but the greed and corruption within financial institutions will probably prevent this. It is likely, therefore, that we are now going through the last spasmodic kicks of this dying elephant of global finance. It seems to me that there are two significant forces still keeping the system going, and the wheels of commerce turning. Both of these are not solutions but are only storing up major problems for the near future. The first is the cheap loans, which as explained above, many will be left unpaid. The second is that many of those, who are lucky enough to have some savings at the moment, are taking those savings out of the banks. Trust for the banks is disappearing rapidly and interest rates are negligible. In many cases the withdrawn money is being used for short term projects or luxury items, most of which will be a draw rather than a contribution to personal and household budgets going forward. The savings are thus disappearing rapidly and the banks can only get more money for their bad loans, if it is printed.

I would like to quote from a comment made by Charlie Johnston,[218] who was a former adviser to President Ronald Reagan, which he made in October 2014:

"In all cases, however, the only real wealth is the goods and services produced by the economy. Ideally, the supply of currency should rise in a roughly parallel relationship to increasing productivity. Any time there is a prolonged distortion to that relationship, the economy is sick. If you have a prolonged period where the money supply is growing much faster than actual productivity, it is a serious cancer on the economy involved. If the issues are not resolved, sudden catastrophic collapse will always come. Some of the more notable examples in the last 150 years have been Germany's Weimar Republic, Pancho Villa's Mexico, most recently Yugoslavia and, in American history, the Confederate dollar near the end of the Civil War. In each of these cases officials were desperately trying to prop up a dying economy by creating more currency which gave the illusion of health for a time, until a series of sudden jolts revealed the currency for the flimsy paper it was and all confidence in its value collapsed. Societies broke apart, wars erupted, rioting spread like wildfire as people would desperately try to trade a wheelbarrow full of currency for a loaf of bread. It is very simple...If production continues to decline while currency supplies continue to rise, there will be a disaster unless it is stopped in time. This is an iron rule."

I have a priest friend in Zimbabwe who employs large numbers of workers, building schools, houses and churches. When inflation really took hold in this country some years ago, he described to me having to take young men with wheelbarrows to the bank in order to take away the currency notes, which multiplied dramatically each week.

How Will The Collapse Happen?

The rise of interest rates is likely to be the significant turning point. This could be the last straw that breaks the camel's back. It could also be something different, however, and something very small, like a small rumour. I noted above, in relation to the tulip bubble of the seventeenth century, that small things can have big effects. I remind myself also that, *Napoleon's retreat from Moscow was started by a louse*. The rumour could be true or false and there is now no need to invent a false rumour as there are plenty of facts in the financial system at the moment, which if enough people know and believe, will bring the whole house of cards crashing down. If I was to say to you that the money you deposited in your bank is no longer there and furthermore is no longer legally yours, you would not get upset because you would not believe it, and you could prove me wrong, by withdrawing your deposit. It depends on the rumour therefore, who instigates it? Who promotes it? And who believes it?

One thing now seems very likely. When the collapse does come, it will be planned. The Global Financial Elite are very much aware of the problems and they believe that they are in control. There is no bank or financial institution, no matter how large, and no country that cannot be destroyed financially within days, if not hours, by this Global Financial Elite.

The Big Short

This is a title of a book by Michael Lewis, written in 2010, describing how renegades, mavericks, manipulators, visionaries, and chancers, foresaw the 2007 financial collapse, bet against the banking system, and made a mint.[219] He had previously written, *Liar's Poker*, which was a book on a similar topic, describing how bond traders in Wall Street, operating in a cloud of unknowing and aided by large numbers of inexperienced young graduates, were packaging and gambling enormous sums of US debts, between an endless parade of rogue traders, and getting outrageous bonuses for their efforts. It should have been obvious that it could not be sustained, but few wanted to believe that the collapse was coming. Michael Lewis has now written several best sellers, a number of which have been the basis of popular films, which includes, *The Big Short.*

In this book Michael Lewis describes how the false valuation of CDOs was one of the biggest problems and the ultimate cause of the financial crash of 2007/8. These are a special type of derivative – (see above for an explanation of the terms). On the 19th July 2007, Ben Bernanke, the Fed chairman, told the US Senate that he saw no more than $100 billion losses in the subprime mortgage market. Two days before, Steve Eisman (described, by a Wall Street analyst, as one of the very few investors, in Wall Street, who knew what was going on in the US financial world), said that he expected losses up to $300 billion in the mezzanine CDO slice of the market alone. The mezzanine CDOs referred to, are those on the 'floor' below the top floor or floors (in the theoretical towers of debt) with a credit rating of double or triple B as opposed to the triple A rating of the top floor. In other words, default on the loans with triple B is more likely than with triple A.

At this time also, investors in the collapsed Bear Stearns hedge funds were told that their $1.6 billion in triple A rated subprime – backed CDOs were now completely worthless. Steve Eisman was convinced that the biggest firms in Wall Street were now unaware of their own risks. Nobody knew what was in, or the real value of, CDOs. CDOs were composed of various collections (traunches) of loans, many already shorted, wrapped up into various portfolios and sold on by the banks. Nobody knew the real value of these various CDOs but, nevertheless, they were sold to gullible investors.

CDOs have been a great source of funds for banks as well as a useful way of passing on financial risks to others. The idea was reasonable enough until greed took over. Then complicated mechanisms were concocted in order to lend larger and larger sums of money to poorer and poorer earners who would obviously never be able to repay these loans. These large sums appeared on the accounts as large loans and they were bundled into CDOs after getting high credit ratings for some unknown reason. In the movie of *The Big Short*, it was clearly suggested that if the rating agencies did not give the banks the triple A ratings required, then the banks just moved business to a rating agency that would. Some suggested that rating agencies had left their posts, were morally bankrupt, and scared of becoming actually bankrupt. Others suggested that the rating agencies were either clueless or crooks. At this stage the whole system was suffering from a significant amount of dishonesty and fraud. The inevitable happened and CDOs became worthless. This was the result of a system built on greed and secular morality with poor policing. The more complicated the systems were the less likely individuals could be blamed and the banks rightly judged that the tax payers could not let them fail. Homes and job losses was not the concern of greedy financial institutions manned by secular minded selfish robots.

Dr. Michael Burry: The story of this interesting man is described in The Big Short. Mike had a medical degree (MD) and he was now working in finance. He had been the first investor to diagnose the disorder in the American financial system in early 2003. He had a glass eye secondary to an injury he got at a football game, when in college. This seemed to be at least one of the reasons for the difficulty he had with social interaction. It was only when his four year old son was diagnosed with Asperger's Syndrome (AS) that he realized that he also had the same problem. His obsessive acquisition of hard facts and his compulsive ability to read the detail in tedious financial statements were all due to his own AS. Ironically, his AS became a "gift" in trying to understand the problems emerging in the US financial system. Mike said, "Only someone who has Asperger's would read a subprime mortgage bond prospectus." Mike eventually made many billions from the financial crisis of 2007 – 2008.

Ireland

In Ireland we are used to rumours. A recent book, published by one of the Government insiders, dealing with the machinations surrounding the bailout of Irish banks in 2010, has been very revealing. After Irish Banks ran into problems in the second half of

2008, efforts were made to sort out a recovery plan with Europe. In early Nov 2008, the Irish Government was negotiating with Mr Olli Rehn, (EU Commissioner for Economic and Monetary Affairs) and Mr Jean Claude Trichet (president of the European Central Bank) and a provisional plan for a four year programme was part of this discussion. Suddenly, "out of the blue", a rumour spread worldwide, mainly from the G20, in Korea, that Ireland had applied for a bailout, which was completely untrue. The source of the rumour, surprise, surprise, was unknown, but it was circulated and accepted widely in the financial press, without question of authenticity. Confidence in Irish shares crashed and as a result huge sums began to flow out from Irish Banks, and a bailout then became inevitable. The Irish Banks lost a total of **133 billion euro** in market and deposit funding.[220] It was the same kind of music, but with a slightly different tune, that the American Banks were dancing with a few years earlier. It was another 'big short'. A number of people 'in the know' made a lot of money by 'shorting' Irish bank shares before the rumour was spread and before the crash. This time Irish taxpayers were paying the piper. It was of course illegal to spread false rumours which could undermine confidence in the Irish banking system, but if these rumours came from some influential people in Wall Street or at the G20, nobody was likely to identify the culprits. Prosecutions never happen so making money at the expense of the Irish was easy. It is likely that these kinds of events will continue in many other countries until the global economic system is either fixed or collapses. The driving force of greed will probably prevent it being fixed, so it will inevitably collapse. Kevin Cardiff, Secretary-General, in Ireland's Department of Finance at the time made the following comment:[220]

"It is one of the saddest things about modern Government that in an era when we speak so much about accountability, transparency, freedom of information, and when real progress has been made in these areas, the unattributed leak, or campaign of leaks, protected by the anonymity of journalists' sources, can be used by often unelected and unaccountable people to damage reputations, to muddy waters and create a sense of crisis to force the pace of decisions that ought to be made in a considered and deliberate manner... Who was in Korea, announcing falsely that the Irish Government had decided to seek a bailout? Who, in Korea or elsewhere, was taking these false rumours and putting them into the hands of media and financial commentators?"

Over the next two years, plans were then gradually put in place for a deal on a bailout. By November 2010, the Irish government was in favour of forcing losses on senior as well as subordinated bank bondholders. The IMF was supportive and 30 billion euro was suggested as the figure to be retrieved from the bondholders. A world leading lawyer with extensive experience in this type of financial retrieval, Lee Buchheit, came to Dublin to help with this project, quietly arranged by the IMF. An international discussion (not reported to the Irish) then took place between Dominique Strauss-Kahn (IMF managing director), Tim Geithner (US treasury secretary), Jean-Claude Trichet (ECB president), and others. Trichet and Geithner in particular were opposed to this solution. It is somewhat ironic that this is the kind of solution that is now being imposed in Europe in 2016, when banks get into financial difficulty. The bailout then went ahead at great cost to Irish taxpayers. The unanswered question remains, could Ireland have avoided the bailout? The answer seems to be that the bailout should not have happened and the ECB President and the US Treasury Secretary, for whatever reason, did no favours for Ireland.

Mr Ajai Chopra was the main IMF negotiator in Ireland's bailout plan. This was at the end of a thirty year career with the IMF. Since retiring, he has severely criticised how the European Central Bank treated the Irish taxpayers. Mr Chopra said that the Eurozone partners had prevented the Irish from imposing haircuts on senior creditors of insolvent banks and that it is unfair to impose the burden of supporting banks primarily on domestic taxpayers, while senior unguaranteed bank bond holders get paid out. This not only adds to sovereign debt, but also creates political problems, making it harder to sustain fiscal adjustment.

Mr Rossa White, chief economist at the National Treasury Management Agency (NTMA) said in the Irish Times (7th Feb. 2011) that the Irish State liabilities were repeatedly overstated by Bloomberg and other media outlets by wrongly using liabilities from International Banks and other financial institutions working in Ireland, which the Irish State had no responsibility for. The debt figures promoted were $880 billion, that is, 410% of the GDP, when the real figure was closer to only 100% of GDP, a figure well less than the average in Europe. Countries like China and Japan, meanwhile, had debt to GDP ratios of between 200 to 300% with apparently no need for a bail-out.

There was one other important event, which is likely to have been significant in the eventual outcome of the Irish negotiations for a financial bailout. This was a secret Trilateral Commission Meeting (part of the Global International Financial Elite) held in Dublin, for the first time ever, 7th – 9th May, 2010. There was a complete blackout on media reporting of this meeting, by those who have complete control of National and International media outlets. It is now almost impossible, however, to keep these meetings completely secret. If we are to believe the unintentional "leaks", a number of headings were on the agenda. Some of the items discussed were, "Change Ireland", "We are deciding the future of the world", and "We need a World Government." One could be very charitable and suggest that the reason the Trilateral Commission selected Dublin in 2010 was to help Ireland with bailout difficulties. Secrecy and control, however, rather than charity is the driving force of the Trilaterals.

Conclusion

The sad news, therefore, is that we seem to be on the cusp of a very major global financial crash. How can a system, which is so poorly regulated, so full of greed, fraud, and general dishonesty stand? The system at the moment is designed to make the rich and the dishonest richer, while the poor get poorer.

In 1985, Cardinal Joseph Ratzinger, the future Pope Benedict XVI, said that the present global economic system cannot survive without a proper ethical and moral discipline. At a public discussion forum on the Church and the economy he said:

"It is becoming an increasingly obvious fact of economic systems which concentrate on the common good, depend on a determinate ethical system, which in turn can be born and sustained only by strong religious convictions. Conversely, it has also become obvious that the decline of such discipline can actually cause the laws of the market to collapse. An economic policy that is ordered not only for the good of the group – indeed, not only to the common good of a determinate state – but to the common good of the family of man, demands a maximum of ethical discipline and thus a maximum of religious strength."

Economies, therefore, like societies, whether global or otherwise, that are based on a secular morality will always fail because greed eventually takes over and the only commandment operating is, "don't be caught". It is not just a house divided against itself, rather, it is every individual trying to outsmart all the other players in the game. As Michael Lewis puts it, it is like a big game of poker between liars. More worrying still is the fact that it is not just the global economy but the whole of society now seems to be drifting into this kind of poker game. I now meet more and more people on a daily basis who try to get money off me by giving me amazing crazy stories – lies, I am convinced. It is a very unhappy time, therefore, for those who want to trust or even give the benefit of doubt to others.

The global financial system will probably collapse and when it happens, there will be lots of hardship. If you believe that this is peddling fiction, then time will prove one of us wrong. The further sad news is that honest democracy and honest journalism seem to be also crashing and dying with the global economy. Technology will help to increase the speed of this collapse and reduce dramatically the number of key people needed to pull the plug – so - batten down the hatches.

Finally, I must say that when it comes to global finance, I am no expert. In fact, I am only a fool, who is trying to make some sense of what appears to be objective evidence.

19. The Final Tapestry

God has put obvious limitations on our intelligence, but none whatsoever on our stupidity.

Father John Corappi S.O.L.T.

Life is a mystery but it is a mystery which has been explained to us. Furthermore, the evidence coming with this explanation has been supplied in abundance for those who, in humility, wish to open their minds and hearts and seek it out. This book has largely been concerned with describing a small portion of this evidence. This book has also emphasized the importance of looking for evidence, analysing it and being led in your path of life by it rather than by feelings or prejudice of one kind or another.

There are different kinds of evidence and in turn different qualities associated with the various aspects of this. In chapter 18, for example, evidence was presented indicating that the global financial system will soon collapse. This, however, is to some extent suggestive but no more than speculative. It could be that the International financial system could be set right, if those involved or those with some influence and responsibility for global financial control, could relinquish the greed and stop playing "liars poker" and "big shorts"[219], as described by Michael Lewis. In this regard it is also interesting that a more recent book by Michael Lewis, *The Undoing Project,* is based on a Nobel Prize winning economic theory developed by two Israelis, which illustrates very well how human decision making is not always rational and not always based on objective evidence. Anybody who has a problem believing this should just observe the number of young girls in European towns and cities at this time, who are spending much time and money, so that they can look like tramps. In trying to overcome obstacles to accepting new evidence, therefore, we must first be aware that we all have an irrational streak which we must guard against as well as our intellectual, psychological, and spiritually blind prejudices.

In chapter 10, evidence was presented indicating that UFOs and alien life forms are real and not imaginary. There is now a very large mass of evidence suggesting that this is true and also that International governments, especially the US, have worked hard at obfuscating and covering up this evidence. The absolute confirmation of alien life forms could easily be done when and if the governments, who have reportedly captured these aliens, would release the evidence for public scrutiny. Until this happens, however, the doubt must remain.

This book has also presented much evidence for the apparitions and associated messages of The Virgin Mary. The order of the quality and quantity of evidence associated with this phenomenon, I suggest, is way above the other two examples quoted, and this evidence is such that it should now be accepted as a reality, beyond all reasonable doubt, by rational humanity. Those who do not accept it at this stage, must be regarded as ignorant of the facts, irrational, or just refusing to accept it for their own particular reasons.

If this book has emphasized one aspect of our human spiritual reality more than any other it is to indicate the profound significance of these apparitions of The Virgin Mary as a direct channel of information, which is opening up more and more, between humanity and God. This seems to be part of the plan of God, who through the person of Jesus Christ, came to live among us by becoming flesh in the human body of The Virgin Mary. Mary has been appointed to intercede for humanity before the Holy Trinity, through Her Son. She is the daughter of the Father, the spouse of the Holy Spirit, and the mother of the Son. She is talking to us and guiding us as a mother and as spiritual brothers and sisters of Jesus Christ, with eternal joy and happiness as a right of inheritance. These communications are now happening on a daily basis in a reasonably public way. We must listen to Her. These apparitions, and messages associated with them, are of supreme importance for humanity, therefore, for the following reasons:

1   They are definite events, not imaginations or hallucinations of the mentally disturbed. This certainty comes from the quality and the quantity of the evidence that goes with them collectively as well as with the individual specific events. The scientific, medical and audio-visual evidence, as well as the evidence received from an enormous number of individuals associated with these events, cannot be explained away by the glib comments of scientists, such as Richard Dawkins or Carl Sagan (RIP). On the contrary, they challenge sincere unbelievers and sincere investigators, who will not be able to find a natural explanation for these occurrences, outside of the spiritual realm.

2   They help to confirm a spiritual reality outside of our material world.

3   They confirm the truth of the existence of God and the authority of this God over the universe.

4   They point us towards the Roman Catholic Church, as the only comprehensive source of the one true teaching about God our creator.

5   They confirm the existence of life after death and that there are three possible destinations for our souls, immediately after death, that is, Hell, Purgatory or Heaven. Only Purgatory is not forever as it is for a period of purification only, on the way to Heaven. The reality of Hell is no small matter for every individual, as well as for their families and friends.

6   They warn of a major chastisement if humanity does not repent and respect God's laws. This chastisement now seems inevitable as a result of the global rejection of God and natural law.

7   The chastisement will have two sources. The first will be chaos of human origin and the second will be direct Divine intervention.

8   They promise major supernatural warnings and signs (some to be announced to the world by visionaries, approximately one week in advance), as a last chance to humanity before the final chastisement.

9   The extent of the chastisement will depend on how humanity responds to these signs, but we are urged to prepare now as the time between the warnings and the chastisement will be short, and there may not be time for many to repent and convert.

10 Before these major supernatural events, we can expect the world to drift into chaos, from man-made disasters, especially war, as well as natural disasters.

11 They remind us, how much God loves us individually and because of this great love He is always ready to forgive us, but we must ask for forgiveness.

12 After the coming chastisements these messages announce a coming transformation of the world as we move towards an era of great peace. "In the end, My Immaculate Heart will Triumph".

A major front cover article in *National Geographic* (December 2015), entitled, *Mary – The most powerful woman in the World*, gives a good secular flavour of the International power and popularity of The Virgin Mary. This article discusses the enormous number of world-wide apparitions, messages, and miraculous healings associated with this *"Mother of God"*.

The author of the magazine article, Maureen Orth, described her 59 year old group leader on a trip to Medjugorje. In 2000, this man was a father of 13 and was riddled with cancer, given a few months to live. He was virtually forced to visit Medjugorje, when he was in the depths of depression, by two close friends. This man described how his anxiety and depression lifted completely when he went to confession on the first night of his visit. During the trip he later met one of the Medjugorje visionaries, "Vicka", and he asked for her help. She put her hand on his head and began to pray for him. His two friends also had their hands on him. He felt a tremendous heat go through his body, so much so, that he and his friends began to sweat. Back in Boston, one week later a scan in the Mass. General hospital revealed that his tumours had shrunk to almost nothing. Since then he has visited the shrine 13 times.

The great mystery is why this overwhelming evidence, associated with these visitations of The Virgin Mary, is almost completely ignored? After all, this is the age of instant communications, instant news analysis and instant confirmation of evidence through audio, video and by other scientific and medical investigations. The failure to recognize this evidence has been discussed briefly in previous chapters. Some of the reasons suggested were the strong anti-Catholic bias in the mass-media, a resistance to belief in the supernatural, and an inherent unwillingness by some to confront the truth, because it scares them and challenges their comfortable life styles. Amazingly, many simply do not want to know, regardless of the consequences. There is also the impression of some great hidden force which is keeping humanity in the dark. This may be due to our collective will and inclination to stay in the dark. Frank Allnutt tried to analyse this mysterious force operating on the human mind in his book, *The Force of Star Wars*[221], where he compared "The Force" made popular in Star War films with a real force for good and evil operating in our world. Catholics might describe this mysterious dark force as a lack of Divine grace. Whatever the reasons are, there is no denying the fuzz of confusion which bathes modern society. This confusion often blinds us from the ability to distinguish lies from truth and evil from good and thus keeps us in the dark. Another way of trying to explain why we are inclined to stay in the dark is that, Satan is always tempting us to become more and more immersed in the world. If we concentrate on the ways of the world, we can begin to forget about the things of God and even begin to resent the unworldly ways of Christianity. Christ reminded us that, "God's ways are not man's ways", and He also told us that "Satan is the Prince of this world".

In order to accept the supernatural and a belief in a personal God, there is a requirement for faith. Faith in turn can only be acquired when there is an openness to accept the supernatural, when there is a willingness to perceive the evidence for the supernatural and when there is a willingness to search for the truth, regardless of personal implications. If we ask, we will receive, if we seek, we will find, and if we knock, the door will be opened for us (Lk 11:9). Faith eventually comes as a free gift from God since it concerns the supernatural, which is controlled by God alone. I mentioned in chapter 9 why I have some hope for the conversion of Richard Dawkins (the well-known Oxford atheist), to Catholicism, because he claims to be passionate about the truth. For someone who sincerely and passionately seeks the truth, like St Paul on his way to Damascus, faith is not far away. Like many others, however, Richard falls down in having a closed mind concerning the supernatural and lacking a willingness to investigate the evidence (in this case the evidence for the apparitions and messages of The Virgin Mary). He prefers to make some glib comments, whilst obviously being in complete ignorance of the facts. If he does ever investigate this evidence, he should be prepared for the shock of his life. **G K Chesterton once quipped that those who believe in miracles do so because of the evidence and those who refuse to**

believe in miracles do so because of faith. As there is no rational explanation for miracles, outside of the spiritual realm, the evidence is simply ignored.

The German philosopher, Arthur Schopenhauer, said that all truth goes through three stages. First it is ridiculed, then it is violently opposed and finally it is accepted as self-evident. The messages from The Virgin Mary are at this time ridiculed by many. Others say that it is scaremongering to suggest that the warnings are real. The truth about these messages, which are coming from God to humanity through The Virgin Mary, will eventually be accepted as self-evident, by both prince and pauper alike. Unfortunately, like the genocide and atrocities in Rwanda, in 1994, (forewarned by The Virgin during the Kibeho messages of the previous decade), by that time it will probably be too late. Most of the population of the earth will have died in a cataclysmic tragedy, as forewarned by The Virgin in Akita (see page 172).

Fatima

The centenary year of the great visitation of The Virgin Mary to Fatima will be celebrated during 2017. These Marian apparitions began on the 13th of May, 1917 and the 13th of October, 2017 marks the centenary of the "great sign" of Fatima which confirmed the supernatural nature of these events (see chapter 5). Over the last century, the implications of these events at Fatima in 1917 for the Roman Catholic Church and for the world have been enormous. Two aspects, in particular, of the Fatima secrets and messages have been discussed at length and many volumes have been written on them. These are:

1. The contents of the "Third Secret".
2. The Consecration of Russia to The Immaculate Heart of Mary.

Many would say, with some justification, that these topics have been over-discussed with little benefit for the Catholic Church or the rest of humanity, while other important aspects of the messages have been largely ignored. These other aspects which need more emphasis are:

1. The importance of living good and holy lives within the confines of natural or moral laws.
2. The importance of making reparation to The Holy Trinity for the evil deeds of humanity, especially for sins against The Sacred Heart of Jesus and The Immaculate Heart of Mary. The importance of the Communion of Reparation on Five First Saturdays.
3. The Importance of Consecration to The Immaculate Heart of Mary in order get Divine protection for countries, homes and individuals and generally to attain peace in the world. (The Fatima messages specifically warned about the dangers to humanity from atheistic Communism that was about to begin in Russia. This Communism did begin in Russia with the October Revolution (1917), coincidental with the final Fatima apparition and the miracle that had been predicted).
4. The importance of recognizing that Hell is one of the two final destinations for each soul after life on earth.

The consecration of Russia to The Immaculate Heart of Mary was a special request from God made to the Roman Catholic Church, through Sr Lucia, the only surviving seer of Fatima, in 1929, at Tuy in Spain. The object of this consecration was:

1. The conversion of Russia and thus the prevention of the spread of Russian errors (Communism) across the world.
2. The promotion of peace between nations.
3. The recognition that peace in the world has been entrusted to The Immaculate Heart of Mary.

The significance of St Pope John Paul II in the downfall of Communism in Eastern Europe is worth considering briefly. On June 6th 1944 (D Day) large numbers of Allied troops invaded Europe in order to defeat Hitler. Millions died in that war. Thirty five years later, on June 6th 1979, the Communist Governments of Eastern Europe were invaded by one man. St Pope John Paul II had returned to Poland for the first time since being elected Pope. It was at this time that the power and influence of this Pope began to be appreciated, in the Soviet Union, and the plan to assassinate him was hatched.

St Pope John Paul II was shot coincidentally, on the 13th of May, 1981 (anniversary of The Virgin's first apparition in Fatima in 1917). The time on the clock at the moment of the shooting was 19:17, in Moscow. The connection with the Fatima message was inescapable for the Pope especially when it was later revealed how the track of the bullets seemed to have been miraculously guided. This event renewed the Pope's interest in the Fatima message and eventually led to his Global consecration to The Immaculate Heart of Mary on the 25th March 1984, in union with the Bishops of the world. According to Sr Lucia this consecration was accepted by Heaven but controversy remains, as the name of Russia was not specifically mentioned in the consecration, and Russia is not yet converted. Church experts are divided on this issue of the validity of this consecration, but when it comes to understanding the mind of God we must expect confusion and disagreement among blind humanity. Fr Gobbi,[3] as well as the famous exorcist, Fr Gabriel Amorth (RIP) and many other well-known prelates said that the consecration was not done properly but this view disagrees with Sr Lucia, St Pope John Paul II and many others. It would seem unreasonable to expect that Russia would be converted overnight and there is no doubting the enormous change which has taken place in Russia since this consecration of 1984.

Mikhail Gorbachev became Secretary General of the Soviet Communist Party in March 1985, one year after St Pope John Paul's consecration. He allowed prominent religious leaders to visit Russia, such as St Teresa of Calcutta. He also granted permission to the 50 million Orthodox Christians and the 10 million Roman Catholics to start opening and repairing their churches, in preparation for the 1,000 anniversary of the Russian Orthodox faith. In June, 1989, exactly, ten years after St Pope John Paul II first returned to Poland, as Pope, this country held their first free election since the Communist takeover.

Some Communist hardliners attempted a coup against Gorbachev in August 1991. This coup was defeated on August 22nd (Feast of the Queenship of Mary). A decision to dissolve the Soviet Union was made and acknowledged in the Belavezha accords, on the 8th December (Feast of Mary's Immaculate Conception). At midnight on December 25th (Christmas Day), 1991, the red flag with the hammer and sickle was lowered for the last time over the Kremlin. The Russian Federation replaced the Soviet Union on January 1st 1992 (Feast of the Solemnity of Mary Mother of God) and freedom of religion was granted to all states. It is surely remarkable that this rejection of Communism had taken place so dramatically and peacefully over a few short years. For further information on the progress of Christianity in Russia, see page 50.

We should learn from Fatima

If humanity had responded appropriately to the messages of Fatima, we were told that World War II and the spread of Communism would have been prevented. Very few knew about these messages at the beginning of World War II, and fewer still appreciated what was necessary to prevent the war. Almost nobody recognized the significance of the second great Fatima sign (the great aurora of the Northern Hemisphere), on the 25th of January 1938. When Hitler and his generals, gathered in their mountain headquarters, saw this great aurora lighting up the sky, they noted that it was a great omen for war. In a similar way today only a tiny percentage are aware of the message of Akita (see page 172), even in Roman Catholic circles. Of those who have heard of Akita, a lot less believe it or give a second thought to its significance. This lack of knowledge, lack of belief, and consequent lack of appreciation of its significance is ironically why the warning of Akita is likely to become a frightful reality. It was no coincidence that the main message of Akita was given on the 13th October, the anniversary of the great sign of Fatima. It was also no coincidence that it was the image of *The Lady of all Nations* that wept human tears and shed human blood at Akita. **The message of Akita is the most profoundly significant warning message ever given directly by God to humanity. It was given by the Mother of God, and was approved as believable at the time by the local Bishop, with permission from Rome.** When God sends His Mother to give a major message to humanity, I think it would be wise for humanity to listen and take note. After all, the destruction of most of the population of the earth is hardly a small matter to concern ourselves with. It would only make sense, for the planet, to take immediate avoidance action.

Sadly it seems that this avoidance action is now unlikely to happen. People prefer to believe that God is not for real. People prefer to believe that secularism is the way forward or that one religion is as good as another. People prefer to believe that the Ten Commandments have passed their "sell by" date, and now there is the freedom to do what you wish. This is the age of disobedience, when rules and laws are made to be broken. This is also the age of foolishness. The final reality is, that if the world listens and responds to the messages of Fatima, Garabandal, Akita, and Medjugorje, the great decimation which now threatens can be prevented, but sadly not enough are responding. It would seem that, like the people of France and Italy (see chapter 11), the vast majority of humanity, are oblivious of the calamity that awaits them.

The Mystery of Iniquity

This is a mystery which dictates that evil leads to suffering. It is a mystery why the good are asked to suffer for the evil deeds of others and Catholics try to explain this with the doctrine of "The Mystical Body". This doctrine says that not only are we all responsible for the good and evil deeds we do ourselves, but also, to some extent, we will reap the rewards for the good and bad deeds of other members of humanity. Suffering in union with Christ, especially for others, is one of the highest forms of prayer and merits great rewards. Roman Catholics are, therefore, encouraged to offer their sufferings for the good of others who may need the sanctifying grace of conversion or healing from illness. All the punishment due to evil has already been expiated by Jesus Christ for those who repent and believe in Him. For those who do not, suffering is inevitable in order to expiate their personal evil deeds. For many unfortunates this suffering can be eternal, as serious evil has an infinite quality, by offending an infinitely good God. Those who refuse to recognize the reality of Hell, are fools (see chapter 7 & 8).

Part of the mystery of iniquity is the suffering associated with the breaking of natural law and the laws of nature. There is an old saying which says, "God always forgives, man sometimes forgives, but nature never forgives". This does not just refer to the effect of atmospheric levels of carbon dioxide on the climate. As well as the six numerical values that regulate the workings of the Universe,[139] the physical laws governing the climate, the movements of the planets and the bond angles in methane molecules etc., there is also a natural law which governs good and evil. Failure to recognize this natural law in the realm of good and evil is the greatest threat to world peace at the moment, even though few recognize it. Natural law limits our freedom to do only what is good. What is being promoted world-wide at the moment as, **"The Right to Choose" to kill unborn babies** is a serious corruption of this natural law with very serious consequences.

The Great Evil of Abortion

The great evils that are currently being perpetrated in the world are about to be expiated. These include, first and foremost, the slaughter of the innocents by abortion, at the rate of more than 150,000 every day. There are also the many other unspeakable crimes in the world, particularly the abuse of children. When Saint Teresa of Calcutta said that the killing of the unborn was the greatest danger to world peace she was deadly serious, as she understood the fruits of evil. The fact that abortion is supported by the World Health Organization, the United Nations, Amnesty International, and many other International bodies, makes this evil all the more shocking. A high percentage of all human families world-wide have now been scarred by abortion. It is a great mistake and a great lie for any woman to think that she can just have an abortion with no consequences. Apart from those who are driven to suicide, damaged psychologically, or driven to addiction, the spiritual damage to individuals and their families is always severe, even if it is often unnoticed. Through indirect contacts with those involved with the abortion counselling and those in 'Rachel's Vineyard' (which tries to heal those who have suffered this tragedy), I have come across some harrowing tales. One of the saddest was the story of a young unmarried father, who committed suicide because he could not bear the loss of his unborn child, and later, the destruction of his own father, who ended his days in a mental hospital, after he discovered the truth about the reason for his son's death. In some "developed" countries one in three women have abortions. Few of them realize before-hand that abortion increases the risk of suicide by six-fold and the risk of mental illness by five-fold, as well as significantly increasing the risk of a number of other medical problems (DeVeber Institute for Bioethics and Social Research). Abortion tears families apart and causes war, because in the words of St Pope John Paul II, it is an unspeakable evil. It is another one of the evil solutions of liberalism and secularism. Abortion is simply murder, and what makes it more heinous is, the fact that it is the murder of the most innocent and most defenceless of all classes of human beings.

In chapter 3, two major errors made by the US Supreme Court were described. These errors were made on the issues of slavery and abortion. The first case was the Dred Scott Decision of 1857 when the US Supreme Court declared people of African descent to be a "subordinate and inferior class of beings" leading to one of the greatest disgraces in the history of US court decisions. The declaration denied the existence of natural rights. The events that followed with Abraham Lincoln, the Civil War and the aftermath, revealed the errors associated with the Dred Scott Decision. In the words of Spitzer,[11] "The consequences were so terrible, that one might think the Court would be careful not to make the same mistake again: yet it has decidedly done this in the Roe v. Wade Decision" for abortion in 1973. There was a great similarity between the legal arguments in both cases. Africans were denied natural rights because they were judged not to be **citizens** and the unborn were denied natural rights because they were judged not to be **persons**. The first duty of all governments and courts must be to protect natural rights and the rights cannot be superseded by the power of the state.

Norma McCorvey (Jane Roe of the famous case of Roe v. Wade) recently died (Feb. 2017). Not many people know about how abortion was legalized in the US, based on lies and legal corruption. The events were based around two US Supreme Court cases, both of which were passed down on the same day on January 22, 1973: Roe v. Wade and Doe v. Bolton. Statements from both ladies involved tell the story:

"The affidavit did not happen the way I said it did, pure and simple. I lied! … Yes, the stated reason for my abortion is based upon a lie, a great lie. So the entire abortion industry is based on a lie." – Norma McCorvey, (Jane Roe) who later became a Catholic and a strong prolife advocate.

"I am against abortion: I never sought an abortion: I have never had an abortion. Abortion is murder. … The Doe v. Bolton case is based on deceit and fraud." Sandra Cano, (Mary Doe).

Generations to come will find it very difficult to contemplate how mothers, living at this time all over the world, could hire killers to kill their unborn babies, while the men of the world approved and the politicians provided the facilities and the laws to permit it. This unspeakable evil will soon be brought to an end, one way or another. Those who promote abortion, (that is, those in favour of direct intentional killing of unborn human life), in any circumstance, are anti-God, anti-Christ and are drifting slowly or rapidly to Hell, unless they repent.

The stark difference between the morality of liberalism and Christian morality is crystallized in the issue of the killing of the unborn. We could even go so far as to say that the next great-war or conflict in the world could be fought on this issue, although few will recognize it as a significant reason for war. St Teresa of Calcutta and Saint Pope John Paul both recognised this danger and this Pope, while in the US, said that, "a nation that kills its unborn does not deserve to survive." A recent published account of the cause of death in the 20th century indicated that, 200 million died from war and oppression, 70 million died from famine, 3.5 million died from natural disasters, and (in the last half of the century) 1,200 million died from induced abortion. Cynical liberalism wants us to believe that these abortions were necessary for "health reasons." Whose health? For certain, these abortions were not helpful for the health of the unborn. **Lest there be any doubt or confusion, it must be stated again clearly that human abortion is the intentional killing of an unborn human being and this intentional killing is never necessary to save the life of a mother. It is pure unadulterated evil and is promoted by those who do not understand or oppose the loving fatherhood of God.**

The extent of the destruction of humanity, whether it is by war, by famine, by natural disasters, by new infectious diseases, by the tipping of the earth axis, or by fire from the Heavens will now depend on how every man and every woman exercise their freedom to choose on this issue of abortion. Although each person is free to choose, **the right** to choose only applies to what is good, not to what is evil. Each person will soon have to make this choice, whether it is by referendum, by sitting quietly doing nothing, or becoming active in the defence of the rights of the unborn. The time for sitting on the fence is passing and each person will now be forced to make a decision. Will you choose to kill and thus decide for Hell or will you choose to let live and thus decide for

Heaven? You have this freedom to choose but remember that ultimately, the only choice is between Heaven and Hell.

The War is Now on

The great drama associated with the election of Donald Trump as the US President leaves us in no doubt that the war is now on. Trump is being portrayed as a lunatic or somebody bordering on insanity by the mainstream media (MSM), but grass root Americans voted for him and are rejecting the lies of MSM. All across the Western World, before the election, Hillary Clinton was promoted as the only hope for a leader of a free world. In Ireland, where I live, all our government political parties, and all our MSM were strongly promoting Hillary Clinton, as the only choice for Americans in the US Presidential election. This was despite the doings and un-doings of the Clintons over the years, now freely publicised in the alternative media sources. This was, above all, despite Hillary Clinton's support, over the years, for partial birth abortion. Abortion has been responsible for the death of at least 50 million unborn Americans over the last forty years and, during that time, Hillary was a strong promoter of abortion in the US and Internationally. If these are the standards we seek for the most powerful leader in the world, it tells us how sick and blind our MSM is, how sick and blind our politicians are, and how sick and blind society in general is. The MSM was proclaiming "foul play" over the Hillary Clinton email leaks, but the problem was not the leaks but the content. There was no publicity of the secret plans revealed that were underway to undermine and create conflict within the Catholic Church.

The election of Donald Trump as the American President, for some of us, has been a little sign of hope, even if he is eccentric, effervescent and unpredictable. One year ago, Putin was identified as the one obstacle to introducing a *One World Order* of liberalism. There were many indications that war with Russia was being planned. Now it seems that there may be two obstacles to the *One World Order* plans, Trump being the second. The leaders of two of the most powerful nations in the world are now openly promoting Christianity and both have a compass for good and evil pointing away from (against) abortion. If Hillary Clinton had been elected, the war with Russia was probably inevitable. It may still happen, but now there is a small glimmer of hope. In winning the Presidential election, Trump has had a major victory, but his greatest challenge is still to come. Can he win the battle with the US secret service? This is the key issue in the months and years ahead. During the Presidential campaign, the FBI was pressured into silence. On which side will they be on now, after the election? It seems that the CIA, during the Obama administration, was deeply embedded with the *One World Order*. One of the essentials for the survival of Trump and his Presidency would seem to be how his relationship with the different branches of the secret service develops over the next few years. We can be hopeful that Trump will remain true to his Christian values, but who can be confident that he will survive as President? Donald Trump and his family need a lot of prayer and the Clinton family need even more prayer.

Two Opposing Forces: There are two opposing forces in this war. On one side are Liberalism, Secularism, Humanism, Atheism and Satanism, being led by the hidden leadership of those in control of the *One World Order.* On the other side, is Christianity and Christian morality, with The Virgin Mary as the hidden leader. Other religions, including Islam, will be swept away as this war progresses and the members of these religions will be forced to choose sides. Islam will be used and destroyed in the process of this war. The Christian Churches who do not accept this exalted role for The Virgin Mary, will also be forced to choose sides, as will every single individual on earth.

Neither Trump nor Putin are angels, but for the sake of all of us and for the sake of peace in the world, let us hope that they are both saints in the making. If these two can work together to promote Christian morality over the next few years, the fruit of this will be world peace. This could be bolstered by the revolution of the many millions of Christian conversions now occurring in China. It is hard, however, to see the *One World Order* leadership submitting easily or peacefully to this major change in Global morality and this is why Global turmoil now seems inevitable. The ground-swell against God is now too much and the *One World Order* Oligarchs are too powerful, with major Global political influence and almost complete Global financial control.

Mainstream Media

The mainstream media (MSM) is now so controlled and corrupt that in matters of national importance, for any country in the world, the reporting has lost almost all credibility. The MSM is now no more than a propaganda tool for a very small elite group with extraordinary power and influence at an International level. The good news, however, is that ordinary citizens, with the help of good journalism in alternative media sources, are beginning to wake up. The MSM is being rejected as a source of truth and in some places the MSM is beginning to decay and implode. Populism is on the rise and it could be due to the perceived corruption, intrigue, and blatant lies promoted in the MSM, by those in power.

Media control is not new. The following quote is attributed to John Swinton, a famous Scottish-American journalist of the nineteenth century, one-time editor of the New York Times:

"What folly is this, toasting an independent press? Everyone present here tonight knows there is no such thing as an independent press. You know it and I know it. There is not one of you who would dare to write his honest opinions and if he did, you know beforehand it would never appear in print. I am paid to keep my honest opinions out of the paper I am connected with. Others of you are paid similar salaries for similar work. The business of the journalist is to destroy the truth, to lie outright, to pervert, to vilify, to fawn at the foot of mammon and to sell himself, his country and his race for his daily bread. You know this, and I know it, and what folly it is to be toasting an independent press! We are the tools and vassals of rich men behind the scenes. We are jumping jacks – they pull the strings and we dance. Our talents, our possibilities and our lives are the property of these men. We are intellectual prostitutes."

The MSM media is now a lot more controlled and a lot more global than in the time of John Swinton. In the 1980's, for example, 50 companies controlled 90% of media in the US but now this 90% is controlled by 6 companies. These are, General Electric, News Corp, Disney, Viacom, Time Warner, and CBS. The magazine, *Christian Order* (February 2017) did a major article on media control. This article noted that, "the soulless corporate conglomerates controlling the media are themselves controlled by the omnipresent and coercive Central Intelligence Agency. – This shocking influence of America's rogue intelligence agency has become widely recognised ever since Operation MOCKINGBIRD, a CIA-based initiative to control mainstream media, was exposed. In a piece titled, 'Who Controls the Media? – The Depraved Spies and Moguls of the CIA''s Operation MOCKINGBIRD,' Alex Constantine provides a neat summary introduction to this vast conspiracy of media manipulation that determines 'news' and official 'truth', at the service of the Oligarchs and their corporate-government empire:

"It is beginning to dawn on a growing number of armchair ombudsmen that the public print reports news from a parallel universe – one that has never heard of politically-motivated assassinations, CIA-Mafia banking thefts, mind control, death squads or even federal agencies with secret budgets fattened by cocaine sales – a place overrun by lone gunmen, where the CIA and Mafia are usually on their best behaviour."

This *Christian Order* magazine further noted that, "In 2014, a former editor of the major German daily, *Frankfurter Allgemeine Zeitung*, confirmed that he and fellow journalists are bribed and controlled by intelligence agencies. He says he went public because the self-designated elites on both sides of the Atlantic are prepping for a war with Russia: using the CIA, the bagmen for America's 'aristocracy', to incite hostility through the media. Though shocking, his allegations are consistent with the CIA's long and sordid history of media infiltration."

The American political scientist, John Mearsheimer and the French politician, Thierry Mariani, both agree that the deposing of, Yanukovych, the President of the Ukraine on the 22nd of February 2014, was nothing other than a 'putsch' (violent overthrow of a government) organized by Washington and NATO. The American, George Friedman, founder and CEO of *Stratfor*, a major private intelligence firm, said that the deposing of Yanukovych was the most blatant coup in history. There was a news blackout on Western aid to Kiev and its neo-Nazi groups responsible for much of the shootings. There was also a complete news blackout on the biggest Western military build-up in the Eastern Europe since World War II. The MSM initially blamed Russia for the crash of the Malaysian airline flight MH17, in July 2014. When the evidence later pointed to the Ukranian American allies being the culprits the reporting changed from "a Russian atrocity" to "a tragic accident".

Judaism

In the final outcome of this battle between the leadership of the *One World Order* and The Virgin Mary, which now seems to be moving rapidly towards a final showdown, the state of Israel will be a key fulcrum point. Those Jews who still believe in the Jewish religion will have a lot of shocks in the near future. In many ways the tradition of Christianity is the tradition of Judaism, which has come of age, and has accepted that the Jewish Messiah has come. The impact of Christianity on Judaism is often forgotten, but it has been profound. The Jews no longer have the Temple, they no longer have priests and no longer offer sacrifices, all of which were the cornerstones of their religion up to the time of Christ. At the moment of the crucifixion, many prodigies happened at the Temple. The two pillars holding the veil fell and the veil was torn. It was also reported that the dead rose and came into the Temple. Up to that time, many strange and unusual events were known to take place in the Temple, especially at the time of sacrifices. These events, which were regarded as miraculous, indicated to the priests of the Temple that God was accepting the sacrifices. After the crucifixion, all these signs mysteriously ceased, and the Rabbis at the time recognized this.[228]

Covenants: In order to appreciate the point we are now at, in salvation history, it is important to have some understanding of the covenants made by God with the Jewish people. This is well explained by Professor Scott Hahn.[91] These covenants were solemn agreements, not just in the spirit of something legal, but also in the spirit of God as a Father making an agreement with his human children. This is the kind of commitment called for in a marriage covenant between husband and wife. Covenants, therefore, are far more binding than would be the case with an ordinary legal agreement. Breaking a covenant with God is regarded as very serious because, by implication, it is a rejection of God as Father.

The first covenant between God and humanity was with Adam and Eve, as the first parents of our race. The second covenant was a household covenant with Noah and his family. The third covenant was a tribal covenant with Abraham. The fourth covenant was with the twelve tribes of Israel through Moses and this was therefore, a national covenant. The fifth was with David as King, making it a national kingdom covenant. With the coming of Jesus, he established the "New Covenant", which is an international kingdom covenant to include Jews and Gentiles (Catholicos). The Catholic Church, therefore, represents the culmination and climax of salvation history to date. It may be that we can expect some kind of "cosmic" covenant at the end of time when the dead will rise and all who have kept faithful to God's laws will join together in the Father's house in Heaven. It may be useful to look at this coming transformation of the world as a preparation for this final event.

The Shekinah: The most significant of all signs for the Jews in the Old Testament was the Shekinah. This was recognized as the visible presence of the Holy Spirit of God. The Hebrew word means "to appear" or "to dwell", meaning that "The Majesty of God" or "The Divine Presence" was with them and became visible. In the Exodus from Egypt, Moses and the Jews were led by this Shekinah sign, in the form of a pillar of cloud by day and a pillar of fire by night. This Shekinah could be found over the Ark of the Covenant in the Temple. From there The Shekinah spoke to the Jewish people through the prophets of the Old Testament and instructed them how to live their lives properly, in union with God. At the time of the prophet Jeremiah, the Jews began to worship false Gods and so broke the covenant with the true God. God then instructed the prophet to hide the Ark. The final result was that the Shekinah disappeared with the Ark, spoke no more, and the prophets stopped teaching. For many centuries before Christ, therefore, the Jews were left without direct spiritual guidance from God.

There was a belief and an understanding among the Jews that when the Messiah came that the Shekinah would also come back and begin to speak again. It was not the Jews who recognized the return of the Shekinah, however, but the Zoroaster wise men, who were led to the Messiah by the Shekinah star. Later there was a Shekinah manifestation to the shepherds, in Bethlehem, near the Crib cave. There were further manifestations during the life of Jesus, such as at the Baptism in the Jordan, the Transfiguration and the Ascension. When Jesus died, according to Jewish writers, the Shekinah rested for a few months on the western wall of the Temple, and from there relocated to the summit of Mount Olivet.[228]

Over the last two decades, pillars of cloud and shafts of light have been photographed at Marian apparition sites, especially at Medjugorje and Betania (in Venezuela). Courtenay Bartholomew, Professor of Medicine in the West Indies, has published a series of these.[229] I mentioned above the possible connection of the Shekinah sign with Garabandal (see page 148) and it is possible that the permanent supernatural signs prophesied for Garabandal and Medjugorje could be a manifestation of the Shekinah. It would be another sign of the visible presence of God with humanity, which would support the material presence in the Eucharist, already with us, in the form of bread and wine. If this were so, it would have very significant implications for believers in Judaism. One way or another, it is likely that The Virgin Mary will have a very influential role in uniting those of both Jewish and Islamic faiths with Christianity, so that all three religions will be able to worship in unity, the one true God, already accepted by these three great monotheistic religions.

Rebuilding the Temple: A number of efforts have been made to rebuild the Jewish Temple, in Jerusalem, but all have failed. Frank Duff (founder of the Legion of Mary) gives a good account of the effort made, by the Roman Emperor Julian, to do this.[230] Julian is often referred to as the "Apostate" as he rejected Christianity.[231] As soon as he took over as Roman Emperor in 361 AD, after Constantine, he immediately set about suppressing Christianity and turning the Empire back to paganism. Many of Julian's family were killed by the family of Constantine, who was a cousin of his, and this was almost definitely the reason for his strong anti-Christian behaviour.

Even though Julian also hated the Jews, he befriended them, as he felt the best way to suppress Christianity was to rebuild the Temple and thus prove Christ's prophecy false (see page 437). In the year 534 BC the prophet Daniel (Daniel 9:26) had also foretold that Solomon's Temple would be abandoned by God and that it would be completely destroyed. The death of Christ would render meaningless and obsolete the sacrifices of the Temple. According to Christian teaching the New Law has now supplanted the Old Law, which will never be renewed. The Jews would not need to offer sacrifices in Solomon's Temple after the death of Christ. It is undeniable that no sacrifices have taken place since his death. Julian recognized the significance of this and thus his efforts to rebuild the Temple.

He put the whole resources of the Empire behind this project. The historical description of the events that happened is corroborated by many historians, and is thus difficult to doubt. Terrible earthquakes, with fire coming up through the foundations, prevented the workers from making any progress. Even the stones of the old foundations were uprooted. The rebuilding efforts were finally abandoned in 363 AD, the same year they had begun. Julian himself admitted defeat and very soon afterwards he was mortally wounded in battle. As he lay dying he was heard to say, "Thou hast conquered, O Galilean". During the earthquakes a large cross appeared in the sky. This was described as luminous at night and dark coloured during the day. Images of crosses were also said to have appeared on the garments of those present, which would not wash out. Many historians have asserted that these manifestations were universally viewed as supernatural, by the world of the day. In these descriptions, Frank Duff quotes in particular, Ammianus Marcellinus, who was the authentic historian of the reign. He was, "a friend, admirer, and companion-in-arms of Julian: a man of affairs, learned, candid, impartial according to all estimates of his character."[230]

It is of interest that the large cross in the sky can be compared with and may have had similarities with a perfect image of a large cross which appeared in the sky, for two days, in mid Atlantic near the Azores, coincidentally, during the days (May 1948) when the state of Israel was getting international recognition. What significance this cross had, if any, is impossible to say. A cloud formation in the shape of a cross is probably not very unusual (see the front cover of this book) but it is unusual for a cloud formation to remain more than a few hours. Those of us who have seen the photographs must admit that the enormous size and perfect shape was impressive. It had the effect of sending all the Portuguese inhabitants of the Azores back to church, during those days. An enthusiastic Christian might suggest that this unusual and enormous cross in the sky indicated that, one day in the future, the cross will be accepted as a great symbol in Israel, when Christ is accepted as the true Messiah.

Why everyone should be a Roman Catholic

There are at least three very good reasons why everybody should be a Roman Catholic:

Firstly, the teaching is based on truth.

Secondly, this Church offers the easiest route to eternal salvation, eternal joy, and eternal happiness.

Thirdly, this Church offers the only hope for world peace.

How does one find what is true? It is very simple: you must seek the truth. He who seeks finds and he who knocks will have the door opened for him. "You will seek me and find me when you seek me with all you heart" (Jeremiah 29:13). You must love the truth and seek it with all your heart. The philosopher, Blaise Pascal, says that there are three classes of people in the world, in terms of belief in God:

1. Those who seek and find God. They are reasonable because they seek and happy because they have found.
2. Those who seek and have not yet found God. They are reasonable but not happy.
3. Those who do not seek and do not find God. They are not reasonable and not happy.

Those in the second category are guaranteed eventually to get into the first category. There is nobody in a fourth category, that is, those who find God without seeking.

Many sections of this book have detailed evidence for the reality of God and life after death. This book has also presented substantial evidence supporting the truth of the Roman Catholic Church (RCC) teaching. The teaching of the RCC is true simply because of the evidence which, in this age of exploding information technology, is now becoming overwhelming. If you are not already a member of this Church, then you may find it difficult to access, assess and appreciate this evidence. Nevertheless, even the most difficult doctrine of all for non-believers, that is, the *Real Presence* of Christ in the Eucharist, is being confirmed more and more by modern miraculous events. At least five Eucharistic miracles, have been described, over the last twenty five years,[232] when scientific laboratories confirmed that Eucharistic bread and wine were transformed into human blood and human cardiac tissue.

The philosopher Peter Kreeft gave an interesting account of his conversion to the RCC.[152] Like most Protestant converts, although he was drawn to Catholicism, he did not want to convert as he knew that his friends and family would be very upset. He kept trying to find reasons for not converting. He could not find a single contradiction to the claims of the RCC. His friends kept telling him that the RCC was the whore of Babylon but, on the contrary, he became very impressed with the lives of the saints and the scholarship of the doctrine in the Church. When he read St John of the Cross, he was certain that it was true, even though he could not fully understand his books. There was nobody of the status of St Thomas Aquinas or St Augustine in the Protestant Churches. As well as all that, he discovered that Protestant objections to Catholic doctrine don't make sense and are often due to misunderstandings. The doctrine of Purgatory makes perfect sense as few of us are perfect when we die.

Peter Kreeft's account of his reading the writings' of St John of the Cross is very reminiscent of Edith Stein (St Teresa Benedicta of the Cross, OCD.) reading the autobiography of St Teresa of Ávila. Edith was born Jewish, on the *Day of Atonement*, 12th October, 1891. Early in her life she lost her Jewish faith and became an atheist. Her brilliant mind was applied to the study of philosophical phenomenology and a continued search for truth. After years of searching, she described that when she read St Teresa of Ávila, she knew that it was true and immediately converted to Catholicism in 1922. Her sister later converted, both became Carmelites (only Edith was enclosed), and were martyred in the Nazi gas chambers. After their conversion, they never again denied their Jewish faith, but said that they had brought it to completion by accepting their Jewish Messiah.

History: Peter Kreeft said that another great reason for his conversion was History. If you could go back to the first and second century, what kind of Christian teaching would you find? Although his Protestant Professors told him that the early Church was Protestant, like many other Protestant converts he found that the opposite was true. The early Church and the early Fathers of the Church used and promoted Christian doctrine as is found in the RCC today. The Mass was celebrated and the *Real Presence* of Christ in the Eucharist was the belief, not only in the first few centuries of the early Christian Church, but right up to the time of Martin Luther. He is a Catholic now, he said, because he wants to be a proper Christian and belong to the Church founded by Christ.

The Nicene Creed: This creed was inspired by the Holy Spirit and gives the method of how the true Christian Church can be identified. The four "marks" of the true Church are: **One, Holy, Catholic, and Apostolic.** The RCC has always preached the same truths in all its branches all over the world. It is Holy because it is set apart to teach the laws of God, but at the same time, it is a hospital for sinners rather than an institution for saints. It is different from the many thousands of different Protestant Churches that have developed due to the private interpretation of the Bible. It is Catholic as it is the same all over the world. In contrast, Protestant Christian doctrine varies from one small church to the next. Finally, and most importantly, it is apostolic. Jesus selected apostles and selected Peter as head. They appointed Bishops as successors and these Bishops exist today with a direct line of authority from the original Church founded by Christ. The Popes can trace a direct line back to Peter.

Sola Scriptura: This is one of the basic teachings of the Protestant Churches. They believe that the Bible is infallible but the Bible does not preach sola scriptura and the Bible says that the pillar of truth is the Church, not the Bible (1 Timothy 3:14-15). The Catholic Church put the Bible together from many books available in the early centuries of the Church. How do we know, for example, that the gospel of Thomas should not belong in the Bible? For no other reason than the RCC said so. It makes no sense therefore to say that the Bible is infallible but the Church that put it together is fallible or worse, even the whore of Babylon.

Science: Scientific support for RCC teaching is massive, phenomenal, and increasing every day. This is mainly through scientific investigations of the miraculous, such as the many miracles of the Eucharist, as explained above and in chapter 4. Another major source of scientific support for RCC teaching is found associated with the apparitions of The Virgin Mary as discussed in some detail in Chapter 5.

The only reason why anybody should believe or be asked to believe something is because it is true. If the evidence points in favour of the RCC being true and as truth cannot be divided, then, to the extent that other religions disagree with RCC teaching, these religions are false, not based on solid evidence, and are thus heretical religions. If Jesus Christ is God, (see page 67 for evidence on this), then Islam must be a false religion. Each person is free to accept or reject the evidence, but remember that there is an obligation of conscience on each person to sincerely search for the truth, which should be based on non-contradictory evidence of one kind or another. GK Chesterton was once asked if he had any argument against Christianity and he replied that there was only one, Christians. The same could be said of Catholicism. The only strong argument against it, at this time, is the behaviour of those who claim to be Catholics.

Peter Kreeft also talks about **the good the true and the beautiful**. He quotes three atheists who converted to belief in God after listening to the music of the St Matthew's Passion by Johann Sebastian Bach.

When Bertrand Russell was dying he was asked by a friendly pastor: what will you say, if you come face to face with God after death? His reply was, "why did you not give us more evidence?" It is a reasonable question. Peter Kreeft suggested the following answer: If God gave us too much evidence, we would be compelled to believe against our will. If there was too little evidence, then even those who seek God would not find Him. Love of the truth and searching for it with all our hearts is the important thing for all of us. Our eternal destination depends on how much we love the truth and how hard we search for it, therefore, rather than on our IQ.

Finally, the RCC teaches the reality of Hell as well as of Heaven. Please read about Hell and Heaven (see chapters 7 & 8) before you decide to ignore the search for God and for truth.

A World Transformation

Reliable prophecy indicates that the triumph of The Immaculate Heart of Mary over Satan and evil in the world is certain. This prediction is intimately connected with the message of Fatima. The Virgin said: "In the end, *My Immaculate Heart* will triumph". It would be great if this triumph could occur peacefully, similar to the transformation and rejection of Communism that began in Russia in the 1980s after the consecration of the world to the

Immaculate Heart of Mary and still continues, but sadly this is now unlikely to happen in the rest of the world.

It is very difficult to comprehend the enormous transformation and changes which are about to take place in the world. The appalling vista which faces humanity, according to Catholic prophecy, does not bear thinking about. This is why few will believe the prophecies described in the previous chapters of this book, and why few will want to consider these events as even a remote possibility. What is predicted is too world-shattering. It seems unnatural and too remote from the reality of the world we know, and in most cases the world we are afraid to change. In many ways, I would also wish that these prophecies were a fantasy and that there could be a less painful way to change human hearts and human thinking. **Unfortunately, according to the reported words of God the Father to Marie Julie Jahenny** (see page 448), **"terrible decimation" may now be the only way.** It is not that God is cruel or that humanity will not get more warnings, but most will not listen, hear, or heed these warnings.

A number of prophecies describe the significant role that a world-wide financial crash will have, at the beginning of the coming tribulation. Of particular interest is the prophecy of the French Poor Clare nun (venerable Magdalene Porzat), who, almost 200 years ago, predicted a time of great sadness and confusion in the Catholic priesthood. She also said that these expected major world problems (described in earlier chapters) would occur when the whole world was bankrupt. Other indicators of these times, which she foresaw were severe weather conditions and severe outbreaks of unknown infectious diseases.

Disasters, natural and otherwise, particularly in the US, could also be a starting point for world turmoil, especially if other nations tried to take advantage of these situations. Remember Teresa

Neumann (see page 84) said that the US would never be invaded, but that it would be brought to its knees by natural disasters.

Where are we now?

In trying to decide where humanity is positioned at this time in eschatological (end-times) terms, we must of necessity refer to the Bible, with particular emphasis on the Book of Daniel and the Book of Revelation, which as the reputed prophetic words of God, is the most authoritative source of information. We are warned by Church authorities, however, to refrain from attempting to apply chronological dates to Bible prophecy, for a number of reasons. Interpretation can be very difficult and many of the prophecies can have a recurring or cyclical validity at different times in the history of the Church. Nevertheless, some understanding of biblical prophecy is essential in trying to make some sense of the veritable flood of modern (some recognized as authentic) Catholic prophecies. Two timelines, in particular, are of special interest at this time and these are also a source of great confusion. These are firstly, the time of the advent of an individual, who will be recognized as the Antichrist, and secondly, the time of the Second Coming of Christ.

The Prophecy of Daniel: The teaching of the Christian Church Fathers are often now referred to as a source of correct belief and teaching of the early Church and this has been the reason for many famous converts to the Roman Catholic Church, over recent decades, such as Professor Peter Kreeft, Professor Scott Hahn, and Marcus Grodi. History now confirms that the "real presence" of Christ in the Eucharist was believed since the time of St Peter and Luther's Reformation was the first major rejection of this.

From the prophetic aspect of The Old Testament, these Church Fathers regarded the prophecy of Daniel (Dan 9) as one of the most accurate for predicting the exact time for the public life, followed by the death and resurrection of Christ. The Archangel Gabriel explained to Daniel that the figure of 70 years given to the prophet Jeremiah for the restoration of Israel should be understood as 70 weeks of years, that is, 490 years. This prophecy indicated that 69 weeks of years were decreed "from the going out of the word to rebuild Jerusalem" to the time of the Messiah. This "going out of the word" was given by the Persian King Artaxerxes in 445 BC at the request of Nehemiah (Book of Nehemiah). The years of the 69th week, therefore, represent 30 to 37 AD.

Abomination of Desolation: It is important to recognize that in Biblical prophecy there are often several layers of fulfilment and some prophecies can be cyclical or recurrent. Days or months quoted can often signify years, as explained above with the prophecy of Daniel. This recurrent prophecy is well illustrated with the phrase, "abomination of desolation". "When you see the Abomination of Desolation set up in the Temple" – spoken by the prophet Daniel, referenced in Mt 24:15-, Mk 13:14- and Lk 21:20- this refers to a number of different events. It refers to the idol set up by the Syrian King (Antiochus IV) in the Temple in 167 BC. It also refers to the time before the destruction of the Temple in 70 AD by the Romans, when the Christians recognised the signs and fled before the desolation. Jesus predicted the destruction of Jerusalem (Luke 21:20-24). "When you see Jerusalem surrounded by armies, then know that desolation has come near. ... flee to the mountains...Jerusalem will be trampled underfoot.. until the times of the Gentiles are fulfilled." The time is given as forty two months (Rev11:2). This period of (42 months or) 1,260 days can sometimes represent 1260 years. 1260 years was a period when Gentiles would occupy Palestine (until the times of the Gentiles are fulfilled – Lk 21:24). Construction on the Dome of the Rock began in 688, that is, fifty years after the Islamic capture of Jerusalem and there is little doubt that this would have been considered an abomination by the Jews. If this represented the beginning of the "Abomination of Desolation", then after 1,260 years we come to 1948 which is the year Israel was restored to the Jews.

The prophecy of Daniel on the "Abomination of Desolation" was later suggested by Jesus as one of the signs of His Second Coming. The Abomination of Desolation here is when the Antichrist takes his place in the Holy Temple and declares himself as God. In Rev 13:5 the Antichrist is described as ruling for 42 months. This agrees with Daniel 9:27 which says that the Antichrist will break his treaty with Israel in the middle of a seven year tribulation period. An image of the Antichrist will also be constructed and those on earth will be forced to worship it. At this stage the Lord will return to destroy the Antichrist (Rev 19:20).

A Summary of the Book of Revelation

This is the last book of the Bible, sometimes called the Apocalypse taken from the Greek word, apocalypsis, meaning revelation. At the time this book was written, everybody in the Roman Empire was obliged, once every year, to burn incense before a statue of the Roman Emperor and declare him as God. When Christians refused to do this, they were severely persecuted. This book was a revelation from God to his persecuted people, given at that time in history. The author, John, describes himself as a prophet rather than an apostle and this book is a book of prophecy. The prophecies of the book were concerned not only with the first century, during the time of St John, but the prophecies also concern the plight of the Church down through the centuries, with many recurring themes and difficulties. The devil, represented by the huge red dragon, will always be persecuting the Church and the two beasts of godless governments and false religions will always be helping the dragon. It is also a book of revelation in that it reveals that Christ was and will eventually be triumphant at every level. He was triumphant at Calvary, is triumphant now and through the centuries by the martyrs, and will be triumphant in the future at the last judgment.

All the various books of the Bible have a particular literary form and we need guidance in order to interpret them properly. Encouraging private interpretation of the Bible, therefore, was one of the sources of great confusion introduced into Christianity by the Reformation. Sacred Scripture reminds us that the pillar and foundation of the truth is the Church (1Timothy 3:14-15) and Sacred Scripture, therefore, cannot be interpreted properly outside the authority invested in the Church by Christ. The literary form of the book of Revelation is particularly difficult to interpret as it uses numbers, symbols and images taken from the prophets, especially, from Ezechial, Daniel, and Zechariah. It has been described as conceptual symbolism coming from the King of kings. It is by far the most difficult book of the Bible to interpret and Catholic scholars differ on many aspects. Many books have been written on the topic of the apocalypse. Some books which I have found very useful are, Apocalypse,[222] Unveiling the Apocalypse[205] and The Book of Destiny.[223] Fr Gobbi[3] also received a number of revelations on the apocalypse which are very enlightening. The Virgin Mary said to Fr Gobbi on 13th Oct. 1987, "I am being sent by God to open this book." She later said on 13th Oct. 1988, "I am opening for you the sealed book, that the secrets contained in it may be revealed." Peter Kreeft[224] points out that we must never interpret a book in the light of our own beliefs (eisegesis, that is, reading in), but rather in the light of the beliefs of the author (exegesis – reading out). When a modernist interprets miracle stories as fables or when a fundamentalist interprets symbols literally, they are reversing the roles of interpretation and belief. It is also important not to confuse symbolism with allegory. In allegory each ingredient has only one meaning. In symbolism there may be many correct meanings, as for example the number 666 (the mark of the Beast) or the term Antichrist. Antichrist can mean a single individual or individuals as well as a spiritual evil force.

The book of the Apocalypse has seven septettes. These are: 7 Letters, 7 Seals, 7 Trumpets, 7 Signs, 7 Angels, 7 Bowls, and 7 Sights. Seven is regarded as the perfect number and thus 666 is regarded as the epitome of imperfection. Three and one half years, or days, or years of days (sometimes referred to as 42 months or 1260 days), is also a recurring number regarded as imperfect by being half of seven. In the beginning, John had a vision of the Throne of God. Around the throne, were four creatures resembling a lion (king of wild beasts), a calf or ox (king of domestic beasts), a human person (king of all creation), and an eagle (swiftest of all birds). God is King of kings, regal, strong, wise, and swift. The creatures had eyes in the front and in the back which symbolize the ability to see the future as well as the past.

7 Letters: John is commanded to write letters to the seven churches in Asia Minor (which is part of Turkey today). The messages in these letters do not just apply to these local churches but to the whole Church down through the centuries. The four main problems identified by John were:

1. **Lukewarmness.**
2. **Slanderous Attacks.**
3. **False Teaching.**
4. **Complacency.**

7 Seals: The first four of the seven seals present the four horsemen of the Apocalypse that symbolize the havoc brought upon people by the godless. The white horse brings war, which brings bloodshed (the red horse), famine (the black horse), and death (the pale green horse). The opening of the fifth seal reveals those martyred for the faith. The sixth seal announced major signs in the elements, such as eclipses of the sun and moon, stars falling from the sky, as well as natural disasters secondary to major earthquakes.

The Mark of the Beast: This is discussed at length by Emmett O Regan in his 777 page tome, Unveiling the Apocalypse.[205] Emmett explains the common custom in Judaism of wearing small portions of scripture (usually the shema of Deut 6:4 as well as other passages) in small leather boxes known as tefillin in Aramaic, now known by the Greek word, phylactery. This was as a result of a literal interpretation of Deut 6:8, which said that, "You shall bind them (the commandments of love) as a sign upon your hand, and they shall be as frontlets between your eyes". It is suggested, therefore, that as the religious Jews wore the commandments of God on their foreheads or upon their hands, so those who are dedicated to the Antichrist will wear similar emblems of dedication.

Emmett O Regan discusses the opening of the sixth seal in Revelation 6:12 (New Testament). He suggests that as the Divine sealing of those faithful to God and the inauguration of the mark of the beast coincide at the same moment in time, we can use the astronomical events described at the opening of the sixth seal to date the arrival of the mark of the beast to humanity. The four astronomical signs quoted at the opening of this seal were an earthquake, an eclipse of the sun, an eclipse of the moon, and stars falling from the sky. The Book of Revelation was originally addressed to seven churches in Asia Minor – now part of Turkey. The best place to see an eclipse of the sun which occurred on the 11th of August 1999 was Northern Turkey. This took place during the peak of a Perseid meteor shower which would fulfil the prophecy of the falling stars. A more dramatic falling of stars also occurred later in mid-November 1999 with a Leonid meteor storm (meteor storms produce thousands of meteors per hour as opposed to just a few with meteor showers). Just six days after the eclipse of the sun there was a devastating earthquake in the area (in the city of Izmit), which was responsible for the death of over 17,000 people. Izmit was the site of the ancient city of Nicomedia which at one time was the eastern capital of the Roman Empire. This was also the site where the Emperor, Diocletian, tortured and decapitated St George and began the great persecution of Christians in 303 AD. The persecution of Christians by Diocletian could possibly be a foreshadowing, therefore, of a persecution still to come under the Antichrist. Finally on the 21st January 2000 there was a dramatic total eclipse of the moon, which could be seen as blood red, over the area where the other events were concentrated, in North-Western Turkey. The four signs described in Revelation 6:12 associated with the opening of the 6th seal all occurred, therefore, in Turkey, in late 1999 and very early 2000 AD.

Many attempts have been made over the centuries to identify Antichrist individuals by applying numbers to various letters in the names of these individuals. Some of these efforts have gone to ridiculous lengths to identify the "number of the beast" which according to sacred scripture is 666. From this approach, Nero was identified as an Antichrist, but so too was President Ronald (Wilson) Reagan with six letters in each section of his name and he was certainly not an Antichrist. By giving a number 100 to the letter A and 101 to the letter B, etc., the sum of Hitler also added up to 666. Emmett O Regan suggests that the internet www is a better candidate for the mark of the beast than any other suggested so far, especially as the Hebrew equivalent of the letter w is "waw", which in turn represents the number 6. This means that www in Hebrew represents 666. In line with the timing of the four astronomical events described above in relation to the opening of the sixth seal of revelation, he points out that the first mobile phone with a wireless application product for browsing the internet (www) was the Nokia 7110, which went on sale during November 1999, that is, at the same time that the astronomical events indicate a time for the coming of the mark of the beast. On the basis of this he also suggests that the mobile phones, rather than "the microchip" (that many Christians get concerned about) may be better candidates for the "anti-phylactery" (associated with the Antichrist) on the hands of modern secular humanity.

Before the breaking of the seventh seal there were two visions. In the first vision there were four angels who were told not to harm the earth until the elect had received God's seal. The vision consisted of the sealing of 144,000 representing the 12 tribes of Israel. The tribe of Dan was excluded and replaced by the tribe of Joseph as it was believed that the Antichrist would come from the tribe of Dan. The second vision was of those in white robes who had reached Heaven by being faithful to God's laws. When the seventh seal was opened there was silence in Heaven for about half an hour. This was the calm before the storm.

7 Trumpets: Seven angels were then given seven trumpets to announce the great disasters to come. The first four disasters would damage the environment directly and evildoers indirectly. The land will be damaged by hail and fire, the sea by volcanic earthquakes, the fresh water by wormwood (a bitter herb) turning it bitter, and the sky by eclipses of the sun and moon. It is of interest that the Ukrainian word for wormwood is Chernobyl. To some extent these are a replay of the plagues of Egypt. The final three trumpets announce three diabolical "woes" to the inhabitants of the earth who are not God-fearing. The fifth trumpet is described as like a plague of locusts, lasting specifically for the life span of a locust, that is, five months. These locusts will cause terrible suffering to those who have not been "sealed" by

God's angels but will not cause death directly. Emmet O Regan[205] notes that the description of the locusts resembles our modern helicopters. The principal angel is a demon in charge of the abyss, called "The Destroyer". The Book of Destiny,[223] first published in 1955, identifies the first woe with a resurgence of domination wars in the Muslim nations, which could describe this time in history (early 2017). This relatively localized conflict in Muslim nations at this time could now progress to a more global situation which could equate with the second woe.

The sixth trumpet announces the second woe. Originally this was the Partian army from east of the Euphrates which came to punish disobedient Israel, leading to lots of deaths. In this woe four demon angels are released in charge of an army of 200 million (from east of the Euphrates river), which will destroy one third of humanity. An army of that size was inconceivable when St John wrote this book of Revelation, but not so today. This could possibly represent the modern Chinese army attacking from the east bringing a resurgence of militaristic atheistic Communism. There is no indication of the time interval between the first and second woe but according to the Book of Destiny,[223] it will be "a time of wars developing into a world-revolution that will deluge the whole world with carnage and bloodshed. The three and one half years of the reign of The Beast will be its climax." In Rev 9:15 it says that the four angels (demons) were released "who had been held for the hour, the day, the month, and the year, to kill one third of humanity." This probably indicates a specific time fixed by the providence of God. The plague of the 200,000,000 conquering army is a punishment for the hostility to the truth of God and indifference to His law and grace. The Book of Destiny says that the second woe culminates in the reign of Antichrist. In Rev 10:4, God gave a special revelation to St John indicating what would immediately precede the coming of the Antichrist but for some mysterious reason, he was not allowed to reveal this to the

Church. It was revealed, however, that there will be special decisions made by the Church which will complete the work of her magisterial office before the Antichrist arrives. There has been some speculation as to what these decisions may be but I like to think that at least one of them will be the declaration of the final dogma on The Virgin Mary. That is, Mary will be declared as "Co-redemptrix, Advocate and Mediatrix of all Graces," as all graces from God come to humanity, through Her from Her Son.

Before the seventh trumpet is blown there are two more visions, like the two visions that preceded the opening of the seventh seal. In this case the first vision is of a gigantic angel giving a secret message to John as well as a message that God would no longer delay in bringing His Kingdom to earth. The second vision is of the "Two Witnesses", who would witness to the truth of the gospel, as Moses and Elijah did, and who would eventually be martyred by the Antichrist. Many will rejoice at the death of these two witnesses as they will not be happy to hear the gospel proclaimed. The rejoicing will only be for a short time, however, as Jesus will overcome the Antichrist and God's Kingdom will be ushered in all over the world. The third woe coming with the seventh trumpet is associated with the seven plagues or bowls of God's wrath – see next page.

7 Signs: God's Temple is opened and John sees the Ark of the Covenant. Today the Divine presence is The Blessed Sacrament in the Church. The first sign is that in the sky of the Woman clothed with sun with the moon under her feet and on her head a crown of twelve stars (representing The Virgin Mary, Rev. 12:1 – dramatically visible in the sky during 2017 – see chapter 16). The second sign is the Red Dragon, which Fr Gobbi[3] was told is now represented by atheistic Communism. The third sign is the Dragon against the Woman's Child and the fourth sign is the Dragon against the Woman herself. The Woman was given the wings of an eagle so that she could fly to safety in the desert for a period of three and one half years. The desert is now represented by the hearts and souls of those dedicated and consecrated to the Immaculate Heart of Mary. In his fury against those who continue to bear witness to true Christian teaching the Dragon will enrol the help of two other beasts, one from the sea and one from the land. The fifth sign is the beast from the sea and the sixth sign is the land beast respectively. These are represented today as secular Freemasonry and Freemasonry within the Church. The Dragon and the two beasts represent an unholy trinity, in conflict with The Father, Son and Holy Spirit. To combat this unholy trinity the seventh sign comes, which is paradoxically, only a lamb. The battle is already lost and won.

7 Angels: These are the Seven Angels of Judgment. The first angel announces the gospel, the second angel warns about the destruction of Babylon (? The US today), and the third angel reminds us of Heaven as a reward for the good and Hell for those who reject God and the laws of God. The next four angels portray the final judgment. Number four and five announce the time and reap the harvest of the good. Number six and seven gather and crush the ungodly.

7 Bowls or Plagues: This is the only septette of the Book of Revelation that is all gloom. The seven plagues are modelled on the plagues of Egypt in the Old Testament. The angels are told to pour these "bowls" upon the earth. The first results in ugly sores, the second turns the sea to blood with the death of living creatures, the third turns the fresh water into blood, the fourth brings scorching heat, the fifth brings darkness, pains and sores, and the sixth dries up the rivers. Unfortunately, like the plagues of Egypt, these plagues fail to lead many of the wicked to convert, but rather their hearts become more hardened. Before the seventh plague, there is again a vision given to John of three unclean spirits, coming from the mouths of the dragon and the two beasts. God then comes like a thief in the night. They are destroyed completely like the wicked Canaanites by Deborah and Barak (Jgs. 5:1-23) and the Midianites by Gideon (Jgs. 7) on the hill of Megiddo (Armageddon) (Rev. 16:13-16). The final seventh event is the destruction of the great pagan city by violent unprecedented earthquakes.

7 Sights: The seven sights concern the fall of Babylon. The first sight was of an angel giving the reasons for the fall, which were immorality and the shedding of innocent blood - (think of the extent of immorality today and the extent of the killing of the unborn). The second sight was of the kings of the earth who were very sad at the fall of Babylon, but for economic reasons only. The third sight was of an angel throwing a huge millstone into the sea to give further destruction to Babylon, - ? by causing an enormous tsunami. The fourth sight was of the saints in Heaven in ecstatic joy over the fall of Babylon. **(Handel had this sight in mind when he composed "The Messiah", between August 24th and September 14th, 1741. The first performance was in Dublin and during the lifetime of Handel all the proceeds from this inspired, immortal Oratorio were used for charitable purposes.)** The fifth sight was of the appearance of Jesus Christ as the conqueror, invincible King and Lord of lords. The sixth sight was of an angel with the key of the abyss where he tied the dragon with a heavy chain. After "one thousand years" (a figurative number), Satan would be released for a short time. In his pride Satan could not admit defeat and he would again try to seduce the pagan nations, Gog and Magog, to battle against the holy nations of God. Finally, the seventh sight is of the last judgment. The Devil and the damned finish up in Hell because they could not admit their evil and refused to ask God for forgiveness.

The Book of Revelation, as stated above, is difficult, if not impossible to interpret chronologically. Nevertheless, many events described are so interconnected that it is possible to recognize some time lines. This is particularly true of the time near the end of the second woe (see page 649). Emmet O Regan[205] lists the events described in the Book of Revelation at that time. These are:

1. The Ministry of the Two Witnesses.
2. The Spiritual Revival / Second Pentecost.
3. The Martyrdom of the Two Witnesses.
4. The Sign of the Son of Man.
5. The Conversion of the Jews.
6. The Fall of Babylon.
7. The Reign of Antichrist.

All these events occur very close together. The conversion of the Jews will not occur until the Gospel is preached all over the world. This world-wide evangelization will be achieved by, and at the time of, the Two Witnesses, which in turn, will lead to a major spiritual revival. These two individuals will then be martyred by the Antichrist.

The Two Witnesses: The Two Witnesses are identified with Elijah and Enoch who were recorded in the Old Testament as being transported bodily into Heaven (Gen 5:24: 2Kings 2:11). Many who believe in a literal translation of the Bible believe that these will come back again in the flesh to fulfil their role in The Book of Revelation. Emmet O Regan has pointed out in his book, Unveiling the Apocalypse,[205] that these two individuals are also based on Joshua, the High Priest and Zerubbabel, the rightful heir to the lost throne of Judah. These two historical figures were responsible for the restoration of the Holy City of Jerusalem, after the Babylonian captivity. The Two Witnesses of the Apocalypse will be responsible for the restoration of the Church after the apostasy period which we are now living through. Christ Himself identified St John the Baptist as another Elijah and Emmet O Regan thinks it likely that The Angelic Pope and The Great Monarch (who will take over the throne of France – see chapter 11) will be the actual Two Witnesses, described in the Apocalypse.

Various saints have spoken about a period of peace before the coming of the Antichrist. Desmond A Birch describes these in some detail.[162] They include St Ephraem, St Francis of Paula, St Mechtilde of Helfta (Saxony), St Vincent Ferrer, and others. They also foresaw the restoration of a French King, who would become a great world leader and the formation of a new very popular and influential religious order during this period of peace. This order will be popularly known as "the cross bearers" (– see chapter 11). This period of peace was generally predicted by some of these saints to be approximately thirty years, during which time the Two Witnesses would be leading the re-evangelization of the world. The reign of the Antichrist would be at the end of this period of peace, that is, towards the end of the second woe described in the Book of Revelation. This period of peace was also recognized in The Book of Destiny by Fr Kramer.[223] The first reign of terror, identified in this book, in the early part of the second woe (see above) will precede this period of peace. The torrent of Catholic prophecies and prophets which have emerged over the last half century describing this reign of terror and associated chastisements suggests that this period of human history, is now about to begin, probably in this year of 2017.

The Sign of The Son of Man: Emmet O Regan points out that the eschatological earthquake, described in the Old Testament (Zech 14:4), occurs as a direct result of the appearance of the Sign of the Son of Man, when "the Mount of Olives shall be split into two from east to west by a very wide valley". This earthquake will be the greatest event in human history (Rev 16:18).

The Sign of The Son of Man was also described by St Faustina, but this event will likely occur in the distant future after the long period of peace. Her description was as follows, "Before the day of justice arrives, there will be given to people a sign in the Heavens of this sort: All light in the Heavens will be extinguished, and there will be great darkness over the whole earth. Then the sign of the cross will be seen in the sky, and from the openings where the hands and the feet of the Saviour were nailed will come forth great lights which will light up the earth for a period of time. This will take place shortly before the last day."

The Second Coming of Christ

There is a lot of confusion at the moment about the term "The Second Coming" which refers to the second coming of Christ. Traditional Roman Catholic teaching uses this term to refer to the return of Jesus in the flesh, as an actual person, at the end of time when all the dead will rise again, both just and unjust, before the Last judgment. After this judgment, the just will go to eternal joy and the unjust will go to eternal punishment (Catechism of the Catholic Church (CCC) 1038). The main source of the confusion at this time is from the common expectation, among many Christians, that a "second" coming of Jesus is imminent. It will help to consider this expectation briefly in order to try to get some clarification of eschatological (end-time) events in the near future.

Although the "second coming" has always been taught in the Catholic Church as a universal event, before the end of time, there was also a wide acceptance, among the Church Fathers, that the power of Satan would be broken before a great period of peace came to the world. A thousand years mentioned for the length of this period of peace is believed by most to be symbolic. Mark Mallett (see foreword to this edition) discusses this expectation of what he describes as a "middle coming of Christ". Mark quotes St Bernard who describes this "middle or intermediate" coming as hidden. Only the elect will see the Lord within their own selves. In His first coming, Jesus came in our flesh and in our weakness: in this middle coming He comes in spirit and power: in the final coming He will be seen in glory and majesty. Emeritus Pope Benedict XVI agrees with this interpretation. St Pope John Paul II also commented on this "Interior Advent", which he said is brought to life through constant meditation on, and assimilation of, the Word of God, rendered fruitful and animated by the prayer of adoration and praise of God, and reinforced by the constant reception of the sacraments.

Mark Mallett goes on to explain that the Church Fathers accepted this coming of Christ in "spirit and power" and it is this manifestation of Christ's power that slays the Antichrist, not at the end of time, but before the era of peace. This new reign of Christ will be established in every nation, when peace and justice will be established throughout the whole world. It will be the reign of Jesus in His saints, who will be living in the Divine Will "on earth as it is in Heaven," in public and private life (see chapter 15 for more discussion on the Divine Will).

Other signs which will be associated with this intermediate coming of Christ are the apostasy or decay of faith, persecution of believers (**the Church will go through a persecution and a passion as Christ did**), wars and rumours of wars, and signs in the Heavens, such as the darkening of the sun and the moon. As explained above, other events that need to have taken place before the coming of Christ are, the conversion of the Jews, the Gospel must be preached to the whole world, and the revelation of the Antichrist.

The Antichrist

There are two broad views as to when we should expect the Antichrist. One view is that he will come on the scene immediately before the final coming of Christ, that is, near the end of the world and just before the final judgment. The second view, which is now becoming very popular, is that the Antichrist will come at a time of great turmoil and apostasy in the Church and in the world. After the defeat of this "lawless one, .son of perdition, .apostate, .robber" there will be an era of great peace in the world and the Catholic Church will spread rapidly all over the world, with the final result of "one fold and one shepherd". According to Mark Mallett (see foreword to this edition), this second view agrees with the time-line of Biblical Revelation and was a common belief among the early Church Fathers, who often referred to this long era of peace as a "Sabbath or seventh day rest". This view is also in keeping with modern revelations and thus has enormous implication for our near future, particularly as some of the signs described in Sacred Scripture that indicate the nearness of the Antichrist are already with us, particularly the growth of evil and error, apostasy from the Christian faith, and war with bloody persecution of believers. See page 653 above, for a list of events before the reign of the Antichrist.

Some of the broad general chronological events associated with the Antichrist are as follows:

1. The rise of the Dragon against the woman clothed with the sun.
2. The Dragon gives authority to the Antichrist. A false prophet forces everybody to worship the Antichrist.
3. Jesus destroys the Antichrist and the false prophet by the "brightness of His coming". Both are cast into Hell.
4. Satan is chained and the Church reigns in peace for an extended period of time.

There are many who believe that the Antichrist is already here and some books have been published to back up this claim.[225] The March-April newsletter of The Order of New Knighthood[226] gives a detailed discussion on messages given to Fr Gobbi[3] suggesting that the time of the Antichrist is very close. This newsletter also points out that it was revealed to Fr Gobbi that another cycle of the 70 week/year Biblical prophecy of Daniel (9:27 and 12:11) began with the apparition of The Virgin Mary in Mexico (Guadalupe) during the winter solstice of 1531. This began The Age of Mary, which is now approaching a conclusion with these "end times". This apparition of Guadalupe was a response to the attack on Catholic teaching by Martin Luther in 1517 and the rejection of Catholic teaching by the English King, Henry VIII in the same year, 1531. Counting forward 62 weeks of years (434) - (see Dan 9:20-27 for explanation of the 62 weeks) we come to 1965, which was the year Vatican II Council ended. The next 7 weeks of years (49) brings us to 2014, which was a period when satanic confusion increased dramatically within the Catholic Church. The doctrine of this Church is now well diluted with New-Age practices as well as liberalism and secularism. The final week of years (7) mark the "end times" which we are now living in and this seven is divided into two halves of 3.5 years, with a midpoint during 2018.

The above news-letter also notes the following, with references, from numerous locutions to Fr Gobbi between 1973 and 1997:

"The true faith will be lost in the world. The Church will undergo a great trial: the man of iniquity will establish himself within it and the Abomination of Desolation will enter the holy temple of God. Satan with his cohorts will triumph in the world and in the Church. The faithful remnant will undergo the greatest trials and persecutions. Fire will descend from Heaven and the world will undergo a great chastisement. The greater part of humanity will be destroyed. The earth and humanity will be purified and renewed. In the end, Our Lady will triumph, snatching victory from Satan's hands. Jesus will return in glory to establish His glorious reign in the world."

The next four years, therefore, could be a re-enactment of the time of great desolation described in Matthew 24:15-. The Garabandal visionaries described the great problems for the world beginning around the time of an invasion with chaos in Rome, when the Pope will have to flee the city.

Referring again to the recurring prophecy of Daniel again (12:10-), it says: "Many will be purified, cleansed and refined. The impious will go on doing evil, none of them will understand anything, only the wise will understand. From the time the perpetual sacrifice is suppressed and the abominable idol of the devastator is installed, there shall be one thousand two hundred and ninety days. Blessed is the one who waits and reaches a thousand three hundred and thirty five days," that is, approximately 3.5 years.

The list of the Biblical events quoted above (see page 653), associated with the advent of the Antichrist is a strong argument, however, against the manifestation of this person at this time, despite the books and many references that argue otherwise. The Antichrist may be coming into the world now but it is more likely that he will not be manifested until after a period of peace (? about 30 years), during which the Two Witnesses will rule and have the true gospel of Christ preached and spread all over the world. For this to happen, the Immaculate Heart of Mary will have to triumph over the efforts of the One World Order. This is very unlikely to happen peacefully.

It was noted above in the Book of Revelation that the eschatological earthquake, described in the Old Testament (Zech 14:4), will occur at the time of the appearance of the Sign of the Son of Man in the sky, and also when "the Mount of Olives shall be split into two from east to west by a very wide valley". This earthquake will be the greatest event in human history (Rev 16:18). These events will be associated directly with the conversion of the Jews. This will also be the time of the Fall of Babylon and the manifestation of the Antichrist, which is not in the immediate future.

The Significance of 2017: There are many pointers to indicate that 2017 is a year of great interest and significance, however, for both the Jewish and Christian religions. The centenary anniversary of the Great Sign of Fatima has already been discussed in detail. 2017 is the Jewish year of 5777. The year is referred to as year 777 as the initial '5' is often dropped and it is also the fifty year anniversary of the six day war, when the Jewish nation reclaimed Jerusalem. It was noted in chapter 16, that not only is the "Star of Bethlehem" coming back but also that a great sign will appear in the Heavens on 23rd September 2017: "And a great sign appeared in Heaven: A woman clothed with the sun and the moon under her feet and on her head a crown of twelve stars."(Revelation 12). This sign, in Catholic theology, represents The Virgin Mary or "The New Eve". It is also, therefore, of great interest that the last previous appearance of this sign in the Heavens was estimated by some investigators to be 5932 years ago, which is around the Biblical date given for Adam and Eve. Others claim that this is a unique astronomical event. The 22nd of September 2017 is also the time of the feast of Trumpets or Rosh Hashanah and is only a few days short of 1260 days (see discussion above page 642, for the significance of this number) from the first of four blood moons on Jewish feast days, which began in mid-April 2014 (? the beginning of these end-times). All these time coincidences may or may not

660

have significance. The three weeks between the 22nd September and 13th October 2017 (centenary of the Great Sign of Fatima) should be noted well, as possibly a time of great fulfilment, and perhaps a great historical pivotal point for the triumph of The Immaculate Heart of Mary.

It is also a real possibility that the Roman Catholic Mass (the Great Sacrifice) will be outlawed at some stage over the next few years. The other big question for us to worry about is: will the tipping of the earth (with accompanying extraordinary winds, earthquakes, volcanoes, and oceans covering the land), followed by the fulfilling of the prophecy of Akita (see page 172), with fire coming from the sky, be within the next few years or after the short period of peace, at the time of the manifestation of the Antichrist? Akita is closely linked to Fatima and both are linked to the triumph of the Immaculate Heart of Mary, which we expect to happen at the end of the Age of Mary. We must expect these events soon, therefore, as the final dramatic act which will selectively but not exclusively destroy evil in the world. In the words of Saint Pope John Paul II, when he was describing the oceans covering the land and millions dying in minutes, he said with his rosary in his hand, "pray, pray, pray, and leave everything to the Mother of God."

In all this drama, let us not forget the complicated but Catholic Church approved (1851) prophecy of La Salette. In particular it is interesting to note the section of this prophecy quoted in the booklet, The End of the World – What Catholics Believe,[227] which says:

"A great country now Protestant, in the north of Europe, will be converted: by the support of this country all the other nations of the world will be converted. Before all that arrives, great disorders will arrive, in the Church, and everywhere. Then after that, our Holy Father the Pope will be persecuted. His successor will be a pontiff that nobody expects. Then after that a great peace will come, but it will not last a long time. A monster will come to disturb it."

It is often suggested that the country referred in that passage above, is England. Just as the defection of King Henry VIII from the Catholic Church, in 1531, marked the year of the start of the Age of Mary (see above), it would be a great sign of the triumph of Mary, if a senior member of the British Royal family was to convert to Catholicism, lead to the conversion of the UK to Catholicism, and then to the conversion of other countries. Certainly, it was well known that Princess Diana, for some years before her untimely death, visited the Carmelite Catholic Church in Kensington, London, on a very regular basis and had developed a great devotion to St Thérése of Lisieux. Princess Diana's mother converted to Catholicism in 1996 and there were indications that she was about to follow in her footsteps if she had survived. This would have had a profound effect on the British people, as the enormous popularity of this Great Lady became so evident at the time of her unfortunate early death. One way or another, the British people, a race for whom I developed an enormous respect during eight years living in the UK, will soon realize that King Henry VIII made a terrible mistake. I wait in hope that the British Monarchy will, in the near future, again become defenders of the true Christian faith.

A Possible Timetable

Nominating dates of days, months or years, when particular events will happen, has never been productive. I resisted doing that in the first edition of this book and although events now seem to be moving rapidly, the best we can do is still guess work based on what reliable visionaries have said, and even these sometimes get the timing wrong or have false statements attributed to them.

Recent history in particular is littered with false prophetic dates and reliable prophets rarely give exact dates as explained in chapter 11.

Nevertheless, there are strong indications that world changing events are very close. The prophecies of Garabandal indicate that Pope Emeritus Benedict was the last Pope before the beginning of the end-times. It was also explained above (page 658) that according to Fr Gobbi, the latest cycle of Daniel's prophecy of 70 weeks of years (490 years) began in 1531 with the apparition of Our Lady of Guadalupe and this also marked the beginning of the *Age of Mary*. We are now living through the last seven years of this time, which is referred to as the "end-times". These last seven years began in 2014 and will finish in 2021, with a mid-point in 2018. Taking these time indicators as a guide, therefore, it would mean that the end-times began the year after Emeritus Pope Benedict XVI resigned. It may be of interest that a much photographed bolt of lightning, hit the dome of St Peter's Basilica in Rome, on the 11th February, 2013, that is, on the day Emeritus Pope Benedict XVI resigned. Was this a heavenly sign of some kind to indicate the approaching *end-times*? We now expect that these *end-times* as well as the *Age of Mary* will end in December 2021 with the *Triumph of The Immaculate Heart of Mary*. The main turmoil associated with this triumph and the transformation of the world towards a belief in the true God, and a respect for God's laws can, therefore, be expected to begin at any moment.

After the *Age of Mary*: The end of the *Age of Mary*, according to many prophecies, will be followed by a short era of peace. This will be a period of approximately thirty years, when the Christian gospel will be preached all over the world. This is described as the sixth era and will come to an end with the manifestation of the Antichrist. This will be towards the end of the reign of the great French King and the "Angelic" Pope, both of whom are likely to die under the direction of the Antichrist. After the Antichrist is defeated the world and the Church will enter a long period of peace when humanity will be living more and more in the *Divine Will* (see chapter 15). At that time, evil will steadily decrease in the world, while the love of God, knowledge, and technological advancement will increase dramatically.

As already pointed out, 2017 is a significant year for a number of reasons. The 13th of October 2017 marks the centenary of the Great Sign of Fatima which could coincide with the end of the time allowed for Satan to have extra power and influence over humanity, in line with the vision of Pope Leo XIII (see page 136). Astronomically, the star of Bethlehem will be making a return in 2017 and will emerge from the constellation Virgo on the 23rd of September 2017 after spending just over nine months there. **It would be nice if we also had a return of three wise Zoroastrian men (Kings or otherwise) who could explain to the Jews and the rest of us, what significance the return of the Star of Bethlehem has on this historical occasion.** At this time also, the Biblical reference of "The Woman clothed with the sun, with the moon under her feet and a crown of 12 stars" will be visible in the night sky. A few years ago, many believed that this time would mark the triumph of the Immaculate Heart of Mary over the forces of the One World Order. Now it looks as if it could be the historical pivotal point when these two forces enter into the final stages of this battle. The end-times, as explained above, would still have another four years to progress up to the end of 2021 when the Age of Mary is expected to end.

The Forties: For those who are now under **forty** years, if they survive, they can expect the human race to be completely transformed during their lives, over the next **forty** years. If the above interpretation of prophecy and the *Book of Revelation* is correct, there will be **two periods of forty two months** that will be particularly difficult, separated by approximately one generation in time (see Revelation 13:5). These will be the times when satanic activity in the world will be at its peak, with the ultimate aim of destroying the Roman Catholic Church. The first of these periods is about to begin, when the satanic activity will be controlled by the spirit of the Antichrist, rather than the Antichrist in person. This will come to an end with the Triumph of the Immaculate Heart of Mary. The second period of forty two months will be, as explained above, after about thirty years, towards the end of the short period of peace. This time the satanic activity will be particularly intense and will be controlled and directed by the Antichrist in person. This will come to an end when Jesus comes in *"Spirit and Power"* to defeat the Antichrist, (see page 656).

These two forty two month periods will be controlled by two sets of Unholy Trinities, in opposition to the *Holy Trinity*. The first Unholy Trinity will be composed of the Red Dragon, which is a resurgent Communism as explained by Fr Gobbi[3] and predicted at Garabandal. Fr Gobbi further explained that resurgent Communism will join forces with two Beasts. These are described as the Beast from the sea and the Beast from the land. These Beasts are represented by secular Freemasons and Freemasonary activity within the Catholic Church, respectively. The second forty two week period will be particularly severe and cruel and will be controlled by the person of the Antichrist. The Anitchrist will be brought to power by the False Prophet, with the help of those who have made a conscious decision to support satanic rule. The False Prophet will insist that the Antichrist be worshipped as God.

The Antichrist will not take over the Papacy, therefore, at this time but the Church leadership will be, confused, scattered and decimated. The Catholic Church will have to go through the period of its passion before its glorious resurrection. It seems, at this stage that a Church schism is very close and with the turmoil in

Rome predicted in Garabandal and by many other prophets, it is very likely that the Pope will have to leave Rome. A "false" church may also be established at that time and the Mass may be outlawed in certain parts of the world during this initial forty two month period, which is due to begin around the middle of 2018. Sr Lucia of Fatima was told that the final battle, at this time, would be against the Christian family unit. We can, therefore, expect that aggressive promotion of homosexuality and abortion will be top of the agenda for *One World Order* forces, which will include the International mainstream media, over the next few years, up to the end of 2021. The predicted Warning of Garabandal will be a very major sign of warning from God (see chapter 12) to encourage humanity to change rapidly, or suffer the consequences. This *Warning* was predicted by the visionaries in Garabandal to occur *"when things were at their worst"* and close to an event, *like a schism*, in the Church.

The second forty two month period, as explained already, will occur after a period of peace, with the manifestation of a particular individual who will later be identified as the Antichrist. He will be brought into power by a False Prophet. He will take over the Throne of Peter, which at that stage may be in Jerusalem, as the *Abomination of Desolation*, and demand to be worshipped as God. According to the Revelation, the second woe will end around the time of the manifestation of the Antichrist (see page 649).

It was described above (see page 646/7) how the four signs associated with the opening of the sixth seal occurred in an area of modern Turkey in late 1999 and early 2,000 AD. These could be described as localized signs, however, and the question must be, can we expect similar signs on a more global scale later or have these events already set the stage for the unfolding of the other great events described in the *Book of Revelation?* The time relationship of the first and second woe to the short period of peace is also difficult to understand. In particular, the timing of the invasion, by the 200 million strong army from the east, described at the beginning of the second woe (see page 649), is difficult to discern. Will this invasion occur soon (over the next few years) or will it be later, at the end of the time of peace, around the time of the Antichrist? If this invasion is to occur soon, then it would mean that the period of peace would occur during the second woe, as the second woe will end with the manifestation of the Antichrist.

The close relation of the Fatima message and the triumph of *The Immaculate Heart of Mary* with **the message of Akita** (fire from the sky – see page 172), and **the tipping of the earth axis**, leading to oceans covering large portions of the world has already been discussed in chapter 16. Sr Lucia of Fatima and St Pope John Paul II as well as other reliable prophets alluded to this catastrophe of the tipping of the earth. The gravitational pull of a large Heavenly body has been mentioned as a possible reason for this. The big question is, when? How near are these events? The triumph of *The Immaculate Heart of* Mary also seems to be linked with the messages of Garabandal and Medjugorje and all this would suggest that the tipping of the earth and the fire from the heavens may be the final act within the next few years, which will ensure the triumph of The Immaculate Heart of Mary over the major evil influences in the world. If we are now at the beginning of the "second woe" as outlined in the Book of Revelation then a possible timetable of events could be as follows:

Global turmoil will begin soon. This could be kicked off by a global financial crash, or the assassination of a little known apparently insignificant politician, or a myriad of other reasons. This could be associated with the announcement of the first of the Medjugorje secrets. The Garabandal Warning will follow soon after an invasion and chaos in Rome, "when things are at their worst." This will be followed within a year by the Great Garabandal Miracle and the occurrence of perpetual Permanent Signs of the presence of God, in different previously selected parts of the world, including Garabandal. At this time also, around the time of the Grabandal Warning and Miracle, there may be an invasion by China, with an army of 200 million, as described in the Book of Revelation but as discussed above this could also be delayed until the time of the Antichrist.

It is possible that the return of the Star of Bethlehem in 2017 could indicate a kind of mystical coming of Christ at this time, with His power being completely manifest, in approximately 30 years time, with the defeat of the Antichrist. This would occur after the short era of peace, and after the triumph of the *Immaculate Heart of Mary*, a time when the Christian gospel will be preached all over the world. For those of us who are unlikely to be around in 30 years time, it would be nice to believe that the tipping of the earth and Akita events could also be delayed to the time of the Antichrist, as suggested by Emmet O Regan,[205] but that may be wishful thinking.

A Russian Invasion: It was made clear in chapter 11, that the invasion of Western Europe by Russia, has been mentioned many times in Catholic prophecy. The impact of the consecration made to the *Immaculate Heart of Mary* by St Pope John Paul II, in 1984, is impossible to discern. There is no doubt that President Putin is now one of the most active global leaders promoting Christianity and ironically, at this time in European history, it is the Western European States that are promoting cultural Marxism, under a veil of liberal democracies. Putin, however, may be just using Christianity to promote his own agenda. The Russian Orthodox Church (ROC) has been controlled, directly or indirectly, by the state for many centuries and there is no reason to believe that this is not still so. Certainly Aleksandr Dugin, who advises Putin, belongs to a strict ROC group and he favours establishing a new

Russian Empire that will wage war against American and European liberalism. Nevertheless, Putin is strongly pro-Christian and now seems to be opposed to abortion and on the side of natural law. The opinion of some is that Russia will be used to punish Europe for the rejection of God, and natural law, especially for the killing of the unborn. The statement by The Virgin *of Garabandal* that the major prophesied events will happen, "When Communism comes back", could refer to a resurgence of Communism in Eastern Europe, or the Gramsci variety of cultural Marxism that is now world-wide, or a Chinese variety of Communism.

An Unusual Photograph

This picture was circulated widely many years ago. The story goes that a man took a photograph of a statue of Our Lady of the Roses, on 14th Sept 1971, with a Polaroid instant camera. The image above is said to have mysteriously appeared on the film. Saint Jacinta is now the youngest non-martyred saint in the Catholic Church. She was one of the Fatima visionaries and was canonized on 13th May 2017 – just as this book was about to go to print. She had warned during her life that by 1972, evil would have increased significantly in the world. A New York visionary, Veronica Leuken (R.I.P.), was apparently told that this was a miraculous picture which had hidden within it, the date of the beginning of a global Chastisement for Mankind. I reproduce the image for interest and discernment only, rather than making any claims of its authenticity.

When the name Jacinta is read at a 90 degree turn, as it appears on the side of the picture, the figures two, three, and eighteen can be clearly deciphered from top to bottom. This may indicate the date, 2nd March 2018 (2/3/18). There are two good reasons to believe that this picture is not an authentic prophecy. Firstly, it is difficult to believe that God plays this kind of game with humanity and secondly, the visionary involved was at one stage condemned by her local Bishop for proclaiming heresy. Nevertheless, this picture is almost 50 years old now and because of the perceived nearness of major world events, the date may not be too far away from the mark. As they say in some parts of Ireland, "nosaigh an aimsir" (time will tell).

In summary, therefore, all the indications are that the triumph of the *Immaculate Heart of Mary* is very close. Global events in the very near future will ensure that this happens. Because the secrets of Fatima, and the message of Akita, are intimately connected with this triumph, it is not difficult to believe that the tipping of the earth with the accompanying fire from Heaven (both of which now seem inevitable in the near future) could be the final act in this drama, despite how remote and unreal all this now seems. The extent of destruction and death will be based on the free choice of humanity to accept or reject God's laws. The exact significance of the return of the Star of Bethlehem in 2017, to coincide with the centenary of the great sign of Fatima on the 13th of October is not clear.

What can you believe?

This book, I hope has challenged you to think a little outside of your normal daily routine. We are all accustomed to live in our own little world and to some extent our rat race has also become our rut race. If what you have read has lifted you a little out of your rut and helped you to see another aspect of the "real" world then I hope you consider that your reading time has not been wasted. Many, I know, especially non-Catholics, will find what has been said about Fatima, Akita and the *Immaculate Heart of Mary* difficult to believe or even to consider it as part of a "real" world. It only becomes part of the real world for those who try to come out of the mainstream information rut and begin to look at the evidence. The simple question for each person to answer is: are the apparitions of The Virgin Mary real substantiated events or are they simply imagination? The correct answer will be found by looking for and investigating the evidence. The implications of this evidence for you and your family will be profoundly important, going into the future.

I have quoted Peter Kreeft previously in this book when he said, "Truth trumps everything."[152] It is ironic in this time, when we are all suffering from information overload, that finding truth has never been more difficult. "Fake-news" is now appearing more and more as part of the news headlines. One of the greatest sources of this fake-news is found in the new social media outlets especially youtube. Every Tom, Dick, and Harry, as well as Jill, Beryl, and Bernadette, are putting their stuff up on youtube. We already know that we cannot always believe what we see in print or get from the mainstream media, but we must now be doubly careful about what we hear and see on youtube. Many sites and stories are designed to be completely fictitious in order to trap the gullible for sale promotions or other reasons. The Western World is now knee deep in fake news and the tide is rising. Corruption is continually crawling and creeping into society. If it continues soon, I fear, that "liar's poker" will be the only game in town. It is spreading from International finance (see chapter 18) into all normal daily encounters and transactions, including those that are supposed to be "legal". But who can be surprised, as this is the inevitable consequence of a secular morality, where survival of the fittest is promoted, where the driving force is selfishness and greed, and where the only error is to be caught and to have the lies exposed.

This age of rapid information sharing is throwing up many new stories which are not just fascinating but some at least, are probably true. These stories are pointing towards a time in the near future of great strangeness or transition, which will open up many new experiences for humanity. One example is that more and more major ancient pyramid structures are being discovered. The latest I have come across is a huge pyramid structure in Romania buried by many ancient flood deposits similar in age and size to the structure in Bosnia, described in chapter 17. The source of shafts of electromagnetic radiation, recently described as coming from the tops of pyramids around the world, is also fascinating and unexplained. On the other hand, a pyramid recently described in Antarctica now seems to be no more than a normal mountain with a pyramid structure. This mountain has given rise to many fake news stories and conspiracy theories concerning demons, extra-terrestrials, and the remains of previous prehistoric civilizations, all of which are unlikely to have any basis in fact. Nevertheless, it is a common question among those who trawl youtube for interesting news items to ask, what is going on in Antarctica?

Rapidly changing attitudes: This is also a time of rapidly changing attitudes as the information-mountains are opening minds up to new ideas and experiences of all kinds. For the first time, some are waking up to the reality of evil, such as the recent Dutch Financier who had no belief in God or Satan and found the gatherings he was invited to, for "Black Masses" with naked ladies, no more than amusing. He came to his senses, and went public, however, when he was asked to get involved with child sacrifices.

Large numbers of Muslims are beginning to convert to Christianity at this time for all different reasons and millions of Chinese are converting in what has been described as a Christian revolution in China. It is now estimated that there are 120 million Christians in China and at the present rate of conversion, will soon become the most populous Christian nation. The Russian state is now openly promoting Christianity and at least 10% more Russians now believe in God than the average of European countries. In his book, *Last Testament*,[233] Emeritus Pope Benedict describes a meeting with Putin in these words:

"He speaks perfect German. We didn't go very deep, but I certainly believe that he is – a man of power of course – somehow affected by the necessity of faith. He is a realist. He sees how Russia suffers from the destruction of morality. Even as a patriot, as someone who wants Russia to have great power again, he sees that the destruction of Christianity threatens to destroy Russia. A human being needs God, he sees that quite evidently, and he is affected by it inwardly as well. He has now even, as he gave the *Papa* (Pope Francis) an Icon, made the sign of the cross and kissed it."

In the West, Christianity has been largely rejected but the traditional base of Communism in the East now seems to be reverting to Christianity. This represents a great challenge to the *One World Order*, trying to promote a world that ignores God.

Doom and Gloom: Some time ago, I began to meet with a few friends at the week-ends and over breakfast we discussed current world affairs with a special emphasis on "end-time" (as in the end of this era, rather than end of the world) events. My daughter dubbed this group, 'The doomsday club'. I also heard of two individuals who chaired a similar group in another part of the country and became known as, "doom and gloom". I am acutely aware, therefore, that discussing end-time events is not popular and carries a major credibility deficit. As fake news stories increase and confusion about what is true and false increase daily, then the big question for you the reader of this book is, therefore, how much credibility and importance you can place on the many end-time events described and discussed in this book.

The first point I must make is that, in my experience, those who have an interest in end-time events are not full of doom and gloom. On the contrary, they are full of joy and hope. They generally agree that the long-term future is very bright, in fact better than ever before, but choppy seas are ahead which must be navigated. Secondly, anybody who thinks that the world is in a good place at the moment and will only continue to improve, with no major hiccups, is living in a "cloud of unknowing" and in a false reality. Each individual will have to decide for themselves where the truth lies. This book has presented some evidence and now it is over to you, the reader, to respond in whatever way you consider appropriate. If you decide positively that the world is on the brink of some major transforming events, it would only make sense to make some preliminary preparations or at least to keep a more watchful and urgent eye on world affairs.

What can you do?

This book is a call to repent and return to the God of love. It is a call to wake up. It is a call to stop living in a false reality and stop living the lie of secularism, which blinds you from the calamity ahead. Please try to answer this call. Above all if change is needed, don't wait too long. Don't wait for the major signs, as by then it will be too late for many and there will be great chaos and confusion.

The Value of Consecration: A number of times, over hundreds of years, Jesus and Mary have asked for consecration to the *Sacred Heart of Jesus* and the *Immaculate Heart of Mary* as a protection from different kinds of disaster. On the 13th July 1917, The Virgin Mary showed the three child visionaries of Fatima a vision of Hell. The children said, "We could see a vast sea of fire. Plunged in the flames were demons and lost souls.." The Virgin Mary said:

"You have seen Hell where the souls of poor sinners go. In order to save them, God wishes to establish in the world devotion to my *Immaculate Heart*. If people do what I ask, many souls will be saved and there will be peace. The war is going to end, but if people do not stop offending God another, even worse will begin in the reign of Pius XI. (note: he was not yet Pope). When you see a night illuminated by an unknown light, know that it is the great sign that God gives you that He is going to punish the world by means of war, hunger and persecution of the Church and of the Holy Father - (this was the so called great aurora of 25th January, 1938, except that it was not a normal natural aurora, with the sun as the source of light. This aurora had two sources of light as may happen with two very large nuclear explosions). To prevent it, I shall come to ask for the **consecration of Russia to my Immaculate Heart** and the devotion of *Communion of Reparation on the First Saturdays* of the month (She returned to Sr Lucia on 13th June 1929 to make this formal request). If people attend to my requests, Russia will be converted and the world will have peace. If not, Russia will spread its errors throughout the world, fomenting wars and persecution of the Church. The good will be martyred, the Holy Father will have much to suffer, and various nations will be annihilated. In the end my *Immaculate Heart* will triumph. The Holy Father will consecrate Russia to me. It will be converted and a period of peace will be granted to the world. In Portugal the dogmas of faith will always be kept.."

As explained in chapter 5 (see page 132), the consecration of the world to *The Immaculate Heart of Mary*, made by Saint Pope John Paul II, on March 25th 1984, in union with Catholic Bishops around the world, as requested at Fatima, had an immediate effect on Communism in Russia. This has already been discussed earlier and there is a difference of opinion on how adequate this consecration was (see page 617/8). Unfortunately, this consecration was done late and could have been done better by world Bishops. Despite this, the fall of Communism was dramatic and although the conversion of Russia has still not been achieved, major strides have been made with President Putin and we can say that Russia now seems to be a lot more Christian than much of the rest of Europe. The consecration, therefore, although late, had a profound effect. A number of attempts have been made to do this consecration of Russia as requested by The Virgin Mary, since the first attempt by Pope Pius XII in 1942. Revelations to Fr Gobbi[3] suggest that it should still be renewed and improved again so as to get the maximum effect. Many believe that this will happen after much blood has been spilt.

Nevertheless, when the new nuclear submarines in Russia have chapels, so that Mass can be offered, when very large numbers of churches and monasteries are re-opening in Russia, when teachers are complaining that it is now hard to teach secularism in Russian schools because all the textbooks are promoting Christianity, when a young girl-band are sent to prison for an extended period for singing pop songs in the sanctuary of a Moscow Cathedral, because they were desecrating the national morals, and when the President attends Mass and retreats and openly promotes Christianity, we must admit that the recent changes in Russia have been dramatic. We must also remember that although, by the wish of The *Holy Trinity*, consecration to *The Immaculate Heart of Mary* opens the flood-gates of Divine grace to unbelievers and believers alike, the full benefits of this will need to be earned by each individual opening their own gates and doors to their hearts so that this grace can pour in. This is done by living holy lives of prayer, especially with the Mass and rosary, reparation, reception of the sacraments, and respecting human life, particularly unborn life.

Historically it should also be noted again that similarly, the delay in consecrating France to *The Sacred Heart of Jesus*, as requested by Jesus, left that country unprotected against revolution in 1789 (see page 133). This request was made through Saint Margaret Mary Alacoque on June 17th, 1689, to King Louis XIV. Exactly 100 years later to the day, June 17th 1789, the National Assembly of the French Revolution stripped King Louis XVI of his power. The consecration of France which was made by King Louis XVI, just before his death, will, according to Catholic prophecy, have the effect of restoring the monarchy to France in the near future and through this a future King of France will play a major role in restoring world peace.

Two further comments noted in the recent Order of New Knighthood newsletter[226] concerning conversations between Jesus and Sr Lucia of Fatima are worth noting.

The first concerned the delay by the Church of consecrating Russia. Jesus said: "They have not chosen to heed my request. As with the King of France (Louis XVI, in 1792), they will regret it and then do it, but it will be too late. Russia will have already spread her errors throughout the world, provoking wars and persecutions against the Church. The Holy Father will have much to suffer."

The second was a response to a question from Sr Lucia as to why the consecration was necessary for the conversion of Russia. Jesus said: "I want My whole Church to acknowledge that consecration as a triumph of the Immaculate Heart of Mary so that it may extend its cult later on and put the devotion to the Immaculate Heart beside the devotion to My Sacred Heart. Pray much for the Holy Father, he will do it but it will be late. Nevertheless the Immaculate Heart of Mary will save Russia. It has been entrusted to Her."

A good way for Catholics to prepare for the coming global chaos and transformation of the world, therefore, is to have themselves, their families, and their homes, consecrated to *The Sacred Heart of Jesus and The Immaculate Heart of Mary*. This consecration can be compared with having the houses and families marked with the blood of the lamb, during the final plague of Egypt, in Old Testament times. If this consecration is lived out in the Eucharistic life style, as promoted by the Alliance of The Holy Family International (AHFI), then this family will have great protection during the coming world turmoil. One should try to wear some emblem of this consecration, such as the brown scapular, and renew some form of simple consecration on a daily basis. One of the simplest forms of consecration prayers to The Virgin Mary is that used by the Legion of Mary, "I am all yours, my Queen and my Mother, and all that I have is Yours."

The Lady of All Nations: The Virgin Mary revealed herself to Ida Peerdeman in Amsterdam in 1947 under the new title of The Lady of All Nations.[60] She revealed a new image of Herself and a new prayer which has now been approved by the Church. She said, "Under this title, and through this prayer, I may deliver the world from a great world catastrophe". It was through miracles associated with a statue of this image that Our Lady of Akita became known to the world. The message of Akita was delivered on the 13th Oct. 1973 connecting Fatima, The Lady of All Nations, and Akita. The Virgin Mary asked us to spread her image and the prayer among all nations, in what she called "A Worldwide Action of Redemption and Peace". She said that this worldwide action is a requirement and a preparation for the new Marian Dogma… "Go with great ardour and zeal about this work of redemption and peace and you will behold the miracle". This dogma will be the greatest Marian dogma and will be a solemn proclamation of the truth of faith that Mary is the Coredemptrix, Mediatrix and Advocate for all nations. It will begin a new Pentecost in the Church and in the world. The spreading of the devotion to The Lady of All Nations, therefore, is a good way to try to prevent or at least mitigate, the catastrophe approaching the world.

Prayer to The Lady of All Nations

Lord Jesus Christ,
Son of the Father,
Send now Your Spirit over the earth.
Let The Holy Spirit live
In the hearts of all nations,
that they may be preserved
from degeneration, disaster and war.
May the Lady of All Nations,
The Blessed Virgin Mary *
Be our Advocate,
Amen.

* This line is a slight change from the original (suggested by Rome, before approval).

A World of Irony

This world is full of irony. It is ironic that at a time when all kinds of information is now freely available on tap through the internet, facebook, twitter, skype and so much else, humanity is ignoring and missing the most important information. The whole population of our planet are now standing at the edge of a precipice and the majority are about to fall over the edge. They are almost 100% unaware. It was a great irony in the past, how the centre of the empire that tried hard to cruelly suppress Christianity at its beginning, should become the centre of a Christian empire. It will be a much greater irony in the future, when a new Roman Empire will emerge, after this eminent human cataclysmic tragedy, and conquer the whole world for Christ. This great irony in the world was well recognized by St John of the Cross in his Ascent of Mount Carmel (see page 230). When Pilate asked Jesus at His trial, **What is Truth?,** he was not aware that the answer was hidden in his question – **It is he who is before you.**

QUID EST VERITAS?
EST VIR QUI ADEST

Efforts are now being made to kill God again, by secularism, liberalism, and evolutionary materialism. This time, however, it is men who will die, not God. Many will die and with these deaths will also come the death of truth, reason, morality, freedom, and human dignity. Humanity is working tirelessly with the help of International bodies such as the UN, WHO and the European Union to create a society devoid of Christianity and alien to God. Humanity will fail, but more than half the population of the earth will die before this mistake is acknowledged. This is a society about to crumble. The disintegration will be a great drama of life and death, reminiscent of the Colosseum, except that the whole world will now be the arena. In the end the Secular Empire will again fall and the Nazarene will again conquer. That is for certain. Who can be blind enough not to see it coming? Who will be foolish enough not to accept it this time? All will eventually have to accept it sooner or later, one way or another. "At the name of Jesus every knee shall bow, in Heaven and on earth and under the earth, and every tongue confess that Jesus Christ is Lord to the Glory of God the Father" (Phil 2: 6 - 11). One of the most poignant moments during exorcisms, according to the, now deceased, chief exorcist in Rome, Fr Gabriel Amorth, is when the possessed individual is forced to kneel, at the name of Jesus. It has already been explained that the only religion with acknowledged power over evil spirits, is Christianity.

The situation in the world at this time has many similarities with the late 1930's and can again be described by the following extract from the Encyclical of Pope Pius XII, *Darkness over the Earth*:[235]

"Many, doubtless, in thus abandoning the commandments of Jesus Christ, failed to realize that they were being cheated by a plausible imitation of truth, tricked out with fine phrases. This rejection of Gospel teaching was cried up as emancipation from a yoke of slavery. They did not guess what would follow, when the truth which sets us free had been exchanged for the lie that makes slaves of us. In repudiating God's law, so fatherly, so infinitely wise, and Christ's commandments, breathing of charity, uniting men together and drawing their minds to things above, they did not reflect that it would mean handing themselves over to a capricious ruler, the feeble and grovelling wisdom of man. They boasted of progress, when they were in fact relapsing into decadence: they conceived that they were reaching heights of achievement when they were miserably forfeiting their human dignity: they claimed that this century of ours was bringing maturity and completion with it, when they were being reduced to a pitiable form of slavery. They had not the wit to see that any human effort to substitute for Christ's law some base model of it, must prove altogether empty and unfruitful: - vanity was the end of their designs."

The Divine Will: In order to be mature and live out our full human potential we need to be educated, not only in the secular fields of science, the humanities and art but also educated spiritually. The most astounding revelation on the love of God for humanity has been the revelations on *The Divine Will* as explained in chapter 15. Through this new gift of "The Divine Will", God is preparing humanity to regain the status and gifts that were lost by our first parents through original sin. The final mystery for us is to try to understand how God's love works for us in our lives. *The Divine Will* is a call to the human creature to return to the order, to the place, and to the purpose for which it was created. It is only through the official approval of the Roman Catholic Church that we can believe this revelation, begin to understand it, and begin to live it. This, in no small way, should emphasize for us the importance or recognizing the ultimate infallibility of this Church, and the importance of submitting to its authority, which comes directly from God.

The Prophetic Message

The message from Catholic prophecy for future events is clear and stark. Unless humanity rapidly changes course towards the God of love, we are heading for disaster. The storm is already gathering and the thunder of a terrible conflict is now near. We are in a count-down to world chaos. The final word must be, – PREPARE – prepare spiritually, mentally and physically. We are all brothers and sisters in the family of humanity and we are all called to love and support one another, especially in the troubled times ahead. I dread to think of the depression, the shock, and the suicides that will overtake us when the going gets really rough. The object of this book is not to alarm or upset but rather to alert and inform readers, so that they will know, what is about to happen, and can prepare. Small actions now can prevent a lot of suffering later. It would be nice to believe that all is well and that reason and goodness will overcome the difficulties. All may be well for those who love God and love others, but for those who reject God, all is not well, and Hell beckons unless they learn to repent and seek forgiveness. Try to accept God's messages for what they are, that is, God's messages and not some human thinking. The clear message must be that repentance and prayer can prevent suffering for you, your family and for others.

Because the Akita message is true, because it is largely ignored and because God does not make idle threats, the annihilation of much of humanity is unfortunately likely to become a reality. *The Immaculate Heart of Mary* is our great hope. The proclamation of the final Marian dogma of, *"Mary, Coredemptrix, Mediatrix and Advocate of all Graces"*, will mark a turning point for humanity over the forces of evil. Eventually, when all this hurly-burly is done, and this battle is lost and won, there will be one fold and one shepherd. At that stage, everybody will know the truth, but, at that stage, it is likely that only one of every three will survive to pick up the pieces and renew the face of the earth.

Trial in a Time Warp

There are many things about our life and about the Universe we live in, that will always be a mystery for us. After all, it is only very recently that it became known that 95% of our Universe is made up of dark energy and dark matter, which is invisible. From reading chapter 10, you may agree that there is likely to be to a lot more intelligent life forms in the Universe and in fact humanity may be the least intelligent. We are also likely to learn a lot more about time and travel within the Universe in the decades to come. Steven DiBasio, writing on a section called "breakaway" science, *Nexus,* 2014[243] referred to a statement made by Ben Rich, former director of Lockheed Martin's Advanced Development Programs or "Skunk Works", while speaking to Los Angeles School of

Engineering Alumni Association, in 1993. He said: "An error in the equations" has been discovered and corrected, so that it will be possible to travel to the stars. He added further that: "these technologies are so locked up in black programs, that it would take an act of God to ever get them out to benefit humanity." I have a feeling that this act of God will come and it will be soon.

Life for us now seems to be in a time warp and perhaps could be described as a "trial in a time warp." This time warp was well illustrated by St Padre Pio on a number of occasions (see page 102). On the first occasion he was praying for his parents, who were long dead, and his friend who discovered the reason for his prayer expressed surprise that his parents were not yet in Heaven. St Pio replied that they were in Heaven, but only because of all the prayers he would be saying for them in the future. On the second occasion St Pio's doctor asked him to pray for a young girl patient of his, who was very dangerously ill, and he wanted to read him a letter from her mother. St Pio dismissed him, however, and said that he would hear it later. The doctor was next called away for days on urgent business and when he returned to his office he found the letter on his desk and immediately set out to read it to St Pio, even though he worried that at that stage, his young patient may have died. When the doctor suggested that the prayers may be too late, St Pio explained that he could still pray for the happy death of his great grandparents who were dead for almost 100 years. He further explained that the Lord did not need his paper bureaucracy to respond to prayers and with the Lord, there is no past or future, everything is an eternal present. When the doctor returned home, he discovered that he had already received a letter from the mother thanking him profusely for getting St Pio's help as her daughter had dramatically improved and was now well again - (Pedriali G., *Padre Pio de Pietrelcina, Una figura del Nostro Tempo*).

This book has encouraged you to base your life on evidence, and has particularly pointed towards the evidence for the apparitions of The Virgin Mary and the reality of Hell. This will point you in the right direction for eternal joy and towards the truth, which is found in the Roman Catholic Church, despite all its flaws and weakness. Remember (see page 282) that St Pio once famously said to a communist who refused to believe in the existence of Hell, that "You will believe in it when you get there." Take everything you read and hear in the mass-media with a "gráinne salainn" (pinch of salt) as it is usually very anti-Catholic and thus, in terms of God, anti-truth, and is leading humanity astray. Our final great effort must be to try to: Act justly, Love tenderly, and Walk humbly with the Lord.

Crossing a Threshold

We are now living in the most extraordinary time in the history of humanity. We have reached a great pivotal point, a turning point, a purification point, and a "crossing over" point, for the human race. Over the next generation, there will be a great transformation. This will occur during a period of great peace lasting about thirty years. There will be two forty two month periods before and after this period of peace, when satanic activity will be rampant and in control all over the world. At the end of the last forty two month period, the Antichrist with his False Prophet will be vanquished by Jesus Christ "through the brightness of His coming".

During this transformation, there will be three great destructive events, as well as many other major but less significant incidents. This will lead to the death of many people. The number who will die will depend on how rapidly humanity returns to the law of love. This means loving God, loving and respecting God's laws, and loving each other. These three events are, in likely chronological order:

1. The invasion by a 200 million strong army from the East.
2. Tipping of the Earth on its axis.
3. Fire falling from the Heavens.

The estimated number of those who will die now stands at two thirds of the population of the earth. Our only hope for a peaceful transformation is that Trump and Putin can work together to promote and renew Christianity in their respective countries and in the rest of the world. If conversion to Christianity, in China, continues at its present rate, this also gives us some reason to hope for peace. We can hope that more and more political leaders will begin to realize that the secular morality, promoted by the *One World Order*, will lead to disaster and must be rejected. We have been told by many recent prophetic messages, however, that a chastisement is now inevitable. All that remains is the question, how bad will it get?

Many young and not so young, alive at this time, will witness this great transformation. It will be a transformation from wars, evil, decadence, and greed on a grand scale to a great peace, tranquillity, and charity on a grand scale. It will be a transformation from living under the tyranny of satanic forces to the joy of living together as part of the Family of God, as epitomized by the loving relationship of Jesus, Mary, and Joseph. It will probably also involve crossing over a threshold to a new appreciation of other intelligent life in the Universe, with all that this will involve in the decades and centuries to come. Finally it will be a transformation that will gradually lead humanity to live more and more in the *Divine Will* and lead to the restoration of the gifts lost after the great mistake of Adam and Eve. God's Will for humanity will be done.

A Final Summary

Finally, therefore, the position and urgency of the message from Catholic prophecy can be summarized as follows:

1. The Catholic Church has the fullness of the truth. Other religions have some of the truth.

2. The message of Akita is a warning directly from God to humanity. It says that most of humanity will be annihilated if people and nations do not repent and stop offending God.

3. Up to now, almost 100% of people are not even aware of the message of Akita. The responsibility for this rests largely with believing Catholics who were given the message (which was approved by the Church in Japan), who are largely ignoring it, and not making others aware of it.

4. The realization of the Akita warning is a logical consequence of a failure to respond to the Fatima messages.

5. The Akita message is in keeping with the prophecies through the centuries and with statements from modern Catholic prophets.

6. The new revelation from Sr Lucia regarding the interpretation of the Fatima secrets on the tipping of the earth is likely to be connected with the prophesied events of Akita. Because of the reliability of Saint Pope John Paul II and Sr Lucia, we can take it, therefore, that the tipping of the earth in the near future is very likely to become a reality and will result in great devastation, unless there is a major rapid global repentance and conversion to Catholicism.

I can only urge you, therefore, to repent, pray and prepare, so that you and yours will have a better chance of surviving what is coming, and living into the great period of peace. The best measure of your preparedness is the quantity and quality of your prayer, as this will also be a measure of your love. The era of peace will be a time of a new Pentecost, when Jesus Christ will rule as the *King of All Nations* and Mary His Mother will rule as The *Lady of All Nations*. In the end, our only ambition should be to get to Heaven rather than Hell, and bring as many others as we can to Heaven with us.

If you are not a believing Roman Catholic and you want to live your life based on evidence and truth, I hope that after reading this book you will decide that the only way to go, is to follow the teachings of Jesus Christ. Let us remember the Biblical reference, John 6:68 after hearing the difficult doctrine of the Eucharist, when many disciples were walking away and Jesus asked the twelve, will you also go away? Peter retorted, "Lord to whom shall we go? You have the words of etrnal life". Christianity poses the perpetual question for all of us; how much are we prepared to suffer for the sake of loving God and loving others? It is not easy but it is the route to salvation and eternal joy. We must all try to carry our personally designed crosses with dignity, recognizing that we are very fortunate not to have the crosses of others, which would be far too heavy for us.

At the beginning of this book it was discussed how the outcome of the struggle between good and evil within each person can impact not just on the individual but also on society generally. It may be fitting, therefore, to close with the well-known story of the Cherokee Indian Chief who was explaining to his grandson about life and how it was really a continual fight between good and bad wolves. Bad wolves are selfish, greedy and are prepared to kill to get control over other wolves. Good wolves are peace loving and always helping to feed other injured wolves and work for the good of the wolf pack. He explained how inside each person there is also a good and a bad wolf fighting. The little boy was very interested, as usual, on his wise old grandfather's stories. He had one very important question at the end of this story. Which wolf would win the fight going on inside himself; would it be the good wolf or would it be the bad wolf? The reply that came was; the wolf you feed.

Finally, I must tell you that I am only a fool. I am a fool for lots of reasons but in particular, I am a fool for not loving my God more and for not loving and helping others more. The longer I live the more this foolishness is haunting me. I know that after I die, this foolishness will become my permanent regret. At this time, I consider myself very privileged to be aware of the revelation on the *Divine Will* (chapter 15) and I now need to try to spend the rest of my life trying to live in it. If this fool's book has been of value to you, please encourage others to read it.

20 - APPENDIX

Radiofrequency Electromagnetic Fields (RF-EMFs)

In the first edition of this book, I included a short appendix on new developments in science. In this edition I have chosen to include a short discourse on the dangers of Wi-Fi and "dirty" electricity to human health. There is now a large volume of scientific literature accumulating on this subject. For some reason/s, however, this information is not penetrating into mainstream media reports and because of its significance, I believe that it needs to be discussed and highlighted, even if only in a very small way.

The connection between electricity and magnetism has been known since 1820, when Oersted discovered that an electric current in a wire will deflect a compass needle. Later, in 1831, Faraday showed that a changing magnetic field can produce a current. RF-EMFs are artificially produced by all modern wireless technologies as well as radio waves that run along electricity wiring, to a greater or lesser degree, depending on the quantity and quality of the wiring. This applies therefore to electric power-lines, generators, wind-turbines and solar energy technology and other electric equipment. It also applies to all wireless communication systems, such as mobile phone antennas and mobile phones, cordless domestic phones, computers, broadband routers, baby monitors, and smart meters etc.

Electromagnetic Spectrum with wavelengths in metres

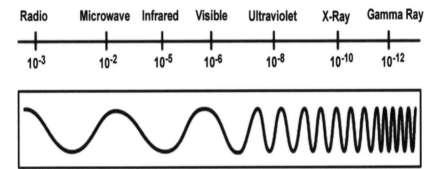

All waves described in the electromagnetic spectrum, have special characteristics that are used to describe them.

1. The first characteristic is the wave **frequency** which is measured in cycles per second. The number of cycles per second is often referred to as Hertz or Hz for short, after the German scientist, Heinrich Hertz (1857 – 1894). This frequency is often measured and noted as Kilo (KHz), Mega (MHz), and Giga (GHz) to denote a thousand, a million, and a billion Hertz respectively. High energy is associated with high frequency and low energy is associated with low frequency. High energy radiation such as gamma rays and x-rays as well as some high energy ultraviolet (UV) radiation is often referred to as ionizing radiation as it carries enough energy to remove electrons from atom and molecules. The lower energy radiation, with lower frequency, such as visible light, infrared, and radiofrequency (RF) radiation, which includes microwaves as well as radio waves, is referred to as non-ionizing radiation as the energy is only enough to heat or cause

rotation in atoms and molecules, but not enough to dislocate the electrons.

2. A second characteristic is the wave **amplitude.** This describes the height or power of the wave which can be non-variable (that is static or polarized) **or** variable (that is composed of different waves with similar frequency but different amplitudes).

3. A third characteristic is the **pulse rate** of the wave. This describes the rate at which the power or amplitude changes and is also measured in Hertz or changes per second.

RF-EMFs are in the 30KHz to 300GHz frequency range. This range also encompasses microwaves, which are described as in the range 300MHz to 300GHz. All electronic gadgets that transmit wireless data emit microwaves.

The very rapid development of new communication technology, based on microwaves, in recent decades has given rise to a growing interest in health and safety issues associated with this technology. The worry about health issues is stimulated by a growing number of individuals, some of whom I know personally, who are claiming to be clinically unwell when in the vicinity of, or closely in contact with, some of this new microwave technology. There is no denying that this technology is bringing great convenience and great potential for the development to many new useful areas of human progress, by using these developments in communication technology, but we do now need to ask the question, what are the dangers and what are the health and safety implications? This is especially important at this time when microwave technology is being developed at an increasing rate. The so called fifth generation (5G) technology is now being launched in some countries which will mean that more and more people will be exposed to higher intensity radiation, usually without their knowledge or consent. It is also now emerging that there is great individual variation in how we can be affected by this radiation. At this stage most individuals are described as non-sensitive, while others are described as electro-sensitive or electro-hypersensitive. Sensitive and hypersensitive individuals can suffer from a wide variety of medical symptoms, such as, fatigue, headache, sleeplessness, impaired learning, memory loss, depression, paranoia, suicide tendency, etc. It has been suggested by some that those who are "sensitive" may be the lucky ones, as they can begin to protect themselves by re-locating or changing their exposure to RF-EMFs in other ways, whereas, those who are "non-sensitive" may be sitting on a "time bomb" of medical problems in the future. The bottom line is that this technology has great potential for the future progress of humanity (and for making a small number very rich), but we are largely ignoring the very important health and safety aspects. To get the balance right, the safety aspects need to be investigated more and the ordinary individual street user needs to become more aware of the risks.

Dr. Samuel Milham is a physician-epidemiologist in the US who has a large number of scientific publications on the health related effects of electricity. In 2010 he published the second edition of his book, *Dirty Electricity*,[236] which deals with this subject. In one of his early studies he detected a correlation between radar exposure and leukaemia. In a paper published in 2001, acute lymphoblastic leukaemia (ALL), a common leukaemia in two to five year old children, was strongly correlated with electrification spreading across the US from urban to rural areas in the middle of the last century. In 2004, a study of a cluster of cancers, in a Middle school in Southern California, led to the conclusion that "high frequency voltage transients" (called "dirty electricity" by the utility industry) was a potent universal carcinogen. Dirty electricity travels along on the usual sixty cycle sine wave of alternating current (AC), as high frequency voltage transients between one and two hundred kilohertz. These can occur along electric wires anywhere and are caused by interruptions of current flow and by arcing and sparking. Dirty electricity is also increasingly found in ground currents returning to utility substations. These ground currents are not very well understood, or investigated, and may also have implications for plant and animal life. Ambient dirty electricity is said to "couple capacitively to the human body" and induce electric currents in the body.

Dr Milham argues that the increased incidence of various diseases associated with electrification happened so gradually that it went un-noticed and the increase was regarded as "normal diseases of modern civilization". In the US, during the 1930s, urban death rates were much higher than rural rates for cardiovascular diseases, malignancy, diabetes, and suicide. Rural death rates were also significantly correlated with the level of residential electric service within the different States. Dr. Milham has said:

"We are electrochemical soup at the cellular and organ level. Think of ECG (electrocardiogram), EEG (electroencephalogram), and EMG (electromyogram). We evolved in a complex **EMF (electromagnetic field)** environment, with an interplay of natural terrestrial and extraterrestrial EMF sources, from solar activity, cosmic rays, and geomagnetic activity... **I believe that man-made EMFs, especially dirty electricity, are chronic stressors and are responsible for many of the disease patterns of electrified populations"**

Dr Milham quotes a study on exposure of rats to non thermal, pulsed and modulated microwaves at a frequency of 2450 MHz. This was a very good quality study supported by the US Air Force, in the late 1970s, which cost $4.5 million. 18 cancers developed in 100 exposed rats with 5 cancers detected in the control group. The exposed rats had significantly higher levels of B and T lymphocytes, compared to controls, and Dr Milham hypothesised that the microwaves caused chronic immune stimulation, which allowed the cancers to develop. There were also seven benign adrenal pheochromocytomas detected in the exposed rats compared to one in the control group. Dr Milham then looked at the figures for human pheochromocytoma, in Washington State. He noted that the figures increased approximately four fold between 1997 and 2007, a time when cell phones were becoming popular. In the same time period the national US figures for this tumour doubled.

Dr Milham further notes that dirty electricity, "helped explain the fact that professional and office workers, like the school teachers (from the school study in Southern California, noted above), have high cancer incidence rates. It also explained why indoor workers had higher malignant melanoma rates, why melanoma occurred on part(s) of the body which are never exposed to sunlight, and why melanoma rates are increasing while the amount of sunshine reaching the earth is stable."[1] The relatively short latency for melanoma and thyroid cancers in the school studied in California suggested to Dr Milham that these tumours may be more sensitive to the effects of dirty electricity than other tumours. In this context, it is interesting that these two tumours have the highest rate of increase in the Western world.

Dr. Milham has noted many other correlations between various tumours in those exposed to "dirty electricity" and radio frequency (RF) microwaves. These include a cluster of rare Ewing's sarcoma associated with radiofrequency radiation from a powerful US Air Force antenna on Cape Cod and an increased incidence of many different types of tumours in Nantucket County. Decreased birth rates in humans and animals have also been associated with dirty electricity. A study in Canada has reported that police officers who hold radar guns on their laps have a seven times expected risk of testicular cancer. He emphasized particularly that large generators produced significant amounts of dirty electricity and speculated that the cause of the increased levels of diabetes and obesity found in many small islands, using generators for power, may in some way be associated with this source of electricity.

Donna Fisher has reviewed the health problems associated with Wi-Fi, which she refers to as, "The EMF Plague", in two articles in Nexus magazine.[237,238] Donna quotes Professor Konstantin Meyl, described as a modern-day Nikola Tesla, when he said, "Only a half-knowing company would allow sale of devices that produce sparks in nature in the midst of perhaps the most important biological window for humanity." He believes that 2.45 GHz is an important biological frequency window that nature uses in cell communication. Not only do microwave ovens use this frequency, but it is also used in some cordless phones and baby monitors.

Donna Fisher also quotes Dr Magda Havas, Associate Professor of Resource Studies in Ontario, Canada, and a world expert on EMF. Dr Havas points out that, "Non-ionizing radiation increases free radicals in the body indirectly (unlike ionizing radiation which increases free radicals directly), by interfering with mechanisms that neutralize free radicals. Free radicals are carcinogenic. Therefore by interfering with the body's ability to repair free radical damage, microwave radiation is also carcinogenic." Dr Havas has also said: "Putting Wi-Fi in schools: allowing cordless phones that radiate constantly to be manufactured: placing wireless baby monitors near an infant: using a wireless tablet, smart phone or computer while pregnant: holding a cell phone next to the head and keeping a cell phone in a bra or hip pocket or under a pillow: placing cell phone antennas near homes, schools and on hospitals: metering electricity, water, and gas with wireless smart meters and designing smart appliances for the home, will be viewed by future generations as dumb technology generated by greed for a population that is largely ignorant of the consequences. We need to protect the health and wellbeing of future generations, because without them there is no future! If we don't do it...who will?"

Dr Martin Blank[239] explained how electrons in our DNA conduct electricity and because DNA is coiled, in many varied ways, within the nucleus, it responds to electromagnetic radiation in a wide range of frequencies across the electromagnetic spectrum. The view therefore that RF-EMFs do not have biological effects is not correct and these effects can be thermal or non-thermal. Donna Fisher pointed out[2] that according to Dr Blank, the section of the DNA controlling the cellular response to EMF has now also been identified and is referred to as the "EMF Domain". The particular stress protein controlled by this section of DNA is identified as heat shock protein - 70 (hsp70). Mobile phone radiation has also been shown to change the expression of hsp27 and change the overall pattern of protein phosphorylation, which can change a variety of cellular signal pathways.

Potentially, therefore, exposure to electromagnetic radiation could be responsible for, or contribute to, a wide variety of diseases. As early as 1990, Robert O. Becker in his book *Cross Currents*,[240] said, "..the scientific evidence is absolutely conclusive: 60Hz magnetic fields cause human cancer cells to permanently increase their rate of growth by as much as 1600 per cent and to develop more malignant characteristics." In his earlier book, The Body Electric (1985),[241] Dr Becker discussed in detail the effects of electricity and magnetism on the body of humans and animals. Effects ranged from "abnormal natural" fields of solar magnetic storms leading to increased psychiatric illness, to varying degrees of stress and stress hormones up to brain cell death, produced in response to different strengths of experimental magnetic field exposure in animals. Even small electric fields found in a typical office leads to an increased level of the neurotransmitter, acetylcholine, in the brainstem, which can activate a subliminal distress signal.

It was pointed out by Dr Martin Pall, Emeritus Professor of Biochemistry, Washington[242] that one of the primary non thermal effects of EMF on cells is the activation of voltage–gated calcium channels (VGCCs). Large concentrations of intracellular calcium are the result, leading to free radical production and oxidative stress. Intracellular nitric oxide (NO) is increased which interacts to create peroxynitrite. The peroxynitrite and free radicals damage DNA and may lead to disease. Dr Pall also says that diseases such as amyotrophic lateral sclerosis (ALS), Parkinson's disease, and Alzheimer's disease (AD) are also caused by excess calcium in the cells. The Bioinitiative 2012 Report said that extra low frequency magnetic field exposure can increase peripheral amyloid beta protein, which is a risk factor for AD. This report also notes that there is also good evidence that melatonin protects against AD. Donna Fischer notes that there is strong evidence that long-term exposure to EMF is associated with decrease in melatonin production. Dr Pall has expressed worry about the role RF-EMF may have in disturbing the blood brain barrier (BBB) and contributing to these diseases.

In 2011 the International Agency for Research on Cancer (IARC) classified mobile phone radiation as Group 2B, "possibly carcinogenic". This is distinct from 2A which is "probably carcinogenic". Some studies have shown a very low but increased risk of brain tumours, especially gliomas (malignant) and acoustic neuromas (benign) associated with mobile phone use. In other words more research is needed to assess and quantitate the risk. The EU-Reflex project (European Union Risk Evaluation of Potential Environmental Hazards From Low-Frequency Electromagnetic Field Exposure) has shown that cells exposed "in vitro" to cell phone radiation exhibit chromosomal damage well below the exposure guidelines of the World Health Organization. It would seem, therefore, that new safety guidelines need to be established.

Anthony Hughes (info@natural-medicine.ie) gives a very good summary of the problems. He notes that 35% of the population are described as "electrosensitive" to some degree and that 3% to 5% are estimated to be severely "electrosensitive". The basis for this categorization, however, was not stated. Some of the many points he has listed are as follows:

Research since 1929 has shown that the use of microwaves for communication causes harm. Published work now runs into many hundreds of studies. Insurance underwriters have denied insurance policies for health effects of EMR in schools. The safety standards for microwave radiation were based on thermal effects only. The 2012 "Bio-initiative Report" indicated that new safety limits must be established. There is even less awareness of the great dangers of DECT phones (Digital Electronic Cordless Telephones or cordless domestic phones) and Tetra (Terrestrial Trunked Radio) a communication system used by police and other emergency services. Tetra uses a pulsed frequency of 17.65 Hz which is close to a key frequency of the human brain of 16Hz. Man made EMR is a polarized form (in contrast to natural EMR) which potentially is a lot more dangerous. The 5th Generation Microwave technology will increase the public exposure to this radiation dramatically without any accompanying safety investigations or regulations. It represents **"The largest Biological Experiment ever."**

Finally, Donna Fischer, in her article in Nexus magazine[237] (2017), also mentions the work of Dr Martha Herbert, a paediatric neurologist at Massachusetts General and Cindy Sage, co-editor of the *Bioinitiative* reports of 2007 and 2012, who have outlined a wide range of autism symptoms that match known symptoms of wireless exposure, including genetic damage to sperm, calcium channel mutations, and inflammation. Dr Martin L Paul has commented that "there are at least 10 different research groups which have argued that EMF has an important role in the autism epidemic" (video at http://www.donnafisher.net), acting mainly via calcium channels.

The Pandora Project: There is good evidence, mostly gleaned from war prisoners, that electromagnetic radiation was being investigated for military purposes, in Germany, during World War II. In 1962, the CIA discovered that the US Embassy in Moscow was being bombarded with electromagnetic radiation. The object of this, which was disclosed later, was intended to produce blurred vision and loss of mental concentration. As a result of this, the US initiated the Pandora Project to investigate this so called "Moscow Signal" and US military research on RF-EMFs has gone on since that time. All countries are now aware of the military potential of electromagnetic radiation as a weapon of war. Much of what has been discovered remains secret, especially the experiments associated with mind control. Enough is known, however, that leaves no doubt about the dangers associated with this radiation when it is misused. For example very low frequency can cause psychological and other medical problems such as, 4.5 Hz causing paranoia, 6.6 Hz causing depression and suicide, 8.0 Hz causing sleep problems, 11 Hz causing anger, 25 Hz causing blindness etc. All of this has enormous implications for health and safety, especially in an environment where truth and trust is not always what it should be.

Covert Military RF-EMF Research

The little that is known about this area of research is both "mind-blowing" and scary. This is reviewed on a regular basis in the magazine, *Nexus*.[243,244] As explained above, the major problems come from extremely low frequencies (ELF), but higher frequencies have the same effects if pulsed or modulated in the ELF range.

Elana Freeland[244] also describes a variety of electromagnetic antipersonnel weapons, referred to euphemistically as "non-lethal", being used by military. Take for example, "the high power microwave (HPM) projectile known as active denial system (ADS) that pulses electromagnetic radiation at 95 GHz, boils molecules in and under the skin and melts body organs, or the Long Range Acoustic Device (LRAD), an absolutely silent sonic weapon ("directed sound communication system") that launches a thermo-elastic wave of acoustic pressure at high frequency (2.5 Khz) in a 30-degree beam which silently screams into the inner ear by bone conduction. A turn of the LRAD dial can cook eyeballs and organs." Elena also says that now, "the line between civilian and military has been erased and we are all living in the battlespace. Private security firms, mobsters and lowlifes contracting with the intelligence community are doing its dirty work so that congressional oversight can be avoided."

The same article describes US special forces wearing magnetoencephalograph scanners (MEGs) known as "thought helmets". These correlate brainwave patterns via a remote crystalline computer whose software reads and translates spoken words and silent thoughts. A former US navy engineer, Elanor White, is quoted as saying, "For the first time in history, one human being, from hiding at a distance, can control the thoughts and actions of another by way of undetectable hypnosis, using still-classified electronic technology. These devices have totally disabled the world's justice systems... Zero evidence weapons make revenge crimes routine and easy."

Elana Freeland finally says, "Loss of freedom of thought means much more than the loss of a republic. It means the loss of civilisation and what it is to be human. These costs of sleeping in our chains of comfort and convenience are too much to pay."

Reducing the Risks

In 2013, the Israeli government issued guidelines for Wi-Fi use in schools. Wi-Fi was not permitted in classrooms for children below the first grade, limited to three hours per week for first and second grades, and limited to eight hours per week for third grades. In 2015, the French Government issued similar guidelines for childhood Wi-Fi exposure. These legal guidelines suggest that children under three years should not be exposed to Wi-Fi with exposure minimised for those under 11 years, and Wi-Fi routers should be switched off when not in use.

Graham/Stetzer (G/S) meters, oscilloscopes and magnetic meters are used to measure the magnetic and electricity problems. In measuring "dirty" electricity, ideally readings should be under 50 G/S units. Most homes have under 100 G/S units, whereas, schools have an average of 700 G/S units in the experience of Dr Samuel Milham.[1] Dr Milham has suggested one easy way to detect higher frequency radiation in your environment is to use a small portable AM radio. Putting the radio near fluorescent lights, dimmer switches, computers, broad-band routers, copy machines, TVs etc., will help you understand the quantity of dirty electricity produced from the on/off switch of the apparatus exposed to the radio. Energy in homes produced by solar or wind can add to the quantity of dirty electricity due the inverters needed to increase the voltage. Light emitting diode (LED) bulbs are much less of a problem than fluorescent bulbs. Wind farms are associated with low frequency sound waves and dirty electricity from their inverters.

For now, it is a matter of trying to balance the risks to health with the convenience and advantages. The relative risks are not at all clear, but more and more risks are being highlighted as the use of this technology advances in exposure time, variety and load quantities. Dr Milham[236] has suggested that exposure to dirty electricity at above 2,000 GS units for six hours, for 180 days, increases cancer risk by 25% but he has also mentioned some screenings where he detected an exposure of 20,000 GS units. The worry is that the damage may be cumulative (as with solar radiation etc.) and we may be sitting on a powder-keg of disease yet to be manifested. When we become aware of some of the risks, it may already be too late. Infants (born and unborn) may be particularly vulnerable. Evidence to date seems to suggest that it is a good idea to scan homes, for hot spots of dirty electricity, and to make sure that there are no brains (young or old) sleeping at night close to these hot spots.

In the meantime let us consider that humanity was lucky that the HIV virus was not spread by droplet infection. We were also lucky that the SARS virus was not more contagious. We were luckier still with 'mad cow disease' when we were being assured by Government experts that prions would not cross the species barrier and were feeding their children hamburgers to prove it. At the same time, those who worked with prions knew very well that they crossed species barriers. It could have been the biggest medical disaster in history. If the 5th Generation communication networks are installed all over the place, I am informed that although the communication rate will be 1,000 better, it will increase the "electrosmog" exposure by a factor of 10, usually without the knowledge or permission of local populations. The advantages of better communications could be seriously out-weighed by the health implications of RF-EMFs. It is my impression that this is a serious issue that demands more attention from health and safety considerations.

After all that, I am still a supporter of this new communication technology. It has contributed so much to the pleasure and efficiency of modern living, but it is important to get the balance right and to know and quantitate the risks. I would seriously question the wisdom of 5G installation, however, without a lot more safety data. Areas where 5G is now being installed should be observed carefully for surges in particular disease patterns. Companies promoting these services may be supporting political parties but they should be asked to fund universities or other independent organizations to do health and safety analysis on their systems. At the very least all wireless technology should only be promoted, installed and sold when there is clear accompanying information on the characteristics of the radiation being produced, so that safety can be more easily assessed when needed.

The following points are worth noting as immediate action that can be taken to reduce exposure:

1. Protect children from exposure as much as possible. Keep the baby monitors well away from the baby.
2. Switch off the WiFi when not in use.
3. Promote and use Fibre-Optic technology, where possible, as an alternative to Wi-Fi. Use direct wiring where possible.
4. Check your home for any hotspots of "dirty electricity" and sleep in the part of the house with poor Wi-Fi reception.
5. Live well away from mast transmitters.

I will finish with a personal experience with mobile phone use. In my former life (before I retired) part of my job was to give clinical advice on the use of antibiotics. On Friday afternoon, in particular, I was often on the mobile phone for long periods, sometimes going into hours. One Saturday morning, about 10 years ago, I awoke suddenly and I could hear a loud sound of my heart beat (blood flow) in both ears. I thought that a serious aneurysm had developed overnight. All other clinical signs were normal and I felt well. I thought it may be due to excess black tea which I took in large volumes (it has good anti-oxidant properties). I stopped drinking black tea to no avail. My son suggested that it may be the phone and he got me a lead with an ear piece. Within three days use the noise in my ears stopped completely. Six weeks later the lead got caught in a door-way and the phone was back on my ear. The noise came back within a few days. I continue to use the mobile phone all the time (what would I do without it?) but now I keep it far away from my head.

I am grateful to John Waigel and Carmel O Sullivan for their helpful suggestions with this discussion.

BIBLIOGRAPHY

1. Richard Dawkins, *The God Delusion*, Bantam Press, 2006
2. Pope John Paul II, *Veritatis Splendour*, Catholic Truth Society 1993
3. Don Stefano Gobbi, *To the Priests, Our Lady's Beloved Sons*, (not for sale), 1998, available from the world-wide movement.
4. Cardinal Karol Wojtyla, *Farewell address at the Eucharistic Congress in Philadelphia,* 1976.
5. Pope John Paul II, Address to pilgrims in Fulda, Germany, Nov. 19th, 1980, *Vox Fidei*, 10, 1981.
6. F William Engdahl, *Seeds of Destruction- The Hidden Agenda of Genetic Manipulation*, Global Research, 2007.
7. Daniel Estalun, *The True Story of the Bilderberg Group*, North American Union Edition, TrineDay (www.TrineDay.com), 2005
8. Patrick J Buchanan, *The Death of the West*, Thomas Dunne Books, 2002.
9. Austin Fagothey, S J, *Right and Reason – Ethics in Theory and Practice,* Tan Books, Second Ed. 1959.
10. Peter Kreeft, *A Refutation of Moral Relativism – Interviews with an Absolutist,* Ignatius Press, 1999.
11. Robert J Spitzer, S J, *Ten Universal Principles – A Brief Philosophy of Life Issues,* Ignatius Press, 2011.
12. Nicky Gumbel, *Questions of life*, Kingsway Publications, 1995.
13. C S Lewis, *Timeless at Heart, Christian Apologetics*, Fount, 1987.
14. C S Lewis, *Mere Christianity*, Harper Collins, 2001.
15. C S Lewis, *Miracles*, Harper Collins, 2001.
16. Pat Collins C M, *Expectant Faith*, The Columba Press, 1998.
17. Joseph Cardinal Ratzinger with Peter Seewald, *God & The World*, Ignatius, 2002.
18. Joan Carroll Cruz, *Eucharistic Miracles*, Tan Books, 1987.
19. Frederick A Reuter, *Moments Divine*, Tan Books, 1995.
20. Michael H Brown, *Secrets of the Eucharist*, Faith Publishing Company, 1996.
21. Francis Johnston, Alexandrina-*The Agony and The Glory*, Tan Books, 1982.
22. Johannes Steiner, *Therese Neumann*, Alba House, 1967.
23. Pere Michel Tierney, Martin Blake, and David Fanning, *Marthe*

Robin, Catholic Truth Society, 1999.

24.   Fr Raymond Peyret, *Marthe Robin*, Alba House, 1983

25.   Michael H Brown, *The Bridge To Heaven*, Marian Communications, 1993.

26.   Joan Carroll Cruz, *Miraculous Images of Jesus*, Tan Books, 1993.

27.   Joan Carroll Cruz, *Miraculous Images of Our Lady*, Tan Books, 1993.

28.   Albert J Hebert, *The Tears of Mary- and Fatima, Why?*
       Private Publication, available at P.O. Box 309, Paulina, La.70763

29.   Sr Briege McKenna, O.S.C., with Henry Libersat, *Miracles Do Happen*, Veritas, 1987.

30.   Colm Keane, *Padre Pio – The Irish Connection*, Mainstream Publishing, 2007

31.   John McCaffery, *The Friar of San Giovanni*, Darton – Longmann & Todd, 1978.

32.   Fr Marcellino Iasenza Niro, *The Padre, Saint Pio of Pietrelcina – Testimonies*, Our Lady of Grace Capuchin Friary, 71013 San Giovanni Rotonda, 2007.

33.   Mieczyslaw Piotrowski & Christopher A. Zakrzewski, *The Radiant Holiness of Padre Pio, Love One Another – No. 4*, Society of Christ, Michigan, 2005.

34.   Jim Gallagher, Padre Pio – *The Pierced Priest*, Harper Collins Publishers, 1995.

35.   Fr Edward D O Connor C.S.C., *Marian Apparitions Today – -Why so Many?*, Queenship Publishing Company, 1996.

36.   Benedict Joseph Ratzinger with Vittorio Messori, *Ratzinger Report*, Ignatius Books, 1985.

37.   Warren Carroll, *Our Lady of Guadalupe*, Christendom Press, 1983.

38.   Francis Johnston, *The Wonder of Guadalupe*, Tan Books, 1981.

39.   Alma Power-Waters, *St Catherine Laboure and The Miraculous Medal*, Ignatius, 1990.

40.   Joan Carroll Cruz, *The Incoruptibles*, Tan Books, 1977.

41.   Fr Patrick O Connor, *I Met a Miracle*, Catholic Truth Society, 1970.

42.   Ruth Cranston, *The Miracle of Lourdes*, McGraw-Hill 1955.

43.   John De Marchi – translated by I.M. Kingsbury, *Fatima from the beginning,* Missoes Consolata, 1950.

44.   Francis Johnston, *Fatima – The Great Sign*, Tan Books, 1980.

45.   Judith M Albright, *Our Lady at Garabandal*, Queenship Publishing Company, 1992

46. Ramon Perez – Translated by Annette I Curot Mathews, *Garabandal – The Village Speaks,* The Workers of Our Lady of Mount Carmel, Inc., 1981.

47. Eusebio Garcia De Pesquera, O.F.M. – Translated by Gerard Suel & Otto Miller, *She Went In Haste To The Mountain*, St Joseph Publications – Cleveland 1970.

48. Barry Hanratty, *Saint Padre Pio and Garabandal*, Garabandal Journal – Jan / Feb, 2008, Garabandal Journal, P.O. Box 1796, St Cloud, MN 56302 – 1796

49. Pearl Zaki, *Before Our Eyes*, Queenship Publishing Company, 2002.

50. Fr Jerome Palmer, O.S.B., *Our Lady Returns to Egypt*, Culligan Publications Inc., 1969.

51. John Bird, *Queen of The Ukraine*, 101 Foundation, 1992.

52. Josyp Terelya with Michael H. Brown, *Witness – An Autobiography*, Faith Publishing Company, 1991.

53. Kibeho – Africa – *Mary Speaks to the World* (video), Marian Communications Ltd. – Cleveland, 1988.

54. Immaculee Ilibagiza with Steve Erwin, *Our Lady of Kibeho*, Hay House Inc., 2008.

55. Fr Michael O Carroll, C.S.SP., *Medjugorje – Facts, Documents, Theology*, Veritas, 1986.

56. David Baldwin, *Medjugorje*, Catholic Truth Society, 2002.

57. Mirjana Soldo, *My Heart will Triumph*, CatholicShop Publishing, 2016.

58. Francis Mutsuo Fukushima, *Akita,* Queenship Publishing Company, 1994.

59. Ray Burke, *The Two Pillars,* Kolbe Publications – Cork, 1998.

60. Josef Kunzli, *The Messages of The Lady of All Nations,* Queenship Publishing Company, 1996.

61. Johnnette S Benkovic, *The New Age Counterfeit*, Queenship Publishing, 1993.

62. Randy England, *The Unicorn in the Sanctuary*, Tan Books, 1991.

63. Randall N Baer, *Inside The New Age*, Huntington House Inc. 1989.

64. Pontifical Council for Culture & for Interreligious Dialogue, *Jesus Christ – The Bearer of The Water of Life*, Vatican publications, 2002.

65. James Hitchcock, *What is Secular Humanism?,* Servant Books – Ann Arbor, Michigan, 1982.

66. *The Truth about Reiki – A Warning To Catholics*, Catholic Response to the New Age, P.O. Box 8340, Rathmines, Dublin, 2006.

67. Gary H Kah, *En Route to Global Occupation,* Huntington House Publishers, 1991.

68.   Gar H Kah, *The Demonic Roots of Globalism*, Huntington House Publishers, 1995.

69.   Two Hearts Media, *Conspiracy against Life,* Two Hearts Media – Philippines, 1996.

70.   Ted Flynn, *Hope of The Wicked – The Master Plan to Rule the World,* MaxKol Communications – Virginia, 2000.

71.   Bro Charles Madden, O.F.M., *Freemasonary*, Tan Books, 1995.

72.   Jim Shaw & Tom McKenney, *The Deadly Deception,* Huntington House, Inc., 1988.

73.   Fr Andrew O Brien with Brian Lee-Johnson, *Make Yourself an Ark*, Private Publication, Dalgan Park, Navan, Meath, Ireland.

74.   Gerald Winrod, *Adam Weishaupt*, Emissary Publications, 1937, quoted by Gary Kah, (67).

75.   *Winston Churchill*, Illustrated Sunday Herald, Feb 8, 1920- quoted in – Review of the News, Jan 26th 1972.

76.   John Coleman, *Conspirators Hierarchy: The Story of the Committee of 300*, available from 2533 North Carson St, Suite J – 118, Carson City, NV.

77.   Cliff Kincaid, *Global Bondage – The U.N. Plan to Rule the World*, Huntington House Publishers, 1995.

78.   Pope John Paul II, *Evangelium Vitae*, Veritas, 1995.

79.   John Bird, *What Once Was and What is to come*, McCrimmon Publishing Co. Ltd., 2003

80.   Edward Connor, *Prophecy For Today*, Tan Books, 1984.

81.   Michael Day – translation of: *A Story of a Soul – The Autobiography of Saint Thérése of Lisieux,* Tan Books, 1997.

82.   St Teresa of Avila, *Interior Castle, Tan Books*, 1997.

83.   St Teresa of Avila, *Way of Perfection*, Sheed and Ward, 1977.

84.   John McGowan, *A Fresh approach to St John of The Cross*, St Pauls, 1993.

85.   *St John of the Cross* – compiled by Don Mullan, A Little Book of John of the Cross, The Columba Press, 2003.

86.   Fr G. M. Cussen, O.P., *Prayer, The Breath of Life*, 1986. Private publication, now available with permission from Benedictus Books, 9 North Main St, Cork.

87.   Robert Faricy SJ and Lucy Rooney SND, *The Contemplative Way of Prayer,* The Mercier Press Ltd., 1986.

88.   John Gillespie, *The Key to Powerful Prayer*, Kilkenny, Ireland, Ph. 00353 56 7721739.

89.   Brian O Hare, *The Miracle Ship*, Crimson Cloak Publishing, 2013.

90. Frances Hogan, *A Path to Healing a Nation*, The Columba Press, 2013.
91. Scott Hahn and Leon J Suprenant Jr, *Catholic for a Reason – Scripture and the Mystery of the Family of God*, Emmaus Road, 1998.
92. Scott Hahn, *Hail Holy Queen,* Darton – Longman & Todd, 2001.
93. Scott Hahn & Jeff Cavins, *Our Fathers Plan*, Ignatius Press, DVD set, 1996.
94. Scott and Kimberly Hahn, *Rome Sweet Home – Our Journey to Catholicism*, Ignatius, 1993.
95. Marcus C. Grodi, *Journey Home,* Queenship Publishing Company, 1997.
96. Patrick Madrid, *Surprised by Truth*, Basilica Press, 1994.
97. Scott Hahn, *The Lamb's Supper – The Mass as Heaven on Earth*, Darton – Longman & Todd, 1999.
98. Scott Hahn, *Reasons to Believe*, Darton – Longman & Todd, 2007.
99. Pope John Paul II, *Salvifici Doloris*, Vatican Press, 1984.
100. "Anne" – a lay apostle, *The Mist of Mercy – Spiritual Warfare and Purgatory,* Direction for Our Times (directionforourtime.com), 2006.
101. Fr Frederick William Faber, *Purgatory*, Tan Books, 1993.
102. Fr Paul O Sullivan, O.P. *Read me or Rue it*, Tan Books, 1992
103. Maria Simma with Nicky Eltz, *Get Us Out of Here!!,* Private Publication by Nicholas Maria Eltz with White Lily Gallery, *Medjugorje,* BiH, 2002.
104. *Spiritual Diary – Selected Sayings and Examples of Saints*, Daughter of Saint Paul edition, 1962.
105. Fr Edgardo M. Arellano, *Victimhood – Hope of the Present Crises*, Two Heart Media – Deleware, 2003.
106. Fr Edgardo M. Arellano, *How to win your Spiritual Warfare – Exposing the Enemy*, Two Hearts Media – Deleware, 1994.
107. Gabriele Amorth, *An Exorcist Tells His Story*, Ignatius, 1999.
108. *The Exorcism of Emily Rose*, Ignatius Press, DVD, 2006.
109. Leon Cristiani translated by Cynthia Rowland, *Evidence of Satan in the Modern World*, Tan Books, 1974.
110. Fr Carl Vogl, *Begone Satan*, Tan Books, 1973.
111. Fr F. X. Schouppe, S.J., & Thomas A. Nelson, *Hell and How to avoid Hell*, Tan Books, 1989.
112. Saint Alphonsus Liguori compiled by J. Schaefer, *What Will Hell Be Like?* Tan Books, 1988.
113. Sister Josefa Menendez, *The Way of Divine Love*, Tan Books, 1981.
114. Fr Edgard M. Arellano, *The Life and Teachings of St Veronica Guiliani*, Two Heart Media – Deleware, 2006.
115. *Catherine Emmerich on Hell, The Dolorous Passion of Our Lord Jesus Christ,* Tan Books, 1983.

116.   Fr Robert J. Spitzer, S.J., *Healing the Culture*, Ignatius Press, 2000.

117.   Peter J. Kreeft, *Catholic Christianity*, Ignatius Books, 2001

118.   Peter J. Kreeft, *Angels and Demons – What do we really know about them?* Ignatius Press, 1995.

119.   Dinesh D'Souza, *Life after Death, - The Evidence,* Regnery Publishing, Inc. 2009.

120.   Peter J. Kreeft, *Because God is Real*, Ignatius, 2008.

121.   Jeffrey Long, MD., with Paul Perry, *Evidence of the Afterlife – The Science of Near-Death Experiences,* Harper Collins, 2010.

122.   Eben Alexander, MD., Proof of Heaven – A Neurosurgeon's Journey into the Afterlife, pub by Simon & Schuster in US and Piatkus in the UK, 2012 (New York Times best seller).

123.   Colm Keane, Going Home: Irish Stories from the Edge of Death, Colm Keane, Capel Island Press, 2009.

124.   Michael H. Brown, *After Life: What it's like in Heaven, Hell, and Purgatory*, Queenship Publishing, 1997.

125.   Todd Burpo with Lynn Vincent, *Heaven is for Real: A little Boy's story of His Trip to Heaven and Back*, W Publishing Group, 2010.

126.   *Tenderly Loved, What is there beyond that which is here?* The original was in Spanish (Qué hay más allá de este aquí ?) Published by, Apostolic Society Sons of the Divine Will, St Cloud, Florida, USA, 1994.

127.   J. M. Van Den Aardweg, Gerard, *Hungry Souls,* Tan Books, 2008.

128.   Howard Storm, *My Descent into Death*, Clairview, 2000.

129.   Albert Einstein, *Relativity*, Crown Publishers Inc., New York, 1961.

130.   P.C.W. Davies & J.R. Brown, The Ghost in the Atom, Cambridge University Press, 1986.

131.   Jim Al – Khalili, *Quantum – A Guide for the Perplexed* Weidenfeld & Nicolson, 2003.

132.   Jerome J. Langford, *Galileo, Science and the Church*, St Augustines Press – Indiana, 1998

133.   Wallace Johnson, *The Death of Evolution,* Tan Books, 2000.

134.   Francis S. Collins, *The Language of God – A Scientist Presents Evidence for Belief*, Wheeler Publishing, 2007.

135.   Michael J. Behe, William A. Dembski, Stephen C. Meyer, *The Proceedings of The Wethersfield Institute – Science and Evidence for Design in the Universe,* Ignatius Press, 2000

136.   Richard Dawkins, *The Blind Watch Maker,* Penguin Books, 1986.

137.   Joseph Cardinal Ratzinger, *In the Beginning: A Catholic Understanding of the Story of Creation and the Fall,* Eerdmans – Grand Rapids, Mich., 1986.

138. Michael J. Behe, *Darwin's Black Box*, Touchstone – Simon & Schuster, 1998.

139. Martin Rees, *Just Six Numbers – The Deep Forces That Shape the Universe*, Phoenix Paperback, 1999.

140. Roger Penrose, *The Emperor's New Mind*, Oxford University Press, 1989.

141. Pope John Paul II, *Truth Cannot Contradict Truth*, Address to the Pontifical Academy of Sciences, 1996, (L'Osservatore Romano, October 30).

142. Pope Benedict XVI with Henry Taylor, *Truth and Tolerance*, Ignatius Books, 2004.

143. Stephen M. Barr, *Modern Physics and Ancient Faith*, University of Notre Dame Press, Indiana, 2006, p213.

144. Stephen Hawking, *Godel and the end of Physics*, Lecture for the Dirac Centennial Celebration, Cambridge, July, 2002.

145. Richard Dawkins, *The Selfish Gene*, Oxford University Press, 2006.

146. Alister McGrath with Joanna Collicutt McGrath, *The Dawkins Delusion*, Society for promoting Christian Knowledge Books (SPCK), 2007.

147. Fr Robert Spitzer, *Finding God through Faith and Reason*, EWTN Global Catholic Catholic Network, DVD set, 2006.

148. Michael J. Murray & Alvin Plantinga, *Reason for the Hope Within*, Eerdmans, Grand Rapids, Mich., 1999.

149. Clifford Longley, *London Times, 1989* quoted in The Proceedings of The *Wethersfield Institute*, (118 p65).

150. Stephen Hawking, *A brief History of Time*, Bantam Books, 1988

151. Hilaire Belloc, Essays of a Catholic, Tan Books, 1992.

152. Peter J. Kreeft, *7 Reasons to be Catholic*, talk on CD, Lighthouse Media.

153. Fr Edgardo M. Arellanno, *Conference of Alliance Of Holy Family International, Maynooth*, Ireland, 2007.

154. Micheal O Searcoid, Department of Mathematics, University College Dublin, Ireland, 2008.

155. Joseph Cardinal Ratzinger – with Peter Seewald, *God and The World*, Ignatius Books, 2002.

156. Dom Columban Hawkins O.C.S.O., *A Handbook on Guadalupe*, Park Press Inc., 355 6th Ave. N., Waite Park, MN 56387, 1997.

157. Fr Miguel Guadalupe, *The Seven Veils of Our Lady of Guadalupe*, Queenship Publishing Company, 1998.

158. Leslie Kean, *UFOs – Generals, Pilots, and Government Officials go on Record*, Three Rivers Press, New York. 2010.

159. Bret Lueder, *A UFO Hunter's Guide*, Watkins Publishing, London, 2013.

160.   Neil Arnold, *Shadows in the Sky – The Haunted Airways of Britain*, The History Press, 2012.

161.   *She went in haste to the mountain, Book three, page 138,* St Joseph Publications, 1981.

162.   Desmond A Birch, *Trial, Tribulation & Triumph – Before, During and After Antichrist,* Queenship Publishing Company, 1996.

163.   R Gerald Culleton, *The Prophets and Our Times*, Tan Books, 1974.

164.   Yves Dupont, *Catholic Prophecy – The Coming Chastisement,* Tan Books, 1973.

165.   Fr Albert J Hebert, S.M., *Prophecies – The Chastisement and Purification,* Private Publication – available at P.O. Box 309, Paulina, La. 70763, 1986

166.   Fr Albert J Hebert, S.M., *The Three Days Darkness,* Private Publication – available at P.O. Box 309, Paulina, La. 70763, 1986.

167.   John Bird, *A Storm unleashed from The Waters of the Abyss,* Private publication by John Bird, 2005.

168.   Michael H Brown, *The Final Hour*, Queenship Publishing Company, 1992

169.   Michael H Brown, *The Trumpet of Gabriel,* Faith Publishing Company, 1994

170.   Michael H Brown, *The Tower of Light*, Spirit Daily Publishing, 2007.

171.   Mary Alice Dennis, *Melanie,* Tan Books, 1995.

172.   John Bird, *The Eldest Daughter of the Church*, Videoset of Four (No 4) – SJB/Westernhanger Productions, US, 1997.

173.   Germain Giraud, *Marie Julie Jahenny* – The Breton Stigmatist, available at rue des Ileaux, 85670 Palluau, France

174.   Comte Paul Biver – Translated by Fr John O Connor, *Pere Lamay*, Tan Books, 1973.

175.   Fr Michael O Carroll, C.S.S.p., *Victim for Christ the King – Sr Marie du Christ Roi*, Private Publication, 2000.

176.   Eddie Doherty, *Wisdom's Fool – A biography of St Louis De Montfort,* Montfort Publications, 1975.

177.   Sister M. Faustina Kowalska, *Divine Mercy in my Soul – Diary*, Marian Press – Stockbridge, Mass., 1987.

178.   *Oceans of Mercy*, DVD, Divine Mercy Publications, Dublin, 2005.

179.   Anne – a lay apostle, Climbing The Mountain, Direction for Our Times, 2005.

180.   Anne – a lay apostle, *Serving in Clarity*, Direction for Our Times, 2008

181.   Fr Philip Bebie, C.P., *The Warning,* 101 Foundation, Inc. 1987.

182. Luis Eduardo Lopez Padilla, *El Gran Aviso De Dios – Al termino del Pontificado de Benedicto XVI y despues del cisma*, Appartado Postal 44 – 149, Colonia de Valle, Mexico 03100 D.F., 2005.

183. Middle East Media & Research Institute, Muslim American Leaders: *A Wave of Conversion to Islam in the U.S. following Sept. 11*, Nov. 16, 2001.

184. Daniel Ali & Robert Spencer, *Inside Islam: A Guide for Catholics*, Ascension Press, 2003.

185. Joel Richardson, The Islamic Antichrist, WND Books, 2009.

186. Joel Richardson, Mideast Beast, WND Books, 2012.

187. A Shiite Encyclopaedia, (on line), www.al-islam.org/encyclopedia/ chapter 6b Oct. 1995.

188. Walid Shoebat with Ben Barrack, *The Case for Islamophobia,* Top Executive Media, 2013.

189. John F Harvey O.S.F.S., *The Truth About Homosexuality*, Ignatius Press, 1996.

190. J Bancroft, *Homosexual Orientation: The Search for a Biological Basis*, British Journal of Psychiatry 164 (1994):439.

191. J Money, *Sin, Sickness, or Status?*, American Psychologist (1987): 397

192. Family Research Institute, P.O. Box 2091, Washington, DC 20013 – 2091, 1993.

193. Siegel, JM et al. *The Prevalence of Childhood Assault.* Amer. J. Epidemiology1987: 126: 1141 – 53.

194. Cameron P *Homosexual molestation of children / sexual interaction of teacher and pupil.* Psychological Reports 1985: 57: 1227 – 36.

195. *The Causes & Context of Sexual Abuse of Minors by Catholic Priests in the United States, 1950 – 2010*, John Jay College Research Team.

196. *Gays in the Clergy*, Newsweek, 23/02/1987.

197. Greg Hadfield, *This is Just a Start, Say the Activists*, The Daily Mail, 18/03/1995.

198. Atila Sinke Guimaráes, *The Catholic Church and Homosexuality*, Tan Books, 1999.

199. Edward O Connor, C.S.C., *Living in The Divine Will*, Queenship, 2014.

200. Hugh Owen, *New and Divine – The Holiness of the Third Christian Millennium*, pub by John Paul II Institute of Christian Spirituality, P.O. Box 798, Woodstock, VA 22664.

201. Rev Joseph Leo Iannuzzi, Std, Ph.D., *The Gift of Living in the Divine Will in the Writings of Luisa Piccarreta*, St Andrew's Productions, Pittsburg. PA. 2013.

202. Rev. Joseph Leo Iannuzzi, Std, Ph.D. *The Kingdom of The Divine Will,* Angelus Communications, UK, translation.

203. Maria Rosaria Del Genio, *The Sun of My Will*, Libreria Editrice Vaticana, 2015.

204. Sergio Pellegrini, *Saints in the Divine Will*, Pious Associatíon "Luísa Píccarreta Little Children of the Dívíne Wíll", Cartotecnica Graziani sas, Via della Macina, 62, CORATO (Ba), 2005.

205. Emmet O Regan, *Unveiling the Apocalypse – The Final Passover of the Church,* Seraphim Press, Belfast, 2016.

206. Carmel of Saint Teresa, *A Pathway under the Gaze of Mary*, World Apostolate of Fatima, USA, 2015.

207. *The Timing and Spatiotemporal patterning of Neanderthal disappearance,* NATURE: 2014, Aug 21st: 512:306 – 309.

208. LaViolette, Paul A, *New Findings at the Bosnian Pyramids Complex*, Nexus: 22 (Dec 2014 – Jan 2015) 51 – 59.

209. Cremo, M A and Thompson, R L, *The Hidden History of the Human Race,* Bhaktivedanta Publishing, 1996.

210. Frank Joseph, *Before Atlantis: 20 Million Years of Human and Pre-Human Cultures,* Bear & Company, Rochester, VT, USA., 2013.

211. Hancock, Graham, *Fingerprints of the Gods – The Quest Continues,* Century Books, 1995.

212. Jobling, M A , Tyler-Smith, C., *The human Y chromosome: an evolutionary marker comes of age,* Nature Reviews 4:598–612, 2003.

213. Carter, R W, *The Neutral Model of evolution and recent African origins,* Journal of Creation 23(1):70–77, 2009.

214. Richard J Dewhurst, *The Giants Who Ruled America,* Bear & Company, Rochester, VT,USA.,2014.

215. Jim Vieira and Hugh Newman, *Giants on Record: Hidden History of the Americas,* Nexus: 23 (Feb – Mar 2016) 43 – 48.

216. Fr Brendan Purcell, *From Big Bang to Big Mystery*, Veritas, 2011.

217. Leigh Skene & Melissa Kidd, *Surviving the Debt Storm*, Profile Books, 2013.

218. Charlie Johnston, *CharlieJ373 – blog-* October 2014.

219. Michael Lewis, *The Big Short*, Penguin Books, 2010.

220. Kevin Cardiff, *RECAP – Inside Ireland's Financial Crisis*, The Liffey Press, 2016.

221. Frank Allnutt, *The Force of Starwars – unlocking the mystery of the Force,* Bible Voice Inc., California, 1977.

222. Fr Albert Joseph Mary Shamon, *Apocalyps*e, Faith Publishing Company, 1991.

223.   Fr Herman Bernard Kramer, *The Book of Destiny*, Tan Books, 1956.
224.   Peter Kreeft, *You Can Understand the Bible*, Ignatius, 2005.
225.   Daniel Michael Giovanni, *The Antichrist is Here - And The World Must Prepare,* CreateSpace Independent Publishing Platform, 2015.
226.   *The Order of New Knighthood of Our Lord and His Holy Mother*, Newsletter 54, March-April 2017. P.O. Box 49, Miltown D.S.U. Monaghan, Ireland.
227.   Emmett O Regan, *The End of the World – What Catholics Believe*, CTS, 2014.
228.   Fr James L Meagher, D.D., *How Christ Said The First Mass,* Tan Books, 1984.
229.   Professor Courtenay Bartholomew, M.D., *A Scientist Researches Mary, The Ark of the Covenant,* The 101 Foundation, 1995.
230.   Frank Duff, *Virgo Praedicanda*, Legion of Mary, Dublin, 1967.
231.   Abbot Giuseppe Rioociotti, *Julian the Apostate*, Tan Books, 1999.
232.   Catholic Voice, 26th Feb., 2017, Athy, Co. Kildare, Ireland.
233.   Peter Seewald, *Benedict XVI – Last Testament*, Bloomsbury, 2016.
234.   *Proceedings of the International Conference of Exorcists*, "Fraterna Domus" – Rome, 20th – 25th October, 2014.
235.   Pope Pius XII, *Darkness over the Earth*, Catholic Truth Society, 1939
236.   Samuel Milham M.D., M.P.H., *Dirty Electricity – Electrification and the Diseases of Civilization, Second Ed.*, iUniverse, Inc. Bloomington, 2010.
237.   Donna Fisher, *Wi-Fi, cellphones and DNA damage*, Nexus magazine, 24/02, 15 – 20, 2017.
238.   Donna Fisher, *The EMF Plague*, Nexus magazine, 24/03, 19 – 25, 2017.
239.   Martin Blank, *Overpowered: What Science Tell Us About the Dangers of Cell Phones and Other Wi-Fi Age Devices*, Seven Stories Press, 2014.
240.   Robert O Becker, M.D., *Cross Currents: The Promise of Electromedicine, The Perils of Electropolution,* Tarcher, New York, 1990.
241.   Robert O Becker, M.D., Gary Seldin, *The Body Electric – Electromagnetism and the foundation of life,* Harper Collins, 1985.
242.   Martin L Pall, *Electromagnetic fields act via activation of voltage-gated calcium channels to produce beneficial or adverse effects,* J. Cell. Mol. Med.,17/8: 958-965, 2013.
243.   Steven DiBasio, *Mind Control in the 21st Century,* Nexus, Vol 21, No 4, 2014.
244.   Elana Freeland, *Directed-Energy Weapons for Political Control,* Nexus, Vol 21, No 6, 2014.